On Loving Women

JAMES MOORE

On Loving Women

HelixEye Books
Farmington, Connecticut

PUBLISHED BY
HELIXEYE BOOKS
222 MAIN STREET, SUITE #142
FARMINGTON, CONNECTICUT 06032
HTTP://WWW.HELIXEYE.COM

USE OF HELIX NEBULA AND SPIRAL GALAXY PHOTOS COURTESY OF NASA AND ESA.

FIRST EDITION, FIRST PRINTING JUNE 2012.

COPYRIGHT © 2012 BY JAMES MOORE

ISBN-13: 978-0-9742845-3-8

ALL RIGHTS RESERVED. NO PART OF THIS BOOK MAY BE REPRODUCED, SOLD, SCANNED, COPIED, TRANSMITTED OR MADE AVAILABLE BY ANYONE OTHER THAN THE PUBLISHER OR AUTHOR IN ANY FORM OR BY ANY MEANS WITHOUT PRIOR WRITTEN PERMISSION BY AND APPROPRIATE FINANCIAL COMPENSATION PAID TO THE PUBLISHER ACCORDING TO A WRITTEN CONTRACTUAL AGREEMENT AGREED TO BY THE PUBLISHER IN ADVANCE. ALSO FORBIDDEN IS THE STORAGE, USE IN ANY WAY, OR PROMULGATION OF ANY PART OF THIS BOOK BY ANY INFORMATION STORAGE AND RETRIEVAL ENTITY - WHETHER A COMPANY OR INDIVIDUAL - WITHOUT PRIOR WRITTEN PERMISSION FROM OR CONTRACT WITH THE PUBLISHER. UNAUTHORIZED DISTRIBUTION OF THIS BOOK, PUBLIC POSTING OF ANY OF ITS CONTENTS (ON THE INTERNET OR ELSEWHERE), OR SHARING OF ITS CONTENTS, VIA EMAIL OR ANY OTHER MEANS, IS ABSOLUTELY FORBIDDEN - WHETHER DISTRIBUTION IS DONE FOR COMPENSATION OR NOT. BOOK REVIEWERS MAY, OF COURSE, QUOTE VERY LIMITED PORTIONS OF THIS BOOK IN CONFORMANCE WITH FAIR USE PRACTICES.

HELIXEYE IS AN IMPRINT OF MYSTIC RIDGE PRODUCTIONS, INC.

PRINTED AND BOUND IN THE UNITED STATES OF AMERICA.

Library of Congress Cataloging-in-Publication Data

Moore, James, 1961-

On loving women / James Moore. -- 1st ed.

   p. cm.

Includes index.

Summary: "Techniques, anatomical discoveries and other information are provided to those whose goal it is to become a great lover and partner to a woman"--Provided by publisher.

ISBN 978-0-9742845-3-8 (alk. paper)

1. Sex instruction for men. 2. Sexual excitement. 3. Sexual intercourse. 4. Female orgasm. 5. Women--Sexual behavior. I. Title.

HQ36.M66 2012

613.9'6081--dc23

                          2012013951

*Dedicated to my awesome wife,
without whose love, devotion and support
this book would not have been possible.*

Table of Contents

Why Read This Book?	1
Women Don't Leave Great Lovers	15
One Of The Great Lover's Greatest Secrets	19
Sex Vs. Lovemaking: Putting The Love Into Lovemaking	23
The Long-Term Lovers' Unique Challenges	31
A Higher Love: The Spiritual Side To Lovemaking	41
Becoming The Type Of Man Women Desire	45
A New Way Of Thinking	53
Romance & Affection 24/7	59
What You Don't Know About Hygiene & Grooming	69
Is She Faking It?	79
Achieving The Ultimate Control	93
MEDICAL BREAKTHROUGHS WITH PREMATURE EJACULATION	129
Forget "Foreplay:" That Concept Makes Men Bad Lovers	130
Seduction, Wettening, Arousal, Orgasm: The 4 Sexual Processes	132
WHEN SHE NEEDS HELP GETTING & STAYING WET	141
The Art Of Seduction 24/7	145
Excite Her With Sexy Visuals	155
Erotic Talking For Sexual Results	163

Table of Contents

Female Sexual Anatomy — 175
- HOW THE VAGINA "TENTS" WITH AROUSAL — 190
- INTRODUCING THE FEMALE SEXUAL ANATOMY — 194
- NICHE, NOOK, V-SPOT, VAGINAL BALL & RING, AND CLITORAL RING — 195
- THE DEEP TRIGGER, NEXUS, FORNIX & NOOK — 196
- INTRODUCING FEMALE EJACULATION — 209

Play Her Like An Instrument (Through Feedback) — 225

Kissing For Effect: The Art of Kissing — 229

Oral Sex That Will Drive Her Wild — 233

The Art of Loving Touching — 259

Breast Orgasms, The M Spot & More — 281

The Shocking Facts About Positions — 297
- WARNING: A PENIS CAN BE BROKEN — 315
- THREE BEST POSITIONS TO GIVE HER DEEP VAGINAL ORGASMS — 331
- YOUR POSITION AFFECTS WHERE YOU ARE INSIDE HER — 340

Cocksmanship — 341
- VULVA LOVE TECHNIQUES — 355
- MORE SHALLOW LOVEMAKING TECHNIQUES — 364
- UNDERSTANDING MOTION-INCHES: G-SPOT TECHNIQUE EXAMPLES — 371

After The Lovin' — 381

Location, Location, Location — 383

Edgy Titillations: Sex Toys, Masturbation & Gentle Bondage — 389

Choosing The Right Lovemaking Furniture — 411

What Now? — 417

Glossary — 419

Index — 429

> "Should anyone here in Rome lack finesse at love-making, let him try me - read my book, and results are guaranteed!"
> - 1st Century B.C. Roman poet Ovid in The Art of Love, Book I

Why Read This Book?

☯

*T*his book almost didn't happen. The only reason this book exists is that a girlfriend dogged me for *two years* to get me to write a book on **love**making, **romance** and **women**. She kept after me, saying, "You *have* to teach other men what you know about women!" And she'd take me to bookstores to *show* me there was a need for this book. She'd bring me to the sex books aisle and say, "See? These books are good but *none of them talk about what you know!*"

I laughed off her suggestions for quite awhile. After all, didn't famed poet Ovid wind up *scandalized* and ultimately *banished* from the Roman Empire in 8 A.D. for writing the *Ars Amatoria (The Art of Love)*? And attitudes on talking about **sex** haven't changed much since then. Today's sex writers are marginalized and trivialized for daring to discuss the same juicy subject that got Ovid in trouble. It's still largely taboo. That made me think twice about writing *On Loving Women*.

But others - ex-girlfriends and *male friends who'd sought my advice on sexual matters* - were also telling me, "You *have* to write a book!" They said I had *unique knowledge* I needed to pass on to others so they too could become *great lovers*.

Ovid's Art of Love, German Edition (1644)

Most recently, my *wife* has been after me to complete *On Loving Women*. (It's taken a lot of encouragement to finish this ambitious project.) Just the

Why Read This Book?

other day, my wife (who understandably has had some misgivings about my revealing intimate details involving former lovers) pleaded with me, "You *have* to finish *On Loving Women! **It's an important book!**"* (And she's a PhD. So *she knows books.*)

Why does my *wife* believe in *On Loving Women?* She's told me repeatedly that this book contains *new* material that *no other book has covered.* More important, *she says that it will help innumerable men find happiness as the awesome lovers and great partners they'll become as a result of reading it.*

I can't tell you how much I was moved by my wife's endorsement. It got me back to writing after a hiatus.

...But then came the *clincher*. My Dad, upon reading my manuscript, suddenly got serious and - in one of those rare revealing moments that touch you greatly - he confessed wistfully: ***"I wish I had read this book about 50 years ago!"*** *I knew then that I had to get this book out there.*

SO MANY GUYS NEED SEXUAL ADVICE - EVEN SOME FAMOUS ONES

But there were other factors that convinced me to write *On Loving Women*. There was an article in *The Post Gazette* of New Jersey on November 29, 2005, for instance, that revealed that *Chris Martin*, the lead singer of *Coldplay, might need some coaching on sexual matters to find happiness in his relationship.* The article said:

> The British rocker...holds hostage the heart of one of Hollywood's sexiest leading ladies, Gwyneth Paltrow. Yet, **the rocker recently confessed that he had wished someone had given him tips on sex during his younger years.**
>
> Martin said that as a young man with uncontrollable urges, **he had not known a lot about the art of lovemaking and often dreamed of someone to give him practical advice on the subject.**
>
> *"I didn't really know what I was doing, I wanted someone to explain it to me,"* Contactmusic quoted him as saying.

More recently, accusations were made in a high profile breakup that a famous bon vivant and playboy might be suffering from the all-too common problem of **premature ejaculation** (for which I provide solutions in the chapter, "Achieving The Ultimate Control" on page 93). These stories of **sexual problems** that lead to **relationship disasters** are not isolated.

The general need for a book like this became painfully apparent recently at a concert in Westhampton Beach, New York. There, a well-known singer-songwriter shocked me and my wife with tales of **sexual unhappiness**. And he sang *break-up songs* of the *saddest* sort. He sang of having been **cheated on** a lot. He'd had a *lifetime* of **unrequited love**.

On Loving Women

He clearly had problems in the romance department. To which my wife commented, "See? He needs your book!" (I had not yet finished *On Loving Women* and she was trying to get me to complete this *massive undertaking*.)

Even the joke the performer told had sad overtones in the **sex** department. Actually, it sounded more like a *confession* than a *joke*. It went like this:

> "A wife calls to her husband, 'Come to the kitchen, quickly!' So he runs to her and she says, 'I need sex! Right now!' So he asks, 'Why do you need sex?' And she says, 'My egg timer's broken!'"

I laughed with the audience for a *nanosecond* before I realized that this "joke" was *nothing* to laugh at. The guy in the "joke" was a **premature ejaculator**. And, by inference, my wife and I surmised that *this* performer's *love life problems* had to do with **premature ejaculation**.

"He needs your book!" my wife whispered again.

The performer, strangely enough, then shouted, "*Sex!* Who likes *sex?*" - to which I and *just one other guy* applauded. (So puzzling! *Just two of us?*) To which the performer wryly replied: "Having it only *occasionally* then?" To which one of the concert-goers shouted, "Once a week!" The performer, looking offstage, then shouted (presumably to his lover), "Darling, can we manage once a week?"

Once a week? *Really? Only* once a week? Was this the norm?

My wife and I were struck by how **sexually unsatisfied** this educated and sophisticated Hamptons crowd seemed to be! And we were shocked by this *revealing* concert banter (bizarre as it seemed). *In its outspokenness it revealed an urgent, important and* widespread *problem.*

People in today's world are largely unhappy and unfulfilled when it comes to their love lives. And without a happy love life, they're miserable. They're living tragic, empty lives. And, as the songwriter's songs proved, their lives are filled with anger *and* bitterness *over it.*

After listening to the sexual banter, my wife concluded: "They **all** need your book!" *This* is how she convinced me to finish *On Loving Women*.

It became clear to me that there was a *legit* reason to write this book - and possibly even an *urgent need* for it. But it's taken me *eight years* to get this project done, believe it or not! It's been a monumental effort.

I've Helped So Many Others - Including Premature Ejaculators

But what makes me *qualified* to write such a book? If you knew my background and what I've achieved as a **lover** and **researcher**, I believe you'd agree I've earned the **street cred** that's made me many guys' favorite

3

Why Read This Book?

unofficial sex, romance and relationship counselor.

For one thing, *I've helped innumerable men get over their **sexual problems**, over the course of several decades.* My advice enabled them to become the lovers they'd always wanted to be, and in so doing, win the hearts of the women they loved and achieve happiness in their relationships.

I really can't say how the men who have sought my **sexual advice** knew I could help them. But **I've always been the guy everyone turns to for sexual help.** Even in college, guys would knock on my door for advice. I told them the ins and outs of **female sexual anatomy** and shared some of my secrets in driving women crazy sexually. *I taught them about **their own bodies and minds - information that's crucial to becoming a great lover**.* They all - to a man - said how incredibly *impressed* they were with how much I knew about **women** and **the art of love**making.

Another of my *proud achievements* is that I've had *great success* in helping men with **premature ejaculation** overcome that *relationship-threatening condition.* I taught them to achieve the *ultimate control in bed* through some super-effective **methods** and **training exercises** (that I'd originally invented for myself) **that train a man to last inside a woman as long as he (or his lover) desires, without coming.** (I'll share these with you later, in the chapter on *control*.)

In fact, *one of those men - a former neighbor - was one of those who was after me to write this book*. Why? My advice had *transformed* his life.

He'd had many sex-related problems. He blamed the failure of his marriage on premature ejaculation. He was also short on *carnal knowledge*. In fact, he didn't know much about *women* at all.

After his divorce, we'd go to a movie and instead of getting out of my car immediately when I'd drop him off at his apartment, he'd spill his guts. He shared the pain of his failure to live up to his wife's expectations as a lover. And he asked questions about **women** and **sex**.

I counseled him gladly for several months. He soon afterward reported that my help had enabled him to have a successful relationship with an awesome woman, who turned out to be the love of his life. No longer handicapped by **sexual inadequacies**, he won her heart. Now they're married and they're fabulously happy. In fact, *they toasted me at their wedding, telling*

On Loving Women

everyone ***I was the man who'd made it all possible***. *That's* the kind of help I'm offering you in *On Loving Women*, to achieve similar results.

Another person among the many I counseled was a house painter who'd been hired by my friend Earle. During a break, he painfully admitted he was having a problem in the sack. *He was in love with a woman but he was disappointing her as a lover. He could not last very long inside a woman. He was demoralized and didn't know what to do.*

I listened intently as he told his tale of frustration and sadness to Earle. He apparently did not think I could help him (I was a young man at the time), so he ignored me. He felt *Earle* had the answer to his problem.

But when I realized Earle wasn't prepared to respond, I chimed in with my prescription for the painter's problem. I taught him the powerful **control exercises** I'd invented that he could do at home (which I mentioned before). Very impressed, he said to Earle (both of whom were Black):

"Can you believe a *White boy* is the one who's helping me with this?" (To him, this was the highest compliment he could give me.)

Smiling very proudly, Earle responded: "*That's* my son!" (Earle was like a father to me.)

I Can Help You Too

What does this mean to you? *Because of my track record and the information I've gained in helping other men I believe I have a lot to offer in helping just about any man master the art of **love**making. And, after reading this book, I hope you agree that On Loving Women is your path to becoming a great lover...a lover who knows every inch of a woman's body - inside and out...who knows how to win a woman's heart and keep her wanting more...who gives his woman **Earth-shaking orgasms every** <u>time</u>* - and ***multiple orgasms*** - *including **vaginal orgasms*** *(every time),* ***breast-induced orgasms, and exotic orgasms*** *such as **ones brought on by vocal suggestions**...who knows everything there is to know about **female ejaculation** and can make her **ejaculate great gushes of love juices**...who knows* <u>every</u> *orgasm **trigger, wetness and wideness trigger and erogenous zone** in her body...who never gets boring...the kind of **man** and **lover** a woman*

Why Read This Book?

desperately craves and won't ever want to leave.

A book like that was referred to reverently in the High School movie classic *American Pie* - in the scene in which Kevin desperately calls his older brother for *sex tips* now that he's gotten a girl interested in him:

> **Kevin:** *I was thinking maybe you could give me some advice, brother to brother. I thought you might know a trick or something to make her...*
>
> **Brother:** *Orgasm? Is that all that you're interested in? Trying to get your girl into bed?*
>
> **Kevin:** *No. It'd be good to be able to return the favor. It'd be nice to know she enjoyed things as much as I do.*
>
> **Brother:** *That's good. That's what I wanted to hear. <u>Now</u> you <u>qualify</u>.*
>
> **Kevin:** *Qualify for what?*
>
> **Brother:** *My man, you just inherited "the Bible." It originally started as a sex manual, this book that some guys brought back from Amsterdam. And each year it got passed onto one East student that was worthy. It's full of all sorts of stuff that guys have added over the years. You have to keep it a secret and return it after the year.*

That's what I was shooting for in writing this book. I wanted to put together the kind of rare comprehensive and well-respected book that, like Kevin's "Bible," men pass down to others as a sort of *Holy Grail* of **sexual knowledge** because of the incredible insights it reveals...because it unlocks the *mysteries* men have had for ages about **women** and **love**making... because Kevin's not alone in hungering for such knowledge.

On Loving Women hopefully fits that bill because it contains more than *three decades'* worth of **sexual secrets** I've collected through **hands-on experimentation**, *intense research* and **love**making **experience** involving **hundreds of women**.

LET ME BE YOUR MENTOR - AS OTHERS HELPED ME

I was very curious about **sex** even as a young boy. I wanted to know *everything* about it. My goal from an early age was *to become such a great lover that most any woman I wanted to be with would desire me, big time.*

But who's going to teach you that kind of thing? That kind of knowledge is hard to come by. Few really great lovers have written books. Writing is, after all, a different talent than making love and both skills don't always reside in one person. Plus, we're living in one of the most sexually *repressed* of times. Lurid images are everywhere but useful *sexual information* is not happily passed along.

On Loving Women

So where did I go for sexual advice as a youngster? Like many kids, I first turned to my father. You know what he told me?

He said, "You get a tickle and then you **ejaculate**." That was the *sum total* of what he had to say. So like an idiot I went to the bathroom that night, stripped down and stood there waiting for that "tickle" to happen. It didn't take long for me to realize my Dad hadn't told me the whole story.

That only left me hungering for more information. I wanted the *key* to knowing what women wanted you to do sexually. I was impatient for my first sexual encounters to occur and I wanted to be *good*. No - I wanted to be *great*. Even as a kid. That was my big goal.

I found some clues walking home from junior high school one day when I found a sexy newspaper, wilted by the rain, by the side of the road. Full of *erotic stories*, it gave me a glimpse of what **sex** was all about. Yet it raised as many questions as it answered, so it only made me eager to learn more.

Fortunately, right around the corner from my parents' house was a family who welcomed me as one of their own. I was the original latchkey kid. I came home to an empty house. So it was welcome news that there was a kid around the block who wanted to play basketball after school. Even better - I discovered *his father Earle had a treasure trove of sex manuals*.

And Earle, who came home from work in the mid-afternoon, became like a father to me. A *mentor*. I mention him because *he was kind enough to teach me what a father should teach his son about* **sex**. So I had a leg up so to speak on the other boys when it came to knowing what to do during my first sexual experiences.

Well I know of no better way to repay Earle (and others along the way who helped me in my quest for carnal knowledge) than by becoming a mentor in a similar way *to you*. That's why I am passing along to you many of the secrets I've learned, so you too can set fireworks off with just about any woman, and win over the woman of your dreams, forever.

SOME OF THE KILLER FEATURES IN THIS BOOK

But how is this book different from the rest? Why another book on the **love***making arts?* **There are topics in On Loving Women few if any other books have dared to tackle.**

For one thing, I'm offering you a very personal approach, with **no-holds barred descriptions of some of what I've done to blow my lover's minds, sexually**. In reading other books, there were not many that gave me the feeling the authors were great lovers themselves. There was no "meat."

Why Read This Book?

Perhaps that kind of thing was too controversial at the time. In *On Loving Women*, you'll get **juicy details**. *During the course of writing On Loving Women, after* **love***making, I often recorded, in detail, the awesome* **sexual techniques** *I'd just used to drive my lovers crazy, so I could pass these along to you. So now you can* emulate *what I've done with great success, with your lover! (I also wrote down many telling comments my lovers made, so I could share these with you too.)*

On Loving Women also reveals some of the *incredible* **sexological breakthroughs** I have made regarding the **female sexual anatomy**. Having been **university-trained in biological research**, I took it upon myself to do my own *informal scientific studies* into **female sexual anatomy** over the decades through *practical experiments* with *scores of lovers,* in my quest to become the **perfect lover**. The result is that I've made some pretty hot *anatomical* and *sexual discoveries* along the way, some of which have been confirmed by recent scientific studies. And I've developed some phenomenal *new* ways to thoroughly thrill a woman sexually.

So there is information in this book even experienced sexologists and scientists will find of interest - such as **the identification of orgasm triggers, wetness triggers, erogenous zones and orgasm boosters never before documented** *(to my knowledge). And* **instructions on how orgasms can be produced with the slightest of touches or penetration. And revelations on how orgasms and great gushes of love juices can be brought on simply with the heat and pressure of a** motionless **erection or finger.**

All of this information is meant to enable you to become *the very best lover you can be. The more you know about the female body, the better you can knock the socks off your lover.*

If you don't discover at least one new **sexual hot spot** in here - such as her **Niche, Nook, V-Spot, M Spot, vaginal ball, vaginal ring**, or any of the others I introduce in *On Loving Women* - I'd be *shocked*. If you don't learn at least one **killer new sexual technique** *that will thrill and impress your lover beyond belief,* I'd be *highly surprised*.

On Loving Women

I will also teach you new concepts about *your own body* - insights that are *essential* to your reaching your **sexual potential**. (One of my lovers, in fact, praised me for this: "You know more about a *man's* body than most men know, too!")

Along these lines, I believe the chapter on *control* - mentioned earlier - will be recognized as *one of the best ever*, containing some of the **most effective solutions to premature ejaculation and other control issues** ever published. There you will learn **exercises, essential information, skills and techniques that will enable you to last as long as your lover wants you to**.

And I think you'll love the **cocksmanship** chapter, too, which covers new territory. *It shows you graphically, in intimate detail, how to use your **cock** artfully to give your lover not just **multiple orgasms** and **vaginal orgasms** but also the **biggest** orgasms of her life - even **instantaneous** orgasms occurring with your first insertion! (Yes, you can bring on **vaginal orgasms,** every time, **without** clitoral stimulation**.** I'll show you how!)*

Another benefit of this book: *While some of my methods require **deep penetration**, I've also invented many techniques that men of all sizes can use to give their lovers incredible orgasms - with only shallow penetration. Those are in here too.* So that, I'm sure, will be of great help to many men.

In On Loving Women, *you'll find tested and proven **sexual techniques** that will absolutely drive her crazy! And many involve **sexual hot spots** your lover will be surprised to find she has!* Use these and she'll be convinced you're sophisticated in the **love**making arts.

*Do you know how to give her **vaginal orgasms** (without touching her clit)?*

*Do you know how to do that without **deep penetration** and maniacally fast cockwork? That's in here.*

*Do you know **which positions produce the biggest vaginal orgasms?***

*Do you know her **vagina** grows in size during the **arousal process** and do you know what significance that has to you, as a lover?*

*Did you know **her vulva is a rich sexual zone, separate from her vagina**? That's in here too.*

*Do you know how to make her absolutely wet the bed with great fountains of love juices in moments of **ecstasy** - with your **fingers** or **penis**? The whole subject of **female ejaculation** will be of interest to both men and women. My experience with a wide range of women proves that **most women can be made to ejaculate**. And this is a **natural** and **desirable phenomenon** all lovers of women need to know how to produce.* That's in here too.

Why Read This Book?

I've Earned My "Degree"

Now some scientists might question my **credentials** since I have no university degree in sex-related subjects (hopefully, after reading this book, they *won't*). But in my defense, I've been with *hundreds of women* since I became sexually active at 17. And **the number of women I've known sexually (upon which I base my observations) far outstrips the number that most scientific studies have used as their data groups**. Another advantage I've had over most scientists in learning *how best to sexually please a woman* is that **I have decades of hands-on experience that no scientist can ever hope to accumulate, in studying the female body**. Scientists are ethically *barred* from being *active participants* in their studies. Yet *how else can you really get to know women, sexually?*

After all, if you want to learn how to play the guitar, would you rather take lessons from a *guitar manufacturer* or *Eric Clapton? Right. Eric.* And *I've made an awful lot of lovers super happy. So I have the* **experience** and **street cred** *to show you how to do this too.*

And this fact caps my **sexual "resume"**: *No long-term lover has ever left me. And all the women with whom I broke up returned afterward to ask me to take them back. I think that's an impressive record.*

So that's *another way* this book is *unique*. Here, you'll be taught by someone who's proven himself over and over again to be an expert in the art of **love**making. With the people who count. *Women*.

When it comes to **love**making, it seems to me an expert has the most **credibility** if he or she has more than enough **actual experience** in the field, to know of whence he speaks. So that sets this book apart, too.

Yet scientists can certainly play a big role in furthering the **art of lovemaking** - at least indirectly. *Smart lovers of women* are always eager to learn about the latest *scientific discoveries*, which they can then integrate into their approach to **love**making, to thrill their lovers even more. So I will also introduce you to some of the most exciting and most recent **scientific sexual studies** whose findings will help make you a better lover. That's in here too - knowledge that has helped me please an untold number of women as they'd never been pleased before.

It's Also About Becoming The Kind Of Man Women Desire

But becoming a **great lover** women would die for involves a lot more than just being great in bed! That's another aspect to this book that makes it unique - the chapters on how to become the kind of **man** women want to settle down with *forever*. I'll talk about this, too, because it's *key* to

On Loving Women

making women *desire* you.

So *On Loving Women* is not just about **sexual techniques**. Because *that alone does not make a man a **great lover**.* Being a **great lover** requires you to *walk the walk*. It's a *lifestyle*. It's about being a **good partner**. *I'll also help you become the kind of **companion** a woman wants.* On Loving Women will school you in the little-known **secrets** you need to know in order to become *the kind of man that **attracts women** and **keeps them wanting more**.*

And actually, I'd like to help you become something that I feel is even *better* than being a *great lover*. I'd like to help you become a **great lovemaker**. A **great lovemaker**, by my definition, is such a **great romantic, lover, partner and man** that his <u>every</u> *act makes a woman fall in love with him. Over and over again. After every **love**making session. After every kindness he shows her. After every thoughtful deed he does for her. In the way he looks after her and takes care of her. In the way he makes her feel like a woman. Every day he graces her life.*

THIS IS ABOUT WINNING A WOMAN'S HEART & *KEEPING* HER HAPPY

Along these lines, I need to add that this book is not about screwing around. (There are enough books about that. And I don't think most men would be satisfied doing that forever anyway.) **Yet I believe my goal reflects what most men are looking for, which is: to give you the skills and information you need in order to win the heart of the woman you love and please her forever - whether you've found her already or not.**

First of all, *studies* show *men in devoted relationships* **get more in the way of sex** and **are more happy** *than others*. Plus - whether you're *monogamous, a swinger, polyamorous* or even a *Lesbian* - *most lovers of women want to know how to attain a* **happy and strong long-term sexual relationship with a desired lover** *(even if that woman is just considered that person's "primary squeeze"). And that's what this book is all about.*

Yet, as most lovers of women will eventually find out, *making one woman happy forever is a lot bigger challenge than attempting to thrill a stranger you'll never see again, in a one-night stand.* So we'll look at this challenge and how to beat it. *This is apparently where many lovers of women fall short, from what I'm told - even married men. They don't have the skills or knowledge to be thrilling beyond one lustful first encounter or, at the most, a few months of limited tricks.*

So On Loving Women is not just for a man who is seeking the love of his life. This is for all men - including those who are married or in long-

Why Read This Book?

term relationships - who need help in the love and romance departments. The challenge just begins once you've won a woman's heart. Then you need to keep the home fires burning, so your relationship doesn't die on the vine and end prematurely (as all too many do). That's where all too many men fail. So in On Loving Women, I'm providing you with all the skills and information you need to make a long-term loving relationship work, forever.

...And, now that I think of it, this book might be *especially timely* given the fact that many lovers of women in our *loveless world* (of **hooking up** and **empty homes**) now reportedly are desiring a higher, long-term love. And many have come to the realization that in order to do so they need to learn how attain the *higher skills* and *sophistication* women crave.

Yet another unique feature:

Because I'm a true romantic (as I believe most *women* are), my approach emphasizes the **love** in **love**making. In fact, one fellow author who writes about *romance* and knows about this book told me:

> "I like that - you're putting the **love** back in **love**making. And just as Dr. Ruth is the authority on **sex**," he predicted, "you will become known as the authority on **love**making!"

(From his mouth to God's ears, as they say!)

As you'll find out, there's a huge difference between **sex** (which most people and all *animals* practice) and **love**making. In this book, you'll learn the *art* of **love**making. That practice will set you apart from the rest. **Love**making is on a **higher level** than **sex**, taking women to **higher heights of ecstasy, pleasing** women **far more**.

Another plus of this book: **I've interviewed hundreds of women in researching it**. I think you'll find their comments on what they want in a man and their complaints about the shortcomings of most male lovers are crucial to your ability to understand women. For instance, **you'll find out about the secret designations women use to rate men as lovers!** (Don't you want to know what women say behind your back? After all, how else can you improve if you don't know what women want?) That's in here too.

I also think you will love the chapter, "Is She Faking It?" on page 79. This solves an age-old riddle that dogs a lot of guys - with concrete methods you can use to ferret out the answer: is she or isn't she?

Bottom line: My wife and I agree that if this book helps even just *one person* find **sexual happiness** or it helps just *one couple* make their relationship work, then the long (and sometimes tedious) effort writing it

On Loving Women

was worthwhile.

On Loving Women is a <u>detailed</u> and <u>personal</u> account of someone who's made a **science** and **art** of **love**making. I've devoted my life to it.

So come along with me on a fantastic journey to becoming the man and lover *you want to be*. The kind *your woman* wants you to be.

Now is this the sexual *Bible?* This isn't the only book you should read. But you just might find this to be the most *effective* book you've ever gotten your hands on. The kind of book you'll want to share with others too.

I hope you'll agree with my Dad, my wife, past lovers and men I've helped achieve happiness with women that your path to success is right <u>here</u>. This book is full of awesome new discoveries. Everyone - including scientists - should learn something incredibly useful.

So - check it out. Leaf through the pages. I think you'll find very quickly that this book can *tremendously* change your love life for the better. And isn't that a goal that's worthy of your time and effort? Perhaps you'll find that this book was <u>the</u> very book that *you and I had hoped to find as kids - the Holy Grail book that makes everything clear and gives you the knowledge and skills necessary to become one of the celebrated great lovers of women; one who's highly desired and sought-after,* **who no woman would ever want to leave**.

...One final note: Market research shows *there's a tremendous demand for this book among <u>women</u>*. **Many women who have been surveyed have said they will buy a copy for their partners to read**. (If that's not an **endorsement**, I don't know what is! Women obviously want their lovers to know what's in this book!) Now, if you are one of those whose woman has given you On Loving Women, please understand that this act was done <u>lovingly</u> by your lover in order to make your relationship work. She is telling you: "What I want is in this book!" Isn't that great? Now your job couldn't be simpler! If that's the case, this book holds the key to your finding happiness in love and **love**making and to your making your relationship work. The answers to your questions are right <u>here</u>, in your hands.

And if you love your woman and want to do everything to make your relationship as exciting and happy as it can be, to <u>last forever</u>, then you should be <u>glad</u> your lover got this for you. She's telling you that she wants to help you become the man and lover she wants to be with, and <u>stay</u> with - to find happiness with <u>you</u>! She wants you to perfect the art of romance and **love**making so your intimate times together can be incredible, to propel your relationship to the heights. What greater <u>gift</u> could she give you?

Why Read This Book?

...You know, in a joke on the *Tonight Show* a number of years ago, Jay Leno noted: "A study was done and 11% of Americans surveyed said they'd be willing to give up a *kidney* for great sex." (Ouch!) That reveals:

- ⚥ How **important** great sex is to some people
- ⚥ How many Americans feel they're **not** getting great sex
- ⚥ How **impossible** those 11% feel it is to obtain great sex
- ⚥ How many Americans are clueless as to **how** to have great sex
- ⚥ How few realize that there's something even **better** than great sex - that is, great **love**making (as you'll find out)

Good news for that study group: *the true solution to the problem is in your hands*. And, thankfully, this book costs far less than a *kidney*. But given the *premium* women place on *great sex*, I hope you will agree with my wife that this book's *true value* is *far greater* than its cover price!

...So now it's my pleasure to hand down to you much of what I know about **women, romance, female sexual anatomy, biological sexual processes** and **lovemaking** - the product of decades of **sexual R&D** if you will. I am confident it will help you dramatically in capturing the heart of the woman you love. And it will teach you how to make her so happy that she will never dream of leaving you.

P.S. Before we get into the nitty gritty of *the act*, there are essential *lifestyle, attitude* and *mindset* issues you must comprehend before you can become a **great lover**. So in the next few chapters, I'll reveal these **secrets**. They are the necessary *foundation* upon which everything else rests. So please don't skip any of the *lifestyle, attitude* and *mindset* chapters, all of which are *crucial* to your success with women.

P.P.S. There's a lot that goes into a relationship, including **chemistry**. *You cannot win every woman's heart - no man can. (Nor should you try.) Part of finding happiness with a lover is in being discriminating in who you choose to go out with and in finding the perfect match for your specific needs, desires, personality, background and so on. But what On Loving Women will do for you is to make you as ready as possible to achieve success by teaching you how to become the kind of lover women crave - the best lover you can possibly be. I guarantee you will LOVE this book!*

> *"A great sex life is not just the symptom of a passionate relationship, but is also a major factor in creating it. Great sex fills our hearts with love."*
> *- John Gray, in Mars And Venus In The Bedroom*

Women Don't Leave Great Lovers

"**I miss your cock!**" said the handwritten note placed under my windshield wiper. It was from a beautiful blonde I'd broken up with. She wanted me back.

She had said she was in <u>awe</u> of my "control" (my ability to make love for a long time and come only when I want to). She had never been with a lover like me.

What her note really was saying was that she missed the great lovemaking **she'd experienced with me**. And that's why I was getting note after note from her, asking me to return.

If you want to know why you should learn to become a great lover, *that's* one reason why. **Women do not leave great lovers**. (That is, *if you're also the kind of man and partner they want to be with*, as well. We'll talk about *that* in later chapters.)

Women *crave* **great lovers** just as you do. And they're hard to find. So if you can learn to become one, you'll be valued and sought after, big time.

Another lover said to me once:

"You're the only man I know of who can go on and on forever. No other man I've been with could do that. I'm sure there are other men out there who can do that, but I've never met them. So...I guess you're <u>stuck</u> with me!"

(I wrote down what she said, in secret, shortly after she'd left the room. I wanted to pass it along to you, as further **proof** of what I'm telling you here.)

Along these lines, a different girlfriend related a conversation she'd had with a girlfriend who asked her:

Women Don't Leave Great Lovers

"How's it going with your boyfriend? I hear you're back together!" (She'd known I'd broken up with her a couple of times, but she'd kept coming back to me.)

"Sure are," my girlfriend replied.

"The sex is great, isn't it?" her friend said, with a wink of the eye. *"Too great to leave,* isn't it?"

"Mmm hmmm!" my girlfriend responded.

"That's the way it is with me and my husband," her friend continued. "I don't ever want to make him mad! The sex is too good!"

So there you are, guys. Proof that **women don't leave great lovers**. And that's the biggest *benefit* of being a great lover.

And here's a fact that *proves* the power of *great* **love**making which bears repeating:

I have not been left by a long-term lover ever. And I'm going back more than 25 years. I should add that this demonstrates the power of great **love**making coupled with the power of being a great partner (as you will see - that goes hand in hand).

This is especially incredible because, being a perfectionist, I am admittedly not the easiest person to get along with. But I've had a much easier time than the average guy attracting women and keeping them happy because I've devoted my life to mastering the twin arts of **love**making and **romance** (much of which I'll share with you in On Loving Women).

More proof of the power of *great* **love**making lies in the **feedback** I've received from my lovers. Here's just a sampling of what women have said to me over the years after I knocked their socks off in bed:

"You've spoiled me for other men!" (Two different lovers said that!)

"Where have ***you*** *been hiding?!"*

"I'm not letting ***you*** *out of my sight!"*

"You're an awesome lover! But I guess every woman's told you that!"

And by the way - you're not a great lover until many women have told you that you are! It's the woman's point of view that matters here. Only women can be the judge of this.

(Because *all women are different*, you need a greater depth of **skills** to know how to please a lot of women than you need to please just one. But if you're reading this book to learn how to please the *one* woman in your life, that equation is good news, actually - it means it shouldn't take you

On Loving Women

as long to achieve your goal as it would if you instead faced a *lifetime* of trying to impress *many* women sexually in a journey to *find the woman of your dreams!* For you, only *one* woman's opinion *matters*. All the better.)

But please take me at my word:

I don't mention all of this to boast. A **great lover** cannot afford to become an egoist. The act must be *selfless*, not *selfish*. Plus - *the minute you get egotistical about your **love**making skills is the day women will stop finding you attractive*. That's how it works. So we don't want to go there!

My reason for passing along real comments made through the years by my lovers is to show you that:

*If you master the art of **love**making it will vastly increase your chances to win the heart of the one you desire most, and <u>keep</u> her wanting to be with you <u>forever</u>*. But don't take my word for it.

Mars And Venus author John Gray expressed this very same idea in *Mars And Venus In The Bedroom*:

> "Advanced bedroom skills are required if a man is to provide his partner with the sexual fulfillment she requires. The more traditional bedroom skills men and women have used for centuries are outdated. It is not enough for a man to have his way with a woman. She wants more."

Advanced bedroom skills. *That's what <u>this</u> book is all about.*

Flip side (as you will learn, from the comments made by women I quote throughout this book): <u>Women do leave bad lovers</u>.

The media, in fact, reflects this truth as well as <u>encourages</u> it. Witness Season 6, Episode 2 of TV's Sex & The City, in which Samantha complains to Carrie that Berger (her new boyfriend) is a <u>lousy</u> lover. She then declares she's going to <u>leave</u> him because of it:

> "Fuck me badly once, shame on you. Fuck me badly twice, shame on me!"

Any woman watching that show got the message loud and clear: Smart women should <u>leave</u> bad lovers.

And if you want further proof of my contention that *women don't leave great lovers* (but they leave *bad* ones), there are plenty of credible of surveys that support what I'm saying.

For example, the *Atlantic* (February 4, 2012) reported that, of the *women* who answered a Match.com survey of 5,000 singles, **"50 percent would dump a guy for being bad in bed."**

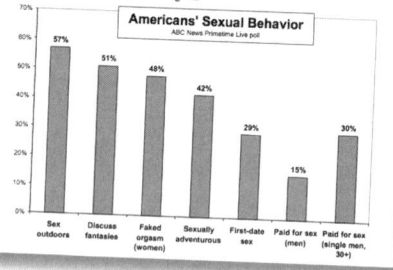

Women Don't Leave Great Lovers

And an *ABC News Primetime Live* **American Sex Survey** of 1,501 randomly-called adults in 2004 concluded that:

> *"People who are satisfied with their sex lives are considerably more likely in turn to be satisfied with their overall relationship...Moreover, people who aren't satisfied with their sexual relationship are by far the most likely to cheat on their spouse or partner."*

And they had the numbers to back up that determination:

> *"Specifically, among those who are very satisfied with the sex, 90 percent are also very satisfied with their marriage or committed relationship overall. Among those who are just somewhat satisfied with their sex lives, fewer, 71 percent, are very satisfied with their relationship. And among those who aren't satisfied with the sex, fewer still – 53 percent – are very satisfied with their marriage or partnership."*

If that wasn't clear enough, the study's creators wrote:

> *"[A] regression analysis finds that Americans' satisfaction with their sex lives is a significant predictor of their satisfaction with their marriages or committed relationships."*

So don't underestimate the power of great *love*making. (FYI: I'm talking about great **love**making. Not **sex**. There's a *big* difference (as you will see in the chapter on *Sex Vs. **Love**making*).

And, believe it or not, **women can often tell if you're a great lover <u>within seconds of meeting you!</u>** (But you cannot *fake* the signs they see in reaching this conclusion, so don't even try!)

So the sooner you become a great lover, the sooner you will begin to attract more women than you ever imagined was possible. (But don't be a phony! This has to come across honestly and without effort on the man's part.)

...Long story short - what I want to do for you is to transform you into the kind of *man* and *lover* women are attracted to - the kind women *crave* and *never want to leave*. So let's get you on the right track!

> Kurt Russell as Wyatt Earp proposing to actress Josephine Marcus in the movie "Tombstone":
>
> "I have nothing left. Nothing to give you. I have no money. I have no pride, no dignity.
>
> "I don't even know how we'll earn a living.
>
> "But I know that I'll love you the rest of your life."

One Of The Great Lover's Greatest Secrets

In the movie Hitch, "date doctor" Hitch (played by Will Smith) gets angry when a prospective client requests advice on how to bed a *maximum number* of women:

Vance: I was told that you help guys get in there.

Hitch: Right, but see, here's the thing - my clients actually *like* women. "Hit it and quit it" is not my thing.

Vance: Let me make one thing clear to you, rabbi, I need professional help.

Hitch (getting up to leave): Well, that is for damn certain!

That scene explains where *I'm* coming from. And it reveals one of the biggest *secrets* that makes a *certain kind* of **Casanova** so *desired* by women. *It's* our **love of women**. Actually, no. It's our extreme *love of women*. We *revel* in their company.

Giacomo Casanova

One Of The Great Lover's Greatest Secrets

Now, if you're like me, *unlike the real Giacomo Casanova, you don't want to become a great lover to sleep with a* maximum *number of women.* You want to obtain all the **love***making skills you can in order to win the heart of the one woman you love, forever.* (And the average woman, while attracted to the Casanova *type*, wants a man who is interested *only* in her.)

But it all begins with your **love of women**. *You cannot be the greatest of lovers if you are not truly* thrilled *to be in the company of women.*

Yet I'm not sure this *secret* can be taught. And in fact many men actually seem to *dislike* women! They tell *misogynistic jokes* like this one:

"What's the worst part of being with a beautiful woman? You have to talk to them after the sex is over!"

Very funny. *Ha ha ha.* But that kind of *hateful attitude* prevents a man from becoming a **great lover**. If a woman senses that you *can't stand* being around them except for **sex**, they won't find you *desirable*.

You Can't Fake This

Why are your *innermost thoughts and feelings* so important when it comes to being a *lover? A* woman can *sense* what your feelings, thoughts and attitudes are. They can really *read your mind*. No joke. If you don't believe this then you haven't been around women much.

What does this mean to you as a lover? A woman will *know* whether you love women in general, or *not*. And a *woman wants to be around men who love women*. It's only natural. Who (among heteros) doesn't want to be with a lover who absolutely *loves* the opposite sex?

You know what a *thrill* it is to be around a woman who is *totally fascinated* by you. Why would it be a shock to learn that women want this kind of thing too, from a man? Plus don't forget that in today's world, it's likely that any woman you're with will have *already been with men who love women*. And once they've experienced how *wonderful* men like that make them feel, *they only want to be with lovers who fit that category*.

Therefore - if you *don't* fit that category - we need to turn you around. You need some self-examination. What's the cause?

If you're wallowing in *bitterness* over *past* relationships, that's going to be an *impediment* to your moving on. Women can sense that kind of thing. *Get over it. We've all been through lousy relationships.*

If you haven't yet met a woman who's been really good to you, you have to have faith that someday you will. Those of us (like myself) who have found great women can tell you: *They're out there.* Have *patience. If*

On Loving Women

you prepare yourself for the moment, you'll meet one and win her heart.

If your mother or grandmother or other women in your family weren't very nice, *don't take it out on the women you date.* (You don't get to pick your family.) Again - *trust* me. There are *fabulous* women out there. Nice ones. Loyal ones. *If you look for a woman in the right way, by the right body part - by what kind of* heart *she has - you'll find a good woman eventually.*

Whatever the reason, if you're harboring *past grudges* or are seeing women in the *wrong* light (negatively or as *inferiors* somehow), you have an *issue* that needs to be addressed. It will pose an obstacle to you as a lover. It will keep you from being seen as a **great lover**, and perhaps even as a **desirable man**. Worse, it will become an *obstacle* in your attempt to have *happy relationships* with the women you go out with. And ultimately - if you don't banish *negative thoughts* - it will limit your *choice* of women. Because **self-respecting, desirable women** *don't want to be with men who are not thoroughly* **enraptured by** *and* **respectful of women**.

Women are perhaps God's greatest gift to us. (Isn't that what the story of Adam and Eve was all about?) *The sooner you see women in that light, the sooner you will become more* **eligible** *and* **attractive** *to women.*

A Related Secret

Now along these lines, there's something else you should know that helps make *Romeos* successful: *Our ability to make women feel as if they're the* belle *of the ball, the* star *of the show, the one who* rocks *our world.* I'm not talking about in a goofy, fawning or immature way. I'm talking about in a mature, *appreciative* way.

Occasionally, I'm sure you've been around a woman who makes you feel as if you're the *only* man in the room. A woman who clearly *loves* the company of men in general and your company in particular. A woman who makes you feel she can't *imagine* being with anyone else.

How great did that make you feel? Well, that's how you should make your lover feel. *Make her feel as if the world's dissolved away and you can't imagine being with anyone else. Make her believe she's the most incredible woman you've ever known.*

Romance Is Not Out Of Fashion

Now, perhaps you're confused about this. For awhile, American men were taught the disinformation that women didn't want "old fashioned" **romantic relationships**. And they might have gone out of style temporarily.

But that *anti-romantic fad* was not natural and it disappeared. It went away

One Of The Great Lover's Greatest Secrets

because *most women are hard-wired for a desire of all things romantic.* Thank Goodness! And I'm not speaking only about women in my age group. I met a charming 26-year-old woman recently, who, like many other women before her, agreed with what I'm telling you. She told me decidedly that: *"A woman wants to be the center of a man's attention."*

Are you giving this to your woman? Every day I see men who are not only *not* making their woman the center of their attention but are being out-and-out rude! And strangely enough, they apparently don't realize their behavior is not only offensive, cold and insulting to their *women*, but to *onlookers* as well.

How Your Attitude Toward Women Relates To Lovemaking

You might be asking yourself: *What the heck does this have to do with lovemaking?* As you'll find out, **love**making has many aspects to it. And one of the most important **principles** when it comes to **love**making is: *The way a woman feels about you and the relative desire she feels to make love to you is dependent upon how you treat her and how you think about her.*

So is it any secret why *men who love women* have *much more* **love**making *success?* Or here's a better question: *Why in heck does a man who treats his woman with disrespect or neglect think his woman will later get the hots for him?* Hello!!!! *That's* how all of this relates to **love**making!

Not that your desire for **sex** should be the reason you "treat your woman right," as they say in Brooklyn. You should *want* to be the very *best* person you can be and behave like a **sophisticated, loving gentleman** *without regard to ulterior motivations.* That has its own rewards.

So try this the next time you're in a nightclub or restaurant, or just out on the town: *Never look at other women, or let your eyes become distracted. Look only at your lover - with loving, admiring eyes - as if the women nearby don't exist. Act as if she's the most fascinating woman you've ever met.*

Make her feel *revered*, a woman *loved uniquely and passionately.* Put *incredible* **emotion, feeling** and **passion** behind *every* move and expression you make. If she feels *you love being with her*, then she will likely *love* being with *you*. Conversely, if she *doesn't* get that feeling, she *won't* love being with you and *she won't want to make love to you.*

That's how your **thoughts, feelings** and **attitudes** toward women and your woman in particular relate to **love**making. So keep them *positive* and *loving*.

This is the foundation upon which everything else rests.

> *"Don't go for second best baby, Put your love to the test. You know, you know, you've got to make him <u>express</u> how he feels, And maybe then you'll know your <u>love</u> is real."*
> — lyrics from Madonna's Express Yourself

Sex Vs. Lovemaking: Putting The Love Into Lovemaking

Years ago, I told a girlfriend that my late mentor, Earle, was not an attractive man, yet his (now-deceased) wife was *gorgeous*. Her response?

"It must have been **great sex.**"

Now, that might or might not have been true. I tend to believe it was **great love**making - there's a big difference. (And although my now ex-girlfriend quibbled over this distinction, it was the **love**making that kept her coming back to me for more. It was great **love**making that made her say things like, "You *rock* my world," and "Why don't you just *marry* me?")

The point is: *This* is the premium many women place on **great love**making.

Of course, Earle had other values that appealed to his wife, too, as should any **great lover**. He was a cultured, charming, refined and kind man of many interests, possessing wide knowledge and a keen sense of humor – values you, too, should desire to attain. No woman of any value with a proper amount of self-respect would want to be with a shallow man.

But if - as women like to put it - the way to a *man's* heart is through his *stomach*, I can tell you that *the way to a woman's heart is through* **great love**making. Women may deny this, but it's been my experience that if it's *great*, it might very well *make* the relationship.

So what is **love**making *and why am I so intent on making the distinction between* **love**making *and sex?* That's what we'll discuss in this chapter.

Putting The _Love_ Back In Lovemaking

WHAT IS A GREAT LOVEMAKER?

You need to understand the difference between ordinary **sex** *and* **love***making in order to become a* **great lover***, or as I prefer to put it, a* **great lovemaker***. This book is about great* **love***making. Leave the sex to chimps.*

Sex *can thrill for an hour or two.* **Love***making can thrill for a lifetime. And a woman can* feel *the difference.*

Sex *is a simple physical act even animals can do.* **Love***making is a complex expression of love no animal can hope to do.*

Sex is about lust for someone's **body** *- and the desire is carnal.* **Love***making is about love for* **the person** *you're with - and the desire is to communicate that love, (mostly) non-verbally.*

Sex is about the body. **Love***making is about your lover's soul, heart, mind - the whole person.*

Sex is most often a selfish act seeking self-release. **Love***making is a selfless act, seeking to please your partner.*

All **sex** *requires is a rudimentary knowledge of the physical requirements of intercourse. And making the woman* **come** *is not a requirement.* **Love***making requires much more.* **Great lovemakers** *excel in more than just the physical. And making the woman* **come** *- many times - is of supreme importance. But, more important, making the woman reach* **spiritual** *and* **emotional heights** *she's not achieved before is the ultimate goal.*

It's very easy – for many of us – to *bed* a woman. That's having **sex**. It's a lot harder to win over a woman's **heart** and **mind** and **soul** such that she wants to be with you, forever. That is what you can do through **love***making* (hence why it's called love-*making*). Our goal as **great lovemakers** is *higher*, and so are the (infinite) rewards.

Anyone can make a woman **climax**. Theoretically, a *monkey* could be trained to service someone. But, **sex** without **love** is *not* **love***making*. And, if you're *servicing* your lover through **sex** – simply giving her **physical gratification and release** – you may decrease her tension and make her feel better, but you're not being a **great lover.** You're not satisfying her in a deep way. More important - *you're not making her love you.*

Making **love,** at its best, is about making her **love** you. That should be what you want to achieve . That's a gift you can attain through *great* **love***making*.

If you're only getting her off, then you're an interchangeable commodity. Any normal man can make any normal, sexually-functioning woman come.

On Loving Women

If you don't care whether you're taking her to **sexual** and **spiritual heights** through true **love**making, if you don't care whether she wants to stay with you or not, then this book is not for you. If, however, you treasure the love of one woman, and want to attain her undying devotion and loyalty, then you need to become the best lover you can be. This book's for you.

Sex will not win her heart…***love***making will. And that potential reward alone should motivate you to become a *great lovemaker*.

KEEPING IT REAL

I just saw two documentaries on iconic movie director Elia Kazan in which legendary film director Martin Scorcese and acting icons Robert De Niro and Al Pacino spoke of how Kazan wanted *more* from an actor than just a "natural" performance. He wanted the "real."

In other words, Kazan wanted his actors to reach the heights, the pinnacle of acting, where the actor makes everyone in the audience feel that he or she is witnessing the *real deal*. Actor Alec Baldwin added: "Kazan also wanted to *hit* you." He wanted every scene to *move*, to *affect* the audience.

That describes what most women want through intimacy. They want you to make it *real*. They want you to communicate how you're *really* <u>feeling</u>… *in the moment* (as actors like to say). And they want you to *hit* them with it. *Move* them.

How? Actors like to ask directors, "What's my character's *motivation* for doing this scene?" They need this information to know what *emotions* and *thoughts* should be running through their head - as that character - so their activity on screen or on the stage has the ring of truth and moves the audience in the right way. And in a way, you, as a *lover*, should ask yourself the same question before becoming intimate with your partner.

What's your *motivation?* If you want to reach the *heights* through ***love***making, the answer to that question should always be: *To* **express passionate Love - with a capital "L."** More specifically: *To express all the good thoughts and feelings you're having about her - <u>now</u>.*

> **"With my body I thee revere."**
> *– Wedding vow overheard recently*

ANOTHER BENEFIT OF ENGAGING IN LOVEMAKING

Because your thoughts and feelings will be different for her every day, *using those to determine what you do during* ***love****making will have an added benefit. They will guide you in making gestures of love*. In doing so, you will find yourself being more **creative**. And, with your *inspiration* being *different* every day, you should never have to worry about *repeating* yourself from day to day.

So this approach alone - *tying what you do to how you feel* - should help you avoid the "same-old-same-old" trap.

THE PRICE YOU MIGHT PAY IF YOU'RE NOT A GREAT LOVEMAKER

You want to know how big a deal this is? I'll give you your *motivation, as a lover,* to engage in **love**making rather than *sex*, from another standpoint. I'm going to tell you a true story - all too common - that *dramatically* explains why all of this is important.

This has been a *cautionary tale I've heard over and over again*. Sad but true:

Most of the women I've been with have complained to me that the last man in their life was a lousy lover. (This usually came out during our first few dates - which shows you how upsetting that was to them.)

More important:

They told me they <u>left</u> their last lover in large part because of his lack of bedroom skills. (Most of those women added that they left their husbands or boyfriends because they also fell short as a <u>man</u>. We'll cover that topic in future chapters. Because the consummate lover of women is a man who's made himself desirable in all departments.)

Lesson here:

*If you fall short in the **love**making category you will <u>likely</u> lose the woman you love. Women specifically list a lack of **love**making as being one major factor that causes them to seek someone new. (Not a lack of **sex**, but **love**making.)*

A TRUE STORY: THE FACTS SPEAK FOR THEMSELVES

...Which is where the story I promised you above comes in. It was from one of the women I interviewed for this book. This frank and moving story should forever explain what women expect of you. More important, it should open your eyes as to what's *at stake* if you *don't* provide your woman with a deeply satisfying *love* life.

She was an attractive woman from Chicago in her mid forties and she shook with emotion as she related the very intimate story *of the critical day on which she decided to leave her husband. She wanted me to know what had motivated her to do that.*

On Loving Women

On that day, her husband wanted to visit his parents in another state. She wasn't feeling well so she stayed home, sending him off with the kids to make that trip alone.

That night, feeling better after a long nap, something moved her to put on some sexy lingerie, light some candles and put on soft, sexy music. Looking at herself in a mirror, she began to dance sensuously to the slow song that was playing.

Inevitably, she began to *make love* to *herself*.

"It was then that I realized what was *lacking* in my life and what I craved the most," she told me. "It was **love**making."

And she stopped to make the same distinction I've been making here:

"...Not sex," she intoned. "**Love**making." (And she emphasized the first syllable, "love," in articulating the word **love**making. To her, that said it all.)

Then she dropped the bombshell:

"And I decided that night I would never let my husband touch me again."

*Wow! That's powerful proof of how important **love**making is to a woman.*

*She was getting sex. She didn't lack for sex. But she didn't want sex. She wanted **love**making. She wasn't getting that.*

And, upon reflection, she didn't feel her husband was capable of giving that to her. And without it, she felt it was time for a divorce.

*That shows you the value she put on **love**making. And her need for it. But she's not alone in that regard.*

*There's your motivation for wanting to become great at **love**making. It's hugely important to the woman you love. It's important to the success of your relationship.*

*The true story above demonstrates that a woman understands the difference between sex and **love**making. And most women want **love**making; not sex. So if you don't supply a woman with this crucial female need, she will most likely find someone else who can.*

Trust me. There are millions of tales being told by women like her this very minute worldwide proving this is true.

THE DIFFERENCE BETWEEN SEX AND LOVEMAKING

So what's the difference between *sex* and **love**making? If you listen to songs written and sung by women, you should know. Aretha Franklin sang about it in the Carole King song *(You Make Me Feel Like) A Natural Woman*:

Putting The _Love_ Back In Lovemaking

Oh, baby, what you done to me?
You make me feel so good inside
And I just wanna be close to you
You make me feel so alive

You make me feel
You make me feel
You make me feel like a natural woman

Lovemaking makes a woman feel like...a *woman*. Alive. Sexy. Loved. Happy. Bonded to you. *In love* with you. Overcome with *emotion* that lasts far beyond the event itself. Like she's in a *joyful haze* of **ecstasy**.

Something *significant* is being expressed...and a *beautiful* reaction results.

In contrast, there's no *love* or *romance* behind *pure sex*. Sex is a *mechanical act*, satisfying a momentary *physical* need for release.

For most women, purely physical sex is an empty *experience that leaves them feeling* lonely *and* cold. *Sex* is *not* what Aretha sang about, for sure. It's not the stuff of a woman's dreams.

Lovemaking requires *loving feelings and thoughts* to soar to the **heights**.

This book is about **love**making. More than that - it's about putting the *love* back in **love**making.

I put it that way because:

👎 *I think a lot of lovers lose sight of what their motivation should be in making love; and*

👎 *Without the expression of loving thoughts and feelings, the act becomes meaningless*

Why do you need to know this? You need to get your *mind* straight before you can become a great lover.

Great **love**making is about **nonverbal communication**. You should be telling your lover, through *touch*, how you feel toward her. How much you *care* for her.

In so doing, your actions should be **passionate**. That element makes a *huge* difference. Yet it's lacking in most sexual experiences - according to what most women tell me.

Without this, you just have...**sex**. Physical. Mechanical. A getting off of the rocks. The same thing that animals do. Without artistry, feeling or, ultimately, satisfactory effect. It's nothing special. And it often leaves the participants feeling empty and lonely.

On Loving Women

The best part about engaging in **love**making rather than **physical sex** is that it makes things easy, in a way. Instead of wracking your brain and attempting Olympian moves to put together a performance, you need only let your **emotions** guide you. The difference, to her, will be immense.

Women respond to **feelings**. In communicating **loving, warm, positive feelings** to her, she'll feel **warm, loved, cozy and cared for**. If you **make love** to her instead of engaging in **sex** by rote, she'll feel what you're telling her non-verbally. And *that* will make <u>all</u> the difference in the world.

Among other things, **love**making will give her *the warm fuzzies*. And that's what makes her feel good *during* the event and, more importantly, *afterward*. This is how you create the bonds that bind her to you, lovingly.

Now, along these lines, to prepare you for what lies ahead:

Great lovemakers *spend a lifetime exploring* **female sexual anatomy** *– through intelligent experimentation with their lovers (much as a scientist does lab research) and the reading of the latest medical and sexual books and articles. What are they looking for? More* **orgasm triggers***. More ways to excite their lovers' bodies. Unexplored* **nerve endings***. Better ways to exploit* **biological factors***. Ways to take their lovers to ever higher* **spiritual and emotional heights***.*

They have an innate feel for **the sensual***. This is almost a* **field of science***. They know how to create the* **right mood** *(or more accurately: they know how to make their lovers want to be loved). They know how to talk, to move, to awaken* **a woman's sensuality***. And they can* **empathize** *and* **synchronize with** *their lovers' immediate desires.*

And there's much more great lovers do, including making themselves the very best they can be, to become the kind of man most women desire.

So we need to cover all of this and more. (And we will!)

But for now, if you take nothing else away from this chapter, please **always remember to put the expression of** <u>**love**</u> **into your love**making**. Let** <u>**love**</u> **be your guide.** *It will make all the difference in the world.*

Just ask sexy movie siren Sophia Loren. According to her: "Sex without love is absolutely ridiculous. Sex follows love, it never precedes it."

...But if you really want to be a great lover you should also bear this in mind: **Love***making should be a 24/7 kind of thing. A* **lifestyle***. You should make love to her all day long - figuratively speaking. Master this and you'll endear yourself to her forever.*

An Age Old Problem That Prevents Many Men From Achieving Happy Relationships
And How Lovemaking Offers A Solution

In a world with an **oversexed media** pumping out images of **scantily-clad 20-somethings** it's no surprise that *some older men are having a problem being attracted to women their own age*.

One of my buddies, in fact, newly divorced, admitted to having this issue. He was 50 but he only found women in their 20s sexually desirable.

That syndrome poses a serious problem. It will destroy a man's ability to achieve happiness in long-term relationships.

You cannot keep trading in one 20-something for another as each turns 30 (assuming you can *find* a young woman interested in you - for the *right* reasons - once you're 50 or older). You have to have a mature view to happily grow old with the woman you love.

After all, **love**making is not about finding the best and youngest **body** you can attract. It's about winning the heart of the very best, most <u>lovable</u> **woman** you can...someone with whom you want to spend the rest of your life. She's a rare breed so you must cherish her forever.

I helped my friend get over this syndrome. Here's what I told him:

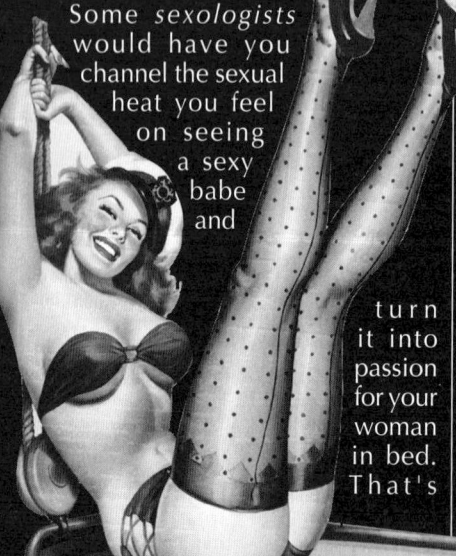

Some *sexologists* would have you channel the sexual heat you feel on seeing a sexy babe and turn it into passion for your woman in bed. That's an idea. But I prefer something else.

Just tune out the noise. Once you've found the great woman you want to spend the rest of your life with, focus only on the love you feel toward *her*.

Those obsessed with *sex* might be attracted purely by physical looks, but practitioners of great **love**making are attracted to the *beauty within* (which is there *no matter what her age is*). And *true beauty comes from within*. We see her heart, her soul, all the giving acts she has done, and so our love grows greater with each passing day. We don't feel our lovers *lack* anything. To us, they're highly *lovable*. *More* desirable with time, not *less*. *We want to make love to our partners because we want to show them how much love we feel for them. We want to make them feel special because they make us feel special and enhance our lives in countless ways.*

Your joy - during **love**making - should come from giving your lover the special intimate pleasures and excitements a woman of her inner beauty deserves. Nothing beats the *sounds* and *sights* of a woman in ecstasy - *no matter what her age*. What's more **erotic**, a bigger *turn-on*, than that?

Lovemaking should be the **non-verbal communication** of how you feel toward her. Her **nipples**, **vulva** and other **erogenous zones** - which do not feel significantly different as she grows older - are just **conduits** to your expressions of **love**. (And they will always be exciting **sweet spots** with which you can send your lover into orbit.)

Plus, **love**making with the *right* woman only gets *better* with time. As your love *grows*, so does your *passion*. And each of you comes to know each other's favorite **hot spots** and **turn-ons** better and better as the months and years pass.

In this way *true love is like fine wine*. The older, the *better*. (And, by the way, women are beautiful at *every* age.)

> "The Torah places great importance on the sexual relationship between husband and wife. Separate from the commandment of procreation is an obligation that a husband has to meet the sexual needs of his wife."
> - Rabbi Howard Wolk of West Hartford, in an opinion piece, "Sex And The Torah," in the Hartford Courant (February, 26, 2007)

The Long-Term Lovers' Unique Challenges

In the book *Couplehood*, comedian Paul Reiser talks about the *challenges* of surprising your mate during **intercourse** after being together awhile:

> "Sexually speaking, when two people first get together, it's easy to be impressive. They've never seen the show before, so every trick is a crowd pleaser.
>
> "'Watch this. You watching? Hey—look at that. Didn't expect that, did you? Of course not. I'm very, very good.'
>
> "But after a while, you run out of tricks. The bag is empty. The lights go up, and you have to tell the truth. "Ummm, that's basically it. That's all I know. Good night everybody....Drive safely."
>
> "You can't even think of what else could be done. You both just accept that this is pretty much what it's going to be for the rest of your lives."

Eeegad! Many a *truth*, as they say, is told in jest. Indeed, the *ABC News Primetime Live American Sex Survey* I mentioned earlier (on page 17) seems to vouch for the idea that *all too many couples are letting the sexual excitement in their lives fizzle out over time*. It concluded that:

> "There is clear evidence in this survey that sex loses its spark over time. Among couples who've been together less than three years, 58 percent call their sex lives very exciting. At more than 10 years, only half as many, 29 percent, say so.
>
> "Similarly, 79 percent of new couples are "very" satisfied with their sex lives, compared with 52 percent of long-term couples. And 87 percent of new couples enjoy sex "a great deal"; among long-term couples it's 17 points lower.

The Long-Term Lover's Unique Challenges

"Not surprisingly, frequency of sex drops as well – at least several times a week for 72 percent of new couples, but just for 32 percent of long-term couples."

So if this is the *norm* out there, we need to do something about it! There's no excuse for it. And I believe *men* have the onus to turn this situation around since, even in this day and age, *the man largely is the one who most actively creates the fireworks sexually*. And women, most studies show, *want* their men to take charge, to make things happen. We are supposed to be the **sexual magicians**. So clearly *many men are falling down on the job!*

Now before you argue that today's world is different and long-term relationships are a thing of the past so you need not worry about pleasing a woman for a *lifetime*, think again. In my experience, *most women want to settle down* - a fact echoed by that ABC News survey, which noted that:

"...three-quarters of...women...say it's more enjoyable to be married than dating."

Lovemaking Can And Should Be More Exciting With Time

Lovemaking need not grow dull over time. In fact, my relationships with women have proven that. A one-time rock guitarist, I've approached **love**making much as I approached playing a lengthy guitar solo. Full of *creativity* and things to say, musically, I never played the same solo twice. And **lovemaking**, on one level, has similarities to music - it is all about using her body as an **instrument**, as a means of **communication**. And there's so much you can do (as you will see, in *On Loving Women*).

Indeed, my past girlfriends all remarked how astonished they were that our **lovemaking** kept getting *better and better* with time. I'll never forget the girlfriend who even shared this intimate detail with her girlfriends. After that admission, her girlfriends, from week to week, requested an update. They'd ask:

"So, has it gotten *boring* yet? Sex eventually gets a sameness to it. Hasn't that happened to you yet?"

And she'd tell them, "No, in fact, it gets *better* every time!"

The interesting thing was that *they refused to believe her*. The men in their lives had apparently run out of ideas, sexually, and had allowed the passion to flame out. So, for these women, sex had devolved into a disappointing, *humdrum* practice. And they never thought that situation would improve. How *sad*.

Unfortunately, that's not atypical. I spoke to many women over the course of several years regarding their past and current love lives in doing research for this book. Do you know what I found? *Practically all of them had become discontented with their lovers.*

This is shocking and appalling. Why is this going on? It is not *inevitable*.

And actually, I could argue that **love**making should naturally get *better* with time, *so long as your love for each other continues to grow.* After all, you should be getting to know her body *better* over time, so you should be getting *better* at ringing her bells. And your *passion* for her should grow as your love grows, so the *feelings* you express should grow *stronger*.

...Perhaps it's like music. Have you ever noticed how most songwriters and composers grew *dull* after the age of 30 or so? Yet there are those like *Beethoven* - whose music became more and more *exciting* over the years and decades. (*That's* how you want to be, as a lover - a **sexual whiz**, always coming up with something new and exciting - and I'll show you how!)

THE "MARRIED MAN'S ROUTE"

So *how do so many relationships instead hit the doldrums, sexually?* Horse racing, of all things, might hold a clue. Jockeys talk disparagingly of fellow jockeys who take the *married man's route*. In other words, the men riding the racehorses after getting married apparently often race too *cautiously* for fear of getting injured. So they don't win many races. They're too *timid* and *complacent* to accomplish much.

There's a parallel to this in **love**making (though not exact), according to the testimony of the many women I've interviewed. It seems that a lot of married men and men in *long-term relationships* assume they have their relationship "in the bag" - that it's so solid that *no further effort is required of them* in pleasing their partners. *They think they have the race won and they need not do anything more to impress or excite their lovers*. Yet nothing could be further from the truth (especially in this fickle world).

Don't forget: your lover is constantly bombarded with images of celebrated great lovers, the Casanovas, the Fabios, the Romeos. She sees these men in TV commercials, in TV shows, in movies, and hears of them in songs. She reads about them in *Romance novels* (and sees them on the book covers).

So if you're not constantly ringing her bell, her fantasies are going to rise up to the level of urgency where she's going to seek her Casanova.

...And speaking of the *married man's route,* many men I've spoken to have *admitted* (at least indirectly) they are taking their sex lives *for granted*. A car dealer, for instance, upon finding out I was writing this book, stuck

The Long-Term Lover's Unique Challenges

out his chest and claimed he no longer needed books such as this one, saying, "Oh! That's for *single* guys. I'm *married*. *Married guys* don't *need* that sort of stuff!" He then laughed, smug and over-confident, as though he *had it made. Has he not heard of the 66%* **divorce rate**?

This would be akin to a rookie baseball pitcher, upon reaching the majors, telling a pitching coach and former Cy Young winner: "I don't need your advice or anyone else's any longer, thanks. I'm in the *majors!"* Yet the truth is that players who reach the majors need advice more than those in the minors, so as to deal with the better players in the majors and the bigger challenges that come with that…and so as to succeed and *stay* in the majors, and, hopefully, improve enough to justify *a long-term contract!*

THE SPECIAL CHALLENGES LONG-TERM LOVERS FACE

The paradox is that, while most men think a long-term relationship or marriage *lessens* their requirements and responsibilities as lovers, the *opposite* is true. In fact, comedian Bill Cosby made that point years ago. With his inimitable sense of humor, he said something akin to:

The hardest person to surprise in bed is your wife.

Your wife (or long-term lover) can get real *familiar* your **sexual repertoire** - if it's limited (as is the case, reportedly, with most men). And if your repertoire is slim, it won't go that far. *What might wow a one-night-stand gal for its novelty or your long-term lover the very first night you're together will not wow those women if you're still doing the same thing the 100th time you're with them.*

That means that if you're married or in a long-term affair, your **repertoire** and **sexual artistry** must be far <u>greater</u> than when you were a carefree single guy. You must become *more innovative* in order to please and delight a wife or lover of many years. You need to put in *more*, not *less, effort.*

If you have a limited "bag of tricks," and you ply the same-old-same-old moves on her with ever-decreasing passion, she's eventually going to start dreaming of someone else. **Great love**making is the way to a woman's heart, my friend, and **boredom** in bed is the surefire way to *kill* your relationship. So is **neglect** and **incompetence** between the sheets.

Your "job" is not *over* because she's lived with you for a number of years or decades even. It's not "over" after you put the ring on her finger. For *it's never too late for her to <u>leave</u> you.*

And many women I've interviewed for this book left their husbands *after 20 or more years of marriage!* And mostly for the same reason: **neglect** in

On Loving Women

the *romance* and **love**making departments.

So I think you now can see that *this is the biggest mistake most long-term lovers make - thinking they no longer have to work on their* **love***making skills. They also err in thinking that any complaints from their wives or lovers about their love lives can be ignored without consequence.*

A Cautionary Tale

One woman who shared her most intimate stories with me for this book eventually got divorced because of this phenomenon. She'd had two children with her husband, but there was something wrong in bed. *After about 20 years of marriage, her husband had yet to give her an* **orgasm***!* (I wish this was an uncommon complaint among women, but it's *not!*)

According to her, *sex would only last "three and a half minutes, from start to finish."* He'd **come** *quickly* and then he'd jump out of bed *without pleasing her*. She'd beg him to stay in bed with her and try to figure out how to make her **come** but he turned a deaf ear to her.

She finally dragged him to a series of *sex therapists* and *psychologists* but he refused to read the sexual material or advice she procured for him, arguing that *she* was the one with a problem and not *him*.

One day, she finally *had enough*...the day he turned to her and said:

"There's just one *mistake* I've made in this marriage..."

(She told me she at first got *excited* upon hearing that. She thought he was finally going to admit to having made a mistake. But that hope quickly faded when she heard the *rest* of that sentence.)

"...I should have made you seek *intensive psychiatric counseling* <u>years</u> ago!"

That was the final straw for her. And I have to say I side with *her*. That was a *terrible* thing for him to say - especially when *he* was the one who was coming up short as a lover.

If a man cannot last in bed more than a few minutes, that's an **impediment** *to pleasing a woman*. And it's the *man's* problem and not the woman's. (You'll find solutions to most control problems in the chapter on "Achieving The Ultimate Control" on page 93.)

If a man cannot make his woman **come**, it's the man's problem and not the woman's. (You'll find innumerable ways to make your love come in many chapters later on, including the ones on "Female Sexual Anatomy" on page 173, and "Cocksmanship" on page 339.)

The Long-Term Lover's Unique Challenges

And if a man doesn't want his woman to leave him, he must own up to his shortcomings and do something to overcome them. (And that's where this book comes in!)

The truth is that most *women are normal. My experience has been that most women can be given* **orgasms** *- and* **multiple** *ones - without much effort.*

And - by the way:

Intercourse ideally should last at least a half hour if not more, as a general rule. *(This is what women want, as you will find out later).*

So unless there are *extenuating circumstances, any good male lover should be able to please his woman in bed.*

THE ONLY WOMEN WHO MIGHT POSE CHALLENGES

The only way you can truthfully say a woman is difficult to please in bed if she:

- ☢ is on **medication** that has bad **sexual side-effects**
- ☢ has terrible **phobias** that make her fear penetration
- ☢ has **mental illnesses** that interfere with a healthy sex life
- ☢ has a **physical problem** or condition, such as **vaginismus** (where an involuntary tightening of the **vaginal muscles** makes it hard to enter her)
- ☢ has suffered **surgically-caused sexual nerve or other physical damage** that limits her **sexual sensitivity** and/or ability to come

But even if you're dealing with one or more of these impediments, a sensitive and knowledgeable male lover can often overcome these legitimate **challenges**. *(I've been with women who had all of these problems and successfully found a solution in almost every case.)*

Said in a different way:

If your woman is healthy and <u>without</u> impediments - the onus is on you to fulfill her **sexual potential**. *And if you don't, someone else will.*

This is the equation long-term male lovers often don't get - again, according to the many women who were interviewed for this book. Some spoke of husbands who, like the car dealer, thought **romance** was only for the pre-marriage courtship phase. Some said their spouses didn't even say "Goodnight" at night, or "Goodbye" when they left for work! Some said their husbands never complimented them about anything, making them feel worthless and unloved. Some said their husbands no longer kissed them.

On Loving Women

Finally, many said their once-passionate *sex lives* had degenerated into once-every-other-week (or less) events. And the **sex** was a *disappointment*.

My talks with *men* about sex over the same period of time, in fact, *validated* at least some of what these women had said. The car dealer wasn't the only one with an attitude problem. Lots of guys seem to feel that a *long-term relationship* or *marriage* justifies *laziness* or outright *neglect* as a lover.

A guy with whom I was playing poker, for instance, scoffed when he found out I was writing this book: "That's *not* for *me*. I'm *married!*" And he proceeded to play cards with a table full of men until 3 a.m. the following morning! This was on a Saturday night when, without work the next day, he should have, by all rights, been making love to his wife!

I could only imagine what his wife would say about him as a lover! What kind of man was he to her? Her *pillow* was more of a man than he was!

I was single and not dating at the time. If I'd had a lover, I'd never have left her alone like that. I love playing poker, but, unlike many others in my generation – men and women alike - *I don't place obstacles in the way of my love life or my relationships. And now that I'm married, you won't ever find me at a casino late at night. That's a special time, to spend with my wife and my wife alone.*

SWINGERS HAVE IT EASIER

So where does all the **complacency** *come from, that makes men neglectful? And why do few realize that becoming a great lover is a* lifelong *pursuit - that one must always be a student, looking to learn more about women and* **female sexual anatomy** *so as to get better and better? (Like anything else, you cannot rest on your laurels. You either get* better *with time or you get* boring. *And you can only get better by studying the latest sexual information and through intelligent experimentation.)*

I think many men lapse into **complacency** because they are fooled by the reactions they get on the first night or two of intimacy with their lovers. I think that's why so few recognize their need for sexual education. Perhaps a woman's tendency to be very loving and tolerant of imperfections and shortcomings also misleads them into thinking they're better than they are as lovers.

The yeoman lover's experience is very deceiving. For it's relatively easy for any simply adequate male lover to thrill a new lover for one night. And it's relatively easy for one virginal lover to thrill another. Everything's new. You're naked for the first time together. That's a big deal. You and she are *really hot*.

Not so much a few months into the relationship. It's not so easy to thrill her many nights later. And this is probably why many women say that few lovers keep the excitement going for more than a few months - at *most*.

I believe *few men understand this*. They thrilled their lovers on the first night, so why can't they do it on the 100th night?

They don't get it. *They don't realize they need to raise their skills to a higher level if they want to be a lover who can thrill a woman the 100th time around - let alone the 1,000th or 10,000th time around. Now that takes skill.* (Which you'll learn here.)

This is what I've heard from innumerable women over the course of the nearly 10 years I've been researching for this book. They say the average male lover quickly becomes predictable. Boring. He has a limited bag of tricks and, in bed, the *same-old same-old* becomes *old* really fast.

LONG-TERM RELATIONSHIPS COME AT A PRICE

That's bad news for the male monogamist, the man who wants his woman to stay with him forever. In other words, **monogamy comes with a price: the need to become better at love**making **than the rest, to keep your lover happy for a lifetime, to make her want to stay with you forever.**

Anyone who sleeps around has an easier time of it. They can get away with a limited palette of sexual "tricks" and a poor understanding of *female sexual anatomy* because their *sometime* lovers won't get to know them all that well. And their sexual encounters will ride on the *first-time lustful excitement* that quickly fades and must give way to something more substantial in a long-term relationship, if it's to work.

So if you're like me - you want to settle down with someone special forever and thrill them for a lifetime - you need to recognize this fact:

The special challenge of the long-term lover is to constantly become better, to keep lovemaking **fresh.** *(And that's what this book is all about.)*

And you should want your **love**making to be **more** thrilling with time, not *less*. **Unpredictable** and **surprising** even. Because *if it's not getting better for her, it's getting worse. What worked last night will not work tonight.* The shine will have come off it. *Newness* brings with it a unique excitement. *Predictability* brings with it a certain *boredom*.

THE CONSEQUENCE OF NEGLECT AND POOR LOVEMAKING

Even worse - **neglect** and **poor love**making lead to **discontent**. And that's something to guard against. Most every woman I spoke to for this book who said she was **discontented** with her man had either already *sought a divorce* or a *break up* or was *contemplating* such a move. *With a lack of romantic attention, their relationships no longer meant much to them.*

Meanwhile, I was struck by the fact that their men were obviously *unaware* of how unhappy they'd made their women by being so sorely lacking in the **love**making and *romance* departments. I often wondered what their husbands and lovers would have *thought* had they heard what their wives and lovers were telling me. They would have been totally surprised. I doubt they'd have been so smug and confident about their relationships had they known the truth.

Or would they? What would the men involved have *done* if they could have heard their wives and lovers detailing their shortcomings? Would they have realized that *they* were in the *wrong*, and that *they needed to dedicate themselves to becoming better lovers – or risk losing their women?*

If this isn't *a wake up call for most every man*, I don't know what is. And even if you're not among the guilty, this is a cautionary tale for one and for all: **If you're not doing all you can to romance and love your woman, she is undoubtedly complaining about you to someone like me. (This is, incidentally, how affairs often begin.)**

Women won't usually tell you if they're disappointed with you, as a man or as a lover. Most are afraid of hurting their men's feelings; or afraid of getting them *upset*. (And, in their defense, all too often men turn off the invaluable feedback spigot by being closed-minded and quick-tempered.)

The point is – while the oft-repeated phrase *"Sex is not the most important thing in a relationship"* might sound comforting, make no mistake: Sex – actually, more accurately, **skilled love**making - is *crucial* to the success of a relationship. Especially to *today's women*, who have *nurtured* their *sensual and sexual sides*.

And if you were thinking, "This book isn't for me, I already know everything," then you are actually *most* in need of it. Because *a truly great lover never feels he knows everything*. In fact, the more a great lover learns, the more he knows how much he doesn't know. An accomplished lover realizes that a lifetime is not long enough to acquire all the **sexual knowledge** there is to attain.

So when recently I heard one poker player claim that poker is "better than sex…and it lasts longer," I was amazed and disappointed. Because I absolutely disagree. On both counts.

The Long-Term Lover's Unique Challenges

Why can't **love**making last as long? It does in my house!!!

Get with it, guys!!! **Love**making, love, romance…and women…are God's biggest *blessings* to us. Try spending the same number of hours you're currently spending with your poker pals or bar buddies in bed, naked, with your lover, and tell me it isn't much more fun!

If you – like the poker guy I quoted above – don't know what to do for hours at a time in bed, stick with me. I'm going to give you a lot of great information that will open your eyes and rev up your love life to the max – for which you'll thank me many times over.

Because I think if truth be told, the reason many men leave their wives or lovers alone to play poker, or go off on hunting or golf trips with the guys, or watch TV endlessly, or simply stop being interested in sex, is that *they've run out of* **sexual ideas**…My hunch is that they know they're not very good in the sack, but they don't know where to turn to become better. So, they run away from their problem.

And if that scenario fits you, don't worry any longer. You've come to the right place. Let's get your love life on the right track. You can do it. All you need is a little help, from a friendly mentor.

It's Like Dancing In A Way

And it's no more difficult than *dancing*. And actually, in some ways, it's very similar.

If you've ever been into ballroom or disco-type dancing, where both partners dance as a unit, you've gotten an inkling as to what's involved in being a great lover. That's right.

The man, as the leader, must constantly think ahead to plan the next moves. To keep things interesting, a good leader tries to mix things up, so his partner finds it creative, surprising even, and fun. If he's a great dancer, he even comes up with dance steps of his own, with a style all his own. If he's not, all of his moves are reminiscent of dance moves you were taught in dance classes.

What you need to know is that it's your duty every time you make love to surprise her. Do something different. Better. Give her *more* **orgasms**. *Bigger* **orgasms**. Different **orgasms**, from *different* **orgasm triggers (many of which you are likely unaware right now)**. Make her come more *quickly. Harder.*

And you'll learn how to do all of that - and more - very soon, in On Loving Women.

Think about it, there must be higher love
Down in the heart or hidden in the stars above
Without it, life is wasted time
Look inside your heart, I'll look inside mine...
I could light the night up with my soul on fire
I could make the sun shine from pure desire
Let me feel that love come over me
Let me feel how strong it could be...
Bring me a higher love...I could rise above on a higher love.
   - From the song "Higher Love" by Steve Winwood

A Higher Love: The Spiritual Side To Lovemaking

To reach the highest **love**making **heights** requires that you *see* **love**making and **love** in the right way. As a means to a **higher consciousness** and **joy**.

This was perhaps what Robert Duvall, as cowboy Print Ritter, was trying to express in the movie *Broken Trail*. His take on **love** described a **yin yang** spirituality:

"Romance is for pikers. I ain't talking about *infatuation*. I'm talking about something way *beyond* romance. *Bone* deep.

"You feel it just between the two of you. Now, if you stub your right toe, the left toe feels it. *Ain't no he or she or you or me.* You're both just *one*."

A Higher Love: The Spiritual Side To Lovemaking

That's what I'm talking about in On Loving Women. **Transcendental love** - and its **expression** in **love**making that takes you to such *heights of ecstasy* that it almost feels like *a religious experience*. This is a thrill I've experienced many times and you can, too, if you approach **love**making from this perspective.

In fact, many of the world's religions see the act of **love**making as a means to achieve a *higher* form of consciousness. As a *spiritual* event.

We all know about the Hindu *Kama Sutra*. That ancient religious guide to life includes a healthy dose of sexuality as means to achieving **a higher state of being and bliss.**

The ancient Chinese Taoists believed in the concept of *Yin Yang*, a religious view that encompassed sex. The **physical merging** accomplished a **spiritual merging**. The man and woman were just two halves of a whole.

In the article "The History of Female Ejaculation" in *The Journal of Sexual Medicine* (May 2010), researchers Joanna B. Korda MD, Sue W. Goldstein and Frank Sommer MD wrote:

> "Ancient Chinese writers wrote openly and in great detail about sex, believing sexual intercourse to be the foundation of life. The concept of Yin and Yang embodies a philosophical perspective of all existence, that heaven, earth, creatures, and forces of nature are all determined by these contrasting but interconnected and interdependent forces that are constantly in motion. Together they are considered to embody Chi, the universal energy. The purest and most concentrated form, Ching is released in women and men at the moment of orgasm."

I like that. The **orgasm** as a *means to tap into the Universe's energy!*

The ancient *Kabbalah* - expressing a mystical form of Judaism - also said the *physical expression* of **love** could be a means to the deepest spiritual fulfillment. *Kabbalah Inspirations* author Jeremy Rosen explains:

> "...the Kabbalah gives sexuality a special place in unifying the physical and the spiritual worlds...On one level this means that sex should involve intellectual, emotional, moral and spiritual aspects. More profoundly, it also means that sexual pleasure is **a legitimate means of getting closer to God.**" [my emphasis]

If you can share that idea with your lover and make her see the potential for the **highest consciousness** that can be achieved through <u>selfless</u> **love**making, then **love**making will become more *meaningful* to her. (As will your relationship.) You must both imagine your souls intermingling as one, the **love**making process, a trip to Heaven.

It then becomes *nourishment for her soul*. It becomes a *necessity*.

On Loving Women

That's what my lover was trying to express one day when she walked over to me and gave me a tender embrace.

"Our **love**making is so **profound**," she said. "It means *so* much."

"It's magic," I said.

"Yes," she replied. "It is truly **magical**."

Our **love**making had *moved* her. It had given her a higher pleasure, satisfaction, a feeling of **Love** with a *capital "***L***."* A feeling of having *arrived* someplace *higher* - and of wanting to stay there forever.

That's **love**making at its best. When you *move* your lover. When you reach her *deeply*. On an *emotional* and *spiritual* level.

Then you've really achieved something. You've bonded like two aimless Oxygen atoms that suddenly join together to form something *bigger* and *better* - an O_2 molecule, *breathable air, an essential necessity*. Your merging creates a *whole* that is *more precious* than the two *halves*, and the two halves are now *inseparable*.

When you've accomplished that, she will *value you* and *your relationship* as much as *life* itself. That's a big reason to seek that level.

But you must give **love**making that kind of *importance*. You must *elevate* it to that level.

How? You need to have a certain kind of **attitude** or **perception**. Great **love**making at its height **requires** a *spiritual awareness*. And an almost **religious devotion** to each other...and you must try to imbue your lover with this view. It is something special. What you share should not be taken lightly. It's an almost miraculous process; the greatest blessing we've been given.

The moment you enter her, you should imagine yourselves physically and spiritually becoming one - your souls opposite poles of a magnet, inexorably drawn together by powerful magnetic forces of passion and love. See yourselves as being brought together by Fate...or a higher power... for Eternity...with the absence of ego. Because a **higher love** is a <u>selfless</u> pursuit. You think of her, not yourself. It's a giving act, not one of taking.

And it should be almost *ritualistic*. Given that kind of *respect*. And *importance*.

To get into the *right frame of mind* you must think of yourselves as *two halves of a whole*. Think of her as the *Yin* to your *Yang*. You were made for *her* and she for *you*.

A Higher Love: The Spiritual Side To Lovemaking

It's a magical mystical moment and that idea should be in your thoughts and feelings. You should envision the whole process as being *mind-blowing* in order to get into the right *mindset*.

Or it might help you think in terms of the way the Bible described it. Isn't the relationship of a man to a woman sanctified, miraculous and preordained in a very special way? *We fit together beautifully because we were created for each other.*

Doesn't the *Song of Solomon* in the *Old Testament* exalt physical love? Doesn't that teach us how fervent our **love**making should be? And how, in our devotion to each other, we find the ultimate happiness?

If you can get in tune with that concept, if you can add a layer of spirituality to your intimate relationship, you will be amazed to find your **love**making brings more satisfaction, contentment and Love.

You are part of her; she is part of you. You are made whole by your coming together.

Isn't that a beautiful way of seeing things? And guess what? If you see it in that way, she will too.

And if you see it in that unselfish way, you've prepared yourself for the most *perfect* **coming together**. (In fact, I've sometimes thought that a ritualistic, respectful, loving and thankful ceremony at the start of **love**making might be sexy and fun - as well as putting the event in its proper perspective.)

It's A Celebration

But, please understand: When I say **love**making should have a *foundation of spirituality*, I don't mean it should be a *somber* event. *Far from it!*

I like the idea of **love**making being a *celebration*. Whether you want to celebrate the miraculous nature of your union in **love**making, or the wonderful fact that you have found each other, or the *gift* of being able to find supreme joy in *coming together as one*...**love**making should always *be a joyous celebration*. This is an idea the ancient Taoists promoted. And I think there's a lesson there for all of us.

Keep that in mind, in your quest to *soar to the Heavens* with your lover, and you'll soon find you're attaining greater joy and satisfaction through **great love**making. Like anything else, what you *invest* in your effort and the *mindset* you bring to it determines the *results*.

> *"I will be your Shining Knight, be your Romance novel hero,*
> *I would risk my life to save yours in a fray,*
> *I would go to battle for you, I would stay with you through fire,*
> *I will love you when the stars no longer shine, my love."*
> *- From the song "Romance Novel Hero" by Rick Brown*

Becoming The Type Of Man Women Desire

There's an old movie, *Double Wedding* with debonair actor William Powell, whose sentiments on what it means to be a **man** are still right on. In this film, Powell's character gets exasperated talking to a goofball named *Waldo*. You see, Waldo wants to *propose* to Irene but he can't *man up* enough to do it. So Powell tries to teach him what being a **man** is all about:

"It's the way you **talk**, the way you **look**, the way you **stand**." And he chides Waldo: *"You look at a woman as if she has a trench coat on."*

That scene is as true today as it was in 1937. Forget all the **sexual role confusion** of the past 50 years. The truth is and always will be that most **women want their men to be...men. Masculine. Confident. Smooth. Sophisticated. Sexy. And a woman wants want you to look at her in a way that tells her you see her as someone who's extraordinarily sexy and special. They want to see appreciation and attraction in your eyes.**

If you've been fooled by all the *unisex crap* of the past half century, *get over it*. Don't be like a super-liberal older friend of mine whose wife has made him a *politically correct* **wuss**. She's trained him to deny there is such a thing as *masculinity* and *femininity* - or any difference between the sexes! So when I told him a girlfriend of mine was **feminine,** he went into a rage.

"Feminine?" he growled. *"What is feminine?"*

"Well," I said, "I'll *tell* you what *Webster's* says about that." Grabbing the dictionary, I read the following: **"'Feminine: having qualities traditionally ascribed to women, as sensitivity and gentleness.'"**

Just for fun (because I suspect his wife is bisexual), I looked up how *Lesbians* described themselves in their singles ads. Guess what I found?

Becoming The Type Of Man Women Desire

Many wrote they were a "butch" (translation: masculine) woman looking for a "feminine" partner! And *vice versa*. So even *Lesbians* see sexual relationships as the natural bonding of *two polar opposites*. That is, even *they* accept and *celebrate* the **traditional sexual roles** - with one partner being *masculine* and the other being *feminine*. We're all in agreement!

So *even today* lovers prefer adopting the *ages-old masculine and feminine role models, even in homosexual* relationships. Even in our cynical, unromantic world. ***And if you don't recognize this, you will fail as a lover.***

If you're not yet convinced, consider this: *I don't see any hetero couples on the dance floor where the <u>woman</u> is leading. I haven't heard of many couples where the <u>woman</u> proposed marriage to the man. I haven't seen any couples where the <u>woman</u> gave the man a diamond engagement ring. I don't know any marriages where the <u>man</u> has taken the woman's surname.*

After a woman's gotten dressed up to go out, she wants you to compliment her on her looks. She wants you to hold her door open for her. She wants you to say you love her. These are <u>feminine</u> traits. (Men don't require this.) And you'd better rise to the occasion, as a man, and fulfill her desires or she'll likely feel you're not man enough for her.

In my experience, most women want you to be **confident**, **sexy** in a **masculine** way (with an *understated power* and *grace*), **capable**, **romantic**, **thoughtful**, **warm, kind, sophisticated** and **a "take charge" kind of person**. If you do not adopt these qualities, you'll likely be seen as a *disappointment*.

The fact is, men who do not fulfill the traditional masculine role are often disrespected by the women they love. My grandmother had a *saying* about such *undesirable* men. They were, she said, *"no one to take to the table."* They didn't supply a woman with the type of *companionship* women desire, and were, ultimately, an *embarrassment*.

The Queen Of Soul Will Tell You

Aretha Franklin hinted at this in a *CBS Sunday Morning* interview when she was asked if men were intimidated by her fame. Maybe, the reporter suggested, men who were attracted to her did not approach her because she was larger than life. Her answer went something like this:

"That may be true. But **real men** cut through all of that."

A lesson from the Queen of Soul. Aretha Franklin is telling you that **women want you to <u>man-up</u>. They're looking for a "real man."**

Think Cary Grant. That man could walk. He knew how to dress. He knew what wine to order. He knew how to look at a woman, how to treat her,

On Loving Women

how to hold her. He was the man every woman wanted to be seen with.

And guys, there's no doubt: *When it comes to **love**making and **romance**, women want us to **lead**. And they want us to be **great lovers who can last as long as they want us to**.* (You'll see *scientific proof* of that in the *control* chapter.) Women want **the complete package**.

OUR BRAINS ARE DIFFERENT!

Hormones are powerful personality shapers. So are the *differences* between women's and men's brains - *physiologically*.

That's right! Scientists have *proven* that women's and men's brains are *different - structurally and biologically. This, I contend, is what shapes women's unique desires and sexual role preferences*, among other things.

The startling scientific findings were announced in the British newspaper *The Independent* in July 2008:

"*Men and women show differences in **behaviour** because their brains are physically distinct organs, new research suggests. Male and female brains appear to be constructed from markedly different genetic blueprints.*"

The Independent quoted a *New Scientist* article:

"*One study, by scientists at Harvard Medical School, found that parts of the frontal lobe, which houses **decision-making and problem-solving functions**, were proportionally larger in women, as was the limbic cortex, which regulates **emotions**. Other studies have found that the **hippocampus**, involved in short-term memory and spatial navigation, is also proportionally larger in women than in men... The mere fact that a structure is different in size suggests a difference in functional organisation,' says Dr. Larry Cahill of the Centre for the Neurobiology of Learning and Memory, at the University of California, Irvine.*"

And - FYI - *your lover's* **hippocampus** *is also associated with* **sex!** (See page 135.) **These scientific studies *prove* and *explain* why women are *different* than men.** Not *better*. Not *worse. Different*. They have *different needs. Desires.* Ways of *seeing* things. And *Amen* to that, brother! *Viva la difference!*

Becoming The Type Of Man Women Desire

THINK CLARK GABLE IN GONE WITH THE WIND

...But you have to understand what that means to you, as a lover. If you're uncertain, go back and watch the famous scene from *Gone With The Wind* in which a drunk Rhett (played by the manly Clark Gable) chases Scarlett around the house after an argument. Catching her at the bottom of the staircase, he holds her and says: *"It's not that easy, Scarlett."* He then puts her in a bear hug and plants a huge kiss on her. She tries to resist him but is not strong enough to do so. He then vows: *"You turned me out while you chased Ashley Wilkes, while you dreamed of Ashley Wilkes. This is one night you're not turning me out."* He then picks her up in his arms and carries her up the staircase. It's obvious *he's going to have his way with her*. (And to the *finger waggers* who might read this: *that was not a rape* scene.)

The next scene shows Scarlett waking up the next morning, *a big smile on her face*. With a contented, *"Mmmmm!,"* she *stretches with satisfaction* and everyone in the movie audience knows what *that* means.

Wow! And say what you want; *that remarkable scene speaks to a common fantasy among women. They want to be swept off their feet.* (I saw a documentary recently in which an actor who'd been in the movie recalled that, *"Every woman watching the film wanted Clark Gable to carry them up the staircase too!"*)

That scene drew some controversy at the height of the Women's Movement. But the dust has cleared, the boxing gloves have come off and guess what? *Women are back to being themselves.* (And thank God!) You can see it in the way women *dress*. Cleavage is stressed. Strappy shoes are paraded about, revealing sexy bare feet. Short dresses show off beautiful legs. But – even more important – you can *hear* the attitude change in what they're *saying* about themselves...and *men*. Women are *celebrating* their *womanhood* and *femininity* worldwide. (Isn't that great!)

But wait a minute. This affects *you* in a way you might not have thought about. *Because as women have become more feminine, their visions of what they want in a man have changed too.* They're not talking about wanting "sensitive" men anymore. They want *masculine* men.

That doesn't mean you have to be a body builder to be manly. And that definitely doesn't gives you the green light to be *insensitive*. It just means that most women desire a man who *enjoys being a man*. One who *doesn't* "celebrate his feminine side." One who knows how to treat a lady.

Don't take my word for it. *Ask women what they want from a man. They'll tell you.* A Santa Fe woman told me recently what *ended* her marriage:

On Loving Women

"We changed over the years. As I got older, my feminine side got stronger. As my husband got older, his feminine side became dominant, too. That didn't work."

GET INTO YOUR MASCULINE SIDE

Another woman, from Tucson, had a similar gripe about her ex-hubbie:

"I was always the one who had to be in control, decide what we were going to do in bed. I don't want to be in control. I want to be treated like a woman."

Get it? Women everywhere are saying the same thing. *Forget the bull about getting into your "feminine side." Get into your **masculine** side!* Don't be a *wimp* or become *feminized* in a wrongheaded effort to seem *overly "sensitive." That's not what most women want.*

There's a great scene in the remake of the Dudley Moore movie *Bedazzled* that demonstrates this. It's where the male lead, played by Brendan Fraser, asks *the Devil*, played by Elizabeth Hurley, to make him a *sensitive* man - because he thinks is what women *want*. So she grants him that wish. Next, you see him on a beach, on a date. He's acting "sensitive," but instead of being pleased, his date is *repulsed*. She sees him as *effeminate*. Within minutes, she leaves with a *manly* man she meets.

Funny scene. But it reflects *reality*, too. *Women want a man to be a man.* Yet - as you saw above - many of the women I interviewed for this book complained about the *lack* of manliness in their men. One said:

"After the Women's Movement came out, men stopped being as assertive romantically as they used to be – as if they were afraid of being called 'insensitive,' or being accused of worse. I long for the way things were before the Women's Movement began, when men weren't afraid to romance you, take charge and seduce you!"

There's a lot to be learned from that cry. And I say that because I see a lot of confused men out there. They don't apparently understand what *role* they should be playing in their women's lives. They don't seem to know what they need to do as *men* to please their women. Every day. All day.

And the average man (according to what I've been told) deals with his confusion by becoming *lazy* at playing the role of the *man* and *lover*. The trouble is, *a lazy man and lover will eventually be put out with the cat.*

Don't you see that there's a reason why sales of those steamy *Romance novels* you see in every drug store, bookstore, airport shop, and convenience store are reportedly going *through the roof? Those books, featuring a masculine guy sweeping a woman off her feet represent a deep-seated desire in most women.* So take a few lessons from those books.

Becoming The Type Of **Man** Women Desire

The guys in those books aren't concerned about appearing politically correct or "sensitive to women." Don't get me wrong – *you must always be kind and loving to women*. But you must never make yourself a *wuss* for fear that someone will criticize your sexual moves. As you can tell from the Romance novels, *women want a man to make advances* (if the man is one to whom they're attracted). And *women want men to provide them with a romantic, sensual, sexy lifestyle*.

The heroes in Romance novels, for one thing, know how to **seduce**, **romance** *and* **make love** *to a woman. They exude* **confidence, masculinity, testosterone** *and* **sexuality.** (You can too. No matter who you are.)

The women in Romance novels are "taken," in a loving way, by the male heroes of the stories. In the face of the *Romance novel hero's* **sexual power**, the female character cannot resist him. Even if she tried. The female leads *swoon* and want to be made love to, spontaneously, *upon first meeting these men*. Their **manly, sensual and sexual presence** is that compelling.

This should tell you something. *Something's lacking in the lives of the millions of women who read Romance novels*. And it also tells you that women want **romance** and **passion** as well as a **great lover**. They want a man who makes them *crave* his **love**making.

Like the Romance novel heroines, a woman wants you to *desire her passionately - as if you cannot help yourself because you're so overwhelmed by her charms*. And like the Romance novel heroes, you should never take your woman for granted. Your **passion** should never cool. And you should strive to be a cut above the rest.

There might be a few *dominatrixes* who want *submissive* men, but they're in the *minority*. The truth is that *most women dream of men who take control and sweep them away with a tidal wave of* **passion**. As the date coach (played by Will Smith) in the movie *Hitch*, counseled:

"Basic principles: no woman wakes up saying: 'God, I hope I don't get swept off my feet today.'"

The popularity of the Romance novel among women is worth noting for another reason. *Yes, these books might be expressing their dreams. But they are also teaching women what the ideal man is all about.* So they'll be measuring you against the Romance novel heroes they read about.

Guys – it's your job to be your lover's *Romance novel hero*. *In* and *out* of bed. And part of this equation means you need to *take charge* of making the *romance* and **love**making work; to take *control* and make *magic* happen.

And when making love, *think of yourself as a* **love**making **dancer**. On the

On Loving Women

dance floor, the man *leads*. The same thing is true in *sex*. *The man **leads***. On rare occasions your woman might take control. But in my experience this doesn't happen often, with most women. A woman is not *biologically* or *socially* conditioned to be the aggressor in **love**making.

Ask any woman – she'll tell you. Most times, she wants you to be prepared to lead, be the *creative* one, the one with *ideas* and *moves* to satisfy her. And she wants you to lead in such a way that the **love**making will be an *incredible* **experience**. And in leading the **love**making *"dance,"* you need to set the right **mood**, make the experience **sexy** and **exciting**, and make your woman feel like a highly desirable, super-sexy woman.

Being Handy And Helpful Is Sexy Too

But you also need to be an ***all-around*** lover. Always **considerate**. Always **loving**. Always a **good partner**. Especially when <u>not</u> making love. This is what Madonna was telling you in *Express Yourself* when she sang:

Long stem roses are the way to your heart
But he needs to start with your head
Satin sheets are very romantic
[But] What happens when you're not in bed?

A woman wants to feel *loved* and *cared for*. She wants you to do for her what she feels a *man* should do. And *that includes being <u>handy</u> and <u>helpful</u>* around the house, to help make the house a <u>home</u>.

One day my wife, for instance, told me she'd excitedly told her co-workers what I'd done around the house the night before: "You know what's **sexy** about him?" she told her co-workers breathlessly. *"He fixed two of our toilets last night!"*

"That's nothing," said a co-worker. "Tell us when he *cleans* the toilets."

Without missing a beat she responded: "He did that too!" (I did.)

"He's a *keeper*," said another co-worker, genuinely impressed.

Get it? That's part of what *you* need to do, as a *man, to make your woman feel <u>loved</u> and <u>cared for</u>*. (An added bonus is that it's *sexy* to her!) If you don't believe me, try it and watch her reaction!

That's right. She used the word *sexy* to describe my *handiwork!* And she enjoyed *watching* me doing the repair jobs! I've seen this kind of behavior in other women before. They are actually *turned on* by watching men *being resourceful* and doing *physical work! Sex often follows your good work.*

But you earn a much bigger benefit when you pitch in around the house. She'll become a better partner. She'll pitch in more. And she'll become

more womanly, more feminine. Believe it or not, this is absolutely true. It might take some time, but the transformation is remarkable. So get with it!

AND WOMEN LOVE SWEET TALKERS WITH THE GIFT OF GAB

And, by the way, are *you* **positive** and **confident?** And *do you have something to say?* My mentor Earle taught me years ago that women want to be around **charming, sweet talking** men with the **gift of gab**. For *sweet talking*, Earle recommended finding an outstanding feature to *compliment* the woman about. But, he warned, it needs to be something *unusual* that no one else has praised, ad infinitum. For *gab*, Earle was *well-read*, so he always had something *interesting* to say. Staying *interesting* is *especially* important for the married guy or long-term lover. Grow dull as a person and you'll dull her interest in you sexually. **(That's the flip side of how her mind works as a sexual organ. If she sees you negatively, she will cease being sexually attracted to you.)** And **make her laugh**. Women are attracted to men who make them laugh. Create a **fun atmosphere.**

It also helps to be *smooth*. One girlfriend validated this idea when she told me one day, "I bet you impressed a lot of women with the way you undo a *bra* with *one hand!*" *Being suave turns women on.* Work on it.

Being talented at something helps, too. **Women are turned on by men who demonstrate a mastery of music, athletics, dancing and other interesting pursuits.** So if you have a talent, do it well. She's watching.

So...can you **make her feel special, valued and loved**, grace her world with **happiness**, **support** and **kindness, entertain her** and *then* **rock her world as a lover** (*after* fixing the toilets and caulking the skylights)? Are you fun, romantic, masculine, confident, sensual, cultured, sophisticated, well-read, well-dressed, nice-smelling, conversant with the opposite sex, caring, helpful, handy, capable, a **connoisseur of women**, a **suave** man who knows his way around a woman - physically, emotionally, spiritually...a man who makes his woman feel good about herself (making her feel *desirable* and *attractive*), a man who exudes confidence, masculinity, sensuality and sexuality? **This is what she wants!!!** You must be a *desirable and lovable man* if you want her to desire you *sexually*.

I'm not talking about grovelling or being smarmy. Think *James Bond*. Or *Sean Connery*. Be *cool*, as they say. But never *cold*.

You don't have to achieve the impossible. *Just become the best person you can be. If you can't be everything I described above, become everything you can be.* That's a worthwhile goal in and of itself. In improving yourself you'll develop more **self respect** - and that's attractive to women too!

> *"When it comes to sex, the most important erogenous zone is between your right ear and your left ear."*
> *- from God Never Blinks by Regina Brett*

A New Way Of Thinking

Bobby Jones, one of the world's greatest golfers, is famous for noting that, "Competitive golf is played mainly on a five-and-a-half-inch course... the space between your ears."

It's no different in **love**making. *Your most important sex organ is your* **brain**.

I know that some wise people have expressed that idea already. But few have explained what that means. I will try to do that here. Because *you cannot become a great lover if your* **thought processes, attitude and overall mindset** *are off*.

Even when it comes to the deed itself, you need to understand this:

Mindless **sex** quickly becomes *boring*. You don't want to be someone who can thrill a woman on a first-night basis but quickly grow dull with repeat performances that disappoint.

The number one lesson you must learn is that **great lovers** *think*. They use their **brains** to choreograph great **love**making sessions. They plan ahead, they use their creativity.

On one level, you're trying to out-think your lover. *A great lover anticipates what his lover thinks he will do and he does something* **else** *instead*.

My mentor Earle taught me when I was a teen to respect **women's brains**

A New Way Of Thinking

as being *superior* to men's. He was fond of saying:

"When you're thinking A, B, C, she's thinking X, Y, Z."

That's important to understand as a lover of women. She's thinking, too. *More than you.*

While you're merrily going on about sex, she's *anticipating* what you might do. If you're predictable, you're dead meat. She'll think less of you.

*So you always must **surprise** her.* To do that you must think...be creative... never repeat what you did recently.

Maybe you might recall how exciting it was when the *Beatles* came out with a new album. We raced to the store to buy it because we never knew what they were going to come up with. Every record was different, new, fresh. They were always getting better, pushing forward.

That's ideally how you should be as a lover. And how do you get there? With your **mind**.

Now I won't leave you hanging in the dark. I'll lay it all out for you in this book, what you should be doing. But I need to get your mind on the right track first.

How Your Brain Processes Women

Great lovers also view women in the right way. They have a **loving**, **kind** and **appreciative attitude** toward their lovers. More important, they're *forgiving*.

Someone who's not **forgiving** is unkind. And women *don't want to be with unkind men*. Keep this phrase in your head: *To err is human, to forgive, divine.* That's how you want to be toward you, don't you?

You cannot produce great **love**making if your **head** is in the wrong place.

Why Lust Screws You Up

Another thing:

*If you're coming from a lustful way of looking at women, you need a new way of thinking if you want to become a **great lover**. If **love**making to you is what takes place between the sheets, you need an attitude adjustment.*

If women to you are sex objects and you cannot help but leer at every one who walks by, you need to increase your awareness of what love's all about. You need to become more savvy about what makes women tick and what they're all about. You need to get more mature about what a mutually satisfying sexual relationship is all about.

On Loving Women

Love**making** is a *lifestyle*. And it's a healthy one. Not prurient.

Relax, though. I'm not taking the anti-male radical feminist line here. And I'm not telling you that you should not get **hot** over seeing *sexy images*.

What I'm saying is you can't be a **great lover** if you see women the wrong way. That hurts you more than anybody else.

Hear me out. For starters:

Looking at women lustfully instead of lovingly and humanely can help lead to premature ejaculation problems. (I cover that topic in detail, by the way, in the chapter, "Achieving The Ultimate Control" on page 93.)

It also can turn you into a leering letch. One of my relatives is like that, and I cringe for his wife's sake whenever he sneaks a look at every scantily-clad woman that walks by. He often tries to cover for his sins by complaining loudly that the women are not dressed properly but it's obvious to everyone around him that he's pleased they're showing some skin and he's lamely trying to cover up the fact that he's a letch.

That's a real unattractive trait. And, trust me, women pick up on that.

I'll give you another example of why a lustful mindset backfires on you. My wife and I saw a major TV talk show host recently make a fool of himself with Kirstie Alley (of *Cheers* fame). He was a *horn dog*. From the moment she came on the set.

"Look at that!" my wife said disdainfully. "His hands are all over her!"

During the interview, he was hitting on her nonstop. He kept making lewd comments and touching her in an obviously lustful way.

He was practically coming out of his chair, leaning over her lecherously. *She leaned way over to her right in response.*

"Look at that!" my wife said, annoyed with the host. "She's avoiding him!"

Lechery is **unacceptable behavior** *and women hate it*. It's produced by *a lustful view of women*. He might as well have hung a sign on his neck saying, "I'm horny!"

Kirstie was dressed in a low-cut sexy dress and she looked great. But he reacted to her as if she was a whore, looking for quick and easy sex, not as the fabulous person she is. She's witty, she's funny, she's fun. But all this guy could do was drool. He didn't realize it, but it was painfully obvious.

When the interview came to an end, Kirstie coolly shook the host's extended hand and then quickly leaned to her right to talk conspiratorially with her TV reality show dance instructor. She wanted nothing to do with

A New Way Of Thinking

the talk show host.

A **great lover** of women is not a *horn dog*. He's a **sophisticated gentleman** who makes women want him by the way he treats them, by the way he looks in their eyes, by the way he talks to them and shows them how enamored he is of them. **It takes the correct mindset to become that kind of man.**

And along these lines, yes, women, especially in today's world, are going to dress super-sexy on occasion. They're allowed to. So don't *gawk* for chrissakes! You should never debase or embarrass yourself by slobbering over them.

Always be the gentleman. Think Cary Grant. Clark Gable. Sidney Poitier. Sean Connery. James Bond.

Man up. Be the one who makes her melt. That's your proper healthy, mature role. *And treat her like a lady - always.*

Here's another point: Women who dress in a *sexy way* want to be loved. Plus, when they dress that way, *it gets them* **hot**. That's to *your* advantage.

You can compliment them on looking great. But don't make raunchy references to whatever that's showing. That only makes you look bad, low class.

Lust Doesn't Work In The Sack

Also - a *lustful attitude* is the *worst* **mindset** to bring to the bedroom. It leads to very unsatisfying sex for her.

Let me give you a what-if to explain why:

What if your woman saw you only as a sex object. She lusts for your body. That's what sex means to her. So every time you're together, looking out only for herself, she quickly jumps on top of you, bouncing wildly until she comes in a few minutes. She then rolls off you, content. She later gives you a hand job after she recovers, almost as an afterthought.

Romantic? *No way*. Fun? *Unh-unh*. Satisfying? *Not on your life*.

That's a *lonely* experience. It's *cold*.

Is that what you're giving women in bed? If you lust for their bodies and that's what it's all about to you, that's exactly what you're giving them.

If it's all about you and your lust for her body, what are you communicating? Selfishness? Coldness? That's what you're broadcasting.

Don't tell me I'm a prude. I love women as much as the other guy.

On Loving Women

But *lechery* only hurts *you*. It damages your ability to relate to women as they would like you to. With respect. With appreciation for who they are.

Women see through a lustful veneer. And it's totally unattractive. (Remember how we all wanted to puke when Jimmy Carter, President of the United States and a married man and father told *Playboy* magazine he sometimes had *lust* in his heart?)

Acknowledging that a woman is sexy or beautiful is one thing. That's natural. Coming off like a jerk-off is another.

Put your eyeballs back in your head. You've seen naked women before, right? Don't give off the wrong vibes. Horny is seen as sleezy to women.

You want a finer image than that. (And knowing how to strike the proper image is part of being a great lover.) You want her to respect you. You want her to *love* you. Show her your values are in the right place.

Gentlemen's eyes don't stray. Especially when they're with their women.

(My wife agrees. She commented, "Straying eyes are the worst!")

There's nothing more *insulting* or *unappealing* than a lover whose eyes are all about the room, leching for others in the room.

Make her feel she's all that matters to you, that she's the only person in the room with you. Make her feel she's special. That's how you want your woman to be with you, right? *This comes from having the right mindset.*

Plus - a lurid attitude hurts your ability to relate to women properly. Many men who see women as objects of lust and not love become intimidated by sexy, confident women because in their minds these women are all-powerful and..."up there" above them. In a higher class. Almost like rock stars you can't approach.

That keeps the men who see women that way from making the moves they need to make to attract desirable women. It produces a crippling fear of rejection.

Or they choose the wrong partners - based upon looks and not the person. Personally, I'd rather be with a small-chested woman who's an angel than be with a big-chested woman who's a bitch. But that's just me.

I'm also talking about this: Men who see women *pornographically* or *lustfully* instead of lovingly cannot connect with women on a human level. Because real women are far different than those who are depicted in come-on sexy ads, movies, TV shows, billboards, music videos and magazines.

Women are *three dimensional*. They're *people*.

A New Way Of Thinking

You're not going to find women like the ones you see in the media, sex kittens who are ready to service you like some prostitute, without strings. And thank God about that, too. Who really wants that, in the long run?

Being a **great lover** does not have anything to do with being *sleazy*. It has everything to do with being *classy*.

"The primary reason for loss of interest is that... women don't feel romanced and understood in the relationship."
- John Gray in Mars And Venus In The Bedroom

Romance & Affection 24/7

I remember the time a partner of mine, away on a business trip, phoned to tell me what she loved about me:

"One of things I love about you is that, when we're walking, anywhere, you reach out right away and take my hand! *I love that*, how you always want to hold my hand!"

Why do I mention this? **Romance is a necessary precursor to love**making.

How often do you hold hands with your lover? Do you do it while you drive? And don't tell me you drive a stick, so you can't – you can (I've done it). Do you do it when you're sitting at a restaurant? Do you do it when you're walking? Do you do it at the movies?

And – do you do it the right way? (Like anything else, there's a way in which to hold hands.) Do you do it with **affection? Feeling?**

The reason my partner loved what I did was not so much the physical action but also **the feeling of love** that came through my hand...the **feeling** it gave her of **being loved and being secure**...the **feeling of closeness and togetherness** it produced...the electricity that was generated due to the **passion** that came through...And the fact that I made **romance** a *constant*.

If you don't do that, you might find your lover's complaining to someone else about you. One of the women I interviewed for this book, for instance, criticized men *like her husband* "who don't pay attention to you during the day, don't *say* anything *nice*, don't *do* anything *nice*, aren't **romantic**, don't *touch* you even, and then expect you to be in the mood to have sex with them the minute they jump in bed. *It doesn't happen that way.*"

AN ESSENTIAL EVERYDAY ACT: THE SHOWING OF AFFECTION

And, while we're at it, let's talk about the overall topic I'm hinting at: the concept of **showing affection**. This needs to be a daily part of your life. And your acts of affection must *say* something. They should nonverbally communicate that you love her.

As you saw in an earlier chapter, *women's brains are physiologically different than men's* (refer back to page 47). This explains why a woman seems to operate on a *different* level than you. She interprets your physical actions *emotionally*. It's like a language to her.

You do something physically and she knows right away what's behind it. If it's love, great. But if you take her hand just to fulfill what you see is a woman's need (and it's not fun for you), she's going to interpret how you feel right away and not like it.

You might as well not do anything for a woman if you're doing it out of a sense of obligation; she'll pick up on that right away.

So, when it comes to acts of affection, understand: *It's not the physical act that's important; it's the* **feeling** *you're communicating.*

Now, if you don't like holding hands or showing other signs of affection, you need some self-examination. If you truly love women and you've chosen a great partner that you really love, be a man and show her.

This kind of thing should come naturally. And, if it's not natural to you, it will be in time – if you get in the habit of doing it. If you have warm feelings toward your lover, let her feel them in a way she understands.

If you're not showing your affection because it embarrasses you – publicly and privately – then you just need to get over yourself. This is part of being a grown-up. This is part of being a real man.

Not long ago there was a series of beer commercials on TV that suggested romantic, considerate and affectionate men were not real men. A huge beer can clobbered this kind of man on the head in one of those spots.

What was his sin? Lovingly calling his wife "sweetie" on the phone. And his buddies in the commercial accepted that as being proper punishment.

So I understand the peer pressure that might be making you afraid of being affectionate in public. But if your buddies are giving you a hard time about your acts of affection toward your woman, the solution is to find other buddies.

They're losers if they act that way. And what kind of relationship do losers

On Loving Women

have with women? Not what you'd want. I can tell you that!

If you'd rather please your buddies and be cold toward your woman, then reconcile yourself to living life alone. Because some man will come along who has no problem showing her affection and he'll take your woman away.

Now I've seen that some men have deep-seated psychological problems that prevent them from showing affection. If that describes you, please see a therapist. You're missing out on a beautiful thing.

Now, you might be saying to yourself, "What does this have to do with **love**making? I bought this book to learn about **love**making!"

It's true; the traditional view of things is that **love**making is sex and sex is purely a physical act that exists in a vacuum. But the truth is:

The quality of your sexual experiences with your lover depends upon the quality of your relationship. *If you want the best, most happy, most loving relationship possible, you must think of* **romance** *(which includes* **acts of affection***) as being an all-day, every-day kind of activity. Actually, think of romance as a* **lifestyle***.*

THREE CAUTIONARY TALES

This brings to mind an episode of the wonderful TV show *Shalom In The Home* with Rabbi Shmuley. It was about a troubled family whose husband and father – a firefighter (I mention this because this is considered a caring profession) – was absolutely tearing his family apart by his inability to show affection to his wife and kids.

They all felt unloved because he could not bring himself to hug them. He wouldn't even simply *touch them* in any way. Nor would he say, "I love you." Because of this, **his wife was about to leave him** and his daughter hadn't spoken to him in months. Plus, behind his back (unbeknownst to him) **his own daughter was urging his wife to seek a divorce! All because he could not or would not show them any affection.**

Get the point? How could there be great **love**making in that relationship when the wife was practically over him? Wouldn't happen.

Great **love**making – or even good **love**making – cannot happen when the woman doesn't, for starters, love you. What goes on *between* sexual sessions matters a *lot*.

So, ask yourself: *Am I making my woman love me because of the man I am when we're not making love? Or am I neglecting her and turning her off to me?* (It's either one or the other.)

This reminds me of the story a very beautiful and intelligent woman in her early forties related. She bemoaned her defunct marriage, and her story echoed those I'd heard from the lips of many other women. She said:

"The reason my marriage fell apart is because my ex-husband felt that once we were married he didn't have to or want to work at the relationship anymore.' That's what he told me!

"There was *no more* **romance** once we got married…He told me he no longer needed to seduce me, that he 'had me' now – but that's wrong!…

"One thing I tried to tell him was that I needed him to touch me more… but he didn't listen to me!"

She wanted "flowers for no reason…for him to tell me I was the one he loved more than anyone else, that I was special to him," but he did not realize how deeply a woman needs romance. Therefore, she felt neglected. And she said, **"I finally didn't even feel like making love with him anymore."**

The **love** was gone. Killed by **neglect**. Killed by a man who had not a clue as to what a man should do for the woman he loves – every day, all day, all the time. Killed by a man who had allowed the **romance** to go out of his relationship, and who didn't even listen to his woman when she spelled out, in plain English, what she desired, as a woman.

Along these lines, there's a message, loud and clear. Men:

Do not ignore the often softly-spoken requests of your lovers, when it comes to love, romance and **love***making. These requests are often actually needs that must be met.*

If your lover tells you what she wants, something you aren't giving her now, *she's actually doing you a favor. She's giving you the chance to redeem yourself.* So you should be thankful instead of resentful when she gets up the courage to hip you to something you're neglecting.

Unless you want your relationship to end, don't ignore her requests for something more. She's saying *I cannot live without this.*

You ignore her pleas, it's a deal-breaker. Sooner or later.

That brings to mind the time when an executive at a prestigious club told me she was terribly disappointed with her singer-songwriter husband. She had told him many times for *years* that she wanted him to write a love song for her. *But he never did. A few months later, I heard she'd left him.*

What would it have taken for him to have penned a tune for her?

On Loving Women

SOME GREAT IDEAS IN THE ROMANCE DEPARTMENT

Speaking of which - if you have the talent and inclination, **write a love song for your lover**. There's nothing more **romantic**. And write the lyrics carefully and beautifully to show her how passionate you are toward her. Reveal it to her with excitement, as the thoughtful gift it is. Sing it for her. Better yet - record it for her, so she can pop it in her car stereo before or after work and be reminded of how much you love her. It doesn't get any better than that!

Or **write poetry for her**. Not baloney. Write it as well as you can. Quality stuff. With *unique* romantic and loving sentiments; about her. With *details*, to show her you notice and appreciate every little thing about her.

Or **make a romantic dinner for her**. With candlelight. And sweet music. But make it a gourmet meal. Something you know she loves.

Or do something else, something romantic that fits your unique talents. **Give her a great massage!** Don't tell me you don't know how. There are great books that teach you how. Read one. There are few things that please a woman more than a wonderful **sensual massage**. But you have to know your stuff. Half-hearted massages are just annoying.

Women still hope for and appreciate the old standbys too - **chocolates** and **perfumes**. For *no reason*. That takes such little effort. Yet I know of many men who have not given their wives chocolates or flowers for many years. It's pathetic. *It hurts their own relationship. And it hurts their wives' pride.*

Thoughtfulness goes a long way. If that's not been your path, wake up.

A **great lover** of women develops the skills that are necessary to **romance** women. If it takes reading hundreds of poems to learn how to write them - or just quote them when the occasion arises - you do it. If that takes learning an instrument to write a love song for her, you do it. If that means taking a cooking class to learn how to wow her, you do it.

James Bond is a fictional character but there is many a truth in the way he is able to bed women. *He's cool and sophisticated. He knows what wines to order with dinner*. If you don't think that impresses most women, you're wrong. (Maybe you should consider subscribing to a wine magazine or taking a wine class. That's a smart move for a man devoted to the *love*making arts. Do you know your Cabs from your Chiantis?)

Romance is a necessary precursor to lovemaking. **And part of this involves showing her you're a sophisticated lover. Romantic. Caring. Someone who loves women, and her in particular. Who understands**

Romance & Affection 24/7

women and has learned what it takes to make them happy. Who has schooled himself in areas that enable him to please women and make their lives nicer and more fun.

Most men don't need constant **romance, affection and reassurance**. But make no mistake my friend. *Women* ***do***. And you absolutely have to understand the **psyche** of women. A woman needs to know, every day, all day, all the time, that:

- *You see her as desirable, as a woman - so* **compliment** *her (and make your praises specific - but not the obvious ones others might tell her a thousand times a day)*
- *You care for her - express this with* **acts of affection**
- *You think she's absolutely fabulous - smile often and show her you're having fun just being with her through your behavior and comments*
- *You can't think of anyone else with whom you'd rather be - this means you don't talk about anyone else*
- *You don't see any other women in the room when you're with your lover - this means your eyes and focus are always on her*
- *You're listening to every word she says - you need to prove this by reflecting back to her what you've heard her tell you*
- *You think of her and miss her when she's not there - bring back something nice or call her to tell her you miss her*
- *She makes you* **hot** *for her, sexually - tell her at some point every day*
- *You love her company - tell her something nice like, "Do you know how much I love you?" (with a warm smile)*
- *You want to be close to her before and after sex, too - physical acts of affection go a long way, especially cuddling*
- *She's attractive - you especially need to point this out after she's dressed to the 9s for you when you're going out*
- *Your life revolves around her and depends upon her - let her know how much you appreciate her; thank her for acts of kindness*
- *You love her deeply, passionately - this needs to be expressed in fervent squeezes, pats on the butt, and so on, throughout the day; verbally, with those magic three words, "I love you;" and through passionate* **love***making (peppered with passionate verbal expressions)*

And when it comes to **affection**: *Never underestimate the value of hugs, affectionate kisses (as opposed to romantic kisses), hand holding, an arm around her shoulders, pats on the back, simple touches, the words "I love you," and other non-intimate expressions of love.*

The flip side of that is that *the lack of those expressions will doom your*

On Loving Women

love life. And it will threaten to end your relationship. Hence:

Lovemaking 101 Rule #1: *If a woman doesn't feel love from you in the course of everyday life, she's likely not going to be in the mood to make love with you. The feeling's not there.*

Lovemaking 101 Rule #2: *If a woman doesn't feel like making love to you, she will eventually not want to be with you.*

A woman sleeps with you and stays with you only if she loves you – the "you" that she experiences when you are *not* making love. If you are not **lovable** during those times, she won't feel like making love to you later on.

A woman might go through the motions (while fantasizing about someone else). But she'll eventually likely leave you if you are not *lovable*.

A LACK OF ROMANCE KILLS RELATIONSHIPS

One of my partners and I came together largely because of this kind of thing. She had been married to a man who, over the course of many years, showed her no **affection**. After nearly 30 years of this, she finally had enough of it. She left her husband for me. (Don't be angry with me, though. I did nothing to encourage it. I was as surprised as her ex- that she chose to leave him.)

Her husband was shocked when she told him she wanted a divorce! After <u>all the years</u> they'd been married he thought he was in like Flynn. After all the decades she tolerated his bad behavior he must have thought she'd stay no matter how neglectful he was!

Once she told him the relationship was through he halfheartedly tried to make changes he thought would please her. But it was too little, too late. *Lose a woman's heart and you'll likely lose her forever.*

…And - going back to the story I told you at the start of this chapter - *a good measure of how well you're doing as a man and a partner to a woman can be found in how often your lover tells you what she loves about you.* If she *rarely* or *never* does this, then you're not doing enough to make her feel special and loved. **If you're making your woman happy, she'll tell you.** You have to **earn** a woman's compliments. You have to be the man and lover she's dreamed of. There's nothing like hearing your lover praise you as a man. But it doesn't come by being a couch potato. It comes from *being a good partner, making her life beautiful and doing giving acts freely*.

So, this is where you need to be honest with yourself. If your woman is not effusive with praise of you as a man and lover, you need to get up to speed – and quickly (before it's too late).

Romance & Affection 24/7

TOGETHERNESS IS WHERE IT'S AT

When's the last time you took your lover out to a great play? To a fabulous museum (very romantic!)? To a sports event (if she likes it)? To an outdoor concert? The symphony or opera (if she likes that)? To a vineyard or winery (if she's into wine)? A happy and classy piano bar with a lively entertainer?

If she's into dance, there are some really awesome troupes out there. Take her to a sensuous dance performance by Pilobolus or Momix. Or go to one of Cirque du Soleil's romantic shows. Man if that doesn't put her "in the mood" I don't know what will!

Is she an outdoors kind of woman? Take her skiing (if she's into it; you can take lessons if you don't know how). Take her kayaking or canoeing (so fun!). Go camping if she's into that. Take her to a quiet romantic getaway for the weekend. Golf together. Join a coed softball or volleyball league.

If you don't know anything about cultural activities or sports and she's into those things, then no matter. There are books and courses that will teach you what you need to know. Get cracking! That's the kind of thing great lovers do!

When's the last time you took her to a nice women's clothing store and bought her a fabulous dress, or sweater, or jewelry? Get her something she would love. The gift doesn't have to be expensive, by the way, to make her day. Just thoughtful.

In fact, romance and thoughtfulness doesn't have to cost a cent. Here's a sampling of *free* romantic activities that will stir her heart (if done with a *light loving attitude*):

♡ *Take her to the beach (scores you lots of points)!*
♡ *Take bike rides together (that's too much fun!). (Don't have bikes? Buy them! Good bikes don't cost that much. Or rent them!)*
♡ *Go for long romantic walks, hand-in-hand - in beautiful parks; by a lake, river or an ocean; or in the mountains (somewhere special).*
♡ *Walk the dogs together (if you have them); dog-friendly beaches or parks are especially fun.*
♡ *Take her to a free outdoor event you know she'd like. Many cities and towns offer free summer concerts, dance performances, plays and other special events. Bring wine and cheese while you're at it.*
♡ *Take her to a free concert at a museum.*
♡ *Take her somewhere to watch the sunset! (Don't forget the wine!)*
♡ *Gaze at the stars from your deck, balcony or a blanket on your lawn.*

On Loving Women

♡ Find a gorgeous secluded spot along a river to picnic; or bring some wine and cheese and just savor the sounds and beauty of the water.

♡ Take her to an art gallery. That can be real romantic. (But do your homework first; make sure the artwork is pleasing and not disturbing!)

Sharing fun activities together is another great way to make love to her mind. And togetherness makes her heart grow fonder.

COMMIT RANDOM ACTS OF AFFECTION & THOUGHTFULNESS

Are you paying attention, incidentally, to her tastes in food, wine or liquor, clothing, perfume and jewelry? *That's what romantic men do.* That's part of your job as a **great lover**. What does she like? *Dislike?*

And if you're a loving, caring, and giving man who loves his woman, all of this should be *a labor of love*. Done gladly. That is, being the kind of man your woman wants should be done with a sense of joy and pride. If you feel it's drudgery, then you need a *huge attitude shift*.

Today's woman is not willing to put up with what her mother put up with. If you want to keep your woman, you have to be the kind of man she wants. You have to be a good partner, affectionate, and a caring, skilled lover.

Never forget: **There are men out there who know how to make a woman feel special. If you're not one of them, your woman will eventually find a man who is. Women want a man who makes them feel special.**

And – FYI: *Acts of* **affection**, like **hugs**, benefit *you*, too. There's nothing more healing or energizing or satisfying than a hug. If you can't feel the exchange of warmth, love and energy when you hug your lover, then something's wrong. If two people love each other, their hugs (when done long enough and with enough passion) should leave them feeling as if they have a halo of happiness and love surrounding them. And medical research has shown that hugs and other acts of affection actually improve your health. It's so easy to do. And it doesn't cost a cent.

So get into good loving habits. But do it right. Do *acts of affection* freely and *regularly* through the course of a day. But do them *with* **feeling**. Let her know how you really feel toward her. Let her know she's loved. A *lot*.

And through these deeds, let her, in the way you do them, know that you appreciate her. You have no idea how important that is to a woman.

They talk about the "laying on of hands," in a religious or medical sense, of how desirable and beneficial this is to a person in spiritual need or a patient who needs healing. The same principle applies to the lover – she needs you to "lay on the hands." Do it and watch what happens.

Romance & Affection 24/7

A foot rub at the end of a hard day goes a long way. A neck or shoulder massage works wonders too.

Or just reach out and hold her hand. While you watch a movie, TV, play, lecture. While you take a walk or drive. While you sleep.

And, by the way...spooning at night is likely one of her favorite romantic activities. Some women also like it if you tenderly hold one or both of her breasts while doing so (*motionless*).

...*You see, romance doesn't have to cost a cent to count a lot.*

Oh - and being **considerate** is part of this picture. Help her with the dishes, do the lawn and the laundry - especially if she's busy or ill. Cook her favorite dishes for her. Make her chicken soup when she's not feeling well. Put her to bed early if she's tired or sick. Bring home something she told you she loves or wants.

Thoughtful acts *show her you think about her. They show her you* **care**.

Make her coffee the first thing in the morning. Bring it to her in bed.

Go food shopping with her (if she likes that). Or if she does the shopping, greet her at the door and bring in the packages for her. Offer to do an errand she needs to do.

You know the most romantic thing ever? Just enjoying being together. Doing <u>anything</u>.

Don't be cloying. But be available, helpful, giving, caring, thoughtful, loving, considerate, affectionate, romantic. In a <u>manly</u> way. <u>Be</u> there for her. Show her you've got her back.

...You know, shortly after I started writing this book, my lover at the time told me that one of girlfriends had asked her if she'd *read* it. She excitedly told her, "I don't have to read it. **I'm <u>living</u> it!"** The point is – don't talk the talk. *Walk the walk.* **Make your woman happy. Make giving her romance and affection a 24/7 kind of thing. It doesn't end after you've first won her heart. It's that simple. It's that easy. And if you love her, you'll do it <u>happily</u>. Then watch what happens. The rewards won't only be hers. She'll <u>love</u> you for it!**

(And FYI: The five most romantic things to do to her in bed? Gaze in her eyes. Hug her. Kiss her. Caress her all over. Tell her you love her.)

> *"Pornography is supposed to arouse sexual desires. If pornography is a crime, when will they arrest makers of perfume?"*
> *- Movie director Richard Fleischer*

What You Don't Know About Hygiene & Grooming

Years ago a woman who knew I was writing this book was after me to put a chapter in here about, in her words, **hygiene**. I told her I was indeed planning on writing a chapter on that very subject.

But it took months before it dawned on me to ask her this question:

"Just curious," I said. "Why is this issue so important to you? What do you want me to tell men in this chapter?"

She sighed deeply.

"It's just that my ex-husband and I used to have knock-down drag-out fights about this. For example, he'd pet the dogs just before bedtime and I'd ask him to wash his hands before he got into bed but he refused."

The reason it was so important that he wash his hands? She didn't want him putting his fingers inside of her if they were dirty.

That's an incredibly sensitive issue to a woman. A woman could suffer major health consequences if the germs on your dirty hands cause an infection inside of her. That's no joke.

But her husband didn't get it. Or he didn't want to.

"I think it was a control issue," she posited.

That's a major reason why he's now an **ex**-husband.

Now unless you want to become an **ex**-lover, maybe we should have a

What You Don't Know About Hygiene & Grooming

chat about **hygiene** - and while we're at it, **grooming** too. Obviously *this is a crucial issue to women.*

Hear Me Out

Perhaps you're the consummate gentleman, sophisticated in every way – including all matters of **hygiene**. Then, you might feel this chapter is not for you. Perhaps it's not.

Skip this if you feel you're totally on top of it.

However, I have been told by many women over the course of 30+ years that many men do fall short in this area.

And an eHarmony survey of hundreds of thousands of its members (released in February 2011) found that poor hygiene was among the Top 10 deal-breakers for women.

So, bear with me to make sure you're not unwittingly turning off your woman as many men do, by being unaware of what women want men to do in the way of maintaining their bodies.

Bad Hygiene Kills Relationships: Real Stories

Just recently, a woman in her 70s told me this story about a boyfriend she'd left many years before:

"Johnny never brushed his teeth and he had terrible breath. I hated kissing him."

"Couldn't you suggest, in a diplomatic way, that you wished he'd take care of his bad breath problem?"

"I told him – many times. I'd say, "Did you brush your teeth today?"

"He'd respond, "I brushed them yesterday," and he'd laugh. "Or he'd say, "What are you telling me, that I have bad breath?"

On Loving Women

"I'd say, "Yes!" But he wouldn't do anything about it!"

"I'm surprised you put up with that," I said.

"Yes, and I was with him for seven years!"

Johnny's **bad breath problem** tortured his lover. It was a *turnoff*. The man was an adult. You'd think he would have known how to take care of himself. You'd think he'd be aware of what women want from a man in the way of cleanliness.

But he was sorely lacking. And because of that, Johnny was seen as a lesser man, ignorant even. An undesirable lover.

She left him and all she could think of for years afterward was his bad hygiene. Not the way you want to be remembered, is it?

And you can bet she told every female friend about Johnny's bad breath. Not the kind of reputation you want, is it?

Bad breath is one of many hygiene deal-breakers. It's no joke.

There's no excuse for it. **Brush** after every meal. **Floss** after every meal. (Stuck food creates unpleasant odors.) Use **mouthwash** too. (Swish it around in your mouth for 15-30 seconds, or it won't work thoroughly.) *Do all of this before making love, too!*

An early-morning brush and mouthwash is a good habit, too, because that way she won't shun your early-morning kisses. Bad breath and sticky teeth are especially a problem if not treated when you first awake.

If you're on the road and you can't brush or mouthwash, try: a) a sprig of parsley if available at mealtime (that works wonders - keep some on hand at home just for clean breath purposes!); b) parsley-based breath pills or others that act on your stomach to reduce odor sources there; and/or c) breath mints or sprays (I don't use sprays anymore, though, because they've gotten a negative connotation, associated with womanizers).

...Here's another story: A woman in her 30s complained to me that her lover never clipped his nails.

"That's so nasty!" she commented. "Especially long toenails on a man!"

...Another woman complained that her boyfriend didn't change his underwear every day. (Yech!!!)

If you're ticking off your woman on matters of **hygiene**, *you're not going to be seen as sexy, sensitive or sophisticated. In fact, you're likely to be making your woman dream of being with someone else. And, like the women above, your lover will be complaining about you to other people!*

What You Don't Know About Hygiene & Grooming

Trust me. If you're being insensitive on this issue, she's definitely complaining about you to her girlfriends. So you're creating an image problem for yourself that will have larger ramifications possibly for years to come! Others (who, unbeknownst to you, know about your bad breath or ugly long nails or smelly underwear) will see you in a negative light.

SMART LOVERS LOOK FOR EFFECTIVE COLOGNES

If you aren't using **cologne** to your benefit, shame on you. Today's **sophisticated man** wears **cologne**.

I'll never forget the time one of my lovers, shortly after we'd gotten involved, cuddled with me and gave me this compliment:

"Mmmmm! You even smell good!"

She then asked me what I was wearing.

If a woman does that, she's telling you that you're being everything she wants – to her you're a great lover and *a sensuously appealing man*.

It also indicates she's been with many men who don't smell good. She's also saying your cologne is the perfect turn-on.

If you'd have heard all the compliments women have given me over the years about how nice I smell, you'd realize how important this is to today's women. And I can't tell you how nice it sounds when your woman coos, "Mmmm! You smell soooo nice!" What it says to me is that my cologne is sensual, *sexually enticing* and even *arousing* to her.

The right cologne can be very *seductive*. And – if you don't wear cologne – some guy who does might come along and, with a whiff of his cologne, he might win her over. (It also speaks of sophistication to her.)

It's a competitive market; you must muster all the wiles you have at your command.

So…what do you need to know about buying a cologne?

Number one, don't buy a cheap scent, or an aftershave. You want a quality cologne. Mine – I alternate between two right now, and I sometimes actually mix them – generally cost about $50 for between 3.4 to 4.2 fluid ounces. Yes, it's expensive, but it lasts a long time and it's very important to the way you come across to her. A sexy scent is like an aphrodisiac. And it says worlds about you.

You don't need to buy more than one cologne, but you should try as many as you can in order to find the one that will be your *signature* scent – the one that says *you*. You need to try it on, too, on your skin, because your

On Loving Women

unique body chemistry changes the way each cologne smells.

If you can find an *uncommon* scent, one that's especially appealing, that will go a long way with a woman. Ask the salesperson for help if you're not sure.

Women have a much sharper sense of smell than men do. And one of the first things your lover does upon meeting you is to identify your scent and evaluate it – if it's a quality aroma, uncommon and wonderful, she'll think of you more *highly*. And, if she encounters someone else wearing that scent, she'll instantly think of you.

But don't go cheap. In the old days a cheap aftershave lotion sufficed. Those days are gone.

Women are much more sophisticated today. If it's a cheap, unpleasant scent, or one that overpowers and sickens her, you're going to turn her off.

On the flip side, *avoid buying the most fabulously popular scent of the day*. Ask the salesperson what colognes are *overly* popular so you do *not* buy one of those. Otherwise, you're going to smell like every other man and not accomplish what you want to accomplish with your cologne – namely, *imprint your own fabulous scent on her consciousness.*

My mentor, Earle, taught me years ago, to be aware of potential body odor problems and to ensure that I always smelled nice. He wore **colognes**, which he mixed himself.

That's smart. Earle was a real **ladies man**.

If you want to be desired by women, you need to apply a *quality cologne* after every shower or bath. I also like to apply cologne to my neck and torso just *before going to bed, before making love,* and at *times when it's possible (but not certain) my partner might want to make love.* For that reason, for instance, I'll apply it when first going to the john after a night's sleep; women often like having sex before work.

And, by the way, colognes only last so long. Few last more than an hour or so, at most.

So if she's coming home from work and you haven't applied a cologne in hours, spray yourself just before she arrives (just enough – not too much; a man with too much cologne is almost more offensive than one who smells from body odor). If you have a spray bottle, spray it once (about 4-6 inches away) on your neck and once on your belly. (You want her to enjoy going down on you). If you're using cologne without a sprayer, put your finger over the end of the top, turn it upside down to wet your finger, and use

What You Don't Know About Hygiene & Grooming

only the moisture clinging to your finger. Dab it on your neck and belly.

Women are highly scent-oriented. If she loves the cologne you use (and that's a big if), you'll be surprised how much this will work in your favor toward making her desire you all the more.

Your scent will play on her mind, be a source of memories that are rekindled when she encounters colognes wafting in the air throughout the day, and be **a turn-on that makes her want to make love to you more than she otherwise might.**

It's your job to find nice scents. Go to a quality store and ask the gal behind the counter to let you sample the better colognes. Ask for her point of view. You'll ultimately want to have at least three great scents from which you can choose each day. If you use just one and she's likely to grow tired of it.

And make sure she likes them. (She'll tell you. If she doesn't compliment you on the scent, it's not a keeper.) Also:

Try to choose colognes that are not worn by every man. You want to smell unique. *Avoid the strongest ones, too.* A woman's nose has been proven biologically more sensitive than a man's, so she will probably hate the scents that arrive before you do.

WHY HANDS AND NAILS CAN BE DEAL BREAKERS

There's a great line in the Paul Newman movie *Hombre* that probably goes over the heads of most men who hear it. It's where a sexy woman tells a man she's just met, "Your nails are so clean!" It's a **turn-on** for her.

I experienced a similar event. Years ago a woman, on our first date, took one of my hands in hers and marveled, "Your hands! They look so young! And they're manicured!"

Well, no, they were not manicured. But because I take care of my hands, it made her excited.

It's obvious *women appreciate that.* Yet I believe very few men think about their hands.

It's not even on their radar. Few men have a *clue* as to how much women really *care* about their hands.

A typical woman will scrutinize your hands before you make love to her. She'll watch to see if you wash them before coming to bed.

And, yes, women are concerned about your *nails*. Women watch to see if you trim your nails *regularly* and *carefully*.

On Loving Women

Why? This is very important:

They want to know there are no sharp edges that might cut them internally when you enter them with your fingers. Nail cuts inside a **vagina** are very painful. They can also cause nasty *infections*.

Nails should be kept short, well-trimmed and clean at all times. If they're long and dirty (or worse, full of fungus), she will be disgusted and she'll probably decide you're ignorant, uncouth and undesirable. Even if you manage to establish a relationship when you have a nail problem, she'll be bugged every time she looks at your horrible nails. It'll work against the mood when you're intimate.

It makes sense:

Your fingers will sooner or later be inside of her. **No woman wants you touching her most intimate places with dirty hands or fingers whose nails are razor-sharp.**

So, be honest:

Are you washing your hands *immediately before making love?* Make sure you're using warm or hot water, too! If you come to bed with cold hands, that might tick her off. It will provoke a negative reaction at the least.

Are you trimming your nails so they are smooth, short and *round* (edge-free) in front? In doing your nails, be sure to cut off the rough edges on each side of every nail. Use the curved center portion of your nail cutter for that. Afterward, feel them to make sure they feel completely smooth.

Also, during your shower or bath, after your hands have been soaking in the water for some time, push back your now-softened cuticles so they're neat and attractive.

These acts are so easy and fast to accomplish. And there's a huge payoff if you do all this:

It says to her you're a sophisticated and caring lover. It says to her you're worthy of her affection and devotion. And it says to her you love her.

Trust me. You'll score big points for keeping your hands clean and your nails trimmed before engaging in intercourse.

SPECIAL NEEDS IF YOU'RE UNCIRCUMCISED

If you're **uncircumcised**, you need to be more proactive on cleaning yourself regularly. Daily in fact. And possibly before sex too.

The foreskin produces and collects within its folds a substance called **smegma**. Its purpose is to lubricate the **glans**. But **smegma** quickly develops a *smell*. And it also is a great collector of *germs*.

In fact those working to reduce the incidence of HIV in Africa have found that male circumcision reduces the transmission of HIV by 60%! *That should tell you something.*

I'm not campaigning for **circumcision**. What I'm saying is:

Pull back your **foreskin** and clean it thoroughly *daily* and *before sex*. Keep yourself smelling good and your lover free of disease.

It's the considerate and kind thing to do. For your lover. She will appreciate it.

PUBES, BALLS, PERINEUM, ANUS

Smells also tend to accumulate in your **pubic hair** and in your **anal region**. It's a no-no to let this happen.

I can't forget the time I took a lover from behind only to have some *unpleasant anal smells* waft up to my nose. Big turnoff. It lessened her attractiveness to me. And it reduced my desire to use that position.

Lesson here: Wash your **pubes, balls, perineum** (the patch of skin between your **balls** and **anus**) and anal region every day. Possibly before sex too. Smells can build up during the day and a morning shower's effect may have long worn off by the time you're about to make love.

A **great lover** does this for his lover. A *smart lover* does this for himself - so as not to turn off his lover or make her think less of him or be less attracted to him.

Avoid the negatives!

Odors can be a **deal-breaker**. They can also make her less likely to go down on you. If you're wondering why she doesn't go down on you very much and you haven't paid much attention to your hygiene, that could be why.

A friend of mine from the Philippines asked me years ago: "Do you wash yourself after you go to the bathroom? With a wash cloth?"

At the time I didn't. She told me that the Filipino people did that and she was curious why Americans did not.

She has a point. And, actually, since I started doing that, I feel dirty if I cannot wash myself afterward. Tip: Keep some Handiwipes in your pocket or wallet. That will enable you to wash yourself before making love wherever you are.

On Loving Women

MATTERS OF THE COCK

And word to the wise (if you like **blowjobs**): Clean your **cock** – after peeing…and with every shower. If you taste bad, she's not going to want to go down on you.

PUTTING YOUR BEST FOOT FORWARD: ON FEET

A final word on **hygiene**...about your *feet*.

If your feet have nails so *long* they've become claws…if your cuticles are so ugly they're painful to look at…if there's *dirt* or *sock fuzz under your toenails - or fungus*…if they have *athlete's foot*…if your feet *smell*… you're looking for trouble. That could eventually turn her off so badly it'll become a serious issue, and it might even end your relationship.

You love it when she goes barefoot; it's a turn-on, right? Make sure your feet are a turn-on for her. Although women might not get turned on by your feet, they will definitely be turned off by your feet if you don't take care of them. (And some *will* get turned on if you go around barefoot if you're taking care of your feet! So don't miss out on that possible plus.)

SO AS NOT TO BREAK THE MOOD OR CAUSE PROBLEMS...

A side tip: Always go to the bathroom (if needed) before making love to her. Don't be afraid to affect the mood; only kids are in a rush to get it on. Plus, if you don't, you might accidentally pass gas during the act or lose your erection due to a need to pee! Use the excuse, too, to brush your teeth, use some mouthwash, wash your butt and put on some cologne - in erotic places.

You can handle this smoothly and even playfully.

"Hold that idea, honey," you could say. Or the childlike, "Baffroom break first! Be right back!"

Do it with a smile. She'll probably go to the john too.

ON GROOMING: DRESS FOR HER

On *grooming*: Not so very long ago, there was a quirky TV show *Queer Eye For The Straight Guy*. One of my partners got me to watch it.

The title was a bit of a turnoff but the show was great. The "Fab 5" of queer guys were a team of fashion and decorating experts who helped many a straight guy strike the right fashion statement in becoming super attractive to his mate.

With a great sense of humor and style, these fabulous guys helped many

What You Don't Know About Hygiene & Grooming

men in need to find happiness in their relationship. Through the reactions of the straight men's women after the makeover, they proved that if you look your best - through great clothes and hairstyles - you will thrill your lover, bond more tightly, make her love you more, and have a more romantic and happy life together. This fits in with my theme.

If you look like a schmuck you're not going to turn her on. You want to look like a *sophisticated, sexy man*. Even when going casual. Think *style* and *fit*.

You know how unkempt women are a turnoff? These days women are looking at unkempt men in the same way.

Spend some money on nice threads - especially for when you take her out. But don't let your daily duds be a turnoff either. They're supposed to seduce her (if you're smart)!

If you can't get straight on *fashion issues*, ask her to shop with you. (And always pay attention to her comments about what you wear, with an eye toward learning what she likes.)

Or find a good salesperson at a quality clothing store who can give you good advice. (But make sure she likes what you purchase!)

My mentor Earle used to point to Cary Grant and Sean Connery as models of how a sophisticated man should dress. Their clothes were "cut," he'd say (in other words, their suits and formal wear fit their bodies supremely; tailor-made). They always looked good.

If you don't think that turns women's heads, you're looking to lose your partner to a more well-dressed man.

How your *hair* looks matters too. Shop around and find a stylist who makes you look your best. And if you're going bald, consider shaving it all off (that often looks best).

But find out how she wants you to look. Every woman is different. Does she like your hair long, short or in-between?

I cannot emphasize this enough: *Dress for her.*

Does she like you in *sweaters* (with nothing on underneath)? Many women like this look. It's sexy, it makes them want to reach under your sweater to touch bare skin? Does she like V-necks or crew necks? *Find out.*

And FYI: If you can access old episodes of *Queer Eye for the Straight Guy*, check it out. I think you'll learn a lot. (Don't laugh. Those guys had a keen sense for what a straight guy should wear.)

> Carrie: Still faking it?
> Miranda: Yeah. [Men] can rebuild a jet engine, but when it comes to a woman... What's the big mystery? It's my clitoris! Not the sphinx!
> Samantha: It's not their fault! [Vaginas] don't come with a manual!
> - From TV's Sex & The City (Season Two, Episode Four)

Is She Faking It?

Who can forget the hilarious scene in the quintessential romantic comedy *When Harry Met Sally* where Meg Ryan's character (Sally) fakes an orgasm in the middle of a diner to prove to Billy Crystal's character (Harry) it's easy for a woman to do so?

That comes after the conversation in which Sally suggests that Harry's girlfriends might have been **faking** their **orgasms** with him. To which Harry, full of bravado, replies that it's ridiculous; no woman's **faked it** with him.

"How do you know?" asks Sally.

"Because I do," replies Harry with disdain.

"Right. That's right. I forgot. You're a man."

"What is that supposed to mean?"

"Nothing. It's just that most men are sure it never happened to them and **most women at one time or another have done it** so you do the math."

"You don't think that I could tell the difference?"

"No."

She then proceeds to writhe and *simulate* an **orgasm**. "Yes! Yes! Yes!" she shouts, gasping, pounding her hands on the table while everyone watches, mesmerized. "Oh God! Oh God!" she shouts and feigns completion.

A waiter then approaches an older woman sitting in a nearby booth. Having watched intently, she tells the waiter: *"I'll have what she's having."*

...Along these lines there was also the *Seinfeld* episode ("The Mango")

Is She Faking It?

where Elaine reveals she *faked* her orgasms with Jerry.

JERRY: You faked it?

ELAINE: I faked it.

JERRY: That whole thing, the whole production, it was all an act?

ELAINE: Not bad huh?

JERRY: What about the breathing, the panting, the moaning, the screaming?

ELAINE: Fake, fake, fake, fake.

JERRY: I'm stunned, I'm shocked! How many times did you do this?

ELAINE: Um, all the time.

Jerry later whines, "But I'm so good." (Often what most men think.) So Elaine tries to make Jerry feel better: "Jerry, listen, it wasn't you. I just didn't have 'em back then."

...Those were two funny scenes. But they expose a *prevalent* problem.

Why do I *know* this is true? Many of my lovers have told me they'd **never** been given an **orgasm** by prior lovers. It's clear that *many men are not skilled enough to give their women* **orgasms**.

And that's undoubtedly one reason why many sexually dissatisfied women are *faking it*. Indiana University's *National Survey of Sexual Health and Behavior* (released in October 2010), for instance, reported that:

> "About 85% of men report that their partner had an orgasm at the most recent sexual event; this compares to the 64% of women who report having had an orgasm at their most recent sexual event."

The study concluded that those numbers imply that up to 21% of women are *faking* their orgasms. (The survey respondents were largely college students, by the way.)

I think the true statistic is much higher. The ABC-TV *American Sex Survey* I introduced on page 17 said that *48% of their female respondents* had **faked an orgasm** at least once.

Another troubling statistic: *just 30% of the women said they had an orgasm*

every time they had sex. The 2011 *Playboy* Reader Sex Survey's numbers were worse: *59% of the women in that poll said they had* **faked orgasms**.

This is not good. There are *consequences* when a woman feels the need to *fake it*. The ABC study concluded:

> "...people who aren't satisfied with their sexual relationship are by far the most likely to cheat on their spouse or partner."

Syndicated columnist Ian Kerner agrees. In a recent column, he wrote:

> "...in my experience as a sex counselor, women who fake it consistently are also more likely to eventually stray...in search of sexual satisfaction."

Not surprising. In fact, many of my lovers have told me that they had *left* men because those lovers had failed to please them sexually.

Understanding A Woman's Motivation

And I can relate to why a woman might fake it. *I once faked an* **orgasm** *- and got away with it, too!*

Why? *To get it over with*. She was a lousy lover. She was like a dead fish. *It was such a drag that I didn't feel like continuing. In fact, I broke up with her shortly afterward.*

That experience gave me an insight into why some women resort to this tactic: to bring a quick end to *boring* or *incompetent* **love**making while trying not to hurt their lover's feelings.

It also demonstrates how important a warning sign a symptom like this can be. If your lover is faking it, your very relationship could be at stake. You cannot afford to *miss* or *ignore* this **red flag**. So we need to discuss all the possible reasons a woman might *fake it* and how you should react.

It's A Prevalent Bedroom Fear

By the way, if you're thinking your partner is faking it, you're not alone. Most men at some point in their lives fear their lover is faking it in bed.

The bad thing is that in the face of this fear, a man's imagination goes into overdrive. That inspires *thoughts* that can pose a threat to a relationship (and often needlessly). If you suspect your lover is faking the "Big O" you're likely to jump to conclusions and think you're a lousy lover (and/or feel *she* thinks you are). This can hurt your self confidence and sexual performance. Or it might make you angry. (And that would be regrettable.)

You also might conclude that your partner is being dishonest with you. Like a cancer, this suspicion can produce negative emotions that can destroy the foundation of *trust* essential to the success of any relationship.

So before you wreck your relationship on a hunch and lack of information, take a deep breath and relax. Let's look at this issue calmly.

Digest the information in this chapter before you act on your impulses. You might be misreading the situation and drawing the wrong conclusions. That might lead you to make wrong-headed accusations you'll regret later.

It is true that if she's faking it *might* mean your relationship is in jeopardy. She might not be getting what she wants from you in bed. (But if that's the case, don't you want to know it?) But it also might point to something else.

Is She Or Isn't She?

But, first things first. Are you really sure she's faking it? From what I hear, **most men do not know how to tell if their lover's faking it or not - which leads to nagging fears** (no doubt made worse by Meg Ryan's brilliant faked **orgasm** in When Harry Met Sally). That makes things more difficult.

So the question then becomes: How can you address this issue if you're not sure there's a problem? Fortunately, I can clear up that concern. *I've given you some useful tips on page 84 on how to tell if she's faking it*. Please read that section carefully.

But let's assume you're *sure* she is pretending to come. What should you make of it? And how should you handle the delicate issues motivating her to do that? Well, it depends upon the ***underlying reason***.

Problems Of Her Own That Might Make Her Fake It

Just because a woman's *faking it* doesn't necessarily mean *you* are to blame. There are many factors that can lead women to fake orgasms due to problems that have nothing to do with you, such as:

- ⚠ she has a **physical problem** (pain; nerve damage from surgery; physical damage from a hysterectomy)
- ⚠ **medication** *is interfering with her response (some drugs including epilepsy medicine, SSRI anti-depressants and birth control pills can dull a woman's sexual sensations and even prevent orgasms)*
- ⚠ she has **psychological problems** (phobias perhaps about being entered)
- ⚠ **she's not been honest with you** about her desire to be with you (she's really in love with someone else; or she's gotten involved

On Loving Women

with you to get back at someone else)

⚠ **something is temporarily bothering her** and she can't get in the mood (but she doesn't want to create a scene or spoil your fun by telling you)

⚠ she's experiencing **decreasing sensitivity in her genitals due to age**

⚠ there's a **sexuality issue - she's a closet Lesbian** and does not like hetero sex (some Lesbians unfortunately use men as "beards," to pretend to be straight - to please their moms, fit in, or attain career advancements, among other reasons)

⚠ least likely but possible nonetheless: **she could be a transsexual with orgasm difficulties** (this, of course, could be a **deal-breaker**)

Some of these problems cause women to fake it *all the time*. These are the ones I'd worry about most. *Some* of these problems, like temporary upsets, cause women to fake it *occasionally* (those are less worrisome; with time, the cause may pass - but you still need to get to the heart of the problem).

The point is, until you find out what the **underlying reason** is, be *kind* if you suspect your lover's faking it! Given the range of possible reasons, you need to find out what's going on. *Something's wrong* and *you need to* **do** *something about it*.

How Should You React If She Is?

If you are sure your lover is putting on an act in bed, that kind of thing is no fun for you or her. It's demeaning for both of you. And it reveals that there's a huge obstacle in the way of your achieving *sexual happiness*.

But it's difficult to figure out whether she's pretending in bed because *you're* not cutting it as a lover or *she* has issues. So you need to have a heart-to-heart conversation about it. That's where you begin: with a *loving* talk.

Be especially nice. You might to blame for the problem. Or there might be a medical issue that requires sensitivity and sympathy on your part.

(Continued on page 86)

IS YOUR LOVER FAKING IT?
Here's How To Tell: Be A Detective!

I'm the kind of guy who gets pleasure from pleasing his partner. So if a woman were to fake it, that would take a lot of the enjoyment out of sex for me. It would be a drag.

I can only recall encountering this once. There was a woman I dated briefly who exhibited this trait. It might have broken us up had her terrible temper not done so.

From the first time we'd had sex I noticed something unusual. She wasn't making any noises!

That made it hard to tell if I was pleasing her. I was getting no verbal feedback. Plus, it was a huge disappointment.

A clue as to what might have been going on came from an unlikely source. Around this time I saw the *Lesbian* movie *Kissing Jessica Stein* and a scene in that film seemed to echo my situation.

This was where the *Lesbian* complained to the otherwise-straight woman she'd temporarily won over as her lover: "How come you don't make any sounds when I'm making love to you? You seem to be enjoying it when I go down on you but I never know."

That struck a chord with me and made me wonder:

Was my lover a closet *Lesbian* who, like the straight woman in the movie, didn't feel comfortable during sex because she was going against her type? (In other words, was her lack of verbal responses a clue that she wasn't into hetero sex?)

Another clue: she always wanted to end sex quickly. And she did it by unrealistically pretending to ***come***, either by exhaling loudly or by going limp all of a sudden when she was on top.

When I raised the issue she denied she was faking it, which made it difficult to get beyond the problem. I suspected she was faking it for one of two possible reasons: to hide a debilitating medical problem or perhaps indeed she was a *Lesbian* (there were reasons to suspect this).

*It's important to know if your woman is having **orgasms** because you want to: a) be sure you're pleasing her; and, b) find out if there's something wrong.*

How did I know she was faking it?

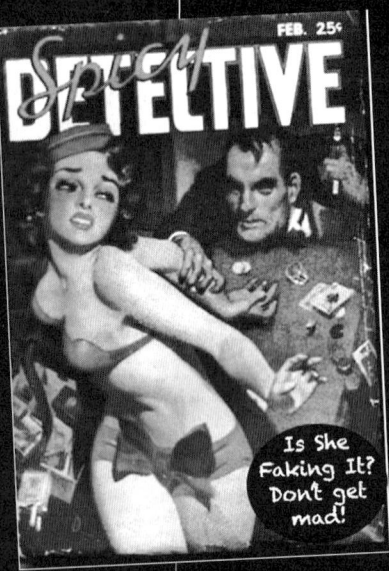

The Biological Facts

First, her **orgasm simulations** were pretty poor. Second, there was none of the typical biological feedback an **orgasm** produces.

A woman's **orgasm** goes on for 30 seconds on average. A strong one could last minutes. It does not come and go in a split second, as her **simulations** did.

And **orgasms** literally "blow her mind." See the latest scientific discoveries about this on page 138.

A woman does not **relax** during an **orgasm**. She's at the height of muscle tension and in a frenzy of nerve activity and sensations. Yet her **put-on climaxes** were gestures of **relaxation**!

Other evidence? Here are just some other telltale events that were missing:

- ⚠ her **vagina** did not change markedly during her feigned climax - it did not increase in diameter, wetness or temperature (all of which occur normally)
- ⚠ her **vagina** did not tense up beforehand nor did it spasm or contract during the supposed event (all the involuntary muscle movements that occur)
- ⚠ there was no downpour of hot **vaginal fluids** at the moment she indicated she was climaxing, as so often happens (and there was no wet spot on the bed)
- ⚠ her **G-Spot** did not swell up
- ⚠ her body's muscles did not tense up - not in her **neck, face, chest or arms**
- ⚠ her **breathing** did not increase (quite the opposite)
- ⚠ her **heart rate** did not increase dramatically
- ⚠ there was no **rash**; her skin did not turn red anywhere (not on her neck, face or chest, for example, which is so typical)
- ⚠ there was no **recovery period** after the event; she needed no time to get over the orgasm as is typical (except with nymphos)
- ⚠ she seemed no different after the supposed **climax** than she was beforehand

(For more on this see page 137.)

Smoking guns. Something was wrong. But what? We'll never know. Call this *The Case of the Missing Orgasm*. (Had the relationship lasted longer, I would have had to unravel this riddle.)

If any of this sounds familiar, you have an issue you need to resolve.

Is She Faking It?

(Continued from page 83)

Possible problem: *Some women will deny they're faking it even when they are.* That could make finding a solution tough.

That could mean the problem is *hers*. Or it could be your lover is denying there's a problem because *she fears a confrontation* or *she doesn't know how to break it to you diplomatically*.

The good news is that a woman in this category will eventually open up to you if you reassure her you won't react badly to constructive criticism. This is why I urge you to be *patient* and *persistent* if something's wrong.

IF IT'S YOUR PROBLEM, MAN UP

Unfortunately, all too often a woman fakes it because the *man* is not up to par. So if that's the truth in your situation, my first word of advice is:

Don't blame her for your inadequacies! The worst thing you could do is to get upset with her if you're the one with the problem.

Take a deep breath and pause before you make a fool of yourself and make the situation worse. If you try to pass the blame along to her when in truth it's all *yours*, think of how *ignorant* and *arrogant* you'll seem to her!

You can't fool her with bluster. She's likely been with men who can make her come. If you're not one of them she's likely wondering why you can't (and she's probably *annoyed* with you and/or *disappointed*).

Plus, before you (wrongly) say something unkind to her, you need to understand that if she's faking it because *you're* not cutting it as a lover, she did it to be kind to you. Her *faking it* was her way of being diplomatic; to avoid hurting you. A woman who *fakes it* because her lover is inadequate or lacking in some way does it *to spare her lover's feelings*.

THE SOLUTION MIGHT BE EASY

Bear in mind that your failings might not be from a technique standpoint. Maybe it's something that's *easily fixable*.

Perhaps she'll say you have *body odor*. There's a *simple solution* to that problem: you simply *shower or bathe often*. Or perhaps you talk too much. Simple solution: you *listen* more. Or maybe you don't set the proper mood or tease her enough before sex. Solution: you *learn* to do these things.

Keep an *open mind*. And be prepared to *work* on getting over your shortcomings, *whatever* they are, whether it's *easy* or *difficult*.

TAKE IT AS THE GIFT THAT IT IS

If she says it's your fault, you can either see this in a negative or positive

On Loving Women

light. I would hope you'd respond to that news as if it as a **gift**.

It is a **red flag** that you're not cutting it as a lover. Without this **wake up call**, you'd likely lose her. A woman who fakes it is an unhappy lover. (And women have a right to be picky, just as you do.)

It's true there's an outside chance you two are just incompatible in bed. But that's unlikely.

Most often your lover is telling you the truth if she says you're falling short in one area or another (unless she's *mean-spirited*, that is - but I'm assuming you're with a *loving* woman). A woman knows when a man is doing something wrong, sexually, so you should *respect* her feedback.

Even if you've pleased other women and you're simply not ringing your current lover's bell, so to speak, it's still your problem. If you love her and want her to love you and stay with you, you need to fulfill her unique needs.

It doesn't matter if past lovers liked you just as you are. You need to please the woman you're with. And *all women are different*.

It is true that there are women who are more difficult to please than others. But that's what this book is for. It teaches you how to satisfy them, too. In my experience, a good lover can figure out how to knock the socks off even the most challenging of lovers.

So *thank your lucky stars* if you've discovered she's faking orgasms - *especially* if your lover is doing it because *you're* not up to snuff. See this as a welcome **alert** that gives you the *opportunity* to **do** something about it *before it's too late*. You still have *time* to *make an effort* to *improve* and *save* the relationship.

START BY INITIATING A LOVING TALK

The solution? If your lover is faking the *Big O*, here's what I suggest:

Find a quiet and appropriate time to calmly and lovingly talk to her. Perhaps prepare a romantic candlelit dinner if you're good at that, or take her out to an elegant and romantic restaurant. Suggest to her that you both dress up for it.

Then, over wine perhaps, tell her you know that you haven't yet been the lover she's hoped for - but you are intent on becoming that man. Tell her you *know* she's been faking it. *Put her at ease* by saying *you know it's your problem and not hers*.

Tell her it hurts to know she fakes it because you want to be her dream lover and her faking it means you're not pleasing her. Then promise that you will do what it takes to become a better lover so she never feels the need to fake it anymore. Tell her that you've *already begun a* **plan of action**.

Here's Your Plan Of Action

Now tell her excitedly that you've found a great new book (this one), and you're studying it intently. (You should probably *show* her the book, too. She'll undoubtedly be impressed that you chose to read *On Loving Women* and you'll win some extra "points.")

Explain that you've just started reading this and you know it'll make your love life much better with time. Add that you're eager to try out some of the techniques you've already learned from *On Loving Women* the next time you two are in bed - *starting on that very night*.

But make sure you can back this promise up. Before you have this talk, you should have read enough of this book to really wow her the next time you're together. Make sure, at the very least, that you've read the sections covering **female sexual anatomy** and **orgasms**. (And you should have made a mental list of several great **love**making **scenarios** you can pull off that night, leaving the final choice of which scenario you'll use to the last minute, letting the mood of the moment be your guide.)

Tell Her: "I'm Your Student!"

Now tell her that you plan on becoming her *student*. Say *you're going to study every inch of her body*. (That should send a chill down her spine!)

Tell her you're going to tickle her from head to toe until you find every sweet spot on her body - areas that make her **hot**, and spots that are out-and-out **orgasm triggers**. (Then make sure you follow through with this promise, in the days and weeks ahead. Explore her body with your fingertips, lips and tongue, paying close attention to her reactions to your touch. If she sighs, wriggles, moans, reacts as if you just set her on fire, you've found another **sweet spot**.)

And because you're behind the eight ball so to speak, *ask her to be patient with you* as you go about this **learning process**. Then, *she won't be as quick to get as annoyed with you during this learning phase as she might otherwise*. Plus, this humble request will *endear* you to her.

But don't let the talk get too serious or dark. Make the sexy joke that you'll need "lots of practice!" She'll appreciate the good humor and the implied vow that you'll make an honest effort to improve. And further lighten the mood by promising her the "homework" will be *fun*. (Then be *true* to your promise.)

On Loving Women
ASK HER FOR SOME SEXY HELP

More important - *tell her that, as her student, you will need some help - in the form of* **advice** *and perhaps even some* **practical demonstrations**. (This undoubtedly will win her over - and **titillate** her, making her imagine the sexy possibilities! You're *making love to her mind.*)

You can ask her for some starter advice right away or you can wait for this until you have time for intimate relations. And your first request might be:

"Please tell me what you need from me to make you come."

(FYI: Don't expect her to teach you everything you need to know in order to become a *great* lover. This won't happen. But she might give you a few good tips. And she might even have some suggestions that have nothing to do with technique. Maybe she'll tell you that you're not setting the proper *mood* she needs to feel sexy, for example.)

Then, when you're alone together and ready for sex, ask (in a sexy, loving way) if she'd mind giving you some **practical demonstrations**. A woman will not likely be able to show you how to make her come vaginally or by any other **non-clitoral orgasm triggers** I'll introduce to you in later chapters. But she can definitely teach you how to use your fingers to give her **clitoral orgasms - something most women know how to give themselves.** (That's a good place to start anyway. Her **clitoris** is your easiest route to making her come. It's **Love**making **101**. Later on, you can try to make her come with the other **hot spots** you'll learn about in this book.)

Ask her if she'd mind masturbating for you. Or ask her to *masturbate during sex* while you watch and learn. Or ask her to *take your fingers and (placing them on her* **clitoris**) *move them the*

way she wants you to touch her. Explain that you want to *study* what she does to achieve an **orgasm** so you can later do it yourself.

If you're lucky, she'll agree. You'd be surprised; even the most conservative women tend to find these ideas sexy and fun. And if she does, don't waste that event getting hot over it. *Watch* what she does very carefully so you can use the same technique on her later.

Every woman has her own personal preferences when it comes to how she likes her **clitoris** stimulated for an **orgasm**. So watch:

- **Where** *she likes to pleasure herself: is it directly on her clit, or to the left, right, top or bottom - or somewhere else?*
- *The amount of* **pressure** *she applies: is it soft, medium or hard?*
- *The* **speed** *at which she moves her finger(s): slowly, moderately or really fast?*
- *The* **type of stroke** *she prefers: is it circular, straight down or up, or something else?*
- **How intensely she "attacks" the place she likes best**: *is it almost detached or is it fervent and heated?*
- **Whether she stretches her labia open and/or pulls back the hood of her clitoris.**
- **Whether she touches any part of her genitals other than her clit.** *Does she insert a finger inside herself (and, if so, how?) and does she stimulate her* **labia**?
- **Whether she multi-tasks.** *Does she touch any part of her body other than her genitals? Does she stroke her* **legs** *or* **nipples** *simultaneously, with her other hand, for instance?*

She'll likely consent to do some sort of demonstration for you and appreciate your request because she knows you're sincerely working hard to become the lover she desires. *Once she's shown you the way, though, don't ask any more questions or ruin the mood with idle chatter.*

RULERS MAKE BAD LOVERS

By the way, there are other reasons why a woman might fake it for which you are to blame.

For example, *if she's ticked off with you she might fake it.* So let's be honest: Are you being loving with her or not? Do you always treat her well?

Your *attitude* might be the problem. (Remember the Fleetwood Mac song, *Gold Dust Woman* in which Stevie Nicks sings: "Rulers make bad lovers; you'd better put your kingdom up for sale"?) A pissed off woman might let you have your way with her but then fake it to get back at you for being unkind. If that's the case, you need an attitude adjustment. Seek counseling if you need help doing this.

Your lover might also fake it *to get it over with* because:

⚠ *you have bad breath*

⚠ *you're not seducing her properly*

⚠ *she has serious misgivings about you, as a man or partner*

Hopefully this book will help you get beyond all of these problems. The *hygiene* and *seduction* chapters will help you with the first two complaints. If she's not totally happy with you, though, you'll need to find out why and see if there's something you can do to turn that around.

But What If The Problem Lies With Her?

OK - but what if she's the one with the problem? We discussed this possibility earlier in this chapter. Here's my take on this:

- *if medicine she's on keeps her from climaxing, suggest she see if there are alternatives that don't harm her sex drive*
- *if she has an innate physical or medical problem that has prevented her from having an orgasm her entire life, that can be a tough nut to crack (in some cases the cause can even be a mystery to the medical community); you'll need outside help to resolve this*
- *if something has happened due to aging to lessen her sex drive and feeling, medical intervention might be necessary; but with patience, resourcefulness and effort, you might be able to surmount this problem yourself (with the ideas in this book)*
- *if surgery (such as a hysterectomy) has compromised her nerves and her sexual response, you might be able to get beyond this by experimenting with techniques in this book coupled with patience (I did, in a situation like this; greater stimulation, more multi-tasking and a prolonging of sex helped in achieving a solution)*
- *if she has a psychological problem that prevents her from enjoying sex, this requires outside help and can be a difficult problem to surmount*
- *if she's really not into you (she's asexual; in love with someone else; turned off by you for any reason; or she's a closet Lesbian), that's a likely deal breaker (but thank goodness you found out!)*
- *if "she" is really a transsexual and cannot come in the traditional ways a woman who was born a woman can...that's for you to decide*

Have a heart if she's facing a medical problem. Try hard to find a solution. It may take patience. It may take a visit to the doctor. It may take hard

Is She Faking It?

work. But your patience will be rewarded. She will love you more for it.

The Most Benign Possibilities

There are two other reasons a woman might *fake an **orgasm**,* by the way: She's too tired for sex or she's not in the mood (but she's too shy to tell you or doesn't want to put you off). She'll then fake an orgasm to protect your feelings (she doesn't want you to feel you've failed).

If you discover your lover is doing this, thank her for her being so considerate but tell her (lovingly) you'd prefer that she told you when she was too tired or not in the mood for sex. Tell her you'd rather do it when you're both up to it.

Yes, she was being kind and polite, but this kind of behavior can lead to resentment on her part and mistrust on yours. Plus, if she gives you false feedback that can lead to misunderstandings that hurt her in the long run: she's misleading you about what rings her bells, leading you later to engage in behavior that's ineffective. (Plus one-sided sex is ultimately no fun!)

Give her an easy out: Tell her that whenever she's too tired for sex she can always request a rain check. She'll love you for that!

The Path That Lies Ahead

OK - so maybe you've been hit on the head with the reality that you have a lot to learn about women. Now it's up to you to work hard to get up to speed. The good news is that you will find the information you need right here in *On Loving Women*. Especially study the chapters on *female sexual anatomy, cocksmanship, fingerwork* and *oral sex*.

Speaking of which, here's a great tip to get back in her good graces quickly if you're not yet pleasing her in bed: *She's likely to forgive you for all past wrongs if you learn how to give her great oral sex!* So before all else, read the *oral sex chapter* and learn to become an artist with your tongue. If you produce fireworks that way, it'll buy you the time you need to get up to speed on everything else.

The truth is: *a skilled man can make most any (normal healthy heterosexual) woman come.* And once you're done studying this book (if you've done your homework and you apply the knowledge you've gained here), no woman should ever feel the need to fake it with you - at least for any reason that might be related to you.

(P.S. One final interesting fact: That ABC-TV American Sex Survey found that, "blondes are a little less likely than other women to always have an orgasm, and a little more likely to have faked it.")

*"I've been with thousands of men, again and again -
They promise the moon.
They're always coming and going and going and coming,
And always too soon."*
         - Madeleine Kahn as Lilly Von Shtupp in Blazing Saddles

Achieving The <u>Ultimate</u> Control

In 1990, rock star Sting set the standard for **sexual longevity** when he claimed he could "go on for *five hours*" with *tantric* sex techniques. Well, you can understand why everyone then thought *tantric* sex was "the *way*."

But that proved to be a prank. In a *Daily Mail* interview (December 30, 2011), Sting's wife said his claim was just "a drunken boast." (Sting, in fact, admitted to the BBC in 2004 that he did not have "a *clue*" what *tantric* sex involved.) Trudie Styler blamed rock promoter Bob Geldof for floating the false claim in an interview:

"At one point, the journalist asked how long they could go for, and Geldof said he was a three-minute man, but, as Sting did yoga, he could probably go for hours. And Sting said "Well, haven't you heard of tantric sex?"

Said Styler: "...suddenly, I was doing it all day long. Well, *if only!*"

Well shame on Geldof for fibbing and - worse - for not becoming a better lover! But the truth is you *can* learn to last a very long time inside a woman before you come. Not necessarily five hours, but easily *one to three hours (as*

93

Achieving The _Ultimate_ Control

I've done innumerable times - to which my partners can attest). You can even make a night or whole day of it, with multiple sessions, once you train yourself to be able to have **multiple orgasms**.

And you don't need to learn tantric sex practices to do so. I mastered **sexual longevity**, developing my own way of making love seemingly forever, *20 years before I'd heard of it*.

It's all about **control**. This became clear to me in my early 20s when I bedded a beautiful blonde who was my doctor's receptionist. After giving her the ride of her life for more than two hours, she proclaimed it was the best sex she'd ever had. And, she marveled, "You have such great *control!*"

That's when I realized there was a name for what I had perfected - **great control.** I had spent years training myself to last a long time inside of a woman. But, she gave a **name** to my quest and talent. And her expression of astonishment and *awe* showed that it was something women *crave*.

The good news is that **great control** is something most men can acquire, with a bit of homework. (I'll show you how!) Yet - from what I've heard from many lovers, innumerable other women, and many *men - few men do*.

Not good. Because every guy absolutely *must* have this essential skill, with the sophisticated, experienced and *demanding* sex partners he'll encounter these days. Without it, a woman will be disappointed, dissatisfied and likely to stray.

THE SAD STATE OF AFFAIRS

Recent scientific studies have confirmed what I've heard from many women. The picture is dismal:

Actual and Desired Duration of Foreplay and Intercourse: Discordance and Misperceptions Within Heterosexual Couples

S. Andrea Miller and E. Sandra Byers
University of New Brunswick

One hundred and fifty-two heterosexual couples reported their actual and ideal duration of foreplay and intercourse, as well

ORIGINAL RESEARCH—EJACULATORY DISORDERS

Premature Ejaculation: An Ob[servational Study of Men] and Their Partners

Donald L. Patrick, PhD, MSPH,* Sta[...]
Raymond Rosen, PhD,† David L. Ro[...]
Margaret Rothman, PhD,‡‡ and Car[...]

*Department of Health Services and Epidem[...]
University School of Medicine, Beachwood[...]
Minneapolis, MN; ‡Robert Wood Johnson M[...]
††ALZA Corporation, Mountain View, CA; ‡‡J[...]
§§Johnson and Johnson Pharmaceutical Ser[...]

Corresponding Author: Donald L. Patrick,
Washington, 1959 NE Pacific St., Box 35766
Donald@u.washington.edu

ABSTRACT

ORIGINAL RESEARCH—EJACULATORY DISORDERS

Changing Paradigms from a Historical DSM-III and DSM-IV View Toward an Evidence-Based Definition of Premature Ejaculation. Part I—Validity of DSM-IV-TR

Marcel D. Waldinger, MD, PhD,*† and Dave H. Schweitzer, MD, PhD‡

ORIGINAL RESEARCH—EJACULATORY DISORDERS

Canadian and American Sex Therapists' Perceptions of Normal and Abnormal Ejaculatory Latencies: How Long Should Intercourse Last?

Eric W. Corty, PhD, and Jenay M. Guardiani, BS
School of Humanities and Social Sciences, Penn State Erie, The Behrend College, Erie, PA, USA

DOI: 10.1111/j.1743-6109.2008.00797.x

On Loving Women

Scientists have proven conclusively that <u>few men last long enough to please their women in bed</u>.

A 2005 study into men's staying power funded by Pfizer produced astonishing results. Led by Netherlands neuropsychiatrist Dr. Marcel D. Waldinger, 500 couples from five countries (The Netherlands, UK, Spain, Turkey and the US) used *stopwatches* to clock how long the men involved lasted during **vaginal sex**. The disappointing conclusion:

The median length of time before the men came was just 5.4 minutes! And so we know that there are a sizable number of men who cannot reach even that sad result. In fact, on collegesextalk.com University of Maine Human Sexuality professor Sandra L. Caron paints this bleak picture regarding **premature or early ejaculation**:

> "...it is the most common male sexual dysfunction, especially among younger men. Fifty percent of young males report early ejaculation and one-third of adult males report they ejaculate more rapidly then they would like."

After his highly respected *stopwatch study* involving nearly 1600 men (in 2004), University of Washington researcher Donald L. Patrick (and other scientific colleagues) wrote in the Journal of Sexual Medicine that:

> "Premature ejaculation (PE) is the most common male sexual dysfunction, affecting approximately 20–30% of the male population at any one time."

Worse, Patrick reported that few of these men are getting help:

> "Currently, available data suggest that only 1–12% of males self-reporting PE receive treatment for their dysfunction. This may be attributed in part to the very personal nature of the condition, the hesitancy of both men and physicians to approach and discuss the topic, and the lack of awareness of treatment options for PE."

How Long Do Women Want It To Last?

Looking at the broader picture in their study of 152 couples (published in the Journal of Sex Research in 2004), Canadian researchers S. Andrea Miller and E. Sandra Byers showed that **there's a huge gap between how much intercourse most women <u>want</u> and how much they're actually getting.** (And this study did not include couples whose men had premature ejaculation problems) They concluded:

> "The ideal duration of foreplay and intercourse were significantly longer than the actual duration for both gender."

One of their points was that **a woman's sexual satisfaction** is at least partly based upon whether her man is able to last as long inside her as she'd like. But, they noted, *this is not happening in most relationships*. In other words, *there are a lot of dissatisfied women!*

The men who responded to the study said they were able to last an average 8 minutes. Their women said it was actually less - about *7 minutes* (the median length of time men not suffering from PE lasted in *Patrick's stopwatch study*, by the way).

Interestingly, the men in *Miller and Byers' study* said they wanted intercourse to last longer than the women did! Men *wanted* it to go on for at least 18 minutes. The women desired *at least* 15 minutes. *That's more than twice what the women reported they were getting.*

But if those preferences are truly the case, that's actually good news. Because with the information you'll get in this chapter you should *easily* be able to last 15-20 minutes.

But even so, that's not long enough by my standards. I've often told women I've dated over the years (as a tease, before we had sex): "I think anything less than an hour is a quickie." And that's honestly how I feel. (As have most of my partners.)

A less-than-scientific online poll by Dr. Keith Ablow suggests that many others agree with me.

Dr. Ablow reported that:

> **"Fourteen percent of men wanted sex to last 10 minutes or less, 50% wanted sex to last 30 minutes, and 36% wanted it to last 1 hour or longer. For women, the figures were 18%, 52%, and 29%, respectively. Overall, over 80% of men and women wanted sex to last 30 minutes or longer."**

I can truly say that **great sex** *requires a much longer duration than even the scientists understand is ideal*. The fact is that, generally speaking, **the longer the sex, the greater the experience, the deeper the satisfaction and the bigger the orgasms will be** *(if done well)*.

You'll reach greater heights with *longer **love**making* than with *shorter **love**making*. That's been my experience, over and over again, over the course of more than three decades of **love**making.

My partners have all experienced that truth. And they have been won over by it.

CAN YOU HAVE TOO MUCH SEX?

So I have to laugh at some of in the scientific world who warn of those who might want, in their opinion, *too much* sex. Those sex researchers sound like they've never experienced prolonged or great sex.

In 2008, sex therapists Eric W. Corty and Jenay M. Guardiani did what they called, "A random sample of members of the Society for Sex Therapy and Research," and reported their results in the Journal of Sexual Medicine.

The consensus was that "too short" sex lasted 1 to 2 minutes, "adequate" sex lasted 3 to 7 minutes, "desirable" sex lasted 7 to 13 minutes, and anything longer than 13 minutes was "too long."

Too long??? This is what they had to say:

> *"Miller and Byers found that women and men desired intravaginal ejaculatory latency to be around 14 to 18 minutes. This is longer than what most sex therapists think of as desirable for coitus and is verging into territory that many experienced sex therapists consider too long. Lay expectations seem to be out of synch with reality and this desire for longer latencies can be problematic."*

Yet they admitted:

> *"At the same time, we want to note that Patrick et al. found that the highest percentage of men reporting the greatest satisfaction with sexual intercourse were those with intravaginal latencies of 10 minutes or longer."*

In other words, men experiencing *longer* sex have *greater* satisfaction. So, while Corty and Guardiani make fun of what they call "the fantasy model of male sexuality" and worry that sex longer than 13 minutes might be... oh my!...*problematic*...may I suggest that they just might need to read this book?...And get a decent love life!

I'm beginning to think the scientific world needs to interview me (and other men like me...and our *women*). And they need to get with it!

GREAT LOVEMAKING REQUIRES TIME

*Great **love**making **requires** that you be inside your woman, most times, at least a half an hour if not an hour or more. You cannot reach the heights in a short time. (I talk about this more in another chapter.)*

*Less than a half hour is definitely a **quickie** and is not to be done every day!* There's a place for quickies but they should be done only occasionally.

At the extreme, I've been known to make love for two to three hours or more, with partners who loved that. And, for the worry wort (and perhaps inexperienced) scientists who would warn you away from lengthy sex, I can testify:

There were no ill effects to worry about after making love for long periods of time. Far from it!!!

Achieving The <u>Ultimate</u> Control

THE COOL GUYS POINT OUT THE WAY

Even before I'd had sex I knew as a teen that I wanted to develop supreme control as a lover. And one of my childhood heroes convinced me that this was highly desirable, in a magazine interview I read in the early 1970s.

In that piece, the interviewer related how he excitedly told Led Zeppelin frontman Robert Plant that fans were making love to his eight-minute-long song *Stairway To Heaven*. But instead of being impressed, Plant objected.

"That's not **long** enough!" he said, or something to that effect.

Another hit song that impressed me in my teenaged years was James Brown's *Get Up (I Feel Like Being A) Sex Machine* in which he exhorted:

> *Get on up...*
> *Stay on the scene...*
> *Like A Sex Machine...*

Listening to that, I knew I wanted to be like *him* some day. That was obviously the ideal - *to be one of those men who can last forever who the ladies go for big time*. (I'm not sure about the "machine" part, though.)

Heck, when I got into jazz in Junior High School I found that even the king of smooth cool mainstream music, Nat King Cole, was preaching the same standard in his song *Straighten Up And Fly Right*:

> *Straighten up & fly right,*
> *Straighten up and stay right,*
> *Straighten up & fly right,*
> *Cool down, papa, don't you blow your top!*

So even as a kid I knew that this is the widely acknowledged gold standard of the male lover: *Be a master of control. To please your woman.*

And this makes even more sense when you understand that, most times, you should make your woman come (at least once if not more) *before* you do. (I talk about the importance of this in a different chapter.)

HOW LONG CAN YOU LAST?

So, based upon all of this, let's be honest. Now that you understand what's too short and what's ideal, how do you measure up?

If you're only lasting *five minutes* inside your lover, you might fall into the *median* category of male lovers, but *you're disappointing and frustrating your partner*. You now know that scientists say most *women want you to last at least 15 minutes if not more*. If you believe Dr. Keith Ablow, *most women actually want you to last at least 30 minutes or longer*.

On Loving Women

In my experience, *most women want more than 30 minutes*. And the most important thing to keep in mind is: *the quality of the **love**making goes up generally with the amount of time spent doing it* (within reason; I'm not encouraging you to seek Olympic records every time you couple together).

On the other end of the scale, you now know that if you cannot last more than one or two minutes, you probably are suffering from a clinical case of premature ejaculation. If that describes you, it might help to know that Dr. Waldinger and other researchers have divided those suffering from PE into two groups, from a medical standpoint.

One group is curable without medication and suffers from **temporary PE**. The other has a **chronic "dysfunction"** requiring medication to improve.

If you're in the latter group, you might need *medical treatment*. But look on the bright side: the good news is that new treatments now exist that might help you. (Look for my sidebar on some of the hopeful new medicines now available at the end of this chapter.)

Wherever you fit in the spectrum of lovers, however - whether you're doing OK but you're seeking the ultimate control or you are falling far short of the mark - I'm going to give you some incredibly powerful advice, insights and super helpful exercises in a moment. And that should be all you'll need to acquire the staying power women admire and crave! (It will be for most men.)

I think I've *earned* the right to make those statements because I've helped so many men over the years get beyond their control limitations. (I gave details in the chapter, "My Street Cred"). So I know I can help you.

In helping others, I also found out how much most men don't know about women...and *themselves*. In fact, you might be surprised to find out that we're going to have to talk about *you* in this chapter - about your *body, brain and psychology*. Because, if you have control issues, there are apparently many things you don't understand about *yourself*.

I Can Relate To Your Issues

One reason I understand a lot about my body and how to overcome **control problems** is that I spent many hours working to do so (years before I'd ever been with a woman). Even from my earliest experiences **masturbating** I made up pseudo-scientific games to improve my ability to last. I knew even as a kid - always the Romeo - that I needed to prepare for my first sexual encounters if I wanted the women in my life to value me as a lover. (I'll share some of those very effective games with you soon.)

Achieving The Ultimate Control

Then, in my earliest experiences with women, I tested various techniques I and others had developed in order to last as long as I wanted to in the sack. (That's how I discovered that Masters and Johnson's "squeeze technique," widely touted in the 1970s as the best solution for **premature ejaculation**, did *not* work (at least for me). Whenever a woman used that method - squeezing either end of my erection when I thought I was going to come and she didn't want me to - it only made me come faster. So I will tell you right now: that's *not* one of the methods I'll recommend here!)

We all start somewhere. I realized early on that a man's sexual awakening poses its challenges.

*All of us **come** too fast when we first become sexual. So all of us must work to overcome this natural tendency.*

It's because I taught myself (and so many others) to overcome control problems that I can empathize with you. And I can say with confidence that the wealth of personal information and techniques I have acquired and developed over the course of more than three decades of **love**making will help you too.

As you will see, your path to getting over your control issues will involve your:

- ♂ Processing **new insights** (including those about your own body)
- ♂ Practicing the **exercises** I will give you to attain control skills
- ♂ Using my **practical methods during sex** to stave off **orgasms** if you experience any moments of crisis while inside the **vagina**
- ♂ Following some **general rules** that will help steel you for longer sessions and
- ♂ Changing your **mindset** (so your thoughts about and attitudes toward sex are in the right "place")

#1: Understanding The Frenulum

OK. Let's start at the beginning. Let's talk about your **penis**, because it's one of *two* organs that most often cause **control problems** (the other organ being your **brain**). And one tiny part of it is undoubtedly causing most of your control difficulties. You've probably not heard of it. Few have.

It's your **frenulum**, or if you're **circumcised**, let's call this your **frenulum area**. (In some cases, circumcision removes part or all of the frenulum.) Actually, to simplify things, we'll call this - and the **nerves** associated with it - your **"Trigger."** (You'll see why this name is appropriate in a minute.)

Rather than try to describe what it looks like and where it is, it's easier to show it to you in the artist's rendition below:

It's a rather nondescript area, roughly a small "O" of flesh between the cleft in your **coronal ridge**. It looks different in every man but its effect is the same.

It's connected to *highly sensitive* **nerve endings** and is *the most reactive area on your* **penis**. That's why it can pose a **control problem**.

It's a potent **orgasm trigger** *and I believe* **it's responsible for the "hair trigger response"** *associated with* **PE**.

That's right. If you have **control problems**, your **Trigger** is one of the most likely *culprits*. This can easily and quickly set off your **climax**.

This is also the area most men - especially newly-sexual young men - stimulate the most in **masturbating**. If that describes you, *you've inadvertently been* training *yourself to come quickly!*

As a teen my **Trigger** seemed to be naturally hot and tickly, ready to fire off at any moment. I think that's how nature sets us up. I remember noticing this fact and thinking: *I've got to do something about this!*

And I came up with solutions I'd like to share with you. Bottom line: *We have to tame our* **Triggers** *before we can achieve higher levels of control.*

The journey to achieve the most **supreme control** begins there. It's a necessary **first step** in the process we need to go through in grooming ourselves to become *great lovers*.

The truth is that without your **Trigger**, you'd have a much easier time controlling your **orgasms**. But obviously you would not want to surgically remove that area. So what can you do?

#2: Stopping Your Trigger From Firing Quickly

You *can* achieve a sort of virtual *Triggerectomy*. For a start, here's what you need to do:

Don't stimulate your Trigger when masturbating. You've probably been giving it your primary focus when jerking off, stroking it directly. (Don't feel badly; we all start off doing that, as kids.)

Whether you've realized it or not, you've been **sensitizing** your **Trigger** more and more by doing that, making it ever more responsive to the touch. That's got to stop if you want to put an end to the **easy tickle response** you've been provoking from it, leading to the habit of coming quickly.

You have to physically train your **Trigger** to cool down, so *you're* in control of it. I'll show you how to do this (below). Then I'll show you how you can also take your **Trigger** out of the picture so to speak *mentally*.

To do all this, I need to give you some exercises. Then we'll talk about how to get your mind on the right thought patterns. Control, as you will see, is mostly *mind over matter*. Because most of this is in your head!

#3: Masturbation The Smart Way

In the movie *Y Tu Mama Tambien,* Luisa tells her two young male companions: *"You two need to stop whacking off, and work up some resistance!"*

I immediately scribbled that quote on a piece of paper upon first hearing it so I could share it with you. It was so insightful.

For most men without **PE** (**premature ejaculation**), **masturbation** can almost be done any way you want. And that's how most men do it.

"You're just busting your nuts," one of my older friends told me. His opinion was that it did not matter how quickly you jerked off.

But if you have control problems, *it matters a lot*. As Luisa suggested (and I agree), *this is one way* **PE** *develops; from jerking off way too quickly*.

It leads to a destructive addiction. It accustoms your body to coming too quickly. I believe it actually creates an autonomic nerve response that takes on a life of its own.

And, unfortunately, over-eager whacking off seems to be a common habit among men. *No good*. If you're doing that, you're not even *enjoying* the process! What a waste!

So am I telling you there is a *right* and *wrong* way to **masturbate?** You bet. It begins with having the right goal in mind, namely:

You should use masturbation as an exercise in developing staying power. You should be acclimating your cock to be less sensitive to the touch so it can last longer before it feels the urge to come.

If you're in a steady relationship and you have no control issues, masturbation becomes less important and possibly nonessential. But **for those with PE, masturbation as a means to improving one's staying power is an absolute must.**

So, along these lines, how do you do it? I mentioned this before but it bears repeating. In fact, let's call this <u>**the first rule of smart masturbation:**</u> **Do not touch your Trigger during masturbation. This is the best way to get it to cool down.**

Instead, touch or massage your **shaft**, your **scrotum**, your **perineum** (the skin between your **balls** and your **anus**), your **thighs**, your **nipples** - anywhere that's sensitive or pleasing to the touch. Imagine that your lover is touching you and not yourself. But preferably keep your focus on parts that are not **orgasm triggers**.

In **getting your mind off your Trigger** and onto other body parts, you will find that the anticipatory urgent tickle that is probably right there when you start masturbating now will be reduced. Eventually, with time, you will find it's virtually nonexistent.

It's a matter of **expectations**. Your mind expects you to touch your **Trigger** and to come quickly as you have before. So the tickle will be there until you teach your mind that you will not continue with that habit.

If your **Trigger** doesn't anticipate your touching it, its nagging call to come will disappear. You will have turned it off by ignoring it. Trust me.

Here's <u>**the second rule of smart masturbation**</u>**: Light tickling is out. Especially never play the game of seeing how lightly you can tickle your Trigger (or any other orgasm hot spot) in order to come. Otherwise it will take less and less pressure to set off your orgasm and your problem will grow worse.**

The lighter you touch yourself, the more sensitive your nerves will become. This is a natural biological response. And this is no good for those with PE.

The *opposite* is true, too. *The more pressure you apply in stimulating yourself, the more indifferent your nerves become.* This is the good news. This is what you must do to calm your **penile nerves** down, to make them less prone to firing off an orgasm. Moderate pressure is probably the best.

<u>**The third rule of smart masturbation:**</u> **Slow down! Don't be in a heated rush to come.** Along these lines, **do not allow yourself to do quick jerks or strokes until the very end** (once you've decided it's all right to come).

The faster you stroke, the more quickly you come. This should be obvious.

So keep the stroking and massaging to a moderate or slow pace. Actually, a **non-rhythmic** style would work even better. It's when you set up a *rhythm* that the tension that can lead to a climax starts to build. So stay away from **rhythmic** strokes until you're ready to come.

The fourth rule of smart masturbation: Don't be goal-oriented. That is, don't make your orgasm the be-all and end-all of what you're doing. Enjoy the process.

Savor all the feelings you experience when you touch yourself. Delight in the feelings of being hard and sexually hot. Those sensations should provide a mind-blow in and of themselves.

#4: THE LONG SELF-TEASE EXERCISE

Speaking of which, here's a powerful exercise you should do every time you do yourself that should produce great success. Let's call this the **Long Self-Tease exercise** (just so you have something to call it if it comes up in conversation with your lover, friends or others).

I played this game as a teenager and it worked wonders toward preparing me for the real deal. It taught me how to gain total control over my orgasm (and even the *size of my erection!*).

It also *desensitized me* toward *images of naked women* and *erotic prose*. That is, it removed the *unhealthy overheated reaction* adolescents get when seeing or reading **sexually provocative stimuli**, which in and of itself can lead to **PE**.

The idea of the Long Self-Tease exercise is to prolong the delicious "agony" of being sexually excited as long as you can without coming. You "torment" yourself sexually as long as you can. You're seeing how long you can *put off* your **orgasm**.

So the first requirement to do this properly is:

Allow enough time for masturbating now that you're onto this new "program." Do not masturbate if you do not have the appropriate amount of time available to include this exercise.

And here's the key to the exercise: I want you to use a **timer**.

For your first sessions, set it to go off in about 15 minutes (the *minimum* amount of time the *Miller and Byers study* women desired **vaginal sex** to last) - IF that's a difficult goal for you. If it's not, set it to go off at 30 minutes or some other amount of time that seems desirable but not yet doable.

When the timer goes off, you're on your own. You can make yourself come or prolong the exercise further, to see how long you can go.

#5: The *Big As You Can Get* Game Pays Big Dividends

To mix things up in doing the **Long Self-Tease Exercise**, *you can play a* <u>side game</u> *of sorts (one I used to play), the Big As You Can Get game, which is amusing, educational and productive:*

In the Big As You Can Get game, you see how big you can make yourself!

I've discovered this biological fact and this game will demonstrate it to you too: **it takes at least 15 minutes to a half hour of stimulation for your erection to arrive at its most swollen state.** *Doing this game will translate into greater pleasure for her later on* (as you will see in a second).

In doing the **Big As You Can Get game**, your goal is to do whatever you can to increase your hard-on's size until you've achieved your maximum best. (Do it with patience, though; *gradually*.) Here's what you do:

While doing the **Long Self-Tease** exercise, your job is to pay attention to every change your body goes through. Especially watch how **your erection continues to get bigger and bigger over time**.

In other words, simple prolonged teasing will gradually increase its size. But there are various activities you can do to produce greater swelling:

Squeeze the muscles in your bottom. That should make your hard-on enlarge. Sometimes that increase is only momentary but often it maintains itself. **This is a good thing to know because you can do this during sex to make your erection bigger!**

Put a mirror in front of you and just enjoy watching the physical changes you put yourself through during this process. That alone should excite you enough to attain your largest possible size.

Other ways to make your **hard-on** larger: With one hand, squeeze your **erection** gently (without touching your **Trigger**). Push it forward gently (without causing pain). Tease the **glans** (its head). Pull up on it with the same kind of force you'd put into a handshake - stopping before this becomes painful. Tickle your balls.

You can even do this by using <u>the power of your mind</u>, by thinking of yourself in a sexy situation. For example, you might imagine you're at a resort where a bunch of sexy topless babes surround you and strip you in order to have you sexually. They giggle and marvel at how *big* you're becoming. Or pretend you're a contestant on a sexy game show where the man who makes his erection the biggest wins. Choose whatever fantasy works for you. (*The art of fantasizing should be part of your bag of "tricks"* as a lover by the way. Your mind can produce results - **even during sex** - that nothing else can.)

This kind of observational game *gets your mind off **orgasmic thoughts**.* The more you can learn to tune out thoughts of your own orgasm and concentrate on other aspects of **sex** (such as a finer appreciation of its many amazing aspects), the better.

The lesson here is: **The longer you can put off your climax, the bigger you will get.** (And notice how much bigger your orgasm is too!)

Along these lines, **this game might even help make you become bigger during sex**. *It will at least acclimate your body to lasting long enough inside a woman so you can reach that state of rigidity that makes you the biggest you can be.* (Remember, it takes about 15-30 minutes to reach that fabulous state.) And the bigger you are, the more sensations she'll feel.

#6: THE CLEAR FLUID GAME TEACHES YOU PATIENCE

Let's add some more fun to this. Let's talk about the **Clear Fluid game**, which you can play whenever you want to (if you want to mix things up).

The **Clear Fluid game** has important benefits. It will train you to get your mind off your orgasm. Plus, it will help you develop an attitude of **patience**, *which is essential to overcoming control issues.*

With enough arousal, any man can make his **cock** drip **clear fluid**. It's **pre-ejaculate** produced by your **Cowper's gland** (located internally at the base of your penis). That **slippery lubricant** is fun to play with. *It will appear if you tease yourself long enough. And you can use it to provide extra non-orgasmic pleasure by spreading it all over your body parts.*

Here's how you use it in playing the **Clear Fluid game:**

Tell yourself you're not going to start touching yourself all over until the clear fluid starts dripping from your meatus (the hole at the end of your cock). Tease only your meatus and or your glans (the head of your penis) until the fluid begins to appear.

Tip: **Wetten the end of your finger with saliva at the start. For some reason, that seems to quicken this process.** (*In doing so, too, notice how much nicer a wet finger feels than a dry one. You'll want to remember this when you finger your lover during sex!*)

Once the fluid appears, take a drop of it and rub it slowly over the head of your cock. **Be fascinated by all the sensations you're producing.** Your **glans** is tickly but it's not typically an **orgasm trigger** and so you can put off your **orgasm** by focusing on that part while still experiencing sexual thrills.

On Loving Women

Bear in mind that the production of that **clear fluid** that leaks out of you is often a sign you're approaching **orgasm**, though. So when it first arrives, back off whatever you're doing for a moment and stop touching yourself. Or touch a part that's less likely to make you come than whatever you were touching before.

Touch the back of your shaft. That's pleasing (but beware - that can make you come if you're not careful; so touch it in a non-orgasmic way, without too much pressure).

Or touch your **nipples**. They can be very sensitive and, when touched by a woman, they can prove to be *orgasm triggers*. So it wouldn't hurt to play with your **nipples** from time to time to get used to that kind of stimulation *without allowing it to lead to your climax*.

A side benefit to this is that later on when your lover tickles your **nipples** during **sex** you won't get overexcited. You'll be used to accepting the pleasant sensations you get from them without expecting them to send you over the top.

See how long you can keep up the **Clear Fluid game**. The fluid increases your pleasure in doing the **Long Self-Tease Exercise**.

Another bonus in doing the **Clear Fluid game** regularly is that it will get your body in the habit of producing this helpful fluid during **sex**. That helps provide the **lubrication** you need for **prolonged sex**. That's *huge*, especially if your lover has wetness issues (perhaps from age or medical condition).

#7: THE DESENSITIZATION EXERCISE

Once the **Long Self-Tease Exercise** becomes second nature to you, move on a similar exercise with a more ambitious goal.

The need for this was brought out in the TV sitcom *Seinfeld* in "The Contest" episode. (That was the one where everyone got involved in a *"master of your domain"* contest to see who could hold off longest without *succumbing to some sexual influence* and masturbating.)

For what was the impetus for the contest? George was caught **masturbating** by his mom because...

> GEORGE: My mother had a Glamour magazine, I started leafing through it..
> JERRY: "Glamour"?
> GEORGE: ..So, one thing led to another..
> JERRY: So, what did she do?
> GEORGE: First she screams, "George, what are you doing?!

Achieving The **Ultimate** Control

My God!" And it looked like she was gonna faint - she started clutching the wall, trying to hang onto it. I didn't know whether to try and keep her from falling, or zip up.
JERRY: What did you do?
GEORGE: I zipped up!

That was funny. But the truth behind it is not, for men with control problems. Our society has bred into many men a Pavlovian-style knee jerk reaction to **sexual stimuli**. You see a sexy woman in a magazine, you need to **jerk off**. And fast.

So *we need to counteract this* **automatic response syndrome that rules you** - *the uncontrollable urge you feel to come upon seeing or reading commonly-found sexy material.* Otherwise one source of your control problems will forever plague you.

One effective way to defeat your **automatic response syndrome** is with my **Desensitization Exercise**. Or you could call this the **Master of Your World exercise** or the **Contest exercise** if you prefer. This is kinda sorta a similar challenge to the one in *Seinfeld's* "The Contest." Here, though, you're putting off your *orgasm* and the *time frame* is greatly constricted.

To do this:

You need to set up a sexy activity to combine with relaxed masturbation. You can look at pictures of **naked women** if you like. Or read **erotica**. Or watch a **sexy film**.

Preferably choose something that normally leads you to jerk off and come quickly. **We want to deaden that response. So adding sexy material to a slow masturbation exercise will help disarm the power it has over you. It's contributing to your control problems and we need to put an end to that**.

You're also going to use the **sexy material** to propel your **sexual excitement** - to keep you **hard** and **in the mood** - even while **blunting its effect** in making you want to **come**. It's OK to get **hot** seeing something **hot**. It's not OK to then have to run and **jerk off** quickly, though. Certainly not if you want to be **master of your world.**

OK, so you've got your **sexual stimuli** set up for the **Desensitization Exercise**. What do you do now?

I recommend you start by simply looking at or reading whatever **sexual material** you've chosen to use. Do this for a good long while. *Don't even remove your clothes yet.* Just *appreciate* the images you're looking at or whatever you're reading.

At some point you can start removing clothes. You should make *this* a game, to help prolong the **Desensitization Exercise**.

How should you do it? Take off a piece of clothing with each minute that goes by. Or tell yourself you'll remove more clothing when you see another set of breasts or whatever. Or peel down to your skivvies once you pop a boner. Or wait until you see a wet spot appearing on your pants to strip down to your underwear. Only get **nude** when you think you've spent a sufficient amount of time appreciating the sexual material.

Once you're nude, prolong this portion of the **Desensitization Exercise** further by keeping your hands off yourself for as long as you can. Just love the *incredible feeling* of being a *hard, naked, sexual man*. Come to see that as a reward unto itself. Stay at that excitement level and get into all the tingles and other pleasurable titillations that come your way.

Keep the nude non-touching portion of the **Desensitization Exercise** going for at least 10 minutes or more. And don't be in a rush to end it.

Then, you can go ahead and **slowly tease** yourself. **Savor every moment**.

But keep whatever you choose to do to yourself (tickling, massaging, stroking, etc.) to a **non-orgasmic** level for some time. Keep the pace slow and manageable. Keep the intensity moderate so you're never at risk of coming. And keep viewing or reading the **sexual material** you've chosen.

If you ever feel a crisis coming on, immediately stop what you're doing. Spend a little time cooling down until you know you can handle more teasing. **Keep this up as long as possible before you give in to the need to climax**.

You could use your timer to set a specific (ambitious) duration of time you want to let go by before you allow yourself to come, as you did in the **Long Self-Tease Exercise**. But I'd prefer you rely upon your own self-discipline at this point. Once you've graduated to the **Desensitization Exercise**, it's all about teaching yourself how to develop and exercise **willpower**.

In fact, try this too: *I want you to sometimes end the Desensitization Exercise <u>without climaxing</u>. Here's your most powerful lesson: seeing you can take or leave the act of coming*. You won't believe the results.

...Now all of the exercises and games I just gave you will help you master the skill of control. *They will get you used to being hot without feeling the need or even the desire to come*. **In setting your timer to go off after longer and longer time periods as you master each duration goal, you're learning that you can control whether your climax comes on or not**.

Also, the **Long Self-Tease Exercise**, the **Desensitization Exercise** (aka the

Achieving The Ultimate Control

Contest), the ***Big As You Can Get game*** and ***Clear Fluid Game*** all will build up your **confidence**. That alone is a powerful force in conquering **PE**.

#8: Handling The Unique Challenges The Vagina Poses

But going from **mastering control** during **masturbation** to achieving success in controlling yourself *within a woman's vagina* requires more information. Being inside of her presents its own challenges.

Her **vaginal heat**, **tightness**, and **wetness**, *for instance, are pleasurable forces to be reckoned with*. And that's not to mention the delightful changes that occur within her during her **orgasm**, including the **muscle throbbing**.

You can anticipate these happening and *brace* yourself. But that doesn't always work.

And other **sexual influences** can come into play. Her **sexy reactions**, verbally and otherwise, can be enough to send you off to the races so to speak.

In fact, some women are real touchy-feely *before* **intercourse** *begins* and that in and of itself might test your sense of **control**. (A college buddy came to my dorm room one night seeking my solution to that problem.)

So let's take a look at methods you can use *before and during* **love**making to cope with these factors and thwart any **"Oh no!" moments** you might experience. Then we'll get into **mindset** and other issues that are important.

#9: Some Women Will Pose Greater Challenges Than Others

First, let's look at a fact you might not have known:

Every woman will have a different effect on you. Controlling your **orgasm** will be easier with some than with others. My mentor Earle warned me about this years ago but it took many years of experience to fully understand how to process it.

This means that even if you've achieved years of having **great control**, you might find that one woman sends you over the edge too fast. The first time you're with her, *bam*, you come within a short amount of time. You're naturally embarrassed. And it makes you fear you're back at the beginning - a man with control problems.

Maybe her body is your idea of the ideal sexy body and that sets you off too soon. Or maybe her pussy gets especially wet or hot and that makes you lose control. Or it's really tight.

Or maybe her techniques work too well on you. Or maybe she gets on top and works you too hard from the get-go. (We'll talk about how to handle that on page 116, by the way.)

#10: New Partners And The Effects Of Celibacy Can Test You

Or maybe your fear of coming too soon is the result of having a *new partner*. You haven't had sex for awhile and you're now experiencing the extra excitement that comes with anticipating the first time together.

Being with a woman after a long period of **celibacy** *inevitably makes you more prone to coming sooner than you'd like. That is, at least during the first one or two times you make love to her.*

You need to understand this. It's natural and nothing to worry about - so long as your control skills kick in after the early thrills of being with her for the first time or two wear off.

If you'd like, you could say something like, "Oh wow! I don't usually come that fast! But you're so *sexy!* Just looking at your body made me want to come." Then promise her: "Next time, though, I'm going to show you how good I can be. I'm going to make you come several times before I do."

The important thing to understand here is:

It's not out of the ordinary to have a setback or two with a new partner. That doesn't define who you are.

Hopefully, with the techniques in this chapter, you can think your way through occasional challenges with flair.

#11: Dealing With "Oh No!" Moments

However, maybe you're *new* to the concept of *control* and *any* woman you'd be with would present a control challenge. Maybe the idea of a naked woman is so exciting to you that you fear you can't go the distance, now or ever.

You're living in fear of those **"Oh no!" moments**, the crises when you're with her and suddenly you feel you might **come** before she wants you to. (Or before *you* want to. Either is preventable.)

All of us who have achieved total control over our bodies have had to deal with "Oh no!' moments, especially when first honing our **love**making skills. And all of us have had to get over the adolescent type of excitement that pushes us over the edge before we get very far. It's all part of the **learning curve**.

I remember a time as a boy when *putting on a* **condom** was a challenge; the pressure from it made me want to come. But I developed the skills, methods and mindset that enabled me to get beyond that tendency (and

Achieving The Ultimate Control

I'll show you how too).

What you require most, among other things, is a change in your *attitude* toward sex and women. We'll get to that in a minute.

But for now the first thing to remember is:

Don't freak out when you feel you're in an **"Oh no!" moment**. *You can conquer it.*

How? We'll start with what I call the **Sphincter Relaxation Technique**.

#12: THE SPHINCTER RELAXATION TECHNIQUE

The **Sphincter Relaxation Technique** is an exercise you can do while you're making love to prevent a climax from occurring. *Preferably you should do this before an "Oh no!" moment develops; that should prevent that kind of thing from happening.* But *the* **Sphincter Relaxation Technique** will still often help you even when you're arrived at that moment of panic and you need to prevent an orgasm from triggering.

It really works (if you do it properly and before you're too far along the path to a **climax**)!

In my experience, there's a biological connection between my **orgasm** and **tension in my sphincter**. (That's the **muscle** you can squeeze to close your **anal canal**.)

If it's *clenched* (as I believe it tends to be when you're having sex), it somehow participates in the **orgasm process**. As a young man I noticed that I felt a tickle down there before I came.

I also noticed that I could *stave off a* **climax** if I *relaxed* my sphincter muscle and concentrated on *opening and widening* my **anal canal**. That greatly reduced my likelihood of coming. It worked time after time - not 100% of the time, but almost.

So that's what you have to do. And do it from the outset, the moment you enter her. Because I've found that *if you manage to do this - relax your* **sphincter** *and open your* **anal canal** *from the get-go - it's easier to keep it that way to avoid losing control.*

It takes some doing. You're moving your hips or other body part to make love and you simultaneously have to relax your bottom.

With a little mental effort you should be able to do this. It'll become easier with time, too.

Once you see that **the Sphincter Relaxation Technique** works you'll then also have a certain level of **confidence** that will contribute to your control skills. *Knowing there's something you can do to stay in command of things negates any* **performance fear** *that can help bring on a climax.*

Another advantage to using **the Sphincter Relaxation Technique** is that it concentrates your mental focus on your **sphincter muscle**. In doing that, you're forcing yourself to think of something *other than* the sexy babe you're with and the great way her **pussy** feels. That lessens the impact those **orgasm-inducing influences** might otherwise have on you. (We'll talk more about the power of thoughts in a moment.)

#13: THE *SHORT DIVERSION* METHOD

Another method I used with great success to avoid coming when I did not want to is what I'll call my **Short Diversion Method**. How do you do this?

You simply pull your cock out of her the moment you feel you are on the road to a climax. This requires some finesse, though, so your lover doesn't react to it negatively. That's where the diversion comes in.

To give yourself "cover" (that is, to make it seem as if you didn't pull out to regain control, which might be perceived as a drag by your partner), immediately do something to her she loves. In other words, make it seem as if you purposely stopped making love to her with your penis so you could tease her further.

Going down on her always fits that scenario. She won't complain about your doing that!

But if you choose to give her **head**, don't do it to completion. You're not really giving her **cunnilingus**. You're just allowing your **cock** to cool down a bit so you can attain composure enough to reenter her for the long haul.

If she looks at you funny at you when you pull out or says, "What are you doing?" or something like that, you could say:

"I'm not ready to give it to you yet. I'm going to make you wait. I want to make you good and hot for my **cock**."

Then dive into her **pussy**. She won't question you further; I can guarantee that!

Tease her **vulva** artfully with your **tongue** for a few minutes and then reenter her whenever you've recovered from being too sensitive. Do that smoothly though. You could ask her playfully: "Should I put my **cock** back inside you or should I put my **tongue** back between your **legs**?" That would get many women hotter and eager for you.

An alternative to the above would be to pull out *very briefly* and then reenter her (within seconds) - *if* that works to cool you down. If it does, then work that in-out kind of thing into a rhythm (pull out, push in, pull out, push in) so she thinks it's what you wanted to do (as opposed to what you *needed* to do to calm down). Pulling out quickly can be very titillating to a woman, if you work it into an effective in-out motion.

#14: The Pause Method

Another way to get a grip on things is with the **Pause Method**. With this approach, you simply hold still inside her. If you do this right, it can be done as a very **romantic** gesture or as a **teasing** means of *driving her crazy*.

If you have extreme control problems, by the way, I would recommend you do the **Pause Method** at the very outset. The beauty part is you can make this a **big tease** - especially when doing it from the get-go. She'll get hotter and hotter until she can't take it anymore. The hotter she gets, the closer she is to climaxing.

For those who instead experience only occasional **"Oh no!" moments**, however, this works great at any point in the process in allowing you to *regain* **control**. Doing so in midstream, though, might surprise and disappoint her unless you provide cover for your suddenly pausing.

Either way, it helps to tell her (in your sexiest voice) something like: "Mmmm. It feels so good just to be inside you."

You can give her a **bear hug** and *kiss her neck*. Tell her you paused in order to relish the moment. (That's your cover; you don't want her to think you're actually holding on for dear life, so to speak. It's a plausible explanation because it does feel good to stop and enjoy the pleasures that come simply from coupling.)

Be **suave**. Tell her how much *you love her*. If you need more time, say something like: "I wish we could just stay like this forever."

Then, when you feel you can continue, start small. Move slowly. Minimize your range of motion. That will help you maintain composure.

#15: Stay Within Yourself

Speaking of which, have you ever heard the phrase **stay within yourself**?

When I was first learning how to play lead guitar, I made the common mistake of trying to play faster than I was able to at the time. That's when a friend of mine told me to stay within myself.

That advice went a long way. If you keep to a pace or a set of skills you can handle, you have a much better shot at success, whatever you're doing.

On Loving Women

The same thing with **lovemaking** - especially if you have control issues. **You need to find and stick to a pace and rhythm that you can handle.**

We all have our comfort zones. Stay within yours.

It's the **pace and rhythm** that can test your control skills the most. **Choose a "groove" (a rhythm, intensity, range of motion) which doesn't over-stimulate your penile nerves - one that is "safe" versus one that would lead to quick ejaculation. Choose a speed that you feel you can do forever without losing it.** *You want to start off, most times, rather slowly.*

If she tries to speed things up, say, "No, honey. Let's keep things *slow* for awhile. This is too good to rush."

#16: Choosing Positions That Enable You To Last

Another great ruse if you are struggling with control issues is to choose positions that don't push you closer to your orgasm. One smart idea:

Pick positions where she's least able to control the pace and motion.

For instance, the **sideways positions** work well in this way (you will learn more about these in the chapter on **positions**). They let you easily **pull out** and **keep your penetration shallow** too, which also will help you compose yourself.

Achieving The Ultimate Control

The worst positions for you if you're grappling with control issues are the woman-on-top positions. There the woman has control and, if she's enthusiastic, she can send you over the top. Suggestions:

Try to discourage her from going too fast when on top (in a very loving way). You might try saying something like, "C'mon, baby, let's slow down and make this last." If that doesn't work, though, don't get mad or upset. (Some women love being on top and they have a right to do so. They also like going wild up there.) Here's what you do:

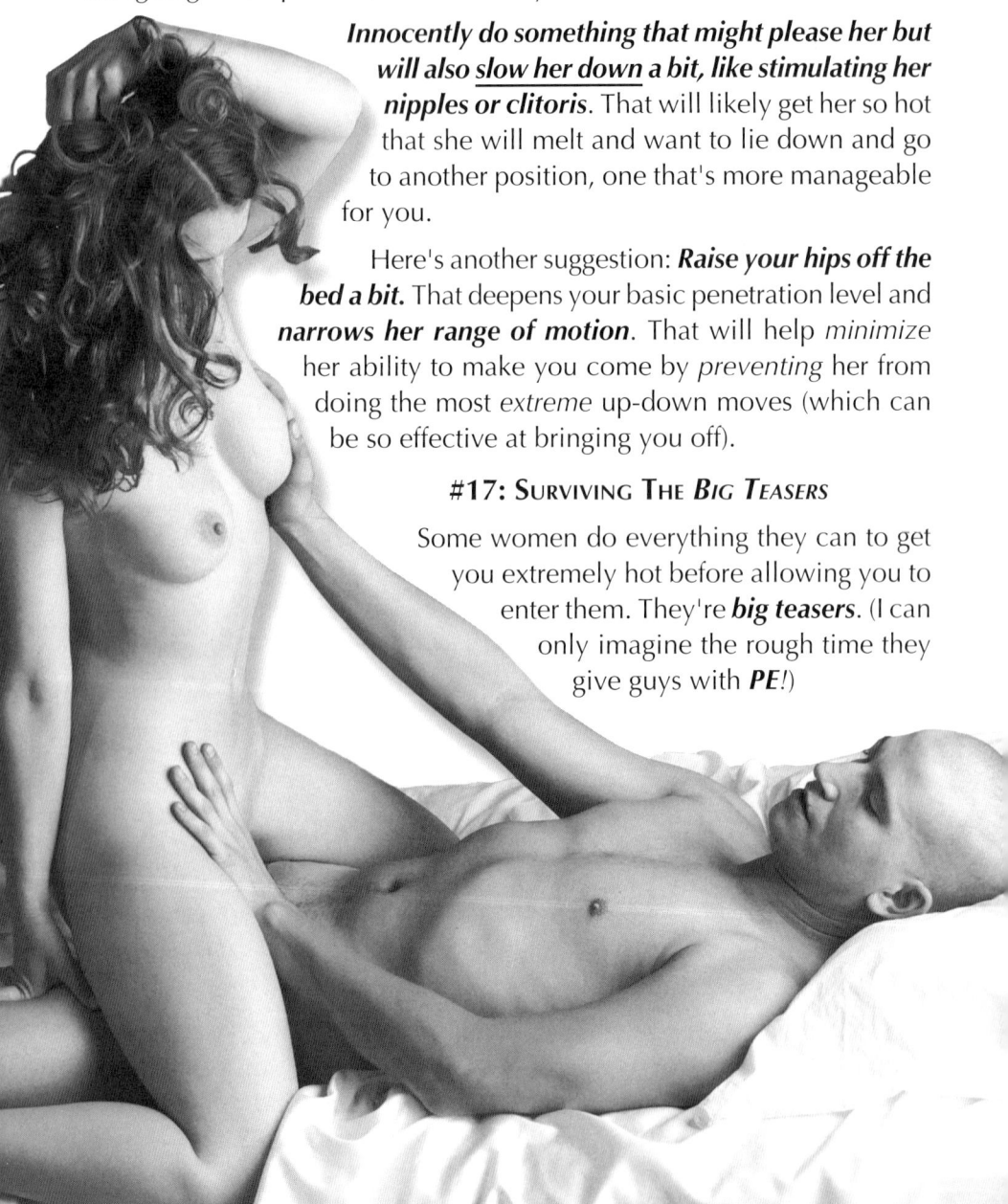

Innocently do something that might please her but will also <u>slow her down</u> a bit, like stimulating her nipples or clitoris. That will likely get her so hot that she will melt and want to lie down and go to another position, one that's more manageable for you.

Here's another suggestion: **Raise your hips off the bed a bit.** That deepens your basic penetration level and **narrows her range of motion**. That will help *minimize* her ability to make you come by *preventing* her from doing the most *extreme* up-down moves (which can be so effective at bringing you off).

#17: Surviving The *Big* Teasers

Some women do everything they can to get you extremely hot before allowing you to enter them. They're **big teasers**. (I can only imagine the rough time they give guys with **PE**!)

On Loving Women

I had a buddy in college, in fact, who complained to me about this.

"She pulls on me forever, man," he said, obviously upset, "and she's tickling my balls and then she sucks my cock for awhile before she lets me enter her. By then I'm so hot I shoot off inside her really quickly!"

Here's what I told him:

Until you've developed the **highest degree of control**, you have to be *proactive* with this kind of woman. *You have to gently resist her efforts to take control at the outset.* If this means you have to grab her hands nicely at the outset before she can grab a hold of you, then you must do that.

Then, one thing you could do is go down on her. No woman will resist that! Then you're in control and you can enter her whenever you like.

Other strategies with this kind of woman:

- *If she's into **gentle bondage**, do it. Get fuzzy handcuffs at an adult toy store (let her pick them out ideally). Put them on from the outset (preferably so her hands are above her head), placing her on her back, so she cannot touch you. Or use her bathrobe's belt (if it's soft) or one of your ties to tie her hands (comfortably). Then tease the heck out of her until you're ready to enter her.*
- *Tell her you want to **blindfold her** for fun. Tell her it will make her more sensitive to the touch. Then she's less apt to try and touch you. Then make her good and hot before entering her.*
- *Tell her you want to **give her a sensual massage**. (Use nice scented massage oil.) She'll relax and you can work her all over until you know she's wet and then you can enter her when you like.*
- **Take control playfully**. *Wiggle your finger (in a "no" motion) and say: "Ah, ah, ah! Today **I'm** in control!" Then hold her hands down on the bed and you control the action.*
- *Throw her over a table, the bed, the hood of your car, whatever. Then **take her from behind** where she cannot easily touch you.*
- *Push her tenderly back on the bed so she's lying on her back and **position your body below her waist so she can't touch you**. Kiss and tongue her **legs, feet** and **toes**. <u>Suck</u> her **toes** and she'll go crazy. Take your time. When you're through with that, she'll be hot enough for you to enter her - when **you're** ready.*

Ultimately, though, you need to increase your **control skills** so your woman can do whatever she wants to you without the risk of your coming. If she likes touching you for a long time before *intercourse*, you need to allow her that pleasure.

Achieving The *Ultimate* Control

#18: Mind Over Matter For The Ultimate Control

Now as you might know, the world's greatest yogis have proven the power of the mind in accomplishing amazing feats. So I don't think it would be controversial if I told you that great **love**making, too, is all about *mindpower*. This is especially is true when it comes to the art of control.

And I can testify to that firsthand. Because I was able to **out-think** all the **normal control problems** we all have to confront as **adolescents**. And brainpower is what has enabled me to achieve the ultimate control. I can go on literally forever without coming if I wanted to - and you can too, if you spend the same amount of time I spent perfecting my skills.

Let me share what I know with you about brainpower so you too can *master the art of control*. It's all in your mind. The **brain** is all-powerful.

Because, think of it:

Isn't your **brain** creating your control problem in the first place? Isn't your mind telling you to come because of some sexy stimulus? Doesn't your brain chatter tell you *omigod her vagina's so wet or tight or hot,* or *she's so sexy,* or *I can't hold back my orgasm?*

We have to train your mind to look at sex and women in a more mature and positive way. That means you need to have the right attitudes and thoughts prior to and during sex.

In times when you're not having sex you have to turn off your tendency to get overexcited because of sexual ideas or images. During sex we have to get your mind focused on matters other than your **orgasm** *and* **orgasm triggers**.

How do we do that? What **thought processes** work for one man might not work for another, but let me give you a list of ideas from which you should find at least a few good ones that should get you on the right track:

1ST: Take Back The Power

Men with a *lack of* **control** often need an **attitude adjustment**. I say that based upon what I recall from my teenaged years and the conversations I've had with the many men I've helped.

They give women far too much power over them. They see women as all-powerful **seductresses**, **sex kittens** who can make them **come** just by showing some flesh or giving them a hot look. And they feel they're necessarily overwhelmed by a woman's touch. It's too much to handle.

If that describes you, you're seeing sexual relationships in the wrong way. You're taking on the wrong role.

The **woman** is supposed to swoon; *not you*.

I partly blame the media for this syndrome. The sexy ads, movies, music videos and prurient TV shows that make it seem like women have a sort of *reverse Svengali effect* on men. The message in the images says:

Women are confident **vixens** *who can make men* **come** *in their pants just by striking a sexy pose in peekaboo clothes.* This *all-pervasive image* creates a *false sense of reality* in a man's head.

Thoughts are *powerful* things. A friend of mine told me of a man who allegedly froze to death when he was locked in the back of a truck after he was told it was a freezer truck (whereas the temperature was actually above freezing). This story may be allegorical but yogis and others have in fact achieved amazing things through mind power.

The point is: **You need to tune out the lustful thoughts created by the media implying you're powerless in the face of a sexy woman.** That's just noise. They're presenting false images.

Don't give a woman too much power over you. Don't tell yourself a woman is a potent seductress you cannot resist. You are in command of your mind. Put those thoughts out of your head.

If you are making yourself feel that way, you cannot give most women what they want. Plus, you'll prime yourself for coming.

2ND: YOU CAN MAN-UP

The truth is: **Most real women want their men to be in control. They want their men to sweep them off their feet.** They want their men to have the **cool self assurance** and **sexiness** that makes them want to drop their panties. *They* want to be the one *overwhelmed* sexually by their partner. Most women like the feeling of being "taken." They don't, by and large, want their *men* to be made *weak* by them.

And don't you see what women are giving you in having those desires and fantasies? The **power**. Most real women are **handing** it to **you. You** have the power.

You might not realize it yet but it's true. We talked about this earlier. Why do you think *Romance novels* are the biggest selling books today? And why do you think those covers most often feature Fabio or someone like him as opposed to, say, Woody Allen or Peewee Herman?

In these books **confident men seduce** women with their **masculine** *charms*. Women are made powerless simply by their presence. Don't you see what effect these books have on women and what their popularity reveals?

Women are being <u>trained</u> by these books to melt in the presence of a self-assured, sexy man who's comfortable in his own skin. They're being taught that this kind of man has the power to make them desire him carnally. And they read these books because <u>this is what they want</u>.

So *wake up to that reality*. And adjust your mind to it. It is, after all, a beautiful thing.

And as my mentor Earle was fond of saying: *"If she gives you* **the woman***, take it."* In other words, if she's happily taking on the **traditional female role** of wanting to be "taken" by a sexy man, run with it. Take that role. And the good news is that most women are happily giving that to you.

3ʳᴰ: AFFIRMATIONS & VISUALIZATIONS

And you can do that. **Yes** you can! *You must tell that to yourself.*

If you ever were on sports teams you know how powerful the right thoughts can be. And they often come in the form of affirmations - although sports people refer to them as pep talk. Or they talk of "psyching themselves" into a **winning** frame of mind - and they truly believe that leads to a performance that makes winning **happen**.

Translating that into what you must do as a lover:

That doesn't mean acting macho or phony. It means **be confident in your manhood**. Believe in yourself as a lover.

It means you should tell yourself positive affirmations, to make what you want to happen come true:

You need to tell yourself that you can and will last as long as women want you to. You can and will knock their socks off. Tell yourself **you're going to show her what kind of man you are**.

And if you can add **visualizations** to that, all the better. Many success coaches will tell you there's real power in *visualizing* something you want to occur, as if it's already happened.

Visualize yourself making your woman come over and over again, fully in charge of the situation. A man in control. Loved all the more for it.

4ᵀᴴ: YOU'RE IN CHARGE OF YOUR THOUGHTS

Also understand: You can control the level of excitement in your

head. That's where many control problems stem from. Getting yourself overheated before the get-go.

It's like coming to a footrace exhausted because you already imagined you ran the race...and *lost*. That's a defeatist attitude, isn't it? So is giving in to thoughts of your "losing" (coming) before the *love*making begins. *But you can put an end to those **defeatist thoughts**.*

For one thing, that means *tuning out the voices in your **brain** that assign the woman way too much influence in the early going.* The "I can't believe this is happening!" voice. The "I can't believe she's doing that to me!" voice. The "look at that *amazingly sexy **naked woman*** next to me!" voice. The "omigod, she's touching me there!" voice.

You must come to see those as negative, counterproductive and false thoughts. Then you must replace those thoughts with proper, confident and truthful thoughts.

Remember that song years ago, Rico Suave? Kind of funny now and dated but still...it might help put a similar (less silly) image of yourself in your head. Be the **cool suave lover**, the **Don Juan**.

In your mind see it this way: **You're** getting her hot, **not** the reverse.

And the truth is: **Women do get hot over sexy, confident men.**

5ᵀᴴ: It's Not About Your Orgasm

And you may have heard this before:

You must not be goal-oriented as a lover. Great lovemaking **is not about rushing to arrive someplace.**

Your orgasm isn't what it's about. It's about enjoying all the roller-coaster-like thrills you get. It's the amazing titillations you experience, changing from moment to moment, that make lovemaking **so incredible.**

In other words: **Don't be orgasm-oriented**. There's so much more to **love**making than that.

In fact, to me my **climax** is almost a *drag*. It's the *end* of an incredible **process** (at least a temporary end, for those of us who are multi-orgasmic). I want the mind-blow to go on forever...or at least a reasonably long time.

That's one reason I suggested that you occasionally do the **Desensitization Exercise <u>without coming</u>** - *to show you the myriad pleasures you can get during sex during* **the awesome pre-climax phase**. *And I wanted you to see that* **if you prolong the pre-climax phase as long as possible, the sensual rewards are at least as good as those you get from coming, if not better.**

Achieving The <u>Ultimate</u> Control

That should have given you an awareness, too, of all the hot sensations you should consciously *luxuriate in* for as long as you can, by holding off your orgasm. What an incredible high you can achieve!

6TH: LOVE IS A DRUG

When Roxy Music singer Brian Ferry sang **Love Is The Drug**, he wasn't far off the mark when he crooned:

> Oh oh catch that buzz
> Love is the drug I'm thinking of
> Oh oh can't you see
> Love is the drug for me

Do you realize how many **drug-like chemicals** are produced by your **brain** and other organs during **sex**? (Especially **great sex**.) Some are said to be as powerful as **opiates**. They actually have *pain relief* and other incredible benefits. Those are chemicals that are released *before* **oxytocin** - the chemical that helps bring on your **orgasm**, the chemical **PE** sufferers are addicted to - is secreted by your **brain**. That is, *you can get off on these* **naturally-produced drugs** *if you put off your climax.*

You've heard of a "runner's high"? These are actually the chemicals that produce it. And they also produce what we need to realize is a "**lover's high**." **Endorphins** produced during **love**making, like **acetylcholine, dopamine** and **norepinephrine** are said to have similar structures to **morphine**. Indeed, **dopamine** and **norepinephrine** can induce a "**drug-like dependency,**" according to Michel Odent of London's Primal Health Research Center. (So, Robert Palmer was right on the mark when he sang of being **Addicted To Love**.) Another drug-like chemical released during sex, **phenylethylamine**, has been said to produce bliss and excitement.

How does this relate to mind control? In this way:

You can take your mind off the urge to come by focusing on the stimulating virtual "high" you get from the drug-like chemicals your body creates during sex. And if you preoccupy yourself with non-orgasmic thoughts - as you would do if you consciously took pleasure in the euphoria brought on by your own body's natural "drugs" - you will lessen your likelihood of coming too early.

7TH: HARNESS THAT LITTLE VOICE IN YOUR HEAD

Another reason not to rush toward an **orgasm**:

Your **climax** won't be anywhere near as big or as pleasurable as it would be if you put if off as long as possible. You should have learned this in doing the **Long Self-Tease** and **Desensitization Exercises** (if you completed them successfully).

So let that little voice in your head sternly remind you of this if you find yourself losing control. I'm talking about the negative character in your brain that often criticizes you (one of my vocal coaches used to call it by the name **"Otto"**).

Let it sober you up like an AA meeting, telling you: "My **orgasm** would suck if I had it now; it wouldn't feel very good." That might very well do the trick.

8ᵀᴴ: IT'S NOT ABOUT YOU

It's also not about you. It's about **her**. So *take the focus off yourself*. This alone will help you gain control over your body.

And this is not a modern discovery, that **your lover should come before you do**. *That's what* **great male lovers** *do - completely satisfy their women before they let themselves wind down.*

This was understood in ancient times. Roman poet Ovid referred to this more than 2,000 years ago in **The Art Of Love: Book 2** when he wrote:

"...take care not to cram on sail and outrace your mistress..."

You will not please your lover if you always come before her. Most women want to experience most of their **orgasms** while their men are still inside them. *That feels best to them; and it propels them to bigger climaxes.*

So - here's where **mind control** comes in:

Have that little voice inside your head sober you up before you give in to an early urge to come by reminding you of this. Have it be like a smack in the face, saying: "No; it'd be crummy to come now - she'd be so disappointed...or even pissed!"

Hopefully your body will respond to that kind of intervention and your nerves will calm down. It's not supposed to be a selfish act, **love**making. It's all about her. And in reminding yourself of that, perhaps you'll get back to the place where you need to be, attitudinally, in being the man your woman wants.

Delight in being the **man**. Get off on giving her what she wants.

9ᵀᴴ: TUNE OUT HER REACTIONS

And here's another major control issue that needs to be addressed:

A woman's sexual reactions are what sends many men over the top.

So learn to tune out her moans and screams (close your ears to it). Don't

look at her tantalizing body reactions either (close your eyes). Don't be surprised or thrown off when her pussy gets wetter or hotter.

It's natural to empathize viscerally with what she's feeling. If this is the case, *you must tune out this* **sensory information**.

Think of something else, even if it's a voice in your head saying, "I'm not going to pay attention to what's going on." Or perhaps repeat the mantra: "I'm really going to give her a good ride and show her how good I can be."

10TH: THINK OF THE MECHANICS

But if that doesn't work, there are other ploys you can use to get your mind off her reactions and your orgasm. One super way is to **focus your thoughts on the mechanics of sex**.

Concentrate on what you're doing physically (while not losing the feeling you're expressing – always remembering that ***love**making is* **nonverbal communication**). If she *likes* what you're doing, see if you can *repeat it over and over* as *exactly* as you can.

Look down at your body. What parts of you are moving and how are you propelling them? Are your knees moving? Your feet? Your hips? How?

Once you've figured that out, try to keep your motion as consistently the same (in your depth of penetration, range of motion (or "motion inches"), angle, rhythm and intensity). It's not easy to do, but it's important to master this.

The **mental process** *takes your mind off your own excitement (which helps you achieve greater longevity). But there's a more important benefit:*

Repetitive motion is often the best way to make your lover come. So you want to become a "machine" when you've noticed that your partner is responding big time and will likely come if you keep doing what you've been doing **exactly as you've been doing it**.

11TH: THINK OF SOMETHING THAT'S NOT SEXY

And if all else fails in your effort to stave off your climax, "Think of England," as the Brits are wont to say.

If all you can think of is your fear of coming too soon, guess what happens? It's like trying not to think of a white elephant.

So in the early stages of surmounting your **control issues**, it's OK to force yourself to think of something that's not sexy at all, to tune out your fears (and any stimuli that might send you over the top). You can look around the room, for example, and study an object of interest; ask yourself questions about it, such as: "I wonder how they made that?"

I resorted to this control tactic a number of times as a teenager before I achieved a very good level of **control**. One time I even forced myself to think about a funeral that was coming up! (That worked well, by the way!)

The idea is to turn your thoughts toward anything innocuous, to get your mind off the sexual activity and your own excitement, at least temporarily. Usually, it won't take long before you've settled down and you can bring your thoughts back to her.

Anything like that is OK, in the *short term. That is, until you can master the art of control in better ways.*

And **as long as she doesn't sense your mind is on something else**. So keep your mind diversion game brief and do it with finesse so she doesn't catch on to what you're doing.

Momentary Setbacks

Whatever the cause, don't be thrown if on a rare occasion you **come** too soon. You will overheat occasionally. Sometimes, for instance, an illness can make you more prone to come quickly. Or maybe something or someone got you hot prior to making love to your honey.

It happens. And, actually, you might be surprised to find that she might even be **pleased** if you lose your control once in a blue moon. She might see that as a tribute to her sexiness! (And play into that. Tell her you lost it because she made you too hot!)

It's all right. If you've learned the lessons in this chapter well, you will be able to think it through or work your exercises and get it together for the next time.

And take heart in this fact:

The very *knowledge* that a woman is a challenge for you helps you prepare for the next time together. You'll be able to **anticipate** the factor that sends you over the top and **blunt it**.

How Much Is Enough?

Yes, if you work hard at this as I did many years ago, you too will master the art of control. You will be able to go on virtually forever. For hours. For as long as you can physically keep it up. No threat of coming.

So should you then go on forever? For hours and hours? Every time? When is enough *enough?* When do you stop?

You might have noticed at the very start of this chapter that I did not say

Achieving The *Ultimate* Control

the art of control was about lasting **forever**. That's because it's **not** our goal.

In my experience, only *college coeds* and **nymphomaniacs** want you to go on for what seems like forever - hours and hours, all night long. That's great when you're a college kid and you don't have to wake up refreshed for work the next day. Once you've got a steady job, though, the idea of going on "forever" is neither attractive to her or you. And if you've ever been with a **nymphomaniac** you'll understand why seemingly *unending* sex on a *daily* basis can become a **nightmare**. You don't want to go there. Plus predictable behavior (as in everyday marathons) becomes *boring*.

This is important for you to understand: **You should only last as long as your woman wants you to.** For one thing, women like the feeling of making you come; they enjoy your **orgasm**. If you don't play the game and come when they indicate they want you to (even if it's far short of when you wanted to), they will feel you're not being excited by their bodies, or that they're not sexy to you, or that you don't like their **love**making. *No good!* And just as you feel it's a drag when it's especially hard to make a woman **come**, *she'll hate it if it's difficult for her to make you* **come**.

Plus, women sometimes physically get *sore* inside and want the **love**making to end while it's still pleasurable. If you go beyond this point you will piss her off. (You wouldn't know that she's sore; she will probably not tell you. That's a huge reason to *stop* when she gently lets you know - verbally or otherwise - that it's time to come.)

In addition, **every work of art must have a natural and proper end**. She doesn't want a mindless marathon. Who does? (This was probably one of my sins in my late teens and early 20s – going on for *too* long.)

At some point, it'll have been just the right amount of **love**making for her. ***That's when you shoot off the fireworks and celebrate your time together by collapsing in each other's arms. For the overall effect to be nice, your* love*making must have a nice and timely end.***

Now since I can go on practically forever without coming, I learned long ago that I have to do something to bring the event to a proper end while making my lover *think* she's "gotten" to me and pleased me too. (There's nothing my lover can do to make me come because I can control myself under all conditions. So I have to give her the *pretense* that she can.) So here's what I've done:

Whenever my lovers have done something indicating they want me to come, such as touching my **balls** *or sucking my* **nipples***, I have pretended their action made me hot enough to come. That's when I go for the "okey* *doke"* (as a friend of mine used to say); *I do whatever it takes to come.*

Upon seeing me come after whatever they did, my lovers then inevitably *repeated* that gentle hint the next time we were having intercourse, when they wanted the sex to a nice end.

It's actually great to get that kind of signal going. That way, you don't have to guess when your lover thinks it's time for a sweet finale.

If you don't do this, you will make **sex** *an unpleasant chore. It's important, though, that she never know you're only* **pretending** *she's making you come. If she did, it would spoil what you've just set up - the perfect signal for knowing when you should* **come***.*

Now You Have The Correct Mindset For Maximum Pleasure

Now once you've mastered the **art of control**, you'll see the amazing effect. She'll be on you like white on rice. This became clear when a lover said to me (I kid you not - I wrote it down afterward!):

> *"You're the only man I know of who can go on and on forever. No other man I've been with could do that. I'm sure there are other men out there who can do that, but I've never met them. So I guess you're stuck with me!"*

...And by the way...*Have you become* **master of your world** yet? Keep working at it. You will. **Every man can master the art of control.** Before long, your lover will be telling you what great control you have. And think of how proud you will be of yourself!

...And in so doing, *you will then be able to get a maximum amount of* **pleasure** *from* **love***making. Because* **my strategies** *will make you an* **aficionado** *of* **sexually stimulating sensations and their related pleasure***. You will learn just to slow down and* **enjoy the ride***.* Isn't that what it's all about?

And isn't that what the Pointer Sisters' song *Slow Hand* pleads for?:

> *I am tired of fast moves, I have got a slow groove on my mind...*
> *...I want somebody who will spend some time,*
> *Not come & go in a heated rush...*

But I'll leave the last word to Ovid (from **The Art of Love: Book 2**):

> *Believe me, love's acme of pleasure must not be hurried,*
> *But drawn insensibly on.*

MEDICAL BREAKTHROUGHS FOR MEN WITH PE

Recent Scientific Studies Offer Hope For The Most Extreme Cases Through The Use Of Medications

New scientific research suggests that some men suffering from **premature ejaculation (PE)** might benefit from medical help.

These are men who cannot last more than a minute or so within a woman and who are now medically described as having a "dysfunction."

In his article *Advances in Treatment for Premature Ejaculation* in the *European Urological Review* in 2008, for instance, Netherlands neuropsychiatrist Dr. Marcel D. Waldinger wrote that since the 1990s new drugs have given doctors hope in treating the most severe cases of PE:

"Research has been conducted by clinicians and neuroscientists, and has remarkably been performed with little financial support from pharmaceutical companies. In a considerable number of studies, it has been shown that daily use of some **SSRIs** and **clomipramine** delays **ejaculation** most effectively, and that the initial side effects diminish and even disappear after about three weeks."

He listed as examples of these medications **paroxetine, sertraline, citalopram and clomipramine**.

He said **tramadol** also has shown promise in two studies.

He expressed reservations, however, about **PDE-V inhibitors**, which he apparently sees as being effective only for men with erectile dysfunction.

"As the **PDE-V inhibitors** have no effect on the actual **ejaculation** time, these drugs are not useful in men with lifelong **PE** and no erectile difficulties. However, there have been some publications in which **PDE-V inhibitors** are recommended for men with lifelong **PE**. However, the methodology of these studies is rather weak."

He also was skeptical about **topical creams and sprays**: "A few studies have demonstrated that **lidocain-** and **prilocain- containing creams**, such as **local anaesthetic (EMLA) cream**, may delay **ejaculation**. However, few men with **lifelong PE** report much success using **EMLA creams**..."

Consult your doctor for the latest information.

> *"There's nothing better than good sex. But bad sex? A peanut butter and jelly sandwich is better than bad sex."*
> *- Singer-Songwriter Billy Joel*

Forget "Foreplay:" That Concept Makes Men Bad Lovers

*F*oreplay as a concept should be *outlawed*. This has given way too many men the crazy idea that non-intercourse activities should be done as a *separate* act, at the start, *just long enough to get her hot* and *only before penetration begins*.

The concept of "***foreplay***" as a means of getting to the "real deal" - an act you're supposed to want *more* than anything else (namely ***intercourse***) - has led many men to see **non-intercourse and pre-intercourse activities** as *obligations* that are *not fun*. It has also, I believe, led many men to give all **non-intercourse activities** (including everything revolving around the exciting **arousal process**) *short shrift*...which might explain why *one of the most common complaints among women is the brevity or complete lack of "foreplay"* (translation: **non-intercourse sexual activities**).

The solution to this complaint is actually to *banish* the idea that there is something called **foreplay** that comes *before* **sex**. Instead you should see *all* types of acceptable **sexual activities** as *equally* desirable, that occur not in any particular *order* or *hierarchy* but as the passion moves you.

You need to think of **love**making as a *unified* event, a *continuum* - not separated into parts. It's my feeling that women complain so much about a lack of **foreplay** because men have seen it as something they should do *quickly*, like a *necessary evil*, only to then abandon anything they associate with it once their **cock** is positioned to enter their lover. **Activities commonly associated with "foreplay" are not lesser pursuits you do only in the first few minutes that you then avoid later on.**

So, regarding **foreplay**: *Just forget this word.* It's destructive, mentally,

Forget "Foreplay": That Concept Makes Men Bad Lovers

to your ability to be a **great lover**. For one thing, the concept of a pre-sex time called **foreplay** gives you the incorrect impression that **pre-intercourse activities** are of lesser importance, like a foreword to a book, and that what comes next is what *really* counts. Plus, it fools you into thinking that the activities lumped under the category of "foreplay" should be done *quickly* and then *end,* not to be done again once penetration has begun. And it gives you the mistaken notion that you should rush into *penetration*. That's often foolish. In fact, if you're smart, you'll sometimes devote more time to teasing her or in pleasing her orally or manually than you will on intercourse. And sometimes you'll avoid intercourse altogether, to shake things up and keep her guessing.

In any event, artful lovers through the generations have long known that **love**making should be a beautiful *undivided* process - without dreaded and laborious requirements or urgently necessary end goals.

***Love*making *is not just about penetration*...**this should not be 100% of what you do. **And non-penetrative activities should not be confined to a brief and hurried pre-intercourse period (otherwise known as "foreplay") or to a lesser status. And once penetration has begun, it should not necessarily be exclusively what you do.**

Most **love**making sessions should be long enough where you'd want to mix things up, with time spent enjoying each other in ways that *don't* involve penetration. **Oral sex, manual sex, creative non-penetrative sex (using non-traditional body parts such as forearms or legs, or involving sex through clothing or while clothed)** and **erotic activities** (including massages, toy play, food play, role playing, a change of venue, etc.) should be considered as options at any stage in the process, befitting her desires.

Plus - if you're really good - you should be able to **multitask** (something we'll talk about later). That is, you should be able to titillate her in more ways than one at a time. During **intercourse**, your mouth and hands are free. So are your legs, your feet, your arms, your body. (And in later chapters I'll show you how to use them during **intercourse** to make her **orgasms** bigger and more frequent!)

The most important thing to take away with you from this chapter is this: ***Love*making *is not a two-stage process where you quickly warm your lover up with a brief pre-sex event ("foreplay") and then move on to penetration.*** That unfortunate and wrong-headed concept is the root of many of men's problems in bed. So banish it from your mind.

Once you do that, you'll find that the way of the modern lover is so much more interesting, sexy and fun!

> "As he began to move, in the sudden helpless orgasm there awoke in her strange thrills rippling inside her..."
> - From Lady Chatterley's Lover (1928) by D. H. Lawrence

Seduction, Wettening, Arousal, Orgasm: The Four Sexual Processes

Sexologists Masters and Johnson announced they'd created a four-phase "human sexual response" model of sexual physiological changes in 1966.

They argued lovers necessarily go through each of these phases in order: *excitement, plateau, orgasmic,* and *resolution. But I respectfully disagree.*

To me, their "plateau phase," the last-minute *tension* before an **orgasm**, is really just the *start* of an *orgasm*.

And their "resolution phase" - a *relaxation period* after a **climax** - seems superfluous, misleading even and possibly irrelevant. Most women can go from one orgasm to another without such rest. Some men, such as myself, can do this too. And, anyway, *why name what you do <u>after</u> sex?*

Also, I object to the notion the act can be separated into separate "phases" rather than it being a **continuum** of events. It's usually a *one-step process* toward a **climax**, kind of like a smooth golf swing after the backswing. You slowly accelerate to your follow-through. Hold and repeat.

But it can also include explorations *without* an **orgasm** taking place. Adolescents often do this kind of activity before they're ready for **intercourse**. But fully-sexual adults also choose to make this an occasional

Seduction, Wettening, Arousal, Orgasm: The Four Sexual Processes

part of their lives. To spice things up. Nothing like a tease to make the day hotter and the eventual orgasm bigger. (We'll talk about that later.)

And at any point during the unified **continuum**, your *focus* can be on any one or *more* of *three types of activities*, depending on what you want to do.

For instance, **love**making can either begin with **arousal** or **wettening** (a separate yet sometimes *concurrent* activity). Here's why I separate them: *different organs often define those activities.*

Plus, if you're **multi-orgasmic**, you can *keep* your **erection** after coming (or spring back in minutes) and continue on from there!

Oh - and quickies? I'd say your focus is purely on the *orgasmic*. Maybe with some artificial lubricant to get by the *lack* of *arousal* or *wettening*!

And soon you will be introduced to a hot spot that can make a woman get *aroused*, *wet* and *come* at the same time - almost *immediately!*

THE FORGOTTEN (NON-PHYSICAL) SEXUAL PROCESS: *SEDUCTION*

Another flaw in the old way of looking at things was that Masters & Johnson (and others) forgot to consider a crucial human sexual process: **seduction**.

It's true that **seduction** is mostly a non-physical activity. It primarily targets her <u>mind</u>. **Yet without the mind involved, sex cannot occur.**

Why those well-respected sexual research pioneers did *not* include **seduction** as *an important part of the sexual* **continuum** is a puzzle. Granted, **seduction** usually takes place before you get naked so you cannot always <u>see</u> its physical effects. And some feel sex does not take place before you strip naked. (Didn't the TV sitcom Seinfeld suggest that sex begins "with the appearance of the nipple"?) But that's just wrong.

Now in the 1970s psychiatrist Helen Singer Kaplan of the Human Sexuality Program at Weill Medical College of Cornell University came close to suggesting this. She invented a three-stage sexual model that went: **desire, excitation, orgasm**. But *desire's* not a *process*. **Seduction** is. (Yet she was right in including a woman's *mind* in the **sexual continuum**.)

Seduction <u>creates</u> desire, an essential element in a woman's mind. Desire then brings on sexual impulses and behavior. So I think it's clear that **sex begins when seduction has begun. Seduction** is a <u>necessary</u> **love**making **process. And it needs to come <u>first</u>.**

Plus, like the other **four love**making **processes** I've suggested, **seduction** *can stand alone. It doesn't need to lead to nudity or physical touching.*

On Loving Women

*Indeed, sex through **seduction** - as I will demonstrate - can actually begin <u>hours</u> before intercourse or orgasm takes place!*

And it's been proven that **seduction** can be *a potent form of making love, in and of itself*. Words can work powerfully on the **brain**. The **brain** then releases **sexually potent chemicals that** *produce physical sexual effects in your lover; they also change her mood and way of thinking - instilling powerful needs, making her amorous.* (In fact, *some Svengalis or expert lovers can make women* **come** *through seductive suggestion alone!* **Seduction** *is the only* **sexual process** *they need.*)

You can bring on the wettening and arousal processes purely through <u>seduction</u> - *with the sound of your voice, the words you say and the sentiments you express, your touch, your appearance, your cologne, and so on. (I talk about this in greater detail elsewhere.) And the* **seduction process** *jump-starts the* **three <u>physical</u> processes** *and makes them more intense.*

*Furthermore, y***ou cannot have great sex without going through the process of seduction.** **Desire** *must be at a significant* **level** *to produce* **passion** *- an essential element in great* **love***making.* **Seduction** *can produce that result.*

And it doesn't have to start just before the physical **love***making begins. You're planting seeds, making her desirous and ready - perhaps hours later.*

You've undoubtedly heard that women need to be *in the mood* for them to *want* sex. Although that's been trivialized or forgotten in these tech-savvy and somewhat antisocial times, it's a crucial consideration. The **seduction process** is a part of what goes into putting your lover *into the mood*.

The mood translates into a *state of mind* that's *conducive* to sex. **The physical changes we discussed before will not occur if her mind's shut down to sex.** You need her **mind** on your side for it to want to produce all those great chemicals which *facilitate* sex (see page 135 for details). *They* are *necessary*. They *allow* sex to occur (*and without them, bruising occurs*).

A woman's *mind* also must be thinking *good thoughts* of *you*, as a man, if you want *great* sex. If you've been unkind or grumpy, she might not see you in a good light. If she doesn't see you in a good light, *the chemical releases in her brain that might produce desire will not likely take place*. Without those *chemical releases*, her thoughts likely will not be of sex.

Conversely, if you've made her feel *lovingly* toward you, her **brain** will produce drug-like chemicals that **relax** and **arouse** her. Those **aphrodisiacs** will give her feelings of **longing** for you. That will make her **want** sex. And

Seduction, Wettening, Arousal, Orgasm: The Four Sexual Processes

that will make her **hotter** and more **passionate** for you *during **love**making*.

*Without that **passion**,* great *sex cannot occur. And* passion *begins in the brain. So **seduction** should start long before you want to make love to her.*

So every man needs to be schooled in the art of **seduction**. While most men I'm sure think **seduction** is the province of the female, nothing could be further from the truth.

In fact, **seduction** can and should be done in a very masculine way. If you've seen a James Bond movie, you should know exactly what I mean.

While James Bond is a fictional character, the men who played that role showed you exactly how to get a woman hot for you. In a *sophisticated* way.

I will cover *the art of seduction* in a later chapter. Don't skip that!

THE THREE PHYSICAL PROCESSES OF LOVEMAKING

Beyond **seduction**, **love**making consists of **three** other **possible processes**. These are associated with the *physical* side of sex: **arousal, wettening** and **orgasm**. I say "possible" because **you can engage in one without including the others. (These processes often feature but don't require nudity.)**

You will need a thorough knowledge of **female sexual anatomy** to take her on a wild and wonderful journey through any one or all of *the three processes*. You'll want to get familiar with her body parts because:

...*You will need to know what body parts* **arouse** *her and what happens during the* **arousal process**. (So you can make your lover experience all the incredible sexual changes a woman can go through.)

...*You will need to know what parts make her* **wet,** *her* **wetness triggers, for the wettening process**. *The wetter the better! You cannot* **penetrate** *her unless she's wet,* made so either by her own lubrication - which is preferable for its safety, plentiful supply and efficiency - or by artificial means, including your own **saliva** or store-bought **lubricants**.

(We'll discuss **artificial lubrication** later. But a great lover knows how to make her wet by physically manipulating areas that can bring on lubrication (I'll teach you how). In later chapters, by the way, you will find out how to make her wet *simply through the use of your voice or by kissing her!)*

...*You will need to know her many* **orgasm triggers**, *including ones I've discovered, to bring on her* **orgasm process**. Along these lines, you will want to know about her **female ejaculation triggers**. These bring on **female ejaculation**. You will want to produce this pleasurable event during her

On Loving Women

orgasm if your lover's capable of this, as most women are.

We'll cover all of her fascinating parts in a later chapter so you know how to do all of this.

THE ROLE HER BRAIN PLAYS

All **four love**making **processes** are choreographed by the ***pleasure centers*** in a woman's ***brain***. This is why *you should think of her brain as **her most important sex organ**.*

This is why **you must learn to make love to her mind.** *(I will show you how in later chapters.)*

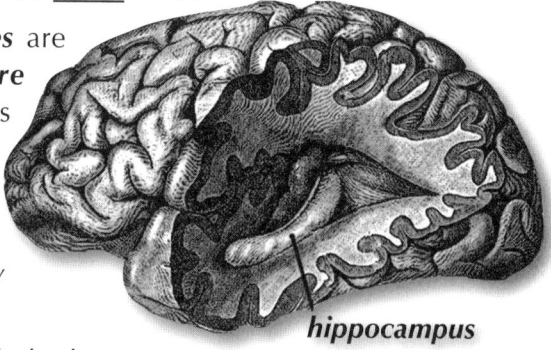

hippocampus

Her ***brain's pleasure centers*** include obscure areas like the ***hippocampus***, ***pituitary gland*** and ***hypothalamus***. And places like the ***nucleus accumbens*** and ***ventral pallidum*** (subcortical regions) and ***orbitofrontal cortex*** and ***anterior cingulate cortex*** (cortical regions) among others. (The ***ventral pallidum*** is hard to show graphically.)

In response to sexual stimulation, they produce a kaleidoscope of amazing chemicals. These include ***neurotransmitters, hormones***, and opiate-like ***endorphins***.

Actually, *three of her systems* are involved. Her ***nervous system*** (her brain and nerves, which control everything), ***endocrine system*** (glands that release hormones into the blood), and ***vascular system*** (blood vessels).

These systems collectively secrete and deliver *de facto* drugs and nerve impulses throughout her body. Those in turn produce euphoria,

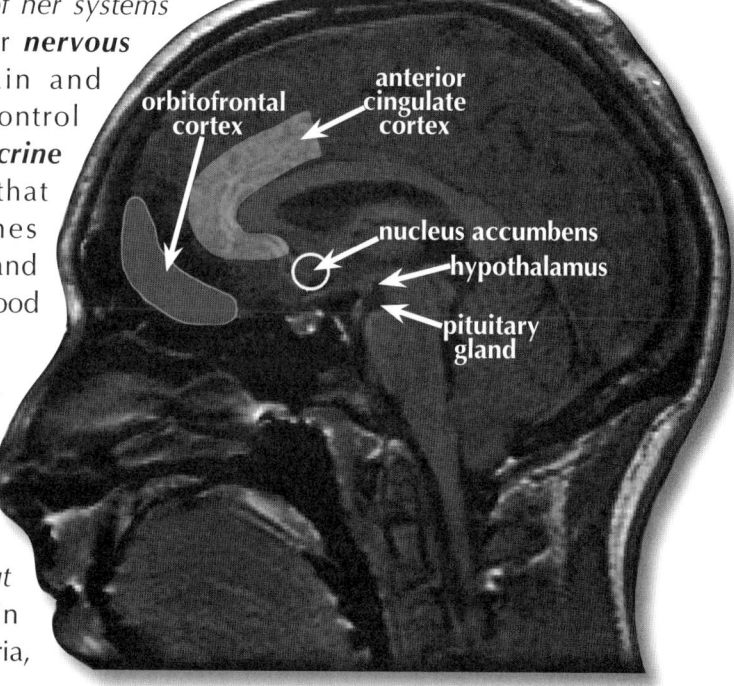

Seduction, Wettening, Arousal, Orgasm: The Four Sexual Processes

have pain killing qualities and anti-depressant effects. They produce a kaleidoscope of pleasurable *feelings* in your lover as well as **telltale physical changes**.

These *changes* are what you want to *produce*. And so you should be *looking for* the **telltale physical changes** *especially* to gauge your success in bringing about this incredible internal sea change in order to please her.

Physical Changes With Arousal, Wettening & Orgasm

So let's look at the *physical changes* you can produce in your lover during the **four sexual processes**. (You won't probably be naked during the preliminary process, **seduction**. So you might not have access to visual or other feedback. But then again, you could sneak a feel to see if she's wet if the opportunity arises or look to see if her nipples are erect, for instance.)

*You should be **looking** for one or more of these **physical changes** to gauge how effective your efforts are during any of the sexual processes.* Here are the most important, grouped by the *process type (for body part locations, refer to the anatomical charts on page 192 through page 194)*:

- *Arousal*
  - ♀ her **nipples** become erect; her **breasts** grow; her **clitoris** gets hard; her **labia minora** swell causing them to spread apart (they also become darker); her **G-Spot** engorges and increases in size - much of this due to an increased blood flow
  - ♀ her **vagina** will "tent" - the **rear two-thirds will lengthen** dramatically (to almost two times its normal measurement), her canal will widen (or "go wide" as I put it), ballooning to accommodate your **penis** (see this graphically on page 188)
- *Wettening:*
  - ♀ **love fluids** will come from her **vaginal walls** and **Bartholin's glands ducts** (these are on the outside); with deep stimulation a gush of fluid might come from deep inside her
  - ♀ you will feel juices inside her **vaginal canal**; liquid also will become visible as a glistening moisture on her **pussy lips** and then a stream of fluid dripping from the bottom V of her **vagina** (her **fourchette**)
  - ♀ her **vaginal canal** will get hotter (in some women so much that it might make you feel the urge to come too soon)
- *Orgasm:*
  - ♀ a woman's **orgasm** can go on for minutes; the length of time varies depending on the amount of time spent during stimulation, the type of stimulation and the quality of the **love**making but the average duration is 30 seconds (in other words, a woman's **orgasm** does not typically end quickly)

On Loving Women

- ♀ once you've triggered her **climax**, there will be a preliminary 5-10 seconds before her orgasm fully flowers; during this time her muscles will tense (throughout her entire body; even her toes will likely curl), her nipples will become erect, her **areolas** (the red circles around her **nipples**) will <u>decrease</u> in diameter, a red **rash** will appear (typically on her face, neck and chest), her body will contort, her **vagina** will grow wetter and hotter, her **labia** will grow darker and her **G-Spot** will grow larger
- ♀ the **outer third of her vaginal canal** will constrict (it will feel tighter) as her **climax** begins; with the full force of her **climax**, it might tighten so much as to partially or fully push you out of her
- ♀ the **inner two-thirds of her vaginal canal** will lengthen and widen (you will feel this taking place, around your **erection**)
- ♀ once her **orgasm** begins her **vaginal canal** will be flooded with juices, she'll have regular **muscular contractions** in her **vaginal walls, pelvis, anus and uterus** (scientists have determined the **contraction rate** during her **orgasm** will be 8-13 per second)
- ♀ her **heartbeat** and **breathing rate** will become more rapid
- ♀ her **clitoris** will disappear within its hood
- ♀ **nerve impulses** will cause **muscle spasms** which in turn will cause her body to uncontrollably writhe
- ♀ she might **ejaculate** bursts of fluids from her **Skene's** and **urethral ducts** - even **before** her **orgasm** fully explodes (not every woman can **ejaculate** but many more can than are experiencing **ejaculation** now - I'll teach you how to produce this in the section on **female ejaculation**)
- ♀ **telltale sign** with a woman who had **breast reduction**: the **surgical seams** harden and become more visually apparent

YOU WILL REALLY BLOW HER MIND

And here's a startling fact: a recent study suggests that *parts of women's brains <u>shut down</u> - at least temporarily - during the orgasm process.*

THE TIMES
THE SUNDAY TIMES

Archive Article — Please enjoy this article from The Times & The Sunday Times archives.

From Times Online
June 20, 2005

Women fall into 'trance' during orgasm

From Mark Henderson, Science Correspondent in Copenhagen

The first brain scans of men and women having sex and reaching orgasm have revealed striking differences in the way each experiences sexual pleasure. While male brains focus heavily on the physical stimulation involved in sexual contact, this is just one part of a much more complex picture for women, scientists in the Netherlands have found.

The key to female arousal seems rather to be deep relaxation and a lack of anxiety, with direct sensory input from the genitals playing a less critical role.

The scans show that during sexual activity, the parts of the female brain responsible for processing fear, anxiety and emotion start to relax and reduce in activity. This reaches a peak at orgasm, when the female brain's emotion centres are effectively closed down to produce an almost trance-like state.

EXPLORE HEALTH
> EXPERT ADVICE
> HEALTH FEATURES
> MENTAL HEALTH
> ALTERNATIVE MEDICINE
> CHILD HEALTH
> HEALTH CLUB

In a widely-publicized research project in 2006, Netherlands neuroscientist Gert Holstege and colleagues at the University of Groningen in the Netherlands used a positron emission tomography (PET) device to scan a dozen **women's brains** while experiencing a **climax**.

They themselves were surprised

Seduction, Wettening, Arousal, Orgasm: The Four Sexual Processes

by the results. According to the Scientific American in "The Orgasmic Mind" (May 15, 2008), Holstege's research team found that:

> "...when a woman reached **orgasm**, something unexpected happened: much of her brain went silent."

The areas most dramatically affected are apparently a woman's **pleasure centers**.

> "Some of the most muted neurons sat in the left lateral orbitofrontal cortex [pictured on page 135], which may govern self-control over basic desires such as sex. Decreased activity there, the researchers suggest, might correspond to a release of tension and inhibition. The scientists also saw a dip in excitation in the dorsomedial prefrontal cortex, which has an apparent role in moral reasoning and social judgment—a change that may be tied to a suspension of judgment and reflection."

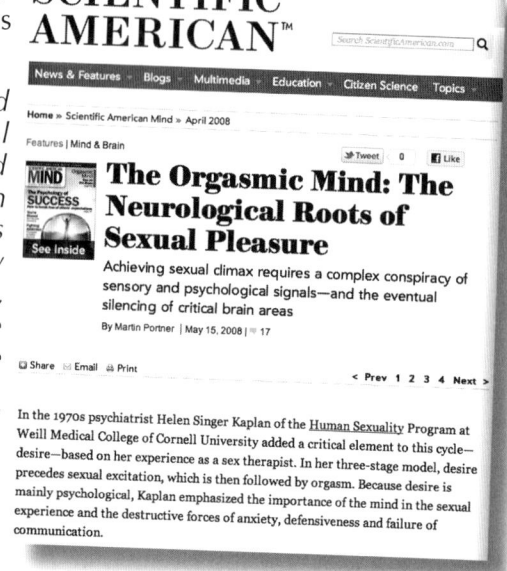

Holstege went on to shock scientists at the annual meeting of the European Society for Human Reproduction and Development in 2005 by announcing:

> "At the moment of **orgasm**, women do not have any emotional feelings."

What does this mean to you? That a **real orgasm** has a **tremendous effect on a woman - from her mind on down**. It's not a light or surface kind of thing. You might find that helpful to know when, for instance, trying to figure out if your lover is faking her orgasms.

What Arousal Is All About

OK. Some final advice about the three main physical sexual processes - the ones you need to correlate with your knowledge of a woman's body, or her **female sexual anatomy**.

Now the **arousal process** should be the process in which you languish the <u>most</u> during **love**making. The arousal process is about *exciting* her. Raising her heartbeat. Her fever. Titillating.

It should not be goal-oriented. Except to give her pleasure. With one exception - and this is important:

> The **arousal process** is what makes her **vagina go wide. You should never enter her until you're sure this has occurred or you'll hurt her. This is another reason - besides wetness issues - to take your time before penetration. (See page 188 for more on the vaginal "tenting" process.)**

And most times the **arousal process** should include what I call **The Big Tease**. That means you take your sweet time in slowly, slowly, slowly getting her hotter and hotter, by degrees.

You want to do **The Big Tease** because *the longer and more exciting the arousal process, the more powerful, exciting, long and satisfying her orgasm will be.* (How great her **climax** will be also depends upon what you've done to get her there and what you do to bring her off, but the **Big Tease** can play a big part in it.)

Arousal activities can include *penetration* or *not.* So be creative. (For instance, my mentor Earle told me he would often suck his wife's **nipples** for 30 minutes or so to fulfill both the **arousal** and **wettening processes**.)

You can devote your attention to just about *any* part of her body during the **arousal process.** Nearly every part of her body can be stimulated to give her tingly feelings to turn her on. Plus, **her skin** - which is **everywhere** - is **her largest sex organ.** Don't neglect that!

During the **arousal process**, you'll want to give her a wild ride of physical and emotional changes. That journey is a reward in and of itself.

So don't rush it. You'll be cheating her out of a beautiful experience.

What Wettening Is All About

You'll often want to get the **wettening process** going early on because *even fingerwork is made easier when your lover is lubricated. A slippery surface is not only easier to work; it also increases the sensations she will feel.* (Try tickling your **Trigger** with a dry finger, then a wet one. You'll see what I mean. The wet one feels better and makes you hotter!)

You don't *need* to start with the *wettening process* though. This is where my way of seeing things frees you up. If you want to tease her *non-lubricating parts* first, as with an erotic massage, then you can start with the *arousal process.*

If you're confused, let me explain. It's true that *wettening* requires that you *arouse* body parts that make her emit love juices. But I'm differentiating *wettening* from *arousal* techniques because **wettening hot spots** are often not high up on the list of **erogenous zones** in their *erotic effect.*

WHEN SHE NEEDS HELP GETTING & STAYING WET
The Pros & Cons of Artificial Lubricants & Saliva To Supplement Her Own Natural Lubricants

There will be times that your lover needs some help with lubrication. Even if she's young and nubile. Especially if you engage in prolonged sex.

A great male lover is expected to anticipate this problem (by sensing her dryness) and deal with it effectively so she doesn't experience any irritation or pain. If you hurt her regularly because you fail to act when she's dry, she will come to dread having sex with you.

And as she gets older, **female dryness** becomes a common issue. Middle-aged women often experience a decline in lubricity due to lower hormone levels. Post-menopausal women sometimes have **hormone replacement therapy** to maintain their ability to get wet naturally, prevent **vaginal inelasticity** problems and preserve their **desire** for sex. But that comes with *cancer risks*. Not good.

Some medications can also lead to dryness. So can **hysterectomies** and other operations.

Whatever the reason for her dryness, when it comes to helping your lover stay wet through the years I highly recommend two options.

The first and easiest choice is always **saliva**. You or she can provide it. It'd be best, though, if you did this. If you wait for your lover to do this you're at a stage where she's probably already experiencing discomfort and possible chafing pain that might not go away for the rest of that lovemaking session. She might also be annoyed with you by that point.

For **saliva**, you just go to your mouth for a wad and rub it either on your **shaft** during **penetration** or on the inside of her **vaginal canal** if you're not inside her (for whatever reason). It's best not to interrupt the lovemaking if you're already inside her.

But **saliva** doesn't last that long. Plus, there's a "yuck" factor.

I prefer using a natural **oil** such as **olive oil**. (Corn oil also works.) I've checked with *physicians* and verified it is a safe and healthy choice.

It lasts the longest of any lube I've tried. It does stain, though, so be careful in applying it. But it can degrade latex. So if you're using a **condom** for **birth control**, then perhaps try **animal skin condoms** in conjunction with the **oil**, if disease is not a fear). Keep a stylish bottle filled with **olive oil** by the bed, so it's easily available during sex. And buy a smaller bottle to take some oil with you for making **outdoor sex** and sex away from home more fun.

When it comes to other choices, a warning: **Do not use petroleum-based lubricants inside of her vagina.** Once inside, it's hard to safely clean them out. Plus they can change **her internal body chemistry** and cause disease.

They are approved for **anal sex** if you're into that. But *they destroy latex*. So don't use them in conjunction with **condoms**.

Water-based lubricants are also on the market but they often dry out. And if they have a **spermicide** they might taste bad on her. If scented they can cause irritation too.

I'm also not sure if all their ingredients (such as **glycerin, propylene glycol, and methyl paraben or propyl paraben** are totally safe.

Check with your doctor.

On Loving Women

One example would be her *outermost vaginal walls*. If you tickle or massage them they will release **mucous-like lubrication**. They will not help make her come though. And they often lose their erotic effect after the first half a minute or so of stimulation. She'll quickly want you to move on to more *arousing* places.

The parts you'll excite during the *arousal process*, however, have the potential to take her to the *edge* of an orgasm if not *over the top*. (But some hot spots do have both functions - *wettening* and *arousing*. And you often can use her **orgasm triggers** for *all* **three physical sexual processes**.)

Now the old way of looking at sex was to have you perform a short act of "foreplay" - essentially a *wettening* process - before jumping right into her pussy and going to town. Sophisticated, artful lovers through the generations, though, have long known that's the wrong way of going about what should be a beautiful and undivided *process* or *continuum*. (Plus there's another factor to consider before entering her: her **wideness**.)

Yet the truth remains that <u>**you should never enter her until she is thoroughly wet.**</u> *(Verify this by feel - lovingly - or visually.) You will hurt her otherwise. Plus, the experience will be unpleasant to her.*

It's very important to understand this, too:

Wettening activities should not <u>end</u> after penetration. You should repeat these periodically <u>throughout</u> lovemaking *whenever she could use some more lubrication. The smart lover does this <u>before</u> she becomes dry.*

You *always* must **keep lubrication going**. A **constant, nice flow of lubricant** makes prolonged sex **easier, more exciting and less likely to end prematurely due to chafing**. (See the sidebar on **artificial lubrication** and **saliva** on page 140 for when you need extra help.)

WHAT THE ORGASM PROCESS IS ALL ABOUT

Finally, let's talk about the **orgasm process**. It includes the big payoff, so to speak - her climax. But it also includes everything that might occur leading up to it, including:

♀ her pussy getting hotter, wetter and wider
♀ her **vaginal muscles** tightening and her **vaginal canal** narrowing
♀ her body tensing and contorting
♀ her neck and chest getting a red **rash**

But that's not to say that what happens next - the **climax** - is predictably the same. It's not. **Orgasms** vary greatly in **size, quality** and **duration**. They can even be *crummy* if you *rush* them or are *clumsy* or *unskilled* in

Seduction, Wettening, Arousal, Orgasm: The Four Sexual Processes

producing them. **Orgasms** also differ in the way they **feel** to her. It depends on *what organs you stimulated* in producing them and *the method you used*. Orgasms also vary in the **type** and **number of body parts** that are **involved**. **Different nerves** are responsible for **different orgasms**.

My lovers have often expressed wonderment, in fact, about the many *types* of **orgasms** I made them feel. Their feedback helped make me aware of this phenomenon. One, for instance, marvelled about the deliciously novel orgasm I'd given her the night before: "When I came, *it started at the base of my spine and it went like this* [she showed me with her hands that the feeling quickly expanded], *and then whoosh!"*

> **"There are all kinds of orgasms. Are you giving her The Big O or a crummy one? They vary in size, quality and feeling."**

So what does this mean to you? It's up to the man to consciously produce a myriad of types of **orgasms** your woman will love. She knows they're "out there" and she wants you to let her experience them all. *Variety*, after all, is the spice of life. Women also expect great lovers to give them *new* types of climaxes they've never felt before. (I'll show you *how*.)

But it's also important that you only produce **climaxes** that *please* her. Not ones that *disappoint* or leave her *unsatisfied* or *frustrated*. You should be able to relate to this. Haven't you been with a woman who is in such a rush to jerk you off that your **orgasm** is very surfacy and almost a non-event? I've even had frustrating experiences where the woman didn't keep the stimulation going long enough through the **orgasm process**. So I had to stroke myself to try and get completion. And that often didn't work. It felt like I didn't come. These were strange and very unpleasant half-climaxes.

So here's what I want you to take from all of this before we move on to mind-blowing information on how to rock her world: *Don't assume that just because you made her come that you knocked her socks off. You might, in fact, have <u>displeased</u> her!* Try and judge the quality based upon her telltale physical changes. But the final arbiter is always your lover. **If she doesn't express how great an orgasm was - verbally or otherwise - chances are it wasn't that great**.

You want to give her the biggest climaxes ever. *I'll show you how*. We'll explore all of her exciting **hot spots**, in the **Female Sexual Anatomy** chapter. Then we'll look at a variety of incredibly effective **techniques** and **positions** in several other chapters, with which you can thrill her *every time*.

But first, I will teach you *everything* you need to know about how to make a woman **hot** for you and *keep* the home fires burning, every day, *forever*.

> *"Venus yields to caresses, not to compulsion."*
> - Publilius Syrus, a 1st B.C. Roman writer of maxims and favorite of Julius Caesar

The Art Of Seduction 24/7

One of the sexiest songs ever was the Peggy Lee hit "Fever" - sung as if in the throes of sexual passion by the **ultimate sexually satisfied woman**:

You give me fever - when you kiss me,
Fever when you hold me tight.
Fever - in the morning,
A Fever all through the night.

Though more than 50 years old, that still song sounds fresh and gets everyone hot. Because it rings true as to what a woman wants: A lover who keeps her *hot* for him, 24/7, who can *please* her like no one else.

*And if you want to be that man, then, beyond possessing great **love**making skills, you have to master the **art of seduction.** As the song implies, the **art of seduction** is not just for single guys wooing someone new. Because if you're married or in a long-term relationship, you have to **keep the home fires burning!** That's where the **art of seduction** comes in. (And FYI: If you feel you're not getting enough at home, this could be the area where you're falling down on the job!)*

You have to keep her turned on. You have to make her want you. If you're a dull presence in her life, where's the *sexual attraction* for her? Keep this in mind: She's seeing images of seductive guys on TV, in movies, online and elsewhere. She's meeting sexy guys during the course of her day. And if you're not *sexually seductive* like those guys (in your own way), she's going to think something's *missing* in her life. Worse - *she might become vulnerable to men who <u>know</u> how to seduce women!*

We'll talk about *seduction and the single guy* a bit later but first let's answer this question: How do you seduce a woman *within* a relationship?

The Art Of Seduction 24/7

You can't stop being sexy, sensual or romantic just because she's made some sort of commitment to you. Commitments can be *broken*. *Your job, through seduction, is to keep the relationship* **sexy, fresh, fun**... *and* **hot**.

THE 24/7 TURN-ON - WITHOUT TURN-OFFS

You should be seducing her 24/7, as a lifestyle. A woman will not want to go to bed with you unless you've laid the groundwork, throughout the day.

How? Be a *tease*. Be **thoughtful**, **loving, romantic, kind**. Be the kind of man she's attracted to, the kind she finds lovable and sexy. And *avoid behavior that turns her off to you.*

Whatever you do generally should be **playful, subtly sexy** and even **deniable** when possible. It's often best if a **seduction** is not an obvious pitch for **sex**. Not that over-the-top seductions aren't called for on occasion. We'll talk about those too. Whatever suits your personality. But, above all, keep it *masculine*. Be *manly* about it.

USING YOUR LOOKS AND CLOTHES TO SEDUCE HER

Start by putting your best foot forward. The better you look, the more she's going to want to jump your bones. *Good looks seduce women.*

There are scientific studies that back up what I'm saying, such as a study done by William Lassek of the University of Pittsburgh and Steven Gaulin of the University of California, Santa Barbara. Published in the September 2009 issue of Evolution and Human Behavior, they concluded:

> *"Using data on males aged 18–59 years from the third National Health and Nutrition Examination Survey and including other relevant variables, fat-free mass (FFM) and/or limb muscle volume (LMV) are significant predictors of the numbers of total and past-year self-reported sex partners, as well as age at first intercourse."*

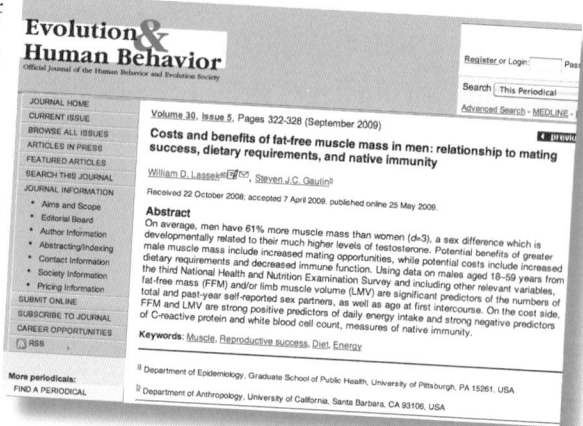

In other words, according to them, *muscular men seem to bed more women and lose their virginity at an earlier age than other men*. But you don't have to be a muscular hunk. Other studies have shown that women are attracted simply to *handsome* men - and no matter what you're born with, you can do much to make yourself look as **handsome** as possible.

On Loving Women

Flip side: **don't be a schlump**. Think of it: If your woman walked around in baggy unisex athletic warm-up clothes all day, I don't think you'd find her too alluring. So why would you think she'd be turned on by unattractive clothes you might wear?

Part of seducing her 24/7 is making sure you look as sexy as you can. Smart men wear *sexy* and *sensual clothing*. I wear *soft* clothes, for instance, because women not only *like* the way they look, they like the way they *feel*. Women can *tell*, just by *looking*, how *soft* clothes are. And they have the urge to *touch* **soft clothes**. They get *turned on* by them. I'm not joking.

So when you're shopping for clothes, *feel everything you're thinking of buying before you try anything on.* Choose only the *softest* shirts, sweaters, and trousers. Even soft *khakis* can do the trick, if they look nice.

And learn how to dress. Along these lines, if you really want to *seduce* a woman, for example, here's a great tip: *Cashmere sweaters - worn without anything under them - are surefire turn-ons for most women.* I'll never forget the time a date reached out and stroked my cashmere sweater (and my chest), purring, "You wore a nice soft sweater so I'd touch you, didn't you?" *Man if that didn't teach me a lesson as to what to wear for women! What's sexier than having your lover - or the woman you want to be your lover - caress your clothing, a smile on her face, obviously turned on by it?*

I was a little embarrassed one day, in fact, when a *married* woman reached over and felt my shirt, noticing, by *sight*, that it was made of a soft fabric. She then shouted to her husband: "Bob! Feel his shirt! See how *soft* it is!" It was obviously a turn-on to her (she kept stroking my chest!) and *she wanted her husband to wear one like it*. I felt badly for Bob momentarily. He wasn't happy his wife had gotten the hots feeling my shirt. But then I thought - his wife wouldn't be touching another man admiringly if *he'd* been considerate enough to dress attractively for her. He was a *schlump*. And if you're a *schlump*, you're going to pay the price.

So **Seduction Lesson #1: Dress seductively.** A good clothing store salesperson can help you with this. Or you might read men's fashion magazines, for a sense of style. This is a good practice for both single guys and men who are already in relationships. This kind of thing might not be a *quick-acting* **seduction** - you might have to patiently wait for the results. But then again, **slow seductions** are often the *sweetest* kind. (You'll see!)

Make Things Happen

Seduction Lesson #2: You have to make things happen, sexually.

Men in long-term relationships often complain they're not getting enough.

Women do too. But **it's the man's role to make things happen**. If you're not getting enough, you're probably not being *seductive* enough.

Want some morning sex, for instance? Stir it up with a sexy comment!

For example, one time a girlfriend awoke one morning saying, "I have a confession to make. I fell asleep during the movie last night. Can we watch it again today?"

"Sure," I said. "But I have a confession to make, too." And I left a pregnant pause to *pique her curiosity*. I was creating a sense of *antici...pation*.

"What?" she asked.

With a smile and all the charm I could muster I said: "I popped a *boner!*"

"Oh!" she said, closing her eyes and stretching her body sensuously back as if I'd just given her an **orgasm**! Once she'd recovered from the shiver my words had sent through her body, her reply was priceless: "Waste not, want not!"

She then reached down to verify that my words were true. (They were.) And that set off a morning of rollicking hot sex.

...So *be bold*. Be *sexy*, in a *boyishly charming* way. *Get things going by playful and sexy* **verbal seductions**. It's up to you! Even in this day and age, *women most often want their men to seduce them*, not the reverse!

SNEAK ATTACKS: SUREFIRE SEDUCTION

Seduction Lesson #3: Don't underestimate the power of an occasional sneak attack late at night, in bed.

I remember a day when I awoke at 6 a.m., early than I'd wanted to. My lover at the time was still asleep. She wouldn't need to get up for work for another hour. That's when I decided to attempt a seduction simply by using the *power of touch. In a strategic place. Touching without moving.* A **sneak attack**.

She was sleeping on her left side, her legs drawn up. I got into a similar position near her and *I gently cupped her left butt cheek with my right hand. In doing so, I let the meat of my hand and my pinky slip between the cleft of her* **vulva**. *And I just rested it there, pressing it ever so slightly against her.*

It wasn't long before she started wriggling. Soon she was wiggling her hips to rub her *vulva* on me. I could feel it getting wet. *That began one of our most passionate* **love***making sessions ever.*

That's how you *seduce* your lover. *That's* how you get her in the mood.

On Loving Women

*That's how you make her feel you're **man** enough to make the right moves. That's how you get her going in a way that few women would resist.*

A **sneak attack** like that has a *powerful effect. A stealthy bedtime seduction when she's asleep makes her extremely hot from the get-go for some reason. And it makes her come faster.* (Try it and see!)

That's the *power* of **seduction**. And that's fun, sexy and memorable. She will love you for it!

The beauty of making the first move and doing so when she's so vulnerable is that *she will anticipate your doing it again*. And *desire* it. *So it will make her hot for many mornings to come!* Even in the half-sleep that comes with the arrival of the sun. She'll be hoping you do it again!

See? Seduction doesn't take much. Sometimes all it takes is a *simple touch*. In *the right place*.

The nice thing about the **sneak attack in the middle of the night** is that it's *a subtle approach*. One that she can *resist* if she wants (but she won't) by removing your hand from her body or by rolling away from you. It provides you and her an out. And it's not *overtly* sexual. *She can choose not to respond to it at all if she's not in the mood.*

You're not making her wake up and pissing her off. She's *choosing* to interrupt her sleep for some **love**making. That makes it all the more sweet.

Sneak attacks add two elements to your relationship:

- Excitement - your taking the initiative in turning her on in ways she will find hard to resist helps fulfill her fantasy to be "taken" by a sexy man
- Unpredictability - this is the sure thing to keep your relationship from becoming dull

SEDUCING A WOMAN TO BED FOR THE FIRST TIME

What about **seduction** for the *single guy* who wants to get the **love**making going with a new woman? **Seduction Lesson #4: In seducing a woman into bed for the first time you should patiently make her desire you.**

As a single guy, I always preferred seducing the woman I wanted to get involved with *slowly*, over time, so *she* made the first move, that one that led to our first time in bed together. That called for patience. But it was fun and it made a lot of sense. In fact, it's the **preferred way**.

You want her to want you. And you don't want to make any moves that might turn her off, so, in leaving the choice of when first to go to bed up to her, you avoid that possibility.

That's not to say you shouldn't *nudge* things in that direction! You should!

Do acts of **kindness**. Be a **sexy, loving masculine presence**. Make love to her mind (which I described in an earlier chapter). Make subtle moves. Caress the back of her neck while watching a movie. Put a hand on her knee or thigh (once you've got a read on her and you know she won't object). Give her a kiss on the **neck** or a **sexy kiss** at the end of a date, full of promise (we'll talk more about *kissing* in a later chapter)...

OVER-THE-TOP SEDUCTIONS

That being said, sometimes a little **over-the-top proactive seduction** is what is called for. So **Seduction Lesson #5: Sometimes a single guy hoping to make love to a woman he desires needs to take a risk and be bold.**

For instance, a dating situation in my mid-20s where I and my date were kind of stuck in neutral...I was seeing a school teacher in upstate New York but we'd not gotten much beyond French kissing even though we'd become good friends and golf buddies.

One day, I decided to try something *bold - something that would have been inappropriate had I not already laid the groundwork for it, had we not already had a relationship that felt comfortable and seemed to be heading in an intimate direction*. What I'm about to describe - for the single man - is obviously a *risky* move and not recommended without similar groundwork having been laid.

On this night, she and I had just returned from playing golf and we were in her apartment (which happened to be on the floor below mine). When she started cooking dinner, I made my first move. I asked her if she minded if I took a *shower* at her place. Although I lived just upstairs, she *happily* invited me to do so - which was a positive sign of sexual interest, I felt. Plus, I figured it might make her *think* about me, in the shower, *naked*. I was working on her mind.

It felt very **sexy** to get naked for the first time in her apartment even though it was behind closed doors, in her shower. So when I came out of the shower to find there were no fresh towels, I came up with an idea on the spur of the moment.

I walked out of the bathroom totally nude. She was cooking and hadn't looked my way. In my deepest, smoothest baritone voice, I called attention to myself, casually saying, You have no towels in the bathroom."

She turned around and her reaction upon seeing me was priceless. "Oh!" she moaned, clearly overcome by the seduction. And she said no more. She walked over and gave me a big hug and the sexiest, most **cock-hardening kiss**...and we wound up eating dinner late that night. The seduction, needless to say, had worked its magic. That was our first night together.

Peek-a-boo Seductions In Long-Term Relationships

But that kind of thing works best for *single* guys, where the shock of the first incident of nudity can move the relationship forward. Nudity can work for a man already in a relationship, too, but the same shock factor that comes with the initial glimpse of nudity won't be there. And it might seem too obvious a ruse.

So **Seduction Lesson #6: When it comes to nudity, subtle seductions often work best for the man in a long-term relationship.**

Once you're involved with a woman, just walking around topless and barefoot while doing chores around the house might work better as a seduction than total nudity (even if it takes longer for its effect to work). One of my girlfriends told me she got hot whenever I wore just jeans and nothing else - especially while doing handy work.

And nothing beats **spooning** with her in bed (naked). Even if nothing comes of it immediately, it will work on her mind and eventually lead to more sex (especially late night and morning sex) than you'd have had otherwise. It's a different kind of **sex**, too - more *urgent* somehow.

...I'll give you more killer ideas on *how to use nudity to get more sex and hotter sex* in the next chapter, because that topic deserves its own chapter.

Slow-Acting Seduction By Suggestion

But turning her on often requires nothing more than a few well-placed *words*. This fits in with what I've been telling you about how you should be **making love to her mind**. Pique a woman's **curiosity** and you will drive her wild...Which takes us to **Seduction Lesson #7: Words can be as potent in seducing her as nudity.**

For instance, you might try a **slow-acting seduction by suggestion**. You can promise something sexy as she leaves for work, for example - as in, "When you come home, I'm going to do something special for you." Let her guess what that is. Or, if she's into erotic talk, get more detailed; whisper in her ear: "Mmmm. My tongue wants to go exploring between your legs when you get home!" *I've never known such a promise not to melt a woman - and cause her to be hot, wet and eager for sex when she returns home after work.*

Try it! But do it in a **smooth, sophisticated, sensual and loving way**. But avoid corny and adolescent kinds of remarks. Talk to her in a mature, confident way. **Seducing her by suggestion** is a great ruse that works most every time - when done *right*.

Single men would do well to follow this advice, too. Arouse a woman's interest with clever sexy banter and provocative comments that appeal to her *curiosity* and *imagination* - two very powerful forces in a woman. This is the way to fan the flames of her desire.

A textbook *classy* lesson in how to do this? The way Cary Grant (as Roger Thornhill) woos Eva Marie Saint (as Eve Kendall) in the Hitchcock film *North by Northwest*. Seated at the same dining table in a train, Thornhill, attracted by Eve's beauty, cleverly tosses out what would be the equivalent of a lover's fishing hook. He playfully suggests to Eve that he has an *intriguing problem*. She's now **hooked**. *A woman can't stand* **not knowing something** *presented in a way that's irresistibly interesting*.

What's his problem, she wants to know (her eagerness to find out clearly intense at this point)? His answer?: Smiling nicely, taking his time to answer, dripping with sexiness, he explains that *he finds it hard not to be "dishonest" around beautiful women*.

What a great, provocative opening! It *beguiles* her while revealing that he has a *sophisticated wit*, an *easy sensuality* and a *confident sexuality*. She asks him, "*Why?*" In toying with her, her eagerness grows. *Every woman would have asked that question - he got her* curiosity *going!* And her inquiry opens the door to his next, more bold tease:

> **Roger Thornhill: The moment I meet an attractive woman, I have to start pretending I have no desire to make love to her.**
> **Eve Kendall: What makes you think you have to conceal it?**
> **Roger Thornhill: She might find the idea objectionable.**
> **Eve Kendall: Then again, she might not.**

He hooked her with intriguing and edgy thoughts. In just a few minutes of conversation, he created *desire* in her for intimacy. Why? *She now knows he's a good lover, by his verbal sophistication and masculine confidence*. He's *made love to her* **mind**, *which makes her want him sexually*.

This was obviously a fictional encounter, but this is how it's done. You **make love to her mind** with playful *sexual fishing*. **You throw out an acceptable teaser to provoke interest. If her response is positive, you find a way to tickle her fancy further.** *Sophisticated repartee* like the above can work wonders - *if your overall presence appeals to her. Everything about you should* **charm** *her*.

On Loving Women

*You want to tickle her mind so she **believes** you're the man she's always dreamed of - so she later says (after your first time in bed), "I knew you'd be a great lover!" This is a line I've heard many times. It's because I did the groundwork to make love to my lovers' minds. The key is to get a woman's mind working, with an easy charm, so she visualizes herself being wowed by you in bed. Those thoughts will then percolate in her brain and often make her want to be with you surprisingly <u>quickly</u>! She'll likely tell you afterward, "I've never slept with a man so quickly before!"* **In making love to her mind, you create intense and impatient <u>desire</u>.**

Casual Seductions

Sometimes just turning on a sexy TV show or showing her a romantic chick flick can do the trick. (Yep!) That's another way to *work on her mind*.

One night, for instance, my then-girlfriend and I were cuddling on the couch after dinner and I casually chose to watch an episode of *Sex and the City* after going through the channel menu - knowing how sexy that show can be. *Within 10 minutes, she was groping me through my jeans.*

So, **Seduction Lesson #8: Sometimes it's best to find a sexy influence you can casually expose her to, like a sensual TV show or movie, if you know its effect will be that of an aphrodisiac.**

Quick-Acting Seductions

Now **seduction** is usually best done with *patience*, allowing her to respond in good time to your ruse. But when you're in a relationship, sometimes you want to heat her up *quickly*. So:

Seduction Lesson #9: Stripping her can have a powerful effect. The act of *stripping her* can be an extremely persuasive and primal act, when done well - and when done only on occasion. The shock of the spontaneous "attack" is what makes it work. *Don't in any way simulate a rape situation, though*. This should be all about *runaway lust and passion* - and that's how *she* should perceive it.

Undressing her immediately after she returns home from work can work especially well because of the surprise nature of it. When done with the right **timing** and **attitude** (**suave, classy and with powerful masculine sexual energy**), this can have an incredibly powerful effect on a woman.

Keep Her Purring

And **Seduction Lesson #10: Always keep her on simmer - all day, most every day. Don't let the flames burn out.**

Example: A girlfriend of mine came out of shower and I walked up to her and gave her a passionate hug. (I was clothed.) A naked woman feels vulnerable in a sexy way when you do this. And as I did so, I ran my fingernails up and down her spine, knowing the sexy shivers it would give her. Her reaction didn't disappoint.

"You keep me purring all day long!" she cooed.

And that's *exactly* what you want to do! (One good variation of the ruse above would be to gently cup her buttocks or a breast in your hand, through her clothing, when you kiss her passionately as she leaves for work.)

Dress Her Up, Take Her Out

Seduction Lesson #11: One way to keep her purring is to take her to places where she feels the desire to dress up - hopefully in a sexy way. Because, general rule (FYI: *big tip* here): *when women dress seductively, the clothes they wear not only get you hot...they make your lover horny too!*

Sexy clothes make your lover **feel sexy**. So look for opportunities to encourage her to dress in a sexy way. *She'll be hot for you when you come home more than not! You'll have more sex - plus, in making her feel attractive, you'll satisfy her need to be admired, physically and sexually.*

Playful Seductions

Finally, **Seduction Lesson #12: *Seductions don't have to be deadly serious. If you've got a playful nature, use it to your benefit.***

Example: One night, as my girlfriend got ready for bed in the bathroom (many years ago, when the Red Hot Chili Peppers were still appearing onstage wearing just an athletic sock over their genitals), I stripped down and put a tube sock over my "stuff."

When she came out of the bathroom and, with a double take, saw my provocative outfit, she smiled and said, "What are you doing?"

Jumping on the bed (as a subtle invite to her to do the same), I replied, "I'm a Red Hot Chili Pepper!"

And, boy was I ever that night! *That's* how you do a playful seduction.

Word to the wise: Ultimately, the best approach is to **seduce without seducing**. *That is, without being obvious or lewd about it.* **Plausible denial** *is the operating word. In the example above, I didn't touch her or initiate sex. I made* her *do that.*

And that's what seduction is all about: making her **want** *to make love.*

> "Lots of women tell me I'm their idol."
> - porn actress Jenna Jameson

Excite Her With Sexy Visuals

You've undoubtedly heard the propaganda that *men* get excited by **sexually-charged visuals** (such as images or films showing nudity or sex) but *women* do *not*. As history will show, a whole generation of men *bought* that mean-spirited nonsense and *became worse lovers as a result.* (They became timid.) And that **disinformation** is still floating around today, producing confusion in men that *handicaps* them as lovers of women.

Here's why I mention this: *If you believe the baloney that women don't respond to the sight of a naked man, you're not going to use your own body or other sexual visuals to spice up your relationship as you should.* So let's put it to rest!

Where did this ridiculous fallacy come from? Wikipedia offers this clue (see http://en.wikipedia.org/wiki/Lesbianism_in_erotica.):

> "Some lesbians and bisexual women object to all pornography on feminist grounds. Since the end of the 1980s "Lesbian Sex Wars", however, lesbians and bisexual women are more likely to have positive views about erotica and pornography. Some lesbians are even consumers of mainstream pornography..."

Whatever the origin, the mistaken notion that women are *not* made hot and eager for sex by **erotic visuals** was exposed as a falsehood by the prestigious

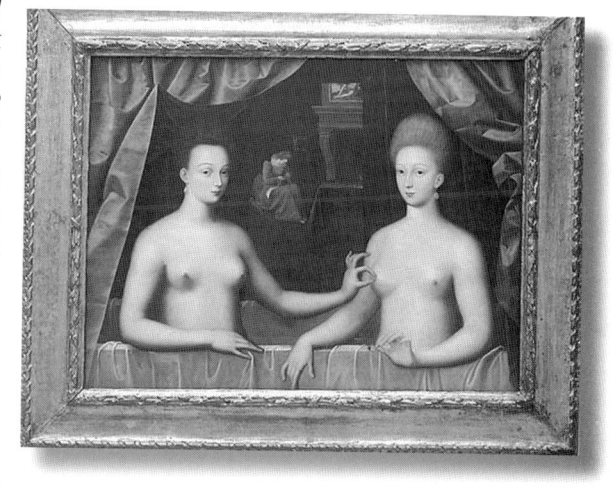

Excite Her With Sexy Visuals

Scientific American in the article "The Orgasmic Mind" (May 15, 2008):

"...sexual imagery devoid of emotional connections can arouse women just as it can men, a 2007 study shows. Psychologist Meredith Chivers of the Center for Addiction and Mental Health in Toronto and her colleagues gauged the degree of sexual arousal in about 100 women and men, both homosexual and heterosexual, while they watched erotic film clips... **Heterosexual women's level of arousal increased along with the intensity of the sexual activity largely irrespective of who or what was engaged in it. In fact, these women were genitally excited by male and female actors equally and also responded physically to bonobo [apes] copulation.***"*

And there have been *numerous* other scientific studies in which sensing devices were placed on women to chart any sexual physical changes that occurred while they watched sexual images or films. **Study after study has proven that erotic visuals make women wet, their hearts beat faster, their genitals swollen, their nipples erect - biological proof those visuals made them hot for sex.**

That's no surprise to me, though. My experience has been that most women have a secret __desire__ and/or __need__ to see sexy images from time to time. That's important for you to know because **that desire needs to be fulfilled.** And you need to fulfill that aspect of her sex life - her *need* for *sexy visuals*. It's part of a healthy sex life and the human experience.

I've witnessed scores of lovers get aroused by visual stimuli (I gave examples in the last chapter). I've gotten *verbal* confirmation too. One lover told me, "I like looking at you (naked)." Another said: "When I see your **cock** hanging down in the morning, I need you inside of me."

Further proof: One divorcee I interviewed for this book told me her husband had only given her *one* **orgasm** in *two decades* of marriage. Why did he succeed that *one* time? *They had just seen a romantic film (about a primitive South American tribe) featuring lots of* __nudity__. **The visuals sexually excited her so much, she said, that once in bed afterward, "I came in four seconds**.*"* **The many scenes of joyously naked people had** __primed__ **her to come.** "It was the sexiest movie I've ever seen!" (FYI: Keep this in mind in choosing the movies you watch!)

On Loving Women

So it's clear that women are just as excited by sexy visual stimulation as men are. You need to understand this indisputable fact if you want to maximize your success in sexually satisfying your woman.

Honest female role models will vouch for that. Self-described sex-positive feminist Carlin Ross blogs, for example, that:

> "**We [women] are visually stimulated...**we *are sexual creatures... and we deserve pleasure.*"

What does this mean to you? You must provide the visual excitement your lover <u>craves</u>. (And P.S. If you don't, she might be inclined to satisfy her desire for sexy visuals elsewhere!)

But you can work this to your benefit. What better way to <u>make love to her mind</u> (to make her hot for you) than through visual suggestion?

SOME REQUIREMENTS TO MAKE IT WORK

How? It's easier than you think. And I will give you some great ideas you can try out on your lover. But **you cannot excite your lover with visuals without some sophistication**. Be **confident** and **comfortable in your own skin, in your nakedness**. And be **smooth**. Most times you'll want to choose a ruse where you have a **plausible deniability**. That is, if it's *obvious* to her that you're *trying* to turn her on with a visual *stunt*, it might *backfire*. You need to have the attitude that you *don't care* if she doesn't take the bait. (And don't let her sense you're putting out "bait.") Be *cool* as they say. **Don't do anything to draw attention to yourself - verbally or otherwise.**

And be willing to let it go. If she doesn't get turned on by your ploy, move on to something else (*asexual*) as if you were unaware that what you were doing before had sexual connotations. Even more important: have *patience*. Sometimes it takes awhile for your visually provocative seeds to flower. They grow best in a *loving atmosphere* of *kindness* and *affection*.

HOW PATIENCE CAN PAY OFF

For instance, years ago I had a sweet girlfriend who would lovingly bring me a hot cup of coffee in bed the first in the morning. One morning, with a groan, she awakened and said apologetically, "I gotta get to work." She was implying that she would have *preferred* to have stayed in bed with me.

I was in the mood for love, though. So when she returned with the cup of Joe, I coolly and strategically sat up, carelessly allowing the tops of the sheet and blanket to lie just above my crotch, exposing my bare torso. She could see the tops of my hips. The covers were that low.

We sipped our coffee, sitting up against pillows we'd propped up against

Excite Her With Sexy Visuals

the headboard and didn't say that much. I put my arm around her and she leaned against me, putting her left hand on my belly.

The placement of her hand made me feel that maybe the visuals were working their magic. But I wasn't sure if she'd succumb to the seduction since she had to get to work. And I had to be respectful of her possible need to leave for work without making love. *So I couldn't be the one who made the first move.* (That might actually have backfired.) So I went about casually seducing her, beginning by massaging the sensitive back of her neck with one of my thumbs. She responded with a sigh and her body relaxed sensuously - a sign she was melting inside. I kept drinking my coffee, though, as if unaware I was turning her on. This provided me with a **plausible deniability**. *I wasn't making any overtly sexual moves.*

I put my coffee down to better massage her head and she collapsed in relaxation, her head on my belly, sighing. But *I continued the pretense of not expecting or wanting anything more* - even as I gently brushed her hair off her forehead in a way I knew would provoke *sexy tingles*. About 15 minutes after I'd started the turn-on she responded in the most delightful way. Moaning, she pulled the covers down and gave me the most incredible **head** (after which I returned the favor, of course). *Nice.*

So *that's* how you do it. *Casually. Carelessly.* With a *sexy sophistication, nonchalance, loving-kindness* and *patience*.

CATER TO WHAT SHE SAY SHE LIKES

Sometimes all it takes to pull off a visual turn-on is to pay attention to what your lover tells you. One of my hottest recollections along these lines goes back to my late 20s when I was driving a hot stand-up comedienne I'd met recently to her next gig. I was wearing soft khaki pants whose shape - unbeknownst to me - enhanced the bulge in my crotch area.

This visual, it turns out, drove my date wild. Sporting a sexy smile, she suddenly reached over and patted my genitals with her left hand, saying, "I just *love* that sexy bulge a man gets in his pants!"

Oh *man*. I nearly drove off the road! Due to our rush to get to her gig, though, I had to wait until that night for our first tryst together. But even after the car incident, I decided to use a *visual ruse* to get things going. It was our first date and I wanted to appear the gentleman. Asking her permission to sleep in the buff (explaining that underwear hurts me if I wear it overnight), I promised not to make any moves on her and she bought the scenario. I then gave her a quick look at me before getting into bed and it wasn't long before I felt her hands upon me, initiating sex.

This doubly *confirms the power visuals can have on women, in making them eager to make love.* And I was no dope. After that experience I repeatedly wore the pants that had visually gotten her hot - especially when I knew we'd be on the road where she could once again get a *good look* at the sight that had made her so horny. It worked every time.

The lesson here is: *Cater to whatever visuals turn your lover on.*

AND DRESS SCANTILY...IT WORKS!

Don't always wait until your lover tells you what turns her on visually, though. Be *proactive.*

One time, for example, I decided to surprise one of my girlfriends by serving her breakfast in bed *bottomless.* Before bringing up the food, I put on a tight black top she told me looked sexy on me and I removed my pants, underwear and footwear.

"Welcome to the *bottomless waiter cafe,* madam," I said with a French accent and a sense of humor as I entered our bedroom. You should have seen the look of complete surprise on her face! I prolonged the tease, mentioning all the food options this "cafe" could provide her, while cautioning her she could "gaze at but not touch" the waiter.

By then, though, she was groping my cock. I kept the waiter role going a little longer until she pulled me into bed for some very hot nooky.

Wow did that turn her on! Talk about turning on the *passion!* That led to the most intense, rollicking time we'd ever had in bed! Oh...and after we'd made love, she smiled and cooed, "I *really* liked the bottomless waiter thing!" **That's the power of sexy visuals.**

THE SEXY "WELCOME HOME" SCENARIO

You might also try the "welcome home" scenario. Some years ago I was feeling amorous when I heard my girlfriend arriving home from work. So, I quickly removed my shirt, shoes and socks and ran downstairs to let her into the house. Then, *casually* unlocking the door from the garage (as if I had not *run* to the door but had instead *ambled* there and was simply doing her a favor), I smiled and kissed her at the top of the garage staircase.

"You're half naked!" she said, in a sexy voice.

In my best breathy-husky voice, I replied, "Well, it's kinda *hot* in here."

It wasn't long before she had the rest of my clothes on the floor.

I *knew* this kind of "outfit" might turn her on because a prior lover (to my surprise at the time) used to get hot seeing me dressed that way. But

Excite Her With Sexy Visuals

for her, there was another requirement to make it work. She needed to see me doing heavy housework dressed that way. It was the action of my muscles lifting or moving something that clinched the seduction with her. Another lover got hot when I got *sweaty* from work. ("You're *sweaty!*" she'd coo. And then she'd inevitably initiate sex.)

SEX HER UP WITH SEXY ARTWORK

And by the way, **sexy artwork can have a desirable visual impact on your lover too**. Example: I was on vacation with a refined woman when we happened upon an art gallery filled with sculptures of naked men. Blushing and wearing a big smile, she cuddled against my chest.

"I feel like making love to you," she whispered, laughing.

"Let's get that sculpture!" I suggested.

Seeing her reaction, I realized that having that sculpture in our house would be a great idea. *It would make her hot for* **love***making on a frequent basis*. It would *sexualize* her more.

"No!" she said, pulling me away from the sculpture playfully.

Her reaction acknowledged the powerful sexual effect the sculpture was having on her. She was smiling from ear to ear and laughing with my repeated suggestions that we buy the bronze *aphrodisiac*.

I wasn't kidding about getting artwork that turned her on. I was impressed by its *aphrodisiac* effect. *So I decorated our home with seductive artwork (in private places, for her eyes only) to make her amorous more often.*

And if you witness the same phenomenon, word to the wise: **Purchase the sculpture, painting, photo, or whatever that makes your woman hot!** Or take her occasionally to a sexy art gallery or museum with sensual paintings! Don't *fear* her sexually charged reactions to naked men in works of art. That's not akin to infidelity. We all react that way to sexually provocative visuals. It's *human*. And *desirable*. *You* get the benefits!

CAUTION: VISUALS REQUIRE THE ELEMENT OF SURPRISE

Now, word to the wise: When you find a visual ruse that makes your lover hot for you, don't run that idea into the ground. Visual turn-ons work best with the element of *surprise*. They need to be used sparingly or they'll grow *predictable* and ultimately **boring**. So you need to develop **a wide range of visual scenarios**. The greater the shock value, the better.

THE REVERSE VISUAL TEASE

And now that you know that *visuals excite your lover,* how about a visual tease *in reverse*? **Tease** her by *denying* her the visuals she craves!

One night, for instance, I gently tied my lover's hands with the belt of her robe (loosely enough so she could remove it) so I could tease her without interruption. But *I stayed clothed* while I undressed her and spent an hour teasing her (without making her come).

Guess what happened! She repeatedly begged, "Let me *see* you."

"You want to see me **naked**?" I asked. She urgently nodded her head.

The lesson: **Not** seeing my body *made her very hot*. The *anticipation* of seeing me nude *drove her wild*. Remember that. *Try* it.

A few weeks later, I again tied her hands with the robe belt but this time I got *naked* before I mercilessly teased her for an hour or so. A few days later she said, "You know what really made me hot that night? *Watching* you. *Seeing* how *hard* you were." *I rest my case.*

OTHER WAYS TO CATER TO HER NEED FOR SEXY VISUALS

And the sky's the limit when it comes to finding ways to satisfy your lover's craving for **sexy visuals**. With one lover who told me she *loved* looking at my penis, I'd sometimes hand her **olive oil** and ask her to massage my **cock** with it to get me ready for **love***making*. That gave her more eye time. Another lover would stealthily and hungrily watch my cock as I got undressed for bed (I could see her doing this from the corner of my eye). So I'd *linger* outside the bed - finding something extra to do while naked - to maximize her peekaboo time (while I pretended not to notice her stare). Sometimes I'd also plump up my member a bit in the bathroom beforehand, knowing that it would look more enticing to her.

IF SHE ADMITS TO VISUAL TURN-ONS, PUSH IT TO THE MAX

Best case scenario: *Your partner might reveal her desire to see you in a sexy way.* Push that gift to the max!

One demure professional, for instance, once gave me **see-through silk thermals** as a Christmas gift. I immediately modelled them for her, which led to her groping me, followed by some of the best **love**making ever. Another girlfriend, a perky California blonde, gave me revealing *tiger-pattern and leather thong underwear* (when thongs were in fashion), which also led to incredible **love**making sessions. **These are magical items!!!**

If you're lucky enough to have this kind of thing happen, *don't let these sexy clothes linger unworn in the closet!* **Your lover has given you the best and quickest way to get her really hot for sex, so use them to steam up your relationship. You'll have <u>more</u> sex and <u>hotter</u> sex!**

Excite Her With Sexy Visuals

With the **see-through thermals**, for instance, I once donned them *furtively* (pulling the underpants *tight*, for *maximum visual effect*) and called my lover to the kitchen for lunch. She moaned when she saw what I was wearing. By the time I'd asked, "What do you want for lunch," it was clear it was *me*. (And boy was the **love**making passionate!) I remember her getting *especially* excited, too, when I *showed* her I could pull my **hard-on** out of the **vent hole** and make love to her *with the outfit still on*. Another time, I wore the **see-through underwear** while we played a board game in bed - not letting her touch me until the end. *Man did that lead to hot sex!!!*

Walking around in a *thong* at unexpected times had a similar effect on the girlfriend who bought me those. Appearing thusly in her home office once, she grabbed my balls and cooed, "Do you know what *that* does to me?" She then *showed* me. That ruse always led to <u>hot</u> **love**making.

(Warning: I could wear the see-through long johns and thong to get those lovers hot for sex because *they'd* given me those *edgy outfits*. If *I'd* bought these *outlandish accoutrements* myself *not knowing what turned my lovers on*, the outfits might have seemed *too obvious* - or perhaps *gay*. So *don't wear those kinds of things without her input.*)

The Power Of Sleeping Nude

...Now, finally...I'm not sure if I need to suggest this to most men...I'm thinking most of you probably sleep in the buff, as I do...but if you're *not* doing that, *get with it!* One of my girlfriends explained why this is smart. Looking at my nude body one morning, she laughed and said, *"You know, we wouldn't have half as much sex in the morning if you wore pajamas!"*

Looking Good For Her Pays Off

Admittedly, visual ploys work best if your lover finds you attractive. So, if it's possible, stay in good shape and dress to attract. That's part of being a good lover. But you should find this bargain acceptable, since I'm sure you'd prefer it if your lover kept herself looking her best for you.

Exciting her with sexy visuals is just one of many strategies you should use to keep your relationship exciting, growing, vital and viable. And although this is not a traditionally *male* ruse, it's so much *fun!* Just because you're in a relationship doesn't mean you shouldn't make things happen. Use **sexy visuals** to create excitement and *have more sex!*

And here's another reason to do so. The ABC-TV *American Sex Survey* I first referred to on page 17 said that, "couples who sometimes "wear something sexy" are more likely, by 12 to 16 points, to enjoy sex a great deal, to be very satisfied with it and to call it very exciting." Enough said.

> *"There's nothing more dangerous than a boy with charm*
> *He's a one stop shop, makes the panties drop*
> *He's a <u>sweet-talkin'</u>, sugar coated candy man*
> *A sweet-talkin', sugar coated candyman"*
> *- lyrics from Candyman sung by Christina Aguilera*

Erotic Talking For Sexual Results

Words, vocalizations and sometimes even just **the tone of your voice** (if it's *deep* and/or *sexy*) can act on a woman like nothing else. They can make her **hot** for **sex** and act as **orgasm boosters** or even **orgasm triggers!**

In fact there have been cases of women allegedly coming as a result of a man's voice or words. Someone I worked with in radio claimed a woman told him she had experienced an **orgasm** listening to my voice on the radio.

Rose Martelli, in a piece on menshealth.com, documented something similar:

> "My friend Colleen, a 30-year-old actress, once had a full-on **orgasm** when her boyfriend sneaked up behind her and, mock Isaac Hayes-like, jokingly intoned in her ear, "Awww, yeah, smooth jazz, CD 101." What's even more surprising is that there's an explanation for Colleen's reaction: The ear canal is highly sensitive to vibration. "Eastern sex techniques--some of which are based entirely on chanting--have proved it's possible to have an orgasm just from sound," says Barbara Carrellas, a New York City-based sex educator."

I had a fascinating date once with a woman who'd claimed she'd spent the prior six months as a *sex slave* to a man and women (by *contract!*) and that *the man had trained her to come in response to his vocal commands*. And I honestly believe her story.

I can honestly testify to making women hot for sex through my words, vocalizations and verbalizations, as well as made them come much faster than they would have without those efforts. One woman specifically told me she liked how I talked to her just before she came because it helped to send her over the edge quicker. (And she requested that I keep doing that.)

Fortunately, it's rather easy to make your lover **wet, aroused and horny** in this way - and to bring on a quicker **orgasm** - if you know how. Plus - the truth is (as you'll find out for yourself) - *women want you to talk sexy to them*. In and out of bed.

Erotic comments, suggestions and **sexy sounds** can have a **sexual power** you wouldn't believe is possible. And if you're not **erotic talking** or **making sexy sounds** while making love (or if you're not doing it *properly*), you're not fulfilling your lover's **sexual potential**.

You saw in earlier chapters how *the right words can make her want to make love to you*. But you might not realize how potent the **right words** and **tone of voice** can be when **making love**. We're taking the concept of **making love to her mind** one step further.

Some refer to this as "talking dirty," but there's nothing dirty about it. And don't be shy about doing this. <u>Most</u> *women get off on* **erotic talk** *in bed. And they admire a man who knows how to turn them on in this way.*

Words are very important to your success as a lover. And to making your relationship as hot and interesting as it can be. And the gift of sexy gab is a necessary component to keeping your relationship's fires burning forever.

I've witnessed *proof* of this time and time again over the years. And all it might take is **one key word** that sets your lover off. For instance, I've found that most women practically swoon when you say the word "fuck" in the right way. It needs to be said playfully, nonchalantly, smoothly and/or in a sophisticated way, done with the right timing and element of surprise - like the time years ago when I told a lover, with a boyish charm:

"I don't think we can play golf today, because of the weather…but we can *fuck!*"

Her response? Do you think it put her off? No!!! It *turned her on* - with **physical manifestations!**

"Oh…" she replied, sighing, *her body collapsing as if she was melting.* "Do you know what that does to me? *I get* ***a buzz in my vagina*** *when you say things like that!"* (This was a *conservative*, even *religious* woman!)

PHONE SEX

Avail yourself of this power when you're on the phone, to turn her on and make her hot for you later, eager to return home for sex. (I'm not specifically referring to **phone sex**, which is a *physical* act, but to the power of **words**, **vocal sounds** - like "mmmm!" - and your **tone of voice** over the phone. If you want to read a fully detailed and complete account of *real* **phone sex** for *ideas*, though, read the chapter recounting that in Layla Shilkret's hot anthology, *Baring It All*.)

These days, I do this kind of thing unconsciously. It's become natural to me. For example, I wrote down this conversation I had a number of years ago with a former lover, in which there's an important lesson:

"I love you," she said toward the end of our phone conversation.

"I love you," I said, my bass tones vibrating the air.

"I love how that sounded."

That piqued my interest. She didn't say, "I love how those words sounded." Or, "I love how you sound." So I decided to ask for details. "How did that sound?"

"As if you were *already* **in** *me*."

The lesson? *During intimate conversations, imagine yourself already inside of your lover. I guarantee she'll pick up on it and be turned on by it.*

Another example:

Sometime ago, over the phone, I told my lover at the time what I was going to do her later on. We'd talked about art before, so I said something like:

"*I want to do some artwork of my own, on your soul. I'd like to shape it until it reaches an explosion of pleasure.*"

"Write that down for me!" she said. "What you said was incredible!"

Words have power. Work on her mind – well before you get naked together. She'll be ready for you before you've unbuttoned her blouse.

TEASING SEX TALK

...And during the course of the day, **tease** her with casual sex talk. For instance, I had just entered a relationship with a beautiful German girl years ago when, during our first time in the shower together, I casually mentioned that my shower massager had been my "girlfriend" when I was in between relationships.

"You can use a shower massager to get off?" she asked.

"You bet," I said, smiling broadly.

She handed me the shower massager. And all I can say is it's fun to put on a show! Just shows you what might happen when you tease with talk.

Erotic Talking - For Sexual Results

THE FEELER-OUTER TALKING TEASE LINE

Even when you're in a relationship, sometimes it's best to feel your lover out to see what her **relative eagerness for sex** is before you go to the next level. I call this **the feeler-outer talking tease line (or "fott" for short)**.

This kind of thing helps prevent your ministrations from being seen as a *nuisance* or *unwelcome*. If she's open to *sex*, your **fott** will also serve a second purpose - seducing her into wanting you sexually.

For instance, one day one of my lovers and I were eating lunch in our robes (and nothing else). It was laundry day and most of our clothes were on the floor waiting to be washed. I was feeling randy but I didn't know if she was in the mood or was preoccupied with work that had to be done. So I used this playful **feeler-outer talking tease line**:

"I'm going to tell everyone you're keeping me *naked* by leaving the dirty clothes undone!"

She smiled and said, "I did that on *purpose*."

Well, that was the *perfect* **feeler-outer talking tease line response**. She *bought* my *suggestion of sex* - replying *positively* and *suggestively* even.

Yet I didn't act on her willingness right away. I let the sexy suggestion percolate in her mind awhile. The thought of lovemaking was undoubtedly making her amorous. I was *making love to her mind*. So I nodded and walked away.

Later, when I heard her loading the wash again, I asked her suggestively, "Have room for one more item?"

Smiling suspiciously (knowing I was wearing just the robe), she purred, "Yes! You have something else I need to wash?"

"Yes," I said breathily, dropping my robe on the floor. "This," I continued, handing the robe to her. She laughed. I knew by her reaction I'd turned her on. But I kept up the mind game, the tease.

"Thanks, hon," I said, and promptly walked upstairs to my office. It wasn't more than a minute or two before she was at my door, giving me a look.

Walking up to her, toute nu, I coyly asked, "Is there anything I can do for you...or to you?" She *groaned*. She *groped me*. The **sex** it led to was incredible. And it was all made possible by a **feeler-outer talking tease line**.

FEELER TEASE LINES & SEXY BANTER FOR SINGLE MEN

Single men would do well to also learn the skill of creating **feeler tease lines** that can make things happen. A single man, after all, especially needs to intrigue the woman he loves, to kindle the flames of desire in her mind, making her *need* him *sexually*.

You can pique a woman's interest with **clever sexy banter** and **provocative comments** that *arouse* her **curiosity** and **imagination** - two very powerful forces in a woman. These are all powerful tools in **making love to her mind**.

You make love to her mind with playful *sexual fishing or, if you prefer, verbal sparring*. **You throw out an <u>acceptable teaser</u> to provoke <u>interest</u>. If her response is positive, you find a way to tickle her fancy further - or, with an implied invitation, you make your move, most often starting with a kiss.**

If she's showing an interest in you on a date, find openings in the conversation where you can coyly **tease** her. If she tells the story of a man who was a jerk with her, touching her too much on a first date, for instance, I would say, "That would never happen with me." Then wait for her to ask, "Why?" (She'll find it impossible *not* to.) Then, with a sophisticated smile, say, "I always wait for the woman to make the first move." (*True* in my case.) That will impress her with your sophistication - and *motivate her to make a move if she's interested (and probably sooner than later)!*

Talking To Her During Sex

But how do you use words and vocal sounds *during* **sex** to make the experience more hot, sexy, fun and memorable? I'll give you a few suggestions (this topic could fill an entire book).

#1: Tell her, in your most sensuous and sexy way, what you're about to do to her that day - or another day - in advance.

For instance, during sex I told one lover, in a **velvety bedroom voice**:

"The next time I make love to you, I'm going to set the alarm clock to go off in two hours. Then I'm going to tease you for those two hours *and not let you come* (not even touch your clit), until the alarm clock goes off!"

She groaned and **came** right then and there!

One of the most sexy things you can do is to tell your lover what you're going to do to her, sexually, *in advance of doing it*. But you have to do it *sensuously* and *suavely* - and with the ultimate masculine confidence. And let's add another important layer: say it *lovingly*. One more essential element to make this work: *you have to promise something that's sure to get her real hot.*

With one lover, I remember luring her into the bed after teasing her all day, visually and verbally. Oiling myself up so I could enter her sooner

Erotic Talking - For Sexual Results

than later, I could tell she was enjoying the scene.

"Like what you see?" I said, with the deepest sexiest rumble I could muster naturally. She just moaned and writhed. The sexy talk had primed her for sex. I knew I had her in the palm of my hands. So that's when I gave her my promise of things to come:

"I'm going to give you my **cock** and make you **come** real hard...and I'm going to put my **tongue** between your **legs** and make you **scream**," I offered. She threw her head back, eyes closed, her body stretched taut and she moaned again. "What would you like first?" I asked. "I won't do either unless you tell me what you want."

To my amazement, her body grew taut and I soon felt a gush of wetness on my right hand, which had been near her crotch. She'd already come! And all because my words had gotten her there!

I kissed her **face, neck and chest** all over, passionately. "That's my sweetheart!" I said over and over. But after I'd allowed her a brief respite, I asked her the same question again. "What would you like first? My **cock** or my **tongue**? I won't do either unless you tell me what you want."

"I can't decide!" she finally replied after some time. But then she pulled my **cock** and made me move so she could rub her **vulva** with my **glans**. *That led to some of the hottest* **love***making ever - the* **passion** *inspired by my promise of things to come* (and the effect that had on her mind, her imagination). And by the way, by the time I went down on her (after she'd already come many times, vaginally), she came in *seconds*. *The verbal teasing I'd done had worked its magic.*

Another suggestion: If you're **sensitizing her to your touch**, to make her **come** with *the slightest of touches* (which we'll discuss in a later chapter), then try telling her, in your sexiest voice, *before* **sex**: "I'm going to sensitize you so you come at my slightest touch." That will, believe it or not, actually intensify her experience and make her more reactive to whatever you choose to do. (Keep it light, though, in keeping with your promise. And don't increase the intensity.) *Talking like a* **Svengali** *in this way is very sexy to her, too - and makes her more likely to surrender to your suggestion.*

A few other ruses that make women hot: Tell her how many times you're going to make her come that day. Or tell her you're going to push her to her limit, to see how many **orgasms** *she can take before she passes out. Or tell her how hard you're going to make her* **come***. (Then follow through.)*

#2: Talk to her about what you're doing to her and suggest that she

must need to come.

The following conversation along those lines worked so well that my lover at the time asked me to <u>repeat</u> it to her!:

In my sexiest deep voice I intoned, with a groan in my voice: "See what my **cock** is doing to you? I know you want to come! I've stripped you **naked**, and now I'm going to make you come! See how hard your **clit** is? No woman could resist what I'm about to do to you…Let it go!…If I had a big **cock** up me like this, I'd really wanna come…"

She **came**, *before I was done repeating it!*

Another example of how to do this; describe what changes she's going through, as in: "Someone's getting **wetter**!" (Or **wider**, or **hotter**, etc.)

#3: Engage her in conversation by asking questions.

For example, I've asked lovers something like, "Does that feel good, honey?" Or, more specifically: "Does my **cock** make you feel good?"

And also: "Do you feel like **coming**?"

Questions like that make her focus on the sexy things you're doing to her. That helps bring on her orgasm more quickly and makes it bigger than it might be otherwise.

#4: Play into her fantasies.

For instance, if she fantasizes about "being taken" (she'll tell you she does, this won't be a mystery), hug her tightly during sex or hold her hands down above her head while telling her something like, "I've got you now! And I won't let you get away…until you've come at least 3 times!"

#5: When you feel her body tensing, close to her climax, egg her on to bring it on faster and harder.

When you start getting the **biofeedback** indicating her **orgasm** *is about to begin* (which I told you about in, "What The Orgasm Process Is All About" on page 141), try the playful comment, "Mmmm! Someone's about to come!" The fact you *know* she's about to **come** will blow her mind!

Or draw on your *inner* **Svengali** and in a **sultry voice**, **lovingly** urge her on: "**Come** all over me, honey. I know you want to. Let it go!" Repeat that mantra over and over in the right way and she'll **come** in **seconds**.

#6: Let out some moans and groans. Utterances. And writhe. Wriggle.

It's important to let her know how **love**making makes you feel - audibly and visibly. You know how hot you get when you hear your woman moaning and groaning during sex, and when you see her rolling around

Erotic Talking - For Sexual Results

in a state of ecstasy? *She desires the same from you.*

Women don't like **nonreactive** *men.* Stevie Nicks made that clear in the Fleetwood Mac hit "Gold Dust Woman" when she scaldingly sang:

"Lousy lovers -- pick their prey
But they never cry out loud."

And it behooves you to allow yourself to moan and groan in keeping with the spontaneous feelings that come over you because - as you can see from its effect on you, when she does it - you can get her even hotter by doing so. A woman finds it sexy when you react audibly and visibly to her touch. **Sounds, utterances, screams...your body writhing**...they're all very *exciting* to her.

In other words – *don't be a stick in the mud!* Imagine if you were making love to a woman and she was totally *unresponsive*. Wouldn't that be a *drag*?

Don't be a drag. Let out how you feel. She'll love you for it.

I don't know how many times women have told me how *sexy* they thought I was for being so *responsive* during *sex*. "It's a big **turn-on**!" more than one has said.

But do it *naturally*. Don't put on fake feelings, sounds, body reactions. If it's not real, that's a letdown – and she'll sense it from the get-go. Women are good *bullshit* detectors. Always be *honest*, and *do what comes naturally, within your personality.*

But, *if you're* **repressed**, that's going to be a problem with women. Get over it. *It's not unmanly to react to your woman's attentions.* In fact, *it's very* **primal** *and* **masculine**, *to* **roar**, *so to speak, with pleasure when your lover's doing you.*

#7: And, finally, the easiest of all things: Express your honest sexiest feelings, thoughts, reactions and emotions. Whatever comes into your mind - said passionately.

These are examples of comments I've made to my lovers:
♡ *"You feel so good inside."*
♡ *"It feels so good to be so deep inside you."*
♡ *"Oh...your* **pussy** *feels* so *good!"*
♡ *"I feel so close to you."*
♡ *"I'm so hot for you!"*
♡ *"Oh, baby, does my* **cock** *make you hot?"*
♡ *"Feel how hard you made me? You've gotten me so excited!"*

On Loving Women

♡ *"Oh, baby…I love you so much."*

♡ *"Oh, look at you! You look so beautiful when you're hot! I'd love to have a painting of you…looking just like this!"*

These were **heartfelt** thoughts that came to me at the time. They came from a place of total honesty, and said with total sincerity and passion.

If you cannot do this with sincerity and depth of feeling, do not attempt to talk to your lover. If you sound forced, dishonest or insincere, it will backfire. But, hopefully, that doesn't describe you. You should feel affection and/or love for your lover. You must have felt something for her if you're in bed with her. You should be able to express that in words – whatever you feel comfortable saying. Say it in your own way.

Even if you're just feeling a sexual attraction, express that. You might say: *"I feel like coming when I look at your body!"* That's something I told a lover. And it's a nice thing, something a woman might want to hear – it tells her she's desirable in your eyes, and sexy.

If you think your lover wouldn't like this kind of thing, think again. Many wives I interviewed for this book specifically complained to me about this. They are upset that their husbands don't talk to them in bed.

I mentioned this to a former lover some years ago and she commented: *"I've said that [to men] many times myself: 'Talk to me! I want to see myself through your eyes.'"* (But they didn't cooperate with her. Go figure! This is fun stuff!) Then, in referring to our lovemaking that morning, she added: *"I loved what you said to me this morning…It added to the heat…***Don't ever stop talking to me [during sex]!***"*

Above all else, you should always find a good time to tell her you love her. And you might try an even more **sexy ruse**. One of my lovers really got off on my saying this as I entered her: *"Tell me you love me."*

Your **words** are like powerful caresses to her, causing sensations of their own, just as titillating as what you're doing to her with your body – if you know what to say, how to say it, and what tone of voice to say it in.

The miracle of the union of a man and woman through **intercourse** is arguably the most mind-blowing, exciting experience you'll ever have. <u>Not</u> to talk during it would seem <u>odd</u> to most women. They'll wonder, how could you not feel like expressing yourself verbally as all of the amazing emotions and feelings course through your body?

A woman would see a non-communicative lover as someone who was not very moved by the experience. She would wonder why there's

Erotic Talking - For Sexual Results

an apparent lack of **passion**. In addition, she'd likely find a quiet sexual experience boring and empty.

She wants to know a number of things, verbally, during the process:

☞ **Reassurance** that you're having sex with her out of a sense of love and desire, rather than just to get your rocks off.
☞ The **depth of your feeling** for her.
☞ The **passion** you're bringing to the event.
☞ That, in sharing this intimate act, **it's engendering in you an even deeper love for her**.
☞ That **her sexuality (her sexiness) and beauty in all its glorious nakedness is really thrilling you** and has gotten you hot for her.
☞ That a **greater bond** of **love** is being created between you in the doing of it, and that you want to make love to her like this not just today but for the rest of your life.

WHAT NOT TO SAY

Now perhaps we should talk about what you should never *say* during *sex*, too...and what *attitude* never to express...

Never get insecure and ask a woman how *well* you're doing. And never engage in a running conversation seeking self-assurance, such as: "Do you like this? Or should I do it faster? Lower? Or do you prefer this?" Comments like those spoil the mood. And they would only piss her off and make you come off like a real clueless beginner; *unsophisticated*.

And in talking sexy to a woman, never *gush* or make it seem she's *above* you. A case in point: Remember the hit song, "She's So High" by Tal Bachman - with these lyrics?:

"'Cause she's so high...High above me, she's so lovely
She's so high...Like Cleopatra, Joan of Arc, or Aphrodite
She's so high...High above me
...What could a guy like me ever really offer?
She's perfect as she can be, Why should I even bother?"

That's **a good example of what not to think or say**. If she hears you say that, or hears the *implication* in your voice or attitude, she'll begin to *believe it* and someday *she'll go off with someone else*. **Never** imply that your woman is *above* you, or that you're *amazed* she's with you, or that you're so *lucky* that a woman like her might *deign* to be with someone like *you*. These are *negative* thoughts and statements; *unattractive* to a woman.

Billy Joel, I believe, expressed that feeling about his relationship with *Christie Brinkley*. Publicly. She undoubtedly heard the interviews where

On Loving Women

he put her *above* him! Lyle Lovett copped the same self-deprecating attitude when he was with Julia Roberts. Where are those couples today? *I rest my case.*

You must always talk to your lover as an *equal*. You should **not** *worship* her and for God's sake, don't ever use that word! A confident and worthy man *adores* his lover. He *loves* her. He feels she's the **yin** to his **yang**. *You're two halves of one whole. She completes you and you complete her.* And *if you follow what I'm suggesting in* On Loving Women, *she should wind up needing you at least as much as you need her.*

Don't forget – a **great male lover** brings a lot to the table. Don't discount your role in **love**making. More often than not, yours is actually a more *active* role than hers – in the planning, the choreography, the performance, etc. (There are exceptions, and women sometimes play the aggressor or dominant partner, but, in my experience, these cases are vastly in the minority.) You lead, like a male dancer leads, and, therefore, the quality of the experience rests on you. If you're great, *you will rock her world.* And, *if you're great, don't negate in your mind the importance you play in her life.*

Hopefully, at some point, having absorbed and put in practice much if not all of what I talk about in *On Loving Women*, you'll come to respect yourself more and have a **confidence level** that is palpable to her (which is **really sexy** to women). And you'll adopt an attitude (not *conceited*, of course) that would never lead you to fawn over or place your woman *above* you - neither in your mind nor in verbal expressions to her, an attitude which will bring about the death of a relationship. Women do not want a man who is *inferior* to them. It's not very **manly** to play the *wimp*, either.

TALKING TO HER ABOUT THE SEXUAL EVENT LATER

...But let's get back to what you <u>should</u> do, in talking to her about **sex**. One more word of advice: *Always talk to her sometime afterward about how great the sex was the night before (or that morning), telling her, in your own way, how great it was and how special. This is a sexy, fun thing to do,* and, more important, *it is a necessary part of solidifying that experience in her mind as having been a romantic and memorable event in your lives. It also gets her hot all over, thinking about what you did to her.*

More important: *until you do that, a woman might wonder why you didn't comment on your most recent sexual experience. She might doubt your heart, mind and soul was really into it.*

A woman wants to know the event lingers on in your mind afterward, as a treasured memory. She wants to know that it was so important and significant to you that you can't stop thinking about it, and that you value the memory of it as much as she does. It also gives her the "warm fuzzies," which helps bond her to you and solidify your relationship. Do not underestimate the importance of this necessary ritual.

Word of caution about everything I've taught you in this chapter: *Talk to her in your own way. Don't parrot my words - that won't work. Say whatever suits your personality and reflects your true feelings. Make it your own.*

Finally...do all of this because *it's so sexy and so much fun!*

> JERRY: So there you are. You've got a nice girl and a clean apartment.
> GEORGE: Yep. There's one little problem.
> JERRY: Sexual?
> GEORGE: Yeeeaaah...Well...I've never really felt confident...in one particular aspect.
> JERRY: Below the equator?
> GEORGE: Yeah.
> JERRY: Nobody does. You know, nobody knows what to do. You just close your eyes and you hope for the best.
> - From TV's Seinfeld ("The Mango" episode)

Female Sexual Anatomy
(Including Newly Discovered Orgasm Triggers!)

It's incredible to me that most people today are still *in the dark* about **female sexual anatomy**. It's even more amazing that *scientists* and *accomplished lovers* (such as myself) are still discovering undocumented **orgasm triggers, sexual nerve connections, wetness triggers** and other **erogenous zones!**

And looking back on it, we were *really* in the *sexual Dark Ages* when I was coming of age in the early 1970s. I was hungry for **sexual information** yet so little seemed to be known at the time.

Even as a teenager I knew I eventually wanted to become a **great lover**. So I devoured every book I could find on the subject. After school, while one of my friends was outside playing basketball, I was in his house reading his father's *sex manuals*. And I talked to every experienced adult who could teach me something about sexually pleasing women. I was dying to know how to knock the socks off my *future lovers*, even in my *first sexual encounters*.

Back then all we were taught was that to make a woman come you should touch her **clitoris**. That's the sum total of it. I don't recall anyone being aware of a woman's **G-Spot** at the time (which, as you'll see soon, shows how ironic it is that we feel we're more "liberated" or knowledgeable than prior generations) - much less <u>other</u> **orgasm triggers**.

From the get-go (at the age of 17, when I began my sexual experimentation with women in earnest), I realized I hadn't been told everything there was to know about **female sexual anatomy**. There were places I had stimulated that were making my lovers *come* yet I hadn't heard about them. *Much of what I was uncovering was not in any book!*

SEXUAL MISINFORMATION AND DISINFORMATION

It became obvious I had been misled by the prevailing **misinformation** and even **disinformation** of that time. For example, the influential *Kinsey Report* in 1953, though well-intentioned, was *full* of **misinformation**. It said a woman's **clitoris** is the "locus" of sexual satisfaction. Conversely, it belittled the **vagina**, saying it was a source of only "psychological satisfaction." Very puzzling, from a respected source. Those misunderstandings were later echoed by Masters and Johnson, who wrote in 1966: "All orgasm involves direct or indirect stimulation of the clitoris." What they were thinking?

Worse, a purposeful **disinformation campaign** helped fuel the **clitoris monomania**. In a courageous ifeminists.com article, "The Vagina Makes A Come-back," Bettina Arndt opines that *extremists who were more interested in gaining political power than obtaining the truth* spread the myth that the **vaginal orgasm** was a falsehood perpetuated by men. She says 1976's *Hite Report* was one example of this kind of *politically-motivated* "clitoromania." She quotes Hite as saying, "The pattern of sexual relations predominant in our culture exploits and oppresses women," suggesting that this quote reveals the book was *a thinly-veiled anti-heterosexual screed.*

THE CLIT AS A POLITICAL WEAPON

Germany-based American psychology professor Stuart Brody agrees. He accuses the clitoris-centrist radical feminists of harboring a hatred of men:

> *"There are certain political subgroups that seem to have an* **anti-intercourse agenda***. They are desperate to portray female sexuality*

On Loving Women

as wholly cliterocentric [for that reason]."

Regrettably, the autocratic *clit-is-everything* propaganda campaign has had terrible consequences. *It has hurt the lives of millions of men and women who believed the pseudo-science that was used to sell it.* In deluding innumerable heterosexuals into thinking the **clit** was the *only source of female* **climaxes**, *the propaganda deprived a generation of men and women of the enjoyment that comes with achieving* **vaginal** *and other* **non-clitoral orgasms**. Many men and women have told me **the clit-is-everything campaign caused them to stop seeking vaginal and other non-clitoral climaxes (for <u>decades</u>) because they were convinced that those types of orgasms were impossible**. How sad!

Some radical feminists even spread the lie that women didn't *like* heterosexual intercourse! I remember discussing this worrisome idea with a friend at my High School when a woman overhearing us thankfully edified us, saying, "Boys, if women didn't like sex, you wouldn't *be* here!"

Along these lines, I hope this chapter will help undo all the damage that's been done in limiting lovers' sexual horizons through wrong-headed or malicious baloney. Because if you want to become a **great lover**, *you need to ignore 50 years of clit mania, anti-male propaganda and mistaken ideas.*

The idea that only a woman's **clitoris** *can give her an* **orgasm** *is insane.* **Non-clitoral orgasm triggers** *were scientifically identified centuries ago. And my lovers have vouched for their existence. (One said, "It's amazing how <u>many kinds of</u>* **orgasms** *you've produced in me! In 28 years of marriage, I had never experienced anything except for one kind of* **orgasm***.")*

Today's Naive Debate Over Vaginal Orgasms

But confusion rages on. Even today, Internet encyclopedia wikipedia states wrongly: "Most women can only achieve **orgasm** through **clitoral stimulation**." Yet that web site includes the **G-Spot** - *another* female *orgasm trigger!* (See the wikimedia graphic on page 176, too, which is full of errors!)

Maybe it's true that many women today *have not* <u>yet</u> *experienced* **non-clitoral orgasms,** such as **vaginal orgasms** *(produced solely by* **penetration***).* But it's not because those women *cannot* achieve them. As professor Brody has suggested, it's likely because *they have not been with accomplished lovers who know how to give them* **vaginal orgasms**.

Professor Brody also suggests that some women have not come **vaginally** because their partners' **penises** did not "fit" the task. I disagree with that. In this chapter, I will show you some exciting ways to make your lover come **vaginally** even if your **erection** cannot reach a woman's deepest regions.

(Continued on page 178)

WHAT'S WRONG WITH THIS PICTURE?

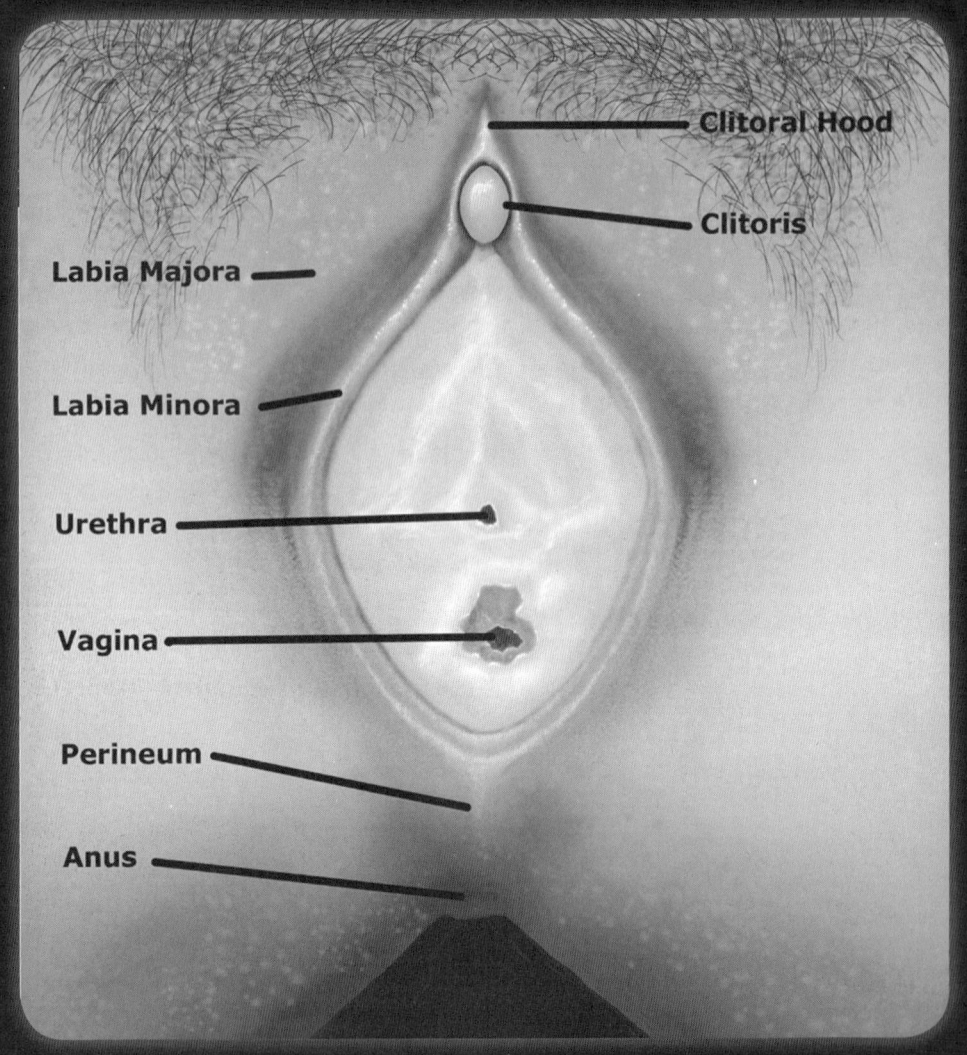

Clitoral Hood
Clitoris
Labia Majora
Labia Minora
Urethra
Vagina
Perineum
Anus

From Wikimedia Commons

The Internet is great for providing easy access to information. Unfortunately, that information is frequently wrong.

For instance, the graphic above contains numerous mistakes. No wonder there's so much confusion out there!

Let's see how many mistakes you can find. You'll find the answers below.

The part labeled "Labia Majora" is pointing instead to skin alongside it. The part labeled "Labia Minora" has the look of her Labia Majora. There is nothing that looks like the Labia Minora. Her "Urethra" as shown is way too far below her "Clitoris" and is actually where her vaginal canal is. It does not show the clitoral body. There is no characteristic "V" of flesh below her "Clitoris" where the labia minora join together. The upside down Clitoris is too large and the hood doesn't cover it as it normally would.

INTRODUCING THE NOOK, NICHE, V-SPOT AND OTHER NEW FEMALE HOT SPOT DISCOVERIES

Vaginal Orgasms Made Easy - For Longer & Shorter Men

Women have been gifted with many different **orgasm triggers,** *so use them all!* Some are located on her outer genitals, some are within her **vaginal canal** and some are found elsewhere (as you'll learn later).

Because **vaginal orgasms** bring about a special kind of fulfillment (since they come about during the intimate act of merging), this chapter contains a special section on how to give her a variety of these. For men of *all* lengths.

Here in the **anatomy** chapter, I'll show you *where* her various **vaginal orgasm triggers** are.

In later chapters, you'll learn how to manipulate them to give her incredible **orgasms.**

How Much Do You Know About Female Sexual Anatomy?

Just for fun, see if you know the five **vulva erogenous zones** in the graphic below. (See the names below.)

In this chapter, you'll learn about these and many others. Some of these are unique to this book, based upon discoveries I've made in three decades of explorations as a lover and researcher. I've found **powerful and quick orgasm triggers** that few if any have documented before. And astonishingly fast **wetness triggers**.

I'll also tell you of scientific discoveries that will help you become a **great lover**.

❶ *Clitoral Hood and Body,* ❷ *Niche,* ❸ *U-Spot,* ❹ *Nook,* ❺ *V-Spot (including, on the inside, the Perineal Sponge)*

(Continued from page 175)

There's another factor to consider, though. Some **medications**, such as **anti-depressants, epilepsy medications** and **birth control pills** can have *orgasm-suppressing effects and interfere with a woman's sexual response.* I personally have been with women who have had trouble climaxing vaginally due to this. But I solved those problems by urging those women to ask their doctors to find prescriptions that didn't handicap them sexually.

The debate over **vaginal orgasms** is just silly. In fact, Professor Brody and two University of Amsterdam associates scientifically *proved* the **vaginal orgasm** is a real phenomenon in a recent study. In their study group of post-menopausal women, *38% reported having **vaginal orgasms** every time they had sex and 33% more reported having them at least half of the time.*

I can testify about this matter firsthand. ***I've given practically every lover I've had vaginal orgasms - with a <u>variety</u> of orgasm triggers I've located inside the vagina. And I've produced vulval orgasms.*** This is what scientists call **empirical evidence** - that is, my successful experimentation with a wide variety of women. In fact, I've discovered **there are up to a half dozen orgasm triggers in the female genitals region!** Some of the **non-clitoral orgasm triggers** I'll introduce to you here, including the **Nook, vaginal ball, vaginal ring** and **V-Spot**, have not yet been described in scientific literature *(as climax triggers),* to my knowledge. Others have been documented but are *not well known* (such as the **perineal sponge**). Yet other **hot spots** that I found *concurrently* with others, *deep in the **vagina***, are shrouded in controversy (their *exact* locations not scientifically known).

...Plus - I've given women **orgasms** *without* even *touching their* **genitals** - such as **breast-induced** and **voice-induced orgasms**. *(More on these later.)*

We're Playing Catch-Up

So why is our world still in the dark about **female sexual anatomy**? It's only in recent years, for example, that scientists have introduced our world to **erogenous zones** like a woman's **AFE zone, clitoral bulbs** and **U-Spot** (something I discovered before it was named). When I first began writing *On Loving Women* years ago, I thought I'd have to <u>name</u> some of those places because it didn't seem as if anyone had identified them yet! And, inexplicably, there's still a debate raging over whether **female ejaculation** is a real and commonplace phenomenon! (It is! See page 207.)

Rutgers neuroscientist Barry Komisaruk explains the paucity of sexual info thusly: "There's no premium on studying pleasure in this society." Fortunately, Komisaruk is helping to clear things up. In fact, he and several colleagues recently completed a study (reported in the October 2011 issue of the *Journal of Sexual Medicine*) that lends credence to the idea that a woman has *multiple* **orgasm triggers. The fMRI study of women's brains showed that stimulation of participants' clitorises, anterior vaginal walls (likely the G-Spot regions), cervical areas and nipples caused "activation" in different areas of the genital sensory cortex! So, they said:**

> *"The present findings provide evidence that, rather than vaginal stimulation being just an indirect means of stimulating the clitoris, vaginal and cervical stimulation...activate specific sensory cortical regions that are distinct from the clitoral sensory projection."*

Translation: **The clit isn't "everything." Vaginal and cervical orgasms are possible if not likely!** The researchers also suggested that **orgasms can be produced through nipple stimulation alone!** These conclusions are reasonable, they said, since **different nerves** connect these areas to the brain. The **pudendal nerve** serves the **clitoris;** the **pelvic nerve,** the **vagina;** **the pelvic, hypogastric** and **vagus nerves,** the **cervix. Thoracic intercostal nerves** send the **brain** sensations from the **breasts** and **nipples.**

...But even with the recent breakthroughs - mine and others[1] - could it be that we're just *rediscovering* what was known *centuries if not eons ago?* Because *in doing my research I've found that there have been major anatomical and other scientific discoveries made over the ages that were somehow* forgotten *with the passage of time! Then, much later, these known facts were "discovered" anew in a another place and time by people who were totally unaware their findings had been uncovered before.*

For example, I believe it's safe to say that most of us in our "modern" world were unaware of a woman's **G-Spot** until the book *The G Spot and Other Recent Discoveries About Human Sexuality* by Alice Kahn Ladas, Beverly Whipple and John D. Perry came out in 1982. And the authors - in their book title - presented the **G-Spot** as a "recent discovery."

But that claim was (forgive me for saying so) *naive.* Yet the history-challenged mass media eagerly spread that **misinformation**. The Associated Press, for instance, published an article on Whipple in 2007 which said:

> *"Early on, she and a former collaborator, psychologist John D. Perry, discovered*

their volunteers had a mysterious, sensual area inside. Researching medical literature, they found Dr. Ernst Grafenberg of Germany had reported in 1950 that women have an erotic zone there that causes orgasm...They named it the Grafenberg spot, or G spot, and created a stir when they reported on it at a medical conference and in their 1982 book..."

The article also quoted a sexuality author as saying,"It [the **G-Spot** book] really furthered the science of women's sexuality and of orgasm quite a bit."

Yet - *no disrespect to the authors of that book, who have done good work* - you can't "discover" something or "further the science" of something that was identified scientifically *many centuries ago*.

Dutch physiologist and histologist Regnier de Graaf discovered the G-Spot in 1672! *(He called it the "female prostate" - which might be the most accurate name for it!)* Some say ancient writers documented it too.

Even more baffling than those who claim to have discovered the **G-Spot** at least three centuries after its true discovery is this: *There are otherwise intelligent people today disputing* the **G-Spot**'s existence!

This is just one example, from the AP story I mentioned before:

"Dr. Brunhild Kring, a psychiatrist at New York University specializing in sexuality issues, said she thinks only some women have a G spot and that only some couples — sort of "sexual athletes" — are able to enjoy it."

Really? Not in my experience. **<u>Every</u> woman has one. And I've proven that it is functional in <u>all</u> healthy women. My lovers can testify to that.**

Yet perhaps there's some twisted political issue behind the **G-Spot** debate. Because, inexplicably, some militant feminists apparently see any talk about the **G-Spot** as a threat to their political agendas! Again, I quote the AP piece:

"Shere Hite, author of the groundbreaking 1976 book, The Hite Report on Female Sexuality, said Whipple's focus on the G spot slowed the drive for women's sexual equality..."

Really? Go figure. From the reactions I've gotten from my lovers by stimulating their **G-Spots**, it seems to me the **G-Spot** is a *gift* to women!

On Loving Women

But even mainstream media outlets have gotten into the goofy **G-Spot** dispute. CNN had this to say in a January 5, 2010 piece entitled "Finding the G-Spot: Is it real?":

> "...this so-called G-spot has never been precisely identified as a concrete biological entity. Scientists are still arguing over what it is and whether it exists at all."

Really? This was based upon a study of 1800 twins at King's College London that concluded:

> "The study suggests that there is no genetic basis for the G-spot and that environmental or psychological factors may contribute to whether a woman believes that she has a G-spot."

But read a bit further and you find the study was laughably unscientific:

[The researcher's] team did not physically examine the women for the presence of G-spots but instead gave participants a survey asking whether they believed that they had a 'so called G-spot'..."

Trust me. *All women have* **G-Spots**. *And anyone can find them.*

Moving onward...get this: **Graaf (the guy who discovered the G-Spot in 1672) also scientifically documented female ejaculation**! *(So why are we debating its existence today?)*

But wait! A recent study by Joanna B. Korda MD, Sue W. Goldstein, and Frank Sommer MD says **female ejaculation** was discovered way before that. In the May 2010 issue of the Journal of Sexual Medicine they wrote:

> "In ancient Asia **female ejaculation was very well known and mentioned in several Chinese Taoist texts starting in the 4th century**...female ejaculation and the Gräfenberg spot (G-spot) are described in detail in most works of the Kāmaśāstra. In ancient Western writings **the emission of female fluid is mentioned even earlier, depicted about 300 B.C. by Aristotle** and in the 2nd century by Galen."

I'm not sure they adequately proved all their points. In reading

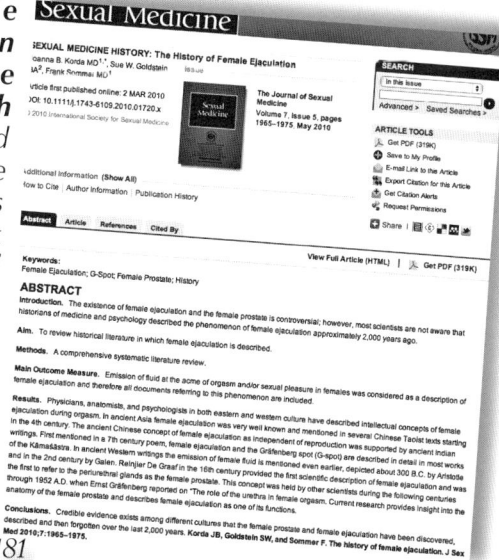

181

their report, I was disappointed to find that they seemed to be bending the meaning of some Chinese phrases they found significant in ancient Taoist sex manuals. They "interpreted" the "Fifth Sign" of sexual arousal - "the genitals transmit fluid" - as referring to **female ejaculation**. Seems to me that phrase might just be a description of **lubrication**. Korda *et al.* also say the instruction to women below, from *Secret Instructions Concerning the Jade Chamber,* alludes to **female ejaculation**:

> "In any event, you must not shake and dance about, causing your female fluid to be exhausted first."

Korda and her colleagues explain: "The author uses the term "female fluid" that can be interpreted as a reference to **female ejaculate**." I'm not so sure. It might be **lubricant**. They're more convincing, though, when they quote the "Ratirahasya" by 12th Century A.D. Indian poet Kukkoka:

> "...at the end they [the females] have like men, the delight, causing swooning of emission"

That does sound like **female ejaculation**. And they note that 16th Century Indian poet Kalyānamalla referred to both male and female **"semen"** (which he called "Kama salila"), which also sounds like the recognition of **female ejaculation** as a legitimate phenomenon, documented long ago.

So it seems that *convincing descriptions of* **female ejaculation** *were published up to 800 or more years ago only to have been forgotten in the intervening centuries.* Yet there are those today who - unaware of the historic references - claim *they* discovered **female ejaculation***!*

Even more foolish - some naysayers are still <u>denying</u> *that this phenomenon is real!* That's incredibly ignorant, as my lovers can attest.

I've made most of my partners in the past 20 years experience female ejaculation. (It took them by surprise because they'd never experienced it before. Plus, they'd never <u>heard</u> of such a phenomenon - which gives me another reason to get the word out about **female ejaculation**, even if others tried to do so centuries ago.)

And the confusion rages on. Some *scientists* still foolishly question whether the fluid that comes from **female ejaculation** is *urine* or not. Even *believers* are unsure of *what organ* the liquid comes from.

Similarly, reports of scientists "discovering" the **clitoris** go back perhaps 2500 years. Yet scientists in more recent eras, apparently *unaware* the clit was already known in ancient times, also claimed they identified it first.

Was the information reported eons ago lost due to decades of sexual repression or ignorance? There's a pattern here.

I mean, didn't we in the United States feel we were an incredibly intelligent and forward-thinking society when the **clitoris** was introduced as something *new* by scientists in the 1950s?

How naive was **that**? *One of the first books off the printing press, **almost 500 years ago**, talked about the **clitoris**!* In **1559** University of Padua lecturer Realdo Colombo's book *De re anatomica* described it as the "seat of woman's delight."

EVEN THE SCIENTISTS HAVE DOUBTS

So it's clear that today's scientists still have a lot to learn about **female sexual anatomy** (even with regard to some of the **female sexual hot spots** that *have* been documented). The more scientific studies I read, the more I realize how *uncertain* a lot of today's theories are.

In some cases the researchers admitted the data group they used was too small (so it was not statistically valid). In other studies, the location of trigger points was not determined scientifically or with exactitude.

Some of today's theories even seem *wrong* to me. One suggests the **G-Spot** is actually part of the greater **clitoral** structure. To me, the position of a woman's urethra makes that theory implausible. And, more important, Dr. Komisaruk's study mentioned on page 179 seems to shoot that down.

OTHER CAUSES OF GENERAL CONFUSION

Adding to the sea of sexual misinformation that's out there is the reality that some scientific findings have been *misinterpreted* by the general public and *distorted* by those who have products to sell.

For example, many web sites indicate the **AFE (Anterior Fornix Erogenous) Zone (or "A-Spot")** is on the "*posterior* vaginal wall" (that is, *opposite* the **G-Spot**). But the highly-private man who *named* the **A-Spot** in 1993, Malaysian physician Chee Chua Ann, recently disputed that obvious misinterpretation in a rare videotaped interview posted on youtube.

"This is completely wrong!" he said. He also disagreed with those who promote the **AFE zone** as an **orgasm trigger**. He sees its value primarily as a means of providing *lubrication* in women with dryness problems:

> "Women, who have poor lubrication response, cannot enjoy sex. I encountered many women patients who complained of dry painful intercourse every time. Conventional methods of treatment did not give satisfactory results. So I started to search for a local reflex mechanism in the vagina to induce lubrication response."

We'll look at this and other **wetness matters** later.

The point is, I hope to clear up as much confusion as I can. And I pray my own breakthroughs, such as they are, will help fill in some gaps when it comes to figuring out what many of us have only just apparently come to realize is a vast playground with many previously unknown pleasure zones.

What Most Men Don't Know

What worries me more than the ongoing **female sexual anatomy** debates among scientists, though, is the fact that what *is* known about the subject still seems to be a mystery to many men. That's become clear in the discussions I've had with the innumerable men who sought my advice over the years - and the complaints I've heard from hundreds of women, who spoke of their lovers' shortcomings in the most intimate terms.

Even today, many women say that most men are baffled as to what to do with a woman's *clitoris!* And although many men have heard about a woman's **G-Spot**, few apparently know *where it is* or *how to manipulate it* to make a woman climax. Fewer still know how to make a woman *ejaculate*.

When it comes to **orgasm triggers** *other than* the **clitoris** and **G-Spot**, women say that *those do not even appear on most men's radar screens*. And other important anatomical areas - **including the exciting areas that generate wetness** (a crucial thing for a lover to be aware of) - reportedly remain unknown to most men.

If I started talking about the **fourchette, vestibule, Bartholin's glands, Skene's glands, perineal sponge** and so on, I'm sure most men would think I was from a different planet. (Soon, you'll be glad you found out about all of these incredible structures!)

That's not to criticize anyone. Few if any are teaching this stuff in high school or college. And that's probably because our society is still very repressed when it comes to sexual matters.

Women Don't Know Everything Either

But men are not the only ones who need to play catch up. I've been told by most of my lovers over the years that I know more about women's bodies than most women do.

I introduced them to **orgasm triggers** they never knew they had. I showed them places on themselves they were unaware of with which I could make them **wet**. I revealed to them the fact I could make them **ejaculate** during an **orgasm**. (And they were thrilled, needless to say, by all of those revelations!)

On Loving Women

Even so, *women are not to blame for being unaware of their many* **pleasure zones**. Some hot spots require a man to set them off to reveal their existence to a woman.

And as I've said before, I believe our culture is really to blame. As advanced and "with it" as we like to think we are, our society doesn't happily pass along sexual information.

So I'm sure that even *women* will find this chapter revealing. If nothing else, *they likely will want to read it so they then can teach their lovers how to locate and satisfy all their erogenous zones (including the ones they didn't know they had).*

Nonetheless, *wherever* you are "at" regarding your state of knowledge about what makes women tick sexually, don't get down on yourself. We all have to learn sometime.

I've devoted a *lifetime* to the subject yet I'm constantly being surprised by how much I *still* don't know! I'm still learning from others too.

But I've had many incredible *epiphanies* I want to share with you. I think you'll find this path of discovery **very** exciting!

Consider this a highly personal, scientifically respectful and unique guide to a woman's body. It's based upon decades of **love**making and *de facto* experimentation with hundreds of women plus *years* of academic research. Strap yourself in!

So...Why Study Anatomy?

Why study **female sexual anatomy**? First, to locate and become familiar with what I call her:

- ♀ **Orgasm triggers** - *the parts with which you can make her come*
- ♀ **Orgasm boosters (new idea)** - *erogenous zones that help bring on an orgasm or make her climax stronger*
- ♀ **Wetness triggers** - *the parts that make her wet*
- ♀ **Female ejaculation triggers** - *places that make her ejaculate out of her Skene's glands ducts and/or urethra*
- ♀ **Pleasure zones** - *sensitive places that titillate but whose stimulation might not lead to orgasms or wetness*

Introducing *Orgasm Boosters*

The concept of **orgasm booster**s is unique to this book. In fact, I believe *it's a new idea in the world of sexual studies*.

Female Sexual Anatomy

And it's an exciting one. With these you can either *speed up* or *intensify* her *Big O!* But *to work,* **orgasm boosters** *need to be used in combination with an orgasm trigger.* And *timing* is everything. Use one or more of these *just before* you want her to come.

I'll identify these as we cover her anatomy in detail.

INTRODUCING *SPECIAL CASE* ORGASM TRIGGERS

One more word on *orgasm triggers* before we delve deeply into *female sexual anatomy*.

That is, there are **special case orgasm triggers** (another concept I believe is unique to this book) that work only:

- ♀ **With a <u>minority</u> of women**
- ♀ **<u>Under certain conditions</u>**
- ♀ **<u>Occasionally</u>**, typically when done in a surprising way (done for the first time, for example, or after a long hiatus and she's not expecting you to touch that special place)

I'll point these out as we go along. (FYI: You and I have these places, too. For example, when I was a single man, I found that my shower massager could help ease the burden of loneliness and keep me from hooking up with the wrong kind of women due to desperation. And during these explorations, I found I could make myself *come* by using it on my balls! (On a very low flow setting.) But - guess what! *I could <u>not</u> produce the same effect every time!* It worked only when done *rarely*. And to date, *I've only been given this kind of orgasm by the shower massager - a woman cannot apparently produce it.* Therefore a man's scrotum is a **special case orgasm trigger**.)

OTHER BENEFITS OF LEARNING FEMALE SEXUAL ANATOMY

Other reasons to get to know **female sexual anatomy**: To know what physical changes you should expect her body to go through

On Loving Women

during sex. *And to show her you're a sophisticated lover who can please her in more ways than just about anyone else.*

Now - just to explain what you're going to learn in this chapter, allow me this analogy: If her body were a car, this chapter would be akin to the manual that shows you where everything is *located*. In later chapters, I will show you how to *drive* the car, so to speak. (To learn *how* to make her come with the **orgasm triggers** you'll find here, you'll want to read the chapters on **cocksmanship, oral sex** and **love touching**, for instance.)

A New Scientific Insight: How Her Vagina "Tents"

First we need to take look at one very important but little-known aspect of her **vaginal canal**. *It needs to be "prepped."*

In an earlier chapter, I told you that a woman's **vaginal canal** grows in size (much as your penis does) during the **arousal process**. (If you didn't know that, don't worry. This is something many *women* are not aware of!)

And if you turn to the two-page spread starting on page 188 you'll learn much of what you need to know about this amazing **tenting** process. We know what goes on with a good deal of precision only because of a recent **MRI** study done in France (which you'll read about on page 338).

But here's what you need to take away from this new awareness:

You now can see, visually, why **you should never enter your lover before her vagina tents** *("goes wide"). Her* **vaginal canal** *is thin and* short *before it tents. So you'll bruise her if you force your way inside her before her* **vagina** fully *expands.*

How can you be sure she's ready for you? You can verify she's **gone wide** by gently and tenderly exploring her either with your **fingers** or **penis**. *If she's still super tight, don't force your way in!*

Enabling You To *Feel* What She Feels

...More really cool information about **female sexual anatomy** (I extrapolated this from what I learned as a premed in college):

Like magic, I'm going to grant you the ability to *know exactly how she feels when you touch some of her intimate places. I mean, what wouldn't you give to know what effect you're having on her?* Wouldn't that enable you to better *orchestrate* what you're doing?

Here's a clue (and this is not widely known):

Your powers of empathy aside, *you already have a pretty good idea of how she feels when you touch her* **labia minora, her clit** *and* **G-Spot**.

(Continued on page 190)

How The Vagina "Tents" With Arousal

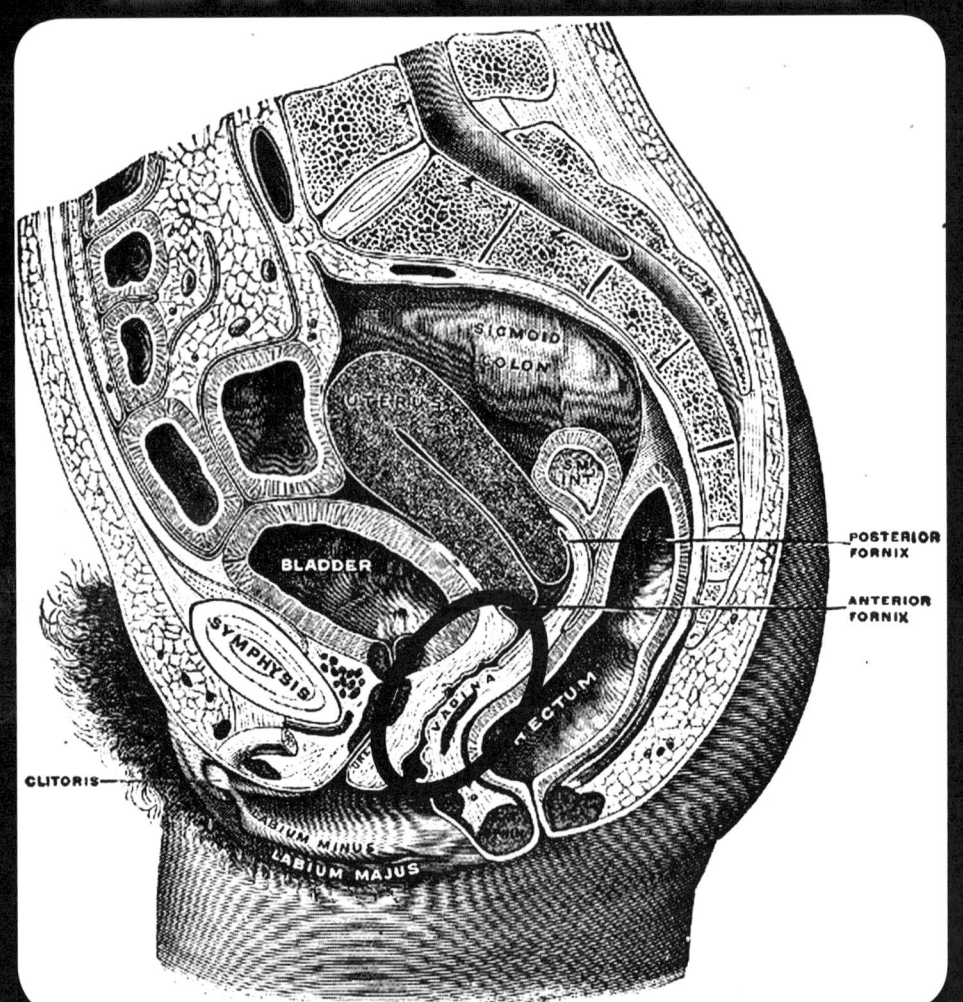

The Vagina At Rest, Untented (From Gray's Anatomy)

The circled area shows what a woman's vagina looks like at rest. Much like your penis, the vagina at rest does not look much like it does in its aroused state.

The *unaroused vagina* is a very narrow passage, much like the space in a deflated balloon. It is only 3-4" long. It is also relatively dry.

Were you to try to enter a woman in this state, it could cause all kinds of problems including *bruising* and *pain*. Even if you used a *lubricant*, the woman physically would not be ready for you to enter her.

This is one reason the *arousal* and *wettening processes* are so important to attend to for awhile before you consider penetration.

Sometimes a woman might get very excited and be ready for you, her vagina "tented" from the get-go (see this on the next page). But this only happens on rare occasions when the thought of sex has been working on her mind beforehand, making her unusually excited.

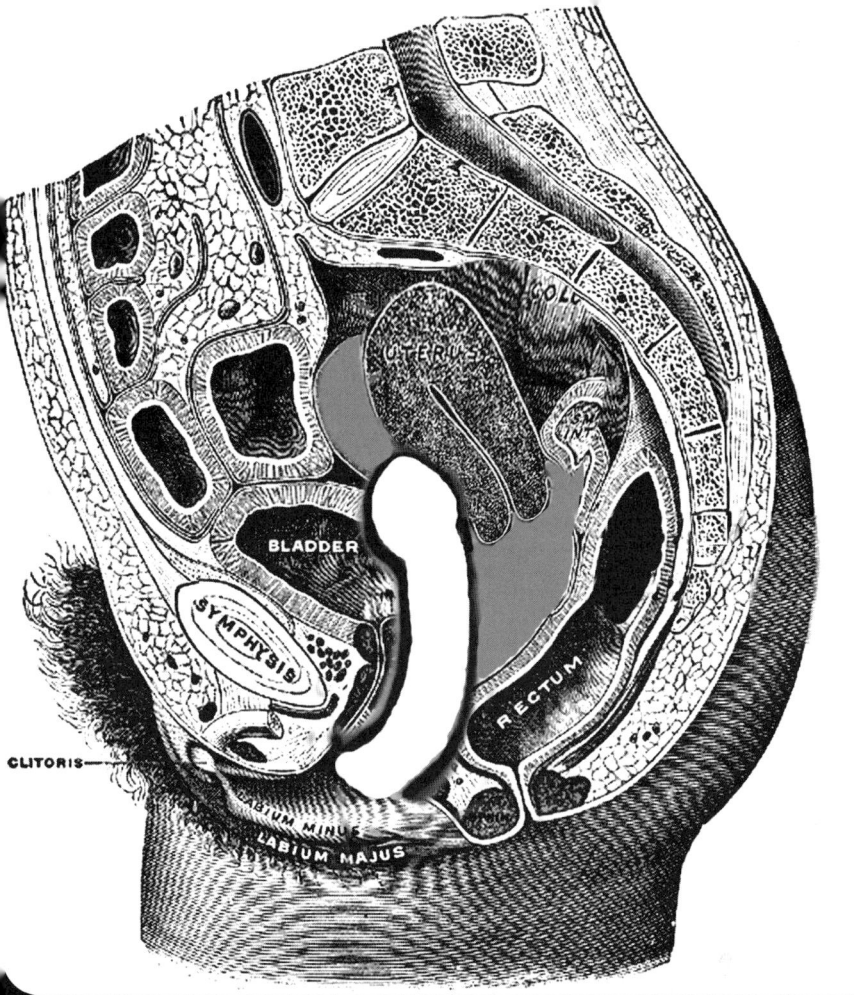

The Tented Vagina: Going Wide In Its Aroused State

The white area (open space) and its black outline (the *vaginal walls*) simulate what a woman's vagina looks like when aroused ("tented"). Like your *penis*, the *vagina* grows longer and wider during the *arousal process*.

The white area is the shape the *vaginal canal* would take on when you enter her from the front, as with the missionary position.

If you'd like to see how the *tented vaginal canal* would look when you enter from behind, take a peek at an artist's rendition based upon an MRI study, on page 338. (You'll see that the head of your erection ends up in very different places depending whether you enter her from the front or the rear.)

That has big consequences when it comes to giving her *vaginal orgasms*.

Depending on your length and her sensitivity in her deepest places, you might find it easier to give her *vaginal orgasms* in one or the other entry methods. (See sidebar on page 329 for more info.)

Female Sexual Anatomy

(Continued from page 187)

Because *they directly relate to areas on your own body!* To understand what I'm saying, let's go back to the womb, figuratively speaking. *Did you know that all fetuses begin as <u>females</u>?* That's right. How does that relate to you? *Some female parts morph into male parts when the fetus is a male! These are often referred to as "homologous" organs. They are biologically similar, originating from the same embryonic structure.*

So she undoubtedly feels much like you do when these homologous organs are stimulated! *These organs have something in common with yours:*

The female fetus' **genital tubercle** becomes her **clitoris**, the **urogenital groove** and **sinus** become her **urethra** and **vagina**, and the **labioscrotal** and **urogenital folds** become her **labia majora** and **minora** *(pussy lips)*. In the male fetus the **tubercle, groove** and **sinus** become the **penis** and the **labioscrotal folds** become the **scrotum** *(ball sack)!* And there's evidence her **G-Spot** is homologous to your **prostate**! (For graphics see page 194.)

So now you already know a lot. Much more than most men do. But what does that tell you? This: You know how great your **homologous** parts feel. *That's undoubtedly how <u>hers</u> make her feel when you touch her there.* So I think *you probably should spend more time stimulating hers - her pussy lips and her **G-Spot**. Her **labia minora** are **orgasm boosters** and her **G-Spot** is an **orgasm trigger**.* Just as a *prostate* can produce a shattering **orgasm** in you, the same is true of her **G-Spot**. Just as her tickling your balls can help bring on your *orgasm*, your stimulating her *pussy lips* can do the same.

And I'm sure you're aware her **clitoris** has been likened to your **penis**. More specifically, I think you should consider it analogous to your **Trigger** (which I introduced to you on page 100). It is an **orgasm trigger**. I tell you all of this because *if you know how you are making her feel you can become a better lover.*

THE UPDATED FEMALE SEXUAL ANATOMY - YOUR PLAYGROUND

OK! With that essential background, let me show you some amazing places on your lover's body (pictured on page 192 to page 195).

You need to get familiar with your lover's many **hot spots** if you want to drive her wild. (*Warning: Some internal anatomical graphics may have a "yuck" factor, but you need to know where to <u>find</u> all her fun parts!*)

LET'S START WITH HER GENITALIA: HER VULVA

OK...So if a smart lover knows he must make his woman **wet** and **wide** before entering her, that means **love***making starts mainly with the outside*

On Loving Women

places. (That doesn't mean you can't slip a finger, preferably *wet*, into her **vagina** during the **wettening** and **widening** period.)

So let's start our look at **female sexual anatomy** by getting familiar with this part of her. I think you'll find her **genitalia** include a few exciting **hot spots** you might not know about.

HER *VULVA* VS. HER *VAGINA*: DO YOU KNOW THE DIFFERENCE?

Let's start with an important fact. *While most people call a woman's* **outer sex organs** *her* **vagina***, this is* not *true. You can either call them her* **genitalia** *or her* **vulva**. (Her **vulval hot spots** are shown on page 192. Her **vaginal sweet spots** are in the two-page spread starting on page 194.)

There are a lot of *sweet spots* to explore in her **vulva**. Look at the graphics on page 194. *Notice how much territory there is, so to speak, between the outer edges of her* **labia minora** *and the entrance to her* **vagina**! And it's rich with **erogenous zones**.

The *difference* between her **vagina** and **vulva** is an *important distinction*. They are two *unique* **sexual zones**. They give her dramatically distinct *feelings*. Your touch upon her **vagina** and **vulva** feels as different to her as her touch upon your **penis** and **scrotum** feels to you.

EVERY VULVA IS DIFFERENT

Another thing. There's a funny but telling scene in the 2005 movie *Boynton Beach Club* in which a bunch of straight-laced old widows are watching a porno video they stumbled upon and one exclaims:

"You know what's so <u>interesting</u>? All the **vaginas** look <u>different!</u>"

Her *shock* shows that even *women* lack a general knowledge about **female sexual anatomy**. *She mistook* **vulvas** *for* **vaginas** *(she misidentified the female genitalia)*. And *yeah! Every woman's* **vulva** *looks different. Dramatically.*

Says Lesbian sex educator Betty Dodson in a video on her wonderful web site, as she sketches **labia minora** onto her **genitals** drawing: "It's different in every woman. It is amazing. Nice full ones. They're my favorite!" (See her Genital Art Gallery for photos and drawings of a variety of **vulvas**!)

Some have huge **labia minora** (*pussy lips*) that pout outside her like blossoming flowers. Some have very tiny lips that are almost nonexistent. Some **vulvas** are very long in height. Some are very compressed.

And **vulval** *variety* goes on from there. They differ in *color*. Some will look pretty to you. Some might appear more *functional* instead. Some have *a* <u>lot</u> *of pubic hair*. Some *not so much*. **Vulvas** vary in appearance by *ethnicity* and *race*, too. **Clitorises** - also part of the **vulva** - vary in *size*.

(Continued on page 196)

INTRODUCING THE FEMALE SEXUAL ANATOMY

The Outer Genitals: Her Vulva

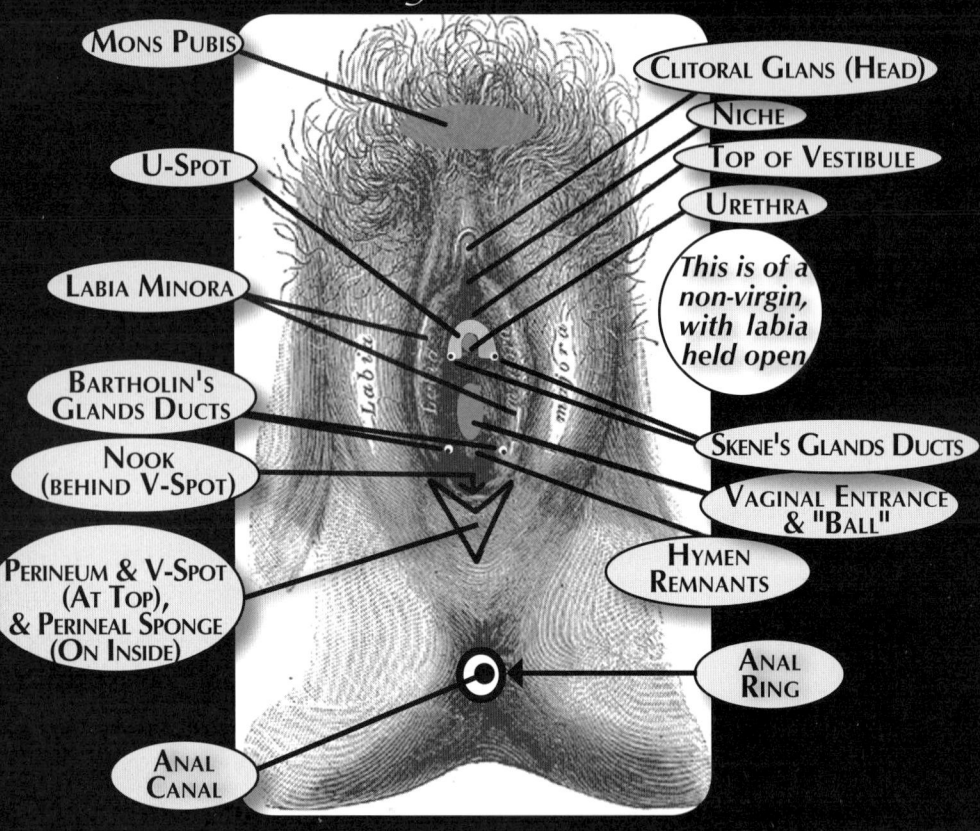

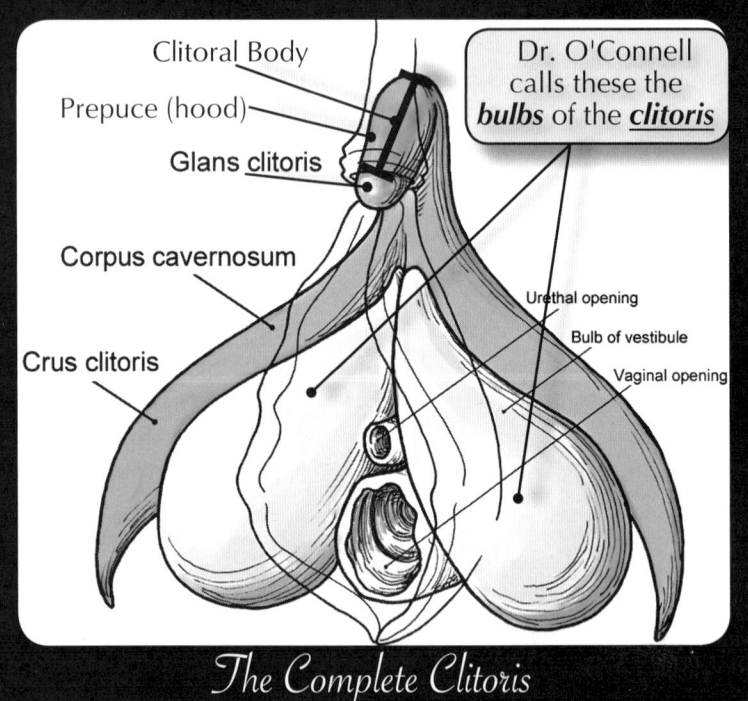

- Mons Pubis
- U-Spot
- Labia Minora
- Bartholin's Glands Ducts
- Nook (behind V-Spot)
- Perineum & V-Spot (At Top), & Perineal Sponge (On Inside)
- Anal Canal
- Clitoral Glans (Head)
- Niche
- Top of Vestibule
- Urethra
- Skene's Glands Ducts
- Vaginal Entrance & "Ball"
- Hymen Remnants
- Anal Ring

This is of a non-virgin, with labia held open

The Complete Clitoris

- Clitoral Body
- Prepuce (hood)
- Glans *clitoris*
- Corpus cavernosum
- Crus clitoris
- Dr. O'Connell calls these the **bulbs** of the *clitoris*
- Urethal opening
- Bulb of vestibule
- Vaginal opening

Introducing New Erogenous Zones

The *Niche, Nook, V-Spot, Vaginal Ball, Vaginal Ring* and *Clitoral Ring*

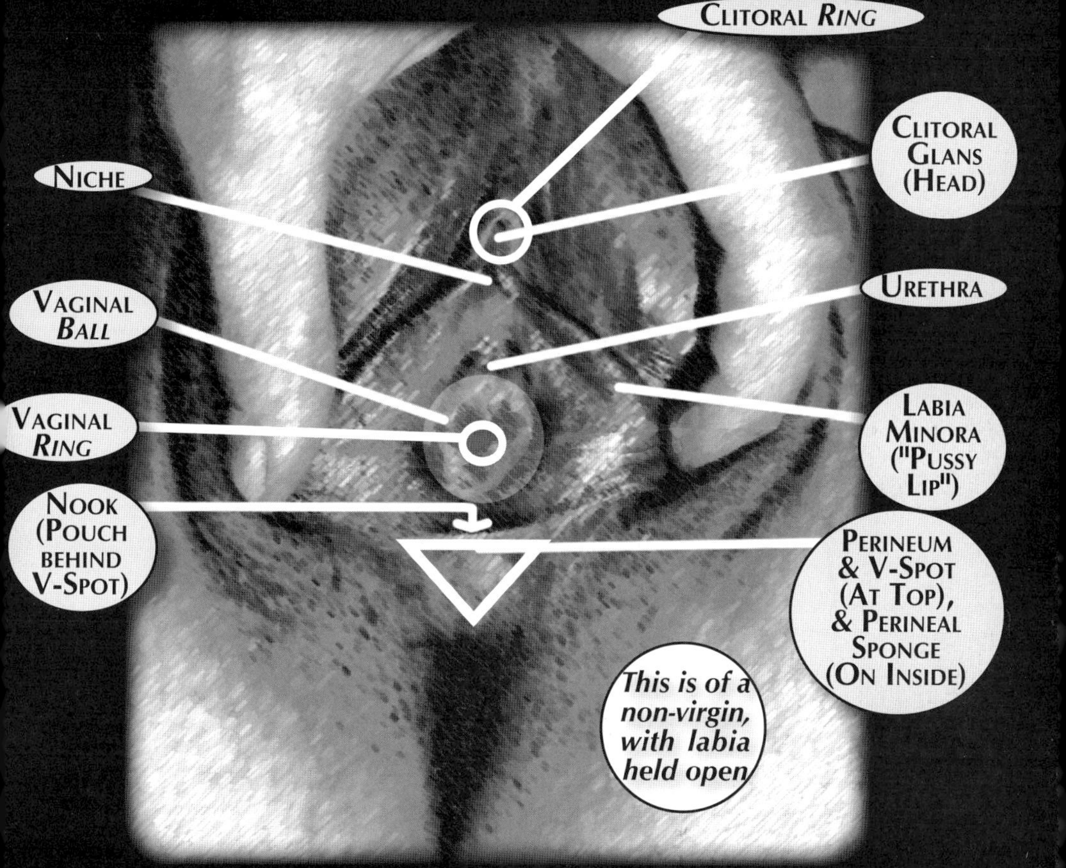

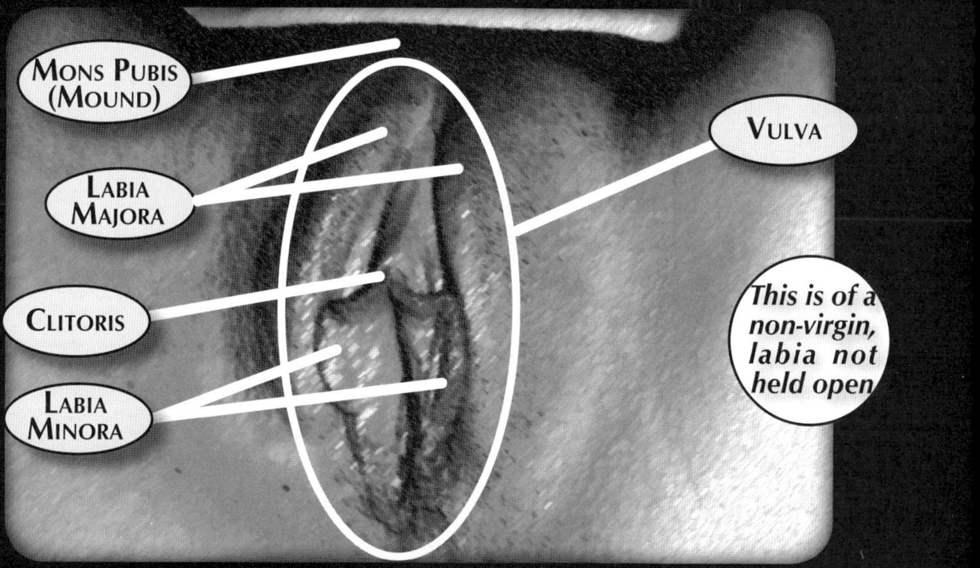

Introducing New Orgasm Triggers
The *Deep Trigger, Nexus, Fornix & Nook*

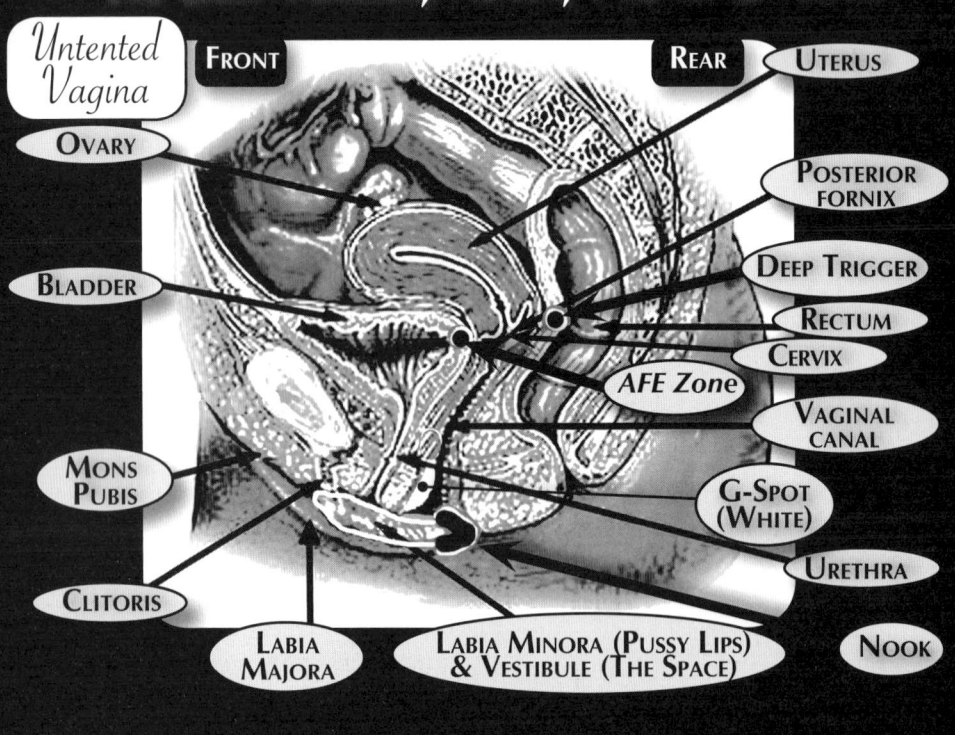

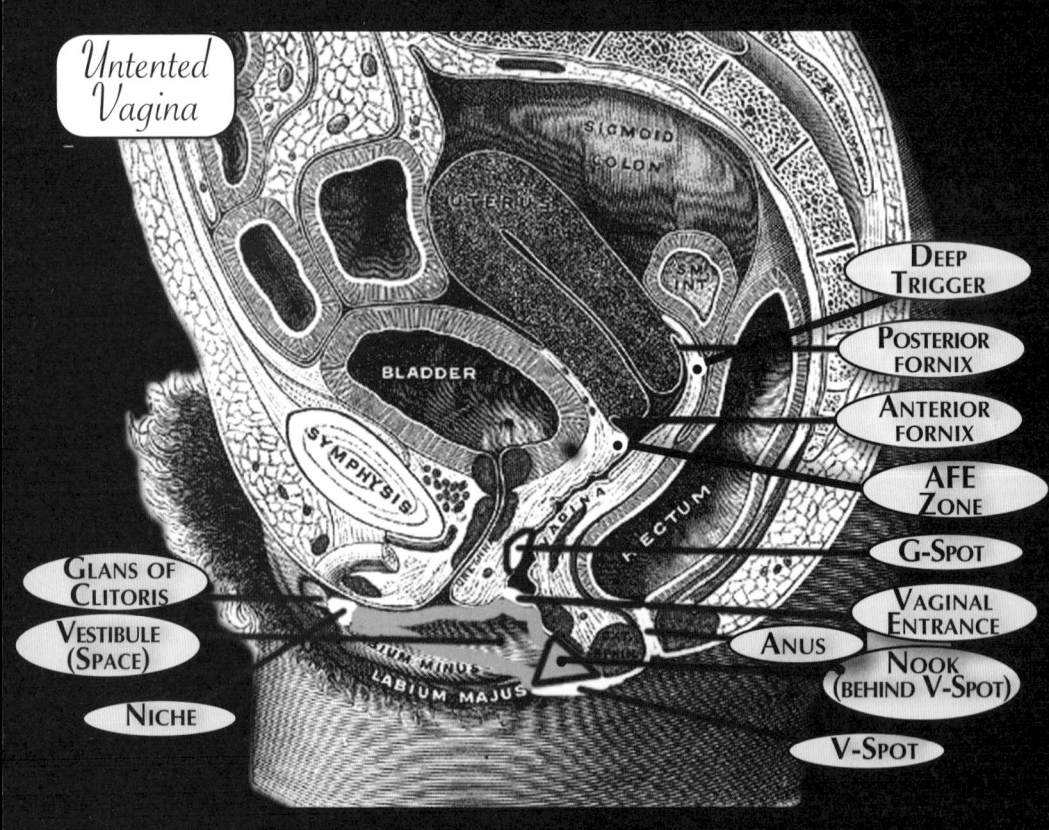

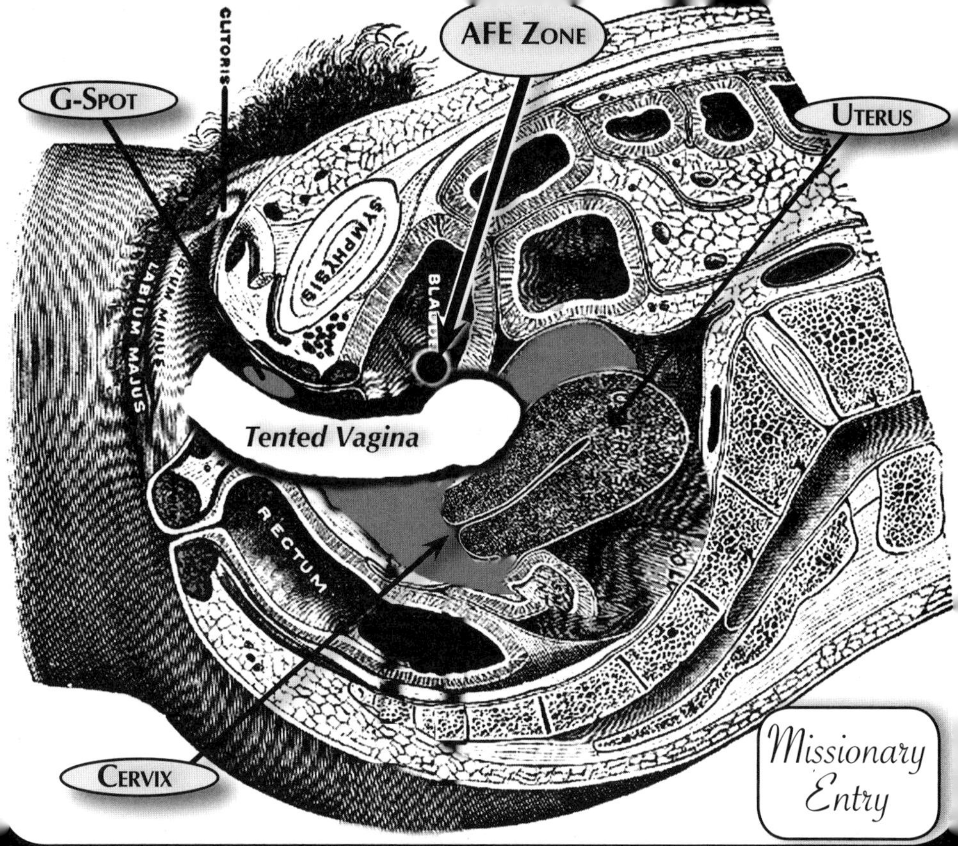
AFE Zone
G-Spot
Clitoris
Uterus
Symphysis
Labium Minus
Labium Majus
Tented Vagina
Rectum
Cervix
Missionary Entry

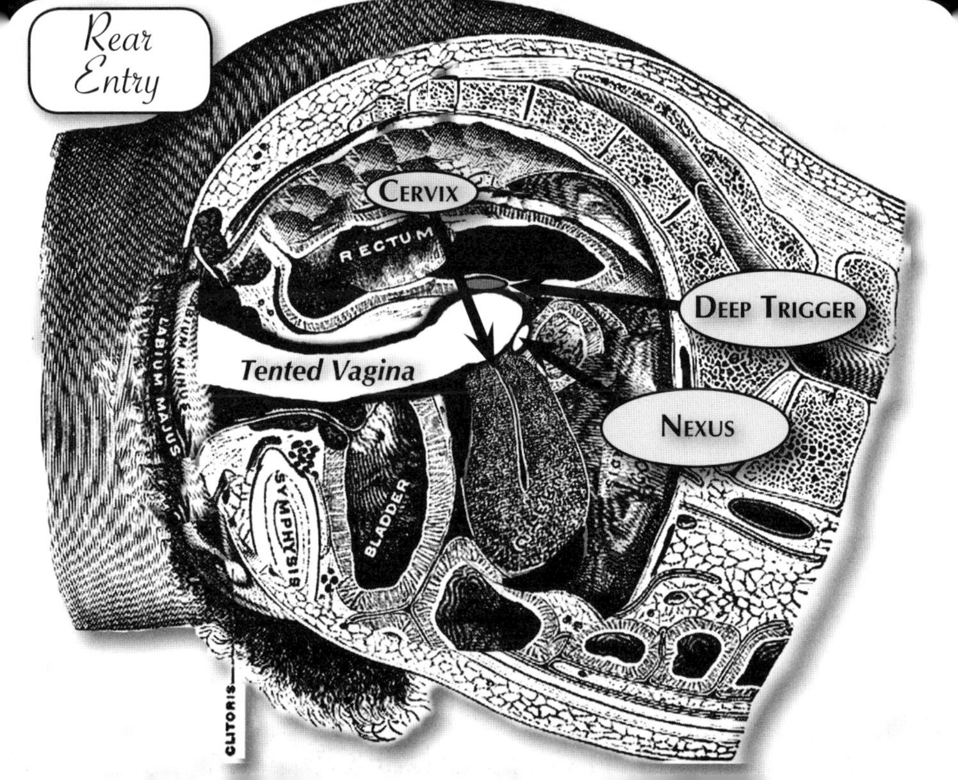
Rear Entry
Cervix
Rectum
Deep Trigger
Tented Vagina
Nexus
Labium Majus
Symphysis
Bladder
Clitoris

(Continued from page 191)

It's *all* good. But you need to know that there's a tremendous variety of **vulval** shapes and sizes so as not to be shocked by what you find on the first night together or think something might be wrong.

I like to think of my lover's **vulva** as a flower. All flowers are *different*. And, best of all, like flowers, they *blossom* as you play with them. How *wonderful*, whatever the shape.

Her Labia Minora For Arousal, Wetness & Widening

Now the first significant **vulval hot spots** we should talk about are her **labia**. We'll focus primarily on her **labia <u>minora</u> (aka her "pussy lips")**, because those are the *sexually reactive* ones. They are also the outermost parts of her **vulva** and, as such, the first **vulval areas** you typically touch. (See the bottom illustration on page 193.)

Her *pussy lips* are really fun to play with. They *swell* with blood (much as your penis does) and *part* in response to your touch. They can grow quite large, in fact, and turn very *dark* in color during the **arousal process**.

As I mentioned before, they're biologically similar to the flesh of your *scrotum*. And you know how great the skin covering your *testicles* feels when it's touched. So you should easily understand exactly how hot she will feel when you tease her analogous parts, her **labia minora**.

And her **labia minora** are super **wetness triggers**. They are especially great for teasing her *before* intercourse to bring on not just the **arousal process** but also the **wettening and widening processes**. (See "More Fun With Her Pussy Lips" on page 277 for some fantastic ways to do that.)

They're also great **orgasm boosters**. Not during the "act" (they're hard to touch during intercourse) but during *oral sex* and when you're doing *fingerwork*. (In fact, I'll give you an <u>incredible</u> **cunnilingus technique** in a later chapter that will absolutely drive her *crazy* using her **labia minora** as **orgasm boosters**. You'll have to peel her off the wall afterward! For that, see "Knock-Her-Socks-Off Head" on page 252.)

Sexual Entrances And Her Labia Minora

But her **labia minora** have a deeper significance. They are one of her three **sexual entrances**. They are the **doors** to her most intimate places.

This is an important concept for you to understand. Biologically speaking, **sexual entrances** (her **labia minora**, **vaginal introitus** and **anal canal opening**) come with *extra nerves* and *unique excitations*. When **initially** penetrated, they provide titillating sensations other body parts *don't*.

This is especially true of the **inner rims** of each **labia minora lip**. So - word to the wise:

Don't rush past her **labia minora** or you'll miss out on giving her the heightened pleasures of being **entered** for the first time. Those extra-tingly feelings **entrances** such as her **labia minora** give her *only happen when you tenderly play with those entrances first before moving on.* It's a biological quirk.

> *"Sexual entrances should be treated differently than other erogenous zones."*

So don't neglect these flower-like organs during sex (as I believe most men do). They're among her most *sensitive* places. They're guaranteed to raise her fever an extra notch and, as you can see, *you can work them to many purposes.* And be *creative!* (For example, see "The Shower Massager As Sex Toy" on page 395.)

But there's something else you need to know about these special **hot spots**. As **entrances** to her body, they also have an **emotional, psychological and spiritual significance** to a woman that you need to recognize.

This crucial knowledge - of the **emotional, psychological and spiritual significance** of penetration, to a woman - will help guide you in becoming a better lover. (For that side of **love***making*, see "Sexual Entrances And Their Psychological Significance" on page 348.)

HER LABIA MAJORA AS PLEASURE ZONES

We should not totally dismiss her **labia majora**, though, as places of interest. (See page 193 for their location.) While they're not **orgasm triggers** or **orgasm boosters**, they are worth playing with from time to time as **pleasure zones** - in conjunction with other **vulval erogenous zones**.

There's an upside down *U* of a space at the top where her **labia majora** meet, for instance, which you can manipulate to give her pleasure. The act of *separating* her **labia majora** will also elicit a moan or two. We'll talk more about this in the love touching chapter.

HER VESTIBULE

Now let me introduce you to a little-known area inside her **vulva** that contains some awesome **erogenous zones** few lovers are aware of. It's a *boat-shaped shallow alcove* biologists call her **vestibule**. (See the graphics on page 194 for its location.)

Scientists have assigned no special value to this *depression*. But as you will see in a minute, it has a *lot* of value in **love***making*. Her **vestibule**

Female Sexual Anatomy

includes some of the most *exciting* places on your lover's body.

INTRODUCING HER *NICHE*

For instance, there's a structure I call her **Niche**. It's located at the top of her **vestibule**. *(See page 193. It's also the white triangle shaded area in the graphic on the right side of page 177.)*

You will find her **Niche** inside an upside-down triangular-shaped protruding *V* of skin where the tops of her **labia minora** join together. Biologists call the *top* of this upside-down *V* her **frenulum clitoridis** or **Crus glandis clitoridis**. The **Niche** is the *skin* inside the *bottom* of that *V* and the *cove-like little space about ¼" to ½" deep inside the **vulva**, just below the sensitive under-surface of the **clitoral glans**. In fact, you can stimulate her **clitoral body** and **glans** from within her **Niche**.

This is an exciting place because *if you manipulate it in the correct way you can make her come while giving her feelings she doesn't seem to get elsewhere. This certainly seems to give her different sensations than direct* **clitoral** *stimulation does.*

I believe her **Niche** *feels to her somewhat like your* **Trigger** *feels to you when it's stimulated. (To learn <u>how</u> to give women* **Niche** *orgasms, see "Introducing the Niche Tickle Orgasm Technique" on page 270.) So I would say her* **Niche** *is a* **special case orgasm trigger***, since its role might be indirect.*

Yet its value doesn't just lie in the fact that it's near her **clitoris**. I believe it has its own set of nerves that - when touched *independently* of her **clitoris** - make it a natural **orgasm booster**.

In fact, this is also a good place to touch simply to start the **arousal process**. A woman will usually respond super-excitedly to your first entering her **Niche**. It feels <u>that</u> good.

INTRODUCING HER *V-SPOT, NOOK & PERINEAL SPONGE*

The *bottom* of her **vestibule** features two other **hot spots** I've identified: her **V-Spot** and **Nook** - plus a third one scientists call the **perineal sponge** *(an exciting* **erogenous zone** *of which few are aware).*

The hot spot I've named her **V-Spot** (pictured on page 192 and page 193) is a flap of skin physiologists called the **fourchette** or, alternatively, her **frenulum labiorum pudendi**; but they did not recognize its *sexual* value. It's the sensitive thin top **V-shaped skin** (where her **labia minora** meet at the bottom) atop her **perineum** (a tickly *flap of skin* that extends from the bottom of her **vestibule** to her **anus**).

On Loving Women

I've been able to give some but not all my lovers **V-Spot orgasms**. So I would call the **V-Spot** a *special case orgasm trigger.* *(Well worth exploring.)*

But whether you can give your lover **V-Spot orgasms** or not, *all* women find this an intensely erotic and titillating area. And during oral sex or finger manipulation it can help bring about and intensify her orgasm. So, during those activities, it's an **orgasm booster**.

But it can also be a **wetness trigger** if you work it right. (To do this I'll teach you my **V-Spot Massage** method in the *love touching* chapter.)

Just Seconds To Wetness And Orgasm

The **erogenous zone** I call her **Nook** is located at the bottom end of a woman's **vestibule**. *That's a good descriptive name for it because is a little* **nook** *or* **pouch** *just outside* the entrance to her **vagina**. (See its location graphically on page 192 through page 195.)

The sexually active part of this cove-like **erogenous zone** is its *bottom*, where you feel you are touching her spinal cord. (I imagine you are touching *nerves* that come from it, at the very least.) Its bottom feels like a *flat ridge* about *an inch or more in length* once your lover's **vagina** is tented.

The best thing about it? **The Nook is both an orgasm and wetness trigger. In fact, it can produce powerful orgasms and a burst of wetness <u>in a matter of seconds</u>** - that is, if you touch it in the right way, with your fingers or the head of your penis. (I give you <u>awesome</u> techniques to do that, in the cocksmanship and love touching chapters!)

The same is true of her **perineal sponge**, an incredible **special case orgasm and ejaculation trigger**. You'll find this fabulously sensitive erectile tissue full of nerve endings and blood vessels on the *inside wall* of your lover's **perineum** (see page 192 for its location). And on page 271 you'll learn a sexy way to manipulate it to make her *come* and *ejaculate* <u>quickly</u>.

Introducing Her Vaginal Ball

Also in her **vestibule** is a very sensitive place I call her **vaginal ball**. If you look at the graphic on page 193 you'll see that this stands out distinctly from its surroundings as a separate structure.

This is an incredible area no one to my knowledge has talked about. Yet it undoubtedly will become one of your favorite places to play with.

I'm talking about the unique spherical rubbery ball of flesh that surrounds the entrance to her **vaginal canal**. It works *amazingly* well as both an **orgasm** and **wetness trigger**. If you stimulate it correctly, you can *easily* and *quickly* make her come, with a *gush* of love juices. Or you can choose to use it simply to make her *wet*.

One interesting thing about her **vaginal ball** is that it is not *stationary* (like her **clitoris** for instance). It *moves* with the contractions of her **vaginal muscles**. You can actually see it moving forward and backward as you manipulate it. Incredibly, it will sometimes protrude beyond her **vulva**.

You'll want to spend a lot of time exploring this area, with your **fingers**, **tongue** and **glans**. I'll give you some great ways to do this in later chapters.

But first find it inside her visually, so you know where to touch her to produce incredible results. While giving her a finger job so she's lost in excitations and not noticing what you're doing, spread her vaginal lips wide and peer inside.

The **vaginal ball** looks different in every woman, but its *distinct feel* gives it away. So give a feel to locate it. Its flesh is firmer than the surrounding skin because of the muscles it contains.

Don't be surprised when it moves back and forth with your touch! She should immediately grow more excited too. (*That* will reveal you found it!)

THE CLITORIS IS NOT JUST WHAT YOU SEE

Now to her **clitoris**. Ready for a shock? Her **clitoris** is *much bigger* than you've probably been taught!

Called by many names over the ages including **columella** ("little pillar") by ancient Greek physician Hippocrates, **landica** (a profanity, exact translation unknown) by the ancient Romans, **crista** ("crest") by 1st Century A.D. Roman poet Juvenal, and **tentigo** (tension) by Andalusian surgeon Albucasis at the turn of the second millennium A.D., it's an organ that's helpful in all *three types of* **love**making *processes*.

Most commonly known as an **orgasm trigger**, it also works in **wettening** her and in slowly steaming her up during **arousal**.

Made of erectile tissue that *swells* with blood when aroused, it was long thought to consist only of a pea-sized pearl-like hard object (that is, in its engorged state, with arousal). That part, which you can barely see until you pull back the **clitoral hood** (or **prepuce**), is actually just the **glans**.

Well guess what? That's just the tip of the iceberg!

And the complete, amazing structure of the clitoris (shown in Figure 1 on page 192) has been known for a long time. For instance, a man known as the "Dean of Gynecologists," Robert Latou Dickinson M.D., revealed this fact in his 1940s-era anatomy book, *Human Sex Anatomy*. In fact, he'd shown the structure in drawings he'd done before World War I.

But he wasn't the first scientist to unveil the true nature of the **clitoris**. Not by a long shot.

Yet the BBC News (and others), not knowing about Dickinson (or anyone before him), announced on June 11, 2006 that someone had "discovered" what others had known for decades.

In the article, "Time for rethink on the clitoris," the BBC News said:

> "For two millennia it was a "little hill" - the meaning of kleitoris, its root word in Greek. But an Australian urologist, Dr. Helen O'Connell, has revealed that the clitoris is shaped more like a mountain than a hill.
>
> "Her work is forcing a rewrite of anatomy books and a rethink among medical professionals...The clitoris rivals the penis in size...
>
> Dr. O'Connell's finding has forced a rewriting of medical texts."

...Well, not really. Dr. O'Connell's work was not radically new. Her *facts* are right but she was *not* the *first* to uncover them. And *Dr. O'Connell* knew that.

In her October 2005 Journal of Urology report "Anatomy of the Clitoris," she acknowledged that anatomist **Georg Ludwig Kobelt** had described the true size of the **clitoris** in the 1800s:

> "The work of Kobelt in the early 19th century provides a most comprehensive and accurate description of clitoral anatomy, and modern study provides objective images and few novel findings."

And, in fact, she says Reigner de Graaf (see page 180) might have been the first to discover the clitoral bulbs, more than 300 years ago:

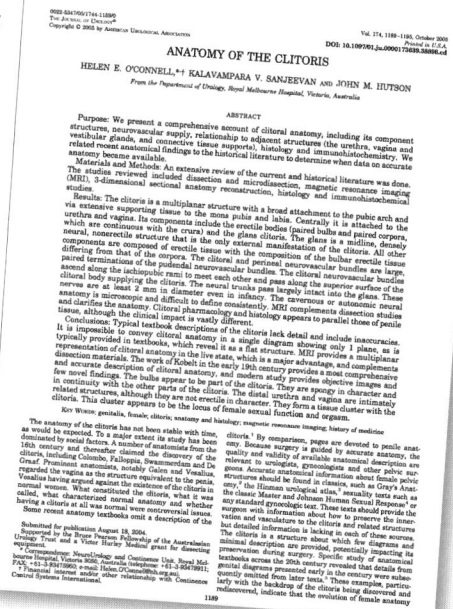

> "De Graaf described the bulbs, calling them plexus

retiformis: "The constriction of the penis (by the female) previously mentioned is assisted in a wonderful way by those bodies..."

She also credits de Graaf with standardizing the name "clitoris."

Along those lines, her report echoed what I've told you about how **sexual information** sometimes gets forgotten:

"...for periods as long as 100 years anatomical knowledge of the clitoris appears to have been lost or hidden, presumably for cultural reasons."

This might interest you, too. She says Kobelt drew these conclusions about what parts of the greater clitoris structure were sensitive to a lover's touch:

"He subdivided the female sexual organs into **active** (clitoral shaft and vagina) and **passive** (bulbus vestibuli, associated muscles, pars intermedia and the glans clitoris) organs."

It seems to me then that much of the greater **clitoral structure**, being *passive* parts, are of less interest to a lover. But there are other lessons to be learned as a *lover* and a *caring companion*:

A *caring companion* will be concerned about what Dr. O'Connell's study said about *pelvic surgery*. She issued this warning in the San Jose Mercury News (July 29, 1998):

"O'Connell also is tracing the nerves and blood vessels that feed into the clitoris, allowing it to swell and engorge during sexual arousal in much the same way the penis does in men. Because they have never been described in detail, **these vital connections are in danger of being severed whenever surgeons cut into the area**."

In other words, *you and your mate had better think twice about any surgical procedure that might cut through areas that might contain the greater part of the clitoris and the blood vessels and nerves that keep it vital*. In a 1998 ABC-TV interview, O'Connell gave examples:

"I guess the common operations that may put these structures at risk would be hysterectomy and incontinence surgery, and maybe even prolapse surgery - to be honest we don't know."

Good to know.

And *from a lover's standpoint*, O'Connell claims:

"The vaginal wall is, in fact, the clitoris."

Are Her Clitoral Bulbs Vaginal Orgasm Triggers?

This, you'll see, is wrong. The *vaginal walls* extend far beyond the *clitoral bulbs*. So I doubt they are responsible for the reactions produced by deeper penetration. And there are in fact scientists who feel the **clitoral bulbs** are *inactive* as *orgasm triggers*.

On Loving Women

And I strongly disagree with O'Connell when she asserts that the **greater clitoral structure** is the source of **all** **vaginal orgasms**. In fact, I believe the recent **fMRI** study I mentioned on page 178 *proves* her wrong.

Perhaps the **clitoral bulbs** have helped bring on the *orgasms* I have given my lovers with what I call the **vaginal ring,** which we'll look at soon...

Non-Clitoral Vaginal Orgasm Triggers

But it's important to point out that O'Connell's assertions about **vaginal walls** and **orgasms** have been disputed by what my *lovers* have told me about *where* they feel their **vaginal orgasms** originate. They've reported, for instance, experiencing **vaginal climaxes** in places that are *too far* from the **clitoris** to have been triggered **clitorally**. And many have told me that "**vaginal orgasms** feel *completely different* than **clitoral orgasms**."

In fact, my experiences tell me *there are a half dozen or so* **non-clitoral** *erogenous zones that can trigger* **vaginal orgasms**. These include her:

- ♀ *vaginal ball*
- ♀ *vaginal ring*
- ♀ *G-Spot*
- ♀ *AFE zone*
- ♀ *Deep Trigger*
- ♀ *Nexus possibly*
- ♀ *vaginal walls possibly*
- ♀ *cervix possibly*

(See "Introducing New Erogenous Zones" on page 193 and "Introducing New Orgasm Triggers" on page 194 and page 195 for their locations.)

It differs from woman to woman but in general I've found that **non-clitoral orgasm triggers** often produce the *biggest* climaxes. Based upon Rutgers neuroscientist Barry Komisaruk's finding (in his recent **fMRI** study) that different **nerves** and **brain sensors** are responsible for the *unique* feelings coming from each of a woman's various **erogenous zones**, the disparity I've noticed in **orgasm size** should surprise no one.

On the positive side, O'Connell's support of the concept of **vaginal orgasms**, however, is important because that provides additional scientific validation for their existence. And it adds to the weight of evidence screaming out at you that **vaginal orgasms** are *real*. And *that* means:

Lovers of women should routinely seek to give their women vaginal orgasms. That's part of your "job" as a great lover. If you're not doing

*that, you're not giving her the whole **love**making experience.*

And - just to undo any misunderstandings you might have: **You do not have to touch her clitoris to give your lover a complete sexual experience with satisfying vaginal orgasms.**

SUMMING UP THE NEWLY-UNDERSTOOD CLITORIS' ROLE

Anyway, the revelation that the **clitoris** is not a *pea-sized object* but a *large organ* rivalling the **penis'** size gives you something to think about and experiment with. The *sexual* side to this is, alas, still new territory (as O'Connell admits).

Perhaps we will ultimately find the **clitoral bulbs** are *not* active in the **orgasm process**. But it's worth exploring.

Tying all of this into the *three processes of **love**making* idea, here are my thoughts:

While the **clitoris** is best used as an **orgasm trigger**, *it can also be used as a tool in teasing your lover during the **arousal process***. But avoid this no-no:

As a rule, *don't bring your lover to the very brink of a climax and then suddenly back off. Unless there's some kind of S&M thing you're doing, she'll probably get very mad at you. If you commit this faux pas, it'll likely make it harder for her to come afterward and her orgasm probably will be unsatisfying.*

Two other **arousal process** tips:

Number one, *some* women find direct stimulation of the head of the *glans* almost painful. It's too intense for them. Ask your lover if that's the case with her. *If your lover's **clitoral glans** is too sensitive for direct touching, devote your attention to the areas surrounding it.*

Number two, *don't neglect her* **clitoral body** and **clitoral hood** (refer back to page 192 to see these parts). They can be used as **orgasm boosters** or as **pleasure zones** during the **arousal process**. (Her **clitoral hood** is like a sleeve of thin flesh surrounding her **clitoral body** and **glans**.) In fact, her **hood** and **clitoral body** can be **special case orgasm triggers** *in some women*. (To learn how to make her come with her clitoral hood and clitoral body, see "The Clitoral Body Massage Orgasm Technique" on page 274.)

THE CLIT AS WETTENER: NOT SO MUCH

...But what about using your lover's **clitoris** as a tool in the **wettening and widening process** goes? Not so much.

While the **clitoral glans** is the best known female **orgasm trigger** in the world and the part of the clitoris that is best in producing her climax, *it isn't your **wettening** organ of first choice*. In fact, there will be times where you'll find you cannot produce sufficient lubrication through *clitoral stimulation* to enter her comfortably. And it isn't the best *vaginal widener* either.

Actually most times you'll find it desirable to *avoid* the clit for as long as possible. That's a smart way to play with her head and make her hotter through the *anticipation* of your going there.

As to *how* to manipulate and/or engage her **clitoris** to make her come; you'll learn all about that in the chapters on **oral sex** (page 231), **positions** (page 295), **love touching** (page 268), and **cocksmanship** (page 351).

Introducing The Clitoral Ring

But before we leave the clitoris, I have to introduce you to something new. I call it the **clitoral ring**. (See it pictured on page 193.)

If you take your middle finger and do wide circles around her **glans**, you'll feel a *rim* that feels like *an almost complete circle of flesh*. At the top, it's the end of her **hood**, surrounding her **clitoris.** *The **clitoral ring's** (virtual) bottom part* is formed by the tops of her **labia minora**.

You'll want to get to know the **clitoral ring**. Rub it the right way and that **orgasm booster** will facilitate the proper *clitoral stimulation* to get her off big time. (See "The Clitoral Ring Orgasm Technique" on page 274 for details.)

Her Oft-Neglected Mound

By the way, you can *indirectly* stimulate her **clitoris** (and other **vulval zones**) by massaging her **mons pubis** (aka her **mound**) with your *palm or fingers*. (See this much-neglected **pleasure zone** pictured on page 192 and page 193.) For more suggestions on *how* to *work* her **mound** to get her hot, see "Using Her Mound To Good Effect" on page 278.

But there are even more interesting **vulval zones** we haven't gotten to yet!

Vulval Wetness Triggers And Other Erogenous Areas

How about places you've probably never heard of, that can make her really wet! Let's talk about her **U-Spot, Bartholin's** and **Skene's glands**. (Refer back to page 192 for their locations.)

Her **U-Spot** is an upside-down *U* of erectile flesh surrounding her **urethra**. I've known of this **erogenous zone** for some time, but it's been generally recognized as such only recently. (FYI: Her **urethra** - like yours - is a **pleasure zone** but not big on *results*.)

On a rare occasion I've made a lover or two *come* solely by manually

Female Sexual Anatomy

or orally working the **U-Spot**. So it just might be a **special case orgasm trigger**. But not all women can come in this fashion. So I disagree with those who claim the **U-Spot** is a surefire **orgasm trigger**.

But her **U-Spot** is a fabulous **orgasm booster** *(as you'll see in the love touching chapter)*. It also might be a **female ejaculation trigger** (although I believe that might be because it's near her **Skene's glands**). So explore this her **U-Spot** especially when you want to give your lover a *quicker* or *bigger* **climax** (while you're also stimulating one of her **orgasm triggers**).

Just below her **U-Spot** are her **Skene's glands ducts** (or **paraurethral ducts**). Her **Skene's glands** are likely one of the **triggers** for the exciting phenomenon known as **female ejaculation**. (See the next page for details.) The skin immediately below her **urethra**, which we'll call the **sub-U**, also helps bring on *excitement* and **female ejaculation** when stimulated in conjunction with her **Skene's glands** (see page 268 for the technique).

Another **vulval area** to which you should give some attention is the region just below her **vaginal ball.** That's where you'll find her **Bartholin's glands ducts**. These appear as little holes to the left and right of her lower **vagina**.

Her **Bartholin's glands** produce **mucus** or **lubrication** with **arousal** and should even produce **wetness** and *titillating sensations* with your touch. So her **Bartholin's glands ducts** *and the sensitive skin that surrounds them* are great to use as a **pleasure zone** and **wetness trigger**.

INTRODUCING THE MULTIPLE EROGENOUS ZONE AREA

Now before we go on to talk about her **vaginal hot spots**, I want to point out something very special about your lover's **vulva**. *It's full of sexual hot spots located within touching distance of each other. (Take another look at the anatomical charts!)*

It's what I call a **multiple erogenous zone area**.

That reality opens up all kinds of possibilities to the creative lover. This means that *when you want to focus on her vulval region you don't have to touch just one erogenous zone at a time.* It's easy to stimulate one or more **orgasm triggers** while you tickle an **orgasm booster** or two **simultaneously**. In fact, you could use techniques that give her **complete vulval stimulation**.

AN IMPORTANT BIOLOGICAL RULE: MULTIPLE SPOTS = BIGGER ORGASMS

Why would you do this? *The answer to that question comes in the form of a biological general rule: The more erogenous zones you touch in bringing on her climax, the more nerve types you'll engage, the more sensations you'll give her, the bigger her climax will be.*

INTRODUCING FEMALE EJACULATION

The widespread story - apocryphal or not - of a man who *left his wife* because he thought she was *pissing* on him during an *orgasm* requires me to discuss **female ejaculation**.

Ongoing debate notwithstanding, this phenomenon is **real**. In fact, scientists noted it centuries ago.

If you're lucky enough and good enough, your woman will emit a gush of *ejaculate* (a clear watery fluid) when you make her come.

Why haven't all women experienced this? Some scientists theorize that a woman must have **Skene's glands ducts** to ejaculate. (Some women lack them.) Those researchers believe those **ducts** are the *conduits* for **female ejaculation**. (Others argue that the **urethra** is also involved.)

But they might be another more important reason why a woman might not ejaculate. *Female Ejaculation and the G-Spot* author Deborah Sundahl says: "The sensation to ejaculate often feels like the urge to pee. That being the last thing any woman wants to do when they're having sex, that gets shut down immediately. And that's what's going on with the majority of women. That is why most women do not ejaculate."

If your lover fits into that category, I have great news. A recent scientific study by Austrian urologist Florian Wimpissinger *dispelled* the notion that **female ejaculation** involves urine. In the *Journal of Sexual Medicine* (July 18, 2007), he wrote: "On high-definition perineal ultrasound images, a structure was identified consistent with the gland tissue surrounding the entire length of the female urethra. On urethroscopy, one midline opening (duct) was seen just inside the external meatus... Biochemically, the fluid emitted during orgasm showed all the parameters found in prostate plasma in contrast to the values measured in voided urine."

In other words: He verified the existence of what de Graaf called the **female prostate** (the **G-Spot**) and said it was the *source* of **female ejaculation**. And he proved that the **female ejaculate** is *not* urine. It's akin to what your **prostate** secretes. You'll learn in later chapters how to produce **female ejaculation** by manipulating the **G-Spot, U-Spot**, and **M Spot** (introduced in the **breasts** chapter).

Tip: Don't fret the **wet spot**. Have a **towel** handy and use a **waterproof mattress cover**.

A corollary:

*The best way to build her excitement as you push her closer and closer to an **orgasm** is to add additional **hot spots** to the mix of **erogenous zones** you're touching.*

Now I call **multiple erogenous zone areas** that contain more than one **orgasm trigger: <u>orgasm trigger complexes.</u>** An **orgasm trigger complex** is my term for **an area with a number of erogenous zones within easy reach of each other that can be stimulated at the same time to make her come.** (FYI: I believe **multiple erogenous zone areas** and **orgasm trigger complexes** are new concepts in the field of **sexology**.) One **orgasm trigger complex**, for example, would be the region where you can set off an **orgasm** simultaneously with a **vaginal orgasm trigger** like her **vaginal ball** as well as **vulval orgasm triggers** like her **V-Spot, Nook** and **perineal sponge**.

You'll learn some killer techniques involving **multiple erogenous zones** in later chapters when we discuss how to work her body to great effect. In fact, this concept will open up a whole new form of **love**making for you. (See "Introducing Shallow Lovemaking Techniques" on page 350.)

For now, though, it's enough that you study the anatomical charts and get familiar with all the nearby hot spots in and around her **vulva** that you can play with <u>at the same time</u>.

GREATER RESULTS THROUGH MULTITASKING

A *larger biological principle* is involved here, though. Each of her body parts - from her *head* to her *toes* to her *sexual organs* to her *skin* itself - produces *different types of sensations* when stimulated. *These feelings add together to produce bigger results when more than one part is involved.* And they produce *different combined feelings* depending on what parts you choose to focus your attention on.

That biological fact screams out for you to **multitask** *(do more than one thing) when you make love. You'll learn to do that in later chapters on technique.*

THE CONTROVERSY ABOUT VAGINAL ORGASM TRIGGERS

I will introduce you in a moment to her **vaginal orgasm triggers**. But first you need to understand something. A number of scientists have begun to suspect an idea that I have been exploring. Namely:

Vaginal orgasms might be produced by nerves liberally spread about inside her vaginal walls and <u>not</u> by one or more distinct "spots." That raises the question:

On Loving Women

Should we then concentrate on a <u>general location</u> rather than try to massage a specific spot of limited size within her to make her come?

There have been a number of neurological studies suggesting this might be the case. These **"vaginal erotic sensitivity"** studies all confirmed the existence of a **vaginal orgasm trigger** but they could not find an exact trigger point. *More scientific studies, perhaps with technology we do not yet possess, are urgently needed.*

*It turns out it's extremely difficult to study nerve function in a **vagina**. Therefore much remains a mystery.*

Along these lines there was a very interesting **vaginal nerve** study done in 2006 of 21 women through biopsies and questionnaires. It was done by Dr. Rachel Pauls of Cincinnati's Good Samaritan Hospital. In her final report in the *Journal of Sexual Medicine*, Pauls wrote:

> "Women possess sufficient vaginal innervation such that tactile stimulation of the vagina can lead to orgasm. However, there are few anatomic studies that have characterized the distribution of nerves throughout the human vagina."

She admitted that today's scientists have "a limited understanding of nerve distribution in the adult vagina." And she lamented:

> "The neurophysiology of the vagina is poorly understood."

Even more interesting - in her conclusion she wrote:

> "...vaginal nerves were located regularly throughout the anterior and posterior vagina, proximally and distally, including apex and cervix. **There was no vaginal location with increased nerve density.**"

That's significant in that it **disproves** the disinformation being spread that a woman's **vagina** has little nerve activity or feeling beyond the first few inches. Now we know <u>the **entire vagina** has significant nerve coverage</u>.

Dr. Pauls' study also contradicts earlier histological studies *done by*

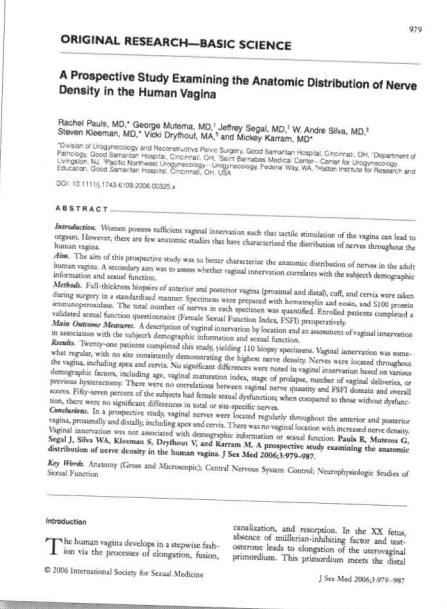

Female Sexual Anatomy

Hilleges, Falconer, Ekmon-Orderberg, & Johanson in 1995 that concluded the **anterior wall of the vagina** has many more nerves than the **posterior wall** (see the graphic here). Instead, Dr. Pauls' conclusions suggest that your lover will experience pleasure from the touch of your **penis** throughout the length of her **vaginal canal**.

The fact that Dr. Pauls found no spots within the *vagina* with *increased nerve density* is food for thought. It doesn't help us in our quest to find specific *orgasm trigger locations*, though.

Maybe it tells us that **vaginal orgasms** are set off by *generalized nerves* located throughout the skin of her **vaginal canal**? I'm not sure.

The only thing *certain* in the scientific world is the **uncertainty**. A 2002 study by Northwestern University Medical School Physiology and Urology Professor Dr. Kevin E. McKenna, in fact, bemoaned that situation.

In the *World Journal of Urology*, he reported that:

"The study of the neurophysiology of human female sexual function is a field still in its infancy. There remain today many important unanswered questions in this area. There have been few studies and much of what is known (or presumed to be known) is inferred from animal studies, primarily in rodents, and by analogy drawn from studies in males."

Therefore Dr. McKenna concluded:

"The control of female genital responses has not been extensively

studied and **significant gaps in our knowledge remain.**"

A couple of studies from the 1980s supported the notion, however, of a **generalized orgasm trigger** along the **anterior wall of the vagina** (see the graphic on the top of the last page).

In 1984, sexological researcher Heli Alzate of Columbia's Caldas University Manizales examined 48 female subjects to try and locate the *source* of **vaginal orgasm**s. Although that sample size was small, he concluded by disputing the existence of the **G-Spot**, arguing in favor of something *bigger* in his report *Vaginal Erotic Sensitivity*:

> *It was found that 45 subjects reported erotic sensitivity located in most cases on the upper anterior wall, and of those, 30 (66.7%) either reached orgasm or requested to stop stimulation short of orgasm. This study supports previous findings indicating that the vagina of most women has a zone (or zones) of erotic sensitivity whose appropriate stimulation can lead to orgasm; it does not support, however, the particular location and characteristics of the vaginal erogenous zone described by other authors.*

Another sexological study of that time, done in 1986 by Dr. Zwi Hoch of Israel's Rambam Medical Center, came to similar conclusions:

> *"The existence on the anterior vaginal wall of an anatomically clearly definable erotically triggering entity, termed "The G Spot", was refuted by our findings.* **The entire anterior vaginal wall**, *including the deeper situated urinary bladder, periurethral tissues and Halban's fascia,* **rather than one specific spot, were found to be erotically sensitive in most of the women examined, and 64% of them learned how to reach orgasm by direct specific digital and/or coital stimulation of this area. All other parts of the vagina had poor erotic sensitivity.***"*

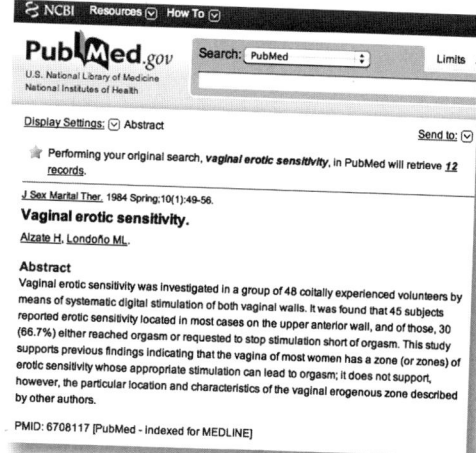

While there might be a *broad area* such as the one Hoch believes exists in the **anterior wall**, I disagree strongly with his dismissal of the *rest of the vagina* as sexually useless. Nothing could be further from the truth.

Also interesting was an MRI study of the human anatomy during *missionary position* and *rear-entry sex*, done by CMC Beausoleil researchers in Montpellier, France in 2002 (about which you'll read more in the positions chapter). That research project (involving just *one* couple) speculated there might be two **vaginal orgasm triggers**, one of which might be located on the **posterior wall of the vagina**:

"We could suggest that...there possibly are two types of vaginal orgasms, **one from preferential stimulation of the anterior vaginal wall** (G- spot?) and **one from deeper preferential stimulation of the posterior wall of the vagina** and cervix (perhaps the posterior fornix?)."

(The parenthetical comments were the researchers', not mine.)

It doesn't appear that they had enough information to draw that conclusion, though. They admitted that the woman in that study did not attain a climax. But they were honest enough to say:

> Obviously, we need to be very careful about this artificial dichotomy of the **vaginal orgasm** before other studies are conducted, because our study was carried out using only one couple and the deductions are hypothetical.

But there's some truth to what they said about the **posterior wall**. In fact, the **posterior wall of the vagina**, in my experience, has an **orgasm trigger** that's *more* reactive than any on the **anterior wall**! (I'm sure you will discover this is true too, once you test out what I'm about to show you.)

And what about their suggestion that a woman's **posterior fornix** might be the trigger for **orgasms** you can easily produce with **rear-entry sex**? (See the **fornices** clearly depicted in the bottom graphic on page 195. They're the spaces to either side of the lip-like firm skin that forms the **ring** around the entrance to her **cervix**.) That's as good a guess as any. (I'll show you where I think that **deep orgasm trigger** might be found very soon.)

I agree, though, with the researchers who suggested that the **vagina's anterior wall** seems to contain *a greater number of* **sexually reactive areas** than the **vagina's posterior wall**. And a <u>larger</u> *sexually reactive area*.

But I also wonder...why do most scientists only talk about the **anterior wall** (top wall) and **posterior wall** (bottom wall) of the **vaginal canal?** What about the **side walls** of the **vagina?** *No proof - but my experience tells me these are especially reactive with* <u>very shallow sex</u> *(which might fit in with Dr. O'Connell's theories on the* **clitoral bulbs***) and* <u>quick, deep, rhythmic penetration.</u>

...Final analysis...here's what you need to know:

The truth is that no one has proven precisely where **vaginal orgasms** *are triggered so no one should pretend they can pinpoint an exact location.* I pursued all available research along these lines because I thought there might be a way to confirm what nerves were firing to set off **vaginal orgasms**. Then, perhaps *exact trigger locations* could be found. (That is, I was hoping the **orgasm trigger locations** I've identified could be *confirmed.*)

No luck. And this nagging question begs to be answered, too:

Is it possible that a woman can feel her **orgasmic sensations** *in places far away from the* **orgasm triggers** *that set off her climaxes? In other words, could it be that a woman thinks her climax originates in one place whereas it was actually set in motion by an orgasm trigger somewhere else?*

This would make pinpointing orgasm trigger locations much more difficult.

I pose this question because I once made a lover come by working her **Nook**. When we discussed that novel orgasm later on she was surprised. She thought I'd been stimulating her **G-Spot!** *(I wasn't near it.)*

Remember all of this when I introduce you to a place I call her **Nexus**. Because that's a place with which you can make her *come* **vaginally**. But she might believe the resultant orgasm is coming from somewhere else (a place I call her **Deep Trigger**).

No matter. What you and I are concerned with is *what locations we should massage* internally to make her come. And, whether or not her **orgasm triggers** are *generalized* or *specific* in location, I've found a number of *specific places inside her* that you can work to set off **vaginal orgasms**.

And that's everything you will need to know about her **vaginal region** to set off all her **vaginal fireworks**, so to speak. Your knowledge of these locations and how to work them, as well as your ability to set off **vaginal orgasms**, will tell the woman you love that you're a sophisticated lover. Or to put it another way - give her **vaginal orgasms** and she'll follow you anywhere.

So let's move on to specifics!

HER VAGINAL REGION

Before we go any further, you should know that her **vaginal walls** are made up of **smooth muscles** (which account for the contractions you'll feel with sexual stimulation and *orgasms*), **nerves** (some of which, at least, trigger **orgasms**, the rest, **sensations**) and **mucous membranes** (which secrete **lubrication** throughout her **vaginal canal**). And their relative *tightness* (that is your relative *fit* inside her - whether her **vaginal walls** are **tented** or not) will *vary* from woman to woman.

Now *lubrication* can happen *gradually* or in a *sudden gush* of **love juices**. You'll learn about several **vaginal areas** that can trigger gushes shortly.

Remember that *it's your job to make her* **wet** *and* keep *her* **wet**. And you should not enter her *vagina* until you're sure she's wet. And, again, you should not attempt **deep penetration** until your tentative explorations confirm that her vagina's **tented (wide)** as well.

INTRODUCING HER VAGINAL RING

We already discussed her **vaginal ball** in the section on her **vulva,** as being **a wetness** and **orgasm trigger**. A protrusion of her **vagina**, it is technically speaking, located in her **vestibule**.

The *second* **vaginal erogenous zone** I want to introduce you to is her **vaginal ring**. This is one of her three **entrances**, about which I spoke earlier. And as such, it is highly **sensitive**.

As you know from the anatomical graphics earlier (on page 193), her **vaginal ring** is located just inside her **vaginal ball**. Surrounding her **vaginal introitus** (her **vaginal entry hole**), this circular half inch or so of flesh is lined with strong **muscles**.

The feel of this *small rubber-band-like ring of muscle* gripping you as you first enter her **vaginal canal** is unmistakable. Yet, to my knowledge, no one's documented it before as the incredible **erogenous zone** it truly is.

The great thing about her **vaginal ring** is that **it's easily accessible by men of just about any size and length** and it's an awesome **orgasm trigger**. It can also be used as a **wetness trigger** instead if you prefer deeper explorations on any particular occasion.

How to produce **orgasms** with it is the subject of the cocksmanship chapter. But let me suggest that her **vaginal ring** calls for **a shallow form of intercourse** I've never read about before. I think you'll be excited to learn all about that later.

It's so easy to make her come with it that it's almost a crime. But it's best triggered (in its *orgasmic potential*) by your **penis**.

HER G-SPOT (OR FEMALE PROSTATE)

I'm not sure why the *third vaginal orgasm trigger* we'll discuss, her **G-Spot** (or *female prostate*), has stirred up so much controversy. It's kind of silly.

I side with **Regnier de Graaf (see page 180)** and other researchers (including respected 20th Century German gynecologist **Ernst Grafenberg** and American researcher **Beverly Whipple**) who have declared it - for more than 325 years - a real entity as a great **orgasm trigger**. It's been my experience that it's a super-reactive area that's easily definable by its prune-like feel and shape.

Confirmation of its existence might be in the way *it responds to the same kind of stimulus that your prostate gland responds to, sexually*. That is, the same kind of stimulation that can make you come with your **prostate** is the same kind that will make her *come* with her **G-Spot**...Which makes sense, after all, since I taught you awhile ago that scientists say these are **biologically analogous organs**. Plus, my lovers have unanimously told me the **G-Spot orgasms** I gave them felt *different* than **clitoral orgasms**.

The *how-to* comes later. But for now understand that if you want to give your lover **powerful climaxes** that produce a *huge gush of juices* and possibly even **female ejaculation**, learn to locate and work her **G-Spot**. (The **G-Spot** is the hands-down best **female ejaculation trigger**.)

This **erogenous zone**, *like her* **vaginal ring**, *is super in that* <u>even men of modest length should be able to reach it and trigger</u> **vaginal orgasms**. *And it responds equally well to the touch of your* **penis** *or* **fingers**. *It's easily found no more than an inch or so inside of her* **vaginal canal** *along the* **anterior (top) wall**. *When swollen, it's about 2-3 inches long*. And by the way, her **G-Spot** is a phenomenal **wetness trigger** too.

HER AFE ZONE

Now to her **deep orgasm triggers**. To follow convention, I will tip my hat to Dr. Chee Chua Ann (see page 183) and call one of them her **Anterior Fornix Erogenous Zone,** or **AFE zone** for short. This is an **orgasm** and **wetness**

Female Sexual Anatomy

trigger you can access **manually** or via **missionary-style intercourse**.

There's definitely a unique **orgasm and wetness trigger** in the deepest regions of her **vagina's anterior wall**, in the *vicinity* of the theoretical **AFE zone**. I discovered it long before Dr. Ann went public with his theory.

But can we *pinpoint* where it is? If you look at the missionary position graphic at the bottom of page 338 you will see three dots where *I* theorize it might be located. Dr. Ann believes this **hot spot** is located in the **anterior fornix** area (see that designation in the spread, "Introducing New Orgasm Triggers," starting on page 194). Again, since no one's scientifically proven the exact location of any **orgasm trigger** *back there*, Dr. Ann's chosen location is open to speculation. *Could it instead, for instance, be on the wall of her* **uterus?** Or the very end of her **vaginal canal?** Without scientific proof, the answer is: *Yes, it could be elsewhere*. But I agree that there's a **hot spot** at that **general depth** and **location**. And that's all you need to know.

The best feature about her **AFE zone** is that *you do not have to use any particular technique on it to cause your lover to emit a gush of sex juices or orgasm. All it requires is your touch in the right location (simply resting your* **glans** *over it would trigger a reaction)*. But notice in the graphics I mentioned above how it moves deeper inside her with **arousal** and **tenting**. And you might even feel your lover's <u>cervix</u> moving upward and a **secondary tenting process** occurring when you simply *touch* her **AFE zone** (pushing in to that area and then resting there *motionless*). That makes finding this awesome area real *easy*.

Warning, though: Dr. Ann's recommendation to use this spot for **vaginal lubrication** is puzzling to me. The liquid you get upon stimulating the **AFE zone** is more akin to water (or the stuff you get with **female ejaculation**) than the desirable *slippery stuff* her **vaginal walls** and **Bartholin's glands** produce. In my experience, it acts to *hinder* movement rather than help.

I'll reveal more about this **hot spot** in later chapters. And I'll give you *sexual positions* that are best in producing **AFE zone orgasms.**

Introducing Her *Deep Trigger* And *Nexus*

There's another **deep orgasm trigger** you need to know about in the **vaginal canal**. And it's even more exciting than her **AFE zone** because it produces apoplectic reactions that are almost unbelievable in their spasmodic and orgasmic intensity.

Without any scientific proof to be had, I can only show you the *general region* where I've produced these shattering climaxes. And in this case, I've chosen to identify two possible locations for this **orgasm trigger**.

I call these the **Deep Trigger** and **Nexus**. These are only accessible during *rear-entry sex*. (See the section called "Introducing New Orgasm Triggers" on page 194 for their locations, graphically.)

While feedback from my lovers indicates women *feel* the **orgasm** produced in this general location as if it's coming from the area I call her **Deep Trigger**, I can tell you I'm focused on massaging her **Nexus** when I trigger it (so at the very least, it's a good ***massage focus point***).

I wouldn't be surprised, though, to find that the ***trigger*** is actually within the **nethermost walls** (the end point) of her **vagina** (that is, within the membrane that's *between* her **Deep Trigger** and **Nexus**). Your **glans** presses against that at your deepest in-stroke. Others think it might be her **cervix**.

But the *exact* location is moot. Again, all you need to know is the *general vicinity* to set off the sexual fireworks.

And the beauty part of this **orgasm trigger** is that it doesn't take long to fire off her **climax** from it once you reach the *right place*. Only a matter of seconds. Perhaps 10-15 at most; sometimes less. **Repeat orgasms** often take a little longer to achieve; perhaps a half minute or so.

She will likely beg you to stop stimulating this area, however, after a few **orgasms** or so. Most women find **climaxes** produced in this way too *intense* to repeat too often within a short period of time.

The Very Best Orgasm Booster: Her *Bottom*

Now let's talk about *non-genital* sexual areas worthy of note.

That brings me to our next anatomical area. Earlier I introduced you to the concept of the **orgasm booster** - a place that either brings on her climax more quickly or makes it much bigger than normal. Now if I had to say what a woman's *very biggest* **orgasm booster** is, it'd be her **anal canal**.

Female Sexual Anatomy

This is an exciting area and one not to be squeamish about. I have not run across one woman who doesn't find this area intensely exciting. Even ones who resist your going there initially will eventually give in to your furtive explorations down there if you're persistent and you introduce her to the pleasures of **anal stimulation** slowly.

When you see her writhing uncontrollably and moaning like you've never heard her moan before, you'll be convinced too.

But I'm not talking about **anal intercourse**. I'm just not into it. (Sorry. I'm not knocking it though. I do have some **anal intercourse** tips for you in "Anal Sex - If You're Into It" on page 377.) I'm talking about ample opportunities to give her sexual thrills through **loving touching** (see page 269 for techniques).

Interestingly enough, her **anal canal** is similar in structure to her **vagina** in some ways:

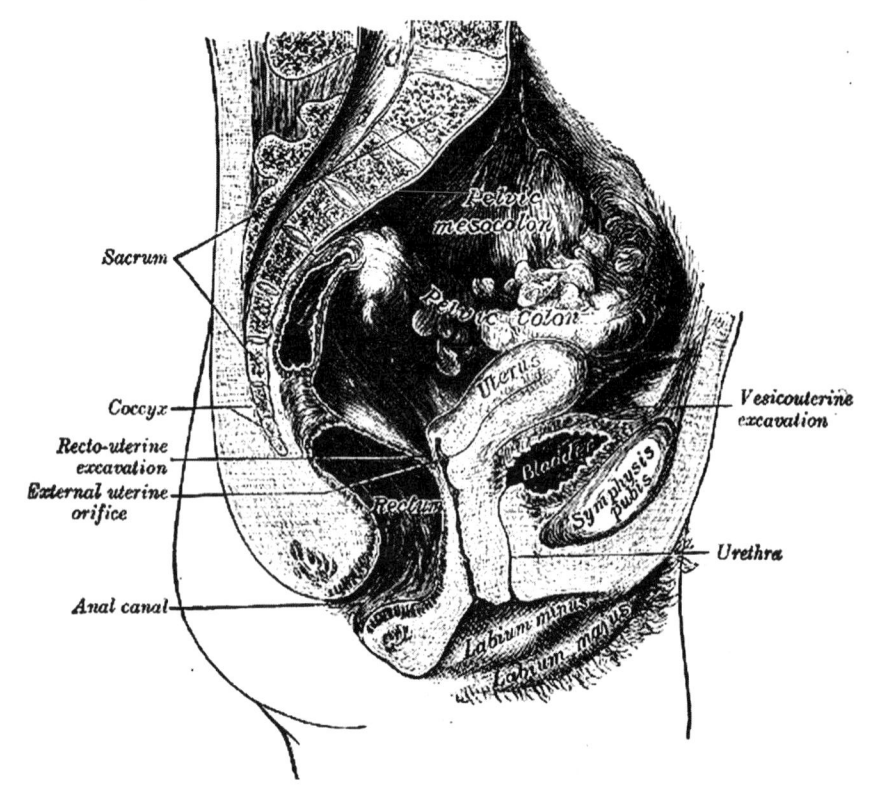

♀ *It has a muscular **ring** at its entrance whose outer flesh and inner inch or so give her distinctly different pleasures*

♀ *As with her vaginal lips, opening her **anal hole** by separating her **butt cheeks** will give her **erotic sensations***

♀ *Her **anal canal** also has incredibly sensitive internal walls*

218

On Loving Women

♀ *It even might contain an **orgasm trigger***

In fact, urologist Kristene Whitmore of The Pelvic Floor Institute has been quoted as saying: "Anal stimulation can trigger **the same nerve pathways as a deep-vaginal orgasm.**" If that's true, a good lover should give this area some attention, for their orgasmic potential. Don't rush into a full exploration of this territory, though, until you know she's into it!

Now some believe **anal sex orgasms** (and **deep rear-entry vaginal orgasms)** are caused by an **orgasm trigger** in her **anal canal**. Scientists refer to the *location* of this *alleged trigger* as the **Pouch of Douglas** or, alternatively, the **recto-uterine excavation** (pictured on the prior page). In a *sexual* connotation, *proponents* of the *alleged* **anal orgasm trigger** call it various names such as the **cul-de-sac, epicenter** and **deep spot**. It's said that the retraction of her **uterus** during sex enables you to reach this place (if you're long enough).

That being said, I suspect the **hot spot** that causes **anal sex orgasms** is actually the **Deep Trigger** I identified as a **vaginal orgasm trigger** in the anatomical graphics starting on page 194. I believe it can be stimulated through the **thin membrane** that separates her **anal** and **vaginal canals**.

Yet perhaps those who believe the **Pouch of Douglas** *is* responsible for **anal** and **deep rear-entry vaginal orgasms** are right. Only time and more scientific research will tell.

But on one level, you - as a *lover* of women and not a scientist - needn't worry about this scientific debate over what **exact orgasm trigger** in what *exact location* gives her an earth-shattering **climax** so long as you know *approximately* where to put your **cock** or **finger** or *a sex toy* inside her to set it off. *This is an important point* - about *this* area as well as *all the other places in the* **female sexual anatomy** *I told you about earlier:*

We don't have **eyes** on our **cocks** or **fingers** to show us *exactly* where we are inside her at any time. And *every woman's anatomy is slightly different*. So (until you've gotten thoroughly familiar with your lover's insides) the most important fact for you to remember is the **general location of the orgasm triggers I've shown you,** *so you can* **explore** around inside her until - **through her reactions** - *you know you have* **found** them. You'll get better over time, too, at using your **cock** and **fingers** as **feelers**.

Of course, once you're in their *general location*, you also need how to know how to *move* in such a way that will *set off* her **orgasm triggers** to make her come. **Orgasm triggers** don't fire off her **climaxes** on touch. That takes some finesse. That's where *technique* comes in. (More on that later.)

Female Sexual Anatomy

Anyway, because of the possibilities raised by this possible **anal canal orgasm trigger** I refer to her **anal canal** also as a **special case orgasm trigger**. *Now my experience tells me that not every woman will come solely through **anal stimulation**. But some will. And it's worth exploring because, if she has a workable **anal orgasm trigger**, you can use it to produce incredibly explosive climaxes.*

...More on this kind of **love**making later...

HER NIPPLES AS SPECIAL CASE ORGASM TRIGGERS

Now few men need encouragement to suck on their lover's **nipples**. But do they spend enough time doing that? And do they do it well enough?

I mentioned earlier how my friend and mentor Earle would always start a sexual session by playing with his lover's **nipples,** continuing this tease for up to a *half hour* or until he knew she was really ready for him to *enter* her. That's a great way to use her **nipples** as a **wetness trigger** and **widening** agent. I'm not sure I'd recommend doing that every time. Seems to me it might get *predictable*. But as a sometime thing, it's a *super* idea. There are few better **wetness** and **widening triggers** than your lover's **nipples** - if you tease them with patience. They don't produce those desirous effects instantaneously.

On Loving Women

But don't stop there. Are you aware that you can give most women **orgasms** solely by teasing their **nipples? Nipple orgasms** are not things you can produce every day; they're dependent upon novelty and surprise and as such they're **special case orgasm triggers**.

But you will blow her mind if you can give her these! So focus on her **breasts** the next time you're together, at the get-go. Take your time and experiment to see if you can bring on a **nipple orgasm**. (Find out *how* in "Breast Orgasms, The *M Spot* & More" on page 279.)

Her **nipples** work fabulously well as **orgasm boosters**, *too*. If her **anal canal** is her *number one best* **orgasm booster** for the *power* it brings to her **orgasms**, then her **nipples** are a close *second*, for how well they speed along the start of those events.

So, as you can see, her **nipples** have a *variety* of **sexual roles**. Don't neglect any of them!

MORE NON-GENITAL ORGASM BOOSTERS & EROGENOUS ZONES

And don't ignore the rest of her body. Her **whole body** should be your canvas.

Her **skin** is her largest sexual organ. A **pleasure zone**, it's great for teasing her during the **arousal process**. Explore every inch of it!

Speaking of which, the **skin of her neck** is especially sensitive - both on the *front* and *back* (each area produces *different* sensations; the **nape** or back is more sensitive than the front). This region is not only one of her great **arousal starters** but it's also super as an **orgasm booster!** Great lovers don't restrict themselves to genitals...they experiment with every one of her fabulous places, to see what results they can produce.

Other great **orgasm boosters** include her:

- ♀ **shoulders** (which especially respond well to your **lips**)
- ♀ **toes** (*suck* one just before she comes and she'll shoot through the roof!)
- ♀ **spine** (*lick* it before she climaxes to give her incredible tingles)

Female Sexual Anatomy

Other great **wetness triggers** include her:

- ♀ **thighs**
- ♀ **feet**
- ♀ **hips**
- ♀ **belly**
- ♀ **knees**
- ♀ **the bottom of her back, just above her butt**

All of the above respond well to kissing, caressing and tongue work. (And don't forget her **lips**, which are great **orgasm boosters** and **wetness triggers**. See "Kissing For Effect: The Art of Kissing" on page 227 for more on that.)

REACHING HER ORGASMIC POTENTIAL

One more thing, anatomically speaking - and this is *really important:*

Most women are **multi-orgasmic**. In other words, they can **come** a number of times within *one* **love**making session. And *they can experience* **multiple orgasms** *within a short time from* **a variety** *of orgasm triggers*. It's up to you to see that she achieves her **orgasmic potential**. (So read on and find out how!) For now understand: *Most times, once is not enough.*

ANATOMICAL DIFFERENCES CALL FOR EXPERIMENTATION

Well now it's time for you to **experiment** with your lover's body. Try to find and work all the parts I've told you about here. Then try to find some other places on her body perhaps no one else has found.

Practically every one of her parts should be considered for its sexual possibilities. Be creative.

But remember: **Every woman is different**. Every woman has her favorite and not-so-favorite places. I've given you the **female anatomical palette**. *Now go study your lover's body to find out what places best ring her bells!*

> "You're my song - music too magic to end
> I'll play you over and over again"
> -Lyrics from "Somewhere In The Night"
> sung by Barry Manilow

Play Her Like An Instrument (Through Feedback)

*B*efore we get into the technique chapters, the nitty-gritty how-to stuff, you need to understand something very important: *All the technique in the world means nothing if you're getting no feedback from your lover.*

That's why you cannot rely upon a list of old moves that worked on past lovers or a cookie cutter guide to **sex moves**. Because what worked for Mary won't work for Jane and vice versa. And the only way you'll *know* what *works* is through **feedback** - her **reactions** *to what you are doing.*

This seems pretty clear. But if it were, there would be many more great lovers. Because *it's your ability to play her like an instrument* - using her **feedback** as your "music" - *that separates the men from the boys.*

You need to be *observant*, keenly aware of every sound and move she makes. **She's giving you a road map to success**. She can lead the way. It might not be the way you had in mind, but if you follow her **positive feedback**, it's a good way. Because it's what she's reactive to, responding to excitedly, *at the moment.*

My great-uncle used to tell me, "Boy, if a door of opportunity opens for you, you'd better be ready to walk through it." That sage advice works well for **love**making, too. If she reacts to your touch with a sound like air escaping from a tube or a steak sizzling, you need to pursue that area further. That's a goodie, at the moment. Linger there for awhile until her reactions begin to lessen. Then find another area on her body to play with,

Play Her Like An Instrument (Through Feedback)

by **teasing** her in other sensitive places until she gives you another major sign you've hit another hot button.

Now later on in this book, I'll give you details - names and locations of *every* **hot spot** you need to know, and how to work them. But if you're just trying to tease her, then just about any place on her body is a good place to start. After all, no woman will turn down an **erotic massage**, if you expertly and slowly touch her all over, awakening all her nerves and making her eager to come.

Now when you're done *teasing her* (I'll show you how later) and you're ready to make her *come*, **feedback** is *especially* key to your success. You need to keenly pay attention to it then because that's what will tell you if you're doing something that will help lead to her **orgasm** or *not*. Let her down off the path to a **climax** and you'll *frustrate* her. (Don't go there!)

In other words, *it's your job to learn how to identify* **telltale feedback** - sure signs you've started the inevitable process that builds to an **orgasm** - so you know whether you're heading in the right direction. Then, you need to know how to **interpret it** and **react** to it.

In this way, *lovemaking* is very similar to playing an instrument. Play an instrument well and it sings. Play it poorly, it screeches or produces no sound at all. In *lovemaking*, her *body* is your instrument. The *moves* and *sounds* she makes are the *music you're producing*. Play her *well* and you'll get **sexy sounds, extreme physical reactions, muscle contractions, epithets** and even **screaming**. Play her *poorly* and you'll get next to *nothing*.

So what should you be trying to produce or looking for as validation, in the way of **feedback?** Here's a starter's list - her:

- **body language**
    - *is she totally relaxed? - no good!* (she's either not in the mood or you're not getting to her at all)
    - *is she kind of saying* **no** *with her hands (as if she wants to push you away from an area you're touching), or is her face grimacing as if you're hurting or annoying her or the feeling is too intense to be pleasurable? - stop what you're doing; try something else*
    - *are her* **eyes** *closed, an ecstatic look on her face? - she's aroused*
    - *are her* **muscles** *tense? - what you're doing is working*
    - *are her* **muscles** *growing in tightness? - a climax might be coming*
    - *are her* **toes** *clenching? - you're getting there (she's working for it)*

On Loving Women

- 👍 is her **back arching**? - you're almost there

☞ **motions**

- 👎 is she not really moving that much? - you might not be getting to her (unless her muscles are clenching, on her way to a **climax**)
- 👎 is she reacting as if you're tickling her? - something's wrong (you might be doing something wrong, or she's not that into you, or she's not in the mood, or she's not into men; you need to find out which of these problems you're dealing with, to solve it)
- 👍 is she **writhing** or **wriggling**? - she's aroused
- 👍 are her motions increasing greatly, as if she's getting out of control? - she's either coming or she's about to (so keep doing whatever you're doing until she stops you)

☞ **vocalizations**

- 👎 do the sounds she's making seem phony? - she might be faking it; for what to do, read the chapter, "Is She Faking It?" on page 79)
- 👍 is she regularly **moaning** or **groaning**? - she's aroused
- 👍 are her **vocalizations** growing in volume? - she's likely getting near to coming
- 👍 is she shouting "Oh God!" or something similar? - she's about to come or very close to doing so, so either maintain what you're doing (if you think it will quickly send her over the top) or switch to something more **intense** or more **effective** to make her come (do not pause or relax what you're doing because she's telling you she wants to come)
- 👍 if she says **"Yes!"** - you're doing something she wants you to continue doing exactly as you're doing it because it's going to make her come

Even more telling is her **biological feedback**. These are the *involuntary reactions* she'll experience if what you're doing is *working*. They are beyond her control (brought on by chemicals produced by her brain and the nerve firings and sex organ responses that result). These include:

- 👄 Her **breathing rate**
- 👄 Her **heart rate**
- 👄 The appearance of red skin rashes (on her face, neck or chest typically)
- 👄 Sweating
- 👄 An increase in her **vaginal** temperature

Play Her Like An Instrument (Through Feedback)

- An increase in her **vaginal** wetness
- An increase in her **vaginal** wideness

For a refresher on these and more, see the *anatomy* chapter.

A Lack Of Feedback Indicates Problems

Now if she's giving you *nothing in the way of feedback, ever*, you need to have a conversation with her. It could be due to a number of things:

- you're doing something wrong or your lovemaking is sub-par
- you didn't set the right mood
- there's something on her mind, disturbing or distracting her
- she's not really into you
- she's on medication that dulls her sexual reactions
- she has a medical issue
- she has psychological problems
- she's not into men

On the other hand, if only on *occasion* she gives you no feedback, you still need to find out what's wrong but the list of possibilities is a bit different. It could be any number of things (some benign, some revealing a problem in your relationship), such as:

- there's something on her mind (an argument or disagreement you had, for instance)
- she's not well
- she's distracted, thinking about a problem in her life, perhaps at work
- she's not in the mood
- you're doing something wrong
- she's impatient to get it over with (perhaps she has to get to work, for example)
- she's hungry or thirsty
- she's getting sore
- she needs a bathroom break
- she might have met someone else she's thinking about
- she's fallen out of love with you

Be kind in searching for the answers to these problems. Hopefully, with love, you can work things out. If a lack of feedback reflects on your lack of **lovemaking skills**, then read on. I'll get you up to speed!

> *"Then it came up to the moment when he kissed me. Well, I thought I was going to faint!"*
> *– Actress Carroll Baker, in the cable TV documentary Clark Gable: Tall, Dark & Handsome, talking about her movie co-star, a legendary great-kisser*

Kissing For Effect: The Art of Kissing

*S*exy women know how to give a **cock-hardening kiss** - one that *blows your mind* and makes you *desire* them *immediately*.

You can and should kiss with the same **sexual power**. If you want to be a consummate lover, you need to learn how to give your woman a *pussy-wettening kiss* - making her **eager** and **ready** for **love**making. That's kissing at its best.

Yet, from what I've heard (from the many women I've interviewed), most men *fail* in the kissing department because they:

- don't know <u>how</u> to kiss
- don't kiss <u>often</u> enough
- don't understand and cannot harness the potential **emotional** and **sexual power** of a kiss
- don't <u>communicate</u> anything
- don't kiss with **passion** or **love**
- don't realize kissing is an <u>essential tool</u> in **love**making

You hear these gripes in many chick flicks and female-oriented

The Art Of Kissing

TV shows. In Episode 5 of the sexy TV sitcom *Cougar Town*, for instance, Courteney Cox's character is *distraught* over this problem. Her man Josh can't kiss worth a damn. His kiss doesn't move her at all. So, over lunch, she delicately tries to tell him he needs to do better:

Courteney: Can we talk about the way you kiss?

Josh: What about? (Courteney bites into a new apple.)

Courteney: Pretend this is my mouth, OK? You want to use less tongue. You're not a cow at a salt lick. It's so sloppy. No one wants that. Pretend that you're a curious little garden snake. (She demonstrates pointed-tongued light tickling of apple.) Your tongue peeks in, gets spooked, and then it's out...

Funny. But there's a serious issue there. **Being a bad kisser can be a deal-breaker.**

One woman I interviewed for *On Loving Women* confirmed this fact. She'd just broken up with a man because of this problem:

"He was a horrible kisser. I broke up with him right after our first kiss. That was it for me."

But lest you get the wrong impression from the tongue lesson above, kissing is not just about *technique*. That was made clear in a pithy scene in the Italian film *I'm Crazy About Iris Blond* (1996) (*Sono pazzo di Iris Blond*) in which a female character scolds her lover over his *passionless* kisses:

She: "You kissed me without love or feeling!"

He: "I gave it everything I had."

She: "Precisely."

And kissing should not just be about passion or getting her hot. A woman looks to your kisses to verify that you love her. She's *interpreting* your kisses for their *meaning*. That was made clear years ago in the 1964 hit *The Shoop Shoop Song (It's In His Kiss)*, whose lyrics went:

Does he love me? I wanna know.

How can I tell if he loves me so?

...If you wanna know if he loves you so, **it's in his kiss.**

So like anything else when it comes to **love**making, you should express warm *thoughts* and *feelings* toward your lover through *how you kiss*. It should be **non-verbal communication.** Of **love**. And **passion**. And **desire**.

And all of that combines to set things in motion. If your lover were a car, kissing would be the *starter* that fires up the *pistons* that power her *engine*.

In other words, you should be *kissing* **for effect**. When done well, you will have made her *wet* (and possibly *wide* too) and *hot to make love* with

On Loving Women

you. *Great kisses can make her so hot and primed to come that she'll come with your slightest touch.* The best kisses can even give her an **orgasm**.

When done *poorly*, though, *a woman is likely to decide you're neither romantic nor a great lover.* A bad kiss can turn her off to you.

So let's get you up to speed. There are **four types** of kisses *you must master:*
- 💋 *Pre-sex*
- 💋 *Pre-intercourse*
- 💋 *Intercourse kisses*
- 💋 *Purely romantic*

Pre-sex kissing at its best is done as a **tease** and **seduction**. It should be the **promise of things to come**. *To make her* **melt**. *To make her want to take her clothes off and make love to you.* If you do it right, she'll likely say something breathlessly like, "Ohhh...you know what that makes me want to do!" A well-placed stealth kiss sprung on her from behind, on her **neck** or **shoulders**, *your hot* **breath** *giving her tingles too*, can do this.

Great French kissing can do the same. *And one way to give pre-sex kisses that produce* **results** *is to pretend you're giving her* **oral sex**. Start by teasing her lips, with the *tip* of your tongue, **simulating the act of cunnilingus**. Always keep the tip of your tongue *wet* as you *tenderly* trace the outlines of her lips, as if you're rimming her **labia minora**. Then *lightly* flick the center of her top lip as if it's her **clitoris**. Only after much teasing should you begin - tentatively - sliding your tongue *beyond* her lips. Even then, *do it* **teasingly**, **slowly**, **sensually**, **delicately** *and ever so* **gradually** *- it's the promise of how* <u>artfully</u> *you'll make love to her.* In doing this, *less is more*. Kiss her right and she'll have a hard time standing...or resisting you.

Pre-intercourse kissing is what you should do *as soon as it becomes clear she might be interested in having sex*. This should be done as a **wetness trigger** and the *final motivator* for her to want you inside of her. And with **pre-intercourse kissing, her whole body is your canvas** - *especially her most sensitive places*: her **neck**, her **spine**, the **small of her back**, her **shoulders**, her **breasts**, her **thighs**, her **earlobes**, etc.

Tongue baths are included in this category. Trace her various body parts with a wet, lascivious tongue to send shivers down her nerves.

Great **pre-intercourse kissing**

will send her past *the point of no return* - the point where she *needs* to have **intercourse** *to put out the fires you've lit.* You want to get her hotter and hotter until she can't take it anymore.

Intercourse kisses are the sexiest and most romantic of all. These are kisses (on her *lips* and *elsewhere*) during **penetration**. These should be designed to help bring on her **orgasm** *and* make it *bigger* than it normally would be. So **intercourse French kissing** should be done as a reminder that *you're inside her*. A confident kiss, full of attitude, *with a tongue that simulates your* **hard cock**, will help send her over the top. You're reinforcing the idea - exciting to a woman - that *you've entered her, and you're in control*. An **intercourse kiss**, deftly done, can also make her feel she's being *double-penetrated* - another idea that's a turn-on to most women. A *passionate kiss* on the lips during **penetration**, with its *energy* alone, also can make her lose control and come. A *kiss simulating* **cunnilingus** can also do this.

Purely romantic kisses are kisses that you give her when leaving for work, coming home, while attending a romantic event, or anytime during the course of the day - when sex is not necessarily an intended result. Still, these should be *passionate* and *a promise of* **love***making to come.* They should communicate that *you love her* and *desire her sexually*. Ideally, they should help make her desire **love***making* later on by getting her hot for you. For greater effect, do them with an *all-engulfing hug* or *well-placed touches on or near her most sensitive areas*.

Kisses to avoid: Pecks on the check and kisses without feeling. These actually have a *negative* effect. Kisses without feeling will tell her you're not that into her. Or that the fires have cooled.

Don't go there. *Keep even your non-sexual kisses* <u>romantic</u>. *Great lovers know that mastering the art of kissing and practising the art daily is one key to keeping the home fires burning.*

> *"My junior high school jazz band leader had a big, bushy beard. One day, though, he arrived at school looking weird. His beard was gone! 'Mr. C!' I shouted. 'Why'd you shave the beard?' He smiled and said: 'It gave my wife leg burns!'"*
> - Layla Shilkret, editor of Baring It All

Oral Sex That Will Drive Her Wild

☯

One of the greatest compliments you can get from a woman is when she asks you for a *repeat performance*.

Some years ago, for example, a girlfriend excitedly asked me to repeat a novel **oral sex technique** I'd used on her the night before. In doing it again - because I never do the same thing twice (and neither should you) - I added a novel twist that drove her absolutely crazy!

Afterward she cooed, "Ooooh! Put <u>that</u> in your book!"

(I did! You'll learn that surefire woman-pleaser in this chapter!)

The lesson in all of this is *a man needs to be a master at oral sex*. Women *crave* it. Actually, they **expect** it from you. And you'd better be good at it!

A woman will *judge* you on how well you do in the **oral sex** department. The better

LIPS: OPEN OR CLOSED?

Stretching Her Pussy Lips Open Gives Her Greater Sensations And Gives You More Options

During *cunnilingus*, you have the option of doing it while also stretching her labia majora (the outer lips around her vulva) widely apart. You can also hold open her *labia minora* (the inner lips around the vaginal hole).

How wide you open either pair of pussy lips is also one of your options. The easiest way to hold either set of her pussy lips open is with your thumbs but if you're coordinated you can use one hand if you like (a thumb and index finger for example).

Stretching her open gives your tongue easier access to her *clit*. It also makes it easy for you to slip your *tongue* inside her *vagina*.

A side benefit in doing this is that it increases the sensations you're giving her. The stretching motion gives her tingles in and of itself.

It also somehow increases the pleasure you give her with your tongue, wherever you touch her. It seems to enervate the *nerve endings in her clit, lips and vulva* in general.

As with anything else, though, you should have a reason for doing whatever you do in *oral sex*. When you open either of her set of pussy lips, you should do it with an intended effect in mind.

At the start, you usually want to start small. Make her hunger for more. (And you have more options at the start than you do later on, once you've set a specific pattern and rhythm she might want you to continue.)

So you might want to begin by feeling around seductively with your tongue (tickling and tantilizing) without opening her lips. Or open her lips slightly and do non-rhythmic teasing and exploration.

As you build toward her *climax*, it's often smart to open her outer lips further and further. Again, the more you open them, the more you excite her.

The stretching action as she approaches her peak pushes her closer to her climax.

One smart way to get her extra excited and more likely to come, then, is to stretch her *outer pussy lips* open to the very *max* (without hurting her) just before you bring her to a *climax*.

It will make her *come* faster and harder.

Another creative idea: shake her *vulva lips* dramatically or pulsate them open rhythmically when you're getting ready to make her come. This too will make her *orgasm* bigger.

One exception:

If you want to make her *come* fast from the get-go (on rare occasions, as a surprise), open her lips extremely wide from the start and really have a go at her *clit*.

(Don't do this often, though. On most occasions, she'll prefer you to tease her awhile before you bring her off.)

your artistry and results, the more she'll value you as a lover.

This is the equivalent of the performer's encore or "crowd pleaser" (as in: it always gets the equivalent of a standing ovation) - evidence of which is found in women's literature and TV shows. For example, there was a scene in TV's *Sex and the City* in which sexy Samantha (Kim Cattrall) complained that her new lover had a *small penis*. Without missing a beat, perky Charlotte (Kristin Davis), replied: "How's he with his **tongue?**"

In other words: **A woman will forgive almost anything if her man is an artist at oral sex.** To a woman, the next best thing to being cocked senseless is being tongued into oblivion.

Yet many women have complained to me that their partners don't give them **head** at all. (Big mistake!) Others say their lovers fall far short in this area. So what are so many men doing wrong?

WHAT ARE MEN DOING WRONG?

According to women, one thing men get wrong when it comes to *cunnilingus* (*oral sex* on her *genitals*) is that *they do it in a "let's get it over with" fashion*. They work feverishly from the get-go to make the woman come, lapping furiously - but dispassionately - with one maxed-out speed.

Imagine if a woman did the same thing to you in going down on you - going as fast as she could from the start, without variation, in a big rush to make you come. Would you like that? Not likely.

A related female grievance is that *some men give head reluctantly, as if they don't like doing it* (a woman can tell). That wins no points. After all, you know what a drag it is to be with a woman who is squeamish about giving you oral sex...so don't be that way with her!

THE "HURRY - I'VE GOT A TRAIN TO CATCH!" SYNDROME

Women also talk of men who are in such a terrible rush to get on with **penetration** that *they only give oral sex for a very short time* - not long enough to even get a woman wet. These men then mount their women like John Wayne leaping onto a horse, as if they have a train to catch and don't have the time to pleasure their lovers properly.

These men apparently see giving head as a necessary evil. They mistakenly think that **oral sex** is only for getting a woman **wet**. And the instant they think she's wet, they're outta there. Wrong!

Look at it this way: If a woman went down on you (getting your hopes up for great head) but then stopped after a few seconds, in a rush to stuff your **hard-on** into her **pussy**, you'd be pretty annoyed, wouldn't you?

Oral Sex That Will Drive Her Wild

That's how she'll feel if you do the same thing to her.

Some women also say *their men have an annoyingly "scratchy tongue."* (For advice on how to avoid this problem see page 235.)

Clitoral Sensitivity And Over Doing It

In helping Layla Shilkret compile stories for *Baring It All*, a sexy anthology of erotic *great lovemaking stories* by women, one contributor voiced two more common complaints to me: "*Men only go for one spot* (the **clit**). And it's really *painful* when they're *right on it!*"

Did you know that *some* women - like the woman I just quoted - find direct clit work *overstimulating* and *unpleasant?* It's true. **Clitoral sensitivity varies** among women. Is *your* woman extremely sensitive there? Find out!

And, about her first complaint: If a woman *only* licked your **frenulum** (the most sensitive part of your **penis**, just below the **head**) and *nothing else* when giving you **oral sex** - wouldn't that be frustrating and unsatisfying? So why would you, similarly, focus *only* on the head of her **clit**?

> "Men go for one spot only (the clit) and it's really painful when they're right on it!"

So *tease* her **labia**, and give some attention to her **fourchette** (the sensitive **V** at the bottom of her **vulva**), her **vaginal canal** and don't neglect her tingly **U-Spot!** (See page 245 for diagram.) ...More about this soon.

Other Problems

Other men, I'm told, make the mistake of not setting up a **steady rhythm** when attempting to make their women achieve a climax. Rock steady repetition is usually what it takes. Many women also gripe that most men don't go down on them often enough (if at all). And all women seem to agree on one thing: Men who are artists at **cunnilingus** are few and far between.

...OK. So now you know how important oral sex is to women and what *not* to do. Now let's discuss what you need to do. Not just to become proficient. But to become an artist women desire.

What Are You Communicating?

First, did you know that a woman interprets everything you do during oral sex? She's thinking: What's he saying to me?

Women are very intuitive and will pick up on whatever is on your mind. A woman also picks up on your thoughts and feelings through your behavior,

WET TONGUE HER!

In doing *cunnilingus* you must *always wet tongue her*. This sounds obvious but apparently it's not. Many women say their men don't get it.

Your *tongue* quickly becomes dry with use. That makes its surface feel abrasive and that's not good in performing *oral sex*.

The *head* of a woman's *clitoris* is covered with sensitive skin and it will get *sore* quickly if you do her with a *dry tongue*. You won't win any points for *scratchy tongue work*!

If you get her *clit* sore she won't *come*. She's likely to get mad at you, too. Worse, she's likely to think you're inept and possibly even stupid.

Fortunately, there's a simple solution. Just remember: *A wet tongue feels better*. It also makes her more likely to come; and faster.

It's the same principle that applies to her giving you head. As you know: *The wetter the better!*

The best way to keep your tongue lubricated is to keep a constant flow of *saliva* going over your *tongue* onto her *pussy*. It'll require constant thought at first to pull off, but it'll soon become second nature.

Another way to keep your *tongue* slippery (this is genius!): Lubricate her *vulva* periodically with *olive oil* (keep a bottle nearby). The oil will get on your *tongue* and make it *super slippery* (a real turn-on to her!). That slipperiness will give her heightened *erotic pleasure* that will quickly send her over the top!

body language, attitude and touch.

So you need to control and concentrate on the thoughts and emotions you're transmitting to her by your actions. Make sure they're the positive ones you want her to receive.

That means your moves should not be purely physical or designed simply to titillate her. She will interpret that negatively. She will feel you're cold and mechanical.

So your ***mind*** should not be blank, unemotional, or focused purely on your physical efforts. (And don't let her catch you thinking about something or someone else! She will know.)

Lovemaking is supposed to be about nonverbal communication. You should be letting her know how much she means to you. She should feel the love.

This is why they call it making *love*. **Every touch must tell her how much you <u>love</u> and <u>desire</u> her.** So put some **passion** into it. Especially during cunnilingus.

Stay focused on loving thoughts and feelings. She needs to sense them.

COMMUNICATE SOME EXCITEMENT

Here's another way to make sure you're sending the right message:

Pretend her **vulva** is fabulously tasty candy - luscious, juicy, sweet, and irresistible. Make believe, too, that you've made this incredible discovery after going days without food.

Eagerly roll her sensitive parts in your mouth as if you want them to melt like candy would. Attack them with enthusiasm, as if you cannot believe how *wonderful* the experience is.

This approach will make your lover feel you're really into it.

On Loving Women

Plus you'll be communicating a positive message - that you are excited about her.

TURN OFF THE CLOCK

Also important: You need to take your time. (Hopefully you'll like doing it! There's nothing like the feel of her **pussy** against your lips!) Turn off the clock ticking in your head. The longer you eat her pussy, the more she'll love you for it and the more she'll scream when she comes.

"You nearly killed me!" gasped a breathless lover recently, after I'd given her more head (and better head, according to her) than she'd ever had before. It was music to my ears. Don't you want to hear that?

Now, how long is enough? I've done it for upwards of half an hour or more.

(Continued on page 240)

HER AROMA: GOOD OR A PROBLEM?

A lot of guys came to me for advice on women when I was in college. I'll never forget the day one of them knocked on my door and sheepishly asked me what women smell like "down there."

I instantly ticked off a few ideas: "You know the chili they serve at the cafeteria?" I replied. "It kind of smells like that." (It was the aroma of the herb cumin primarily.)

"Or," I continued, "it smells a bit like pencil lead. Or, a bit like mild underarm musk, but, in a sweeter, pleasant form."

I sensed that he feared the smell. No good. A man needs to get over this common fear and see a woman's musk in a more positive light.

It's *sexy*.

BAD ODOR

It is true that a small minority of women do have a **bad odor**. In fact a friend recently complained that his woman had this problem. I advised him to suggest she see a doctor.

A **bad vaginal odor** usually means she has a **bacterial or yeast infection**. Other factors (such as **IUDs**) can also spoil a woman's natural odor.

It need not spoil your fun or your relationship. But you cannot ignore the problem. You'll want to mention it to her diplomatically and lovingly at a appropriate time when sex is not being contemplated. Your primary concern should be her health.

That being said, most women take care of themselves properly. Some actually do too much, washing themselves before sex so there's little or no **aroma**.

I had a girlfriend in my 20s, for instance, who insisted on taking a bath before we had sex; she didn't want her pussy to have any scent. The result was disappointing to me. I like the aroma, **her *"cassolette."***

You will too, once you get over any adolescent fears you might have and become more sophisticated. If it's an acquired taste, it's worth acquiring.

There's nothing sexier than smelling her scent on your fingers after sex. Especially if wafts up unexpectedly minutes or hours after you were with her, sweetly reminding you of the special intimate moments you just shared.

A Solution

But if you absolutely cannot get used to the scent, here's an idea: Suggest you both take a bath or shower together before the idea of having sex comes up. Then ask if you could wash her "all over."

In giving her the bath or shower, make it real romantic. Place candles around the bath if there's room. Then take your time with your wash cloth, making the experience fun and sexy for her.

You'll want to wash between her legs but don't make it obvious that that's your real goal in doing all of this. Make it titillating, by massaging her in an erotic way.

In doing so, run a washcloth lightly over her **vulva**. Be sure not to get soap inside her urethra or vagina.

Don't make a big deal of it; just do one or two quick brush-overs with the cloth. Then - to make it sexier - use a **shower massager** to cleanse the area of soap, also using the gentle streams of water to stimulate her genitals. In fact, try to get her excited with the shower massager as you do this.

Another idea:

Give her **head** in the bath or shower (with the water running) if it would lessen your squeamishness.

Oral Sex That Will Drive Her Wild

(Continued from page 237)

And why not? If you do it in a relaxed fashion, you can keep it up indefinitely. It doesn't have to be at a breakneck speed. Choose a comfortable speed and position to avoid lockjaw or strain.

And don't stop until she pushes you away or says, "Stop! I can't take any more!" And even then she might not mind a bit more.

THE CUNNILINGUS ARTIST'S "PALETTE"

Now, as I've already warned you, the worst sin in **love**making - and that includes **cunnilingus** - is to be **predictable**. That's boring. Bore a woman and you're looking for trouble.

The solution? Be *creative*. Your imagination is your only limitation. Try out new techniques, on different areas of her body.

And this is a good rule: *Always do something different from session to session*. That's not hard: Remember what you did to her last time? Don't do that the next time! (If you can't remember, write it down!)

To make this easier for you, I've provided a list of ideas for you below. Just as a painter uses a palette of many colors to create his work of art, you, the cunnilingus artist, have many options on your palette to pleasure your partner orally (for anatomical locations, see page 192 to page 195, or page 245):

Use your **lips** to kiss her private parts and elsewhere. And you have many options here: You can ream, suck, massage or gently apply pressure wherever you want to. (Be sure to wet your lips - and keep them wet.)

Use your **teeth** to very gently give her love nibbles (if she likes this).

Use your **tongue tip** to lick, flick, caress, massage or tease her **pussy lips, U-Spot, perineum and clit**. Use it for shallow penetration and for stimulating the sensitive **V** at the bottom of her vulva (the "**fourchette**"). *Tease her* **vaginal ball** *to absolutely drive her wild!! Or tongue her vaginal ring if your tongue can reach inside her vaginal canal!*

Use the **flattened top of your tongue** to stimulate a larger surface area. Or you can simply *press it* against her. This works especially at the start, where the heat from your tongue alone will give her strong tingles.

Penetrate her with your tongue. Want to blow her mind? **Stimulate her G-Spot (or get as close as you can to it). With the right rhythm, pressure and insistency you can make her come!** Put her legs up in the air or over your shoulders for the best access to her **G-Spot** (see second photo, page 244).

Use your **mouth** to give her hot air tickles, with a light breath. (**Never blow into her vaginal hole, though; that can cause a deadly embolism!**)

On Loving Women

You can **shake your head** back and forth while you press your face against her vulva so you pull and stretch that skin with your head motions.

Your head and body placement can also be varied; different angles bring different pleasures. Two examples:

You can kneel on the floor while she lies back on a bed, for example. Or you can do it *sideways* while she lies back.

You also can perform cunnilingus in a 69 position. This is where you place your genitals next to her mouth while you give her oral sex. This gives her the option of pleasuring you too. That's a plus!

As with other positions, you have a variety of ways you could do this:

You could lie on your back and have her sit atop your face (shown below). Or you could hover above her, on all fours (she'd have to pull your member down to access it while you gave her head.)

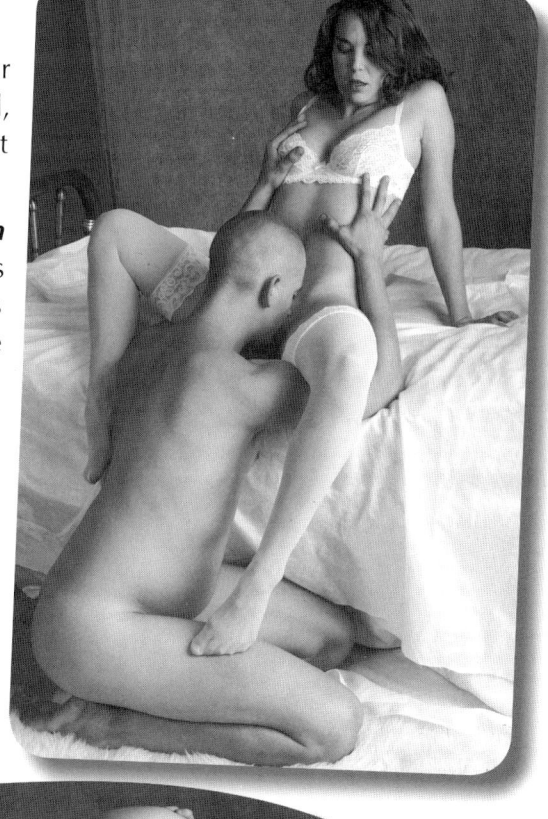

Another way would be with you both lying on your sides.

I personally don't use the 69 position much, except to get my lover more

Oral Sex That Will Drive Her Wild

excited and primed to come. This ruse works well with women who get hot at the sight of your hard-on. (You will know if she gets turned on by looking at your naked body; she'll tell you early on in your relationship.)

You also can vary her body placement - which can make her feel even more sexy-hot and ready to come. Here are some ways of doing that:

You can have her "sit on your face" (you lie on a flat surface while she crouches on all fours above you so her **vulva** is next to your lips), her body facing the same way as yours.

Lying on your stomach, you can **eat her** with her **legs** over your shoulders.

You can pleasure her while she stands up.

Or you can give her **head** from behind with both of you on all fours (see the photo on page 242).

A change in her body position can make a big difference in how sensitive she is to your touch and also how sexy she feels. So be sure to experiment with this; you want to find the positions that turn her on the most!

You also can use your fingers and hands while giving her **head**. As we discussed in the ***loving touching chapter***, ***multitasking*** is a good thing.

You can **rub, tickle, pinch, stretch, pull, massage, outline, knead, hold, touch and shake** just about any part of her **genitals**.

You can give her a **clitoral orgasm** manually while your mouth is elsewhere.

You can also **penetrate** her **vagina** and/or **anus**

On Loving Women

manually while you **eat her** (see the **anal** version of this below). If you give her a **G-Spot orgasm** in this way while giving her a **clitoral orgasm** with your tongue, she'll come harder!

You also can perform oral sex on her in a more general fashion, using her entire body as your canvas.

Give her whole body a thorough going over (and take your time!). Your reward will be the extra-big **orgasm** *you will give her.*

Her **skin** is her *biggest organ* and she has many highly sensitive areas on her body. So explore it all!

Here are some of her many **delightfully sensitive areas:**

- her **buttocks**
- her **inner thighs**
- her **legs** in general
- the small of her back
- her **spine**
- her **neck** (the front and back especially)

Oral Sex That Will Drive Her Wild

- behind her ears
- behind her knees
- the **sensitive skin on her hips**
- her **tummy**
- her **feet and toes**
- her **back**

You also can get her more excited by giving her a show and a feel. Anything that makes a woman hot pushes her closer to her **climax**. And most women are turned on by **visuals**.

For example, many women go crazy at the sight of your **balls** and **cock** hanging down when you're on all fours. So, try this: Strike a **doggy-style pose** when going down on her (angle your body toward her feet; your knees and feet by her head.) Two side benefits of this ruse: She'll reach right over and give you a lot of fabulous handwork! I guarantee it! Also, women become more excited when they touch you - so this trick will make her even hotter when she (inevitably) cops a feel. (Think of how extra-hot you get when you touch her!)

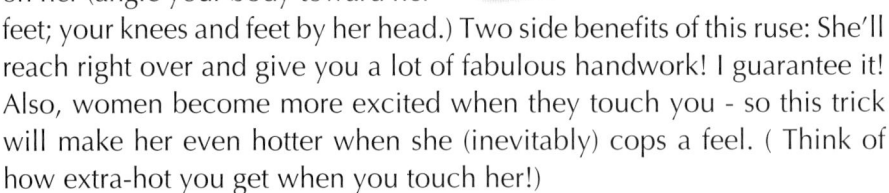

You also can vary a range of other factors, including the:

- intensity
- speed
- rhythm
- <u>range of skin</u> **covered** in a stroke, motion or set of motions
- the amount of motions and stimulation points you include in a repeating pattern (example: you could circle her clit twice, with two fingers, and then quickly pop a finger in and out of her vagina)
- the **path your tongue takes**
- the <u>sounds</u> you make (saying Mmmm! can arouse her; it also vibrates her skin erotically)

And sexy talk can also send her over the top (more on that later).

Finally, you have these options when doing her clit: You can tongue it <u>with</u> or <u>without</u> exposing it by pulling its hood back.

On Loving Women

clitoral hood
Niche
clitoris
U-Spot
urethra
vaginal ball
labia
Nook
V-Spot (fourchette)
perineum
anus

Pulling the **clitoral hood** back is pleasurable to her and produces heightened reactions. This also better exposes her **U-Spot!**

Want to make her come fast? Pull the **hood** back to the max! Want to make it even sexier? *Make her hold her clitoral hood back herself!*

THE HANDS-FREE CLIT EXPOSER

If you want to be really smooth, there's an incredible move you should try; let's call this the **hands-free clit exposer**. It pops the head of her **clitoris** out of its **hood** (which gives your mouth and tongue better access to her **clit** to give her greater pleasure) while leaving your fingers free to stimulate her elsewhere. Here's how to do it:

Press your face and mouth tightly against the skin of her vulva above her clit and move your head upward (while still tonguing her clitoris). That will lift her upper vulva up and pull her clitoral hood back to expose her pearl-like clitoral head for maximum stimulation. (Use your fingers to simultaneously massage, stroke and tease her other sensitive body parts - her **vagina**; **perineum**; **nipples**; **anus**; etc.) It's a move that will impress her by its sophistication and excite her by its effect. **Multitasking** *in this way gives her the feeling she's being done by more than one lover.*

EXPLORE DIFFERENT TONGUE PATTERNS

...So now you've learned many ways in which you can perform oral sex. And there are an endless number of **tongue patterns** you could do, from the simple to the complex.

There are an endless number of **rhythms** you can use in tonguing her (for example: dit-dit-dah - two quick flicks followed by one long lick)...an endless number of non-rhythmic approaches ("going wild," for example, with lots of tongue surface, rapid motion and intense pressure, will often make her come at the appropriate moment, such as after you've teased her into a frenzy)...an endless number of intensities and speeds (a real slow tease done right will drive her crazy, for instance)...an endless variety of ways to stimulate her many parts with your lips, mouth, face...

...And don't forget to dip your **tongue** into her **vaginal canal!** Try circles inside it. Or pop your tongue in rapidly and pull it out just as quickly. Or do rapid triplets. A well-placed, rapid three-flick pulsing of the tongue, with a brief pause in between, will generate sparks!

Feedback Is Key

...And so there's an idea of what your "artist's palette" of options is in pleasing your partner orally. But your "canvas" is not dead to the touch, like a painter's. You're not operating in a vacuum.

In other words, you cannot just do anything on the list I've just given you (mechanically) and call it good head. You've got an "audience." What you do must please her. It must be done with feeling and finesse; and with an empathy for her. You must now try out your "artist's palette" of options on her to see what she likes and does not like.

It's all about exploration. And feedback is key. Pay close attention to how she responds - verbally, visually, biologically. Watch, listen, learn. How are you making her feel? Observe.

That's the only way you'll know whether you've found a technique that's effective on her. Moans, wriggling, an increase in **vaginal wetness** and heat - these are some of the positive clues you'll get when she likes what you're doing. If she doesn't respond to one thing, try another. If she likes something, prolong that (and make note of it; put that in your "bag of tricks" for the future).

Aside from experimenting with techniques, you also should be searching for two types of locations on her body: ones that are **orgasm triggers** (the places you can stimulate to make her climax) and ones that are simply sensitive to your touch (with which you can make her hot).

That's part of your "job," after all - discovering what she likes best. All women are different. Along the way to discovery, of course, you should give up quickly on anything you try that provokes no response or, worse, a negative response.

What To Do If She Doesn't Like Direct Stimulation

Speaking of which: I mentioned earlier that, while most prefer direct tongue work on the clitoris, some women find that annoying or too intense. Here's what you do if your lover is that way:

Tongue areas other than her **clitoris' head**. And don't pull her clitoral hood back.

Do tight circles around the **clit.** Give her tongue work just below her clit (on and around her **U-Spot**), or on either side of it. It's also about drama.

On Loving Women

Drama is partly about setting the stage for a big orgasm. You do this by building her sense of anticipation. You need to make her really <u>want</u> it.

EMPATHY IS IMPORTANT

Now let's add another level of sophistication: The better you are at empathizing with her, feeling exactly what she's feeling (physically) with every touch of yours, the better a lover you will be. And that pertains to oral sex as well as everything else you might do.

Empathizing with your lover while giving her **head** requires an understanding of **female sexual anatomy**. For example, you now know that the skin of her pussy lips (her labia minora) is similar to that of your scrotum. Well, you know how great it feels for a woman to caress or lick your balls. That's how it feels to her when you lick her **labia minora**.

So do to her **pussy lips** what you'd like done to your **balls**. Give them a lot of attention. Start by kissing them. Isn't that what you like done to your **balls** first? Then tickle them with your **tongue**. Or blow her mind by taking each one - individually or together - into your mouth and suck them gently (make sure your lips are wet). Don't give them short shrift.

Try to feel what she's feeling as a result of whatever you're doing to her, at any given moment. That's what empathy is all about. Then you'll know exactly how to proceed - you'll know what she wants next.

GOOD LOVERS USE DRAMA

Drama is also about creating a <u>scenario</u> she understands - in the short- or long-term. Here's an example of a short-term scenario that works: At the start, act as if her **vulva** is too hot to touch. That's the ruse. Put your tongue to it only briefly, without much pressure, and then pull it away quickly, as if you're afraid of getting burned. She'll get the idea and gasp with pleasure! You can even verbalize the idea: "Oooh," you might say. "Your pussy's so hot!" She'll almost instantly get hotter simply because you placed the thought of her **skin** being hot in her mind.

In contrast, a long-term scenario is akin to orchestrating a symphony. You invent a theme or idea that propels an entire **love**making session (or a significant portion of it). It can be stated or unstated.

One such approach - when applied to **oral sex** - would be to tell her you were going to **tease** her mercilessly for an hour before letting her come. For dramatic effect, make her watch as you set your **alarm clock** to go off in an hour. Tell her: "When this goes off, so will you!" (Believe me. You'll send a shiver through her body! She'll get hot and wet with those words!)

Oral Sex That Will Drive Her Wild

Then, start small and build ever-so-gradually. You might choose to tickle her around and near her clit but not on her clit. Or you could flick her clitoris teasingly until she's good and hot; then suddenly move on to other places on her body. Whatever you do, don't go wild on her clit and make her come until an hour's up.

It's A Two-Step Process

Understand: On one level, **cunnilingus** is really simple. Most often it's a two-step process: step one, you **tease**; step two, you **please**.

Teasing is all about getting her hot and aroused, primed to come. **Pleasing** is the process of making her come.

And most times, you should spend much more time *teasing* her than *pleasing* her. Here's where you especially need to be an artist. There is an **art** to *teasing*. And women love great *teasers*.

Becoming An Artist At Teasing Her

For one thing, if you tease her well she'll feel you're "in control." Women want to feel they're being "done."

Plus, the benefits of teasing are huge: The slower you increase her internal flame, so to speak, the bigger her orgasm will be.

If you get good enough at teasing she'll say something admiring like, "Ooooh! That's such sweet torture!" And that's what it is!

At The Start Less Is More

Along these lines, you should not try to make her come from the get-go on most occasions. Begin small. Let her enjoy a slow buildup.

At the start, you just want to light a fire; make her hot. All your efforts should be on "low volume." Soft and not insistent. Not in a rush. You don't have to move too much, or set up any kind of rhythm. The good teaser makes his woman hotter and hotter ever so gradually. Begin by giving her goose bumps simply with the heat of your tongue. Just press it on her - anywhere but her clit. Do light outlines around or near but not on her clit.

There are exceptions to every rule, of course. On rare occasions you'll want to make her come fast - skipping the teasing phase. And sometimes you'll want to go down on her not to make her come but simply to arouse her, for better **love**making. But, most times, the above advice works best.

Hold Off On Giving Her The "Prize"

Accordingly, it's usually best to leave the heavy duty clit work to last.

On Loving Women

That doesn't mean ignoring it altogether, though.

You might tease her clitoris very lightly toward the beginning (without pulling her clitoral hood back). Keep your tongue work soft and fleeting - not enough to push her close to a climax. Then move on to other places.

Or you might decide to totally hold off on giving her the "prize" - not doing any clit work until the very end. The great thing about this approach is that the longer she anticipates your touching her clit, the hotter she'll get.

Play With Her Mind

That's one way of playing with her mind, her biggest sexual organ.

Another way of doing this is to drag out your approach to her genitals when you're ready to focus solely on her vulva or clit (after doing more general body work). Her mind will do half the work for you if you bring your mouth to her groin excruciatingly slowly.

The closer you get, the more her mind is going to imagine what your electrifying first touch will feel like. You'll give her tingles without touching her! And she'll be <u>extra hot</u> when you first apply your tongue.

On Flutter-Tonguing And The Clitoris Phase

...And when you're ready to focus your attention mostly on her clitoris, don't fall into a common trap. Here's where most men, I'm told, tend to go for the "okey doke" - feverishly trying to make their women come fast, usually with flutter-tonguing (a rapid and intense lapping of the clitoris).

Now - don't get me wrong. You should learn this technique. Most women like this a lot if you do it well, with the right tempo and intensity. They will come quickly when you do this properly and at an appropriate time (once they're good and hot) and they will appreciate you for it - if you're not a one-note and do this all the time. (FYI: On occasion, a "surprise attack" with the purpose of making her come fast can be fun. Flat-out flutter-tonguing is great for this. The surprise factor is what makes this work. But do this only rarely; women usually prefer mucho teasing.)

Flutter-tonguing is done with an extremely rapid moving of the tip of your tongue up and down; there's usually a characteristic "thup" sound at the top, where your tongue hits your upper lip. It can be done essentially non-stop, done with a regular rhythm; or you can do bursts of flutter "attacks" separated by short (typically split-second) pauses. You can focus on one spot or move your tongue around as you do this. Word of advice: Don't do this at your maximum best speed from the start. Leave room to increase the tempo if she needs a contrast in speed in order to come.

That being said, women don't want you to be in a rush to make them come. In other words: Flutter-tonguing should neither be done indiscriminately nor exclusively. And, when done, flutter-tonguing generally should come after a long tension-building process (and only when you want her to come).

Flutter-tonguing her every time you give her head is like using an atom bomb to clean your house. There's no subtlety in that. Don't lose out on all the many pleasures you can give her - and you can delight in - if you keep things lighter (pleasures you cannot produce once you deaden her nerves from over-stimulation; once you start applying stronger pressure, she will lose a sensitivity she had previously to light touches). The fact is: You don't have to tongue her at the speed of light to thoroughly satisfy her AND make her come.

Plus, if you flutter-tongue her every time you'll become predictable. Again - if a woman finds you predictable, you're boring her.

THE BUTTERFLY-LIGHT VULVA TONGUE TECHNIQUE

And why be predictable when the possibilities are endless?! And, before we move on to other topics, let me give you a few more great ideas you can try out on your lover (which she's unlikely to have ever experienced!):

If you really want to wow her, try what I call the Butterfly-Light Tongue Technique. The idea with the **Butterfly-Light Vulva Tongue Technique** is to do such soft tongue moves that, if she were asleep, she wouldn't know if she was imagining things or you were really doing something to her.

So, as you might imagine, this involves the tiniest of tongue touches - so soft they're just barely perceptible. Believe it or not, this will make her extremely hot (which is its main purpose). Her reactions will be incredible, given how little you're doing.

Here's how to do it:

Apply the *tip of your tongue* to various places on her vulva, with such little effect that you could almost deny you were doing anything. Use the lightest pressure you can muster. You can either hold your tongue briefly on her, or do a quick on-and-off tease. You can even do micro flicks - so long as whatever you do is no more than scarcely noticeable.

Trust me. This is <u>killer</u>. She'll got so hot so fast you won't believe it. In fact, I've made some women come with this **super-light technique**. (FYI: The **Butterfly-Light Vulva Tongue Technique** won't work very well if you do it every time you give her head. The novelty and audacity of it are what make it work. So only do it rarely, for maximum effect.)

The beauty part is that, by the extreme lightness of your initial touches, you've sensitized her to the max. Her organs will be like plants straining to catch the faintest light.

So, no matter what you do from then on, she'll react more excitedly than she usually would. She'll feel everything more intensely!

THE PULSAR TONGUE TECHNIQUE

One step up from that technique is the **Pulsar Tongue Technique**. A pulsar is a rapidly spinning star. In regular rhythm, you see its light and then darkness. The light has an incredible effect due to the regular rhythm and intensity of the light.

Similarly, the **Pulsar Tongue Technique** is a maddeningly-regular moderate-tempo insistent lick-pause-lick-pause approach directly on top of the (exposed) **glans** of her **clitoris**. But it's more involved than that. Here's an example of how I used it with great effect:

I had my girlfriend sit on my face - crouching above my prone body, her vulva pressed against my mouth. I then used a maximum range of upper tongue surface per stroke - at least an inch - directly on the **head** of her **clit**. These were one-way strokes (up only), by the way. I did this, too, with a lot of pressure and passion.

For some reason the Beatles' *Let It Be* was playing over and over in my head, so I tongued her to that **medium tempo**. (Boy did that work!) It helps to have a song in your head when you want to do something with a **constant rhythm**. I also maximized the effect by moving my tongue at the end of the stroke to the starting position as quickly as I could, so that my tongue was always on her; it was only off her clit a nanosecond between strokes. This made her hotter, transmitting urgency, pushing her close to **orgasm**.

USING A MANTRA TO COMMUNICATE THOUGHTS

I also added a powerful element worthy of note: I repeated a sexy mantra in my head with every tongue stroke: "You're going to come! You're going to come!" Knowing how well women can read our minds and interpret our every move, I'm sure she "heard" that mantra through my tongue work. She came within two minutes.

The novelty of her sitting on my face also played a part in making her come fast (she told me she'd never done that before). And, she commented happily: "My orgasm felt different from up here!" That's why you position your lover differently each time and why you should constantly experiment with her to find ways in which she's never been done before. Novelty creates extra excitement.

THE MIND-BLOWING ECSTASY CLITORIS STEM TECHNIQUE

Speaking of which, do you want a really unique cunnilingus technique that will blow her mind? In the anatomy chapter, you learned that *behind the head (or **glans**) of a woman's **clitoris** is a little shaft or **stem*** (known as the "***body***"). When aroused, this ***stem*** will grow even longer. (You won't be able to see it directly; it's hidden under her ***clitoral hood***. You can *feel* it though, with your fingers, lips, and tongue.)

I've found that many women enjoy having this stimulated. Not *all* women like it; but those who like it ***really*** like it! So you'll want to try what I call the ***Ecstasy Clitoris Stem Technique*** on your lover. Here's what you do:

Using your lower lip, push up on the skin just below her clit. This should let you grasp the end of the ***clit body*** with your lips. Then suck gently to pull the ***head*** and part of the ***stem*** (¼" to ½" of it) into your mouth. Now work it! Take her ***clit head*** and ***stem*** into your mouth as deeply as possible (without hurting her, of course; don't be rough) and use your tongue and lips to stimulate them in every way possible. Pay close attention to her feedback and stick to what she likes most. Try this, for instance: With the tip of your tongue, ream the ***clit's shaft*** as you'd like her to ream the ***shaft*** of your ***cock***. Start softly and only gradually increase the pressure. Experiment; see what she likes best.

Here are other approaches to try, working the ***clit*** and ***stem*** together:

- *Suck on them*
- *Lick them all over*
- *Roll them in your mouth*
- *Pull on them gently*
- *Shake them gently (move your head in a rapid "no" motion)*
- *Massage them with your tongue*

Another approach is what I call **Clit Stemming**. There are two ways to do that. You can run your ***tongue*** along the length of her ***stem***, through her ***clitoral hood***. If you make the tip of her ***clit*** the beginning and endpoint for each stroke, she'll come fast! Or you can *ream* the ***stem*** *(through its* ***hood****)* with your ***lips***, like it's a tiny corn cob - shaking your head back and forth. Experiment with this. It will send her through the *roof!*

KNOCK-HER-SOCKS-OFF HEAD

Now, at the beginning of this chapter, I spoke of a special technique that, when used judiciously, rarely fails to please. And I promised to tell you about it. I'm going to name this the **Ecstasy Vulva Technique**.

With this method, wet, moderately-strong sucking is the primary defining force, but if you're good enough to also give her adept tongue work, you're going to become her friend for life.

The **Ecstasy Vulva Technique** is done with your head sideways to her vulva. First spread her legs far apart. Then place your head so that the lips of your mouth are in the same orientation as the lips of her **vulva**. If you'd like, you can rest the top of your head on one of her thighs (her other thigh resting over your body).

Then, take both of her fleshy **pussy lips** (**labia minora**) into your mouth with a gentle sucking motion. (Her **pussy lips** are made of the same kind of sensitive skin that covers your balls so you might imagine how pleasurable this feels.) Massage them inside your mouth, keeping your mouth really wet. Manipulate them (delicately) in every way you can - just with your lips and mouth - listening to and watching her reactions to gauge what she likes best (so you can do that the most when you're ready to make her come).

You can add some tongue work after awhile. Start by pressing her lips together with your tongue while moving your tongue in a massaging circle. Do this for at least a minute or two before you go for the pièce de resistance.

Now - this is killer - while you're still sucking her **labia minora** into your mouth, use your tongue to add a second front, so to speak. Place your tongue *between* her **pussy lips**, which you'll keep firmly in your mouth, throughout this process. No matter what you do with your tongue from that point on, keep it between her lips.

Start by tonguing the *center cleft* of her **vulva**, keeping your tongue within the upper and lower limits of her **labia minora** at first. Do this for at least a minute or two, to establish the theme of what you're doing.

Then, you can add some variation. You can tongue just one area, like the upside down V below her **clit** (the **U-Spot**), or the V at the bottom of her **vagina** (the **V-Spot** or "**fourchette**"), or you could go up and down her entire crack, making sure to run your tongue over her **clit.**

But - no matter what you do - *always keep your tongue action going between her **pussy lips***. That's what makes the **Ecstasy Vulva Technique** so great. In other words - the tongue strokes to the clit (or anywhere else you can reach for that matter) should start and end between her lips.

As you get closer to wanting to make her come, increase the amount of attention you give her **clit** - again, using longer than normal strokes so your tongue begins and ends between her **pussy lips.**

One important note though: To pull this off, you must breathe through your nose so the necessary sucking action that keeps her pussy lips in your mouth is <u>continuous</u>. The continuous sucking action blows her mind. The warm and wet sensations your mouth gives to her labia minora are also effective in making her extraordinarily hot.

Now Add A Twist

All of this is enough to send her way over the edge. (She's probably never been thrilled in this way before.) And she'll love you for it. But don't do it the same way each time. A great lover never repeats things by rote.

The story I told at the start of this chapter, in fact, was about a lover on whom I'd done the **Ecstasy Vulva Technique** who requested it again the next day. But, to make things interesting, I added a **twist**. This twist - in combination with all of the stimulation the **Technique** provides to so many of her most sensitive areas, simultaneously - produces awesome results. It brought my girlfriend to an ear-shattering climax and made her ask breathlessly: "What did you just DO to me?"

What I did was to wait until she was really hot – after I'd been giving her head for some time, knowing I wanted to bring her to a **climax** – and then **I stuck my thumb inside her pussy (downward, so that the fleshy pad was touching the skin that runs inside from the bottom V of it) while I simultaneously inserted my middle finger into her bottom**. The groans that came from her just from that move alone were priceless. (Mind you, I was still giving her **oral sex**.)

Then I pressed both fingers together, such that each fingertip was resting on the other through the **thin membrane** that separates her **vaginal and anal canals** - moving both fingers in tandem. Sometimes I massaged that **membrane** up and down, with a gentle in and out motion, or I tenderly shook it, or made circles – making sure to express passion with my fingerwork, through the insistency of my touch and urgency of the motion. (Touch is one thing; but, if you can make her feel as if your touch is the *irresistible force* that moves the immovable object, and that her **orgasm** is *inevitable*, then you're really doing something.)

With the fingers of my left hand – while all of the above was still going on – I pulled her **vulva** up and apart to the max. This severe stretching action was done as a means to give her the feeling that an **orgasm** was going to come on soon. (This is a great way to heighten a woman's pleasure; if you can give her the sense that she is being stretched to the limit, it helps send her over the top to her **climax**.)

A side benefit of the pulling up of her **vulva skin** was that it made her **clit** pop out of the top of its **hood**. That gave me better access to it with my tongue. I began furiously lapping at it.

She came quickly and intensely. There wasn't a neighbor within a couple of blocks who didn't hear her come that day.

Where To Do It

By the way, **location** counts, too. You know what the real estate people say: location, location, location. That's a factor in sex, too! One of the great things about **cunnilingus** is that you can spring it on her just about anywhere. And *the more public the place, the more exciting it often is*.

For example, the best **head** I was ever given was in the Jones Beach parking lot - *with security guys driving circles around us, watching everything that was going on (with big smiles on their faces)! The thrill of the scenario, the naughtiness and relative danger of it, made me come harder than I'd ever come before.*

Well, guess what? *That same concept is also effective on a woman.* So why don't you do something like that to her?! (Perhaps in a less public place. I'll let you decide what's appropriate and safe and what's not.)

And do it all around the house, too - in every room! Every room provides a different atmosphere and gives her a different feeling. Often, doing it outside the bedroom is more exciting to her.

When To Do It

Now - from what women tell me - most men relegate **cunnilingus** to **pre-penetration action**. I imagine these men got the wrong idea from whomever taught them the idea of *foreplay* (which you now know I don't like) - that, in fact, cunnilingus is what you do for a short time before "real" sex (a period dubbed "foreplay"). That's just wrong.

My advice on when to do it: any time. Before. During. After. *Also do it when you just want to please her and you have no intention of entering her.*

Use it to shake things up. You don't know how elated she'll be, for instance, if you go down on her after you've just given her a huge orgasm some other way. Anything unexpected works well.

The Thrill of Surprise

Speaking of which - the element of surprise should be in your bag of tricks. It's amazing the effect certain spontaneous and unexpected acts can have on her. They can ramp up her excitement level dramatically. Along these lines, there are surprise "events" and surprise "attacks."

An example of a surprise **event**: Pop your tongue suddenly and deeply into her vaginal hole after you've teased her **pussy lips** awhile. Wiggle it vigorously for a few seconds. Then pull it out just as quickly. She'll moan!

An example of a great surprise **attack** that will knock her socks off: Pull her panties down at the front door the minute she comes home from work. And make her stand up while you give her the best head she's had in her life. That will give her the sexy feeling of being "taken" - especially if you *leave her partly-clothed.* (One caveat: make sure she's in a good mood before you spring this sexy "attack" on her!)

Forcing a lover to stand, by the way, is a great ploy. It's sweetly tormenting. (If you don't know how this makes her feel, ask your lover to give you head while you stand. It's sexy and it makes you extra hot! And it's hard to keep standing the hotter you get, which adds to the **erotic effect**.) And **stripping her** gives her an added thrill.

Make it even sexier? Keep your clothes on. The contrast (you clothed, she partially or totally **bare**) will make her feel more **naked**, vulnerable and hot. The whole effect of all of this will give her a **powerful orgasm**.

EDGY ORAL SEX

One final thing. If you're an edgy lover, pushing the envelope, you might want to explore her <u>outer</u> **anal ring**. They're **pleasure zones**. If you like tonguing her **bottom**, she'll love you for it.

You might want to use a warm wash cloth on her beforehand, though, to cleanse the area. And *do not put your tongue into her* **vagina** *immediately afterward, or you'll risk giving her a vaginal infection.*

GREAT CUNNILINGUS BENEFITS <u>YOU</u>

It works in your favor if you become a master at **cunnilingus**. It's one of the best ways to make a woman love you. There's nothing more *giving*. (And make no mistake: women see it that way and appreciate the gesture.)

Trust me. If you give her great head, as often as she likes, you're golden.

You want her to go down on *you,* don't you?

> *"'You have great hands!' is something I've been told by a lot of women. Many of them also added, 'That's one of my favorite things about you.' This is no small thing to a woman."*
> *- James Moore*

The Art of Loving Touching

The **art of loving touching** is something **unattached men and those in relationships (including married men) need to master**. For the single guy, it could provide the edge that seduces the woman of your dreams into your bed. For those in relationships, it could mean the difference between keeping your lover satisfied or losing her to someone else.

Women have an intense need to be touched. For **affectionate touching**. This is where *massages* come in (by *you*); *loving pats, hugs* and *squeezes* throughout the day; and *cuddling (while watching the TV, for instance)*, for a feeling of closeness. Done with **warmth, communicating love**, it validates their attractiveness. It makes them feel desirable and desired - and *loved*. It relaxes them; makes them feel good.

But they need *more*. They also hunger for **skillful sexual touching** to give them **sexual pleasure** and **satisfaction**. They want to be touched *artfully. Seductively. Sensuously. Tenderly. With feeling.* They know that, when done artfully, **loving touching** can put them in a state of **ecstasy**, taking them to **sexual heights** they'd give just about anything to experience. And they expect their lover to know how to do that. They crave a man with "**great hands**" - and you must fill that need or someone else might.

TOUCHING RUSES FOR SINGLE GUYS

The unattached man needs to understand that a woman's need to be touched is her Achilles heel. It gives you the means to lower her barriers. This could be the very secret you need to know to seduce the woman of your dreams! For example, the offer of a **shoulder** or **neck massage** is often

The Art of Loving Touching

welcomed, surprisingly enough, when done in a gentlemanly cool way. And the *power* of a *good* shoulder massage is *amazing!*

Haven't you ever witnessed the bold suave guys who walk up to a female acquaintance with an **easy masculine confidence** and start massaging her shoulders and neck? What an audacious move! Yet the good ones get away with this bold ruse because their **artful touch** sends **irresistible sexual tingles** down the woman's body, *which lower the woman's normal barriers to being touched publicly and can even make her* **desire sex**.

In fact, I've seduced innumerable women simply by running my thumb lightly up and down the **backs of their necks**, or by lightly **massaging their hairline** or the tops of their heads. Smoothly done while watching a movie or TV show or sitting on the couch, this kind of **loving touching**, when done artfully, can get a woman so hot she'll likely want to sleep with you - much sooner than she would have otherwise!

I'll never forget the lesson I learned watching one of my friends in High School - beloved by all the girls - walk right up to a girl who was dressed in a low-cut top and run his index finger down her neck to grab hold of the pendant of her necklace. I could see the color change in the girl's face as he smoothly lifted the pendant off her skin, just above her **breasts**, and coyly growled, "Nice necklace!" *He made her so hot you could practically feel the heat coming off of her!* The lesson was clear to me: *The right touch, done in the right place at the right time, is disarming to a woman and it could quickly open the door to an intimate relationship.*

And you don't have to be as bold as my friend to use this truth to your advantage. For instance: *Haven't you noticed the surprising feelings of* **shock** *and* **sexual desire** *a new woman in your life gives you the first time she casually touches you in conversation? You* possess the same *power*. So casually touch your prospective lover's hand or thigh or shoulder briefly, in a natural way, without missing a beat in the conversation. You'll send ripples of excitement up her body. Do it as *naturally* as you can. (If it comes off as you're copping a feel, *no good!*) *Pretend you're just touching her to emphasize whatever point you're making.* Do it with *kindness*, with a *smile*.

Another tip: *The offer of a massage can sometimes speed along the development of a relationship.* Few women can turn down that offer, if the timing's right and they find you attractive. So you especially need to learn that skill, as a single guy. (I'll talk about that in a moment.)

LOVING TOUCHING FOR MEN IN RELATIONSHIPS

Now, married men and others in relationships are in a different situation, yet *they're just as much in need of* **loving touching skills**. Because, according to most of the women I interviewed for *On Loving Women*, most men are leaving their women feeling neglected in this regard.

And here's *proof*: Why do you think so many women these days are saying they "need" a massage (meaning they are going *outside the home* seeking massages from *strangers*)? Because they're not getting enough **loving touching** at home - *sexually* or *affectionately*.

You don't want your woman to feel she needs the touch of *strangers* to satisfy her need for **loving touching.** So let's look at some of the many ways you can please her in this way, so she'll not seek outside attention.

Within a relationship, **loving touching** is something that should go on all day long. You need to keep her feeling loved. You also need to keep her **hot** for you. And so *you need* the **sexual touching skills** *that make women thrill, "You have* **great hands***!"*

Women who are not touched artfully or often enough often fall prey to the smooth operators that know how to seduce with a touch. You don't want that happening to your woman! So...when's the last time you made your lover weak in the knees by coming up from behind her and massaging the sensitive skin on her neck or shoulders?

Massages Within A Relationship - To Please & To Learn

And - guess what? Getting back to what I mentioned earlier, you need to listen to the chorus of women begging for a good massage! *Massages -* **Swedish** *or* **erotic** *- are among your best tools in keeping your lover satisfied within the confines of a loving relationship (IF you do this <u>well</u>).*

A **Swedish massage (non-sexual)** is a type of massage that is very *healing* and *calming*. When done purely to relax her after a tough day, it will *endear* you to her all the more. She'll appreciate it no end. You should ideally read some good books on it to learn this art, but basically you're kneading, tickling, rubbing and manipulating her skin in pleasing ways. One tip: *You should generally move your hands toward her heart, to move the blood in the proper direction.*

A good **erotic** or **sensual massage** (done *slowly*, with *patience*, as a **tease**) is a type of massage that makes her *hot for sex*, and more likely to **come** quickly and powerfully once sex starts. You can even make her **come** as part of the *massage. And she'll love you for it.*

The best thing about doing this for her is that, in learning to give her a great **erotic massage**, you will master skills that you should use in touching her every time you make love to her. So:

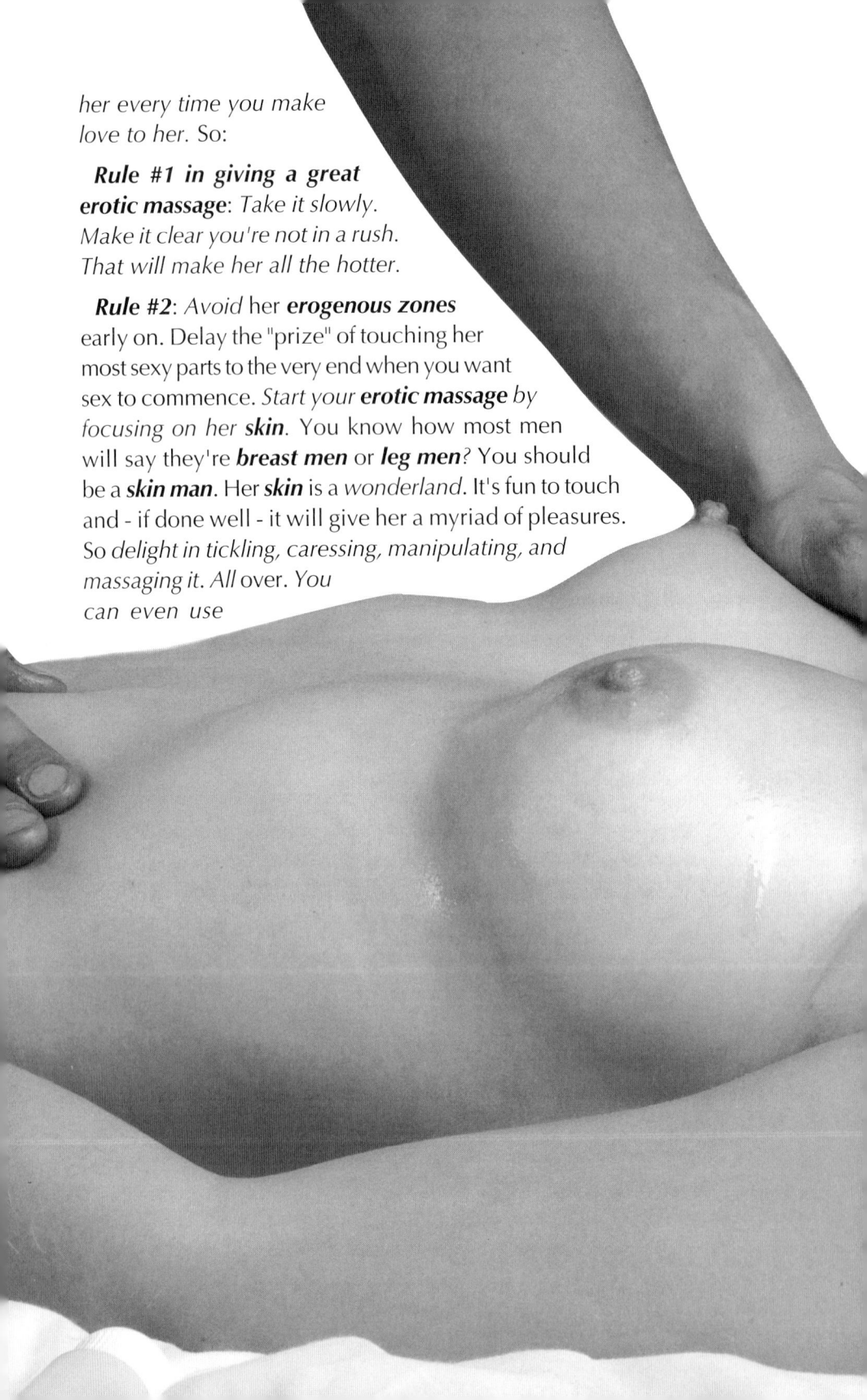

Rule #1 in giving a great erotic massage: *Take it slowly. Make it clear you're not in a rush. That will make her all the hotter.*

Rule #2: *Avoid* her **erogenous zones** early on. Delay the "prize" of touching her most sexy parts to the very end when you want sex to commence. *Start your* **erotic massage** *by focusing on her* **skin**. You know how most men will say they're **breast men** or **leg men**? You should be a **skin man**. Her **skin** is a *wonderland*. It's fun to touch and - if done well - it will give her a myriad of pleasures. So *delight in tickling, caressing, manipulating, and massaging it. All* over. You can even use

A Woman In Ecstasy

objects to **tickle** or **stimulate** her, such as feathers, a soft robe or blanket, her fuzzy slippers or whatever.

Rule #3: *After you've thoroughly teased her skin, then* **approach** *but* **do not touch** *her* **erogenous zones**. *Touch or stroke* <u>nearby</u>; *make her believe you're going to touch them, but then - as a big tease - move away from the parts she most wants you to touch. Get close to her* **breasts, nipples** *and* **vulva** *and then* back off. *This will really get her going! Her* **erogenous zones** *will experience* **sexual tingles** *as if you've* actually *touched them! (It's kind of like a "fake" in football - you* pretend *to go one way but then you go a* different *way.) Sometimes, though, you can brush against her erogenous zones, as if* by accident. *That tease will make her even hotter.*

Rule #4: *Only move on to her* **erogenous zones** *when she's* <u>super</u> *hot (she's moaning a lot and/or begging you to touch her* **hot spots**). *And even then, you'll probably want to take your time in getting her off. (Although I remember the time when I made one of my lovers so* **hot** *with a prolonged* **erotic massage** *that she* came <u>immediately</u> *when I simply placed my well-oiled palm over her*

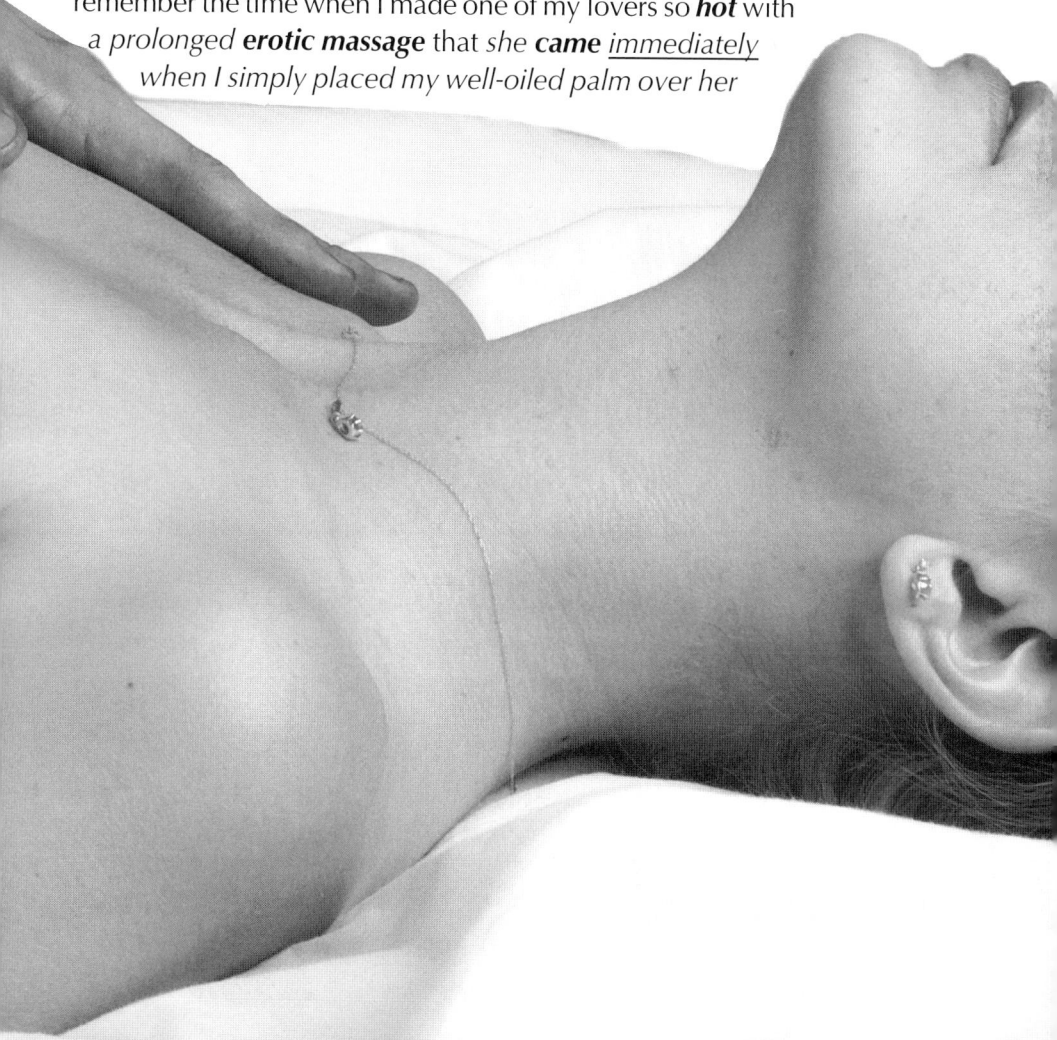

The Art of Loving Touching

***vulva*!**) Or you can choose <u>not</u> to make her **come** immediately, launching right into **love**making instead.

THE MANY KINDS OF EROTIC TOUCHES

But what is **sexual love touching** and having **"great hands"** all about? It's probably one of the most difficult things to teach. It's a *feel*. Remember the first time you touched velvet? You *gently* stroked it, *admiringly*. *That* kind of approach works great as a **love touch**. It's about **touching her with a sensitivity as to how you're making her feel**, concentrating on the types of touches that she responds to best. It's touching her with **tenderness**, sometimes **tickling**, sometimes **teasing**, always **communicating love and a fascination with her body**. And when you're going for her **orgasm**, you should communicate an **urgency, passion, intensity** and **inevitability**.

Now, akin to **volume** in music, **sexual love touches** come in a multitude of *strengths* or **pressure levels** - from **feather light** to **super strong**. Most times it's smart to stay in the **feather light** to **soft range**. In this way you can **sensitize your lover** - making her react more powerfully to your touch and quicker to blow her cork. Her **sexual nerves** become more **responsive** the **lighter** you touch her. So try that!

But what should you do when you want to bring on her **climax?** The most effective techniques in **love**making - the ones that will make your lover come - are most often **rhythmic**. They have a regular *repeating* nature to them, according to a **pace** or **tempo** that can be related to any number of pieces of music you like. So *once you've found a **tempo** that makes her come* (such as with your finger on her clitoris), make a mental note of it and **try to associate it with a song or piece of music you like**. That way, you can easily repeat that tantalizingly effective rhythm on a later occasion (by **conjuring up that music in your head**) to **make her come as quickly as you'd like**. Preferably find a **tempo** that's easy to repeat without tiring, such as a moderate tempo.

And don't violate what I call the **plateau effect**. That is, once you switch to a **fast tempo**, *your touch will lose its effect if you slow down the tempo later on*. Her nerves will be dulled to a *slower tempo* after getting used to a *higher tempo*. She'll then perceive the slowing down as a *disappointment* and will be *less likely to* **orgasm**. (More on the **plateau effect** on page 364.)

The **plateau effect** also pertains to the **pressure** and **range of motion** you use. So **a good general rule** is to *build* in **tempo, pressure and range of motion slowly**...with each **orgasm** you give her, that is. You should think in the long-term, because each of your **love**making sessions should last at

A Woman In Ecstasy

least an hour or so and include *many* **orgasms** for her. In other words, plan on giving her *ever more powerful* **orgasms** - in keeping with the **plateau effect rule** (so she's thrilled ever more to the end).

You Can Ask For Her Help Too

Another idea: You can become good at **love touching** by learning what *specific kinds* of touches *move her*. You can ask her to tell you what touches she likes best and you might get a few good tips. Or you can figure this out *in reverse*: *Study how she touches you during sex and make note of what you like best. What kinds of touches get you hot? Which ones make you come?* Then use those strokes (or *similar* ones) on her! ...Even *better*:

Ask her to give you an **erotic massage**. *Tell her you want her to touch you the way she likes to be touched. Promise that you will study what she does so you can do it to her immediately afterwards. Pay attention to what she does to you so you can then try it out on her when she's done!*

Sexy Ways To Use Lubricants And Lotions

Now would you like to know how to make your touches much more *potent* than normal, producing a more powerful effect on her? Use a **lubricant**.

Lubricants make your touch feel more pleasing to her. Even better, they *enhance* the *effect* of your touch. Her skin becomes more *reactive* to your touch with the right slippery liquids. That enables you to make her *hotter* and *more likely to come quickly*.

One *exciting* way to use a **lubricant** *during sex* is to let it do some of the work for you. For example: **a well-placed drop of oil on one of her erogenous zones** (such as a **nipple** or her **vulva**) **can elicit huge moans from her**. But to produce the biggest results in this way, it's best to do this *early on in the sexual process,* after you've teased her a bit and gotten her hot for sex. *(And make sure you've warmed up the oil in advance. Use your hands or warm water to heat the container.)*

Lubrication goes a long way in facilitating your finger and hand work, too. The whole experience is enhanced.

Saliva can work in a pinch but **the best love touching lubricants** are

The Art of Loving Touching

lotions and **oils**. **Lotions** such as *skin moisturizers* are great for using in *massaging* your lover. But shop for ones with the most *natural* and *healthy* ingredients. However, **oils** are what you should use once **sex** has begun, especially on her **erogenous zones**.

But to use oils in a sophisticated, smooth and romantic way requires some *preparation*. First, you need to shop for one or more **small convenient bottles** to use as **lubricant dispensers** - especially ones that *control the flow* so that you can pour the **lubricant** out *drop by drop*. (Don't use the bottle the oil originally came in if you can avoid it. They're unsightly and not very romantic. Plus, you'll end up with too much oil coming out and occasional spills, which can destroy the mood.)

I recommend you purchase **quality oils** that are *healthy* on her skin. My preference, actually, is for a good brand of *extra virgin olive oil*. (Doctors have told me that this is a safe and healthy practice.) Then **half-fill** the bedside dispenser you purchased and have it positioned for handy use whenever you're making love. (You can even put a nice **scent** in the **oil** if you'd like.) *Half*-filling them helps prevent tip-overs and spilling.

OTHER LOVE TOUCHING TOOLS

Beyond **lubricants**, anything that pleasingly touches her skin can be considered as a **love touching tool**. So don't neglect this potential opportunity to please your lover. That will bring a *variety* to your love life.

Try using feathers, her soft robe (if she doesn't have one, I suggest you buy one for her!) or any other soft clothing she has that she won't mind getting soiled during sex, a soft blanket or bedsheet, her fuzzy slippers, sexy fruit and veggies (strawberries, for example, for their **glans** *shape, or any of the phallic veggies like cucumbers or carrots), your softest ties, a stuffed animal even - whatever you have that might feel great against her* **skin**.

Some of these items can even be used on her **genitals**. *And in so doing, the element of surprise and the novelty of it will help make her orgasm bigger and more memorable. A side benefit to using common household items, too, such as her robe, is that it will later get her hot when she sees the items later on and she recalls what you did to her with them. Nice way to help keep her hot, all the time. That's one of your goals, as I've mentioned - to* **sexualize** *her, keep her hot for you. A woman who's fully realized, sexually, is an awesome companion. Trust me.*

It's all part of working on her mind, **sexualizing** *her and* **sensitizing** *her to* **your touch** *and* **your voice**. *One of my girlfriends once joked, in fact, that, in five years, I'd have her coming simply at the touch of my hand on hers.*

A Woman In Ecstasy

THE POWER OF *FURTIVE FINGERWORK* & *STEALTH ATTACKS*

And there's no better way to keep her anticipating your next seduction than with **furtive fingerwork** in a public place. It works because it's totally unexpected and exciting. She can't scream when she comes, which makes her climax all the more powerful. And **a side benefit for the future is that you've shown her she's always vulnerable to your wiles, which keeps her hot, imagining what you'll do to her next**. It's a smart tactic.

When it comes to handwork technique, let me suggest that here's where you really need to hone your skills - in pulling off **public sneak attacks**, or as I prefer to call them **stealth attacks**.

To do this: You're probably used to using the index or middle finger of your dominant hand on her **clit** but if you can learn to use your **pinky** you will have a better chance of sneaking that finger onto her **clit** and keeping it there long enough without being noticed - by her or potential onlookers. For two reasons: because your **pinky** produces the lightest impression on her, so she might not realize it's there at first; and, if most of your hand is visible and apparently resting innocently on her **thigh**, few would suspect your **pinky** is hidden under her dress, tickling her into oblivion. (The meat of your palm nestled subtly into the **cleft of her vulva** can work great, too!)

I recommend you use a super-subtle approach to **furtive fingerwork** and **stealth attacks** by the way. Do it in such a way that she's not really sure if you're doing something or not to cause the sexual sensations she's feeling - especially at the start. It's deniable, at least at the beginning. In that way, **she won't stop you early on; and once she realizes what's going on, she'll likely be so hot she'll have little desire to stop you!**

To pull off a **stealth attack**, limit your movement to only the slightest motion back and forth or up and down or in circles or in gently tapping her clit. Your touch much be the softest you can conjure. The beauty part is that all **stealth attacks** make your lover twice as hot as normal and produce **huge orgasms**, because of the elements of **surprise** and **audacity**.

This kind of thing is best done when she's put on a dress (especially if she doesn't wear one often), is more dressed up than normal, ideally even in a sexy way (with a shorter dress than normal or a low-cut top). **When a woman is dressed to the 9s and looking sexy, she feels sexy. The clothes will naturally tend to make her horny.** So, on those occasions, she's likely more vulnerable to a **furtive finger attack** - if done in a playful, sexy way!

A fancy restaurant with billowing table cloths (for the extra privacy they afford) is often great for **furtive fingerwork** as is the back row of a theatre.

The Art of Loving Touching

Semi-private is the operational word.

But sometimes **risky ventures** pay off bigger, if you can do them without being noticed. For its sheer audacity, nothing will beat the time I made a girlfriend come at the opera (during the performance, surrounded by well-dressed, well-heeled patrons) by ever so slightly pulling on the skin near her **groin**, through her dress, rhythmically.

I had ever-so-subtly put my hand on her **thigh**, near her **pussy**, and, placing my **pinky** in the crook that runs from her **hip** to her **pussy**, I moved her **skin** toward me and then back so her **pussy lips** would open and close. (After the opera she told me how impressed she was with what I'd done, saying, "I wondered: 'how is he moving that part?'") It took about 10 minutes (increasing the rhythm only slightly) but the resulting **orgasm** was so <u>powerful</u> - because her frustration in not being able to vocalize her feelings was so immense - that she later said it nearly tore her head off. "You're so naughty!" she whispered admiringly. (See "Location, Location, Location" on page 381 for more bold **love**making ideas along these lines.)

Learn To Use All Your Fingers

And by the way, you should become skilled at using every one of your fingers on her. Each feels different to her.

I'll never forget the time I first used my **thumb** on an ex-girlfriend, while making love to her (I was sitting up on my heels, with her lying on her back). Pressing the entire pad of my **thumb** on her **clitoral region** and environs, I made urgent *circles*, kneading her skin while doing so. Her climax was helped along by the novelty of that move and she later praised me for it, cooing, "You're *amazing!*" Nothing beats hearing that.

So *try getting her off (on different occasions) with each of your fingers* - from the **thumb** to the **pinky**. She'll get novel thrills from each.

Want a *fingerwork technique* that's a real *woman pleaser?* Try my **Spread-Lips Clitoris Technique:** While fingering her **clitoris** with your **middle finger**, spread her **labia minora** by inserting your **index and ring fingers** inside each **lip** and pushing outward. That will **expose** her **clitoris** from its **hood** for better access to your **middle finger**. It will also **excite** her in and of itself and *impress* her in its *sophistication.* Try pulling or pushing *upward* with your spread fingers, too. That exposes her **clit** further and stretches it upward, increasing her **pleasure,** which *helps bring on her* **orgasm**.

Fingerwork During Sex

...So as you can see, when it comes to **fingerwork,** it should not be

confined to your sexual efforts *before penetration*. *If your fingers are idle once your **cock** is inside her, you're falling down on the job.* Artful **fingerwork** during **penetration** will accomplish several important things:
- *it will make her **hotter** than mere penetration ever could*
- *it will make her **come faster** than penetration alone could*
- *it will give her a bigger **orgasm***

Now when you do more than one thing at a time, we call that **multitasking**. And that idea is so hot to a woman, all you need to do is say **"multitask"** and she'll likely swoon. *This is what they want.*

Her Multiple Erogenous Zones For The Biggest Fireworks

In fact, in the **anatomy chapter**, I presented a simple *formula*, which I called An Important Biological Rule:

Multiple Spots = Bigger Orgasms

More specifically, **the more hot spots you engage, the more excited she'll get and the more powerful her climaxes will be**. Touch any one of her great **orgasm boosters** when either *fingering* an **orgasm trigger** or during **penetration** and she'll come faster and harder. I'll give you some of the **hottest techniques** you could ever use on a woman in a moment.

But first there's another great way to stimulate **multiple hot spots** for **bigger orgasms**, which I want to discuss. In the section, "Introducing The Multiple Erogenous Zone Area" on page 206, I promised to show you some techniques to take advantage of **multiple erogenous zone areas** and **orgasm trigger complexes** - areas containing *a number of* **hot spots**, which you can stimulate *simultaneously* to produce *bigger* **excitement** and **climaxes**.

A simple way to give her big **multiple erogenous zone** thrills and **orgasms** is through my **Vulva Orgasm Massage Techniques**.

The first type of these techniques are what I call **Covered Vulva Orgasm Techniques**. Here, you cover her **vulva** with either **the side of your hand, the face of your palm, a finger, an arm or a leg** and then rub up and down such that you **stimulate** and **trigger** almost every **hot spot and orgasm trigger** in her **vulval region**. The easiest and most effective means of doing this is with *the meaty side of your hand, the face of your palm or your middle finger*. With *the side of your hand or middle finger,* ease into an *up and down* motion, pressing up against her **vulva** so everything possible (including, ideally, her **labia minora, clitoris, clitoral stem, clitoral hood, Niche, urethra, Skene's glands, vaginal ball, Bartholin's glands and V-Spot**) move up and down with you - slowly moving at first so as to generate some wetness that will facilitate your going faster. (*With your palm*, you should do *wide circles*, which are easier to do. Again, *press against her to move as much skin and as many **hot spots** as you can*.) Pay close attention to her feedback with everything you do and latch onto whatever produces a big reaction; repeat it rhythmically (perhaps speeding up a bit to send her over the top) and she should **come** like mad.

The second type of **Vulva Orgasm Massage Technique** I recommend is my **Vulva Vibrations Massage Method.** This is great just for getting her super-hot if you want to send her into a frenzy - or for giving her **the Big O.** Here, you slip three or four fingers (*not* the thumb) between her **labia minora**, so they're deep enough to rest inside her **vestibule** (see "Introducing New Orgasm Triggers" on page 194 if you need a refresher on its location) - placing your lowest finger (your ring finger or pinky) within the **V** of her **V-Spot**. Then, slowly and tenderly *waggle your fingers back and forth quickly and lightly,* until she gets **wet**. Use that **wetness** to enable you to move a bit faster, with greater ease, speeding up to the level that provokes the biggest rise out of her. The idea is to make her feel as if that area is being **vibrated vigorously** - a great feeling that produces unique **orgasms**.

Killer U-Zone Techniques

*One way to impress her while sending her through the roof is by artfully massaging the **multiple erogenous zone (MEZ)** area containing her **U-Spot, Niche, urethra** and **Skene's glands** during intercourse.* In fact, the techniques I'm about to suggest sometimes also include *a very sensitive tiny patch of skin directly below her* **urethra**, *between her **Skene's glands**, which we'll call her **sub-U**.*

We'll call this **MEZ** her **U-Zone**, since you can cover and stimulate *all* of its various **hot spots** with one finger (or your **glans** if you prefer) *at the same time*. This **zone** is a great **orgasm booster** and **female ejaculation trigger** that - in *conjunction* with an **orgasm trigger** - can help set off *big, juicy* **multiple orgasms**, accompanied by great gushing **female ejaculation**.

Skene's glands
clitoris
Niche
U-Spot
urethra
sub-U
Bartholin's glands

Quick Pressure Point Orgasm Techniques

Incredibly enough - if you already made her very hot, sometimes all you need to do is to *press* a **large finger** (your **middle finger** or **thumb**) or the **head** of your **cock** over the entire **U-Zone** and she might **come** and **ejaculate** within *seconds* with a *flood* of juices.

This is what I call a **pressure point orgasm technique**. You can produce even more reliably quick **pressure point orgasms** with her **Perineal sponge, Nook, vaginal ball** and **G-spot**. *I discovered* **pressure point orgasms** *on my own and they're known by so few that you're sure to blow her mind by giving her one*. I'll give you other ways to produce them in a minute.

...Another way to produce **female ejaculation:** Insistently rub back and forth, in a *short horizontal line*, **from one Skene's gland duct to the other, over her sub-U**. Start with a slow pace. That might be all you need.

Her **U-Zone** as an **orgasm booster:** Touching anywhere within her **U-Zone** - even *without moving* - while also working her **clit** will instantly boost her **sensitivity** and resultant **climax**. Or *rub along* the **outline** of her **U-Spot** while stimulating her **clit**. That should set off a **big orgasm**!

HER BOTTOM - FOR DOUBLE-PENETRATION AND MORE

Now to perhaps the most exciting **multitasking** *method ever (IF she's into it). It's through* **double-penetration***. She'll get the* **biggest orgasms** *in this way.*

Most women like it because it fulfills a fantasy of being made love to by two men. The very best way to do it is by stimulating her **anal canal** *with a finger during* **vaginal penetration** *with your* **cock***. That drives most women* wild!

The deeper you go, the better. And **wiggling** is the **finger motion** that seems to produce the *quickest* and *biggest* **orgasms** - although the old **in and out** also works. See what she likes best. (FYI: Be sure to wash your **finger** before touching her elsewhere afterward because of the risk of **infection**.)

Now if you or she is squeamish about doing that, try simply tickling her **anal ring** *during* **penetration***.* That will set off her climax more quickly and powerfully. You can do it from the outside or poke a finger into it gently, to make *shallow circles* inside her **anal canal**.

Or you can engage that **orgasm booster** instead by separating her **butt cheeks** with your hands during sex (or you could open and close them repeatedly, perhaps *rhythmically*). This will indirectly open her **anal canal**. And *opening any sexual opening creates titillating sensations*. These will often send her over the top.

Now it goes without saying that, aside from **multitasking** with her **anal region** during **penetration**, you can of course focus on that region *alone* to give her thrills. And that's true of the other techniques I'm about to show you. These can be done before, during or after penetrative intercourse.

The Art of Loving Touching

INTRODUCING THE NICHE TICKLE ORGASM TECHNIQUE

Mention doing **fingerwork** during *sex* and I'm sure most men would immediately think you're talking about tickling a woman's **clitoris**. But you'd be denying her a lot of big thrills if you ignored her other great **erogenous zones**. And one reason great lovemakers are valued so much is that they know how to push all their lover's buttons.

Within her **U-Zone**, for instance, her **Niche** can bring on **orgasms** in and of itself. I told you in the *anatomy chapter* that you can tickle or massage the **stem** and **glans** of her **clitoris** indirectly, from *below* her **clit,** to make her come. You do that with her **Niche** and here's how *(I call this method* the **Niche Tickle Orgasm Technique)**:

Place your index or middle finger inside the crevice of her **Niche.** As I mentioned in the anatomy chapter, it's probably no more than ¼" to ½" deep.

Now do a rhythmic and persistent "come here" outward stroking of the end of her **stem** *and* **glans** *through her* **Niche,** *with a* **moderate pace.** *You should push upward from below so her* **stem** *and* **glans** *are engaged with every stroke. (You should be able to feel them through the thin skin that you're manipulating.) This should bring her to a rousing climax fairly quickly, depending on how hot you got her before attempting it.*

THE NOOK PRESS FOR AN INCREDIBLY QUICK ORGASM

Another **sweet spot** most men totally ignore can produce *the quickest and sloppy-wettest of* **orgasms**. And the technique you'll use, the **Nook Press**, is yet another **pressure point orgasm technique**. *(See the* **Nook** *on page 194.)*

It's so easy to produce it's almost a crime. Simply insert your index and middle fingers (or just your middle finger) slowly within her **Nook** and press down on its bottom. Exert continuous medium pressure, with intensity, while keeping the tips of your fingers engaged on her, motionless.

She's likely to come within seconds of your doing this if you do it correctly - if she's sensitive in that location. A great flood of juices is likely to accompany this kind of **orgasm**. If she doesn't respond in this way, try rubbing your fingers along the ridge that you'll find at the bottom of her **Nook** or wiggling your fingers inside that cavity.

The awesome thing about this is that you can give her this **climax** quickly, from the get-go, without prior priming! One of my lovers excitedly explained after first experiencing a **Nook Press orgasm**: *"I orgasmed without being aroused! It was a very different feeling than I've ever had!"*

A Woman In Ecstasy

As I mentioned in the anatomy chapter, though, her **Nook** *is a* **special case orgasm trigger** *and should best be used occasionally, to not wear out its novelty, which is key to its effect.*

The Titillating *V-Spot Massage*

And there's another little-known **erogenous zone** near the **Nook** with which you can thrill her no end. In the anatomy chapter, I told you how your lover's **V-Spot** could be a **wetness trigger** if massaged correctly. Here, you'll learn how. (See page 192 to review where the **V-Spot** is located.)

One way to do so is simply by running a **finger** or your **tongue** over the top *V* of **skin**. Another way is to press this **skin** between your **thumb** and **index finger** and gently pull up - either *stretching* and holding it in place or *pulling* up and down *rhythmically*. Or better, try this method, which I call the **V-Spot Massage**: rub the top *V* of skin between your **index finger** and **thumb** (the skin is so thin you'll *feel* each of your fingers through it), moving your thumb in small circles, with moderate pressure. *That will drive her crazy!*

The *Perineal Pinch* - For Quick Dramatic Results

And here's another **pressure point orgasm technique** for a **hot spot** just below the **V-Spot** that's great for producing **female ejaculation** *and* **orgasms** *in seconds (believe it or not)!* I call this method the **Perineal Pinch**.

Here, you place your thumb on the outside of her **perineum** (the covering skin at the bottom of her vulva) and your forefinger on the inside (atop what scientists call her **perineal sponge**), toward the *bottom* - where this thin flap of skin connects with her body. (See page 193 if you've forgotten where her **perineum** is.)

Now gently *pinch* the **perineum,** using just enough pressure so that you can feel your forefinger with your thumb, through the membrane. Then rub or massage your fingers together - keeping in mind that the most *sexually reactive* part of it is on the *inside*. You can either repeatedly pull up on that thin flap of skin (in a stretching motion) or make circles. If you do this well, she's likely to go through the roof, *coming* and **ejaculating** like you wouldn't believe!

The Vaginal Ball & Bartholin's Glands Wetness Technique

Now as I mentioned earlier in this book, **female ejaculation** does <u>not</u> produce the **slippery kind of wetness** that's a *helpful* **lubricant** for sex. To produce the useful *slippery* kind, nothing beats the **Vaginal Ball Wetness Technique**. And it's quite simple to do! (If you need to refresh your memory as to where her **vaginal ball** is, refer back to page 193.)

Just take a finger or two and either rub her **vaginal ball's surface** - with back and forth motions or in small circles - or make big circles around the entire ball, making sure to include her **Bartholin's glands ducts** on the lower end of your circles (her **Bartholin's glands** help produce the **mucous-based slippery lubrication** you desire during sex). Use moderate pressure and think in terms of massaging the skin. You can also choose to take her **vaginal ball** between your **index** and **middle fingers** (at the top) and **thumb** (at the bottom) and **squeeze, knead or massage** it by bringing your fingers together in the middle and then starting all over again.

If done with the proper *finesse* and *sensuality (that is, not like you're a doctor giving her a medical exam)*, large amounts of **slippery lubrication** should quickly anoint your fingers - helping to make her ready for **penetration**. Some women can also **come** in this way. So consider her **vaginal ball** a **special case orgasm trigger** and try to make her **come** with it!

...Want to *turbocharge* the **Vaginal Ball Wetness Technique**? Slip your finger into her **Nook** while doing it and, pressing your nail against her **perineal sponge**, massage both her **vaginal ball** and **perineal sponge** or **V-Spot**. That will produce a *quick* and dramatically *wet* **orgasm**!

Knock-Her-Socks-Off G-Spot Techniques

Even better - if you want to make her **wet** and **wide** *quickly*, ready for your entrance, nothing beats her **G-Spot** for **fast slippery lubrication** and even **powerful** and **rapid-fire multiple orgasms** - if you know how to "milk" this *awesome* **gland**. If you get good enough, in fact, all you have to do is touch it to produce results.

I'll give you *seven* different ways to drive her wild with her **G-Spot** (every woman will have her own favorite):

G-Spot Orgasm Technique #1: This is the easiest, physically, but you must arouse her beforehand and do it with the right sexy attitude (**not** like an examining physician). It's one of the **pressure point orgasm techniques** I've discovered. I call it **the G-Spot Press Technique**. All you do is take the tips of your **index** and **middle fingers** and press them up against the innermost end of her **G-Spot** with moderate pressure - enough that you can feel her **pubic bone** behind her **G-Spot**. Simultaneously, spread the *length* of your fingers *over her entire* **G-Spot** - *with intense but not painful pressure*. Keep this up until she **comes** - which shouldn't take too long (figure 10-30 seconds). She'll think you're *incredible*. Never fails to impress.

G-Spot Orgasm Technique #2: G-Spot Pulsations. Similar to #1, but here you press on her **G-Spot** with a **pulsating rhythm** - slowly at first, then speeding up, befitting her reactions (hold the pace steady once she starts going crazy).

G-Spot Orgasm Technique #3: This makes her **come** and *really* **wet!** It's what I call **the G-Spot Wiggle Technique**. Here you insert your index and middle fingers so the tips are just beyond the reaches of the **G-Spot,** inside her canal, curled up towards the **G-Spot**. Then vigorously wiggle them back and forth, touching her **G-Spot** on the up-stroke and the *opposite* **vaginal wall** on the down-stroke, until she comes. Start slowly and build in pace. (Press *firmly* on her **G-Spot** on the up-stroke.) This is a killer technique that really wows most women.

G-Spot Orgasm Technique #4: Tickle her **G-Spot** into submission (so to speak) with what I've named the **"Come Here" G-Spot Technique**. You do this by touching the end of her **G-Spot** with the fingertips of your curled index and middle fingers, and then doing "come here" motions or quick lines across the body of the organ. The motion should always and only be **toward you**, and it needs to be done in a *regular rhythm* - even if slowly sped up. This can be done with light to strong pressure, depending on your mood and her preferences.

G-Spot Orgasm Technique #5: G-Spot Circles. Make *insistent circles* around the outside edges of her **G-Spot**, either with *three fingers* (your *ring, middle and index fingers*), *two fingers* (your *index and middle fingers*) or *just your middle finger*. Press *firmly* when doing this. This is the hardest to pull off, physically, but it's worth trying. Again - do it with a **regular rhythm**, even if you pause in between circles or choose to speed it up eventually.

G-Spot Orgasm Technique #6: The G-Spot Tease. Slowly squeeze your middle finger into her **vaginal canal** and stop just beyond her **G-Spot**, pressing the length of your finger against its body, with moderate pressure. Then, as if you're a snake that's been spooked, pull it out quickly - while *maintaining* the same **finger pressure** on her **G-Spot**. Repeat and speed up until she comes.

G-Spot Orgasm Technique #7: Killer G-Spot Crunches. If you can fit your middle finger into her during **penetration** (in a **sideways,** *preferably,* or **front-entry position**) slip it into her **vaginal canal**, upside down, above your **cock**, so the pad of your finger rests on the farthest end of her **G-Spot**. Press *the rest of your finger flat against that egg-shaped organ* with **moderate to strong pressure**. Now either **wiggle your finger** or do **rhythmic pulsations** on her **G-Spot**, *pressing firmly against it on your finger's up-strokes*. Ideally, you want to *move your* **cock** *in concert with your finger;* but move only *very slightly* in and out - just enough to give her the *perception* of motion. If you can pull this off (some **vaginal canals** are smaller than others and your finger won't fit), you will completely send her through the roof! One girlfriend breathlessly told me afterward: "It was **so** intense!"

THE CLITORAL BODY MASSAGE ORGASM TECHNIQUE

Now once you're ready to touch her **clitoris** - which, most times, should be well into the sexual process - you don't need to be predictable about it, going straight for its *head* for direct stimulation. As I mentioned in the *anatomy* chapter, massaging her **clitoral body** through the **hood** can be *very exciting* to her. In fact, you should be able to make her **come** that way.

Here's a method to accomplish that. I call it the **Clitoral Body Massage Orgasm Technique**. To do this: *Gently* place your thumb and index finger on either side of her **clitoral hood**. Start by rubbing your fingers slowly back and forth along the sides of her *hood* (your fingers will go in *opposite* directions). See how she reacts. *Continue* this if she gives you good feedback. If what you're doing doesn't seem to get her aroused, move on to the **hood pull**.

With the **hood pull**, you tenderly pull her **clitoral hood** back and forth, using your index finger and thumb. You should stretch the hood on the back stroke as far as it can go - without becoming painful. You'll see her **clitoral glans** pop out when you're reaching the limits of your **hood pull**.

Gauge her reaction. Choose a *rhythm* and *intensity* by her feedback. *If something you do gets her hot big time, repeat it over and over again.*

THE CLITORAL RING ORGASM TECHNIQUE

You learned earlier that your lover's **clitoris** is surrounded by a sensitive **clitoral ring** of flesh (for a refresher, see "Introducing The Clitoral Ring" on page 205). And you can use this **ring** to give her **huge orgasms**.

In doing fingerwork, you have a choice of any number of patterns. But the *circle* is one of the most effective. And *the rim* of the **clitoral ring** *facilitates your making circles!*

Simply follow the outline of its shape while pressing the pad of your finger simultaneously onto her **clitoris**! Start off slowly and build up to a moderate **pace** and **pressure**. It shouldn't take very long before she's coming like mad.

EXTREME CLITORAL ORGASM TECHNIQUES: SORRENTO & THE CLIT SHAKE

Now what I'm about to teach you is not for all women. Some women's

clits are too sensitive for it. But here are two incredibly popular and effective **extreme clitoral orgasm techniques** you should try when you're ready to make her come, which we'll call the **Sorrento technique** and **the clit shake technique**:

Some necessary background on the **Sorrento technique**: Years ago, I was a guitarist at a swanky nightclub, backing an Italian crooner who sang the famous operatic Neapolitan song "Torna a Surriento" ("Come Back to Sorrento") every night. That song required me to do an extremely fast back and forth style of strumming.

Well, after one of those gigs one night, in bed - as an inside *joke* (for my own amusement) - I got the inspiration to use a modified version of that strumming technique on my girlfriend's **vulva** and **clitoris.** *Holy cow! The neighbors must have heard her coming many blocks away! That quickly became her favorite way to come* **clitorally**. So here's how you do what I decided to call the **Sorrento technique**:

Orienting your fingers along the vertical line of her **vulva**, take your *index and middle fingers* and **wiggle them quickly and intensely back and forth** - but don't let them travel very far in either direction. (Imagine you're strumming *one guitar string*.) The idea is to create a *vibration* kind of effect. (Tip: If you have trouble keeping this up, try using your *thumb* to *support* both fingers - placing your thumb on the **pads** of those fingers.)

The trick is to then bring your fingers just close enough to her **clit** (or the surrounding tissue - to the left or right, or above or below it), so you can apply the technique *lightly*. (You can experiment with stronger pressures if you like, but that might be too intense for her.) You might also want to wet your fingers with *saliva* or *oil* beforehand, to make this work best.

Lubrication would not work for the second **extreme clitoral orgasm technique** I want to share with you, though. Here you want to grab hold of the skin on either side of her clitoris, to move her clit and the area surrounding in tandem, *together* - quickly, either **back and forth** (up and down, or, more easily, to the right and left) or **in circles**. You can choose either to do this by holding her **clitoris** between your **thumb** *on one side* and your **index and middle fingers** *on the other*; or by shaking her **clit** only *indirectly*, through the moving of the flesh surrounding it (avoiding touching her **clit** *directly*). If you're shaking her **clit** indirectly, you'll need to press the skin you want to shake by *pressing it against her body* such that it moves along with your fingers *and* takes her **clitoris** along with it.

The motion is very similar to what you'd use to wipe off a small spot on a window with a wet towel, only faster. Experiment with the placement

The Art of Loving Touching

of your fingers and the range of motion she responds to best.

Now, a word of warning: **the clit shake technique** requires *vigorous* and, sometimes, *protracted* hand, wrist and arm motion, so only attempt this if your muscles can keep this up for some time. Speaking of which, with both **the Sorrento** and the **clit shake techniques,** set a *comfortable* pace. It should be one you can continue for quite some time in case she doesn't come *quickly*. Otherwise, you'll tire and she'll become frustrated if you have to slow down or give up entirely.

CRANBERRY TWISTS AND SHAKES

Two less intense variations of **the clit shake technique** are worth trying with a woman whose **clitoris** is not overly *sensitive*. (Some women can find these variants too intense to bear.) I call these methods the **cranberry twist** and **cranberry shake techniques**.

You start both techniques in the same way - by gently taking her **clitoris** between your **thumb** *on one side* and your **index and middle fingers** *on the other* and **pull up** *very slightly* so you can feel a small part of her **clitoral stem** (behind the **glans**) between your fingers. Then, to do **cranberry twists**, gently and every so slightly turn her **clitoris** one way and then the other (like you're turning the dial on a radio). If she likes it, do it repeatedly and as quickly as she can take it. To do **cranberry shakes**, shake her **clit** and **stem** *delicately*, *very slowly* and *with a very constricted range of motion*. Be sure she likes what you're doing before you try to make her come this way.

MORE GREAT OPPORTUNITIES TO TITILLATE & AROUSE

There are many other ways to give your lover "good vibrations" through **artful fingerwork** - one of which is through **sexual teasing**. And I think Chrissie Hynde of the Pretenders schooled us in that with the sexy lyrics to "Brass in Pocket":

*Gonna use my **arms**, Gonna use my **legs**,*
Gonna use my style, Gonna use my sidestep
*Gonna use my **fingers**, Gonna use my, my, my imagination...*

Sexual teasing is not something only women should do. And **loving touching** is not just about touching her with your **hands**. So don't forget to use your **arms, legs, feet, chest and other body parts** for *teasing*, too (I gave you a few suggestions on doing that in the section, "Her Multiple Erogenous Zones For The Biggest Fireworks" on page 267)! And use your **imagination! Be creative!**

The cool thing is that it doesn't take much to get your lover eager for sex once you know how to use your fingers and other body parts. Here are some interesting ways to do that:

THE EROTIC LIP SPREADING TECHNIQUE

Early on in a sexual encounter, your primary goal is to **arouse** her as well as make her **wet** and **wide.** (You do *not* usually want to make her **come** right away.) Well, guess what? Fingerwork's great for that purpose, too.

In the *anatomy* chapter I showed you that your lover's **clitoris** is a large organ whose **bulbs** extend down along the sides of her outer **vaginal walls**. Maybe that explains why, at the outset of sex, you can make your lover groan with pleasure with a method I call the **Erotic Lip Spreading Technique. This is a great technique for both the wettening and arousal processes.** To do this:

Put your fingers inside her **vagina** *at the center; now delicately and slowly spread her* **vaginal walls** *apart. The* way *you do this is important, though. Do it sensuously. (Not like you're giving her a gynecological exam!) Do it as if you've just made the most incredible discovery. Or do it to give her a sense of anticipation of your entering her - as if you're relishing that thought.*

Hold her lips apart for a short while. Then gently increase the width of the now-gaping hole until it's as wide as it can comfortably get (without causing pain). Maintain the tension for some time (you can also do pulsating contraction-like movements or other creative moves as you like).

Do this until her reactions grow less intense, as they inevitably will (I'll talk about this "plateau" phenomenon in a later chapter). Doing this definitely will stimulate the **clitoral bulbs,** *even if indirectly. Great for getting her wet and wide.*

MORE FUN WITH HER PUSSY LIPS

Three more great ways to get her **wet** and **hot** with her **labia minora** (which as you might recall, are biologically similar to the skin of your scrotum):

The gentle stretch: Taking both **labia minora** between your index fingers and thumbs, tenderly *stretch them away from her body* (but not so much as to cause pain, of course). You can also *massage* and *stroke* them in their stretched-out state. Or simply apply a little *pressure* on them.

The velvet touch technique: Taking both **labia minora** between your index fingers and thumbs, *stroke them as if you're admiring the softness of a piece of velvet.* This will excite her no end!

Inner circles: Separating her **labia minora**, *make circles* around their **inner rims** with one or two fingers. (FYI: This can be done during **oral sex** or while tickling her **clit**, as an **orgasm booster**.)

The Art of Loving Touching

By the way, the **gentle stretch** and **velvet touch techniques** work great as **orgasm boosters** if you can manage to do them during **penetration**. (Yet another fantastic way to **multitask**.)

USING HER MOUND TO GOOD EFFECT

In the **anatomy** chapter I suggested you not neglect her **mons pubis** or **mound**. (See "Her Oft-Neglected Mound" on page 205 for a refresher. For its location, see page 193.) Because it's a **pleasure zone** worth exploring.

In my experience, it's a great place to *massage* in the early stages of the **arousal process**. It can help get her excited in that it can *indirectly* move her more sensitive parts below, making her anticipate your touching those.

I was told by one lover many years ago that she'd been made to come by a prior lover, simply using his palm on her **mound**. I've never been able to reproduce that event but I thought I'd mention it just in case you wanted to give it a try. Here's what I recommend:

In manipulating her **mound**, gently but dramatically stretch it upward so it stretches her **vulva** upward during whatever massage strokes you choose to do. That moves her most sensitive places in a wonderfully erotic way. At the very least, I have found that this helps make a woman **hot** and **hungry for more**, early on in the sexual process. It's a good way to **tease** her.

EVEN SMALL GESTURES CAN PRODUCE DESIRABLE RESULTS

So, as you've seen, loving touching is not just about grand techniques that impress her. It's also about simple titillations.

One last pointer along these lines:

A woman gets a special thrill when you remove her panties and expose her privates. So when you strip her panties off, do it with a sense of drama, to enhance her titillation. Do it slowly and sensually - as if you've been given a gift too delicate to open quickly; with a "what have we here" excitement.

The point is, once you harness the **sexual power** *you can possess by mastering the art of* **love touching***, the opportunities to please your lover and make your love life together more exciting are almost endless!*

> "Because Everyone Loves Breasts"
> - the caption below a photo on a blog by feminist sexpert Carlin Ross, showing a chimp groping a bikini clad babe's breast

Breast Orgasms, The M Spot & More

☯

*I*n my late teens, I made an *amazing sexual discovery*. I was in bed with a lovely young woman who said I'd pleased her in every other way but *one*.

"What do you mean?" I said, feeling badly I'd let her down in any way.

"Well," she began shyly, "one of my boyfriends was able to make me *come* by sucking my nipples and I *really* liked that. Can you do that too?"

Honestly, I didn't know if I could or could not. *I wasn't aware at the time that you could give a woman **orgasms** by manipulating her **breasts** or **nipples**. I'd never heard of or read about such a thing before.* But instead of being hurt or insulted by the suggestion, I took her question as a *challenge*.

"Well, I'll certainly try!" I replied.

Within a month I came up with a way do it. And since then, I've developed *numerous other ways* to give just about *every* woman *incredibly powerful* **breast induced climaxes**. (I even found a *previously unknown* **orgasm trigger** within the **breast**, which I'll reveal to you shortly!)

That's right! A skilled lover can make a woman **come** by stimulating her **breasts** expertly. A woman's **nipple-areola complex** and their **inner glandular connections** are **special case orgasm triggers**.

I anticipate a day when women everywhere will *expect* their lovers to know how to give them **breast-induced orgasms**. Then, all men will be measured by their ability to produce these.

To date, though, few men seem to know about **breast-induced orgasms**, based upon the scarcity of information out there. So: a) your lover's unlikely to have experienced them; and, b) you'll really blow her mind when you

Breast Orgasms, The M Spot & More

show her what you can do with her breasts! Plus, these strong **orgasms** will *shake her to the core* and likely bring on a *gush of love juices* if not **female ejaculation** as well. So: *do this and you'll score points, big time.*

The **breast-induced orgasm** is a *genuine biological phenomenon*. It was given scientific credence by a major university study published in October 2011. See page 294 for more on that. But first, some essential anatomical info:

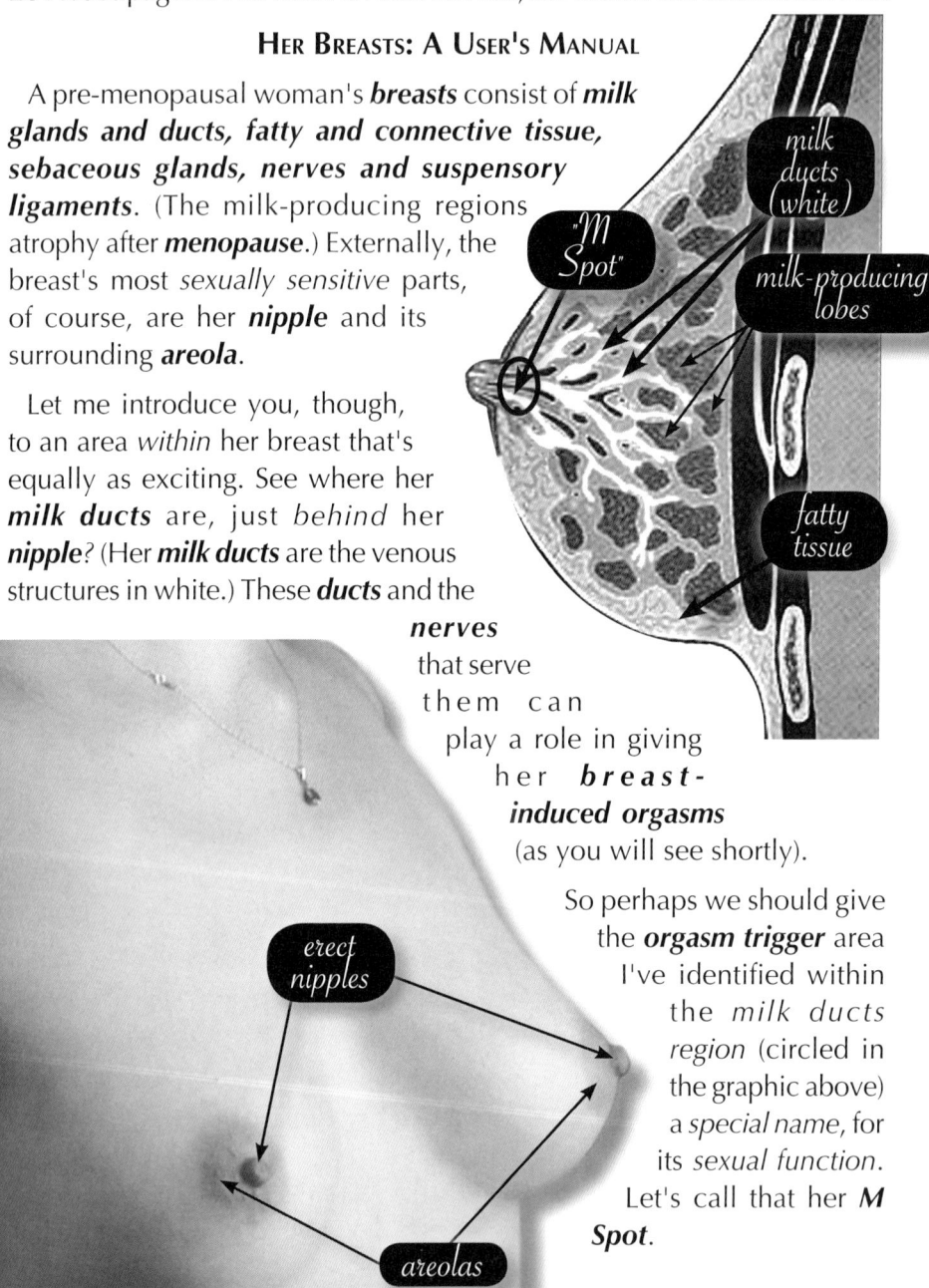

Her Breasts: A User's Manual

A pre-menopausal woman's **breasts** consist of **milk glands and ducts, fatty and connective tissue, sebaceous glands, nerves and suspensory ligaments**. (The milk-producing regions atrophy after **menopause**.) Externally, the breast's most *sexually sensitive* parts, of course, are her **nipple** and its surrounding **areola**.

Let me introduce you, though, to an area *within* her breast that's equally as exciting. See where her **milk ducts** are, just *behind* her **nipple**? (Her **milk ducts** are the venous structures in white.) These **ducts** and the **nerves** that serve them can play a role in giving her **breast-induced orgasms** (as you will see shortly).

So perhaps we should give the **orgasm trigger** area I've identified within the *milk ducts region* (circled in the graphic above) a *special name*, for its *sexual function*. Let's call that her **M Spot**.

On Loving Women

FYI: Her **areolas** (the ring of colored flesh around her **nipples**) undoubtedly have *pimply bumps* on them but don't worry or get turned off by them. They're not pimples or abnormalities. They're **Montgomery tubercles**, part of the **Glands of Montgomery**, which emit oily secretions to help protect the surface of the **nipple** and **areola**. I have no proof, but if they're like her other sexual glands, they undoubtedly are sensitive to the touch - so give them some attention.

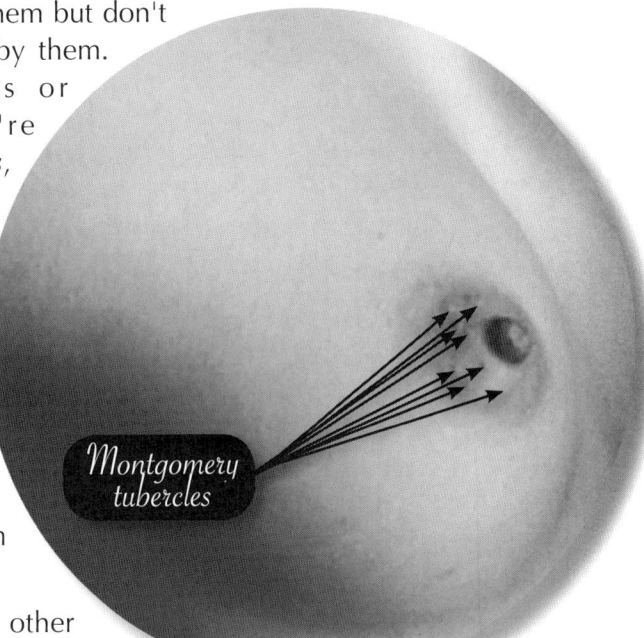

Montgomery tubercles

Now, like most of her other **erogenous zones**, a woman's **breasts** (not just her **nipples**) *swell* with sexual stimulation. So the mere act of touching them sensuously will give her much the same kind of *pleasure* that you experience when you get an *erection*. (You won't be able to *see* her **breasts** grow, though. Your only visual cue will be her pointed **erect nipples**.)

However, the unique pleasure a woman gets from this *increase in breast size* and *hardening of her nipples* occurs only at the *onset* of sexual activity (if your act of *seduction* did not produce this effect already). That pleasurable feeling will fade quickly once she experiences more intense sensations with your stimulation of her most sensitive **erogenous zones**.

*So it's a good general rule to make the most of **breast massaging**, manipulation, (gentle) squeezing, holding and fondling at the <u>start</u> of the sexual process.*

This approach works well, anyway, in helping along the **seduction process**. In delaying touching the parts she most urgently wants you to touch - namely her **areola** and **nipple** areas - you heighten her sense of **anticipation** which, as I've mentioned before, results in getting her **hotter**.

So early on, go *small*. Brush your chest against her **nipples**. Cup her **breasts** tenderly. In fact, one lover said to me, "it gets me excited to see you touching my breasts." *Play on that unique excitement.*

Breast Orgasms, The M Spot & More

KEEP THEM HARD

And, speaking of teasing, a smart lover keeps an eye on his lover's **nipples** throughout the sex act, making sure to keep them **hard** at all times. When they're **erect**, it's confirmation that you're keeping her hot *to the max*.

But more important, an **erect nipple** is *super sensitive*. It sends tingles down her nerves, impulses that in turn help make her **vagina** *wet and wide*, as well as help bring on her **orgasm**.

Plus, you undoubtedly know just how good it feels when your nipples are hard. So *keep that good feeling going in her*.

Interestingly enough, nipple erections are more akin to goose pimples than a swollen gland. They're produced by muscle contractions, not blood.

THE GREAT VARIABILITY IN BREASTS

Now I noted earlier that every woman is different and that you cannot assume that what pleases Mary pleases Jane. Well that's *especially* true when it comes to a woman's *breasts* - that is, from the lover's point of view.

I'm not referring to their endlessly variable *sizes* and *shapes*. That's an aesthetic matter. What I'm referring to is their **sexual sensitivity** and **a woman's preferences** when it comes to **how she would like you to stimulate them** and the **amount of time** she'd like you to devote to them.

Even more crucial - what it takes to make a woman come by stimulating her breasts varies greatly from woman to woman (and not all women can achieve a **breast-induced orgasm** *by the way). The pinpoint location that triggers a* **breast-induced orgasm** *and the type of stimulation it takes to produce it differs from woman to woman. (FYI: Some call* **breast-induced orgasms** *"nipple orgasms" but it's a bit more complex than that. As I noted before, her* **M Spot** *might have a crucial role in setting these off, not the* **nipple**. *In addition, some scientists believe* **breast-induced orgasms** *are actually genitally based; in other words, they might not be* **breast-centered**, *but* **breast-triggered vaginal, uterine or clitoral orgasms**. *At least one of my girlfriends said she felt* **uterine contractions** *when I gave her* **breast-induced orgasms**, *so maybe there's something to this debate.)*

As with everything else in the sexual realm, it will take some *experimentation* on your part to find out what techniques work best on your lover's **breasts**. So let's look at the wide range of possibilities so you can find exactly what rings your lover's bells.

WHERE IS SHE ON THE SENSITIVITY SPECTRUM?

The first thing you need to do is to determine where your lover falls on

the sensitivity scale. This will tell you how much pressure to use.

That is, *are her nipples super-sensitive to your touch,* possibly experiencing pain at times, depending on how much stimulation you apply? *Or are they on the other end of the scale - rather insensitive or numb to your touch,* making it hard to excite her? *Or is she somewhere in between?*

Overly *sensitive* **nipples** require a lot of *delicacy*. You'll need to apply only *light pressure* in sucking or squeezing them. You'll need to use *slow* speeds and rhythms in flicking her **nipple** with your **tongue** or **fingers**.

On the other extreme, a woman whose **nipples** don't respond very much to your touch might require *intense pressure* in sucking or squeezing them, for her to feel pleasure. She might even like light *biting* (but of course be very careful not to cause injury). She'll probably like fairly *extreme stretching* (pulling up on the **nipple**) too, not to mention *fast* rhythms.

WHAT CAN CAUSE BREASTS TO BE LESS SENSITIVE?

There are several factors that might make a woman's **breasts** *less* sensitive to the touch than is normal. The *amount of glandular vs. fatty tissue they have* can affect how sensitive a woman's breasts are. So can the *size* of a woman's breasts, a woman's age, *changes that come with pregnancy and menopause,* breast *sagging,* and *surgery* (such as **breast** *augmentation* - as in the use of *implants* - and **breast** *reduction* procedures).

It's been my experience that women with *large* **breasts** tend to have less sensitivity in their **nipples**, **areolas** and **M Spots** than those with *small to medium sized ones*. And in 1998, researchers at the University of Vienna (Tairych, Kuzbari, Rigel, Todoroff, Schneider, and Deutinger) seemed to confirm my theory. They concluded that there is an *inverse* relationship between **breast** size and *sensitivity:*

> "The cutaneous sensibility of all tested areas decreased significantly with increasing breast size and increasing breast ptosis [sagging]."

They also said: "The nipple was less sensitive in women who had a previous pregnancy."

Sexologist Rachel Ross, MD, PhD was among those who agreed with the study's conclusions. Her explanation for why this might be true appeared in the *Cosmopolitan* article, "The A-Cup Revolution:"

> "Larger breasts have more fatty tissue than glandular tissue, which is the most sensitive part. With smaller breasts, the glands are easier to stimulate during foreplay because they're not underneath a fatty layer."

The study's use of *Semmes-Weinstein monofilaments* in testing sensitivity later came into question. But its conclusions were supported by a Johns Hopkins Hospital and Medical Center study in 2002 (by Mofid, Dellon, Elias, and Nahabedian) using *computer-assisted neurosensory testing*. They also confirmed my contention that *women vary greatly in* **breast sensitivity**:

> "Several findings from previous studies using Semmes-Weinstein monofilament testing were confirmed in unoperated controls, including an inverse relationship between sensitivity and breast size, superior nipple sensitivity when compared with the areola, and significant interpatient variability with respect to static and moving two-point discrimination among women matched according to age and breast size."

What This Means To You

So now you know you're likely to need to be more ginger about applying pressure to a **smaller breast** than you would to a *larger* one. Conversely, you now know you probably need to be more intense in whatever you do to a **large breast** than you would to a small one. In other words - **lighter touching, sucking, stretching and manipulating** likely will work best for the **nipples**, **areolas** and **M Spots** of **smaller-breasted women**, whereas more intense stimulation likely will work best for larger-breasted women.

At one extreme you will find that *some* women with **small breasts** will experience *pain* with the *slightest* of touches. At the other extreme, you will find that some women with large breasts prefer incredibly strong squeezing and never seem to feel pain, even with extreme stretching and pinching; they might even like moderate *biting*.

Lower sensitivity is also frequently a factor among older women, women who have experienced menopause (because the **milk glands**

On Loving Women

atrophy, among other reasons), and among women who have had breast *augmentation, reduction and lift* procedures. So they are also likely to need more from you in the way of intensity to produce pleasure.

THE BREASTS OF WOMEN WHO HAVE HAD SURGERY

Speaking of which, there are many reasons a woman might want to have surgical procedures on their **breasts** and that's their prerogative. And if your lover has had **implants** or **breast reduction** or a lift job, your love for her and interest in her sexually should not be reduced if these operations made her **breasts** less responsive to your touch.

However, if your lover has not had such surgery, you might *not* want to encourage her to do so. You should be aware that breast operations come with *risks* - aside from the likely reduction in sensitivity.

And I don't know about you, but I'd rather have a woman with highly responsive breasts than one with less responsive breasts, given the choice. I'm not hung up on the size of a lover's breasts because to me the excitement comes from how she reacts to my touch.

So I feel the need to pass along some information to you, so you can make an educated choice if you're ever in the position to voice your opinion on a lover's decision whether or not to have surgery.

First, you need to visit the FDA's site on the risks associated with breast *implants*. There they warn, among things:

- **Breast implants are not lifetime devices**; the longer you have your implants, the more likely it will be for you to have them removed.
- The longer you have breast implants, the more likely you are to experience local **complications** and adverse outcomes.
- The most common local complications and adverse outcomes are capsular contracture, reoperation and implant removal. Other complications include rupture or deflation, wrinkling, asymmetry, scarring, pain, and infection at the incision site.
- You should assume that you will need to have additional surgeries

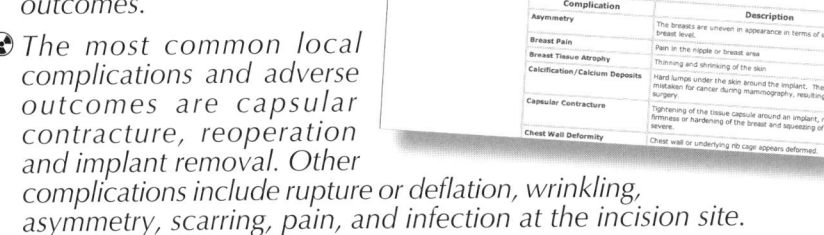

285

(reoperations).

☢ Many of the changes to your breast following implantation may be cosmetically undesirable and irreversible.

If your lover is considering a *breast reduction procedure*, she should visit the web site of the British Association of Aesthetic Plastic Surgeons that in all honesty warns:

- "All of them will involve a **scar** around the areola of the breast."
- **Scars**: "...they will always be present and visible when clothing is not worn and the scars will vary from one woman to another. In some they may be very thin, in others they may stretch and become quite red and possibly ugly."
- "Very few women are able to breast feed following breast reduction surgery as the **nipples are separated from the underlying milk ducts.**"
- "The **nipples are likely to be very much less sensitive following surgery** due to the nature of the cuts and the **nerve** supply and it is quite possible that numbness will extend over part of the breast as well."

The San Francisco Plastic Surgery And Laser Center web site is equally honest:

"Many women who are considering a breast augmentation, reduction or lift are often concerned about how the surgery will affect their **nipple sensitivity**. For some people, breast surgery leads to lost or reduced sensation in the nipples. However, **for others it causes the nipple and areola area to become more sensitive, sometimes to the point of pain**. Usually these changes are temporary, lasting from a matter of weeks to a few years, but sometimes they can be permanent. It all depends on what happened to the **nerves** during surgery.

"Plastic surgeons take great care to protect the nerves found in the breast during any cosmetic procedure. Unfortunately, sometimes nerve pathways are impaired or damaged."

The Marina Plastic Surgery Associates (of Marina del Ray, California) web site is similarly sanguine about the risks of breast reduction surgery:

"It has the same basic side effects as any surgical procedure, and the **nipples can be less sensitive afterwards**."

A University of Brussels study in 2001 (conducted by Hamdi, Greuse, De Mey, and Webster) was even more pessimistic about the affect of **breast reduction procedures** on **breast sensitivity**. They said their results were *unanimously* negative on that score:

Breast innervation was damaged by breast reduction using both the inferior and the superior pedicle techniques. The breast skin had better sensation after the superior pedicle technique while the areola had slightly better sensation after the inferior pedicle technique.

Given all of the above, it seems as if **breast surgery** should only be done if there's a good *medical reason* for it (as in the desire for breast reconstruction after cancer surgery, or the need for relief from extreme back pain due to the weight of **super-large breasts**, for example). And as you can see from the quotes above, even the medical community supports that idea.

...And that's not to mention the **other negative effects of surgery**. I'll never forget how one lover's **breasts** - which had undergone *reduction* surgery - used to *pucker up at the* **surgical seams** when my lover approached her orgasm, making her **breasts** look like footballs. It made me feel sad because *it looked like they'd been mutilated*. And the **scars** around her **areolas**, where her nipple-areola complex had been removed and reattached, were equally unsettling to me.

The **breasts** of lovers who'd had **implants** presented other uncomfortable realities. They *felt hard and unnatural*. Their **nipples** had little **sensitivity**.

Yet my love for the women in my life who'd had surgery was undiminished by that reality. I'm just saying that *if you have the choice*, **don't encourage** *your lover to go under the knife unless there's a really good reason for it*. That being said, such decisions are *hers* alone to make.

And finally, it goes without saying that you should not *leave* a woman because she's had surgery or let that fact lessen your love for her. But you'll need to understand that her breasts will need more intense stimulation.

Are Sensitive Breasts Best?

All of that being said, are the more sensitive breasts *better* than less sensitive breasts? Not really. Each comes with its pluses and minuses.

With really sensitive breasts you have to be very careful not to hurt your lover because she'll feel pain with higher degrees of intensity where a less sensitive woman would not. With less sensitive breasts you cannot evoke a huge reaction with small lip tickles but you can do things to them you couldn't with a more sensitive breast - such as pulling up on the nipples an inch or more, squeezing them hard, rapidly flicking them with your tongue or finger, shaking them rapidly, and so on.

It's true that less sensitivity might mean you cannot give your lover a **breast-induced orgasm**. But you can still make her so *hot* that she'll be on the *verge* of coming. And the difference, in the end, between those two realities is very slight. Plus, whether they are less or more sensitive, each case presents opportunities the other case does not. (You'll see soon.)

And in the final analysis, **love**making is all about pleasing the woman you love - as she is, physically, emotionally and spiritually. You make the most with whatever you have. Plus - as I've said before - **love**making is all about **physically communicating** *how you feel toward her*. The breast is just one means of expressing your love for her. Think of it as *an instrument*, the less or more sensitive ones being *two different types of instruments* to play. So you play them *differently*. It's all good.

A BIG-BREAST ADVANTAGE: THE DOUBLE-NIPPLE SUCKING TECHNIQUE

Oh and by the way, while I've noted that **big breasts** tend to have *less* sensitivity than **small breasts**, they often have a nice advantage. That is, you usually can adjust their **nipples** inward so they're touching each other (or nearly so). Then, *you can suck them both at the same time* - and boy will she like that! That will really send your lover through the roof!

Apparently few men think to do this because one of my lovers expressed surprise as well as gratitude after I performed this feat on her (I wrote down what she said when she wasn't looking, to pass along to you):

> *"When you put both of my **nipples** in your mouth at the same time I nearly came! You made me so hot that I came really fast once you entered me!"*

This was a post-menopausal woman, which made giving her **breast-induced orgasms** difficult if not impossible. But, as you can see, the effect of my **double-nipple sucking technique** blew her mind.

When should do you do this? The **double-nipple sucking technique** works best when done at the end of a *prolonged* teasing of her breasts. *Work up to it*. Build in intensity and then surprise her with it to send her over the top.

How do you do it? Turn her **breasts** <u>inward</u> until *both* **nipples** are close enough to be brought inside your mouth simultaneously. Perhaps first tease one and then the other; go back and forth between the two creatively. Then clamp down gently on both breasts' **M Spots** (the soft flesh below her nipples) to keep her tits in place, putting steady pressure on those sensitive **orgasm triggers *(with your tongue or lips)***.

Now *suck her nipples* **rhythmically**. Or *ream* them. Or *massage* them with your tongue. Do this with *exact repetition* and *duplication of motion*. And do it in a *sexy* way, with *passion* and *fervor*. Act as if you're really *excited* by what you're doing. Then, after awhile, move your lips back and forth rhythmically, *as if you're trying to suck the milk out of her*. Do this really intensely. Then - while still doing that - urgently stroke *both* **nipples** with your tongue, in an *exacting* regular *rhythm* - if you're good at **multitasking**. Take your time. Make it fun. Build on the passion as time goes on, and really try to bring on a **breast-induced orgasm**.

On Loving Women

But if an **orgasm** is not in the offing, keep all of this up while slowly inserting your hard-on in and out of her. It shouldn't be long before she's in the throes of a **big O**.

DOUBLE-NIPPLE STIMULATION

...But what if your lover's **breasts** are unable to be turned so *both* **nipples** are in your mouth? Then you do the next-best thing: ***double-nipple stimulation.*** *This* can be done with virtually *all* women. And doing this will likely excite your lover to the *max* - even possibly sending her over the top. It's a surefire **orgasm booster**.

For **nipple** titillation few techniques excite a woman more than **double-nipple stimulation** - if done *sensuously, artfully, for the right duration, with the right intensity and passion,* and *at the right time.*

As with the **double-nipple sucking technique**, **double-nipple stimulation** *is best done after you've gotten her pretty hot and you want to make her come. It should be done with a sudden onset and intensity. The element of surprise plays an important role in producing quick and big results.*

How do you do it? Use your imagination! You can use your fingertips or the pads of your fingers to squeeze both **nipples** (like a clamp); or do this with your mouth on one and your fingers on the other. Or you can tease both **nipples** with your palms, or flick both **nipples** with your fingers. You can run your fingers in circles around both **areolas**. Or try something new!

Breast Orgasms, The M Spot & More

...But there are three important principles you should follow, regardless of which **double-nipple stimulation** technique you choose to do:

- **Use the same rhythm and technique on both nipples**
- Slowly **build** in **intensity, urgency, speed** and **passion**
- **Take your time - do it until she comes** (either through breast manipulation or through simultaneous vaginal or clitoral stimulation)

The one exception in following the *first* rule above is if you're using your mouth on one nipple. You can't *exactly* reproduce your mouth work on the other nipple so just try to keep the rhythm and the *general type of motion* the same. Example: If you're flicking your tongue upward on a nipple, do a similar flick upward on her other nipple with a finger, palm or arm. If you're sucking a nipple, mimic that sucking motion on the other nipple with your fingers. And so on.

Which Nipple Is The Most Sensitive?

And by the way, did you know that the relative sensitivity of each **breast** is *different*! One **nipple** is often more sensitive than the other - and it's your job to discover which one that is! **In a right-handed woman, it's usually her left breast, and vice versa with a southpaw.**

This is most important when doing mouth work because when you're ready to make her come, it's best to give your attention to **her most sensitive nipple**. That's not to say you should *ignore* the less reactive one. But *move over to the more excitable one when you want to trigger a* **climax**.

How To Give Her Breast-Induced Orgasms

...Now on to the *Holy Grail of nipple work*, the **breast-induced orgasm**. I promised earlier to teach you how to treat your lover to those. Here are a number of ways I've successfully brought them on:

◆ **Grape Circles**: *Imagining her nipples are grapes (somewhat* *delicate - not to be broken)*, take both between the **thumbs** and **forefingers** of each hand and pretend as if you're trying to get their surfaces clean by moving your **thumbs** in circles, pressing the **nipple** between your fingers as firmly as you can without causing discomfort. Keep this up, slowly increasing the speed and intensity, for as long as it takes. Never do this violently or excessively fast.

◆ **Nipple Twists**: *Taking both **nipples** between your **thumbs** and **forefingers**, gently twist them like you're turning the dials of a radio, but go only as far as is pleasurable to her (usually no more than 20°-30°). Do this insistently but at a slow to moderate pace, with a steady rhythm and as much pressure as you can without producing pain. (This might work best with **sensitive nipples**.)*

◆ **M Spot Massaging:** *Dig your tongue into the flesh below her **nipple**, press her **M Spot** between your palette and the top of your **tongue**, and move your **tongue** back and forth with moderate pressure.*

◆ **Extreme "Baby" Sucking**: *Taking her **most sensitive nipple** in your mouth, suck with moderate strength so it gives the illusion you're trying to suck it off her body or draw some milk. Do a rhythmic or pulsating sucking action - much like a baby might do it only more insistently and sensually. For a more powerful effect, also roll her **nipple** with your **tongue** or massage her **M Spot** with your **tongue**.*

◆ **M Spot Pulsations**: *Taking her **M Spots** between the **thumbs** and **forefingers** of both hands, tenderly pull up and away from her body a centimeter or so and then squeeze them softly but with urgency and a moderate regular rhythm, in a pulsating fashion. Adjust the pressure to suit her **sensitivity** level.*

◆ **Nipple Pulsations**: *This technique is the same as the one for **M Spot Pulsations** but you do this holding her **nipples** firmly between your fingers. This works best on less sensitive **nipples**. A more sensitive woman might find this technique to be too intense but give it a try.*

◆ **Deep-Tissue Tongue Lines**: *With one **nipple** in your mouth, lightly squeezed between your **tongue** and **palette**, and the upper portion of your tongue flat against the upper part of her **breast** and **nipple** (facing downward), run the **tip of your tongue** up from her **M Spot** region to the top of her **nipple** repeatedly (using enough pressure to dig into her **breast** to give her **milk ducts** a deep tissue massage - without a downward motion; lift your **tongue** off her **nipple** temporarily between strokes). Do this with an insistent upward motion and steady, moderate rhythm. Try slowly increasing the tempo and pressure as she nears her climax. (FYI: **Deep-Tissue Tongue Lines** can also be done without her **nipple** in your mouth.)*

◆ **Nipple Circles**: *With both **nipples** firmly between your fingers (or one in your mouth), move them in circular paths, pulling the rest of the **breast** along with the **nipple**. Pull up slightly if it pleases her. This technique works best once she's really hot. Your circles (of about 1-2" in diameter, depending on her size and comfort level) can be done in concert with each other or in opposite directions.*

◆ **Nipple or M Spot Clamping**: *Pinch or squeeze both **nipples** or **M***

Breast Orgasms, The M Spot & More

Spots with your fingers with a regular, urgent pressure. Or pinch one with one hand and the other between your **lips**. Even if she doesn't come (and she might), it will push her closer to her **orgasm**! You can vary your **pressure** or **pressure point location** if you'd like, if it pleases her or helps you find the spot that sends her over the top.

♦ **Nipple Pulls**: Holding both of her **nipples** between your fingers, pull upward on each either **statically** or **rhythmically**. How far up you pull on them is dependent on the **sensitivity** of her **breasts** and the **feedback** you get from her. Variation: Pull one up with your fingers and the other with your mouth.

♦ **Nipple Shakes**: When she's very close to her **orgasm**, take both **tits** in your fingers and vigorously shake them back and forth, either from side to side or up and down. Variation: Shake one with your fingers and the other with your mouth (shaking your head to accomplish the motion). This is best done on **less sensitive breasts**.

Every woman is different, so experiment with the techniques above until you find which ones work on your honey. Use *less* pressure and intensity if your lover has *sensitive* breasts, *more* if her breasts are *less* sensitive.

HER BREASTS AS ORGASM BOOSTERS, FOR TEASING & OTHER FUN

But there's something else you need to understand: Breasts also work great as **orgasm boosters**. When you stimulate them *artfully in conjunction with an* **orgasm trigger**, they can make her come *quickly* and *powerfully*. In this way you can *maximize* a woman's **orgasm**. Just *touching* her **nipples** sensually or tenderly holding her **M Spots** lightly when you've gotten her close to coming with another **orgasm trigger** can send her over the top.

But don't use her **breasts** just as devices to make her come. Nothing beats her **breasts** as organs to **tease** her with, to make her real **hot**. And *teasing her into a frenzy is a worthy goal in and of itself.* So every now and then, begin your **love**making session by devoting 15-30 minutes just to teasing her **breasts**. The duration and intensity of this approach will make her **super-hot**, **wet** and **wide**, as well as priming her to **come** quickly with penetration. And in doing that don't forget her **areolas** (which respond well to circular tongue work, outlining their shape). And give attention to the *tops* of her **nipples**, which respond even to light touches of the tongue, fingers, glans, whatever. To enhance the effect, *cup* or *reshape* her **breasts** with your palms, with moderate pressure (you can even pull the skin taut). She'll love it, too, if you gently move her **breasts** in *circular motions*.

You also can drive her wild by teasing her **nipples** *through clothing* - either *before* **love**making (to seduce her) or *during* sex (it's sometimes fun to have her wear something on top during the act, like a see-through negligee or a soft teddy). You can also use something soft - like a blanket or her robe - to *massage* her **breasts**. That can really get her going. The sensations she'll get from your doing this will be different from those you could give her yourself. (An added bonus: This adds *variety* to your **love**making.)

Another thing: If her **breasts** are big enough, see if your lover might occasionally want you to *make love* to her **breasts** - or more accurately, to the *space between* them. (Some women *love* this. Those who do often get a thrill from having you *come on their faces and/or necks* too.) In doing this, you'll find you're rubbing upon her **sternum (breastbone)**. It's *hard* and doesn't feel as nice as her **vagina**. But if you lubricate yourself with *olive oil*, it will feel much better. And make it as **sexy** and **sensual** an event as you can. (Tell her how *good* her **breasts** feel and look, for example.)

Be creative and *have fun*. Experiment with different pressures, motions and techniques. Her **breasts** are a playground with endless possibilities!

...But a final word on **breast size**: Don't get hung up on it. Women of all sizes can look sexy. Plus, the *excitement* comes from her **nipples** and **M Spots**. All women have those. Plus, if she's got **small breasts**, you might be able to get all of one in your mouth. (Try it!) That's too much fun!

Wetter Is *Better*

And don't forget: **Wetter is better! Make her nips wet before touching them.** A little **oil** or **saliva** will multiply the effect of your touches by at least *double*. Just letting drops of oil fall on her nipples will get her hotter.

The Best Reason To Give Her Breasts Lots Of Attention

Finally, here's further motivation to maximize the amount of time you spend titillating her breasts: The web site yourpurelife.com quotes Susan Kellogg, Ph.D., codirector of sexual medicine at The Pelvic Floor Institute at Graduate Hospital in Philadelphia, as saying, "Intense breast stimulation makes your body release **oxytocin**, the chemical that makes you feel love and attachment." And numerous scientific studies have backed that up.

So it's true that *if you stimulate a woman's breasts long enough, she'll feel more* **loving** *and* **bonded** *with you.* (University of Pisa researchers in Italy reached that conclusion in a study done in 2006, for instance. See their report on the right.) *That* should be incentive enough. Because **that's** the higher reward we want from **love**making, isn't it?

A relationship between oxytocin and anxiety of romantic attachment

Donatella Marazziti,[⊠,1] Bernardo Dell'Osso,[1,2] Stefano Baroni,[1] Francesco Mungai,[1] Mario Catena,[1] Paola Rucci,[1] Francesco Albanese,[1] Gino Giannaccini,[1] Laura Betti,[1] Laura Fabbrini,[1] Paola Italiani,[1] Alessandro Del Debbio,[1] Antonio Lucacchini,[1] and Liliana Dell'Osso[1]

[1]Dipartimento di Psichiatria, Neurobiologia, Farmacologia e Biotecnologie, University of Pisa, Italy
[2]Compulsive, Impulsive and Anxiety Disorders Program, Department of Psychiatry, Mount Sinai School of Medicine, New York, USA
[⊠]Corresponding author.

Donatella Marazziti: dmarazzi@psico.med.unipi.it; Bernardo Dell'Osso: bdellosso@hotmail.com; Stefano Baroni: stefanobaroni67@alice.it; Francesco Mungai: mungai@tiscali.it; Mario Catena: mariocatena@interfree.it; Paola Rucci: paola57@hotmail.com; Francesco Albanese: f.albanese@psicoleb.net; Gino Giannaccini: ggino@farm.unipi.it; Laura Betti: betti@farm.unipi.it; Laura Fabbrini: fabbrini@farm.unipi.it; Paola Italiani: italiani@farm.unipi.it; Alessandro Del Debbio: a.deldebbio@hotmail.com; Antonio Lucacchini: lucas@farm.unipi.it; Liliana Dell'Osso: ldelloss@med.unipi.it

Received July 31, 2006; Accepted October 11, 2006.

This is an Open Access article distributed under the terms of the Creative Commons Attribution License (http://creativecommons.org/licenses/by/2.0), which permits unrestricted use, distribution, and reproduction in any medium, provided the original work is properly cited.

Abstract — Other Section

The formation of social bonding is fundamental for several animals, including humans, for its relevant and obvious impact upon reproduction and, thus, survival of the species. Recent data would suggest that oxytocin might be one of the mediators of this process.

A RECENT SCIENTIFIC DISCOVERY UPS THE ANTE FOR LOVERS OF WOMEN
Breast-Induced Orgasms Are Recognized As Real

Sexual history was made with the publication of the October 2011 issue of the *Journal of Sexual Medicine* (which I mentioned earlier, in a different context, on page 178). It wasn't greeted with a big fanfare - as it should have, especially from those devoted to the **love**making arts. And it did not immediately result in a greater awareness of the potential of the female **breast**, among lovers of women - as would have been ideal.

I'm referring to the article in which Rutgers University neuroscientist Barry Komisaruk and his colleagues announced the amazing results of their **fMRI** study of how women's **brains** reacted to the stimulation of various **sexual organs**. Their goal was to map the areas of the **brain** that were activated by the **nerves** from a woman's **clitoris, anterior vaginal wall** (most likely in the **G-Spot** area), **cervix** and **nipples**.

Noting that different **nerves** are attached to each of these **erogenous zones**, they were not surprised that the stimulation of each of these four areas were reflected by uniquely **different brain patterns** in the way of **neuron activation** - even though these patterns were all in roughly the same area, the **genital sensory cortex** of the **brain** (roughly speaking, the very middle of the tops of both **brain hemispheres**, to a depth of what appeared to be an inch or so, give or take).

Their conclusions regarding what they observed with **nipple stimulation** were perhaps the most startling: "Unexpectedly, nipple/breast self-stimulation activated...the region of the **paracentral lobule** [of the brain] that overlaps with the region activated by clitoral, vaginal, or cervical self-stimulation. This finding is consistent with many women's reports that **nipple/breast stimulation is erotogenic and can elicit orgasms**."

While they said this might have been an indirect result of the fact that **nipple/breast stimulation can produce oxytocin**, a chemical that induces **uterine contractions**, they played that possibility down:

"...it is also possible that nipple/breast and **genital sensory activity** converge directly not only on **oxytocinergic neurons** of the **hypothalamic paraventricular nucleus**...but also on **paracentral lobule neurons** of the **genital sensory cortex**."

Translation: When you stimulate a woman's **nipples**, the feelings are transmitted via **nerves** that lead directly to the part of her **brain** that also processes **genital sensations** - and in so doing, that can lead to **orgasm**.

While some of us were aware of this reality years ago, the scientific world's endorsement gives it **credibility**. Knowing this, lovers of women must now realize they need to develop the skills to produce these **orgasms**. They are just as real and desirable as any other a woman can experience.

> Khajuraho, India - "Gentlemen, don't try this at home," jokes the guide as a group of tourists gazes at an erotic relief on a Hindu temple. The sandstone frieze depicts a man standing on his <u>head</u> having intercourse with a voluptuous woman as two handmaidens provide support.
> - From the article "Temples of Passion" by Debra Black in the Star

The Shocking Facts About Positions

Many people think that sex is all about **positions**. The thinking goes: the more you use, the better. The more difficult the position, the better.

There's a scene in the sexy play *O Calcutta*, for instance, in which a female swinger shows a younger woman a deck of playing cards with erotic photos, excitedly explaining that the photos depict "52 positions!"

She wants the younger woman to be *impressed* and eager to try them all. Instead the younger woman, gazing at one of the positions with a look of horror, says: "That one looks painful!"

The scene draws laughs but the young woman's complaint sums up the problem many people have with positions-centered **love**making manuals:

The impression most people get is that lovers must be Olympic-class athletes able to contort themselves into difficult pretzel shapes in order to have great sex.

The Shocking Facts About Positions

Worse, the *positions-based manuals* often leave readers wondering *why* they should use any of the positions.

If you've felt this way about the position-driven books, don't worry. The truth is that *positions are not the be-all and end-all of* **love***making*.

Let me put it this way: A ballet beginner can scrunch himself into a position Nureyev once used, but that doesn't make the beginner a Nureyev. A child can mimic a Barry Bonds batting stance but that will not make the child hit like Barry Bonds.

Positions are like tubes of paint to an artist. They're just colors on your **love**making palette. Just as owning many paint tubes does not make you a great artist, knowing many sexual positions does not make you a great lover.

It's not the position. It's what you **do** *in the position that matters*.

It takes about two seconds to get into a position. The question then arises: Now what are you going to do?

You can have good, bad or indifferent sex in any position. <u>The position doesn't make the lover. The lover makes the position</u>. Understand: **Love**making is what happens *after* you've moved into a position.

However, positions, when used properly, can *facilitate* great **love**making. To that end, you need understand that:

- It matters <u>why</u> you choose a position. You should choose positions with a <u>purpose</u> in mind.
- Each position has its strengths and weaknesses. **Each one orients you inside her differently. You achieve different depths. Reach different places. Trigger different reactions.** You need to know how each position stacks up in each of these ways.
- Some are great for giving her vaginal orgasms. Others for clitoral orgasms. Some are just great for teasing her to make her hot.
- Positions should serve your overall plan. Make sure you are using positions that will make that happen.
- It matters <u>why</u> you choose to change positions. The new position should make things more exciting.
- It matters <u>when</u> you choose to change positions. Do you have a smart reason to leave a position? Do you mine a position for all it is worth or do you annoy your lover by leaving positions too soon?
- It matters <u>how</u> you change positions. Do you do this smoothly? (If you're clumsy you will break the mood.) Do you keep your cock inside of her when changing positions? (That's usually preferable if

On Loving Women

you can do it with skill.)

We'll look at all of this and more. After reading the entire book you'll realize that what I'm talking about here is the art of choosing positions and making position changes to orchestrate a series of sensual effects on your lover that makes your overall **love**making **master plan** succeed. (For **love**making to reach the heights, you need some sort of master plan or prolonged idea, flexible but visualized in your head as a doable rough outline of what mood, pace and result you want to achieve along the way, to create an exciting experience for your lover.)

It's All About Her

Now, in choosing positions you need remember that **every woman is different.** How does this relate to your choice of positions?

Early on in a relationship, you must become a student of your lover. This includes figuring out what her <u>very favorite</u> positions are as well as other positions she enjoys.

Be observant. Experiment with a variety of positions and pay close attention to the sounds she makes, any biological feedback you're getting (such as her pussy getting wetter with a position change), **and any unsolicited comments she might make.**

If you can't learn what your lover's favorites are in this way, though, there's no harm in asking her what she likes best. Just don't do this while you're making love! That would be a real mood breaker. And try not to ask in a way that makes you seem like a real greenhorn. (But, frankly, you're unlikely to get much from this direct approach. You need to be proactive about this. *Pay attention to her responses when in each position during sex.*)

If you instead ignore this learning process and simply assume that your past lover's favorites are your current lover's favorites, boy are you looking for trouble! She'll feel you're using a "move" on her and moves that have been used on other women are about as welcome as the trashy "lines" losers tell women at bars. And if you don't take the time to learn what positions she loves and instead use positions she hates, you'll come across as annoying, inept and insensitive.

If you can't wrap your brain around that, imagine a woman getting on top of you in a position you hate. It's clear she thinks she's doing something great but you're not having fun and you're not giving her any good feedback. You groan because she's hurting you but she's oblivious to your displeasure. Soon, you can't wait for it to end and you've decided to break up with her. Yeah. It's like that.

POSITION MYTHS

Myth #1:
The purpose of using sexual positions is for variety.

The truth is: That's the least important reason. And it's a superficial and ineffective way approach to achieve variety.

It doesn't matter how many positions you use. If you're a dull lover, every position will seem dull to her. If you're a one-trick pony (doing the same pump-and-grind in every position, for instance) your lover won't perceive much of a difference from position to position.

Positions are simply tools to use in lovemaking and not the meat of it. It's analogous to the fonts the editor chose for this book. They are design tools, not the content.

So here's the graphic equivalent of position changes made without rhythm or reason:

If I kept arbitrarily CHANGING FONTS in mid-sentence like a bad lover changes positions for no rhyme or reason *that wouldn't achieve a good kind of variety would it?*

Myth #2:
Great lovemaking involves mastering difficult positions.

The truth is: The most challenging sexual positions are beyond the physical abilities of most lovers. Plus in my experience women are rarely interested in them even if they're physically up to it. Most women see these positions as an unwelcome chore, requiring too much effort.

There's also the fact that difficult positions often make for awkward moments.

And there's another drawback:

There's a biological syndrome that makes the most difficult positions less pleasurable for her. They deaden her nerve responses. If she's holding on tight for dear life, twisted like a pretzel, concentrating hard on muscle coordination, she won't be relaxed enough to come.

Don't choose positions with physical challenges she'll dread. This is not the Olympics. Don't forget: *you could blow the mood by picking positions that are no fun.*

On Loving Women

Now, once you've discovered the positions your lover likes and also her very favorites, these are the positions you will by and large use. (You might have noticed that I differentiated between the positions she "likes" and her "favorites." That's because you should not use her favorites exclusively. I'll explain later.)

FYI: Don't assume that she can list all of her favorites, because if you're a good lover, you'll lead her to find new favorites - ones she's never tried before or ones you use better than her prior lovers.

Another way to discover the positions she likes best is to take into account your lover's emotional makeup and her degree of adventurousness. At one extreme, an emotionally needy or conservative woman might prefer positions in which you are face-to-face so that you can hug and kiss (the missionary position; sitting face-to-face on a seat or flat object; standing face-to-face; etc.). At the other extreme, a highly adventurous woman would want you to use more "thrilling" positions (those that make her feel she's being "taken" or being "naughty," for example; we'll discuss these soon). She'd want you to push the envelope; use daring positions she's never experienced. (You would need a large repertoire of positions and/or a high degree of creativity for this kind of lover.)

Now, in searching for good positions, here's something you might not have known: there's a **synergy** or **feng shui** side to it. *Every couple fits together differently.* Different body types join together uniquely. Therefore every couple has a unique set of positions they physically can and cannot do; positions that work best and positions that work worst.

> "*Every couple fits together differently. Therefore every couple has a unique set of positions that work best and work worst.*"

You need to do some exploration to find the positions that work best for your body types.

If you're very tall and your woman is very short, for example, you might not find it so easy or pleasing to make love standing up. Spooning, however, would work well (see the photo on the next page).

Or, if you have a short hard-on and you're with a big-bottomed woman, you might find some **rear-entry positions** difficult (her **butt** might be getting in the way of **full penetration** in your case). You'd probably have more success doing rear-entry positions standing up (with her bending over something, such as a bed or couch). Or you might want to avoid rear-entry positions entirely.

The Shocking Facts About Positions

Whatever your situation is, don't get upset about the positions you cannot do. Make the most of what you can. Few men can do every conceivable position.

It's a road to discovery. Enjoy the process.

Along these lines, I shouldn't have to say this but:

If your lover doesn't <u>like</u> a position, is physically *uncomfortable* in a position, or she *can't stay in a position very long*, give it up immediately and with good humor. Happily move on to something else, preferably a position you know she'll really like.

Remember: It's all about <u>her</u>. And just as each and every woman has her own unique favorites, she also has unique positions she <u>dislikes</u>. This is mostly matter of personal taste (namely, what she finds sexy); but it also has to do with her physical limitations.

A great male lover caters to his woman - to her special needs and desires. So if she's unable to get on top because of knee problems, for instance, or perhaps her thighs are not strong enough, or she has arthritis, she's older, or is overweight, so what? Do something else.

Never make your lover feel it was her fault for a position not working or get angry with her over this kind of thing. That would not only be unkind, but it would also create psychological barriers that might eventually doom your love life.

On Loving Women

You undoubtedly have limitations, too, which will make some positions impossible. So be understanding. Then she will, too.

Also, if you want to try a new position (especially one that might require physical strength or endurance she might not have), suggest the idea to her first (before initiating sex), in a lighthearted way. Let her know that if it doesn't work, it doesn't matter; you'll simply change to a position you know she'll really love! (And have a backup plan in mind in order to fulfill that promise, just in case.)

So, as you might have gathered, all positions are not all desirable for all lovers. Bottom line: *Go with what feels good to the woman you're with.*

If you noticed that I left you out of that equation, you're right. Here's why: Number one, you will find that she won't like some of your favorites. But, since it's all about her, you shouldn't do the ones she doesn't like – even if some of them are *your* favorites.

And, number two, there will be positions that she likes and you don't. But – because it's all about her – you should gladly do those, too (without complaining or indicating in any way your displeasure).

The whole idea is to rock her world. The reward, in doing some things you're not crazy about, is in hearing her scream enough to alert the whole neighborhood as to the pleasure you're giving her.

The Shocking Facts About Positions

How Many Positions Are Enough?

Now...you're probably wondering how many positions should you plan on using...Answer: however many she likes.

You might be surprised to find that she likes only a dozen or so positions. That's actually not so unusual. With the use of multiple entry choices and position variants (which we'll discuss soon), that will be more than enough.

You don't need 1,001 positions to have a happy and rewarding love life. But you do need to be the master of this domain.

The Onus Is On You

Although you now understand that your woman will be the final arbiter as to what positions you may use, you still have the most active role. It is the <u>man's</u> job to choose and change positions (except on rare occasions when your woman takes control).

So make sure you take charge when it comes to the choice of positions. It's much akin to dancing. The man <u>leads</u>. That's because most women like it that way and, furthermore, they expect this of you. And you must guide her into each position like a graceful male dancer leads his partner through the dance.

In my experience, most women prefer it this way; although Amen to those who sometimes prefer to lead! That can be lots of fun. But don't count on that happening (and don't wait for her to act).

Just as with dancing, leading in bed demands forethought on your part. You must constantly think ahead, be flexible, respond to her feedback and be able to think on your feet. It's no small task.

Let's look at what goes into this process.

Position Types

Rather than being manual-dependent in choosing positions, it will work best if you learn instead to be spontaneous and creative. For that, you need to know the basic options in picking positions.

It's simple. Let's start with the basic types of entry choices, attitudes and positions.

Entry Choices (See photos page 306)

Your choice of positions begins with your **entry choice** - that is, whether you want to do it facing her; from the rear; or, from the side. This choice affects the orientation of your hard-on inside of her and what it massages.

EVERY WOMAN HAS HER FAVORITE POSITIONS

A Few Examples

Side-entry: "I like that best," a lover said. "I can watch you better. I like to watch you while you're making love to me." Some women, though, feel it's unromantic, creating a distance.

Rear-entry: Some women love it. Others feel it's "dirty."

Woman-On-Top: Some women tire easily in this position or find it hard on their knees. Others find it empowering.

Missionary: One lover said "I like that because I can kiss you." It might be the most romantic position but few women would say it's the most exciting.

The Shocking Facts About Positions

(Read page 338 for the latest scientific discoveries on sexual positions.)

Positions where you are facing her are perhaps the most romantic. You can easily kiss her and gaze into each others' eyes. Starting and ending with these are never bad choices for that reason. The missionary position (pictured on the bottom of page 303) is the most popular of these but I find it restricts my range and speed of motion. It's also hard to make her come in that position. One of the many variants I prefer (not pictured) is where I lean to my right or left, holding her body at a 45° angle, where I can tickle her vulva with my free hand and even produce a clitoral orgasm.

Rear-entry positions enable you to massage her internally in ways other positions do not offer - and deeply. You can access her **G-Spot** easily with the head of your **penis**. You can (if you're long enough) massage her furthest reaches. Many women find these positions the most stimulating.

Side-entry positions (like the one below) provide you with another angle of approach that produces different feelings for her. You'll get a tighter squeeze from her canal when you enter her from the side. Depending on the position, her vaginal canal might be shortened too; that makes these positions ideal for men who are on the shorter side (who might then be able to reach and massage her deeper regions).

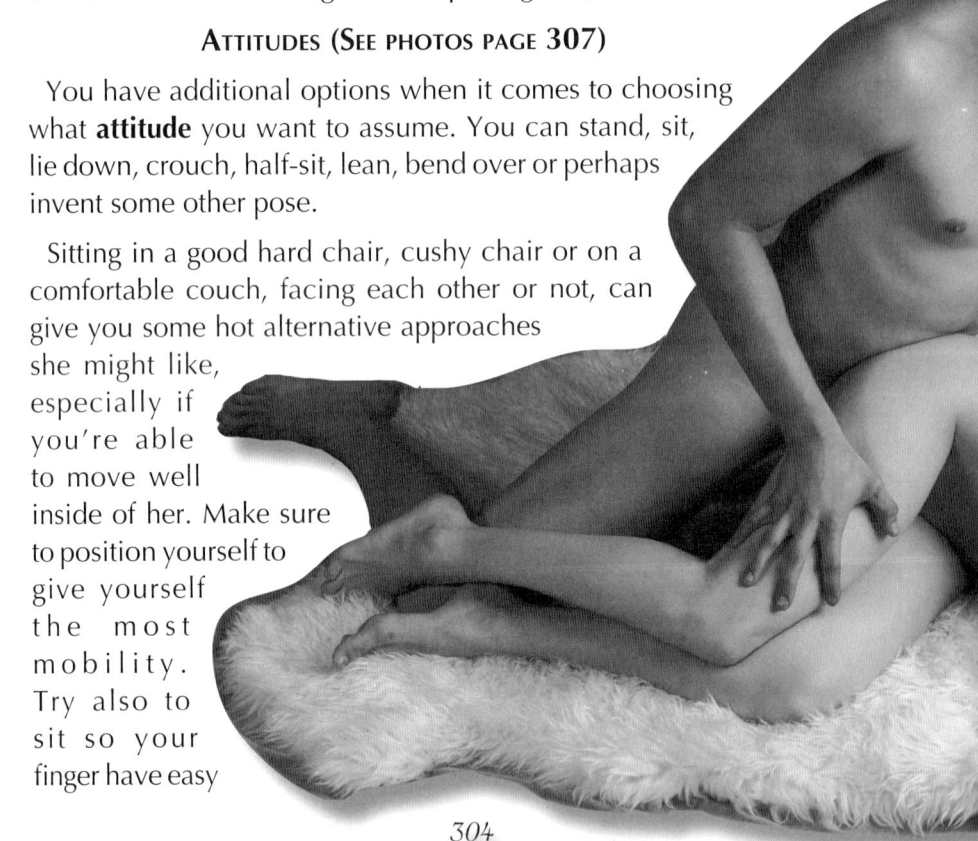

ATTITUDES (SEE PHOTOS PAGE 307)

You have additional options when it comes to choosing what **attitude** you want to assume. You can stand, sit, lie down, crouch, half-sit, lean, bend over or perhaps invent some other pose.

Sitting in a good hard chair, cushy chair or on a comfortable couch, facing each other or not, can give you some hot alternative approaches she might like, especially if you're able to move well inside of her. Make sure to position yourself to give yourself the most mobility. Try also to sit so your finger have easy

On Loving Women

access to her **pussy**, to stimulate her **clitoris**.

Standing can provide exciting positions, especially when entering from the rear. Throw her over a couch, grab her hips and move them in sympathy with your hip movements, work it right and you might have discovered her hottest position. Plus, it feels naughty (often a plus with women). And the feeling of bare feet on a cool floor or cushy carpet helps make this approach super sexy. Doing this in a shower makes moving a bit harder but then give her the shower massager and let her do herself in the process. Nice.

Crouching on your feet or sitting up on your knees when she's lying on her back can give you a lot of bounce from the bed and help provide speed and thrust to your efforts. An added bonus: You might also be able to fondle her clit and make her come that way in these positions.

Experiment with all of the attitudes I listed above. Each option has its own unique pluses.

IN-LINE POSITIONS (SEE PHOTOS PAGE 308)

In addition to your choice of entry methods and attitudes you have many options when it comes to position types. This subject could fill volumes but I'll divide these up into a few categories to summarize your options.

Let's call the first category of positions **in-line positions**. Here, you *face the same way* and *press your bodies closely together*. These are romantic positions because you have full-body contact at all times; the idea is to hug or snuggle throughout the experience.

In-line positions are all rear-entry positions but they are not equivalent in effect (and not all rear-entry positions are in-line positions). Because of the differences in your entry angle, her body angle and muscle tension (which contributes to her tendency to come), her relative feeling of sexiness because of the room location and context, all play a role in making her react to each differently.

Here are some ways you could

(Continued on page 309)

Examples Of Entry Choices

Facing her

From the rear

From the side

Examples Of Attitude Choices

"You can stand, sit, lie down, crouch, half-sit, lean, bend over or perhaps invent some other pose."

Standing

Sitting

Lying down

Inventing A Pose

Examples Of In-Line Positions

(Continued from page 305)
adopt in-line positions:

You and she could both simultaneously: sit; or stand; or lie down. Or you could both: spoon; get down on all-fours; bend over (standing or sitting); or crouch together. If you want to really drive her wild and possibly make her come **vaginally**, the best of these positions might be where you both lie facedown. A close second is where you're both sitting; that's great for its penetration depth and your access to her neck (for kissing and tongue work), breasts and clit.

Full-Frontal Positions (See photos page 310)

Full-frontal positions are kind of the reverse of in-line positions. Here you press your bodies against each other, facing each other. Very romantic.

Take her as she enters the house after work, pressing her body against the wall, holding her hands above her head. That's one of the more exciting full-frontal positions. Bend her backwards over your car hood in the middle of the desert, pinning her hands above her while you straddle her and kiss her neck or lips. That's a "wow" position while still being romantic.

Some missionary variants are full-frontal positions and many allow you better ease of movement. We'll talk about some of these later.

Contrary Positions (See photos page 311)

Contrary positions are those in which one partner does one thing and the other does something else. These are possibly the most interesting positions.

One she'll probably like a lot is where you bend her over a table, counter or the hood of your car (sexy for its coolness on her skin - have her press her body down on it) while you stand or straddle her. You can generate a lot of speed and get great penetration in this way. Plus, your angle of entry and penis orientation will facilitate giving her **G-Spot orgasms**.

The "doggy-style" position is a contrary position: your woman is on all fours while you're sitting up on your knees. (There is a in-line version of the doggy-style position, where you are also on all-fours, like your woman, but this is possible only if your lover is significantly shorter than you.) This is best done on a soft surface or it'll be hard on your knees. Your body types (especially the length of your thighs) must match well, though, for this to work well. Not one of my favorites but some people love it.

Woman-on-top positions give the woman control if she wants it. You can move simultaneously or hold still. If she tires, you can take over entirely. In these positions, your partner could be sitting up or crouching on her feet,

(Continued on page 312)

EXAMPLES OF
FULL FRONTAL POSITIONS

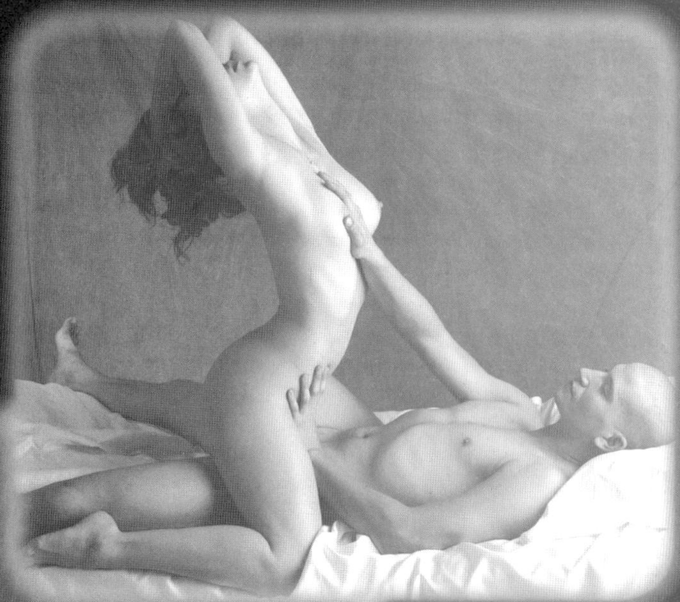

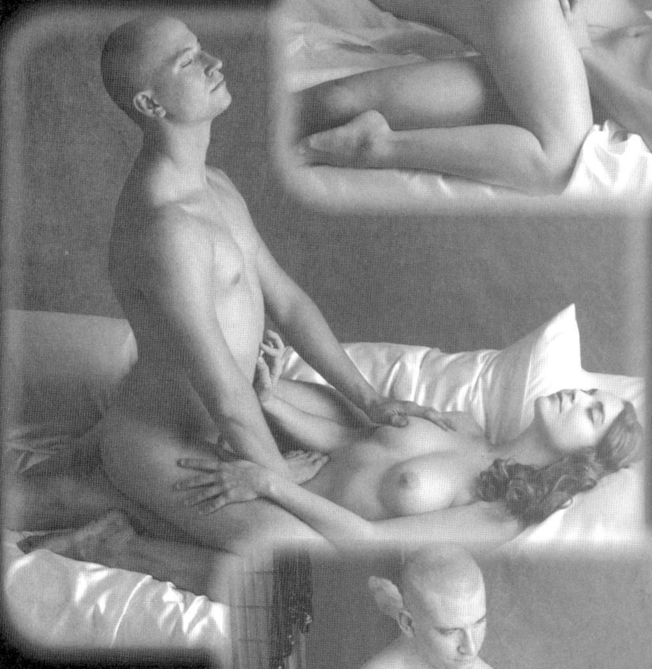

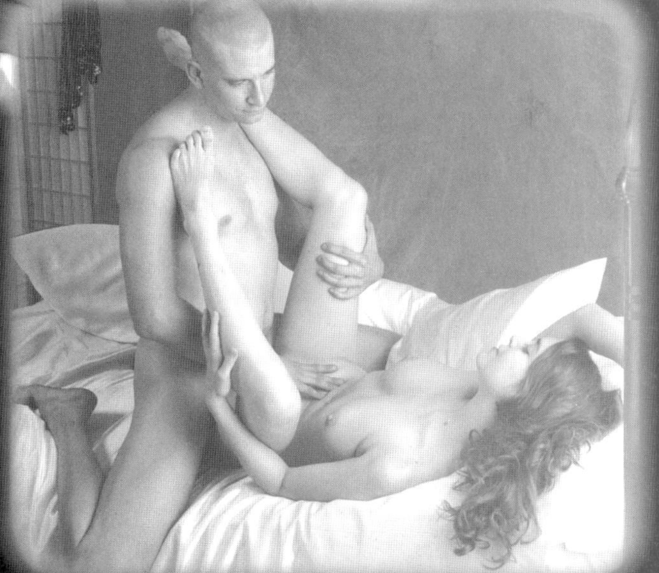

The Shocking Facts About Positions

(Continued from page 309)

either facing you or facing your feet, while you lie on your back. (Tip: Prop your back up with pillows when she's on top, facing you; this will enable you to comfortably suck a tit or kiss her.) Or you could sit up and hug her.

(Woman-on-top positions, though, present a little danger. She can injure you badly in these positions if she's clumsy or unaware of the risks. Read the information on page 313 so that never happens to you.)

Another contrary position is where you sit on top facing her while she lies on her back. (See the middle photo on page 311 for example.) Another fabulous contrary position is where you stand while your lover lies back on a surface that's at your waist height (a bed, kitchen table, counter, car hood or other flat surface), her legs and feet dangling over the edge.

Have fun experimenting, creating different contrary positions. You will discover ones that work well no matter what your body types are.

POSITION VARIANTS (SEE PHOTOS ON PAGE 314)

For more options, explore the many ways you can *vary* each position.

Here are some position variants for the last contrary position I mentioned, for example (where you stand while your lover lies on her back on the bed or some other object); try it while: holding her feet in the air with one hand (you can also suck her toes if she likes that); or throwing her feet over your shoulders (if her legs are long enough; if not, rest her feet on your chest).

The missionary position, which is actually favored by most women, need not be dull. Here's a variation to spice it up: with her legs spread wide and you in between them, reach down with both hands behind her and grab her butt cheeks. Squeeze them, caress them, separate them, gently indirectly pulling open her anus (this gives her erotic tingles) – timing this with every cock thrust you make. Insert a finger, too, if she likes that.

Here are some other ways to vary the missionary position (pictured on page 314): Put your legs outside of hers, so your legs are surrounding her. Or place your thighs directly on top of hers. (These variants might require that you have a fairly long erection. Test them to see if you get adequate penetration.) One super benefit of these variants is that your weight will feel more balanced, making it much easier to move.

Remember - to each his or her own. You have to find the variants best suited to both of your body types and personalities.

But if you're smart, you'll use a <u>lot</u> of variants. For one thing, by simply switching between variants instead of positions, you can happily stay in

(Continued on page 315)

WARNING: A PENIS CAN BE BROKEN

Many lovers are unaware that a **penis** can be broken. (Women in Africa apparently know more about a man's fragile nature than other women. Some there are reportedly being taught how to break a man's **penis** if they're raped.)

HOW IT HAPPENS:

Penile breakage usually occurs in positions where the woman is on top.

A **penis** essentially consists of two tube-like devices that engorge with **blood**, making the organ **erect**.

If your woman goes too far on her upstroke, letting your **erection** *exit her* **vagina**, *and she then comes down hard on it when it's out; or if she violently moves her hips downward when you're not fully inside of her, that severely bends your* **penis** *and the tube-like devices inside of your* **erection** *could rupture.* This will cause extreme pain, swelling, discoloration and an inability to get hard.

A **broken penis** can often be repaired, but **surgery (to repair holes in the erectile chambers) must be done right away or permanent damage might occur** (resulting in **impotence** or a **curved erection**, which can make having **sex** difficult.)

HOW TO AVOID THIS:

Talk to your woman about this (an educated partner will be more careful with you). Ask your partner not to become violently wild when she's on top (both in extreme motion and pace); she especially needs to control herself on the upstroke so you don't pop out of her (suggest that she rest the fingers of one hand on your hard-on so she can make sure you're always in her).

Your lover must avoid severe **downward** *hip movements unless she stops at the top to make sure you're still inside of her.*

You can raise your **hips** to keep your **penis** inside of her if you feel you're in danger of popping out.

You can hold her **hips** down when you feel she is likely to go too far up on her up stroke

You can thrust in time with her, which often slows her down.

If she makes a mistake say (nicely), "Careful, honey; that hurt!" (that should make her more careful)

The best policy is to play it safe. This might spoil some of the fun but, given the risks, a loving partner should be willing to work with you.

TRUE STORY:

I was, in fact, injured during sex in my 20s. My partner went crazy when she was on top of me, which was exciting until I heard a cracking sound that came from my **erection**. It resulted in great pain, bruising and instant **dysfunction** (which lasted two weeks). We rushed to a doctor but luckily the **erectile chambers** were not ruptured and no treatment was necessary. (He warned us to be more careful in the future, however.) Others have been less fortunate.

The lesson is: If you believe your **penis** was *broken* during sex, *you need immediate medical attention.*

After my injury, my partner, being a loving woman, was careful to stay in control when on top so we had no other scares. I missed her wild abandon but the price was too high.

But my experience has had some unfortunate after-effects. Once you've been injured, you get a bit nervous when your partner gets on top. So, I must admit, I now favor other positions.

Yet there's no reason to avoid the woman-on-top positions. With caution and a complete awareness of the facts, they can enhance your sex life.

Examples Of Position Variants

(Continued from page 312)

one position longer than you might have otherwise (without necessitating a withdrawal). That provides you enough time to do what you want to do in each position before you feel compelled to change to something else.

Changing between position variants mimics a complete position change because it varies the angle of your erection and the way your body attitude makes her feel. And here's an example of how you might do that: You could start with what I call the cozy starting position. It's a missionary variant where you're sitting on top of her resting on your heels, bending over to kiss her, your knees drawn up on each side of her torso. This doesn't offer much range of movement, but it's a romantic way to start (and in beginning this way, it allows more time for her arousal phase to mature, so she's good and ready for you once you move into a more functional position.)

Then, when you or she craves more action, you can easily stretch your legs behind you, getting into any number of missionary variants (like the positions pictured on page 314), which allow you greater freedom to work her over to whatever extent you'd like.

...I think it's time now to go beyond the traditional approach to positions for a deeper understanding that will make you a much better lover.

REASONS TO CHOOSE A POSITION

I showed you how to use positions to maintain control in a prior chapter (see page 115). Here are some other smart reasons to use a particular position:

Reason #1: **To fulfill her emotional desire for passionate romance.**

Some positions are just more *romantic* - and not just the face-to-face ones I suggested before. I already described one of these positions before, the **cozy position**. (See two more **cozy-type positions** on the bottom of page 316.)

Any position that lets you hug and/or kiss her while you're making love is a romantic position, such as the one below (a super-sexy and romantic missionary position variant). *Nothing says "I love you" better than when you give her a bear hug and kiss her during sex.* With this variant, you place your legs outside hers, to completely surround her, making her feel

(Continued on page 318)

EXAMPLES OF ROMANTIC POSITIONS

Here's another romantic position, the rocking chair a great choice because its back-and-forth inertia helps power your strokes.

The Shocking Facts About Positions

(Continued from page 315)

enveloped lovingly. But be careful to keep your weight off her. This is a delicate balancing act, but it's something you must learn to do, especially in any of the man-on-top, woman-lying-down positions. Here, you'd be pushing down lightly on the bed with your forearms while pulling your chest backward slightly. (It is true that you need to develop special muscles to perform this deed. It's almost like doing yoga. But, then again, every activity has its peculiar demands.)

Another romantic position is on page 317, doable with any chair, stool or suitable object that might resemble a seat (such as a flat-topped boulder in a romantic and private outdoor setting).

Reason #2: To massage specific areas such as her **G-Spot**, **AFE Zone** or **Deep Trigger**. (See the **anatomy** and **cocksmanship** chapters for details on **hot spot locations** and **cocksmanship techniques**.)

Each of her **hot spots** has its best *positions* for best *access*.

For example, I think you'll find that the **missionary position** and its variants tend to work best if you want to work her **G-Spot** - either to make her **wetter** or to give her **profound orgasms**. **Sideways positions** work second best for this. **Rear-entry positions** are a bit trickier for this - except when standing, as in the photo on the top of the next page, which is *super*.

To give her **Deep Trigger** orgasms, however, you absolutely must enter her *from the rear*. The two positions at the top of page 319 are superior for that.

AFE Zone orgasms on the other hand require that you enter her from the *front* (or, secondarily, *the side*). The **missionary variant** below works well for these, for example. You can propel yourself with your toes, or by rocking on top of her with your torso, or by gently wiggling your bottom.

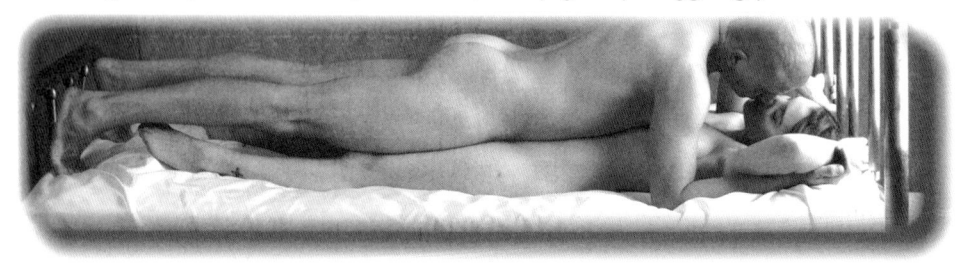

The **missionary variants** on page 314 are also good for this. These naturally position your cock to enable you to massage her **AFE Zone**. Remember - her **AFE zone** offers you two options: it's great simply for making her wetter or for making her come. (Another super **AFE** position is shown on page 414.)

Contrary sideways positions, such as the one on the next page

Examples Of Hot Spot-Specific Positions

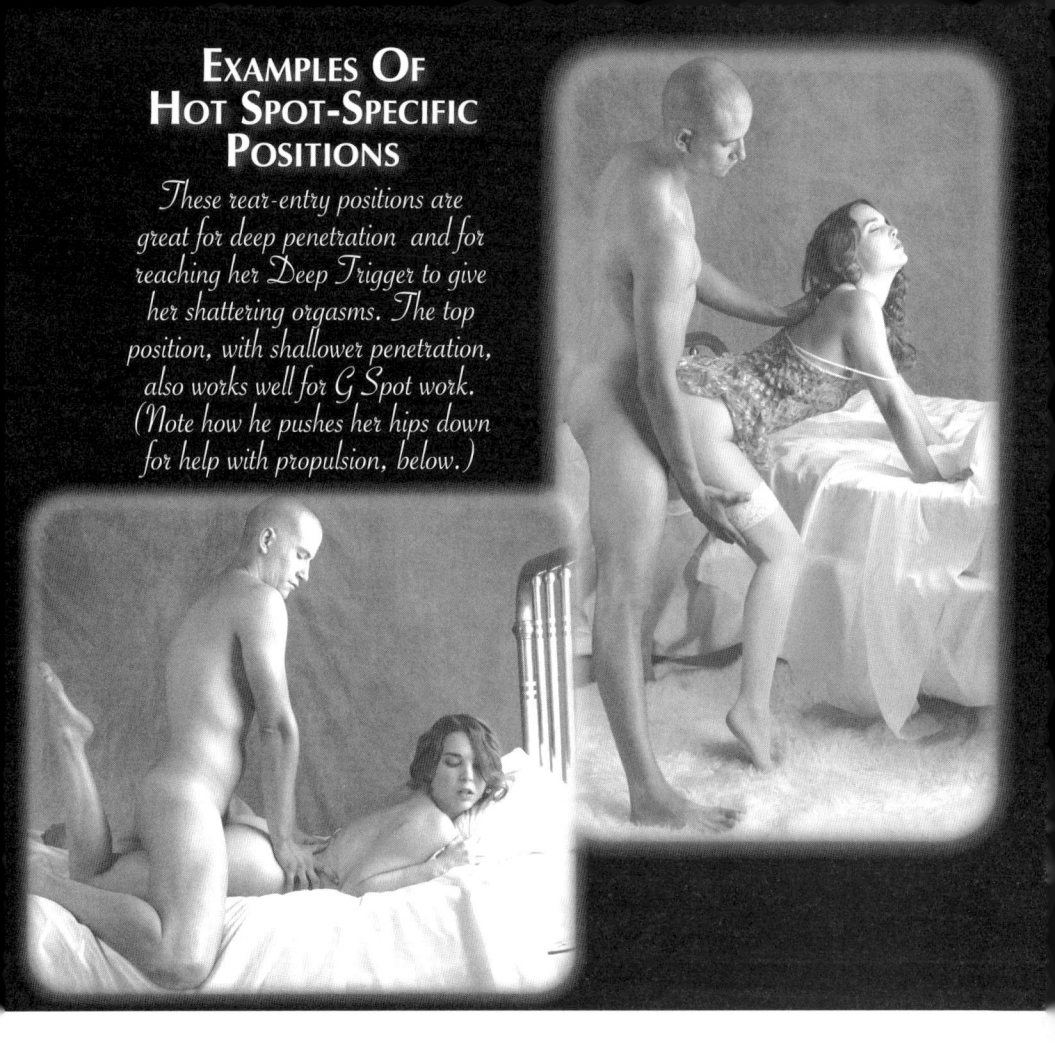

These rear-entry positions are great for deep penetration and for reaching her Deep Trigger to give her shattering orgasms. The top position, with shallower penetration, also works well for G Spot work. (Note how he pushes her hips down for help with propulsion, below.)

(below), and contrary positions where you're sitting up and she's lying on her back (such as the position at the top of page 322) are great if you only want to tease her **vulva** with the head of your cock or if you only want very shallow penetration (perhaps to work her **G-Spot**). These work especially well in the early stages of a **love**making session, especially when

MORE HOT SPOT-SPECIFIC POSITIONS

The position on the right works well for shallow places, such as her G-Spot.

The position atop the next page is great for producing large AFE zone orgasms.

The one below facilitates Deep Trigger orgasms.

shallow, pussy-wettening teasing is what you want to do.

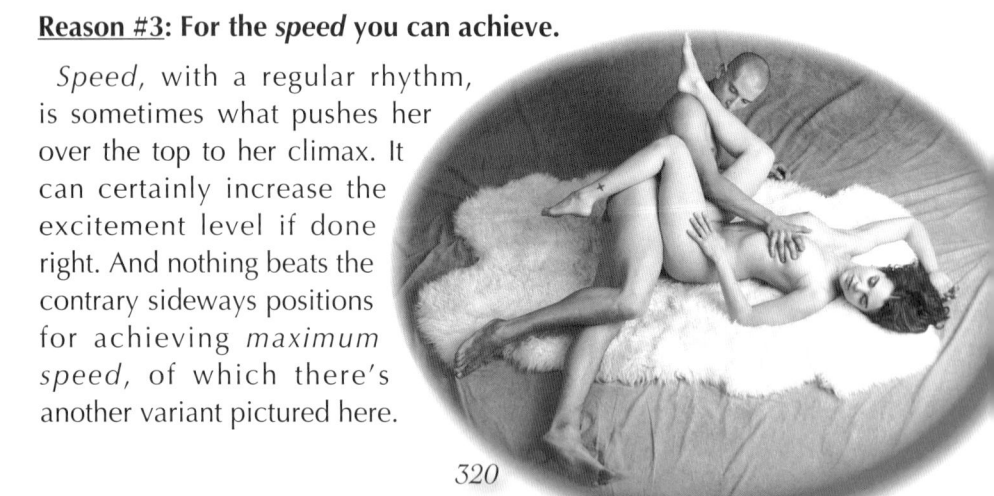

Reason #3: For the *speed* you can achieve.

Speed, with a regular rhythm, is sometimes what pushes her over the top to her climax. It can certainly increase the excitement level if done right. And nothing beats the contrary sideways positions for achieving *maximum speed*, of which there's another variant pictured here.

On Loving Women

Don't go too deep in this position. With her legs drawn up, her vaginal canal is shorter.

Other positions that afford you a good deal of speed include the contrary positions where: 1) you're standing, with your woman lying back on a bed, table or other flat surface, her calves and feet over the side; 2) she's lying back on a bed, couch or other soft, spongy surface and you're sitting up on your knees (in the top two photos here); I suggest you rapidly bounce up and down for propulsion); 3) you're standing, taking her from behind (see page 322); and, 4) you're taking her as shown in the photo to the left, achieving great speed by rhythmically pushing her hips down into the mattress with your hands and then letting up so the spring of the mattress brings her body back up, contributing to the ease and speed of motion.

The Shocking Facts About Positions

Reason #4: For the ability to *multitask*.

As I mentioned in the anatomy chapter, the more sweet spots you stimulate, the hotter she'll get and the bigger her orgasm will be. A sophisticated lover can do many things at once, or **multitask**, no matter what the position. But this is easier in some positions than in others.

For instance, the positions in the two-page spread on page 310 are especially good for the amount of **mouth** access they provide: you can suck her toes, kiss her legs, suck her nipples and kiss her lips. Few other positions offer such a range. The ones on pages 320 and 321 give you easy access to her **clitoris**. Actually, you can *touch* her just about anywhere in these positions. The position on the bottom of page 319 is super too for its multiple **multitasking** possibilities.

The missionary position, in contrast, offers more limited mouth and hand options, due to your need to use your arms or hands to keep your weight off her. It's fine for kissing her lips and neck, though (and limited breast work depending on how your torsos match up).

Some rear entry options are good for *multi-tasking* (see the one above and two on page 323). These are great for easy access to her clit.

The contrary position pictured to the right is also a good multitasking position, for the easy access you have to her clit. This one requires a bit of effort, though, to coordinate. It's probably not for beginners.

On Loving Women

For maximum *speed* you should not multi-task unless you're really good.

Reason #5: For her desire to feel as if she's *being taken*. (See this pictured on page 324 and page 325.)

A minority of women get off on positions that give them the primal feeling that they're being swept away inexorably by a strong, passionate man. The idea is to create the illusion she couldn't get away from you if she tried.

These positions are probably for the uninhibited, though. I wouldn't suggest that you try something like this very early on in the relationship. *And I'd recommend you wait until your lover indicates she's into this before you do it.*

How would she indicate she wants you to make her feel like she's being taken? She might say something like, "Hold my hair like this so you're holding my head down on the bed," while she simultaneously takes your hand and shows you what she likes. Or she might suggest: "Put your hand on my neck and hold me down." That's a pretty clear go-ahead.

Be sure to simulate the scene with a lot of tenderness, to offset any possible dark implications. It should come

The Shocking Facts About Positions

across as a benign form of role playing.

The idea is more akin to pretending you're a strong but loving caveman who's acting out on a strong sense of desire for her (because you can't help yourself; your woman is so desirable). You're simply "taking" the woman you've admired from afar (and she offers nominal resistance because she has secretly admired you). This is the game. The amount of strength you use should be just enough for pretense, and little enough such that she could get away from you easily if she wanted to.

NOTE: You should never enact these "being taken" scenarios with any kind of force. This is not a rape fantasy nor sadomasochism, which is different and, I feel, dangerous to cater to. Don't go there. This is not an invitation for rough sex, either. That's another animal altogether (one that brings to mind the "Preppy Murder" in New York). I'd recommend you steer clear of rough sex at all costs. It's not very loving (and FYI: if a woman ever requests rough sex, it might very well indicate she has a serious emotional or psychological problem.)

And don't take a "being taken" request as an invitation to "really give it to her" (violently shoving your cock in), as some men like to put it. Women refer to this disparagingly as pounding. They see it as artless, bruising and the expression of a general anger or hatred toward women. Do this and you'll be out the door eventually.

Another a word of advice: don't make a big joke out of it. That will spoil the mood and make her feel you're a jerk. You're looking to spend a night on the couch for that one.

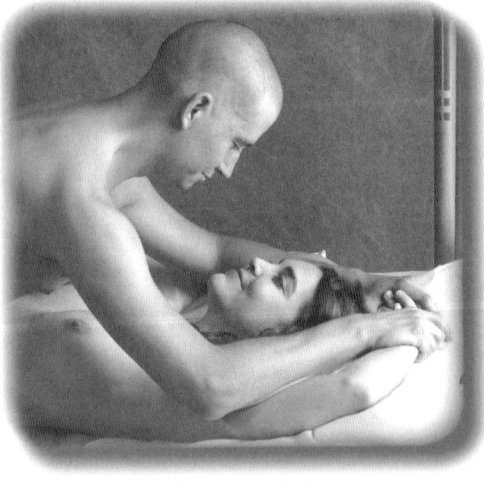

Examples Of "Being Taken" Positions

The Shocking Facts About Positions

Reason #6: For the unique <u>propulsion</u> options the position gives you - especially if they're <u>ergonomic</u> (requiring the least effort on your part, so you can continue that activity for a long time without tiring).

Ergonomic positions often take advantage of **sympathetic motion**, which independently helps provide the energy required to propel your cock in and out. **Sympathetic motion energy** is generated in one of two ways: either from the spring of a bouncy surface (such as a spring-loaded mattress or a shock-stabilized car hood), or the motion of her body. It makes your job a lot easier.

The **wheelbarrow position** is an example of this. This is where you stand by a bed, table, car hood or other object on which your lover is lying back (the object preferably should be hip high) while you hold both of her outstretched legs in your hands. You'd push and pull her legs in rhythm with your in and out motions (generating a **rocking-type motion** with her body and whatever object she's on), the **pendulum-like motion** of your lover and the object she's on combining with your hip wiggling to greatly reduce the amount of energy you have to expend (while also increasing the in-and-out speed you can attain).

The *missionary variant* below is another interesting example of this. Here, by moving your feet back and forth in the air (first pulling your legs close to your butt, then pushing them away from you, repeating this two-part process rhythmically), it's easy to rock the mattress and/or bed back and forth. That *sympathetic motion* will make your in and out motions seem almost effortless.

The *missionary variant* below is also an **ergonomic position**. With this, you'd use your toes to easily propel your body back and forth in a **rocking motion** that would be transmitted to the bed, whose **sympathetic motions** would help make your physical demands that much less.

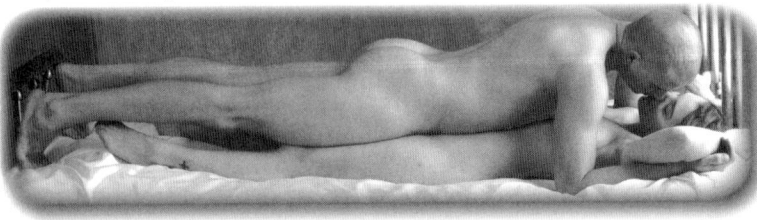

On Loving Women

I also like the positions on the tops of page 314 and page 316, which give you many options for propulsion (propelling your cock). You can butterfly your knees, first sliding them out like they're wings opening up, and then returning them close to her body. Or you can wiggle your hips in and out, or round and round, or up and down. Or you can slide or rock your torso back and forth...Or you could even bounce up and down.

The **rear-entry contrary position** on the bottom of page 321 is another such position. You'd push down on your lover's midsection and then let the mattress spring back up, over and over again, using the natural bounce of the mattress help make things easy on you. (This assumes that you're not on one of the so-called "space age" foam mattresses that have no bounce.)

The **missionary variant** below is also great for **propulsion** (beds with rails or bars, such as mission and brass beds, are great for this). Here, you'd use your hands and arms to pull back and forth, setting up a **sympathetic rocking motion** to make the old in and out a snap.

Ergonomic positions also include those that simply require *the least amount of effort* (i.e., where no **sympathetic motio**n is involved), such as most **woman-on-top positions** or the **rocking-chair positions** on page 323 (for the **momentum** the *motion of the chair* gives you; a **swing** would provide this benefit too).

Every man will have his own personal favorites in this regard. What you should do is to make a mental note of which positions are easiest for you. They're especially useful when you're fatigued or getting older.

Reason #7: For the way it makes her feel.

This is one of the most valid reasons why you might choose a position. This reason often crosses the boundaries of the prior reasons. For example the romantic positions make her feel warm all over; loved.

You might instead want to make her feel all hot and bothered (more aroused) and sexy. In that case, you might use any of the **rear-entry**

The Shocking Facts About Positions

positions; or positions where you're holding her legs in the air; or perhaps the ones where she's on top.

Or she might get excited if you made her feel like she's being naughty. **Doggy-style** is a position often associated with that feeling. Or positions where she's *bent forward over a couch* or *lying back on a table or car hood* (with you standing). The "naughty" effect would be heightened if you "took her" spontaneously immediately upon her returning home from work, leaving some of her clothes on (maybe her shoes, if they're sexy; and maybe her panty hose, especially if they're crotchless).

Some women - believe it or not - also get turned on by being *spanked*; it makes them feel deliciously naughty. I'd suggest that you wait for your lover to ask you for this before you do it. Also follow her lead on how hard to do this. Typically I'd say go lightly - just enough to simulate the act – unless she tells you she wants it harder.

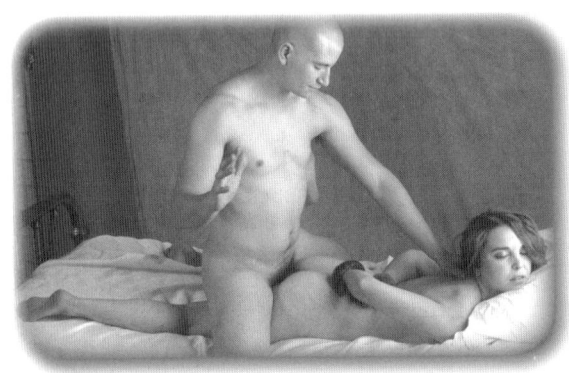

FYI: Women who get off on being *spanked* are not necessarily into *S&M* (sadomasochism). So don't jump to that conclusion and push it too far!

Reason #8: For the ease with which you can give her an *orgasm*.

It's easier to make a woman come in some positions than in others. So you probably want to use those when you're ready to send her over the top.

See the photos on page 329 for the three best positions for giving her *deep vaginal climaxes*. When I say *deep* I mean the orgasms come from **orgasm triggers** in the deepest places of her **vaginal canal** - in her **cervical region**. (See page 194 if you forget where these are.)

And when I say the *best* positions for **vaginal orgasms** I mean they provide the *easiest* route to success. With the right **regular rocking motion** and **complete insertion** just about any man should be able to make his woman come **vaginally** in one or more of these positions.

The **front entry position**s work for just about any man. Even shorter men should be able to make them work because the **vaginal canal** is condensed in length with the drawing up of her legs.

Speaking of which, **G-Spot orgasms** are not hard to achieve in the **missionary position**. Just be sure to keep your penetration *shallow* and

THE THREE BEST POSITIONS TO GIVE HER DEEP VAGINAL ORGASMS

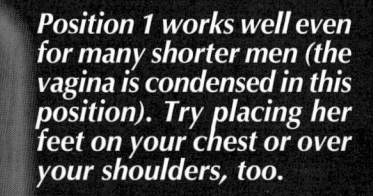

Position 1 works well even for many shorter men (the vagina is condensed in this position). Try placing her feet on your chest or over your shoulders, too.

Position 2 also condenses her vagina's length and is great for most men, for the best vaginal orgasms!

Position 3 (rear entry) requires some length. You must be able to reach the end of her vaginal canal.

Position 1: Man On Top, His Legs Wide; The Woman With Her Legs Up In The Air

Position 2: Man Standing, Woman Bent Over

Position 3: Man On Top, Sitting Up, Knees Butterflied, Woman Lying On Stomach

The Shocking Facts About Positions

your **glans** on her **G-Spot**. (See its location on page 192.) Or use any of the other great **G-Spot** positions I showed you earlier (on page 319 and page 320). But again, stay *shallow* because that's where her **G-Spot** is. (I'll talk more about how to make a woman come **vaginally** in the **cocksmanship** chapter, starting on page 339. Your **motion** and **depth** are key to making her come, as you will see in that chapter.)

Another idea: *She can get off in* **woman-on-top positions** *by rubbing her* **clit** *on your pubic bone. Urge her to try this. All it takes is for her to get as snug a fit as possible with you. Then all she needs to do is wiggle her hips rhythmically while maintaining* **clitoral contact** *with your body.*

Along these lines, here's another approach in picking good positions *once you've decided you want to make her come:*

Choose positions in which it's easy to access and massage her **clitoris** *to* **orgasm**. **Sideways positions** *are great for this (see the top photo page 320).*

Other positions that fit this category include positions:
- *In which she can* **masturbate** *simultaneously (if she's into this)*
- *That allow you to* **multi-task** *(see page 322 to review those)*

Some women will come quickly, for instance, if you've made them really hot and you suddenly suck one or more of their **toes**; or kiss, suck and lick their **spines**, or the backs of their **necks**; or suck one or both **nipples** (as I mentioned in the previous chapter, if you can suck both **nipples** simultaneously in any position - if her **breasts** are *big* enough to squeeze the **nipples** closely together - it will drive her crazy!).

Pacing (i.e., how feverish the sex is and how quickly you want to make her come) is usually your prerogative. So if you want prolonged sex before making your lover climax, then a position that's not so great for making her climax is fine (because that's not your immediate goal).

But when you're ready to make her come, you'll want to switch to one that makes that goal easier.

Reason #9: For the special moves you can do in a position.

I love the positions where you're on your side, **perpendicular** to your

On Loving Women

lover while she lies on her back (as pictured on the top and bottom of page 320). One reason I favor them is that they give you the ability to *quickly* **fill her to the max** with your erection and then *swiftly* pull it all the way out.

This super-quick maximum in-and-out stroke is highly exciting to most women and is hard to accomplish in most other positions. (Do this carefully if you are well-endowed so you don't bruise her by going in too far. If you hurt her in any position she might very well stop you from using that position again. It'll have a negative connotation.)

Reason #10: For the depth you can achieve.

Some positions enable you to go your deepest, *which are especially great for giving her orgasms just through penetration.* (See the photo, right.)

One such position type is one I call the **vaginal canal shorteners (VCS).** These positions are where her legs are drawn up, internally shrinking the length of her canal (as in the photo below).

VCS positions are great for short men. *Long men should stay shallow, though, so as not to hurt her.*

Another great one: she lies on her back, you lean forward on her legs (your chest holding her legs against her body, your hands on the bed supporting your weight) so that her feet are above her head or over your shoulders and her butt is drawn up off the mattress.

If you're of average or less-than-average length and your baby's got butt, you might find the rear-entry position where she's lying facedown on the bed a bit challenging, as far as penetration

The Shocking Facts About Positions

depth goes. So you might especially prefer **VCS positions** where her legs are pulled up toward her chest, which shortens the length of her vagina (such as the top two positions on page 329).

For those with at least average-length erections, some positions that offer the greatest **penetration** include: where you're standing up and she's lying back on a bed or table; where you're standing up and she's standing but bent forward over a couch, table, car hood or other object; and where you're on your side perpendicular to her as she lies on her back.

Reason #11: Because a position is one of her favorites.

We talked about how it's your job to discover which positions are her favorites. Now it's time to use them – whether they're your favorites or not. Often, these positions are the ones in which she has the greatest sensitivity, which make her the hottest and most likely to come.

HOW TO USE HER FAVORITE POSITIONS

So here's one smart way to use her favorite positions:

*Avoid going to her **most favorite positions** too early*. Hold off putting her in those positions until she's *really hot*. Wait until you've been making love to her for a long time and she's dying for one of her most favorite positions.

*You want to **play on her eagerness for them**. You want to **heighten her expectations**, thereby **creating excitement**.*

*If you ignore this rule and use all of her favorite positions at the outset, it'll be all **downhill** from there. There will be no positions left for her to look forward to.*

Or...even better:

*Hold off on using her **most favorite positions** until you want to bring things to a rousing close. Sweet torment is a good overall strategy.*

*Then when you finally switch over to one of her **most favorite positions** after making her crave for seemingly forever, it will make her especially hot. So when she finally comes, you will really send her over the top!*

That's right! *In denying her her **most favorite positions** until you begin her orgasm process, her desire for and anticipation of them will make her orgasm bigger*.

This is the smart way to use positions to orchestrate the whole experience.

Another word of advice: Don't use her **most favorite positions** too much. In fact, use them *sparingly*. Otherwise you will *wear off their effect* in surprising her and making her more excited. Plus, using any position too much becomes boring. And you don't want to bore her!

Worse, if you *overdo* using her **most favorite positions** you might even make her *hate* them! Anything repeated too much becomes old.

So *even if she asks for them every time, resist that temptation*. You can say, "No, let's try this right now," and then do something else. Don't allow sex to become *predictable!* That's a drag.

OTHER REASONS TO MOVE INTO A PARTICULAR POSITION

There are many other valid reasons to choose a position, such as:

- *For the surprise value (make her lie back on a table and you'll see what I mean!)*
- *To appeal to her desire for spontaneity (you might take her from behind, in a passionate surprise "attack," with her pressed against the front door of your house, for instance, her panties pulled down to her knees, her skirt pulled up just enough to allow you to enter her)*
- *To help you avoid coming too soon (for this you'd choose sideways and other positions where she has less control and you can easily pull out or keep penetration shallow)*
- *To make her feel you can't find enough ways to love her (use an unusual position such as the one below, which she might like for the access she gets to your bottom)*
- *To give her a show (One of my girlfriends, for instance, said she liked sideways positions because, "then I can watch you better. I like to watch you while you're making love to me.")*
- *For the novelty of it (see below)*

The position below is difficult to achieve but it's novel. And it's super for women who like having access to your butt. (It's also great for men with **premature ejaculation** issues, as I noted in the chapter on **control**.)

Warning, though: *You need to move into this in a flaccid or half-flaccid state*. Your hard-on will be bent sharply backward. *Don't attempt this*

The Shocking Facts About Positions

position once you're hard because injury might result. Try it after you've already come once but you're ready for more. It's also an exciting way to start things off. It limits your mobility, though, so move on to something else when you're ready for faster or deeper action.)

THE ART OF CHANGING POSITIONS

...Now to **position changing**. Great lovers elevate this to an art.

Don't do this haphazardly. Position changing in and of itself will not satisfy any of your partner's desires. In fact, if you're like most men (constantly changing positions for no apparent reason) she'll find your position changes distracting and annoying. You'll want to avoid that because once she's angry with you good luck making her come!

Stupid or wrongful changes break the mood and take her off the path to her climax. She might even laugh at you. At that point you might as well break out the cards. Here are some examples of stupid changes:

- ☹ *moving to a new position before having spent more than a minute or two in the prior position*
- ☹ *moving to positions you have extreme difficulty getting into, which kill the excitement you've generated to that point*
- ☹ *moving back to a position you've just come from and then doing the same thing you'd done before, giving her a been-there, done-that feeling of boredom*
- ☹ *going from a position where she's on the brink of coming to one in which you have difficulty making her climax*

And you should never make your lover change to a position she perceives as uninteresting or less interesting than the one you were just in. Especially if you want to make her come!

If you're inept or clueless in making position changes, *she will conclude that you don't know what you're doing*. You will have a hard time shaking off that impression, too. That will harm your relationship and could eventually end it.

THE HOW, WHEN & WHY OF POSITION CHANGING

So now's the time to ask yourself: *Do you make* **position changes** *with a goal in mind, or do you do it randomly, without rhyme or reason?* Let's look at what position *changes* are all about.

A sophisticated lover knows how, when and why to change positions. A good general rule is that **position changes** should be made **infrequently, intelligently** and **smoothly**.

Two Ladders To Climb (And Not Descend)

Another good general rule is that **position changes** should be used to **build excitement.** But how do you do this?

For one thing, as I said earlier, you need to catalog the positions she likes (in order of preference). Because once you have that information, you can make smarter position changes. *In changing positions you want to make sure you're going up her ladder of preferences. Not down.*

I don't mean to imply that you should use all the positions she likes or all of her favorites at any one time. That would be dull!

The point is, whatever position you go to should be *higher* up on her list of preferences. Once she's had an orgasm you can back off a bit; you've arrived at a new start. But as you're building toward a climax, stick to this ladder of preference rule.

Smart Reasons To Make A Position Change

Beyond that, here are some intelligent reasons to make a position change:

- *To achieve greater penetration (to stimulate more of her nerves)*
- *To achieve greater mobility and speed*
- *To make her come faster (I told you earlier of positions in which it's easiest to make her come - due to the angle or speed you can achieve)*
- *To be able to do a special, exciting move you can't do in a prior position (such as the maximum in-and-out move I mentioned before)*
- *To make things easier on yourself when you're tired (by using an ergonomic position which requires less energy)*
- *To heighten her excitement level (by changing to a naughty or favorite position, for example)*
- *To awaken her senses by surprising her (as in trying a daring new idea, such as throwing her over the kitchen table)*
- *To achieve greater access to one of her favorite sweet spots (as in taking her from behind, which lets you nicely massage her **G-Spot**)*

For The Position-Challenged

Now if you're not good at changing positions, here are some tips:

- *It's better to stay in one position longer than attempting to change to another clumsily*
- *Use less position changes in general*
- *Make changes slowly and (always) lovingly*
- *Do it with good humor and fun*

The Shocking Facts About Positions

And by the way, while it is true that most women would prefer that you stay inside of them when you go to a new position, this is sometimes not possible and it's not an imperative if this is too difficult a task for you. If you're not too slick at this or you have an infirmity that prevents your staying inside her during position changes, a quick re-entrance can suffice. It's better than attempting something at which you're clumsy.

Or here's an idea: If you're really smooth, you can divert her attention when you have to make a temporary exit by: giving her oral sex (even if just to get her hotter); or by kissing her in sensitive places during the switch-over (on her shoulders, for example, or on the back of her neck); or doing something sexy like showing her your hard-on and saying (in your best Barry White voice): "Look how big you made me!" Make it seem as if you intended to do the diversionary act before re-entering her, that it was the reason for "dismounting" as it were between positions.

ONE FINAL CONSIDERATION: *NERVE FATIGUE*

Before we move on to more important topics, here's one more reason why you might not want but *need* to change positions. Once you've learned how to give her **vaginal orgasms** (through techniques you'll read about in the next chapter), you'll find there are times where your efforts in one position, massaging one particular area inside of her, produce no more results. **Nerve fatigue** has set in (her nerves have been dulled; we'll discuss this more later on). With some women, for example, this sets in quickly when you're in **deep penetration positions** focused on her **AFE zone** or **Deep Trigger**. Easy solution: Just move to a position that has your **cock** positioned to massage a new area, one that has not experienced **nerve fatigue**.

FINAL WORDS

Finally, remember that positions are just tools; they're like a *frame* to a painting. The frame must fit and complement the painting. But it's the *painting* that counts. In other words:

It's not the position. It's what you *do* in the position that matters.

EXAMPLES OF ARTFUL POSITION CHANGES

Changing positions can be done many ways. But you should develop your own style in doing it. Practice makes perfect.

To go from A to B, use your left hand to guide her left thigh to your right, gently rolling her body onto her left side.

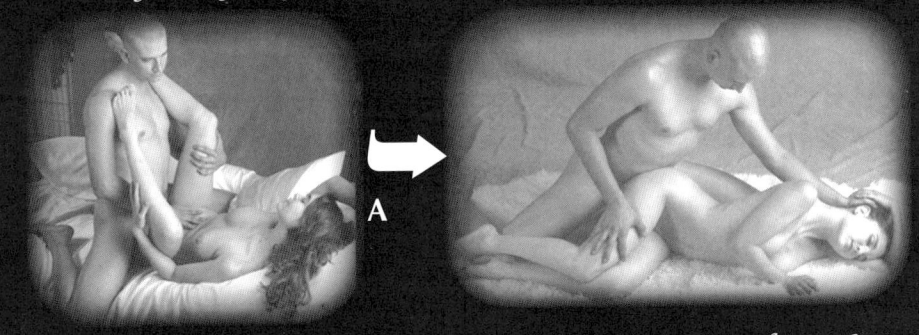

A → B

Rolling moves are great. You can roll from C to D or from E to F below. You could guide her body into the roll. Or you could encourage her to roll with you, saying: "Roll to your left, honey."

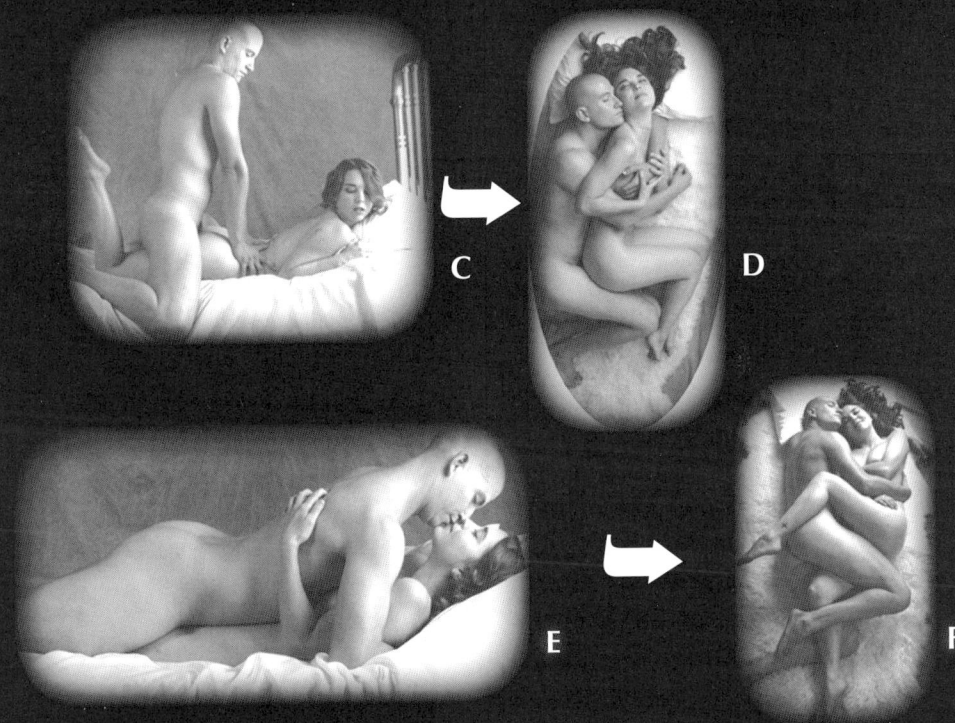

C → D

E → F

How you guide your lover from one position to another depends upon what position you're leaving and which one you're going to. If at first you're awkward doing this, take it slowly.

NEW RESEARCH DISCOVERIES ON SEXUAL POSITIONS

Your entry choice affects where you arrive inside her

In 2002* a French MRI study of a couple having sex in the missionary and posterior positions came to some startling conclusions.

From the rear, the head of your *penis* can reach her most distant reaches (her *posterior fornix*). In the missionary position your *glans* arrives at her *anterior fornix*. So *you're massaging different places inside her with front and rear entry.*

The quintet of CMC Beau Soleil researchers concluded there is "a difference in stimulation, thus the pleasure felt as a result may also be different." They also suggested there are "*two types of vaginal orgasms*, one from preferential stimulation of the *anterior vaginal wall*...and one from deeper preferential stimulation of the *posterior wall of the vagina* and *cervix* (and perhaps the *posterior fornix*)." Because they believe the *anterior wall* has more nerves, they theorized that *orgasms* produced there are *bigger* than *posterior wall orgasms*. (Note: This idea has been disputed. See page 208.)

That seems to give the missionary position the edge. But in my experience it's the opposite. (And my lovers agree.) I've found it's easiest to induce orgasms in *rear-entry positions* with maximum penetration (with the *Deep Trigger* I introduced in the anatomy chapter; see page 194). Plus, they're super *quick* and *powerful*. Maximum-insertion front-entry orgasms (produced by the *AFE Zone or a trigger near it*) are *less* strong.

The study also revealed: Your penis becomes *boomerang-shaped* during sex. And her *vagina* nearly *doubles* in length, "tents" and becomes *convex*.

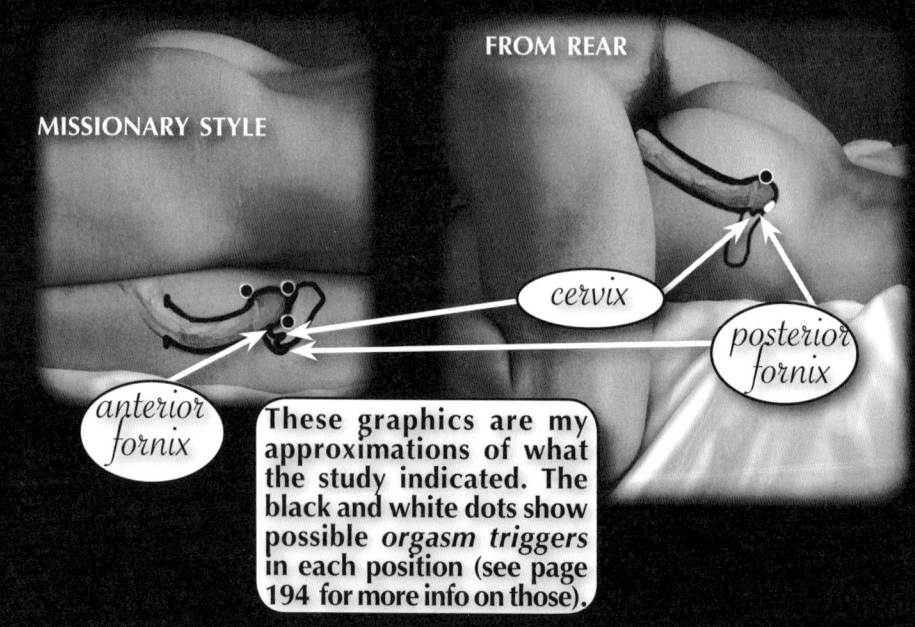

MISSIONARY STYLE

FROM REAR

cervix

posterior fornix

anterior fornix

These graphics are my approximations of what the study indicated. The black and white dots show possible *orgasm triggers* in each position (see page 194 for more info on those).

* See "Magnetic Resonance Imaging (MRI) of Sexual Intercourse: Second Experience in Missionary Position and Initial Experience in Posterior Position" by A. Faix et. al. in the Journal of Sex & Marital Therapy

> *"[Sex is] one of the greatest gifts God has given us. And there can be no marriage if it is not right."*
> *– screen legend Bette Davis on TV's Dick Cavett Show*

Cocksmanship

On one of Oprah Winfrey's last network TV shows (airing on April 11, 2011), she asked actress and author Shirley MacLaine about MacLaine's legendary love life. Her answer was poignant:

"I've had an **awful** lot of lovers," she admitted. Without missing a beat she continued: "I've had a lot of **awful** lovers."

That confirms what many women have told me. According to the fair sex, *most men fall short when it comes to* **cocksmanship.**

And that refrain turns up everywhere. Season 2, Episode 8 of *Sex and the City* ("The Man, The Myth, The Viagra,") featured this commentary:

> Miranda: Guys are such liars!
> Samantha: And 97% of them can't fuck you worth a damn!

That should be a wake-up call. The average male lover is apparently *inadequate*. At least *women* think so. And they're the ones who count.

And they're not afraid to *voice* their gripes. So...what is your lover telling her girlfriends about *you*?

One of my girlfriends told me she and her girlfriends *often* discuss their lovers. They identify men as either **Pounders** (bad) or **Ticklers** (good) - referring to how men use their **cocks**. I was unaware of those designations at the time. Happily, though, she said I was definitely a **Tickler**.

ARE YOU A POUNDER OR TICKLER?

Her point was that women are *particular* about their lovers. *They want men who know what they're doing with their cocks.*

And they don't like **Pounders**. Those are lovers, she explained, who thrust their cocks in violently during intercourse as if they're *angry* or they're trying to *punish* their women. The effect is *jarring* and *unpleasant*.

The **Pounder** shows no finesse or sensitivity toward the woman. So she feels as if she's being *violated*. Because of the *emotion* behind the motion.

Cocksmanship

The impression women get is that the **Pounder** is expressing a repressed dark and anti-female feeling more akin to *hate* or *rage* than *love*. And women don't want lovers who use their **hard-ons** as battering rams, as too many apparently do.

The **Tickler**, on the other hand, she continued, is celebrated for his ability to *tenderly touch, stroke, massage and tickle* his woman into a state of ecstasy. He uses his **erection** as *an instrument of* **positive** *and* **romantic** *expressions*. He communicates **loving** *thoughts and feelings* through sexy physical motions (as I suggested to you in the *Sex Vs.* **Love***making* chapter).

She added that the **Tickler** possesses an almost clairvoyant **empathy** *for what his lover is feeling*. He has learned to get in touch with what his woman *wants*, at any moment. And he *acts* on that knowledge to give her the most sublime and satisfying *pleasures*.

Don't Be A "I Really Gave It To Her" Type

So...let's be honest. Are you the kind of guy who tells his buddies the next day, *"I really gave it to her last night"*? I hear a lot of that.

Sorry, my friend. If that's you, it sounds like you fall into the undesirable **Pounder** category. That kind of approach doesn't usually work well with women. In their minds, it doesn't express *love*.

If you are (in your mind) *"giving it to her"* during intercourse, your lover will likely be among those unhappy women I mentioned before. She'll be *complaining* about you to her girlfriends *just as you are boasting to your buddies, unaware your brutal technique backfired on her!*

So, **Cocksmanship Lesson #1**:

Don't be a **Pounder**. Be a **Tickler**. (We'll talk about how to do this in a moment.) The very idea that you should use your erection to *tickle* her gets you into the right way of thinking.

Don't Be A Stroke, Stroke, Stroker

Another kind of lover women don't want: **Stroke, Stroke, Strokers**.

If what women say is true, most men make love like they're in a *crew* competition. They think it's all about **stroke, stroke, stroke - going in-and-out as quickly as possible, with a steady, rhythmic stroke of a maximum range of motion and force and a lack of focus on or apparent awareness of any particular erogenous zone**. You see this all the time in porno films.

So, **Cocksmanship Lesson #2**:

Unlike *men's crew*, **love**making is not supposed to be **predictable**, **mechanical, artless** or, ultimately, **boring** through **regularity**. There's a time and a place for *rhythmic stroking*, but if you're primarily a **Stroke, Stroke, Stroker**, you'll quickly become a *turn-off*. That becomes *old* really fast.

And you cannot *aimlessly* go in-and-out of her. You need to locate a **hot spot** and *work it*.

Actually, if this describes you, you're giving way *too much* of yourself way *too fast*. If you start off with quick, hard and deep insertions, *where are you going to go from there?*

Making her *come* often involves *increasing* something - *speed, intensity, range of motion, depth* or *rhythm*. But how can you increase *anything* to bring that about if you've been giving her <u>everything</u>, *to the max, from the get-go?*

And there's something else you might not have thought about, if you're a **Stroke, Stroke, Stroker. Nerve fatigue** *quickly sets in with that approach.* Her **nerves** *soon will become* **dulled**. *Then your efforts will feel like annoyances to her. And her* **nerves** *will no longer be able to feel more subtle and tender expressions.*

So, **Cocksmanship Lesson #3**:

In great **love**making, <u>**less**</u> **is often** <u>**more**</u>.

Cocksmanship Lesson #4:

You do not have to go **fast** to get her **hot** or even to make her **come**. Indeed, *you can go very slowly and produce a bigger effect than you can by artless* **Stroke, Stroke, Stroking**.

Cocksmanship Lesson #5:

You do not have to penetrate her **deeply** to make her come. You can engage in **shallow intercourse** and make her **gush** and **come** like crazy. The beauty part? *Guys of just about any size and length should be able to give her* **orgasms** *using the novel* **shallow lovemaking techniques** *I will show you in this chapter!*

Cocksmanship Lesson #6:

You do not have to use much **force**. In fact, *finesse is more effective*.

Cocksmanship Lesson #7:

You do not have to **move** very much to give her an **orgasm**. Indeed, it's often better not to move too far in either direction! And sometimes you

Cocksmanship

can make her come **without moving at all!** (I'll teach you how very soon!)

A Smart Lover Sensitizes His Lover

Putting together all the lessons above and what I told you in the *love touching* chapter, here's **Cocksmanship Lesson #8:**

A smart lover will go out of his way to **sensitize** *his lover so she responds to the lightest of touches and moves sexually.*

How do you do this? The more you keep things to a *minimum*, the more you will **sensitize** her to *lower levels* of **stimulation**, the *less it will take* to *make her come*, and *the easier it will be to make her come* **multiple times**.

What Is Great Cocksmanship?

OK...so you now know what **great cocksmanship** is *not* about. It's not, in general, about *going at a maximum speed and intensity* or *mechanical motions*. That will not do very much (except perhaps *annoy* her).

So what is **great cocksmanship** all about? *It's about using your cock to get her* **hot**, *make her* **come**, *and, ultimately, to* **please** *and* **satisfy** *her.* And - in great **love**making - it's especially about expressing the **depth of passion** you feel and your **love** for her.

Most times (unless you can stay hard after coming), she should come before you and, usually, multiple times. Afterward, she should feel like she's really been *done*. *Satiated*. Sweetly *exhausted*. *Exhilarated*.

But how can you tell if you've given her a complete experience?

If you've totally knocked her socks off, *she* eventually will bring the **love**making session to an *end* by saying something like, "*Mercy,*" or "*I can't take anymore!*" That's the kind of feedback great lovers usually get when they've thoroughly rung *all* their lovers' bells.

So you will *know* when you've become a **great cocksman**. She'll *tell* you.

But how do you *get* there? You've undoubtedly been with at least one great female lover. Didn't she seem to *know* how she was making you feel as she did you? (As if she had supernatural powers to get inside your head, to know your thoughts and exactly what she was doing to you.) You probably felt as if she was messing with your mind. And she probably teased you with such a wicked confidence and knowledge of her **sexual finesse** that her **attitude** *alone* undoubtedly made you much *hotter*.

That's what you want to achieve in using your **cock** on and inside her. She should feel that you *know* what you're doing to her. And she should sense you're *delighting* in masterfully driving her deliciously crazy.

On Loving Women

To do that requires that you know what your **hard-on** means to her. How it *feels* to her. How she *responds* to it. What works best.

And that brings me to **Cocksmanship Lesson #9:**

Most men seem to think *women* have *everything* to offer, sexually, and *men* have *nothing*. Nothing could be farther than the truth.

A woman craves your body as much as you crave hers. And your **cock** has the power to *turn on* her *flames, make her sizzle* and, finally, *bring on a real fireworks show* - if you know how to play with her **anticipations** and **reactions** to every possible move you can make with your **cock**.

Your **erection** is your sexual *magic wand*. It can produce a wide range of titillating feelings in her and **orgasms of many types**. In other words - *you have something of real value to offer her*.

My mentor Earle really wanted me to understand this lesson. He felt it was *key* to having *the proper* **attitude** to become a **great lover**.

In fact, he used to get annoyed at women who acted as if they were giving men everything during sex and men were getting a *gift*. He'd respond to that, as if it was an *affront to his value as a lover*:

"You can't give anyone a *hole!*" he'd comment.

That's a bit harsh and not entirely fair to women, as far as their contribution goes. But his overall point was valid.

Unless she takes the initiative (which, as you know, is not typically the case), *you* (the *man*) are the one who's *giving somebody something* and *making things happen* during **love**making. You have the sexual tool that brings it all about. So don't undervalue what you have to offer as a lover.

All of this screams for **Cocksmanship Lesson #10:**

Don't give it all away - give her all of your **erection** - from the get-go.

Once she's *aroused*, she's desperately *desiring your cock*. That gives her a **sexual fever** you can *stoke* by *prolonging* her **craving**. Play on that.

While we all remember Robert Plant's sexy refrain, "I'm gonna give you every inch of my love," in Led Zeppelin's *Whole Lotta Love*, I'm sure he'd agree that you shouldn't give her every inch *too soon*. (He was on record as being a proponent of lengthy **love**making.) If you insert your member to the hilt too early you'll give away all your *power* - the **sexual effects** you can produce by <u>delaying</u> *entering her* and giving her *complete* **penetration**.

Make her *want it* <u>desperately</u>. Delay, delay, delay giving her your **cock**. On some occasions, even make her *ask* for it (or if she's into it, make her

Cocksmanship

beg for it) before you give her *every inch* of your **hard-on**.

The act of **delaying** works great as a **sexual tease**. Women respond to that *big time*. It produces *powerful results. Women want to be teased. They want you to play with their heads. The* more you *delay giving her everything, the* hotter *she'll get (if you tease her with* skill). And the *hotter she gets, the bigger her resulting orgasm will be.*

Now once the **tease** is *over*, you then need to know how to use your **cock** as a sexual *tool*. Better yet, as an **instrument of expression and titillation**.

How Your Hard-On Can Move Her

Remember what I said about how great female lovers understand exactly what they're doing to you as they do it? This is how *you* need to be, to become a great lover of women.

So *how will your* **erection** *affect your lover,* when used properly? And *how can you best use your* **cock** *to please your lover?*

To know all of this, you must first understand *your* own *anatomy - that is, looking at your* **erection** *as a* **sexual tool**. Your **erection** has a:

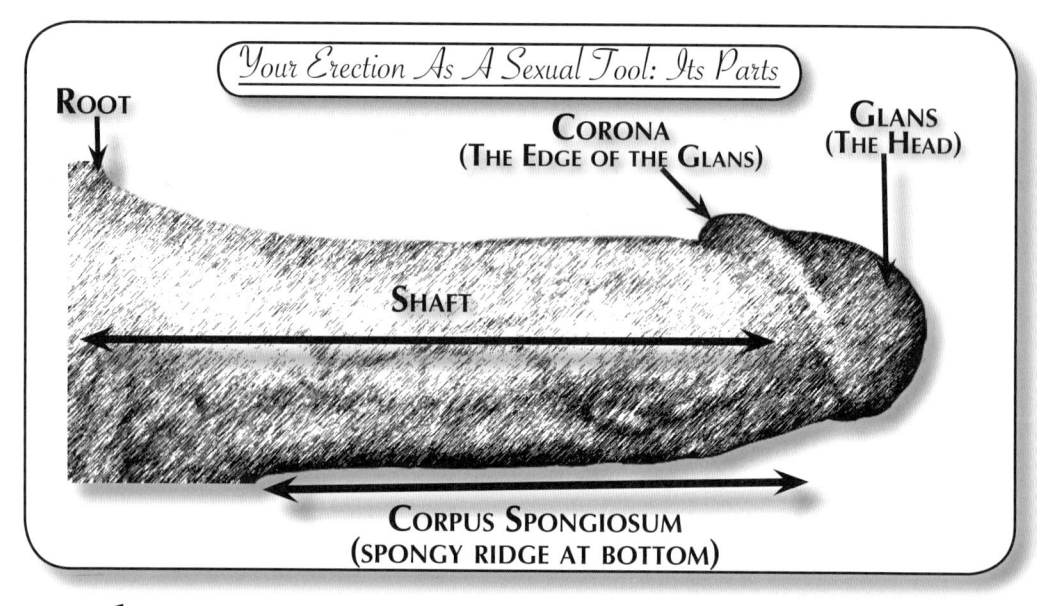

Your Erection As A Sexual Tool: Its Parts

- **ROOT**
- **CORONA** (THE EDGE OF THE GLANS)
- **GLANS** (THE HEAD)
- **SHAFT**
- **CORPUS SPONGIOSUM** (SPONGY RIDGE AT BOTTOM)

- ♂ **Glans** (or **head**), with a <u>corona</u> (the **rounded edge** of the **glans**)
- ♂ **Shaft** (the hard tube that makes up the majority of the **erection**)
- ♂ **Root** (the thickest portion, where your **penis** joins your body)
- ♂ **Corpus spongiosum** - also known as the **Corpus cavernosum urethrae** (the spongy tissue that surrounds the **urethra** to keep it open during **ejaculation**)

On Loving Women

♂ **Corpus cavernosum penis** (*two tubes of* **erectile tissue** *that make the* **penis erect** *and* **hard** *on the* **dorsal side** *(back) of your* **penis**)

♂ **Dorsal artery and veins** (**blood vessels** *along the back of the* **penis**)

Most important is the **head**. And what are the **head's** most important features, to her?

To her, it feels pleasantly **soft** *to the touch*. And it feels wonderfully *warm* to her. That combination of tactile qualities gives her **sexual tingles**, especially when your **cock** *first touches* her **genitals**.

There's an **electricity** about its touch, too - perhaps from the **electrical impulses** in your **nerves** and hers interacting. So she will feel **tingles of pleasure** when you simply *rest* your **glans** against her **erogenous zones**.

Your **glans** is also nicely **plump**. It's the *biggest* part of your **hard-on**.

Add all of your **glans'** qualities together - its *puffy softness, heat, size* and *the tingles it gives her* - and you can see why it makes the perfect *massaging instrument*. It's kind of a sexy, fleshy *cotton swab*. (And you know what *tingles* a cotton swab gives you when you simply insert it in your ear!)

So this is the part you will most want to use to **massage** her **hot spots** and make her *come*. This is also the part of your **erection** you'll most use in *massaging* or simply *touching* her **erogenous** *and* **pleasure zones** to make her **hot, wet** and **wide**.

Two corollaries to this:

You must learn to locate her internal **hot spots** *with your* **glans**, *by feel. Then you must learn how to work those over with your* **glans** *to make her come.* (That's not so difficult, as you'll see.)

But for now understand that *just the touch of your* **glans** *anywhere on her* **genitals** *or within her* **vagina** *will produce potent* **sexual reactions***. Its touch on her* **vulva** *can also make her wet, wide and hot. That's if you create the* <u>anticipation of penetration</u> *by expertly teasing her* **labia minora** and **the opening between those lips**.

Another plus: Your **glans** also will emit a clear **lubricant** *(as I told you in the control chapter). When you see the drops forming at the end of your penis, you should use your glans as a paintbrush to spread it over her* **vulva**.

Why? *You know how your lover can make you more likely to come when she uses lubrication on your* **penis***. This is true in reverse, too. The lubricant you spread on her gives your* **cock's** *ministrations all the greater effect.*

Your **glans** is also *the first part that enters her*. And as your **hard-on's** *fattest* part, it **stretches** her *wide* as it does so. And *stretching* of **any of her sexual openings** or **parts** increases her **arousal level**. *(More on entrances in a moment.)*

Also, if done slowly, **each new millimeter of increased penetration - led by your glans - excites more of her vaginal nerves** which brings about increased **excitement**. So don't rush in or you'll miss out on giving her these feelings. This is yet another reason to enter her and go deeper slowly.

...On to the **shaft** of your **erection.** It also has qualities that can increase her *arousal* and *likelihood of coming*. Number one, it gives off **heat**, and that's a potent **sexual influence**. You know how the *heat* inside your lover's *vagina* gives you the **urge** to *come*? The same thing is true *in reverse*: the **heat** of your **cock** makes *her* want to come. And *you can maximize the heat exchange reaction by holding still or by moving only minimally.*

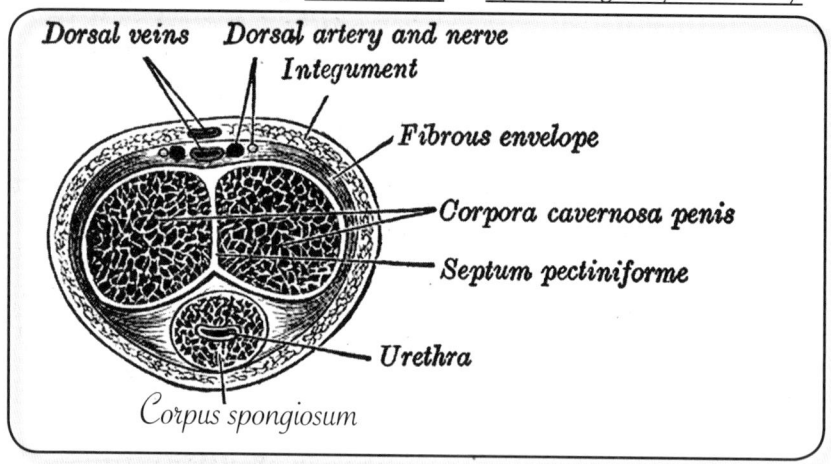

```
Dorsal veins    Dorsal artery and nerve
                   Integument
                         Fibrous envelope
                         Corpora cavernosa penis
                         Septum pectiniforme
                         Urethra
Corpus spongiosum
```

Your **shaft** contains two **corpora cavernosa**, essentially two tubes that fill with **blood** to make the **penis** erect. These are along the back or **dorsal** side of the **penis** and, to your lover, this is what makes your erect penis feel **hard** to her. *(It also transmits body heat, which makes her hotter sexually.)*

Your **shaft**, however, also contains a soft underside, the **Corpus spongiosum** (which we'll call the **CS ridge** for short; this was called the **Corpus cavernosum urethrae** in older anatomy books). This is the *ridge* on the *bottom* of your **erection** that contains your **urethra** (a tube that variously transmits **semen, urine** and **Cowper's gland fluids**). This part of your **shaft** feels pleasantly **soft** (and *sensually* **warm**) to her.

The *hard upper side (dorsal side)* of your **shaft** *(as a voluminous object)* holds her **vaginal walls** open during penetration and provide her *the sensual* and *exciting sensation of being* **filled up**. Think of your **shaft** as a **hard** *balloon*, that stretches her wide. And, again, **stretching actions** - at least when *drawn out slowly* - excite her and make her *hotter*.

To maximize the exciting effect your **shaft** gives her in this way, *minimize movement when you first enter her*. The **stretching action** effect is best produced with a slow *initial* entrance. You can also produce *dramatic stretching sensations* if you rest **motionless** inside of her awhile.

The **hard dorsal side of your shaft** - the *thickest* part of your **shaft** - also contains a **dorsal vein and artery system** that can also give her pleasure when its *rippling texture* passes over her **erogenous zones**. (Which is why the *dorsal side* massages her hot spots - such as her **G-Spot** - better than

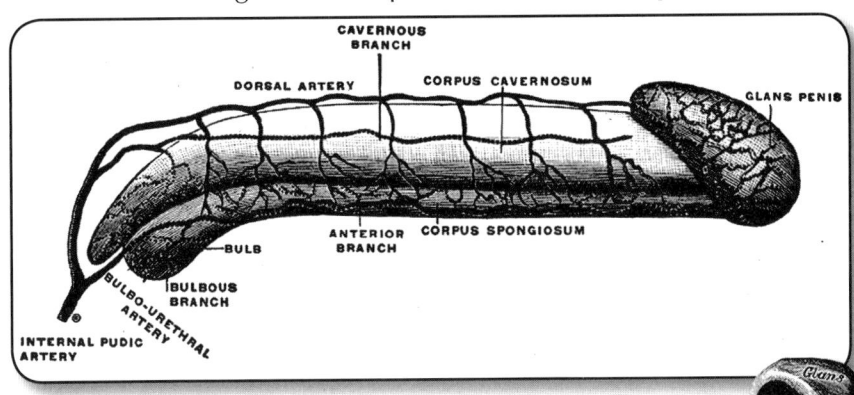

the *thinner, softer underside* of your **erection**. So, for example, when it comes to **G-Spot orgasms**, the **missionary position** is most favorable; that orients your **hard-on** so that the **dorsal side** massages the **G-Spot**.)

Another effect your **shaft** has on her: When *in motion*, it provides *friction* along her **vaginal walls**, which excites her *walls'* **nerves**. When travelling over her **orgasm triggers**, your **shaft** can even sometimes help set off an **orgasm,** although your **glans** is a better instrument to accomplish that. (Your **shaft** will take on a more important role in making her **come** with the **shallow love**making **techniques** on page 350.)

Finally, the **root of your erection** is noteworthy because it's the *thickest* part of your **shaft**. So when you're inside her *to the max*, your **root** will *erotically* and *pleasurably* **stretch** her **vaginal canal's**

Cocksmanship

*outer inch or two. You might even be able to engage her **G-Spot** with it and give her a **G-Spot orgasm** (pressing your **root firmly** against her - **with finesse** (not forcefully) - at **maximum penetration**).*

AN EMOTION IN MOTION

But all of this is *empty* physicality if you don't add an important layer to it: **Love**. As Mae West once said: "Sex is an **emotion** in **motion**." *That's why a mechanical approach to **intercourse** ultimately fails. Women want more from their intimate experiences.*

In other words, when it comes to **cocksmanship**, *you should use your* **cock** *to express how you feel toward your lover.* You should *move* in such a way as to **communicate** *passion* and *affection. Lovingly. Tenderly.*

This is a bit hard to teach. But it's akin to what your music teacher might have advised you when you studied an instrument. He or she probably said at some point: "Once more, **with feeling**." *That's what I'm talking about.*

And *context* is often everything. So - suggestion: If you decide to *go wild*, provide a reason beforehand in terms of *passion*. Tell her how *much* you love her *before* you move vigorously. Then *communicate* how much you *care for, need* and *desire* her (non-verbally) *with every stroke*.

Great **love**making is a **body language**. And, along these lines, don't forget to add lots of *hugs* and *kisses*. And *I love yous*.

SEXUAL ENTRANCES AND THEIR PSYCHOLOGICAL SIGNIFICANCE

But there's an even higher, **spiritual** side to **love**making too. This is crucial to understand, regarding the **female sexual anatomy**. It has **entrances**. You are **entering** her.

A man might not give this much thought but he *should*. Aside from their unique biological effects as unique **hot spots**, a woman's **sexual entrances** have an enormous

On Loving Women

emotional, psychological and **spiritual significance** to <u>her</u>.

I say **entrances** (plural) because - as you saw before - she has a *few; her*:

- ♀ **labia minora** *(they are the outermost doors or entryways to her vulva, through which you first enter her* **sex organs**)
- ♀ **introitus** or **entrance** to her **vagina** *(which, if you think of it - now that you know her vaginal ball is tucked within her vestibule - is a secondary kind of entrance, but an intimate one nonetheless)*
- ♀ **anal canal opening** (if this is a part of your sexual playground) - like the **vaginal canal**, it is ringed with muscular and tingly flesh

You need to understand and respect their *meaning* to her. Only then can you use this reality to your advantage, in pleasing her.

They provide **entry** into her **most intimate** places. And, as such, all of them give her *special* **sensations** and **feelings** *as you* **penetrate** them.

Regarding her **genitals**, her **labia minora** are the *first parts* you must pass in order to be *inside* her. (See the left graphic on the bottom of page 348.)

Biologically, they are the **doors** to her first inner chamber, her **vestibule**. But to *her*, these are the **doorways** into her **inner realm**, through which *you enter not just her* **body** *but her very* **soul** *and* **psyche**. This is how *she* sees it. (One of the many women whose input was invaluable in writing this book, in fact, asked me to make you aware of this. Women feel this concept is *crucial for you to understand* - the **woman's perspective**.)

This is where we, the **lovers of women**, need to part from the *scientists* in our view of **female sexual anatomy**. They think in terms of *biological functioning*. But lovers *need to think in terms of how what we do affects her* **emotionally, psychologically and spiritually** *as well as physically*. We need to know how to *use* all of her *glorious parts* in *sexually satisfying* her.

Given the *significance* women accord your *first entrance* into their bodies, *do not take that event lightly*. Treat it with a kind of *reverence*. **Exalt** the moments you **approach, touch** and **enter** her **doorways**.

Play this concept for all it's worth. Because it's a beautiful thing. Take your time. Savor the moment.

Let her know, through the *delicate* way you first touch her **sexual entrances** that you respect the *emotional, psychological and spiritual significance* she attaches to the event. Let her know, through the *tender* and *loving* way you approach *entering her* that it's an *important* event to *you*, too - her *allowing* you this *intimate* contact *within* her.

So as a general rule, don't carelessly plunge right in past her **labia minora** or the **entrances** to her **vagina** or **anus** and "go to town" with your initial penetration. If you make that mistake, you'll miss out on very special moments and the *emotional, psychological* and *spiritual* **bonding** that can occur when you enter her *carefully, thoughtfully, tenderly* and *lovingly*. (The flip side is that if you don't take your time in entering her she might think you don't *respect* or *understand* the lover's *gift* she's giving you.)

That means you should approach touching her **labia minora** slowly. Tease them, *massage* them or *press against them erotically* before going further. Run your **glans** around their outer edges as if you're drawing lines around them. Use the **head** of your **cock** to tentatively explore the **slit** between the **labia minora.** Go up and down it, *gently*.

It gives her *special excitement* with *the first suggestion* that you're going to *enter her*. She will get *unique tingles* with the anticipation of your *entrance* that you can only create with a cautious approach.

Rush in and she'll not feel that. A *speedy entrance* can also feel *jarring* to her. A*nnoying* and *unsophisticated.* As if you're breaking down her *proverbial doors* rather than easing them *open*. So don't make that faux pas!

Here's an idea that might enable you to strike the right tone in entering her: You might want to pretend you're entering a *crowded* **church**, whose service is *already in progress*. You wouldn't barge in with a lot of noise. You'd *ease* its doors open, with a *reverence* and *respect* for the event that's taking place. *Entering her* that way should produce the right results.

Take your time. Play on her anticipation. Make it significant. Use some drama. Make it a special event.

And, if you remember what I taught you in the *anatomy chapter*, your entering her **vagina** comes *after* you enter her **vulva.** Her **vagina** is snugly located within her **vestibule**; you have to pass her **labia minora** to get there.

So pay respect to *both*. Don't skimp on your attention to either her *first* entrance, her **labia minora**, or her *second*, her **vaginal introitus**.

INTRODUCING SHALLOW LOVEMAKING TECHNIQUES

And I've got a unique way to make sure you give attention to *both* of her **genital entrances**. It's with a fun and very special type of **love**making few men, I believe, engage in.

With the **shallow love**making **techniques** I'm about to show you, men of just about any size or length can give their lovers **genital orgasms** that **satisfy**. (We'll move on to **love**making *techniques that require a long* **member** later.) These **exotic techniques** will take advantage of the existence

On Loving Women

of **multiple erogenous zone areas**, so her **climaxes** will be all the bigger. They will produce **sensations** that are novel to this kind of **love**making, which she'll find pleasantly surprising and satisfying.

We'll start with nine techniques that concentrate solely on her **vulva**, a much-neglected source of fun and pleasure. Then we'll move on to novel ways to give her **vaginal orgasms** without going very deeply at all.

Introducing Vulva Love

Let's start with what I call **vulva love**. This is **a very special kind of love**making - a sensational type of **outside-the-vagina sexual experience**. If you're looking for *novelty* and *variety*, nothing beats this.

In doing this, *you can stimulate most of her **vulva region's hot spots!** You can combine this with vaginal love*making **at any time or it can be satisfying in and of itself, which gives you added versatility as a lover.**

Plus, you can use the **vulva love techniques** I will show you at the outset of your **love**making session (maximizing her pleasure at her **vulval entrance**) while still having the opportunity to awaken her all over again with *entry-type titillations* in her **vagina** later on.

A woman's **vulva** is packed with **sexual hot spots**. (If you recall, it's a **multiple erogenous zone area**.) So it's a place where you can set off **big climaxes by stimulating many erogenous zones at once**.

Introducing Her Vulva Cleft Zone

*The portion of her **vulva** most suited to **love**making is a place I call her **vulva cleft zone** (or **VCZ** for short).* It's a fabulous **orgasm trigger complex**.

This is the area that extends down from her **Niche** to her **V-Spot** (pictured in the drawing on the right).

Her **vulva cleft zone** contains many **erogenous zones** you can engage at once, including her:

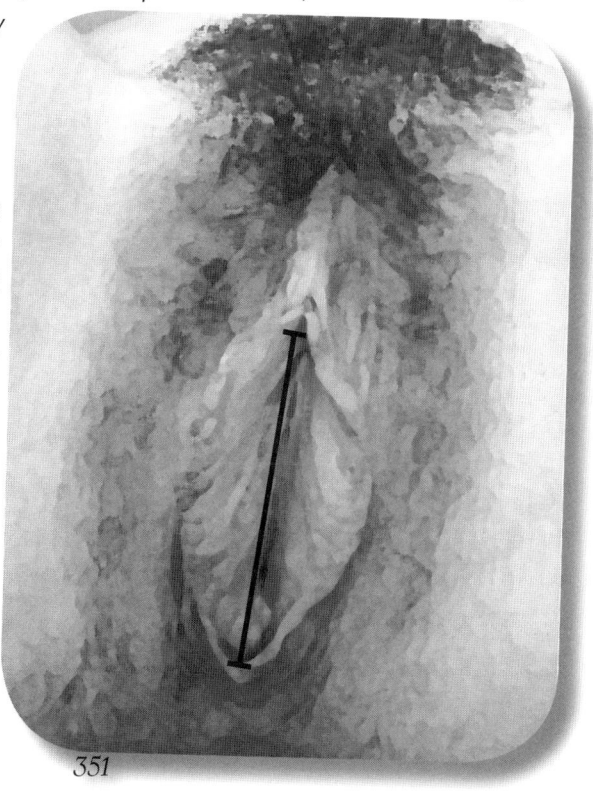

Cocksmanship

- ♀ **Niche**
- ♀ **U-Spot**
- ♀ **labia minora**
- ♀ **Vestibule**
- ♀ **V-Spot**
- ♀ **clitoris** *(which you will stimulate indirectly but you may stimulate directly if you prefer)*

You can also include her **vaginal ball, Skene's** and **Bartholin's ducts**, and **Nook**, depending on your **angle** and choice of **stroke depth** and **path**. (For a review of these **erogenous zone** locations refer back to the anatomical graphics on page 192 to page 195.)

You know what makes your lover's **vulva cleft zone** especially attractive? Its *size* and *shape* naturally hugs and suits your **erection**. It's a cozy place in which you can make love to her. It has its own **lubrication glands**. And it feels so nice against your skin.

When making love to her **vulva cleft zone**, your erection is nestled inside her **vulva**, entirely *outside* her vagina. Your **glans** is pointing up, your **frenulum** touching her **Niche** (or **clitoris** - your choice) at the *top of your upstroke* or *on a constant basis*, depending on the technique you're using.

Other nice benefits of **vulva cleft zone love**making: It will lodge your **hard-on** comfortably within her **vestibule**, which will hug you in a nice way and, with its **wetness**, facilitate smooth *strokes*. It will even serve as a **guide** to keep your **erection** going along the correct path with each stroke.

Let's start with five ways to do her **vulva**, with the *underside* of your **penis** (or **CS ridge**) pressed against and tucked inside her **vulva cleft zone** *(using your hand to hold it against her)*. Most of these - except the **Windshield Wiper Orgasm Technique** - require that you also nestle the **head of your cock** inside her **Niche**. (See page 353 for graphic illustrations.)

Vulva Love Technique #1: The Windshield Wiper

The Windshield Wiper Orgasm Technique works great in bringing on a fairly quick **orgasm**. With this technique, you either lodge your **glans** inside her **Niche** and - with your **hand** - move your **hard-on** back and forth like a windshield wiper, or you can position your frenulum and glans directly over her clit and do this (as pictured on the following page).

If this is the primary **Vulva Love Technique** you're going to use on her, you probably should start slowly and gradually work your way up to a moderate or moderately fast pace. Use her feedback as a guide as to how

Vulva Love Techniques
With Your CS Ridge (Corpus spongiosum) against her Vulva (see page 352, page 355 and page 356 for details)

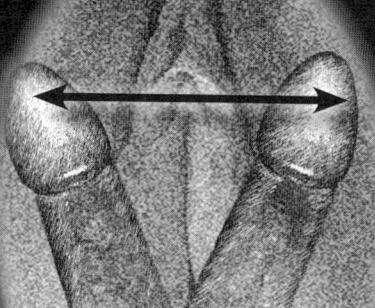

1 The Windshield Wiper

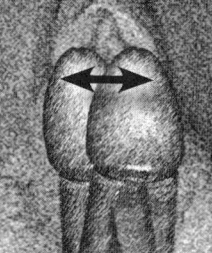

2 The Wiggle

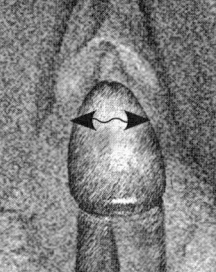

3 The Vibrator

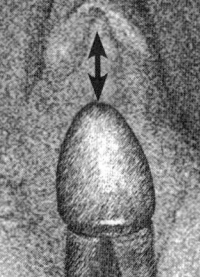

4 The Vulva Slide

5 The Full-On Tease

MORE VULVA LOVE TECHNIQUES
With Your Glans and Back of Your Erection
(see page 356 through page 358 for details)

① ②
NICHE
VAGINAL CANAL
BLADDER
NOOK
RECTUM

(And see page 358 for one more!)

The Niche to Nook Technique

VAGINAL CANAL
BLADDER
RECTUM

The Dorsal Rub Technique

VAGINAL CANAL
BLADDER
RECTUM

The Labia Tease Technique

well this is working on her and adjust your efforts accordingly (depending on how fast you want her to come). You don't have to set up a **regular rhythm** at first, but once you want her to come, you absolutely must.

You might also want to vary the **pressure** you apply on her **vulva** with your **erection**, starting off *lightly* and *increasing the intensity* as her **climax** comes near.

Be careful not to press your **hard-on** too strongly upon her. Every woman has her limits. Watch her reactions for indications you need to back off on the **pressure**.

If you've switched to the **Windshield Wiper Orgasm Technique** from another **Vulva Love Technique** in order to make her **climax**, you might want to start right off with a quicker **tempo** and **regular rhythm**.

Like a windshield wiper, you can also choose to use an **intermittent rhythm**. That is, you can interject **pauses** (typically you'd want them to be no more than *a second* or so). And you can choose to do one, two, three or more *rhythmic back and forth movements* between your **pauses**, as you wish. **Pauses** work even when you want to make her **orgasm** - so long as you build up the **pace** <u>fast</u> enough.

VULVA LOVE TECHNIQUE #2: THE *WIGGLE TECHNIQUE*

The **Wiggle Technique** is akin to a **shaking motion**, which you do within the confines of her **Niche**. (You can also choose to do this directly over her **clit** by the way.) By a **shaking motion** I mean two or three quick **back and forth strokes** of short **length** - as the arrow indicates on page 353.

While you can do this slowly and **arrhythmically** at first as a tease, eventually a **shake-pause-shake** approach, starting slowly and building in **pace** and **pressure**, works best. When you want to make her come, increase the **speed** and **pressure**, keeping your **repetitions** as **exact** and **rhythmically accurate** as possible.

VULVA LOVE TECHNIQUE #3: THE *VIBRATOR*

For the **Vibrator Technique**, you should either place your glans inside her **Niche** or directly over her **clitoris**. Your choice. (You'll achieve different *effects* depending on which way you go. The direct stimulation of her **clit** will lead to a faster climax - but you don't always want to rush things. Also - some women will find the *direct clitoral stimulation* too much; for them, stick to the **Niche** location.)

Then, with your thumb and index finger on either side of your **erection**, you should make your hard-on **vibrate** much like an electric vibrator does - *moving* it *back and forth* <u>*extremely*</u> *rapidly, without moving very far (less than a centimeter) in either direction during the back-and-forth stroke*. Start off, though, at a pace you can take to a *higher* level so you can *increase* your **speed** when you want to make her **come**.

Women *love* this!

Vulva Love Technique #4: The *Vulva Slide*

The **Vulva Slide Technique** is a lot of fun and it's much more like *traditional* **intercourse** than the **Vulva Love Techniques** I just showed you.

With the **Vulva Slide Technique**, you will be moving your **cock** back and forth over a **short distance within her vulva** (indicated by the arrows on page 353), starting and ending with her **Niche**. Rocking her **vulva** with rhythmic hip movements is probably best here.

But as the name implies, you'll want to *slide* your **cock** in doing this. So it requires some "prep work." That is, you'll want to make her **vulva** nice and **wet** by playing with her **U-Spot** beforehand.

Make sure to keep pressing your **CS ridge** against her so your **hard-on** is always snugly within her **vulva** throughout this technique. And, for **complete vulval stimulation**, keep the entire length of your shaft snugly against her so you're massaging sensitive places like her **V-Spot** and **labia minora** with *every stroke*.

Vulva Love Technique #5: The *Full-On Tease*

The **Full-On Tease Technique** is as fun as it is easy to do. All you have to do is position yourself so your **erection** covers her entire **vulva**, with its *underside* or **CS ridge** pressed within the *slit* between her **labia minora**. Your **glans** can either be pressed within her **Niche** or placed atop her **clitoris** *(your choice)*. Once you want her to come, though, you should make sure it has direct contact with her **clit**.

Now once you position yourself in this way, you just tease her by holding absolutely still. It won't be long before she gets so hot that she'll start sliding her **pussy** up and down, working toward her **orgasm**.

Just continue to press your **hard-on** against her, holding still, and enjoy the show. There's nothing more erotic than watching a woman do herself and that's what the **Full-On Tease Technique** is all about!

Vulva Love Technique #6: The *Niche To Nook Technique*

The **Niche-To-Nook Technique** will produce a <u>quick</u> **orgasm** with a *burst of love juices* if done correctly. Shown graphically atop page 354, either you or your lover can do this but it's often more effective if you let *her* handle it.

She should take your **shaft** in one hand and *rub* your **glans** up and down *inside* the top of her **vulva**, from her **U-Spot** up to her **Niche** and back again. Then, after anywhere from two to four repetitions, she should take your **glans** and press it down into her **Nook**, inside the bottom of her **vulva**.

When done correctly, she'll come in seconds once the **head** of your **cock** is inside her **Nook**. Sometimes it takes two or three reps of the whole **Niche-To-Nook Technique** to make this happen, however.

If it works - as it should - you'll find her reaching for your **cock** in the future, wanting to do this again. (FYI: The **Niche-To-Nook Technique** typically works just *once* in the course of any **love**making **session**.) If nothing else, though, it will certainly make her extremely **hot** and **wet**.

VULVA LOVE TECHNIQUE #7: THE DORSAL RUB

The Dorsal Rub Technique requires you to be on top of your lover as you would be in the *missionary position*, but you need to point your **erection** *downward between her thighs* so that the **back (dorsal side)** is resting across her **vulva** (as shown on page 354).

To accomplish this it's best that you are **flaccid** or **semi-hard only** before attempting to maneuver into that position. You would risk damaging your **penis** or causing pain at the very least if you tried to push your **hard-on** down in this way once it's *fully* **erect**.

Still, it's what I'd call an *extreme position*, so you should exercise *caution* so as not to hurt yourself even after you've successfully gotten yourself in place to start with **Dorsal Rub Technique**. (FYI: If you can't pull this off, don't get angry with yourself. Give it a try when you feel ready for it but be quick to switch over to something else, preferably another **shallow love**making **technique**, if she doesn't respond well to your efforts.)

By the way, as you maneuver into position you should attempt to move so as to get her **vulva** *wet*. She needs to be *slippery wet* for this to work. You know now what **vulval hot spots** to tease to make her wet (her **U-Spot, Nook, labia minora, V-Spot** and **vaginal ball**, for instance).

Once in place, move no more than an inch or so up and down, taking care to keep your **hard-on** within her **vulva cleft zone**. *If you can get your* **glans** *into her* **Nook**, *all the better (but if you can't, end your stroke at the bottom at her* **V-Spot**).

As you are now aware, the **back of your erection** has the right texture to best massage her hot spots. It's your job with the **Dorsal Rub Technique** though to make sure the dorsal side of your **cock** is always touching her **clitoris** (that's the easiest **orgasm trigger** to set off in this position, with this technique).

Vulva Love Technique #8: The Labia Tease

The **Labia Tease Technique** never fails to thrill. As you did with the **Niche-To-Nook Technique**, you will be using your **glans** as a massage tool (as shown on page 354).

To do this, take the **shaft** of your **erection** in hand and position yourself so the **head** of your **cock** rests on her **clitoris**. Then *tenderly* begin rubbing it up and down the **slit** between her **labia minora**, ending the upstroke with your **glans** again resting against her **clit.**

Actually, at first, your ministrations with your **glans** can be somewhat **random** and **arrhythmic**, just to get her wet, hot and bothered. But once you decide to work toward her **orgasm**, you'll need to get into a regular **repetitive pattern and rhythm**.

You do not have to go very fast to make her come. In fact, this technique works best at slow to moderate speeds.

So start fairly slowly - as is usually advisable - and see how little it might take to make her come with the **Labia Tease Technique.**

Vulva Love Technique #9: The V-Spot Tease

The last **Vulva Love Technique** I'll show you (pictured here) is the **V-Spot Tease Technique**. This is best done early on, once you've begun to touch her **genitals** with your **member**. When done right, with the proper build-up, it produces a quick **orgasm** along with a *flood of love juices*.

As you know from the anatomy chapter, the **V-Spot** is a thin **membrane** of flesh. What you want to do with the **V-Spot Tease Technique** is place your **glans** inside and atop it and move ever so slightly - really just massaging it without moving away from it - with a moderately slow pace.

At the very least, this should make your lover really wet, if not make her come fast.

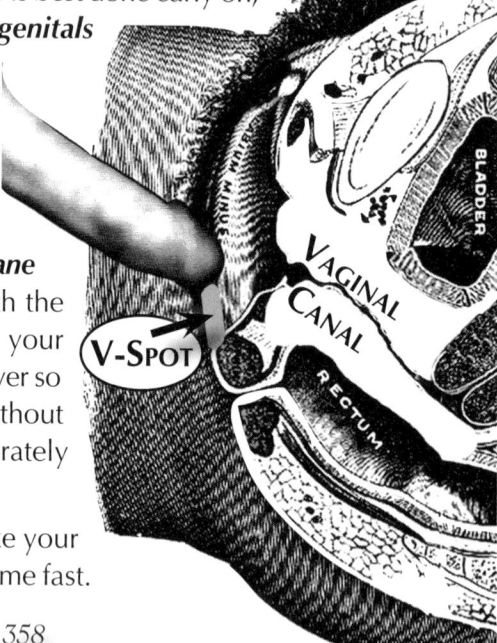

On Loving Women

(P.S. Her **orgasm** will feel unique to her, unlike **clitoral** or other **climaxes**.)

...So those are the nine **Vulva Love Techniques**. But FYI: Don't make love to her **vulva cleft zone** just to make her come. Aside from its *orgasmic potential*, you can use it simply to give your lover **complete vulval stimulation.**

Used in this way, it's great for the **wettening process**, in making her **wet** and **wide** quickly, ready for **vaginal penetration**. It's also great for the **arousal process**, in getting her real **hot**. And another thing:

The creative lover won't just engage in **Vulva Love Techniques** before vaginal intercourse. It's also super for exciting her as a change-of-pace kind of thing now and then even after intercourse has begun - or after she's already come once or twice.

COCKSMANSHIP AND PENETRATION: CREATING EXPECTATIONS

...Now to cocksmanship when it comes to the **vagina** and **vaginal penetration**...

We'll start with the **shallow love**making **techniques** I promised you before. You'll be surprised at how little it takes to make a woman *come*.

A man who's an artist in bed knows that every move he makes creates **expectations** in his lover's head, and he uses this fact to his advantage. (This amplifies on what I talked about earlier in this book, about making love to her mind. Great **cocksmanship** is all about this.)

A man who's not an artist also creates expectations but, because he doesn't realize what he's doing, he constantly dashes those expectations, leading the woman to experience constant let-downs and frustration.

For instance, if it seems as if you're "going for the okey-doke" (as one of my friends would put it), pushing your lover feverishly to the brink of her **orgasm**, she will want to tear your head off if you suddenly turn off the juice when she is in the early stages of coming. You've just spoiled her **orgasm** and her ability to *come* again in the near future. (When a **climax** is killed before it fully flowers a woman's body goes into an uneasy resting period where her **nerves** grow sort of dead to further attention.)

While **teasing** is acceptable, ruining the onset of an **orgasm** is unforgivable. And while your lover's initial feeling would be of frustration, a second more deadly emotion would undoubtedly overcome her: she'd likely feel bored. Initially she'll be thinking. C'mon, jerko, you got me going, now make me **come**! But when you blow it, she'll be outraged and she'll lose respect for you for being such a clod and meathead.

Cocksmanship

That's not to say you don't sometimes want to throw off your woman's expectations by changing course, in a teasing fashion, during the process of **love**making. But this should be done knowingly, with finesse - either with a sexy taunt or a sense of humor - and at the right times. You should *never* back off once your lover's **climax** has already begun.

ONE GENERAL PRINCIPLE IN CREATING ANTICI...PATION

Excepting passionate *quickies* and rare occasions where she's already wet for you, as in the overheated early stages of a relationship, it's much smarter in general to start things off slowly.

In fact, let's call this **Cocksmanship Lesson #11:**

You should not, in general, try to make her come from the get-go through a feverish attack on her **hot spots**. *A* **quick orgasm** *produced with wildly rapid strokes will be* **shallow** *and* **unsatisfying**. *It will occur, most times, before she's* **aroused**! *In other words, you can bring about biological release without satisfying your lover on any level.*

So, for one thing, <u>don't</u> be in a rush to enter her! Savor what most people call foreplay (but which we'll refer to as the **arousal and wettening processes**) during which you want to awaken every nerve in her body through loving and passionate but really slow head-to-toe ministrations.

During this period, you want to *slowly* turn up the heat, so to speak. Through patient *teasing* you want to make her *really* hot for you.

That will set up **expectations** in her mind and she'll quickly become eager for you to step up the pace - but you won't. Make her really want you to enter her before you even think of doing so. No - make her *need* you to enter her before you get close to the act of **penetration**. (And you might not want to let her touch you much during this phase, either - she'll try to do so, to make you go faster.)

The hotter you get her, the bigger the payoff. Drive her wild! She'll be thinking about how much she wants to come and, in making her want it *badly*, her thoughts will make her explode in a more **powerful orgasm**.

THE FIRST-ENTRY ORGASM

In fact - and this may be hard to believe - if you tease her well enough before you enter her, you can make her *climax* in a way few are aware is possible. *You can make her come simply by entering her!* And by inserting just **the head of your cock** inside her **vaginal canal!**

I call this the **first-entry orgasm**, because it's brought on simply by the *very first insertion* of your **cock**. (You've really got to become good at sexy teasing to pull this off!)

To bring this off, you need to make the **wettening process** as *tantalizing as possible*. And - this is essential - you need to get her good and hot *for a good long time <u>before allowing your penis to touch her</u>*. In denying her this thrill you'll create a desire for you that'll make her really hot.

Do whatever you please in teasing her for a long time. Then ever so slowly, as slowly as you can, ease the head of your cock past her **labia minora**. Rest inside her **vestibule** awhile - perhaps on her **V-Spot** or inside her **Nook** (see page 194 for their locations). She might come with that alone, with a *flood* of *juices*. With an expert tease, that's not unusual.

Whether she experiences a **climax** or not with that, though, move on. Ever so slowly enter her **vaginally** - but only so far as the **vaginal ring** (the very outermost ring of *muscle* I described in the *anatomy chapter*). Then rest it inside the **vaginal ring**, motionless. If you've done the **pre-entry tease** long enough and well enough, she should soon *come* with a *gush of love juices*. If not, no matter. Continue your *entry tease*.

(See page 366, by the way, for another kind of *entry-only* **orgasm**!)

ENTRY TIP: A SLOW TEASE IS USUALLY BEST

Speaking of which, a *slow tease* is usually your best approach when entering your lover. It's an incredibly sexy way to start things off – that is, with the ***initial penetration***.

It helps promote a *spirituality* about your *union*, a *sexiness* about it. By *savoring* the moment, you'll both share a feeling of *love, togetherness* and *passion*. It will make the event a *celebration* of the *miracle* of the physical nature of your *union*.

THE VAGINAL BALL AND SHALLOW SWEET PLACE ORGASM TECHNIQUES

Plus, a slow tease at the start lends itself to two other **shallow love**making **techniques** that involve the **outermost parts of her vaginal canal**. You and she will find these incredibly exciting. (See the illustrations demonstrating these graphically, on page 362.)

Her **vaginal ball**, the outer manifestation of her **vaginal canal** (which I introduced to you in the anatomy chapter), is *extremely sensitive* to the touch. (See page 193 if you forget what it looks like.) So it lends itself to something I call the **Vaginal Ball Tease Technique**. *Here's how you do it*:

The simple touch of your **glans** upon her **vaginal ball** may set off a rush of **love juices** and an **orgasm**, in fact. So start by trying that.

MORE SHALLOW LOVEMAKING TECHNIQUES

Vaginal Ball Tease Technique

Shallow Sweet Place Orgasm Technique

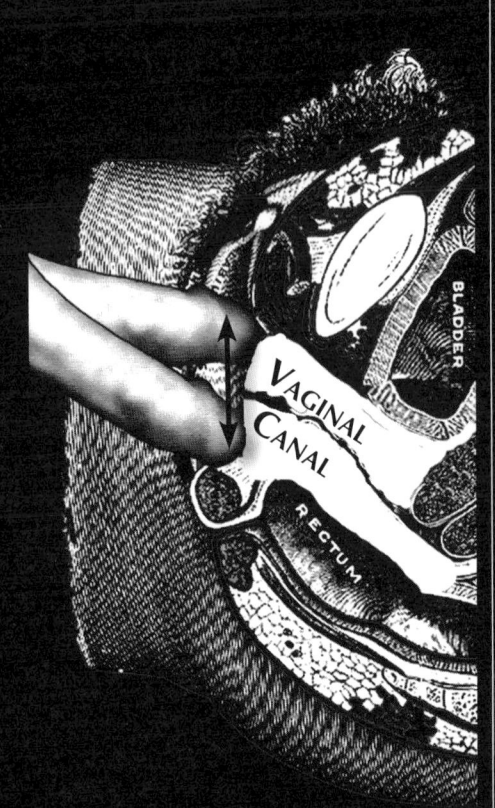

See page 363 for the technique how-tos.

See page 193 for another illustration of the vaginal ring, so you can identify it in order to position your glans inside of it.

See page 361 for the technique how-tos.

See page 192 and page 193 for more illustrations of the vaginal ball, so you can identify it and find its location in order to massage it with your glans.

On Loving Women

That will make her hot and probably wet in and of itself. To make her *come*, you might need to - *cock* in *hand* - move your **glans** up and down delicately (as indicated in the graphic on page 362) over the **vaginal ball's surface** a few times before you trigger a reaction.

Trust me, though. It won't take long - at the very least - to produce a **torrent of lubrication** which you then can use to facilitate other **love**making **techniques**. So give it a try.

The other **shallow love**making **technique** I alluded to above is something I call the **Shallow Sweet Place Orgasm Technique**. It's a surefire **orgasm producer**. This involves a **multiple erogenous zone** that will quickly become one of your favorites - a region I call her **Shallow Sweet Place**. (It might even involve your lover's **clitoral bulbs** by the way, if those are indeed active sexual hot spots.)

Her **Shallow Sweet Place** comprises <u>many</u> **orgasm triggers** and **orgasm boosters** in the *lower half* of her *vulva*. It includes her:

♀ *labia minora*
♀ *V-Spot*
♀ *vaginal ring*
♀ *Nook* (at least indirectly)
♀ *clitoral bulbs* (at least indirectly)

As you might have noticed, the **Shallow Sweet Place** is a <u>mixed</u> **multiple erogenous zone area**. Part of it is a **vulval region;** part of it is a **vaginal region** (the **vaginal ring,** which feels like a rubber band surrounding the entrance to her **vaginal canal**).

That makes it even better. Because it means her **Shallow Sweet Place** comprises **two different kinds of nerves**: **visceral** and **somatic**. So she's getting *a wide range of* **sensations** by its stimulation. The effect of **concurrent multiple orgasm trigger and orgasm booster stimulation** can bring on an <u>incredible</u> climax if you do it correctly.

To get her off using the **Shallow Sweet Place Orgasm Technique**, like the **V-Spot Tease Technique**, requires a *gentle touch* and the *slightest of motions*. You pay homage, so to speak, to each of the <u>**erogenous zones**</u> you pass on your way into her **vaginal ring**, by tickling each (listed above) with your **glans** on your way in.

Don't forget - her **vaginal ring** is one of her **entrances**. So ever so slowly insert the head of your cock inside it at first and **pause** there briefly, *motionless*, to enjoy the moment and *maximize* her *titillations*. (She might *come immediately*, in fact, if you do this right.)

Then start a very slow massaging motion, starting with your **glans** resting on her **V-Spot** and ending with her **vaginal ring**, as shown by the arrows in the illustration on page 362. Then go back to the beginning and do it again.

You can also choose to stay within her **vaginal ring** and move ever so slightly, giving her a tender tickle until she comes.

You and she will love the **Shallow Sweet Place Orgasm Technique**. *Like the* **Vaginal Ball Tease Technique**, *it's best done at the first hint of penetration. After a few orgasms, too, the* **Shallow Sweet Place's nerves** *might fatigue and fail to produce any more* **climaxes**, *so be quick to move on to other hot spots at that point.*

THE PLATEAU RULE

...I think you can see by now that if you make the mistake of entering her in a rush, you'll be missing out on a lot of the pleasures you can give her.

Worse - you'd be violating something I call the **plateau rule**. That is, there are many **stages** in her **arousal process** that you can put her through, *if you take it very slowly*. That is, you can make her *hotter by degrees*, as if you're raising her temperature slightly, slowly stoking her *sexual furnace*, with each *move* you make on her (a *move* being a *protracted* **sexual strategy** - an example of this would be a *long nipple tease*).

As you move on to the next *move* or **sexual strategy, your aim should be to get her excited by just one more degree. So you should choose an activity that's a bit more exciting than the last (in either intensity or pace or number of hot spots you're stimulating or by the nature of the erogenous zone you choose to work over).**

So here's where you need to understand about **the plateau rule - which we can call Cocksmanship Lesson #12:**

In general, once you've taken your lover to a **higher stage or level** in her **arousal process**, you cannot and should not attempt to take her back to **a lower level**. She will no longer feel the same sensations she felt before at that lower level because you previously took her up to and sensitized her to a **higher level** of **stimulation**. Her nerves, once at a higher level, will be dulled to a lower level of stimulation.

She won't feel much, in other words, if you go from one plateau level of excitement or heat down to a less intense level. And it would be highly unsatisfying and frustrating for her. So don't do that.

So - with this necessary knowledge, let's go back to our **slow entry tease** idea. Here's what you should do:

First, *enter her very slowly*. Even if she grabs your **cock** and desperately wants it inside of her, begin by teasing her **vulva** with your **glans**. Not mechanically but *tenderly,* with *feeling*...and with an awareness of how each light stroke, touch and caress of your **cock** makes her feel. Be creative (but keep it *gentle* and *subtle*).

To keep things at **Level 1** on the **plateau scale**, everything you do must be *circumspect* at this stage.

Now, once you've gradually raised her temperature and can practically hear her sizzle from the heat, slowly, slowly, slowly introduce the tip of your **cock** inside her...and then pull it out *immediately*, as if the heat from her pussy was too intense to stay inside it for very long...or as if you were *tantalizing her* with something very, very special.

Make her feel this is an amazingly exciting event by creating a sense of *drama* or *expectations*. Try to be *unpredictable* while at the same time *making her want more* - more of you, more intensity, etc.

And do all this with an *erotic sensuality* - devilish smiles, perhaps, and cooing in her ear. This is where you *talk* to her (as we discussed in an earlier chapter). Tell her how *good* she feels. Make note of the changes you've produced (say something like: "mmm...somebody's wet!").

LESS IS MORE: *SENSITIZING HER* TO THE LIGHTEST TOUCHES

Starting things off *excruciatingly slowly and lightly,* by the way, is a **smart sexual strategy** in that *it heightens the sensitivity of her skin and her nerves*. Your *slightest motion* will be felt with incredible intensity. You're **sensitizing her** so she will react excitedly to the lightest of your touches.

By doing this, you'll engage her sense of *anticipation*. You're playing with her head, making her hotter than she would otherwise be at this stage. She'll be dying to have you enter her. She'll crave her **orgasm**. And she'll come faster - when you're good and ready to make her do so.

OK...so as I suggested above, you've now slowly introduced the head of your **cock** *and then pulled out*. Now...slowly slip back inside her and give her part of your **shaft** too...giving her just an inch or less at before slowly pulling back out again. This kind of tease, again, heightens her desire.

Rest a few moments, with your **glans** against her **vulva**, without moving. (This is delicious!)

Repeat all of this in patiently slow **stages** with *increasing* **penetration**, until you're in *practically to the hilt*.

Your **insertions**, by the way, should be dependent in part on the **biofeedback** you're getting from her. That is – don't progress too quickly if you're not producing growing excitement in her. (By **biofeedback**, I mean *the biological reactions you're getting from her body*. You'll be able to tell if you're accomplishing your goal of making her real hot by her degree of **wetness**, her **wideness**, an *increase in vaginal heat* and by her **body language** - *for example, wriggling* and/or *involuntary convulsions*.)

Is she getting **wetter** and **wetter?** Slip your **erection** in a bit more. If not, continue to work on her mind, through subtle and shallow **cock** work, before going any further.

If you're doing this correctly, you should be producing reactions (**feedback**) that reward your efforts, that indicate your tantalizing approach is *working*. With each *centimeter* you introduce of yourself into her **vagina**, she should be **moaning**, "Oh," or something to that effect; or **writhing**; etc.

The beauty of taking this *slow-tease* approach is that – when done well – it produces expressions of extreme pleasure from the woman, as if you just gave her the most incredible feeling of pleasure she's ever felt. You'll also hear a sense of surprise in her voice – as if she is floored that she's feeling so good, from so little.

Another sweet payoff is that you'll be able to make her **come** with much less effort when you're good and ready to. And her **orgasm** will be *huge*.

THE UNION-ONLY ORGASM

OK...still with me? Here's the best part:

Once you're in just about as far as you can go – continuing to exert a bit of **upward pressure** – you should hold *absolutely still*. Keep your **hard-on** as far up her as you can go, *without moving at all*.

And **talk to her**. Softly, with sexy tones. *In her ear*. Moan, *"Mmm!"* Let her know *how great it feels to be inside her*.

Tell her you want to enjoy the magical moment of being united together before you go any further. *Kiss her* **lips, eyes, face, neck, breasts, nipples**.

Hold her tightly, passionately, perhaps in a *bear hug* (running your arms around her and really holding her closely, as if you can't get close enough).

The amazing thing is, if you've performed this **dance of romance** artfully, she will even *come* one or more times at this point! (Or, perhaps even sooner – from the moment of insertion, **if you slide inside her delicately, as if she's a flower that would be damaged with any more exertion**.)

On Loving Women

When she comes – simply from your **measured penetration,** from the feel of your hot **cock** inside of her, or from the *stretching* and *filling* of her **vaginal canal** by your **erection** – I think you'll agree *there are few things sweeter than that!*

This is what I've named the **union-only orgasm**, which few lovers share. You will be in rarified company if you can pull this off. And it will be such a rush to you and to her! Talk about a *mind blow! This isn't supposed to be possible!*

And by the way, one wonderful feature of the **union-only orgasm** is that *it should work for men of all sizes and lengths. You should be able to access at least two or more* **orgasm triggers** *with this technique, depending on your length* - including her **clitoral bulbs**, tucked behind the outermost inch or two of her **vaginal canal**.

INTRODUCING TARGETED LOVEMAKING

...Now, most times, your **love**making will continue from there. You cannot continue to produce **union-only orgasms**. They work through a novelty effect that's over with their onset.

So what do you do then? Immediately after her **union-only orgasms** you should do what is usually wise after any of her **orgasms** - allow her a bit of down time (unless, that is, you've decided to give her a series of multiple orgasms, which we'll discuss in a moment). Down time can mean you rest *motionless* inside her. Or simply slow down and *avoid* rhythmic activity. Keep it romantic. You can tell her how much you love her.

Then, most times, you will move on to what I call **targeted love**making. Because women, as you know, are multi-orgasmic, you'll be building toward her *next* **orgasm**, by targeting a specific **orgasm trigger** or **multiple erogenous zone area** for your attention.

You can choose - as is often wise - just to make her hotter initially, by first targeting one of her **pleasure zones** (areas that excite her but will *not* make her *come*).

...More on **targeted love**making in a moment...

AFTER AN ORGASM: HOW HER PLATEAU SCALE WORKS

Now it's OK to do *arrhythmic motions* at this point because you're essentially starting a new **arousal process**. That is - *if* you want to build to her next climax *slowly*.

But here's something you need to understand, once she's come at least once:

Cocksmanship

You cannot go back to the *very lowest levels* on her **plateau scale**. In other words, you cannot produce the same *excitement* by doing feather-light **cock work** at this point as you did at the get-go. Her **sexual nerves** have been *dulled* somewhat by her **first orgasm**. Extremely subtle moves at that point will produce very *little* in the way of **sexual reactions**.

So, *after her first orgasm and later ones as well, you should return only to a* **moderate level** *of* **stimulation**. This is the lowest level on the **plateau scale** that will then feel good to her.

INTRODUCING THE CONCEPT OF MOTION-INCHES

Now it's time to talk about what you should do inside her **vagina**. Understand that, unlike with **vulva love** where you used your **shaft** and **glans**, your focus in **cocksmanship** during **vaginal love**making most often should be on your **glans**. You'll produce the best results when using that as a *tool* to <u>target</u> *an area to stimulate* to get her *hot* or make her **climax**.

Along these lines, let's talk briefly about an important concept in **cocksmanship**. It's something I call **motion-inches**.

This is **the range of territory you want to massage inside her with your glans at any one time.** Or put another way, it's *the* **maximum distance** your **glans** moves on *in-and-out strokes - describing the complete start-to-finish* **stroke cycle**. The *distance* you choose to go in **motion-inches** will depend upon what **hot spot** you're working on.

Most often, you should stick to a *small* amount of **motion-inches** in moving your **cock**. It's rarely smart to do a *maximum* amount of in-and-out activity, whether you're inside her **vagina** or making love to her **vulva**. It's indiscriminate and it loses its effect quickly. And the truth is *you usually don't need to move much for maximum effect*. Plus, your motion should be *targeted*. So you'll want to keep your **glans** over or near whatever **erogenous zone** you're working over.

If you're trying to give her a **G-Spot orgasm**, for instance, then **one or two motion inches** would be *more* than enough. In fact, much *less* would do, too, because her **G-Spot** is only one or two inches long. *And if you want to produce a maximum effect in massaging it, you'd only want to cover its length, in a precise, targeted fashion. (See the illustrations on page 369.)*

In contrast, **Deep Trigger** or **AFE zone orgasms** require just a *half* **motion-inch** of *massaging* - or *less!* Actually, simple **pressure** will also do. With her **AFE zone,** try resting **motionless** once in that area. *Rhythmic pressure* works on her **Deep Trigger** - *if you choose not to massage it with a fairly rapid* half **motion-inch stroke cycle** *(which is my favorite approach).*

UNDERSTANDING *MOTION-INCHES*: G-SPOT TECHNIQUE EXAMPLES

Less Is Often More

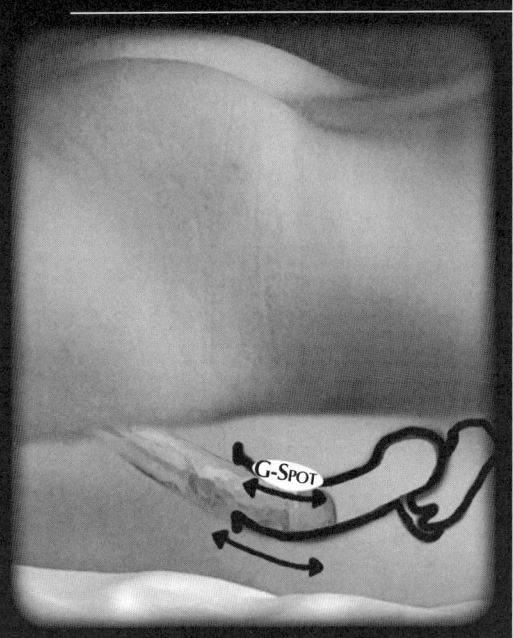

In **love**making, less is often more. And small paths in **motion-inches** (such as the one shown by the double-arrowed **pathway** *drawn just below her G-Spot)* produce the best results in giving her a **G-Spot orgasm**.

For variety, though, try moving another **motion-inch or so**, *quickly* pulling out from the position above until your **glans** rests on her **labia minora**. (The *quick out* motion is primarily what will make her come.) Then *squeeze* in, reinserting yourself to the starting point, resting on her **G-Spot**. (Follow the **pathway** shown below her **vaginal canal**.)

Using Your Corona

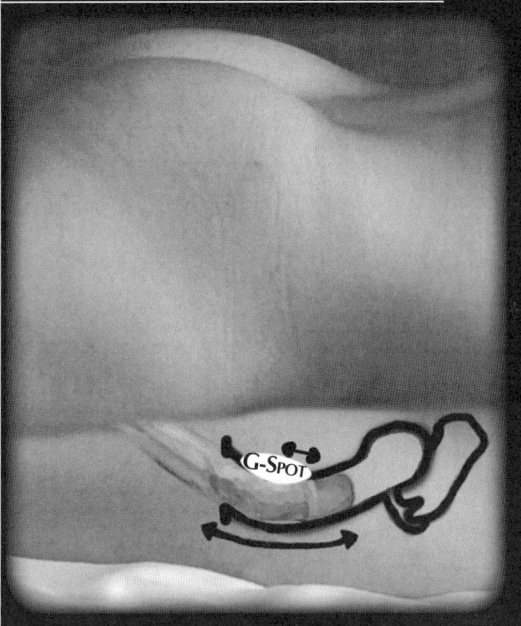

More **motion-inches** will work in giving her an **orgasm** if you use your **corona** to massage her **G-Spot** on its way out and you pull out quickly. (See the **pathway** shown below her **vaginal canal**.) Start with your **corona** resting against the end of her **G-Spot** *(which is fatter than the surrounding tissue)*. On the *out-stroke* stop when your **glans** rests against her **labia minora**.

Or rock her gently with **minimal movement** - a <u>**half motion-inch**</u> (shown by the **pathway** above her **G-Spot**). That will make her come faster; your **glans** is always on her **G-Spot**.

Cocksmanship

Now there may be times when you want to cover more **motion-inches** than just the length of the **orgasm trigger** you're working on. For instance, with the **G-Spot**, you might want to cover 3-4 **motion-inches,** going from its farthest end inside her to (quickly) pulling completely out of her. But I recommend you end such a move by resting your **glans** on her **G-Spot** a second or so before beginning your out move. Your **glans**' heat and pressure will then have a maximum effect on her **G-Spot**. Here's another idea: Move in *just beyond* her **G-Spot** and you can massage it with your **corona on the out stroke**! (See page 369 for details.)

COCKSMANSHIP TECHNIQUES

But you also need the right technique with your **glans**, to massage or tickle her **orgasm triggers** the right way in order to make her *come*. You now know that pounding away is not the way to go. So what do you do?

Use your **glans** as if you're gently trying to wipe a slight stain off a silk shirt. You should give it just enough friction to get that stain off but not enough to cause damage to the delicate material. That analogy should get you on the right track toward using the **head of your cock** as a **massager**.

Other analogies that might get you on the right track: Think in terms of **nudging** an area as if you're gently trying to awaken someone. Or perhaps think of your **glans** as a big **tickler**.

You're trying to generate *friction* with *light* to *moderate* **pressure**. In doing so, make sure to **angle your erection** *properly* so the **greater portion of your glans** is *pressing up against the area you're working over*. (You do this typically by altering the height of your hips.)

To give her **Deep Trigger orgasms** you might want to try **massaging** that **hot spot** with **intermittent pressure**. Because her **Deep Trigger** (accessible only through **rear-entry intercourse**) is located as far back in her **vaginal canal** as you can get, you do not have the luxury of going *beyond* it on your *in-stroke*. Yet the advantage is that you can **press up against it.** And that lends itself to an **intermittent pressure technique** where you **press up** against her endmost wall with your **glans** (if you're long enough to reach it) and then *release* the **pressure**, on and off, *rhythmically*. You're producing more of a *pulsating* sensation than anything else.

Her **Deep Trigger** also responds awesomely well to a **butterfly technique** you'd do with your knees outstretched, causing your **glans** to move no more than **one motion-inch** - the **upstroke** ending with your pressing against her *end wall*. To prevent your bruising her, this must be done with *finesse* and not with pounding. In fact, you can also often produce the same results by thinking in terms of massaging the length of her **Nexus** (a distance of just **one motion-inch** or so). (See page 195 if you forget the location of the **Nexus**.) You can also produce the same results by bouncing up and down on a bed, making sure not to allow your **glans** to move very far inside her. Back off from her most distant wall, her vaginal canal's endpoint, just a bit, and try not to bump against it as you bounce so as to create friction on her end walls - nudging her endpoint gently if you go that far. **Bouncing** is a great **propulsion technique**, on a soft surface that allows for it, because it enables you to go faster than you can with your hips.

You might try another unique **cocksmanship technique** for her **AFE zone** *(accessible only through* **front-entry intercourse)**. That **erogenous zone** often responds simply by your repeatedly pulling out a bit and then pressing your **glans** against it and holding it there *motionless* or pressing forward almost imperceptibly for a few seconds before starting the cycle anew.

Other cocksmanship techniques that give her titillations and sometimes **orgasms** include a **slow squeeze technique** in which you pretend or simulate you need to intensely push your way in to get inside her. This is targeted, though. You should stop at a point where you're resting against one of her hot spots - her **G-Spot**, for instance, or her **AFE zone**.

The **Too Hot Technique** is another goodie, where you enter her up to an **erogenous zone** such as her **vaginal ball**, rest there a second or so motionless, and then pull out **quickly** as if her **hot spot** is *too hot to handle*. Because you can pull out of her faster than you can push your cock into her, this rapid pulling out technique often results in a nice **orgasm**, quickly.

Precision Lovemaking: How To Target Her Orgasm Triggers

But how do you know how deeply to insert your **cock** so your **glans** is positioned precisely over a **hot spot** you want to target? This is only a question in **vaginal intercourse** (you can *see* her **vulval hot spots**, so positioning there can be done *visually*), where you need to find her **G-Spot** and deepest hot spots - her **AFE zone** during **front-entry intercourse** and her **Deep Trigger** during **rear-entry intercourse** - by feeling about with the **head** of your **cock**.

Easy. For her **G-Spot**, first take your index and middle fingers and feel for it along the **top wall** of her **vaginal canal** (as if you're trying to touch her belly button from underneath). It starts an inch or so within her **vaginal entrance** and goes on for about two or so inches. It's egg-shaped and feels spongy and fat, with a prune-like multi-ridged texture.

Once you've located that manually, it should be no trouble gauging how far you need to enter her to engage her **G-Spot**. And once you've discovered how it feels, you should have no trouble feeling for it with your **glans**.

To locate her **AFE zone** and **Deep Trigger**, though, you need to figure out when you're at or beyond her **fornix** or **cervical** area. First of all, a good rule is you should carefully and slowly slide into her about *three or four inches beyond the end of her* **G-Spot** (you will feel your **corona** go over the end, where the fatty tissue gives way to the *flatness* of her *upper wall*).

You'll know when you reach her **AFE zone** because she'll start to go crazy. If you don't get a reaction from her on the way in during *front-entry intercourse* in her deepest regions, keep pushing tenderly until you do. There will be no mistaking it when you're there!

As far as reaching her **Deep Trigger** zone goes, in most women, I feel a "bump" as my **corona** runs over her **posterior fornix** and/or **cervical lip**. That tells me I'm there or almost there. Sometimes I describe the transition as a "pop" because it feels like I'm popping into a rear cavity, beyond a momentary lip of resistance. And this is how you will know you've "arrived" when you're locating her **Deep Trigger**. You might have to press - gingerly - forward from that cavity until you bump (tenderly) against her end wall.

Finally, finding her **vaginal ring** for shallow **love**making should be fairly easy. If you spread her **pussy lips**, you can easily see her **vaginal ball**. (Refer back to page 193 for its graphical representation.) You only want to pop your **glans** into her **vaginal ball** until your **corona** is at its edge and you feel the rubber-band like **vaginal ring** hugging the **head** of your **cock**. To work her **vaginal ring** to give her an **orgasm**, use **minimal motion**.

Choosing The Right Rhythm And Intensity To Make Her Come

Aside from giving her *novel* **orgasms** that require little if any movement on your part (as I showed you before), most times you'll have to set up a **regular rhythm** to make her come - especially *vaginally*. (You'll need to target one of her **hot spots** precisely first, of course, with the **head of your cock**, as we discussed above.)

And, actually, most times, you often need to slowly *increase* a number of factors to give her a satisfying **orgasm: speed, intensity, range of motion (sometimes), depth (sometimes) and rhythm. Not always - a slow steady rhythm is often all you need. But for variety, bear in mind that increasing any of the factors I just listed help push her toward her climax.**

Exact Repetition Is Key

And this is also very important:

On Loving Women

Most times, *to make her **come**,* you'll also have to accompany the **regular rhythm** I talked about above with an **exact repetition** of the **motion** you've decided to do.

*If you deviate from this in speed or execution when she's ready to come, you are going to take her off the path to her **climax** and **frustrate** her. So you must learn to keep doing the same thing over and over again (with **feeling**) once you've decided to push her over the edge with an **orgasm-triggering motion cycle**.*

INTRODUCING <u>WIGGLES</u>, <u>MOTION CYCLES</u> AND NOVEL COCK MOVES

This is true even if the **cycle** you invent includes **novel cock moves**. In other words, a **complete motion cycle** doesn't haven't to be a simple **in-and-out piston-style stroke cycle**.

I'll give you examples of **motion cycles** with **novel cock moves**:

- *Entering her from the front (or **missionary position**) you might choose to do a **motion cycle** starting with your **glans** resting on the outside of her **labia minora**. After a pause of a second or so, you might then quickly insert yourself three or so inches inside her, so you're directly massaging her **G-Spot**, for two **wiggles** (which are **rapid in-and-out stroke cycles of one motion-inch or less - on a straight path or with circular or sideways hip movements** - targeted over a **hot spot**). Then you might choose to quickly pull your **cock** out of her, to rest its **head** on her **pussy lips** again, ready to start the next **repetition** of this unusual **motion cycle**.*

- ***Two steps in, one out:*** *Here you enter her about two inches and pause a second or less and then move in another inch or two; you pause a second and pull back to where you started (your **motion-inches** for each move will vary depending on what **hot spot** you're looking to engage - the move I just described works great, for instance, for her **G-Spot**).*

- ***Shallow in-out twice, one long:*** *Here you enter her only an inch or so and pull out and repeat before going in about four inches (for G-Spot stimulation) and pulling out again. You can pause or not at the apex of each in-stroke if you like, or not.*

- ***One shallow cycle, one long cycle:*** *Similar to the above, with just one shallow in-out-move before doing the deeper in-out move.*

But those are just a few examples of novel moves. Be creative.

LOVEMAKING AS A FORM OF DANCING

Now if you know anything about music, you'll have an advantage in being able to set up **exactly repeating orgasm-triggering motion cycles**. Because what I'm talking about is setting up an **event**, a **movement**, that, like clockwork, *constantly repeats* (keeping your **motion-inches, intensity, cock path** and **targeted location** the same each time too).

A musical beat encourages and facilitates your moving with an **exact repetition of your motion** - as it does on the dance floor. And because dancing is often hip-driven, the idea that you're **sexually dancing** during **intercourse** should help get your hips moving in circles and other interesting patterns that please her. (You don't *need* to propel your **cock** with your **hips**, but you must learn to do so *well* because this is sometimes your best way of **making love**, depending on: your *position*; the *surface* you're making love upon; and the *location* you're in.) Thinking in terms of *dancing inside her* should also get you in the correct *creative* mindset, so you remember to mix things up to avoid becoming boring.

Now you'll want to experiment to find what **rhythm** sets her off with each of her **orgasm triggers**. In doing this, start with an **extremely slow rhythm** and increase it slowly to find **the slowest possible rhythm that makes her come** in each location.

There are several reasons to do this:

☯ *You want to find a* <u>comfortable</u> *pace you can keep up forever so you never risk tiring out*

☯ *You want a pace you can easily speed up if it's not producing results on any occasion*

☯ *A slower approach is often perceived by her as being a sexier pace*

☯ *A slow rhythm is unlikely to produce* **nerve fatigue** *and* **irritation**

Put Some "Head Music" Behind It

And here's a great tip:

One easy way to set a pace and keep it constant is by choosing a **song** *to "play" in your head. But just* any *song won't do. You need to find one that she* <u>responds</u> *to.*

I had a lover, for instance, whom I could make come very easily by positioning my **glans** over her **G-Spot** and then rocking her to the rhythm of the song *Clocks* by Coldplay. (That is, I did **one complete in-and-out move**, a **complete motion cycle**, with every <u>beat</u> of the music.) Worked every time. (*Try* it!)

So - here's some homework for you:

Make a mental list of moderately paced songs that might work in this way *in advance of your next* **love***making session.* Then, during your next time together, see if any of them are exactly at *the* <u>right rhythm</u> *that gets her off.*

On Loving Women

Play each of them in your head and move the head of your cock - by no more than one or two **motion-inches** - to the beat of each song. Try each for 15-30 seconds. If you're getting no feedback indicating she's getting hotter or closer to her **orgasm**, try another until you hit the right one.

Giving Her Multiple Orgasms

Now earlier I told you that *practically every woman is multiply orgasmic*. And so you should be looking to give her *numerous* **climaxes** in any given **love***making* session. How *many* varies per woman, the mood and goals you've set for the session, and the *power* of the *orgasms* you give her.

You need to get familiar with your lover with regard to what satiates her. But you also need to push her boundaries to see just *how many* **orgasms** she can happily have before she's had enough.

In my experience, few women have been given **multiple orgasms** by their past lovers. So it probably will be up to you to test these waters. She might not know her *desires, orgasm potential* or *limits* if she's not been pushed to the max yet. So prepare yourself for a fun process of discovery.

Here are some **cocksmanship tips** in giving her **multiple orgasms:**

- A good general rule: **Once she's had her first orgasm vaginally, she's typically primed to come again, and quickly.**

- **Do not allow a lot of time to pass between one orgasm and your path to another.** *In some cases, with some approaches, with some women,* **no pause at all** *is necessary between triggering one* **orgasm** *and your going for the same type of* **orgasm***, in the very same way. If an* **orgasm** *is real powerful, she might push away from you or her vaginal contractions might even push you out of her* **vagina***. But, in general, it's best to try to get back inside her as quickly as possible and/or go for her next* **orgasm** <u>as soon as possible</u> *(allowing for whatever brief down time she needs - typically no more than five seconds to a half minute), or her nerves will dull down and it'll be harder to set off more* **climaxes** *quickly.*

- Some **shallow lovemaking techniques**, as I mentioned earlier, are only good for one or two climaxes per session - such as the **Niche-To-Nook Technique**. Others, like the **Shallow Sweet Place Orgasm Technique** lend themselves to at least a half dozen, depending on the woman. And the great thing about the **Shallow Sweet Place Orgasm Technique** is that you don't even have to stop between **orgasms**. Just keep a steady, slow rhythm going until she's had enough. Similarly, the first four **Vulva Love Techniques** will enable you to trigger many **clitoral orgasms**; try going without a pause from one to the next if she lets you, for maximum results.

- You should be able to give her <u>many</u> **G-Spot orgasms** with only the *briefest of pauses between each. Her **G-Spot** is relatively immune to **nerve fatigue**. Keep up the same moderate rhythm when going for every **climax** - don't vary it.*

☿ *As far as her deepest **hot spots** go: Giving her multiple **Deep Trigger** and **AFE zone orgasms** is relatively easy once you've learned how to trigger them. You don't need much of a pause between them either. However, since these are so powerful, she'll probably beg you - however gratefully - to stop with these after no more than a half dozen or less with her **Deep Trigger** and no more than three or so with her **AFE zone**. Play it by ear; every woman is different. Because they come on so quickly, however, you should have another **hot spot** in mind to move to once she reaches her limit. To capitalize on the **multiple orgasm wave** she's on and increase the likelihood she'll continue coming quickly and often, do not delay in moving on to another **orgasm trigger**.*

PROPULSION AND ERGONOMICS

As far as methods to ***propel*** your ***cock***, there are *many*. My mentor Earle used to tell me that using your ***hips*** was the *best* means of moving your ***cock***. But I think that mindset is very limiting. My word of advice is:

Always choose the easiest means of moving inside of her, the ***ergonomic*** way. That way *you can continue indefinitely without tiring.*

Here are a few examples of ***ergonomic cock propulsion methods***:

- *If you can find a soft surface with <u>bounce</u>, then **bouncing** is often the easiest way to propel your **cock** in and out, and quickly.*
- ***Spread-eagling your knees**, in an easy, quick <u>sliding</u> motion (moving just **one motion-inch** or so), is often an easy way to make her come in both front- and rear-entry positions.*
- *If you are on a brass bed or missionary bed, you can grab the poles on the headboard with your hands and easily rock her that way.*
- *If you're standing up and taking her from behind, you can grab her hips and pull her back and forth with your hands quite effortlessly.*
- *If you're in a modified missionary position on a bed, you can sometimes move yourself in and out of her easily by pushing her hips down with your hands.*
- *If you're on top of her, position yourself so your thighs are atop hers and use your toes or feet to propel yourself back and forth.*

Again - be *creative*. Even when using your hips. Swivel them. Circle them. Change your ***cock angle*** periodically.

<u>BEFORE</u> "GOING WILD": INTRODUCING THE SECOND WIDENING EVENT

Now sometimes, on rare occasions, you might want to "go wild" inside her - going in and out to the max, with a feverish pitch. If you do it too often you'll lose its effect and you'll seem predictable and artless.

This strategy is often best used when you've got her into a **multiple orgasm phase** and in **going wild** you'll quickly give her a number of new **climaxes**. That's exciting to her.

Going wild is best done when you're inside her as *deeply* as you can go on the *in-stroke* (making sure not to *bruise* her). It's OK to do this sometimes when you're going for your own **orgasm** - if you make it seem as if she's making you lose control or you're overcome with passion (so your wildness is perceived by her in a *sexy* and **loving** context).

But don't try this too early on during *intercourse* because she won't be ready for it. She'll be likely to bruise. I wait until I feel what I call a **second widening event** before I ever consider going wild.

That's right. I taught you about how she goes wide during the arousal process and that you should avoid entering her until that happens. Now I'm telling you about another, less known, phenomenon, where her vaginal canal gets even wider. You'll feel it pull back from your cock and achieve its widest configuration often after 15 minutes to a half hour of **love**making.

That's when more extreme motions become possible, without annoying or hurting her.

ANAL SEX - IF YOU'RE INTO IT

Although I confessed earlier that I'm not into **anal intercourse** (it's just not my thing), I do have some suggestions I hope you'll find helpful if that's something you and your lover enjoy. *(FYI: My advice is absolutely do not engage in this kind of thing unless your lover indicates she wants it. This is a specialized interest not everyone has.)*

Unlike her **vaginal canal**, her **anal canal** contains no **mucous membranes** or other lubrication producers. So you absolutely must use some **artificial lubrication**. For **anal sex**, I believe the preferred choice is *petroleum jelly*. If you don't like that, try *olive oil*. (But check with your doctor on the relative safety of all of this first.) If you're going to use a condom, use one that won't be degraded by the lubrication you choose; or use lubrication that won't degrade the condom you prefer.

Her **anal canal's walls** are also much thinner and more vulnerable to damage than her **vaginal walls**. So be very gentle. Go much more slowly than you would in her **vagina**. And limit your time inside it to no more than about 5-10 minutes max.

Sexually, concentrate on her **anal ring** mostly (the muscular ring around the entrance to her **anus**). And follow the advice I gave you about how to approach her **entrances**. Don't rush the entry process.

Then, *ease* yourself into her **anal canal** very slowly when you want deeper **penetration**. When you think you're deep enough to reach her **cul-de-sac** (the suspected **anal orgasm trigger** I introduced on page 219), set up a slow and steady rhythm with the slightest of motions you can manage. You should only go in and out about a quarter of an inch, if that. Your motion should be similar to how you might delicately finger-rub a silk shirt that has a bit of food stuck on it (you'd massage it gently so as not to tear the silk).

Finally, remember to wash yourself thoroughly or use a new condom if you plan on later entering her **vaginal canal**. That helps prevent the risk of causing a *vaginal infection*.

Savor It...Celebrate It

...If you take anything away from this chapter - and you should have learned quite a lot - it should be this: Lovemaking is not about a rush to having an orgasm. It's about prolonging and appreciating the most incredible gift God has given us.

So just savor being inside of her! Enjoy the ride. There should be no goals in lovemaking, after all.

The best part of lovemaking, for me, are the many pleasures that come before my orgasm (which signals at least a temporary end, which, to me, is a bit of a let down). So prolong it as long as you can. And make it the celebration it should be - of your togetherness, of the mind blow and miracle of your ability to make love.

And speaking of which - if there is a goal, it is to make love. That is, to express your love for her. And to make her love you more and want you more afterward.

So keep the experience loving. Use your cock not just to knock her socks off, but also to express the passionate and deep love and desire you feel for her.

The act of intercourse alone does not suffice. Sex can be an empty experience that leaves her feeling lonely afterward if it lacks this necessary loving component.

And if you ever need to remind yourself, in the saddle so to speak, of what lovemaking requires, just remember this admonition:

"Do it once more...with feeling!"

> "So I sing you to sleep, After the lovin'
> I brush back the hair from your eyes.
> And the love on your face is so real that it makes me want to cry....
> Yes, after the lovin', I'm still in love with you."
> - from "After The Lovin'" (lyrics by Alan Bernstein)

After The Lovin'

*S*tudies have shown that women process **emotions** much better and more completely and quickly than men. It's a biological fact.

Now, ultimately, you will learn to develop your emotional sensitivity…

But – this is crucial – for now, understand that, after **love**making, a woman waits for validation of the experience, emotionally. You absolutely **must** give her **positive feedback** *immediately afterward*…at least once during the day…and then again when she returns home.

Talk about how special it was (if it was). Use your own words, but be specific and honest about what it meant to you. **Not** as a lewd experience, but as an emotionally and spiritually thrilling time. Tell her how beautiful she looked – and you can praise specific parts…or compliment her skin (is it soft?)…

Is her body sensitive and responsive? I once sent an email to my lover telling her how much fun her body was…I said it was "a **love**making playground" – or something to that effect.

Be sure, too, to talk about how much you love her as a person. Again, be specific and be honest. Is she sweet? Fun? Does she give you goose bumps? Take your breath away? Tell her.

Don't gush like a schoolboy. And don't go on forever. Talk like a sexy man…a man who's passionately in love with his woman. Just tell her you were thinking about her…how sexy and sweet she is…how sumptuous her body is…and how much you miss her…and are thinking about her…and can't wait to be with her again.

Was there anything exceptional about the last **love**making experience? Don't forget to mention that – especially if she knocked your socks off by doing something unusually special!

Be playful, sexy and teasing about it if you can find a way. And then you might consider telling her you're going to do something special for her that night (if something special comes to mind – but don't let her in on the secret; you need to create some magic).

However you say it, *make it your own*. Don't parrot my suggestions. Come up with your own observations and say it in a way that comes easy to you. That way it will sound natural and be perceived in a nice way.

Women need this kind of feedback. If you don't provide this to your lover, she is going to be very disappointed and upset. And she'll think you don't really care for her, or value your intimate times together.

This is one area where most men fail. And this is one area that, if ignored, can lead to real discontent on the woman's part - the type of discontent that is relationship-threatening, over time.

If you're not used to being so open and honest about your feelings, and about talking about intimate details, *get over it*. It's part of being a great male lover and mature man. It's sexy.

Start off small…and your confidence will build. As you see how excitedly she's responding to this kind of communication, I'm sure you'll be encouraged to continue giving her regular sexy and/or *loving* feedback after each of your intimate times together.

And you'll get better with time, too. Practice makes perfect. But you're not being graded. Don't be shy! She'll appreciate any and all positive comments.

One last thing. After morning sex, if it's just before work and you're the first one to leave the bed, *be especially sure to sum up the experience in a loving way*. Above all else - *avoid making comments like*, "Gotta run," or "Gotta get to work," or "Gotta shower" as you disembark from the bed. Statements like that will demean everything that came before, as though it was not as important as what lies ahead. You'll make her feel empty, as if she's just had a one-night stand. Word to the wise.

*And sweet Lucretia, so young and gay,
What scandalous doings in the ruins of Pompeii...
And lovely Lisa...You gave a new meaning to the Leaning Tower of Pisa!
-from Cole Porter's song "Where Is The Life That Late I Led?"*

Location, Location, Location

O ne of the *biggest* **orgasms** I ever had was in a Jones Beach parking lot in the middle of the day in the driver's seat of my girlfriend's convertible with the top down and her head between my legs. This was with two young security guys circling our car in their patrol car, smiling approvingly as they watched her give me the blowjob of my life.

I begged her to stop but she refused. And she had me by the balls so I couldn't move.

The *audacity* of it - the *public nature of it* and *my inability to stop her* - added to the excitement and power of my eventual climax. *My head nearly came off when I came.*

Why tell this story? My point is: *Where* you choose to make love produces *different* feelings.

And choosing **sexy locations** to make love is one way to spice up and add variety to your love life (and maybe even experience the biggest orgasms ever). The trick is to do this without getting arrested!

Location, Location, Location

It's your job to experiment with locations and find the ones she finds the most thrilling. Some locations will make her more excited than others. You know how real estate people say it's all about *location, location, location...* Well a smart lover includes **creative locations** in his bag of tricks.

Not every day. Not every week. Not even every month.

But it's smart to scout around periodically to find places for furtive **love**making that provide the added element of excitement, romance, sensuality and novelty that only certain outside-the-home locations can provide. You're not giving your lover a **complete sexual experience** if you deny her the thrills you can give her by making love in fabulously **sexy locations outside the home**. An **exotic location** will make a big difference when it comes to the **sensations** and **orgasms** your lover will get during sex.

Some locations - like **forests** with no one nearby - can be highly **romantic**. They can make you feel really **sexy** - like you're Adam and she's Eve.

On Loving Women

Other locations - like **beach parking lots** - provide thrills **exhibitionists** get off on. (Is your lover one? You might be surprised.)

Still other locations - like **the back of a movie theatre or plane** - feel **naughty** and a bit **risky**. That, in turn, creates a unique excitement - especially when you find your inability to express yourself vocally makes your orgasm that much bigger. (Does your lover crave **risky thrills?**)

Of course, anything can be done to *excess*. I had a girlfriend years ago who *only* wanted to make love in **public places**. *Nowhere else*. While *novel* and *exciting* at first, a *steady diet* of increasingly risky places quickly grew old.

So, like anything else, use unusual semi-public venues only <u>occasionally</u>. But keep this in mind: the bigger the **thrill**, the bigger her **orgasm** (and the fonder the memories). So *choose an* **exotic erotic location** that will **excite her to the max!**

The more *audacious*, the better. Here are **some exciting locations** at which I created **sexy memories**:

Location, Location, Location

- *On a bed of pine needles high up in a beautiful mountain forest*
- *A hotel balcony overlooking a beach, at night, with sexy people in scanty swimsuits watching us as we made love*, covered up enough so as to be able to deny what we were doing
- *The passenger seat of my car on a highway* (I made my girlfriend get **semi-naked** and did her with a **vibrator** we'd just bought her; truckers were honking their horns as I passed them and the idea she was being seen from time to time drove her all the more crazy!)
- *Driving down a crowded city street in the afternoon*
- *A remote cave overlooking a beautiful Southwest city at sunset*
- *The floor of a luxurious bathroom during a private dinner party*
- *Under the table of a swanky New York City restaurant*
- *In my college dorm room*, my roommate asleep near us
- *In the back seats of a movie theatre, with a few people sneaking peeks* (I gave one of my girlfriends the hand job of her life)
- *Behind a woodpile on a forested hill behind a romantic hotel*
- *In the back of my SUV, off-roading it on a mesa in the Southwest*
- *In a friend's pool in the suburbs at night*
- *On a sparsely-populated beach on a summer afternoon*
- *In a teepee at a resort, in a romantic location beside a lake*
- *On my girlfriend's office desk, not far from a storefront window overlooking a crowded sidewalk and street*
- *On the floor of a commercial radio station's broadcast studio*
- *Under the bushes in my parents' back yard*
- *In the parking lot of a night club during a break (I was in the rock band), in the front seat of my car (with the windows fogged up from our breath, so no one could see inside)*
- *At the opera (as I mentioned in the chapter, "The Art of Loving Touching" on page 257)*

Some of the locations I've mentioned (like large forests) are great for having **intercourse**. Others (like **restaurants, planes** and **theatres**) are more suited to enjoying quick **oral sex** or **fingerwork**. That is, **if** the conditions are right.

You need to choose locations with **discretion**. Not every outdoor or semi-public place is *sexy* or *romantic*. Here are some considerations to keep in mind when evaluating a location for its appropriateness:

- *You need a certain amount of **privacy**. If someone can see you, you have to be sure they won't mind or take any negative action.*

On Loving Women

- **Cover up** as much as you can in less private settings. Try to make the activity **deniable**.
- You need to be sure you'll have enough **time** to do whatever act you have in mind before someone might come upon you.
- You need to **find locations that make her feel comfortable** about getting naked and having sex there. (Every woman has her list of likes and dislikes.)
- **Timing** is key. No place is great for furtive sex all the time.
- Err on the side of **caution**. Do not take unnecessary risks.

A Huge Benefit to Making Love In Creative Locations

And lest you think all of this is trivial and silly, there's a side benefit you might not have considered: You can use the choice of a location to solidify your presence in her life, and as a forget-me-not. Nothing solidifies a great love more than through the creation of **memorable romantic moments** you'll cherish and talk about for a lifetime.

Romantic locations are great for **romantic memories**. Others, like **her office desk or chair** (after working hours - if there are no video cameras!) can help create a lasting bond and make for **sexy memories**. From then on, the sight of the chair (and perhaps a lingering aroma) will remind her of you and, like Pavlov's bell, it might continually make her hot for you... as well as bring up some loving memories.

Careful: Some Locations To Avoid

Some locations are not prime **love**making places, though. For example - the **beach** isn't as romantic as it's made out to be. The **sand** makes things difficult. The sea breeze blows it into your eyes and onto her **pussy**. (Not fun!) And then there are the **bugs**...That reminds me of the time I had convinced a pretty young bikini-clad babe at a popular **island resort** to meet me on the beach at midnight, where I played guitar for her. The **seduction** was going really well until we both looked down and saw *thousands of Palmetto bugs body surfing on the sand!* It was disgusting! We *ran* off the beach in different directions. *I never saw her again!*

Water can also pose **problems**. **Pool** and **sea water** can actually make motion difficult inside her vagina. It can act as an *anti-lubricant*.

That being said, go out and be creative. Find some really romantic locations perfect for **love**making and make your own special memories. Keep it **sexy**, **romantic** and **loving**. You'll be glad you did!

Unusual Locations You Might Try
Interesting Venues Where Some Said They Had Sex

"In a hotel pool, while others swam about."

"In a public jacuzzi with others around."

"In my ex-wife's parent's basement while they were home."

"A hospital chapel, while I was a patient."

"Golf course (I wonder whatever happened to the souvenir flag I stole from the 9th hole???)."

"The inside of a huge Caterpillar piece of equipment on a construction site."

"After hours at the zoo in front of the monkey cage."

"In the elevator of the Sheraton Hotel in Shreveport, LA."

"A bathroom of a Starbucks."

"In a church up by the organ."

"On a stone within the Coliseum in Rome."

" A wedding party...we had sex in the bride and groom's bed."

"On a bench after midnight under the trees within view of the cottages at a singles resort."

"In a tanning salon."

"In the back of a New York City bus."

"On the office conference table!"

"On the back of an ATV in the middle of a farmer's field."

" On a motorcycle in an orange grove in Mesa, Arizona."

"On a Zamboni."

"The walk-in closet in my best friend's bedroom, during a party!"

"In a hot tub with people in it."

"On the police station's roof."

Some of these quotes were found on snopes.com, matchdoctor.com, forums.plentyoffish.com, answers.yahoo.com, and www.ivillage.com.

> **"Sexual Bondage"**
> *"The sensual and consensual experience of safe captivity and physical helplessness. A sexual practice in which a participant is physically restrained... as a means of attaining sexual gratification from relinquishing control...*
> *- from definition-of.com*

Edgy Titillations: Sex Toys, Masturbation & Gentle Bondage

Not every woman but a *lot* of women - even *girl-next-door types* - crave some **edgy love**making from time to time. So let's get **edgy** - within the confines of **monogamy** (because I am a **monogamist**). There are a lot of fun and exotic things the **creative male monogamist** can do to spice up his love life - *within the bounds of what his lover desires and enjoys*.

OK. So you sometimes *need* to push the envelope with a woman who desires **edgy scenarios**, but how far should you go? I'll give you tips on how to please this kind of lover, while still maintaining the focus on *love*.

Exhibitionists, Voyeurs, Sex Kittens & Submissives

There are **four types** of lovers who are most likely to want **edgy love**making. You need to understand who they are and what rings their bells in order to meet their sexual needs. Although more common among the swinging and polyamory crowd, there are monogamists who want this too.

The first is the **exhibitionist**. She needs to show herself off, **naked**, to others. The *monogamists* among them will be satisfied to do this without sleeping with others.

The **exhibitionist** will want sex from time to time in **semi-public places**, where there's the **risk** she'll be *seen* by strangers. I provided a list of suggestions for this kind of thing in the chapter, "Location, Location, Location" on page 381. You can also find places on your property to satisfy

Edgy Titillations: Sex Toys, Masturbation & Gentle Bondage

her **special needs** - **in front of a window** perhaps, or **in the backyard**, for instance. (I had a lover in this category who once wanted to make love one night on an empty moving tram at the Epcot Center! *That* I declined to do.)

She's the kind who'd love you to do her with a **vibrator** or **dildo** *while you're driving* and have you pull alongside the big rigs to give the truckers a good look at what you're doing to her. *She's also the kind who could get you arrested, though, so choose your locations and activities carefully!*

Some *safe* suggestions to please this kind of woman:

- Make love in front of a **mirror**. A **cheval mirror** can be brought into the bedroom and put back somewhere else afterward so as never to give away your secret when others visit your home - friends, relatives or workmen. A small **handheld mirror** works in a pinch. Many women get off on watching what you're doing to them.
- **Videotape** your sexual experiences (to watch later on, when making love). The filming and viewing are **erotic activities**.
- Have her **masturbate** in front of you - and possibly in a semi-public place such as the back seat of a relatively empty theatre or plane (more on masturbation for its erotic benefits in a moment)

Some other awesome and safe ways to fulfill her fantasies? Take her to:

- The erotic annual **Burning Man** event in Nevada's Black Rock Desert where anything and everything goes
- A **hedonistic clothing optional resort** where you romp naked and make love outdoors - in full view of other people if you like
- A nice **nude beach**
- A **sex or erotic festival, expo or convention** where participants can attend scantily clad
- The **Carnaval** celebration on the streets of Rio de Janeiro in Brazil, where she can dance topless or go in a revealing costume or flash other revelers
- The sexy **Mardi Gras celebration** in New Orleans, where she can flash her boobs and be provocative just by wearing the beaded necklaces flashers accumulate

That being said, **exhibitionism** can go too far. I once had a lover who was too much for me along these lines. A realtor and daughter of a wealthy family who lived in a mansion on Long Island's posh North Shore, *she only wanted to have sex in public places.* She had something against making love in our home and *refused* to do it! That didn't work for me. Oh well.

The second kind of woman I want to talk about is the **voyeur**. The monogamists among them love you and *don't want to cheat.* But they need to see *other men,* **naked**. So you need to cater to that need.

So allow her to place **statues, photos and paintings of naked men** around the house. Another acceptable idea: go out and buy **porno** DVDs with her or just watch **sexy TV shows** together. Take her to **erotic film festivals** and **sex museums** too. There are **romantic and edgy dance troupes**, too, who sometimes dance with very little if anything on (their performances will *really* get her hot - trust me!). There are *plays* and *musicals* that feature **nudity**. Be proactive and creative in satisfying a **voyeuristic lover**.

And if you're sure she's a monogamist, don't be jealous of the **naked men** whose images turn her on - so long as she gives you all of her sexual attention. Some women require **extreme visual stimulation** to get **aroused**.

Then there are the **sex kittens**. Strap yourself in if this is who you're with. You're in for a wild ride! The **sex kitten** has a lot in common with the **vixen** or **dominatrix** even - but she's not the kind who'll inflict **pain**. She might, however, **tie you up** or put **handcuffs** on you and sweetly torment the heck out of you. (More on these practices in a moment.) She might even want to don a **strap-on** because she feels turnabout is fair play.

She might pull you out of your pants when she's driving and give you a handjob for all to see, on a highway or a crowded city street. She might do that in the backseat of a moving car, with your relatives in the front seat.

She might even push the envelope further. For instance, she might ask to watch you with another woman. (I had a lover request this once. I resisted this idea because I felt it would lead to trouble and break us up.)

If this kind of **sex life** works for you, it can be exciting. She'll often be the one in charge, which can be a huge turn-on (and it removes a lot of the responsibility from you, to keep things fresh). But there's always the danger her needs will blow up into something that threatens the relationship. I'd suggest you keep the reins on her scenarios so they're within the bounds of a **happy monogamistic love life**. It can easily get out of hand.

Finally, there's the **submissive**. This kind of lover delights in being ordered around during sex and made to feel what's she doing is *naughty*.

She *fantasizes* about **being "taken."** This is what gets her off. You might be surprised to find out how many women, in fact, want to **role play** in this way.

If your lover is one of them, she is likely to want some **gentle bondage. More edgy women sometimes want to be a sex "slave" or servant, in a fun, non-threatening, and loving way.** (We'll discuss this very soon.)

Edgy Titillations: Sex Toys, Masturbation & Gentle Bondage

EDGY MASTURBATION

By the way, some edgy pursuits seem to appeal to *all* women. On an episode of HBO's *Real Sex* show some years ago, they did an on-the-street interview with passersby that was very interesting. I doubt most men paid much attention to it. But *it contained a key to satisfying women!*

The question they asked everyone was: "Do you like to **masturbate** *while your boyfriend makes love to you?*" A *crowd* of women erupted in expressions of glee, jumping up and down, shouting a chorus of ***"Yes!!!"***

That being said, most women even today find *masturbating* in front of someone else somewhat embarrassing at first. But once they've gotten over their shyness, most find it is highly erotic and sexually gratifying. So don't be afraid to bring this side out in your lover.

Nothing's *hotter*. You can ask her to **masturbate** for you while you watch. Or you can ask her to jerk herself off (with her **clit**) during intercourse. Or you can both masturbate while watching each other. Even sexier - if she's into **sex toys**, ask her to do herself in front of you with a **vibrator** or **dildo**.

This will help **sexualize her**, too, and make her more fun as a **sex partner**.

SEX TOYS AS AN ADJUNCT TO LOVEMAKING

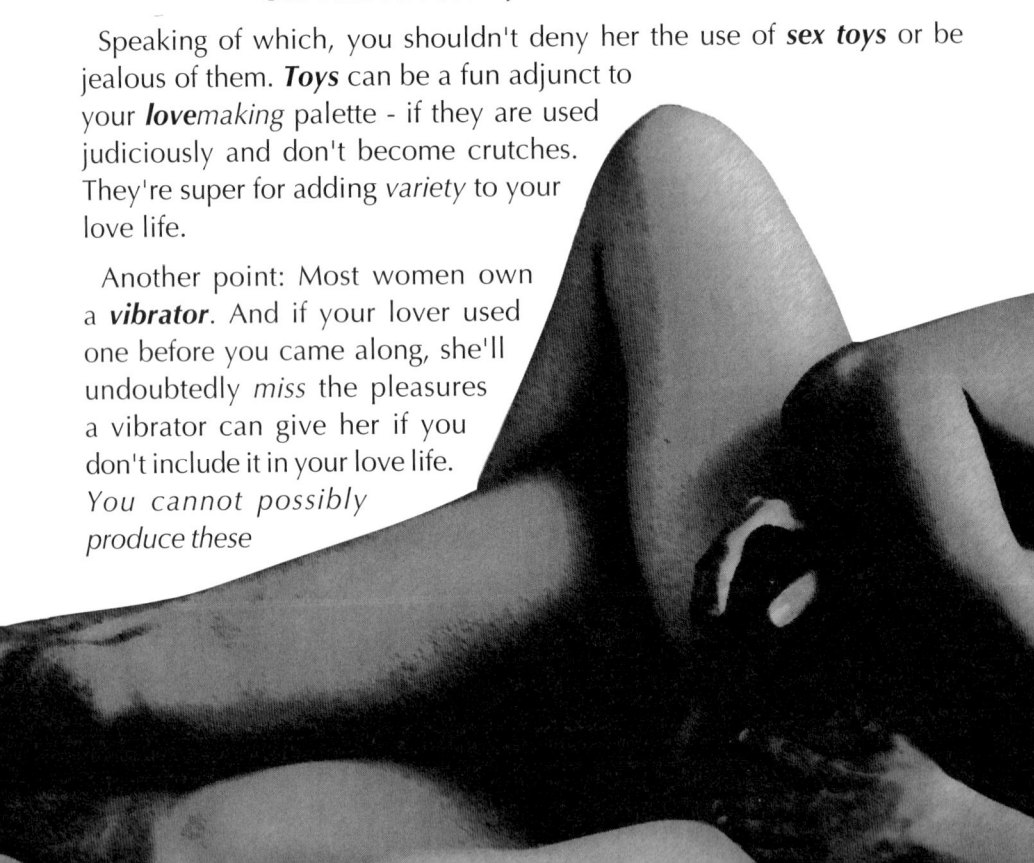

Speaking of which, you shouldn't deny her the use of **sex toys** or be jealous of them. **Toys** can be a fun adjunct to your **love**making palette - if they are used judiciously and don't become crutches. They're super for adding *variety* to your love life.

Another point: Most women own a **vibrator**. And if your lover used one before you came along, she'll undoubtedly *miss* the pleasures a vibrator can give her if you don't include it in your love life. *You cannot possibly produce these*

On Loving Women

feelings and it's not fair to deprive her of these pleasures.

In fact, as a teenager, I'll never forget the day my mentor Earle told me (in a conversation in which he was teaching me about sex) exactly how *he'd used a **vibrator** on his wife the night before. How odd,* I thought - *I'd rather be doing everything myself.* It took me years to realize how *smart* it was to incorporate ***vibrators*** into my love life.

Here's what I found:

- ♀ *It's really sexy to watch your woman using one. You don't have to be a voyeur. You can minister to her in other ways as she uses it.*
- ♀ *She might occasionally want to use hers when you're not home, or not available (maybe you're on the road). Better that than someone else! But, more than that (I'm assuming fidelity is not an issue), we all have the need to **masturbate** from time to time, and you should enable your woman to do it as she pleases. To make it sexier, though, tell her you want her to tell you when she's used it! She'll be thinking about confessing to you as she uses the toy on herself, which will make the experience that much hotter for her.*
- ♀ ***Vibrators*** *can be used as a tool to greater fun on occasion, when you're making love. They won't replace you. They'll simply enhance your times together.*
- ♀ *And you can control the **speed, motion and location**. When you control it, she feels you're doing her, not the vibrator.*

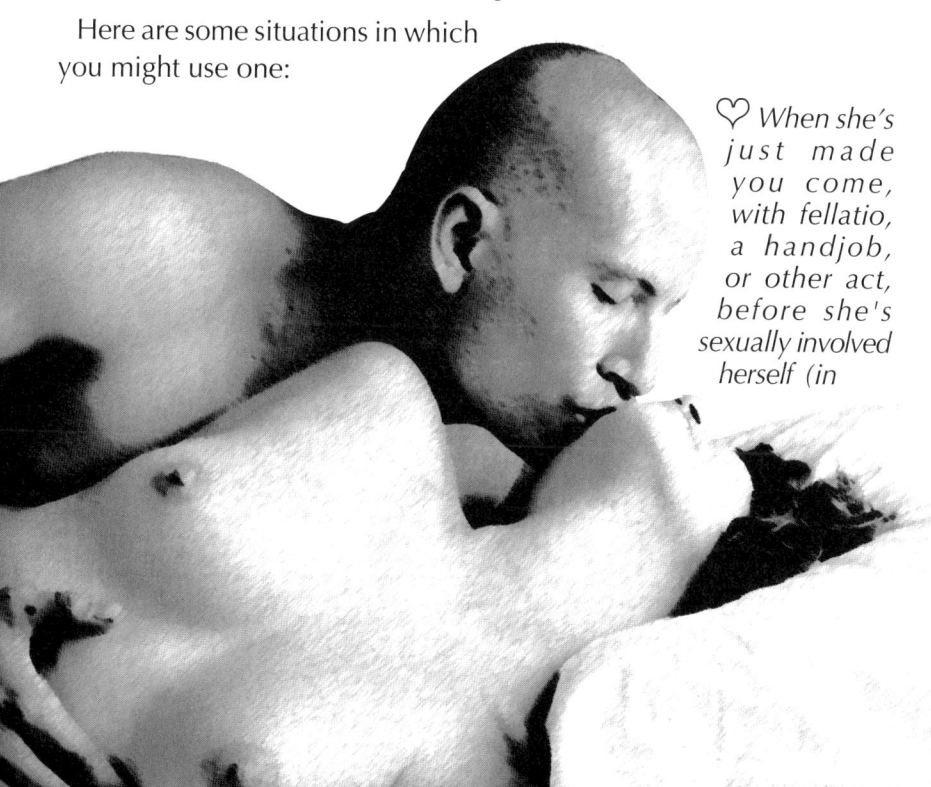

Here are some situations in which you might use one:

♡ *When she's just made you come, with fellatio, a handjob, or other act, before she's sexually involved herself (in*

Edgy Titillations: Sex Toys, Masturbation & Gentle Bondage

other words, she hasn't come yet and undoubtedly has to – there will be occasions where she insists she just wants you to "rest," but, most times most women will want the favor returned)

♡ **When you're tired or ill**, and feel you cannot function but you want to bring her off

♡ When your woman has trouble coming and the **vibrator** makes it easier for her to **climax** (this is a fabulous use for it - but use it only on occasion; and read more on this practice below)

♡ When you're just looking to vary things (try it, for instance, on low speed, on her nipples!)

♡ If she especially loves her **vibrator** and you haven't used it for some time; or if she wants you to use it on a somewhat regular basis to satisfy that specific need (weekly, for instance)

♡ When she wants to use one on you (this can really be hot!)

Some *tips*:

In general, it's best to start at a **slow vibration level**. That might be enough to make most women come, in fact, if you apply the **vibrator** with patience. But if you increase the speed, do it gradually. If you're not at the max, you have someplace to go if you need more intensity to make her come.

Use the **slow tease** method most times - don't go for her **orgasm** right away. Use the **vibrator** everywhere but her **clit** for awhile, for instance. See how hot you can make her. Her **orgasm** will be all the *bigger* for it.

Also – very important -- you need to discover her *comfort level* when it comes to the *highest speeds* (especially when it comes to placing it directly on her **clitoris**). Until you know how high she likes it, ask her, with each increase in speed, how it feels. Back off and make a mental note of what speeds to *avoid* if she has her limits.

Special case advise: With a woman who has **trouble coming**, the temptation is to set the **vibrator** on *high speeds* but that's unwise. With the **plateau effect** (about which I taught you earlier), her **nerves** will become dulled to that high level and subsequently be unable to come from **stimulation** that's at or below that level (she'll need *more*, and the machine can't give much more). More important - *you actually can use the **vibrator** to help cure her of her problems*. You can *sensitize* her so she no longer experiences difficulty in coming *if you primarily use lower speeds*. Believe it or not, her **nerves** will eventually become more *sensitive* in this way. In fact, *the one* **danger in using vibrators** *is that the maximum speeds are so intense that* **they can dull her nerves** *to more* **subtle stimulation**. So try to *avoid the highest settings*.

On Loving Women

Now, there are differences in **vibrators** and you need to know how they vary. Here's a partial list of some you might want to add to your **toy box**:

- 👍 **Vibrating "eggs."** Containing one or two egg-shaped **vibrators**, these are for adventurous lovers. You put them in your **bottoms**. If you're not shy, you won't be sorry you tried these!!!

- 👍 **Long, thin vibrators, non-penis-shaped**. These are less threatening to the average man. Not quite as big as the average **penis** (and not looking like another man), these do the job and can be used either on her **clit, vulva, or inside her vagina** to good effect. They typically have a hard surface and are shaped for function only.

- 👍 **Larger ones, penis-shaped**. Some women prefer the look and feel of cock-shaped vibrators, which tend also to be softer in texture, almost skin-like. Don't be afraid of encouraging her to buy one.

- 👍 **G-Spot vibrators**. Having a curved end, these (coming in many shapes and sizes) are designed specifically to tickle her **G-Spot** (although you might find she'll want to try it on your prostate, too!).

- 👍 **Short thin vibrators and "butt plugs."** Typically for **anal** use, these can be used on her and, if she and you are so inclined, on you as well. Larger **vibrators** might hurt for this use (only women with the wildest sex drives would probably want the big ones inserted in their **bottoms**). Always use **lubrication** when using **sex toys** in this way. **Petroleum jelly** or any kind of **oil** should work well.

- 👍 **Pocket-book sized vibrators**. Shaped innocuously so as to pass inspection at airport security gates, these are meant for a woman's needs on the road, or during the business day. Don't worry if your lover wants one of these. She'll come home even hotter for you, whether she uses it or not – trust me!

- 👍 **"Butterflies" or strap-on clitoral vibrators**. These can be used during sex but they're really great for driving her wild while you're out in public. (Some come with remote controllers!). Very sexy.

WHERE TO FIND SEX TOYS

The best news of all about **sex toys** is that shopping for them becomes an intensely **erotic** experience. If you don't find yourself getting hard or hot as you peruse the myriad of suggestive inventions in all shapes and sizes in the adult store or online, you're in the minority. Her panties will get wet from the excitement, too - and be very eager for sex afterward! That's a bonus of which you should not deprive yourself.

The most fun way to go about this is to find an adult store in your area that seems non-threatening. Some seem sleazy from the outside. Try to locate one that is well-lit, clean and inviting – one that, hopefully, caters

Edgy Titillations: Sex Toys, Masturbation & Gentle Bondage

to couples and nice singles (as opposed to sleazebags). This is important – scout it out well *before* you bring your lover there. You don't want to turn her off to this experience by taking her someplace nasty. (There are, in fact, nationwide chains that operate some of these stores. These might be the best ones to start with.)

Or, if you're a bit shy, you might start by shopping for the few sexually-oriented toys commonly sold by drug stores. Some carry **dildos** and **vibrators** (you'll often see them cleverly placed in window displays). All carry vibrating "**massagers**," with all sorts of attachments that can be used to enhance your sexual experience (these are especially good for **clitoral** stimulation). Or shop online with her, in the privacy of your home.

One very important rule when it comes to **sex toys**:

Let her choose what she likes. Don't impose your desires on her in this area. This is an intensely personal thing and you want her to feel it's romantic. Only she can know what, to her, is sexy, inviting, and the right size and shape.

If you've ever tried a **vibrator**, you know they will give her *unique sensations* and **orgasms** of a kind she cannot get any other way. Why deny her this **pleasure**? It will enhance your love life and she'll love you for it.

A Toy For Double Penetration And *The Biggest Orgasms*

And **the best reason for owning a vibrator? Use it to fulfill her fantasy of being done by two men** (within the borders of your devoted relationship). (I discussed this kind of thing in earlier chapters.) **If** this appeals to her (as it *does* to *most* women), **double-penetration will drive your woman absolutely wild!** You'll give her **the biggest orgasms humanly possible!**

I once did this to a very *conservative, religious* woman. Her reactions were so *incredible* I wrote them down afterward. Here's exactly what she said:

"I **loved** being *double-fucked!* How did you know I'd like it? **Every woman fantasizes about being double-fucked!** Let's do it again some other time!" And she laughed. And she *moaned* over and over for what seemed like an hour afterward. This was a *monogamistic* woman. Then she said (several times): "That was so *nasty!*" (Her *tone* indicated she considered the word nasty a *good* thing, in sex.) "I was *hoping*," she continued, "that you'd do something *nasty* to me today!"

So, as you can see, *you'll score big points doing it!* Here's a super way to do it:

Purchase a *thin* **vibrator** and use it *like a second* **cock** for **double-**

penetration. You'll want a *thin **vibrator*** for this because there's just a thin membrane between her **vaginal canal** and her **anal canal**. *You* will feel the vibrator through it. And if you're of any size, it will press into the **vaginal canal** *too much* and hurt you. If you insert it in her bottom from a **rear-entry position**, you can hold the end of it against your **pubic bone** so it goes in and out of her **anal canal** with the same rhythm with which your **cock** is going in and out of her **pussy**. Prepare yourself for paint-peeling **screams** when she comes! (But P.S.: If you have *control problems*, you might *not* want to do this. You'll feel the *vibrations* and you might come too fast.)

OTHER SEX TOYS

...And of course there are an endless number of **sex toys** you might want to experiment with. One of my girlfriends *loved* **nipple clips and clamps**. They teased her intensely by keeping a constant stimulating pressure on those very sensitive **erogenous zones**. Many women find those too intense, though, so, like anything else, it's all about personal taste and desires.

For you, there are **cock rings** - made to keep men hard who have problems along those lines - but consult your doctor. I'm not sure those are safe.

There are **oils** you can try. Some heat up (but *absolutely do not use these inside her or on your **penis** or **scrotum** - they'll cause worlds of pain*).

THE SHOWER MASSAGER AS SEX TOY

But one of the best **sex toys** ever might already be in your home. (If it's not, run...I say *run* to the store to buy one!) It's a **shower massager!**

Remember in the anatomy chapter where I told you how I used my **shower massager** on my **scrotum** to bring on an **orgasm**? And in that same chapter I told you how her **labia minora** are biologically similar to the skin covering your **scrotum?** Well then why not use the **shower massager** on her **labia minora** to see if you can bring on the same effect? Then turn it on her *clit* for **orgasms** that will blow her mind!

She'll love you all the more it - for being sophisticated enough to know about the joys a **shower massager** can bring *and* for being magnanimous enough to introduce her to these fabulous **onanistic pleasures**. It's a very giving thing to let your partner play with **bathroom sex toys,** which give her feelings you could not possibly produce. She'll appreciate it big time.

And by the way, you'd be making a mistake to see **bathroom pleasures** as taking something away from you, or seeing them as a threat to your manhood. They're nothing of the kind.

In fact, if you're *adventurous* and *sexy* yourself, you will get into using

Edgy Titillations: Sex Toys, Masturbation & Gentle Bondage

the **shower massager** on *yourself* as well. Turnabout is fair play, after all. And, while she's directing the spray on you, or you're using the **shower massager** on yourself while *she* watches, you'll understand why I say that allowing *her* these pleasures is a very giving and *sexy act*.

OK. Now, there are various approaches you can take in incorporating the **shower massager** into your **love**making:

- *You can let her play with it unimpeded by you, and just watch*
- *You can play with her body while she plays with it*
- *You can control the flow yourself and direct it wherever you like*

Each of these approaches is valid and has its place. Go with your feelings as to how you want to proceed. You can always change things in midstream, anyway.

There are a couple of things you need to attend to, though, when it comes to **bathroom fun**:

- First, you need to make sure to heat up the sides and floor of the tub and shower stall before she gets in. (She might likely need to sit or lie down at some point.) Turn the water on hot and direct it over all the parts of the tub or shower stall her body might touch until you're sure no chill remains.
- Second, before using the water on her, you need to test it to make sure the intensity and the heat is not too much. Start off with a light to moderate intensity and heat level to be conservative.
- Finally, always be sure to ask her, "how does that feel?" And really gauge her reaction, to make sure she's enjoying the experience. If she's not, move on to other things.

The **shower massager** is great because you can use it *all over her body*, and at all angles. Experiment with your choice of sprays and try different techniques with the nozzle. You can hold it steady on her (great for orgasms especially). You can shake it violently so the water rapidly stimulates her. Or you can gently move it up or down or back and forth. Use your creativity.

When should you engage in this kind of activity? This is especially fun when you take her into the shower *when no shower was planned.* That brings the element of *surprise* into your **love**making, which is always a plus. And, if you do this frequently enough, an even better benefit is that she'll get hot for you every time she takes a shower and grabs the massager!

THE SEXY SPOUT

There's another **sex toy** that's readily available in your home that you absolutely must try too. It's the **spout** of your **bathtub**. (And if you have a **jacuzzi** or **hot tub**, their **water jets** are awesome **sex toys**.)

To use the **sexy spout** (assuming she's never used one in this way before), first adjust the water so it's just warm enough and not too intense. Have her splay her **legs** open, her **feet** on the wall, pushing her **bottom** to the edge of the bath tub, by the **water spout**, maneuvering her **hips** so that the water flows over her **vulva**. She or you can adjust the torrent so that it builds and builds her excitement until she comes.

I got this idea not too long ago, when I walked in when my then-girlfriend was taking a bath and I saw her sidle up to the **bathtub spout** to get a quick thrill from letting the bath water run over her **vulva**. When she noticed I was there, she hastily backed up, as if she was embarrassed, caught in the act.

She then tried to go ahead with her bath and pretend she hadn't been attracted to the idea of **masturbating** (as I found out later she *often* did in the bath, in her *teenaged* years). Noticing this, I said:

"Did that feel good, when you let the water run over you?"

She smiled a bit shyly, and said, "Yeah!"

I said, "Don't let me stop you," or something to that effect. It was smoother at the time, the suggestion. She didn't know how to take that so I said, "Don't you want to continue?" And she eagerly said, "Definitely!"

It was really hot watching her wiggling her **hips**, trying hard to get the most of the water flow. I played with her **breasts**, sometimes *squeezing* them, sometimes *sucking* them, and she got off in a big way.

This kind of **pleasure** is unique to the **bathtub spout**, and allowing her to indulge herself in this way not only wins big points with her, but it's a big turn-on for you – if you're *secure* enough to let her do this. If your lover is **highly sexual**, she undoubtedly positioned herself in her tub long ago and discovered how *sexy* the water rushing from that water spout or

Edgy Titillations: Sex Toys, Masturbation & Gentle Bondage

jet could be. And if she's experienced this before, she surely craves that feeling again from time to time. But if your lover has *never done this,* she *deserves* to experience the special pleasures this brings.

So - whether or not she did it before - why not *encourage* her to play with your **bathtub spout** or the **jets** of your **jacuzzi** or **hot tub** in front of you! Watching your lover doing this is incredibly *hot*.

Gentle Bondage

Finally, the most edgy of all suggestions. Not for everyone but if your lover has a **submissive** side and wants it, you need to be ready to play the part. That is:

If your lover is into it, you should incorporate some **gentle bondage** into your **love**making. *If* she gets excited by that idea - many women do - then you might also want sex toys such as play **handcuffs** (**not** real ones that lock), **blindfolds** perhaps (that can easily be removed by her) and sexy but easily-removable **bindings** (my favorite are actually her **pantyhose or scarves** or one of my **ties** - they're **sensual**, they fulfill the **pretense**, yet are easy to remove; stay away from **ropes** for their dark connotation).

One of my girlfriends, in fact, *directed* me to do this kind of thing for her. She called me one day with an assignment: I was to get a pair of **fuzzy handcuffs** for her, preferably *pink*. That night, I was to use them on her. She **loved** being **handcuffed, tied, and held down** while I pleased her *sexually*.

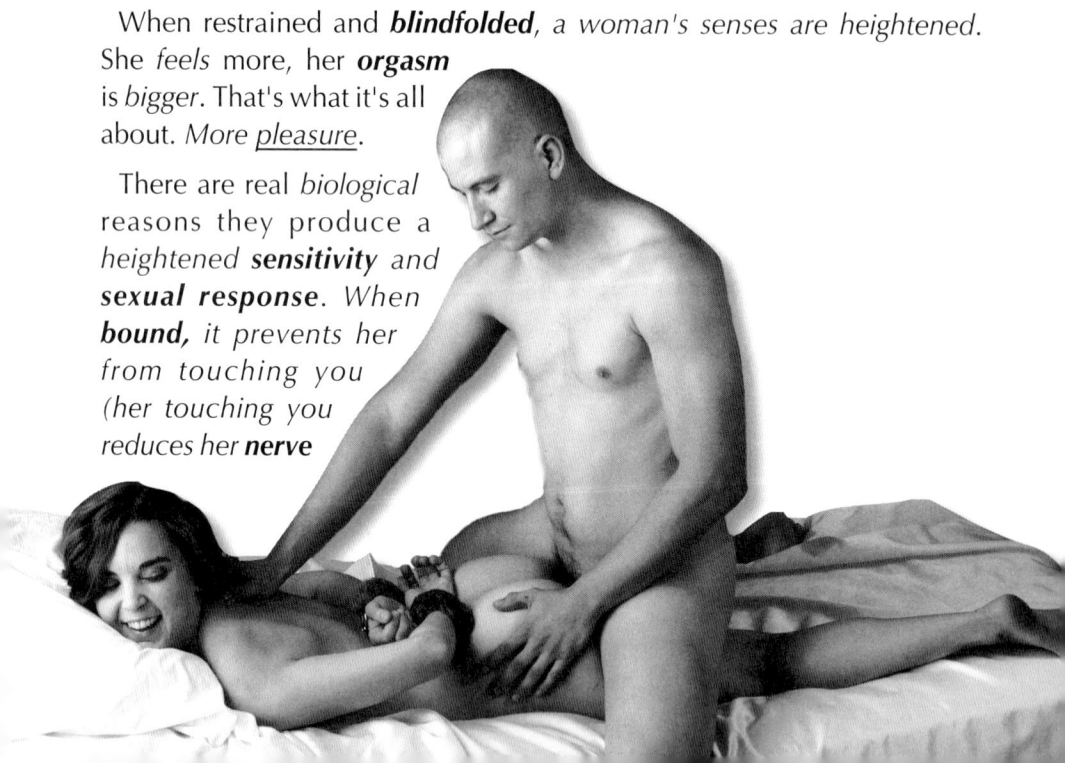

When restrained and **blindfolded**, a woman's senses are heightened. She *feels* more, her **orgasm** is *bigger*. That's what it's all about. More *pleasure*.

There are real *biological reasons they produce a heightened* **sensitivity** *and* **sexual response**. *When* **bound,** *it prevents her from touching you (her touching you reduces her* **nerve** *sensitivity* and *lessens her own enjoyment, through distraction).* When she's touching you, it sends **nerve input** to her **brain** that interferes with the **pleasure** she might otherwise get from whatever you are doing to her. It tamps down the **intensity** of her **reactions**. Perhaps her **brain** cannot handle input from both her **tactile organs** and your touches without turning down the volume on both. Scientists will have to test that theory.

Being **blindfolded** *increases the affect of* **non-visual sensory stimuli** - *in this case, touches and kisses.* The person blindfolded actually *feels more*; her nerves and senses are turned up *high* by the mind, seeking more information with the sense of sight being (temporarily) lost.

Plus, the feeling of *helplessness* she feels when **bound** and/or **blindfolded** creates in her a sense of *surrender*, which forces her to *give in to whatever you're doing to her.* That lets her feel *every ounce* of your stimulation, setting the stage for *big* **orgasms**. It also removes **inhibitions** that might otherwise get in the way of *sexual pleasure*.

So if you're thinking she's a bit *weird* or *kinky* for wanting **gentle loving bondage**, think again. The truth is that there are a *substantial* number of women - hetero *and* Lesbian - who like this kind of <u>innocuous</u> **sex play**. Lesbian feminist sex educator Betty Dodson, in fact, admits to this on her web site, on which she wrote:

> "*My fantasies have ranged from sugary romantic scenarios to thinking up elaborate set ups for bondage where I'm taken advantage of by cruel men. At first I worried about my rape and bondage fantasies, but these were the images that got me really hot.*"

So **gentle bondage** is not just about the **heightened sensations**. There's a **psychological component** - and perhaps a **primal desire** - that makes some women love **bondage**. For instance, a girlfriend who was into being **submissive** told me she liked being handcuffed or tied down for the feeling "of being taken." So **bondage** *plays to some women's* **fantasies**.

We're talking about **fantasies** and **pretend** *play acting* here - <u>**not**</u> *sadomasochism* or *humiliation, which I don't recommend.* I'm talking about <u>harmless</u> *role playing* in order to get a certain unique kind of *gratification*.

The **primal** aspect of this practice became clear to me while watching the sensual but tragic Amazon rainforest movie *The Emerald Forest* many years ago. It was in the scene where a young man, Tommy, abducted as a child and now a mostly-naked member of the "Invisible Ones" tribe, is given a ceremonial wooden club to go and "take" the woman he loves (Kachiri) as his bride.

Edgy Titillations: Sex Toys, Masturbation & Gentle Bondage

Even in this ritual, it's mostly pretense and Tommy knows it. But when he approaches the mostly naked Kachiri and raises the club to ceremonially knock her out, he chickens out in applying it to her head as he's supposed to. He's afraid of hurting her. Kachiri then chides him with a sexy smile, saying something like, "C'mon, if you're going to do it, do it right!"

So he hits her so as to knock her out (or she feigns this) and he carries her off into the forest to make love to her. The thing that really amazed me about all of this was that my girlfriend *loved this scene!*

"Wasn't that *romantic?*" she cooed. "He swept her off her feet!"

There was a similar scene in the movie *Tarzan and His Mate* from 1934 with Johnny Weissmuller and Maureen O'Sullivan. In the original cut - now hard to find - Tarzan *strips* Jane naked in throwing her into a pond. He then swims after her. Sex was only *implied* due to the prudish times.

So *that's* what it's all about. *This* is what women want you to *emulate* with **gentle bondage**. And there's no reason why you can't play along with a fantasy like this, *so long as it's just play acting*, **without any pain, violence, anger, or threats**. Women who get turned on by **gentle bondage** don't want to feel unsafe; they want the *pretense* of this *fantasy*.

The *fantasy* of theirs is one of a *desirable* man who is so passionate for them, he decides to *take her,* spontaneously. She, in this *fantasy*, finds herself unavoidably turned on by sudden desire for him as he *takes her*. This is purely for the feeling of **surrender** and **helplessness** that comes with it and the subsequent **joy** and **excitement** that a man who's **romantic**, **sexy** and **desirable** is involved. So keep everything along those lines.

Gentle bondage (and I emphasize **gentle**, in that this is all to be faked, not done in a serious, harmful or threatening fashion), can enhance your love life (if and only if your partner requests this - **I do not recommend you bring this into your lives unless she does so, in one way or another**).

Fetters (such as **ropes, sexy toy handcuffs, chains, panties tied around wrists and ankles**, etc.) should always be done in such a way that your lover can easily get out of her bonds if she wishes. (**Handcuffs** should only be of the *toy* variety that feature an easily accessible button release mechanism and do not require keys to be unlocked.) And, you must always be swift to release her (without hesitation) when asked if she can't do so herself. This is a *pretend* exercise, not meant to accurately simulate a real scene of abduction, which is sick. Keep it **loving**.

You're a **Fabio type**, intent on giving her a good time, **not** a serial killer. Keep it **loving**. Do that, for instance, by talking to her *teasingly*. Say: "I've

On Loving Women

got you now!," keeping the tone **playful**, **reassuring** and **non-threatening**.

Though it might sound extreme to some, it's really not. **Bondage** is a little bedroom secret of both heteros *and* homosexuals.

There's a Lesbian sex expert, in fact, who makes a *living* teaching women how to tie up their Lesbian lovers with ropes. *She's been a featured speaker at many women's groups, nationwide. So this practice must appeal to many women on a deep psychological level.*

So if it makes your lover hot and it causes no harm, why not *oblige* if she's into **gentle bondage?!** Do it by playfully, *pretending* to hold her down with *loosely* and *poorly tied* **scarves** around a bedpost. (The lover I mentioned before, who requested **bondage**, would always *remove* the **scarves** or **handcuffs** eventually. She didn't want them on tight; she wanted the *suggestion* of being a captive.)

Once you have her **hands** tied to something (like the *bedposts*), *slowly* **tease** her whole body, cooing something like, "Mmmmm! Now I can *tease* you mercilessly - take my time about it, and make you super hot!"

Or you can *pretend* to "take her" by *grabbing her hair (tenderly)* as if you're trying to prevent her from fighting off your advances. One of my lovers *requested* I do this - she *loved feeling helpless*. It enhanced the **sexual experience** for her. In other words, *you don't have to actually <u>bind</u> your lover to play this game. You can simulate it.*

In fact one of my lovers, during sex, would tell me, for instance, "Hold me down!" Or she'd say, "Hold my arms to the bed!" That was all it took for

Edgy Titillations: Sex Toys, Masturbation & Gentle Bondage

her to feel wonderfully helpless, in a blissful, **ecstatic state of absolute surrender and abandon** - my holding her arms down on the bed. No bindings were necessary.

Another of my lovers liked to be taken from behind *with her hands held behind her back*, just above her butt. A few of my lovers even got off on being **spanked**. (They requested it.)

But if you're going to s*imulate* **bondage** through *pretend force*, be careful *not* to cause *pain*. Use just enough moderate pressure so she *believes* you're holding her down. If you ever cross the line accidentally, immediately release your grip and apologize, as in: "Sorry, baby! Was that too hard?" Hopefully, though, you'll know how to hold her so you never cross that line.

By the way, in my experience, women like to be the *subjects* of **bondage** more than they want to tie down their men. When done properly, striking the right **primal** chord, it can be very exciting. *Never act violently, never act like an animal, and, above all else, never simulate a rape or threatening situation.* You simply apply whatever restraint she desires, *loosely*, and *play out a big tease* – with a healthy dose of *playfulness*.

It's all about getting your woman *more excited* than she otherwise would. And, once you find she's wetter than ever, and her **vagina** is internally hotter than ever, you'll see that this kind of **sex play** is worth doing *on occasion*.

And, by the way – if she wants to tie you down – go with it. I think you'll find that it will get you going in ways you never thought possible. Somehow your senses are more vivid, the **pleasures** more intense when you cannot move. This is partly what **gentle bondage** is about. In fact, ask her to tie you down and you'll see that what I'm saying is true. It'll be an educational experience for you. You'll better understand what to do when you turn the tables on her.

Important: *Creativity is important in playing these games.* Remember - you're supposed to create an ***illusion*** and fulfill a ***fantasy*** for her. It shouldn't be hard, though, to come up with a lot of fun **scenarios**. Here are some:

Lay a *pillow* or some soft *blankets* across the **kitchen** or **cocktail table** (if it's strong enough to support her weight) and have her lie across it, facedown. Then, tie her hands (with her pantyhose) to the table legs, making sure that the bindings are not stretching her **arms** or putting her in an uncomfortable position. Ask her before going any further if she feels comfortable. You might also splay her **legs** open with soft bindings (perhaps soft **scarves**) that bind her legs to the table legs, loosely.

Or take her out to a **desert mesa**, or deeply into the **woods** (you might need an SUV for this and it's best done in states where you can really get away from people and find absolute privacy). Then *blindfold* her and ask her to step out of the car, telling her all the wonderfully exciting things you plan on doing to her, and the delicious journey you're about to take her on (your talk should be all about *sex* and nothing suggesting danger, violence or anything unloving). Then, with her **butt** gently stuck out and **hands** above her head, use the **toy handcuffs** you purchased together to *handcuff* her to the strap that most vehicles have atop the passenger side doorjamb. You can then either *strip her* partially (leaving some clothes to rest above her head, or at her ankles), or entirely.

Or you could take her to the **bathtub**, and have her sit down inside it sideways, her **legs** over side. *Tie* her **hands** to whatever's nearby. You could then slowly work her entire body over with the **shower massager**.

Or, on a **bed** or **soft surface** like a **bear rug**, *tie* her **ankles** together, but keep her **partially-nude** (leave her top on). Great **entry angles** for this, once you're ready for **intercourse**:

♡ *sideways: her lying on her side, knees bent, feet to your right*
♡ *from the front: you sitting up on your knees, placed on either side of her butt, holding her feet in the air (or over one shoulder)*
♡ *from behind: she lying on her stomach*
♡ *from behind, standing up (with her bending over the bed, her torso resting on the sheets)*
♡ *modified missionary: her legs between yours*

What do you do once you've set up the scenes above?

How about running your **hands** and, later, your **tongue** all over her **legs**, *kissing* every part of them (the backs, sides and tops of her **thighs** deserve a lot of attention, for their sensitivity, and the backs of her **knees**); *tease* her **feet** in this way, too). You might *suck* her **toes**, if she enjoys this. Run your **tongue** up her **spine** then around the back of her **neck**. Give her shivers by running your **fingers** over the tops of her **arms** and **shoulders**. *Kiss* her really, really close to her **vagina** (close enough to feel the *heat* coming

Edgy Titillations: Sex Toys, Masturbation & Gentle Bondage

from it, and *smell* the wonderful *scent*), but back off once she thinks you're going to kiss it. Keep up the **tease** by kissing her **hips** and **stomach**. Kiss, cuddle and caress her **butt**. Prolong this kind of circuitous **teasing** until you're good and ready to initiate **intercourse**.

More Edgy: Pussy Shaving And Role Playing

Want more edgy things to do while she's tied down? *Shave her **pussy*** (carefully!) – *if you've playfully suggested this beforehand and it turns her on.* (I had a partner like this.) Or have her wear an old t-shirt she doesn't treasure and, once she's bound, cut holes in it to let her **nipples** poke out. If you have her wearing pantyhose you know that doesn't have special meaning to her, you could (carefully!) snip a strategic hole in them, over her pussy, for easy access. Do any of these suggestions sensually and they'll make her extra hot!

And you might try some fun **role playing**. One of my girlfriends, for instance, had me meet her at a swanky piano bar one night and pretend to be a stranger who picks her up there and takes her home. That was fun.

When I arrived, I discovered that she was wearing a little sexy black dress *with nothing underneath it (she made a point of flashing me)*. And her outfit was causing a stir! I could see men ogling her; they were absolutely *drooling* over her! And their jaws dropped as I suavely moved in, chatted her up, brazenly suggesting some lewd acts I wanted to do to her. I did all this while placing my hand on her bare **thigh** (casually stroking it ever more provocatively as the night wore on). Whispering in her ear, I told her I wanted to put my tongue between her legs as I carelessly brushed against her **breasts**.

It was fun getting everyone hot watching us. But they weren't the only ones who were made hot by all of this. As we walked out of the bar, I patted her behind only to find that *the back of her dress was soaking wet!* My suggestions had really gotten her going! When we returned home, I immediately lifted up her dress for some really **hot sex** in the garage. Great night!

More Edgy: Make Her Your Sex Servant (IF It Appeals To Her)

If your lover likes being **submissive** sexually occasionally, ask your lover to be your **sex servant or "slave"** from time to time (understanding that turnabout is fair play; *she might then ask you to be her sex servant later on, to which you must readily agree*). Again, that's **if** and only **if** the idea appeals to her. If it does, plan a night's worth of sexy activities for her.

You've probably read those sexy *Penthouse* or other *erotic stories* where a *vixen* orders a man about sexually. It makes for pretty hot reading - but also *doing. This* is the kind of thing I'm talking about but in *reverse*. (Without any hint of meanness. *This must be done* <u>playfully</u> *and* <u>erotically</u> *only*.)

You'd be surprised how *excited* many women get over this kind of **sexual role playing**. I once broached this idea with a girlfriend, suggesting I'd make her my **sex "slave"** that night, but I thought she wasn't turned on by the idea and so I passed on it. But a few weeks later we were on my bed talking about what she might like to do sexually that we hadn't done yet and she shyly curled up in a ball and wriggled and said, "There *is* one thing you promised that we haven't done that sounded fun. You said you'd make me your *sex slave!*" This was a conservative woman talking!

So here are some ideas along these lines. First things first:

You should always broach this subject beforehand, asking her if she'd like be your sex servant for an evening. Let her know it'll be fun. The key is to make it safe, playful, sensual, sexy and fun and always *stop* if she objects to anything or if she's not in the mood to continue. Again, no matter what you do, you always have to keep things **loving**. *Stay far away from anything that would be interpreted as* **mean** *or* **dark**. *You can kill your relationship doing that. Plus, it's not what love is all about.*

OK. So she's agreed. Now, *playfully* order her to *strip* down either to *partial nudity* or *complete nakedness*. If you'd like, you can even have her walk around *scantily clad* for awhile before engaging in sexual activity. Come up with a sexy outfit that would get you both hot. High heels and pantyhose? Whatever rocks your boat. Perhaps she can serve you some drinks or whatever. That can be a real turn on for you both. It puts off sex and allows for a visual tease to build the sexual tension. Plus, wearing next to nothing should get her juices going.

If she's into giving you oral sex (most women will *tell* you if they are), ask her to kneel on the floor and do you while you stand up or sit on the edge of a chair or couch (you can choose to be *mostly clothed* or *naked* yourself). You can either let this suffice for you as far as your **orgasms** go (in other words, you can make her **come** in ways other than traditional **intercourse** - or even go without **coming** on a *rare* occasion), or you can plan on making love to her later on, once you can get another **erection**.

If she's an **exhibitionist**, you can then tell her to **masturbate** in front of you. Perhaps, if you've made her get *topless* and *barefoot* only, you might make her lie down and wriggle her hips until she **comes** in her pants (you can help her by holding her pants up so the seam is tight up against her **pussy**). If she's into this kind of sexy talk, you might precede this by telling

Edgy Titillations: Sex Toys, Masturbation & Gentle Bondage

her something like: "Most people find **masturbating** and **coming in their pants** embarrassing. I'm going to make you do both." Then have her do it. Or you can have her **masturbate** in any of innumerable other ways.

In fact, on occasion you can choose to *deny* her your **cock** - just as the *vixens* you might have read about deny their male subjects their **pussies** (while making the men do themselves, or suffer while they watch the *vixens* do themselves, in a prolonged tease). *Emulate* the *vixens*. Make her lie back in the tub and watch you do yourself (ever so slowly) with the **shower massager**. (And *if* she's into your **coming** on her - as some women are - do that too. I've had some lovers *request* this.) Then make her do herself with the **shower massager**. Or instead you can *stay clothed* (or *partially* clothed) and have her play out various **erotic scenes** (maybe having her do herself with a **dildo** or **vibrator** or acceptable food item). *This is all about taking the* **sexual tease** *to the max.*

Another idea: Make her put on a *robe*, otherwise *naked*, get in your car, put her *feet* up on the dash and then take her for a short sexy drive during which you either use a **vibrator** or your **fingers** to make her **come** (*if* you can do this *legally*). Then bring her home for more fun. Maybe get her *naked* in the *garage* and tie her to the car so her **breasts** and **torso** are up against the *cool surface of the car* (the hood or the window and door), her *bare feet* against the cool surface of the *garage floor*, and take her from behind, perhaps using a **vibrator** to **double-penetrate her** (*if* she's into this).

You might have noticed that in playing like she's a **sex servant** *I've recommended you choose activities you already <u>know</u> she likes. Avoid going beyond what you know she likes because that can backfire.*

OTHER WAYS TO KEEP THINGS EXCITING

Other ways to spice things up:

- ❤ ***Food play*** can be fun. A nice liqueur, whipped cream or chocolate licked off sensitive places like her **breasts, tummy, legs, feet** or **toes**, can give her **erotic pleasures**. (Prepare a wet towel soaked with warm water to wipe her down afterward, before **intercourse**.) **Never put these on or in her vagina of course.**

- ❤ Especially creative lovers will use specialized appurtenances such as **sex swings** (perhaps you can put one in your home discretely). Or a regular **hammock** might suffice, for swingin' fun.

- ❤ Try **anal beads**, which you insert early on and pull out just before she comes, to make her **orgasm** much bigger.

- ❤ Do her with her **fuzzy slippers** or **robe** (or **robe belt**) or other

clothing. Or make her do herself with it. This has an added benefit: she'll get hot later on when she sees the clothing and remembers how you or she used it to get her off.

GOING TOO FAR

All of that being said, when it comes to **pushing the envelope** you might discover that *there are some indulgences you will find impossible to provide*. And that's OK.

I'll never forget the relationship I had with a very nice young woman that ended when she handed me a book of *sadomasochistic erotica*.

"This is what I like," she said to me sweetly, nodding to the book.

I read it. There were women being whipped until *blood* was dripping down their thighs in numerous stories, women in *pain*, women being abused...This went way beyond *playful* **gentle bondage**.

I regretfully broke up with her because of it. *I will never inflict pain or cause harm*. I don't think that's a healthy thing to get into. Sorry.

Gentle bondage *is not about subjugating or hurting your partner* – that's **S&M**, and it's *dicey territory*. I just cannot go there. I don't feel **hurting someone** or **threatening harm** is *loving*.

Another example: One of my dates - on the *first* date - told me she'd been a **sex slave** for a couple - a man and woman - for *six months!* She'd even signed a *contract* with them! *I did not ask this woman out for a second date. I felt she had a psychological problem. Very sad.*

Hardcore slave stuff, with its abject *humiliation* and *servitude, is* **not** what I'm talking about when I talk about **edgy love**making! The hardcore stuff goes way too far in my book. I steer clear of anything that smacks of being demeaning or unkind.

And, by the way - hopefully your lover <u>won't</u> want **edgy love**making <u>every</u> time. If she does, something might be wrong. **Edgy love**making, like anything else, should be done in moderation. And these **good general rules** bear repeating:

♡ **only engage in edgy lovemaking with a woman who in one way or another requests it**
♡ **keep it <u>loving</u>**

KEEPING THE *LOVE* IN <u>LOVEMAKING</u>

One final note. Word to the wise:

If you find yourself always looking for ever bigger *thrills*, I think you'll

Edgy Titillations: Sex Toys, Masturbation & Gentle Bondage

discover you're approaching *dangerous territory*.

Be smart. If you or she feels the *love* is getting *lost* - as it *can* as you get close to the edge of each others' **comfort boundaries** - *avoid* the **edgy stuff**. It can hurt your relationship.

Lovemaking is not about getting as *kinky* as you can imagine. It's about **communicating love**. Always keep things **loving**.

And it's all about *her*. So if she's *not* into **edgy love**making, *don't* go there.

In addition, while **edgy lovemaking** can be a great source of *variety*, I don't think this kind of avenue should be pursued every day. It's for *occasional* **novelty** and **spice**.

Avoid making it an *obsession*. The **love** in the **love**making equation will get lost and a *dark side* will rear its head. By that I mean an ever-increasing hunger for *bizarre practices*, including *humiliation*, *inflicted pain* and other *questionable behavior that can destroy your relationship - or worse*. That's a recipe for trouble. (Ask Bob Crane of *Hogan's Heroes*, or Felix Pappalardi of the rock band Mountain - both of whom were *murdered* because of their *wild sexual proclivities* and, in Pappalardi's case, *the pain it caused his wife*.)

So whatever you do along these lines, please keep things *loving*. And have *fun*. Laughing is definitely allowed!

Keep all of this in mind and you'll do great.

> *"Slide up the edge of the pool table with your legs splayed. You'll be at the perfect height for your pool shark to attack."*
> *- from the Cosmopolitan article, "Hot Spots for Love"*

Choosing The Right Lovemaking Furniture

A great guitarist is finicky about his or her gear – from his or her guitar (down to the wood it's made of) and amplifier (down to the kind of tubes and wiring inside), to guitar strings, picks, sound altering stomp boxes, etc.

You should be too, as a lover. What's your "gear?" Part of it includes your bed (and mattress) and household furniture.

Because most couples still prefer the **bed** to other locations for most of their **love**making sessions, it's obviously important to you, as *a platform for **making love***. It can either help you, or hurt you – both from a **romantic** point of view, and from a technical point of view.

What makes a bed a good **love**making bed?

Let's start with the **mattress**. Great advances have been made recently in mattress construction technology. While some have provided improvements for the lover, others have resulted in problems you might not realize are there until you get the mattresses home.

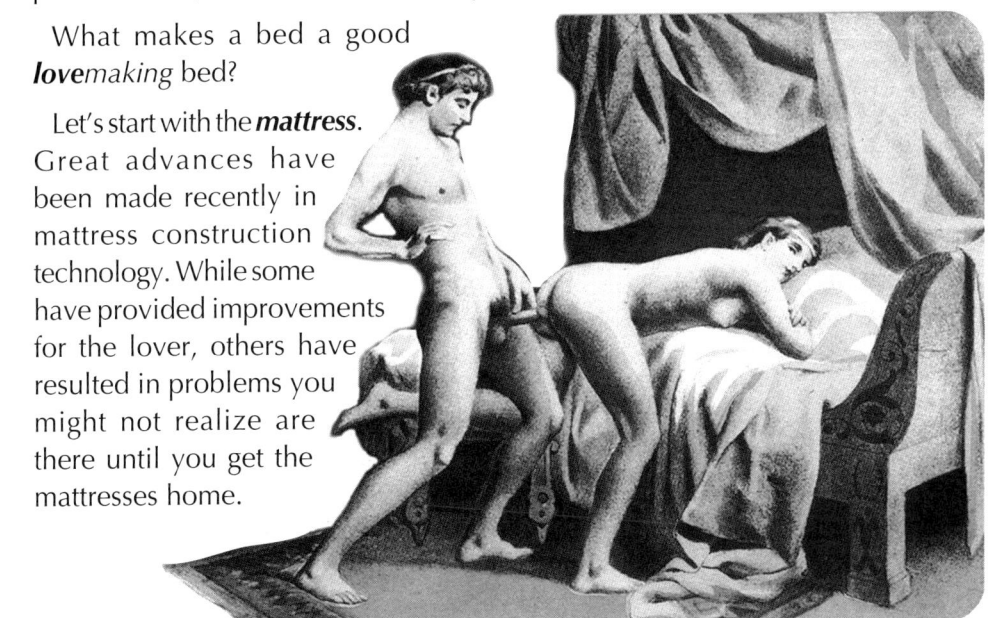

Choosing The Right Lovemaking Furniture

Why is a mattress important to **love***making*? Oftentimes – if you're smart, anyway – you'll use its **springiness** to good effect, to really give it to her, over a protracted time, with a limited effort. The **spring in a mattress** – contrary to public opinion – is actually good. It provides some of the **propulsion**, some of the **energy** you need to give her maximum enjoyment. It also keeps you from pooping out too soon. *Your action* produces a *reaction* (the spring back) in the mattress, which helps *propel your body*, lessens your *fatigue factor* and *makes it easy to do what would be difficult to do on a hard surface*. Try bouncing in position with your partner, and you'll see that, if you choose a comfortable pace, the mattress becomes your friend, and you'll feel as if you could go on forever. Now, try bouncing on a **hard floor**. Ouch! (Not so good for sex!)

A *good, spongy mattress* also lessens the strain on your **knees, legs, feet, arms** and **hands**. In contrast, my **knees** don't do so well after a half hour or so on a **hard floor or surface**.

Now, here's the catch – some **"space-age" mattresses** are being sold, and they're being touted as the best thing since sliced bread. Maybe if you want to eat them (although I don't know about that, either). Certainly not if you want to make love on them. They *fight* you. You *sink into them* – they take the shape of your body – and it's like quicksand. It's worse than being on a floor. On these mattresses, I feel as if I'm almost being held in place – you have to really, really exert yourself to get any momentum going. They're heart attack city.

Also bad are **old mattresses that are way too bouncy** (and squeaky). Nothing kills the romance quicker than the "ee-aw-ee-aw-ee-aw" noise of old springs. And cheap, hard mattresses are killers, too – hard on your knees, no help in the "action-reaction" process.

Pillow-top mattresses, by the way, are great innovations that also contribute in a positive way to your ***love***making experience. They give her a cushy, cuddly feeling, while you – the one who typically does the most work – get a great, soft, bouncy surface to sink into and go to town on.

Great musicians spend a fortune on their gear because they're serious about their art. Yet, most lovers don't spend a dime.

Great lovers, however, do. Mattresses that are fabulous for ***love***making don't cost all that much these days – you can get one for under $1,000, undoubtedly. If you're serious about your art, you'll get one.

Another great thing about the newer mattresses and box spring combos is that *they raise the bed surface higher than the older mattresses did*.

This is super for certain **standing positions** that are hard to do otherwise (unless you have a high, strong **kitchen table**) – the **rear-entry position** where you're *both standing* and she's resting her chest on the bed, and the **front-entry position** where you're standing and she's lying back on the bed.

Those are *two of my favorite positions*, best used *on occasion*, as a surprise. Women love them!

Choosing A Good Bed

As you might have gathered by now, **platform beds** – where there's no box spring, and the whole deal is low to the ground – are not the best. For one thing, without the box springs, you lose a good deal of springiness. You also lose the advantage of the standing up position just mentioned above.

Missionary beds and their variants are great for one thing – for a woman who enjoys a bit of **gentle bondage**, you can easily tie her down to the **bedposts** (unlike **sleigh beds**, for instance). But they're uncomfortable for reading (and you might want to read **erotic stories** to each other), or for watching movies (and you might want to enjoy a *naughty* or *racy movie* on occasion, to warm things up).

I've gravitated to **sleigh beds**, because they're great for everything except the bondage scenario – but that can be accomplished in other parts of the house. (Or, if you're especially into this, you could – as my last girlfriend pointed out – install **hooks** in subtle places.)

But – whatever you do – choose a bed that's **romantic, comfortable for a wide range of activities, and sex-worthy**.

Incidentally, **water beds** – although almost completely out of vogue – were good for the action-reaction benefit, but I really don't know why they were considered great beds for **love**making. They're too uncontrollable. Plus, sea-sickness becomes a factor (no joke – especially for her).

Choosing A F***ing Good Chair

But beds aren't necessarily the best places for **love**making. In fact, I and one of my girlfriends had this Epiphany in a Denver hotel: *Everyone needs at least one* **f***ing chair**.

Our hotel room contained a great, **cushy chair** at *just the right height (this is key)*. We discovered it especially suited one kind of **love**making that was hard to accomplish otherwise - where I'd sit down and she'd sit down on me, facing away.

Thereupon, we went on a mission. We went on a search to find a **f***ing chair** – one that would allow us to make love in a way that nothing else

Choosing The Right Lovemaking Furniture

apparently would.

In fact, our mission became quite humorous.

We'd approach a furniture store and begin an imaginary dialog with an imaginary salesperson as we left our vehicle. It was our little in-joke, our Abbott and Costello routine.

"Do you have a f***ing chair?" she'd say, as if she was approaching an eager salesman.

"A f***ing chair, madam?" I'd say, feigning shock and dismay. "We have many chairs, madam."

"Not just any chair," she'd continue. "A f***ing chair!"

"We have many chairs, madam," I'd reply. "But there's no need for such language. But, if you must, we've got f***ing chairs, couches, end tables – whatever you'd like."

"Not a f***ing *chair!*" she'd exclaim, feigning frustration, as if the salesperson was too daft for words. "A **f***ing** chair!"

And we'd howl with laughter.

The fact is, if a **cushy** arm chair (one with solid sides) can be found whose seat is the right height off the ground (given the length of your legs) so that your woman can perch wonderfully and comfortably in your lap and thereafter go to work on you, then you've found a chair worth its weight in gold. You want one with just the right softness and spring in it so it facilitates **bouncing** (the best way for both of you to move in this position).

There are *not* many suitable chairs around, for making love. Really. You go look, and you'll see. It takes some searching to find a great **f***ing** chair.

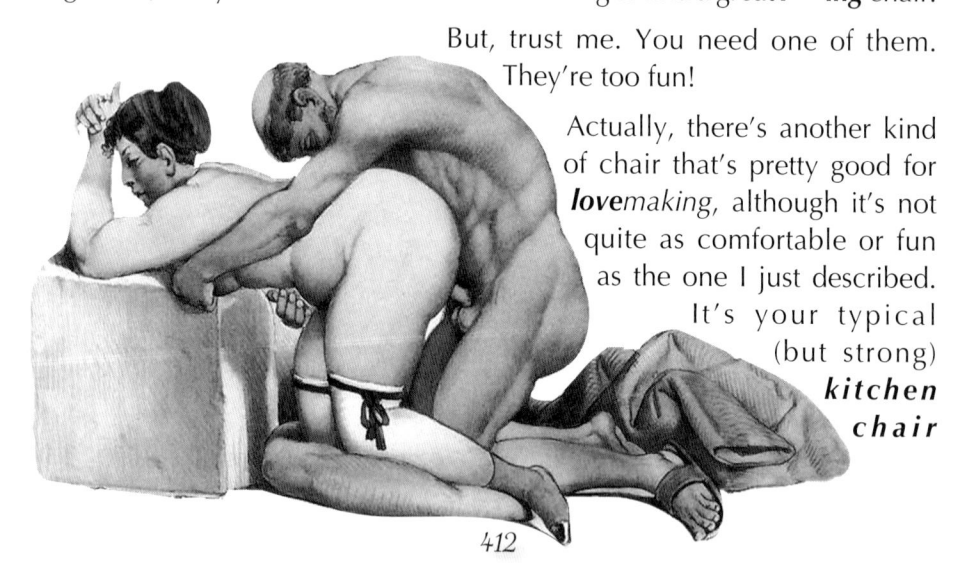

But, trust me. You need one of them. They're too fun!

Actually, there's another kind of chair that's pretty good for ***love***making, although it's not quite as comfortable or fun as the one I just described. It's your typical (but strong) **kitchen chair**

412

(without arms). One that would allow your woman to sit on your lap without strain (so that depends upon the length of her calves and yours), and – either facing you or facing away from you – rock you into oblivion.

One of my college friends was always urging me to find "a great, **hard chair**." I still laugh about it to this day. He was crazy about it – and so was his girlfriend (who's now his wife)!

Tip: You'll find your lover will be more *sexually reactive* (when using a chair) in positions where she's *facing away* from you. I mention this because women tend to want to sit on your lap *facing you* because it seems more *romantic* to them. But resist her efforts to do so. It's less interesting sexually.

If she sits on your lap, facing away from you, it results in **rear-entry sex** and a lot more fireworks! As I told you earlier in the book, she's much more capable of coming **vaginally** in **rear-entry positions**.

Choosing A Good Kitchen Table

A great **kitchen table** is also worth having. By great I mean, of course, one suited to **making love** atop it.

To that end, it needs to be **strong, to support the weight of your girlfriend** – whatever it is. You might want to rest her entirely upon the top (on her back), and enter her while standing next to her (with her legs either over your shoulder, or held back over her body); or you simply might want to throw her torso over the top and take her from behind.

I don't know why this is so sexy, but it really is.

Get yourself a **strong…long…kitchen table**. (And put some **pillows** on top, if she needs them.)

Other Furniture Delights

Ottomans can be great for many positions – especially if they're bouncy. She can sit on your lap, or you can kneel on the floor, have her rest her breasts and head on the top, and take her from behind.

Cocktail tables – if strong – can be used similarly.

Kitchen counters can be good surfaces to rest your lover down on, depending on their height. If you have a ceramic tile floor, all the better (the coolness on her feet makes the location all the more sexy).

They're mostly good for *rear-entry* **love***making,* with both of you standing up and her bending over or laying her torso down on the counter surface. If yours is made of granite or marble or tile or other surface that might be too chilly for her to rest upon, make sure you have a pillow or blanket

Choosing The Right Lovemaking Furniture

handy beforehand, to casually throw over the counter before having her bend over it.

Couches are great – if they're long enough, you can do just about anything on them. *Throw her over the back and take her from behind, standing up (most women love this)*…Make love to her with her lying on her back, or you on your back with her on top. Make love with her sitting on your lap. Or create a position of your own; couches are great for finding **novel and fun positions**. (The one pictured here is great for **AFE orgasms**!)

How do you find a couch that's ideal for **love**making? Try it for size. It should be the right height for her to *lean over,* at the very least.

In some ways, couches are better than beds. A good one somehow angles your **cock** so that you hit her hot spots for their **maximum effect**.

Her **office desk** – or yours – makes a great platform (in the house, or in the office – if that's possible). She'll really think about you all day long if you make love to her enough on her office desk!

Desks are great – if strong – because you can do so much with them. You can have her sit on top and you can eat her **pussy**, while sitting in her chair. You can take her from behind, while she rests her top on the surface. You can, standing, take her while she sits on top, facing you. It's great.

And a desk is a really sexy place to make love. I can't explain it, but it is.

The rest is up to you. Let your **imagination** lead to you discover other delightful furnishings that can become your own **private secret naughty places**…places that will remind you, during the day, of how much fun you have together…places that will eventually make you hot just looking at them (because of the **sexy memories** they'll evoke)!

And that really helps make a relationship special!

> *"Don't stop thinking about tomorrow*
> *Don't stop - it'll soon be here."*
> *- lyrics from "Don't Stop" by Fleetwood Mac*

What Now?

So our journey, for now, comes to an end. But *your **learning process*** should not end here. It should be *ongoing* and *proactive*. You need to *apply* what you've learned in *On Loving Women*. That will take some time. And you should spend each time with her experimenting with new ways to get her **hot** or make her **come**. Never rest on your laurels. Always strive to become better. It's a never-ending process. You'll want to re-read *On Loving Women*, too, from time to time. There's a lot to absorb.

CONTINUE TO LEARN FROM HER, THROUGH QUESTIONS

And if and when your lover *compliments* you, *make sure you always ask "Why?"* When she tells you she "really liked last night" or "you're an amazing man," that's nondescript and open to interpretation. You want to find out *exactly* what she liked about last night or about you, so you can continue doing what she likes and continue down the path that leads to success. *It's amazing what you'll learn when you do this; how helpful the information can be.*

Here, for instance, is an example of a conversation I had years ago with a girlfriend (which I wrote down afterward, to use in this book):

She: *"I really liked last night."*
Me: *"What did you like?"*
She: *"The whole thing!"*
Me: *"Why?"*
She: *"The way you placed your finger over my vulva and just held it there got me really hot. And it was really a great progression [of positions and activities]. You took me from behind and then you smoothly [without pulling out] moved into a [sideways] spooning position, which was so romantic! And the way you built up to my orgasm...the butterfly touching on my clit [I tapped lightly on it] and the way you touched many areas on my vulva...And I really*

What Now?

liked coming together...It makes me come harder when we come at the same time, and it gives me a tickly feeling...Plus the orgasm was spectacular! It seemed like it lasted five minutes (although it probably lasted two to three minutes)..."

What did I learn by asking her to elaborate on her compliment? For one thing, I wasn't aware she liked the **spooning position** that much. She hadn't responded too loudly to it. So I found out I should continue to use that - perhaps even more often than I had before. I also made a note to do the **butterfly tapping** on her **clit** again in the future. **Coming together** - something that isn't seen as an ideal by most lovers - was something I also made a note to strive for in the future, since it gave her such a thrill.

Another day, she said, *"You're really incredible!"* I asked, "Why?" She replied, crying, "Because **you're full of surprises**, and because of the way you make me feel!"

What did I learn by asking "Why?" That she liked **surprises**. *So I made a mental note to be even more **creative** with her.* And she confirmed that I was making her feel wonderful, which was also important information. You need to know whether or not your **love**making efforts are having a positive impact. Only she can validate this. Remember: **You're not a great lover unless your lover <u>tells</u> you so.** (But never let her **compliments** go to your head - **narcissism** does not make for **great lovers**. **Love**making, at its best, is a <u>selfless</u> gift.)

And Now It's Time To Experiment

...Well, it's now time for you to *experiment* with the information you've read, to make your loving relationship as *exciting* and **loving** as it can possibly be. Always remember that **love**making, at its best, should take you to the **spiritual and emotional <u>heights</u>**, and **bond** you closely together, as one. And most of all, **prioritize** your **intimate times** together. Take your time and have *fun* enjoying each other!

By the way, look for me as I do *book tours and public speaking engagements, as well as singles and couples events, retreats, courses, workshops, and seminars*. Hopefully attending one of my events will help those of you who are in a relationship to achieve a *lifetime* of **love** and **happiness** - and perhaps smooth over any problems you're dealing with. Or if you are single, my aim would be to teach you *what you need to do to become the kind of man women crave, to capture the heart of the one you love, forever*. (Applying what you learn, to attain these goals, is up to you, of course!)

Good luck with your **loving journey!**

Index

A

ABC News American Sex Survey 18, 80, 160.
Ablow, Dr. Keith 96, 98.
Achieving The Ultimate Control 93–128.
advanced bedroom skills 17.
AFE zone *See* Anterior Fornix Erogenous Zone.
affection 59–68, 155.
After The Lovin'; what to do afterward 379–380.
alarm clock as sex aid 165, 247.
Alzate, Heli 211.
amazing sexual discovery 279.
anal canal 194, 196, 217, 218, 219, 220, 221, 269, 349, 395.
anal intercourse 140, 218.
    anal beads 406.
    anal sex orgasms 219.
    Her Bottom - For Double-Penetration 269.
    butt plugs, vibrating eggs 393.
anal ring 192, 218, 256.
ankles 400, 403.
Ann, Chee Chua 183, 215.
anterior cingulate cortex 135.
Anterior Fornix Erogenous (AFE) Zone 178, 183, 203, 194, 215, 216, 318, 338, 368, 371, 372, 376, 414.
anterior wall of the vagina 210, 211.
anti-intercourse agenda by political groups 174.
anti-romantic fad 21.
anus 242, 245, 350, 378.
    graphic 194.
    sphincter muscle; as cause of control issues 112.
    special hygiene needs 76.
aphrodisiacs 133, 158.
areola 137, 279, 280, 281, 284, 286, 287.
Aristotle; documented female ejaculation 181.
arms 267, 276, 401, 402, 403, 410, 413.
aroma 238, 239.
arousal process 129, 131, 132, 133, 134, 136, 138, 139, 141, 154, 162, 182, 187, 188, 189, 196, 198, 200, 202, 204, 206, 216, 221, 278.
    arousal starters 221.
    makes her vagina go wide 139.
    What Arousal Is All About 138.
atrophy after menopause 280.
attitudes on talking about sex 1.
attitudes toward women; related to lovemaking 22.

B

back 225, 241, 243, 244, 245, 246, 249.
back pain 287.
bacterial or yeast infection 238.
bad lovers *See also* break-ups, causes
    Why Lust Screws You Up 54.
    horn dogs, leering letches 55, 56.
    inability to show affection 61.
    Stevie Nicks on "lousy lovers" 90, 168.
bad sex 129.
balls 76, 244, 247, 253.
Baring It All 231, 234.
Bartholin's glands 184, 192, 205, 206, 216, 267, 268, 272.
    Bartholin's Glands Wetness Technique 271.
    ducts 136, 206, 352.
    graphic representation 192.
bathroom pleasures 395.
bathtub as a location to make love 403.
beach as a location to make love 384, 385.
bear hugs 114.
bear rug as a location to make love 403.
becoming a gentleman, its own rewards 22.
Becoming Type Of Man Women Desire 10, 45–52.
Bedazzled, scene poking fun at "sensitive" men 49.
bed of pine needles as a location to make love 384.

bedposts 401, 411.
bedroom secret 401.
beds 359, 371, 376, 401, 402, 403, 405, 409, 410, 411.
    mattresses (choosing good one) 410.
    qualities that make a bed sex-worthy 409, 411.
being a good partner 51.
being attractive to women 21.
being bold 146, 148.
being comfortable in your own skin 155.
being confident 155.
being forgiving as important lover's trait 54.
Being Handy And Helpful Is Sexy Too 51.
being kind 144, 145, 148, 149.
being loving 22.
being playful 144, 146, 150, 152.
being sexy 144.
being smooth 149.
being "taken" fantasy 389.
    Clark Gable In Gone With The Wind 48.
    women in Romance novels 50.
big-bottomed women re positions that work 299.
biggest benefit of being a great lover 16.
biofeedback 167, 225, 366.
biologically analogous organs 215.
birth control; orgasm-suppressing effects 178.
biting 283, 284.
bizarre practices 408.
blindfolds 398.
body language 348, 366.
bondage 389, 398–403, 407.
bonding 170, 172.
    through great lovemaking 350.
Bond, James 134.
boring 341, 374.
bottom 393, 395, 397.
bouncing as cock propulsion technique 371.
brain 99, 100, 118, 121, 122, 123, 133, 134, 135, 138, 294, 399.
    as cause of control problems 100.
    Center for the Neurobiology of Learning and Memory study 47.
    differences between male and female brains 47.
    drug-like chemicals it produces 122.
    genital sensory cortex 294.
    hemispheres 294.
    hippocampus; bigger in women 47.
    hypothalamic paraventricular nucleus 294.
    limbic cortex; bigger in women 47.
    most important sex organ 53, 135.
    other chemicals it produces during sex
        neurotransmitters, hormones 135.
    oxytocinergic neurons 294.
    paracentral lobule 294.
    pleasure centers 135, 138.
    study on women's brains during sex 137.
    women's brains 179.
break-ups, causes
    a lack of lovemaking (not sex) 27.
    his feminine side became dominant 49.
    Bad Hygiene 70.
    he felt he didn't have to work at relationship 62.
    I want to be treated like a woman. 49.
    inability to show affection 61.
    he wouldn't write her a love song 62.
    their lover fell short as a man 26.
    the man was a lousy lover 26.
breasts 136, 179, 207, 221, 258, 261, 279–294 (chapter on), 309, 330, 366, 397, 404, 406.
    A-Cup Revolution 284.
    areola 279, 280, 281, 284, 286, 287.
    Best Reason To Give Breasts Attention 293.
    breast-induced orgasms 279, 280, 282, 288.
        How To Give 290-292.
        Science endorses 294.

417

breasts/nipples (continued)
- Double-Nipple Stimulation   289, 290.
- fatty tissue less reactive   280, 283, 284.
- Glands of Montgomery; tubercles   281.
  - glandular tissue; most reactive   284.
- Great Variability In Breasts   282.
- Her Breasts: A User's Manual   280.
- implants
  - complications are likely (FDA)   285.
  - felt hard and unnatural   287.
  - impact on sensitivity   283, 285, 286, 287.
  - will eventually need to be removed   285.
- intense stimulation releases oxytocin   293.
- Johns Hopkins study on breast sensitivity   284.
- milk glands as sexual organs   280, 281, 284.
  - atrophy after menopause   280.
- M Spot   279, 280, 282, 291.
- nerves   280, 282, 286, 294.
- nipples   See nipples (under "N")
- Orgasm Boosters, Teasing & Fun   292.
- pre-menopausal woman's breasts   280.
- reduction operations
  - breasts looking mutilated   287.
  - British Association of Aesthetic Plastic Surgeons warning   286.
  - Marina Plastic Surgery Associates warning 286.
  - nipples less sensitive   283, 285, 286.
  - nipples: separated from milk ducts   286.
  - surgical seams   137, 287.
  - study by University of Brussels: reduction surgery harms breast sensitivity   286.
  - few women can breast feed after   286.
- sebaceous glands   280.
- size and sensitivity
  - Are Sensitive Breasts Best?   287.
  - big breast plus: double-nipple sucking technique   288.
  - large breasts are less sensitive   283, 284.
  - making love to large breasts   293.
  - study by University of Vienna   283.
  - varying sensitivity   284.
- University of Pisa: stimulation = bonding   293.
- super-large breasts and back pain   287.
- surgery
  - can cause chronic pain   286.
  - can hurt nipple sensitivity   284, 286.
  - nerves can get damaged   286.
  - San Francisco Plastic Surgery And Laser Center warns about risks   286.
- suspensory ligaments   280.
- breath, hot, as sexual instrument   229.
- breathing rate   137, 225.
- Brody, Stuart; validates vaginal orgasms 174, 175, 178.
- Brown, James   98.
- bulbus vestibuli   202.
- buttocks   218, 243, 393, 402, 403, 404.
  - separating the cheeks   269.

C

- Caldas University Manizales (Columbia)   211.
- Canadian sexual science researchers S. Andrea Miller and E. Sandra Byers   95, 96, 97, 104.
- cancer   287.
- Candyman; song on what makes a woman hot   161.
- Can You Have Too Much Sex?   96.
- car   389, 403, 406.
- Carole King song A Natural Woman   27.
- Caron, Sandra L.; common male sexual dysfunction   95.
- Casanova
  - secret advantage   19.
  - Casanova type women are attracted to   20.
- cashmere sweaters   145.
- cave as a location to make love   384.
- celibacy as threat to control   111.
- cervix 179, 194, 195, 203, 209, 212, 213, 216, 217, 294, 338, 372.
  - cervical orgasms   179.

- chains as bondage toy   400.
- chair as a location to make love   405, 413.
- charm her   150.
- chest   166, 276.
- cheval mirror as a sex toy   388.
- chick flicks   227.
- Chinese Taoist texts re female ejaculation   181.
- Chi, the universal energy   42.
- circumcision reduces transmission of HIV   76.
- climaxes See orgasms.
- clit   See clitoris.
- clitoris   90, 136, 137, 165, 167, 174, 175, 179, 182, 183, 184, 190, 192, 198, 200, 201, 202, 203, 204, 205, 235, 245, 246, 248, 249, 251, 252, 262, 265, 266, 267, 268, 269, 270, 274, 275, 276, 277, 294, 305, 322, 330, 352, 355, 356, 358, 390, 392, 393, 395, 415, 416.
  - Anatomy of the Clitoris report   201.
  - As A Political Weapon   174.
  - during oral sex to make her come fastest   232.
  - bulbs   178, 192, 201-204, 213, 277, 363, 367.
  - butterfly tapping on her clit   416.
  - clitoral body   176, 198, 204.
  - Clitoral Body Massage Orgasm Technique   274.
  - clitoral ring
    - Clitoral Ring Orgasm Technique   274.
    - graphic representation   193, 205.
  - clitoral sensitivity and over doing oral sex   234.
  - Clit Shake   274.
  - cranberry twist and shake techniques   276.
  - De re anatomica (1559) mentions clitoris   183.
  - glans   194, 274.
  - hood   200, 245, 246, 249, 252, 267, 274.
    - hood pull technique   274.
  - it isn't the best vaginal widener   205.
  - Kobelt, Georg Ludwig; 1800s anatomist, introduced true size of clitoris   201.
  - operations that put it at risk   202.
  - orgasms   175, 203, 215, 242, 243.
    - possibly breast-triggered   282.
  - origin in fetus   190.
  - Reigner de Graaf: standardized name   202.
  - Robert Latou Dickinson M.D.; discussed clitoris' true size in the 1940s   200.
  - size: large organ, rivalling penis   200, 204.
  - some women: direct stimulation painful   204.
  - Sorrento Technique   274.
  - stem   252, 267, 276.
  - If She Doesn't Like Direct Stimulation   246.
- clothing optional resorts: edgy places for sex   388.
- cock   See penis.
- cock-hardening kiss   227.
- cock rings as sex toys   395.
- cocksmanship   339–378 (chapter)
  - act of delaying; great sexual tease   344.
  - anal intercourse   218, 377.
  - arrhythmically   355.
  - slow steady rhythm is all you need   372.
  - Before "Going Wild" wait for Second Widening Event 376.
  - biofeedback as a guide   366.
  - body language as a guide   348, 366.
  - butterfly technique   370.
  - Choosing Rhythm And Intensity To Make Her Come 372.
  - cock angle   376.
  - cock path   374.
  - Cocksmanship Lessons #1-10   340-343.
  - Cocksmanship Lesson #11   360.
  - Cocksmanship Lesson #12   364.
  - Cocksmanship Techniques   370.
  - complete motion cycle   373, 374.
  - complete penetration; value of delaying 343.
  - Creating Antici...pation   343, 360.
  - deep penetration; only when she's tented   214.
  - Deep Trigger orgasms; to produce   370.
  - depth   309, 330, 331, 332.
  - emotional, psychological, spiritual bonding   350.
  - entry angles   403.
  - erection
    - a sexual magic wand   343.

cocksmanship/erection (continued)
    components, as sexual tools   344.
    dorsal vein, artery system illustration   347.
    head (glans)
        as a tickler   370.
        as a paintbrush with clear lubricant   345.
        giving her sexual tingles   345.
        locating her internal hot spots   345.
        nudging an area technique   370.
        perfect massaging instrument   345, 370.
    heat   345, 346, 360, 364, 365, 366, 370.
        makes her want to come   346.
    root will pleasurably stretch her   347.
    shaft; maximize its effect   347.
    most important features, to her   343, 345.
exotic techniques   350–352.
feather-light cock work   368.
finesse   339, 341, 342, 348, 360, 370.
going wild   348, 377.
good massage focus point   217.
how not to enter her   350.
how to enter her   350.
hugs, kisses, and I love yous during   348.
in-and-out piston-style stroke cycle   373.
intermittent pressure technique   370.
Introducing Targeted Lovemaking   367.
her wetness as a guide   366.
less is often more   341.
love, communication   343, 348, 351-359, 375.
Lovemaking As A Form Of Dancing   373, 374.
making her come   341.
    Exact Repetition Is Key   372.
    finding the right rhythm   374.
    Giving Her Multiple Orgasms   375.
    need to increase certain factors   372.
    without moving at all   342.
most men fall short   339.
motion cycles
    orgasm-triggering motion cycle   373.
    novel cock moves (list)   373.
motion-inches
    Introducing Motion-Inches   368.
    Understanding Motion-Inches: G-Spot
        Techniques illustration   369.
multiple orgasms; how to facilitate   342.
pace   352, 355, 356, 358, 359, 360, 364, 374.
penetration
    Creating Expectations technique   359.
    First-Entry Orgasm technique   360.
    increased penetration = more excitement   346.
    maximum penetration   348.
    measured penetration   367.
Plateau Rule   364.
position you must start flaccid   357.
Precision Lovemaking   371.
pre-entry tease   361.
pressure   355, 366, 368, 370.
producing a pulsating sensation   370.
propulsion techniques
    bouncing   371, 376.
    ergonomic cock propulsion methods   376.
Put Some "Head Music" Behind It   374.
range of motion   115.
resting motionless inside of her   347.
rhythm   341, 355, 358, 372, 373, 374, 375, 376, 378.
rhythmic pressure on her Deep Trigger   368.
sensitizing her   365.
Sexual Entrances And Psychological Significance   348.
shallow lovemaking   208, 215, 341, 347, 350-
    359, 361-366, 368, 375.
    Introducing Shallow Lovemaking   350–352.
    shallow vaginal penetration techniques
        First-Entry Orgasm technique   360.
        for vaginal orgasms   341.
        vaginal ring; use minimal motion   372.
        Shallow Sweet Place Technique   361-3.
        Union-Only Orgasm Technique   366.
        Vaginal Ball Tease   361, 362, 364.

cocksmanship/shallow techniques (continued)
    Vulva Love Techniques
        for complete vulval stimulation   356.
        Introducing the Vulva Cleft Zone   351.
        vulva cleft zone (VCZ)   351.
        #1: Windshield Wiper   352–4.
        #2: The Wiggle Technique   355.
        #3: The Vibrator   355.
        #4: The Vulva Slide   356.
        #5: The Full-On Tease   356.
        #6: Niche To Nook Technique   356.
        #7: The Dorsal Rub   357.
        #8: The Labia Tease   358.
        #9: The V-Spot Tease   358.
    she should come before you   342.
    slide inside her delicately   366.
    stretching action effect   347.
    strokes
        depth   352.
        exact as possible   355.
        strokes of short length   355.
        interjecting pauses   355.
        path   352, 373, 374, 375.
        rhythmic/arrhythmic   358.
    targeted lovemaking   367, 374.
    techniques
        for her AFE zone   368, 371, 372, 376.
        slow squeeze technique   371.
        standing up, taking her from behind   376.
        Too Hot Technique   371.
    tempo   355.
    tips   375.
    two types cocksmen: Pounders, Ticklers   339-340.
    what great cocksmanship is not about   342.
    what is great cocksmanship all about   342.
    what works best   343.
    Wiggles   373.
    with feeling   348.
    You do not have to go fast   341.
    You do not have to move very much   341.
    You do not have to penetrate her deeply   341.
    You do not have to use much force   341.
cocktail tables as locations for lovemaking   402, 413.
Coldplay lead singer lacked sex tips   2.
college coeds   126.
collegesextalk.com   95.
colognes; effective ones   72.
Colombo, Realdo refers to clitoris in 1559   183.
comfort boundaries   408.
coming on her   406.
coming together   416.
communicating love and fascination with her body   262.
communicating loving, warm feelings to her   29.
compliments; always ask "Why?"   415.
condoms   111.
    animal skin condoms, benefits   140.
    putting on, as control challenge   111.
    problems with lubricants   140.
confidence   155, 165, 171, 258.
connoisseur of women, being a   52.
control. *See also* premature ejaculation.
    Achieving The Ultimate Control   93–128.
    attitude adjustment   118.
    control problems as adolescents   118.
    Dealing With "Oh No!" Moments   111.
    Every woman a different effect on you.   110.
    exercises   100.
    How Long Do Women Want It To Last?   95.
    How Much Is Enough?   125, 127.
    Long Self-Tease Exercise   104.
    mastering control   110.
    Miller and Byers study   96.
    mind control   123.
    Mind Over Matter   118–128.
    "Oh no!" moments   110.
    problems   395.
    getting over your control issues   100.
control exercises   5, 100.

419

control exercises (continued)
    Big As You Can Get Game   105.
    Clear Fluid Game   106.
    Desensitization Exercise   108.
    Long Self-Tease Exercise   104.
    Pause Method   114.
    Short Diversion Method   113.
    slow masturbation exercise   108.
    Sphincter Relaxation Technique   112.
    use a timer   104.
    without climaxing   109.
corona (of glans penis)   101, 344, 369, 370, 372.
corpora cavernosa; illustration   346.
Corpus cavernosum penis   345.
Corpus cavernosum urethrae   344, 346.
Corpus spongiosum   344, 346, 353.
cortical regions of the brain   135.
Cosmopolitan   284, 409.
couches; as location to make love   405.
    finding a great couch for lovemaking   414.
Cowper's gland   106, 346.
Cox, Courteney; teaches TV boyfriend to kiss   228.
Crane, Bob; as example of how not to be   408.
Creating Antici...pation   360.
Creating Expectations   359.
creating intense and impatient desire   151.
creativity   387, 416.
credentials. *See* qualifications.
Crus glandis clitoridis   198.
CS ridge   346, 352, 356.
cul-de-sac   219.
cunnilingus   113, 232, 233, 234, 235, 236, 240, 241, 248, 252, 255, 256. *See also* oral sex.
    kisses that simulate   229.
    The Cunnilingus Artist's "Palette"   240.

D

Dad; "I wish I had read this book 50 years ago!"   2.
    "You get a tickle and then you ejaculate."   7.
Davis, Bette; valuation of sex   339.
deadly embolism   240.
deal-breakers
    anal region; smell can ruin relationship   76.
    being a bad kisser   228.
    eHarmony poll; poor hygiene   70.
    odors   76.
    smelly feet   77.
deep spot   219.
Deep Trigger   194, 195, 203, 213, 216, 217, 219, 318, 319, 320, 336, 338.
    Deep Trigger orgasms   370.
depth   309, 330, 331, 332, 341, 342, 352, 372.
De re anatomica (1559); mentions clitoris   183.
Desensitization Exercise   107, 108, 109, 121.
desert mesa as location to make love   403.
dicey territory   407.
Dickinson, Robert Latou; and size of clitoris   200.
dildo   388, 390, 406.
disinformation campaign   153, 174, 209.
    bull that women don't get hot over naked man   153.
    myth that vaginal orgasms don't exist   174.
divorce, causes
    he wouldn't write a love song for her   62.
    his lack of proper hygiene   69.
    husband's feminine side became dominant   49.
    husband didn't work at the relationship   62.
    husband showed her no affection   65.
    inability to show affection   61.
    no romance once we got married   62.
    she wasn't treated like a woman.   49.
    why she never let her husband touch her again   27.
Dodson, Betty; on variation in female genitals   191.
doggy-style   328.

doggy-style pose   244.
dopamine   122.
Dorsal Rub Technique; illustration   354.
double-fucked   394.
Double-Nipple Stimulation   289.
double-nipple sucking technique   288, 289.
double-penetration
    A Toy For The Biggest Orgasms   394.
    double-penetrate her   406.
    "Every woman fantasizes about it!"   394.
    using a finger   269.
Double Wedding; on what it means to be a man   45.
drama (use of)   278.
Dress Her Up, Take Her Out   152.

E

ear   345, 365, 366, 376.
Earle, my mentor   5, 7, 23, 52, 220.
    Cary Grant, Sean Connery as role models   78.
    gift of gab   52.
    "If she gives you the woman, take it."   120.
    importance of cologne - the right cologne   73.
    on your value, as a male lover   343, 376.
    use of vibrator on women   391.
    warns: some women pose control challenges   110.
    women are smarter than men   53.
ears   229, 237, 244.
Eastern sex techniques   161.
Ecstasy Clitoris Stem Technique   252.
Ecstasy Vulva Technique   252, 253, 254.
ecstatic state of absolute surrender   402.
edgy female lovers   387–388.
    dominatrices   389.
    sex kittens   389.
    submissive   389, 398, 399, 404.
    vixen   389.
edgy lovemaking   387–408.
    anal beads   406.
    food play   406.
    gentle bondage   398–403.
        can heighten pleasure   398.
        suggestions   402.
    Going Too Far   407.
    handcuffed, tied, and held down   398.
    Make Her Your Sex Servant   404.
    pushing the envelope   407.
    Pussy Shaving   404.
    role playing   404.
    safe suggestions   388.
    sex swings   406.
    should be done in moderation   407.
    videotaping your sexual experiences   388.
    while you're driving   388.
eHarmony survey   70.
ejaculate, female   268.
ejaculation   344.
ejaculation trigger   199, 206, 215.
electrical impulses   345.
emotions   22, 339, 348, 359, 379.
    as a guide in lovemaking   29.
    regulated by limbic cortex, bigger in women   47.
empathy   29.
endocrine system   135.
endorphins   122, 135.
entering her   343, 348, 349, 350, 360, 364, 377, 378.
entrances   346, 348, 349, 350, 363, 378.
epicenter   219.
epilepsy medications; orgasm-suppressing effects   178.
epithets   224.
erectile tissue   345.
erection   105, 132, 137, 340, 343, 344, 345, 346, 347, 352, 355, 356, 357, 358, 366, 367, 370, 405.
    blood vessels   345.
    components as sexual tools   340, 343, 344, 345, 346, 347, 352, 355, 356, 357, 358, 366, 367, 370.
    corona   344, 369, 370, 372.
    corpora cavernosa illustration   346.

erection (continued)
  Corpus cavernosum penis   345.
  Corpus cavernosum urethrae   344, 346.
  Corpus spongiosum   344, 346, 353.
  CS ridge   346, 352, 356.
  dorsal side (back), artery and veins   345.
    illustration   347.
  erectile tissue   345.
  glans (the "head")   344, 345, 350, 352, 354, 357,
      358, 360, 361, 363, 365, 370, 371, 372, 375.
    most important features, to her   345.
    to locate her internal hot spots with   345.
  heat   345, 346, 360, 364, 365, 366, 370.
    makes her want to come   346.
  root; erotically and pleasurably stretches her   347.
  shaft   344.
    dorsal side rippling texture   347.
    provides friction   347.
  shorter cocks can produce vaginal orgasms 175, 189.
  to make your erection bigger   105.
  urethra   344, 346.
  what makes it hard 340, 341, 342, 343, 344, 345,
      346, 347, 348, 352, 355, 356, 357, 360, 366.
    illustration   346.
ergonomic cock propulsion methods   376.
ergonomic positions   326, 327.
erogenous zones   5, 8, 30, 139, 173, 177, 178, 185, 191,
    197, 203, 206, 208, 260, 261, 263, 264, 270, 281, 294,
    340, 351, 352, 363, 364, 367, 368, 371, 395.
  author discovered: Niche, Nook, Nexus, V-Spot, M
      Spot, vaginal ball, vaginal ring 192-195, 280.
  More Erogenous Zones   221.
  multiple erogenous zone areas   208, 351.
  Multiple Spots = Bigger Orgasms   206.
erotic   30, 218, 388, 389, 390, 393, 404, 406.
erotica   108.
erotic activities   130, 388.
erotic effect   256.
erotic festivals   388.
erotic film festivals   389.
Erotic Lip Spreading Technique   277.
erotic massage   224, 259, 260, 261, 263.
  how to give a great erotic massage   260.
erotic pleasures   406.
erotic scenes   406.
erotic stories   7, 404, 411.
Erotic Talking For Sexual Results   161–172.
erotic touching   262.
erotic visuals make women aroused say studies 153, 154.
example of what not to think or say   170.
Excite Her With Sexy Visuals   153–160.
exciting places to make love   383.
ex-girlfriends.
  all asked author to take them back   10.
  No long-term lover has ever left me   10.
  told author, "You have to write a book!"   1.
exhibitionists   383, 387.
exotic techniques   350, 358–365.
expectations   359, 360, 365.
experimentation   37–40, 415.
eyes   224, 366.

F

Fabio
  meaning to women   33–40, 400.
face   166, 366.
faking orgasms
  ABC News Primetime Live American Sex Survey;
      48% of women faked an orgasm 80.
  author once faked an orgasm   81.
  causes; one: many men lack skills   80.
  How Should You React If She Is?   83.
  how to react if you suspect she's faking it 82, 88.
  If It's Your Problem, Man Up   86.
  Indiana University study: perhaps 21% of
      women are faking it   80.

faking orgasms (continued)
  Is She Or Isn't She?   82.
  Is Your Lover Faking It? How To Tell!   84.
  Meg Ryan's faked orgasm in When Harry Met
      Sally; made men's fears worse   82.
  orgasm simulations   85.
  Playboy Reader poll: 59% of females said they'd
      faked orgasms   81.
  Possible problem: Some women who fake it will
      deny they're faking it   86.
  Problems Of Hers That Might Make Her Fake It
    decreasing sensitivity due to age   83.
    medications   82.
    physical problems   82.
    psychological problems   82.
    she could be a transsexual   83.
    she's a closet Lesbian   83.
    she's not been honest with you   82.
    something is bothering her   83.
  red flags   81, 87.
  Seinfeld episode; Elaine faked her orgasms   79.
  solution?   86, 87.
  sounds she's making seem phony   225.
  What If The Problem Lies With Her?   91.
  why it's important to know for sure   84.
  women who fake it likely to stray   81.
  your very relationship could be at stake   81.
fantasies, women's
  being "taken"   167, 389.
  being made love to by two men   269.
fashion issues   78.
fatigue factor   410.
faux pas   350.
feathers as sex toys   261, 264.
feedback   223, 223–226, 226, 292.
  biological feedback   225.
  body language
    back arching   225.
    list   224.
  epithets   224.
  extreme physical reactions   224.
  if she says "Yes!"   225.
  muscle contractions   224.
  screaming   224.
  sexy sounds   224, 225.
  increase in her vaginal temperature   225.
  motions; writhing or wriggling   225.
  telltale feedback; how to react   224.
feedback author has received from his lovers   16.
  "I'm living it!"   68.
  "I really liked last night."   415.
  "I wondered: *how is he moving that part?*"   266.
  "Our lovemaking is so profound."   42.
  "What did you just DO to me?"   254.
  "You can go on and on forever."   127.
  "You have great hands!"   257.
  you reach out right away and take my hand   59.
  "You're amazing!"   266.
  you're full of surprises   416.
  "You're really incredible!"   416.
  "You're so naughty!"   266.
Feeler-Outer Talking Tease Line   164.
feelings   22, 33–40, 39–40.
  women respond to feelings   29.
feet   222, 244, 397, 400, 403, 406, 410, 413.
  as potential deal-breaker (odor)   77.
  bare feet   406.
  need to keep healthy (free of fungus)   77.
  need to trim nails   77.
fellatio   391.
female ejaculation   5, 9, 134, 137, 178, 181, 182,
    206, 207, 215, 216, 268, 269, 271.
  Aristotle documented   181.
  brought on with the heat and pressure of a
      motionless erection or finger   8.
  Chinese Taoist texts mention it   181.
  Deborah Sundahl; reason some women might
      not ejaculate   207.

421

female ejaculation (continued)
  ejaculation triggers 134, 199, 206, 215, 268.
  female "semen"; Kama salila 182.
  Galen; documented female ejaculation in 2nd
      Century A.D. 181.
  History of Female Ejaculation 42.
  Introducing Female Ejaculation 207.
  Kalyānamalla; referred to "female semen"
      (ejaculate) in 16th Century A.D. 182.
  Kukkoka; wrote about female ejaculation in
      12th Century A.D. 182.
  most women can be made to ejaculate 9.
  Perineal Pinch technique for female ejaculation
      and orgasms in seconds 271.
  scientific study by Austrian urologist Florian
      Wimpissinger: ejaculate is not urine 207.
  wet spot; remedies for 207.
Female Ejaculation and the G-Spot 207.
female fetus 190.
female prostate; what G-Spot was called 180, 207, 215.
female sexual anatomy 4, 8, 14, 35-40, 134, 138,
    173–222, 348, 349.
  AFE zone 178, 183, 203, 215, 216, 338.
    graphic 195.
  anal canal
    anal hole 218.
    graphic representation 192.
  anal ring 218.
    graphic representation 192.
  Anterior Fornix Erogenous Zone (AFE Zone) 183.
    graphic 194.
  anus 194.
  areolas 137.
  Bartholin's glands 184, 206, 216.
    ducts 136.
      graphic representation 192.
  breasts *See* breasts (under "B").
  butt cheeks 218.
  cervix 179, 194, 203, 209, 212, 213, 216, 217.
  clitoral bulbs 178, 201, 202, 203, 204, 213.
    graphic representation 192.
    shallow sex might cause bulb orgasms 213.
  clitoral ring; graphic representation 193, 205.
  clitoris 136, 137. *See also* clitoris (under "C").
  cul-de-sac 219.
  deep spot 219.
  Deep Trigger 194.
  earlobes 229.
  entrances
    spiritual and psychological impact 348.
    there are three (listed) 349.
  epicenter 219.
  even women in dark about female sexual anatomy 191.
  female genital responses not well studied 210.
  Fornix 194.
    posterior fornix 212.
  fourchette 136, 184, 198.
  frenulum clitoridis 198.
  Glans of Clitoris 194.
  great lovers study it 29.
  G-Spot 136, 137. *See also* G-Spot (under "G")
  her genitals 345, 349, 358.
  her neck 114, 148.
  her skin; her largest sex organ 139.
  her toes 117.
  Her Vulva Vs. Her Vagina: Know The Difference? 191.
  hippocampus; bigger in women 47.
  hymen remnants; graphic representation 192.
  hypogastric nerve 179.
  Introducing Her Deep Trigger And Nexus 216.
  Introducing New Erogenous Zones: Niche, Nook,
      V-Spot, Vaginal Ball, Clitoral Ring 193.
  Introducing New Orgasm Triggers: Deep
      Trigger, Nexus, Fornix, Nook and more
      194, 203, 216, 217.
  Introducing The Female Sexual Anatomy
      graphics 192.
  labia majora 197.

female sexual anatomy (continued)
  labia minora 136, 345, 349, 350, 352, 356,
      357, 358, 361, 363, 369, 373.
  limbic cortex; regulates emotions
      bigger in women 47.
  mons pubis 192, 193, 194.
  muscles 224, 225.
  muscle spasms 137.
  muscular contractions in her vaginal walls,
      pelvis, anus and uterus 137.
  neurophysiology of human female sexual
      function; a field still in its infancy 210.
  Nexus 194, 371.
    graphic representation 195.
  Niche
    graphic representation
        177, 192, 193, 194, 198.
  nipples 136, 137, 139.
    erect 154.
    Her Nipples: Special Case Orgasm Triggers 220.
    one nipple more sensitive than the other 290.
  Nook 194.
    graphic representation 192.
  Ovary 194.
  pelvic nerve 179.
  perineal sponge 177, 192, 193, 198.
  perineum; graphic representation 192, 193.
  Physical Changes With Arousal, Wettening &
      Orgasm 136.
  Posterior fornix 194.
  Pouch of Douglas 219.
  pudendal nerve 179.
  recto-uterine excavation 219.
  Rectum 194.
  Shallow Sweet Place 361, 362, 363, 364, 375.
    two different kinds of nerves
        visceral and somatic 363.
  Skene's glands 184, 185, 205, 206, 207.
    ducts graphic representation 192.
  skin 176, 190, 196, 198, 200, 206, 208, 210, 212, 221.
    her largest sexual organ 221.
    skin of her neck 221.
  small of her back 229.
  some of her many sensitive areas 243.
  The Very Best Orgasm Booster: Her Bottom 217.
  thighs 222.
  thoracic intercostal nerves 179.
  Urethra 176, 192, 193, 194.
    graphic representation 192.
  U-Spot 177, 178, 192, 205, 206, 207.
    graphic representation 192.
  Uterus 194.
  vagina 136, 137, 139, 140, 345, 346, 349, 3
      50, 351, 352, 359, 366, 368, 375, 377.
    See also vagina (under "V").
    posterior wall of the vagina; most reactive
        orgasm trigger 210, 212, 213.
    vaginal canal 347.
    vaginal nerves 346.
    vaginal walls 346, 347, 377.
  vaginal ball; graphic representation 192.
  vaginal canal 136, 137, 140, 141.
    inner two-thirds 137.
    outer third 137.
  vaginal ring 361, 362, 363, 364, 372.
  vestibule 184, 192, 194, 197, 198, 199, 214.
    graphic representation 192.
  V-Spot; graphic representation 192.
  vulva 345, 349, 350, 351, 352, 355, 356, 357,
      359, 363, 365, 368.
    graphic representations 192.
    Introducing Her Vulva Cleft Zone 351.
  Why Study Anatomy? 185.
female sexual hot spots 183.
female sexuality 174.
femininity 48.
feminists 155, 279.
feminist sexpert Carlin Ross 155, 279.

fetters in sex play 400.
"Fever"; one of the sexiest songs ever 143.
fidelity 391.
field of science 29.
finesse 339, 341, 342, 348, 360, 370.
finger motion 269.
fingers 9, 258, 262, 263, 266-277, 403, 406, 415.
fingerwork 139, 265, 266, 267, 270, 274, 276, 384.
    butterfly tapping on her clit 416.
first rule of smart masturbation 103.
first sexual encounters 174.
five most romantic things to do to her in bed 68.
Flutter-Tonguing 249.
fMRI study 294.
foreplay 129, 130, 360.
    as a flawed concept 129, 130.
    bad idea 255.
    makes men bad lovers 129.
foreskin; cleaning needs 76.
forests as lovemaking location 382, 384.
Forgotten (Non-Physical) Sexual Process:
    Seduction 132.
fornix 194, 212, 216, 372.
    anterior fornix 338.
    posterior fornix 338, 372.
fott 164, 417.
foundation upon which everything else rests 22.
fourchette 136, 184, 198, 234, 240, 245, 253.
Four Sexual Processes, The 131–142.
    a contiuum of events 131.
    choreographed by woman's brain 135.
    telltale physical changes 136, 142.
    three physical processes 133, 134.
fourth rule of smart masturbation 104.
four types of lovers who want edgy lovemaking 387.
Franklin, Aretha 27, 28, 46.
frenulum 100, 234, 352.
    aka "Trigger" 100.
    it can pose a control problem 101.
    responsible for the "hair trigger response" 101.
    the most sensitive area on your penis 101.
frenulum clitoridis 198.
frenulum labiorum pudendi 198.
friction 347, 370, 371.
from behind 402, 403, 406.
front entry 273, 411. *See also* positions.
    where penis arrives inside her 318, 328, 333, 338.
Full-On Tease technique; illustration 353.
fully erect 357.
furniture for lovemaking 409–414.
    Beds. *See also* beds (under "B").
        missionary; great for gentle bondage 411.
        platform beds; not the best 411.
        sleigh beds 411.
        water beds 411.
    What makes a bed great for lovemaking? 409.
    Choosing A F***ing Good Chair 411.
    Choosing A Good Bed 411.
    Choosing A Good Kitchen Table 413.
    cocktail tables; great if strong 413.
    couches
        finding a great f**king couch 414.
        great for AFE orgasms 414.
    cushy chair at the right height 411.
    hard chair; good for lovemaking 413.
    kitchen chairs 412.
    kitchen counters at right height 413.
    mattresses
        old mattresses 410.
        pillow-tops; good for lovemaking 410.
        "space-age"; not great for sex 410.
        springy; desirable for lovemaking 410.
        Why important to lovemaking? 410.
    office desk as a location for making love 414.
    ottomans; great if bouncy 413.
    positions
        facilitated by modern beds 411.
furtive lovemaking 382.

fuzzy handcuffs 398.

G

Gable, Clark
    In Gone With The Wind sexy scene 48.
    as masculine role model 56.
    as great kisser 227.
Galen 181.
garage; as a location to make love 404, 406.
Gaulin, Steven 144.
Geldof, Bob; false story about Sting's prowess 93.
Genital Art Gallery; photos and drawings of female
    genitals by Betty Dodson 191.
genital orgasms 350.
genitals 177, 178, 182, 191, 221, 264, 345, 349, 358.
genital sensations 294.
genital sensory activity 294.
genital sensory cortex 179, 294.
genital tubercle 190.
gentle bondage 389, 398–403, 407, 411.
    can heighten pleasure 398.
    illusion 402.
    only the suggestion of being a captive 401.
    pretend force 402.
    primal desire 399.
    psychological component 399.
    scenarios, suggestions 402.
gentle stretch technique 277, 278.
germs and smegma 76.
Get into your masculine side! 49.
getting naked 385.
Get Up (I Feel Like Being A) Sex Machine 98.
girl-next-door types 387.
Giving Her Multiple Orgasms 375.
Glamour magazine 107.
glands 280, 281, 284.
Glands of Montgomery, tubercles 281.
glans of clitoris 194, 198, 200, 202, 204, 205, 216, 217.
glans of penis 75, 105, 106, 166, 264, 268, 270, 274,
    276, 344, 345, 354. *See also* cocksmanship.
glycerin 140.
God Never Blinks by Regina Brett 53.
going wide; how to verify she's gone wide 187.
going down on her. *See* oral sex.
Going Too Far 407.
going wild 377.
Gold Dust Woman; about "lousy lovers" 90, 168.
Goldstein, Sue W. 181.
good partner 51.
Good Samaritan Hospital (Cincinnati) 209.
good sex 129.
Graaf, Regnier de 201, 215.
    and female ejaculation 207.
    discovered female prostate (G-Spot) 180, 215.
    standardized the name "clitoris" 202.
Grafenberg, Dr. Ernst 180, 215.
Grafenberg spot aka G-Spot 180. *See also* G-Spot.
Grant, Cary
    as masculine role model 56, 78.
    lesson in how to seduce a woman 150.
Grape Circles 290.
great for getting her wet and wide 277.
great hands 257, 259, 262.
    what is having "great hands" all about? 262.
great lovemaker 11.
    a connoisseur of women 52.
    anticipates what his lover thinks he will do and
        does something else 53.
    definition 11.
    empathizes with his lovers' desires 29.
    reads the latest books and articles 29.
    Staying interesting is especially important 52.
    The Price You Might Pay If You're Not A Great
        Lovemaker 26.
    traits 52.
    What Is A Great Lovemaker? 24.

great lovemaking   15, 23, 348.
   a body language   348.
   a significant predictor of satisfaction   18.
   can make gorgeous women go for unattractive men   23.
   field of science   29.
   great skills; you need more than this   143.
   importance of surprise   54.
   involves religious devotion to each other   43.
   requires, most times, at least a half an hour   97.
   the quality of your relationship matters   61.
   think of yourself as a lovemaking dancer   50.
   way to a woman's heart   23.
   when you should enter her   139, 141.
   women desire a great lover   50.
great lovers   37–40, 173, 175, 177, 203.
   a great male lover brings a lot to the table   171.
   and creative locations   382.
   anticipate lubrication problems   140.
   cannot afford to become egoists   17.
   charming, sweet talking   52.
   classy   58.
   have the gift of gab   52.
   have the proper attitude   343.
   impediments to becoming
      behavior that's offensive, cold   22.
      bitterness over past relationships   20, 21.
      hateful attitude   20.
      negative thoughts   21.
   need to ignore anti-male propaganda   175.
   need to take into how what you do affects her emotionally, psychologically, spiritually, and physically   349.
   one of biggest secrets: their love of women   20.
   the way you talk, look, and stand   45.
   they're sophisticated gentlemen   56.
   understand women's brains are physiologically different than men's   60.
   view women in the right way   54.
   What's your motivation?   25.
   women don't leave   15–18.
   you're not one until your lover says so   416.
great orgasm boosters   196, 221, 222.
great sex   23.
great-uncle's advice   223.
great wetness triggers   222.
great women; they're out there   20.
groaning   225.
groin   266.
grooming   70–78.
   Looking Good For Her Pays Off   160.
groove; one that doesn't pose control challenge   115.
G-Spot   85, 136, 137, 174, 175, 179, 180, 181, 183, 184, 187, 190, 194, 195, 203, 207, 211, 213, 215, 272, 273, 294, 318, 319, 320, 328, 330, 335, 347, 348, 368, 369, 370, 371, 372, 373, 374, 375, 376.
   as threat to some feminists' political agendas   180.
   CNN silliness: "The G-Spot: Is it real?"   181.
   debate   178, 180, 207, 219.
   Dr. Brunhild Kring disputes its existence   180.
   every woman has one   180.
   G-Spot orgasms   347, 375.
      missionary position best   347.
      Technique #1: G-Spot Press   272.
      #2: G-Spot Pulsations   272.
      #3: G-Spot Wiggle   273.
      #4: "Come Here" Technique   273.
      #5: G-Spot Circles   273.
      #6: G-Spot Tease   273.
      #7: Killer G-Spot Crunches   273.
      G-Spot Techniques illustration   369.
   G-Spot vibrators   393.
   homologous to your prostate   190.
   orgasm   243.
   stimulating during oral sex   240.
G Spot and Other Recent Discoveries About Human Sexuality, The   179.

H

hair trigger response   101.
hammock; as a location to make love   406.
hand; the side of your hand   267.
handcuffs   389, 398, 400, 401, 403.
handheld mirror; as a sex toy   388.
handjob   389, 391.
hands   401, 402, 403, 410.
Hands-Free Clit Exposer   245.
hard chair for lovemaking   413.
hard floor for sex; drawbacks   410.
hard-on   *See* erection.
Harvard Medical School study on differences between male and female brains   47.
HBO's Real Sex   390.
head; as in oral sex (for her)   233.
heartbeat   137, 138.
heartfelt thoughts   169.
heart rate   85, 225.
heat   345, 346, 360, 364, 365, 366, 370.
   vaginal   403.
heightened sensations   399.
heighten the sensitivity of her skin   365.
her inner realm   349.
her internal body chemistry   140.
her largest sex organ   139, 221.
her most intimate places   349.
her office desk or chair
   as a location to make love   385.
her psyche   349.
her reactions to what you are doing   223.
her sexual potential   36–40.
her very soul   349.
heteros   401.
heterosexual women
   aroused by visual sexual stimuli   154.
higher love; Spiritual Side To Lovemaking   41.
high heels for their sexiness   405.
Hindu Kama Sutra   42.
hippocampus   135.
   bigger in women   47.
Hippocrates   200.
hips   222, 244, 266, 397, 404, 405.
History of Female Ejaculation   42.
Hitch.
   "No woman wakes up saying: 'God, I hope I don't get swept off my feet today.'"   50.
   "Hit it and quit it" is not my thing.   19.
   "My clients actually like women.   19.
Hitchcock   150.
Hite Report; example of anti-male propaganda   174, 180.
HIV; circumcision reduces transmission   76.
Hoch, Dr. Zwi   211.
Hogan's Heroes   408.
Holstege, Gert   137.
homologous organs   190.
homosexuals   401.
honesty   168.
hood of her clitoris   *See* clitoris.
hooks   411.
hormone replacement therapy   140.
hormones   47, 135.
horn dogs; undesirable to women   55.
horny   162, 265.
hotel balcony as location to make love   384.
hot sex   404.
hot spots   9, 30, 139, 141, 142, 177, 345, 347, 348, 351, 357, 360, 363, 364, 371, 372, 376.
   great way to stimulate multiple hot spots   267.
   ones your lover will be surprised to find she has   9.
   using your glans to massage them   345.
Hot Spots for Love   409.
hot tub   397, 398.
how affairs often begin   39–40.
How Her Vagina "Tents"   187, 188.
How Long Do Women Want Sex To Last?   95.

How Many Positions Are Enough?   302.
how men use their cocks   339.
How Much Do You Know About Female Sexual Anatomy?   177.
How Much Is Enough?   125, 127.
how not to react to a woman in a sexy dress   55.
how so many relationships hit the doldrums   33–40.
how to dress   145.
how to get more sex   145.
How To Give Her Breast-Induced Orgasms   290.
how to keep your relationship sexy, fresh, hot   144.
how to make a woman a better partner   51.
how to make your lover wet, aroused and horny   162.
how to use nudity to your benefit (seducing her)   149.
    Excite Her With Sexy Visuals   153–160.
how to get her in the mood   146.
how to seduce your lover   146.
hugs   348, 352.
Human Sex Anatomy; revealed large size of clitoris in the 1940s   200.
Human Sexuality Program at Weill Medical College of Cornell University   132.
humdrum sex   32–40.
humiliation   399, 407, 408.
hurting someone; never to be done   407.
husbands   34–40.
    who neglect their wives   34–40.
hygiene   69–78.
    Bad Hygiene Kills Relationships: Stories   70.
    balls (scrotum) odor can ruin relationship   76.
    cock; if unclean, a woman will avoid   77.
    feet; taking care of   77.
    foreskin; cleaning needs   76.
    nails; why trim them   74, 75.
    perineum; need to keep clean   76.
    pubic hair; need to keep clean   76.
    uncircumcised males; special needs   75.
    why having clean hands is important to her   69.
hymen remnants; graphic representation   192.
Hynde, Chrissie   276.
hypogastric nerve   179.
hypothalamic paraventricular nucleus   294.
hypothalamus   135.
hysterectomies   140.
    risk to clitoris' integrity   202.

I

ifeminists.com   174.
I love yous   348.
imagination   276, 414.
I'm Crazy About Iris Blond (Sono pazzo di Iris Blond); kissing without emotion   228.
impediments to pleasing a woman   35–40.
Important Biological Rule   267.
in and out; finger motion   269, 274.
in-and-out piston-style stroke cycle   373.
incompetence   34–40.
incontinence surgery; risk to clitoris' integrity   202.
index finger   258, 265, 266, 270, 271, 272, 273, 274, 275, 276, 277.
Indiana University's National Survey of Sexual Health and Behavior   80.
indulge her   397.
indulgences; some are impossible to provide   407.
infections
    caused by dirty or untrimmed nails   75.
    risk of   269.
infidelity; bad lovemaking as cause   18.
inflicted pain   408.
inhibitions   399.
inner thighs   243.
innocuous sex play   399.
intensify her experience   166.
intensity   109, 115, 124, 244, 249, 251, 262, 270, 274, 341, 342, 355, 364, 365, 372, 374, 392, 396, 399.
intercourse   *See also* lovemaking and sex.

intercourse (continued)
    ideal duration   36–40.
    intercourse kisses for effect   230.
    multitasking during   130.
    rear-entry intercourse   370.
    shallow intercourse   341.
    why mechanical approach fails   348.
intermittent pressure technique   370.
Internet; spreading misinformation   176.
Introducing Female Ejaculation   207.
Introducing Her Deep Trigger And Nexus   216.
Introducing Her Vulva Cleft Zone   351.
Introducing Shallow Lovemaking   350–352.
Introducing Targeted Lovemaking   367.
Introducing The Concept Of Motion-Inches   368.
Introducing Niche Tickle Orgasm Technique   270.
Introducing Vulva Love   351, 351–358.
introitus   349, 350.
involuntary convulsions   366.
I once faked an orgasm   81.
irresistible sexual tingles   258.
island resort   385.
it's all about her   408.
    positions   297.
IUDs; causes of bad vaginal odor   238.

J

jacuzzi   397, 398.
James Bond; as masculine role model   56.
Jameson, Jenna   153.
Jane   400.
Jay Leno   14.
jerking off   102.   *See* masturbating.
Jewish views on lovemaking   42.
Joan of Arc   170.
Joel, Billy
    feeling he was below Christie Brinkley   170.
    on bad sex   129.
John Gray   15, 17.
    on advanced bedroom skills   17.
    primary reason for loss of interest   59.
Johns Hopkins study; shows inverse relationship between breast sensitivity and size   284.
Jones , Bobby   53.
Jones Beach parking lot; scene of best oral sex   255.
Journal of Sex Research   95.
Journal of Sexual Medicine   95, 179, 181, 207, 209, 294.
Journal of Urology "Anatomy of the Clitoris"   201, 210.
Juvenal   200.

K

Kabbalah   42.
    sexual pleasure to get closer to God   42.
Kahn, Madeleine; song about men who come too fast   93.
Kalyānamalla; referred to "female semen" (ejaculate) in 16th Century A.D.   182.
Kama salila; female ejaculate   182.
Kāmaśāstra (Kama Sutra)   42, 181.
Kaplan, Helen Singer; three-stage sexual model: desire, excitation, orgasm   132.
Keep Her Purring   151.
keeping the home fires burning   12, 143.
Keeping The Love In Lovemaking   407.
Kellogg, Susan; on intense breast stimulation   293.
kindness   144, 145, 148, 149, 155, 156.
kinky   399, 408.
Kinsey Report; misinformation   174.
Kirstie Alley; and leering talk show host   55.
kissing   348, 366, 399, 403, 404.
    a tongue that simulates your hard cock   230.
    cock-hardening kiss; what you need to do, in reverse   227.
    for effect   228.
    four types of kisses   229.
    French kissing   229.

kissing (continued)
    great kisses; power of   229.
    intercourse kisses; what they're all about   230.
    kisses to avoid   230.
    Kissing For Effect: Art of Kissing   227–230.
    pre-intercourse kissing; what it's all about   229.
    purely romantic kisses; what they're about   230.
    sexy kiss   148.
    should be non-verbal communication   228.
    simulating the act of cunnilingus   229.
    to arouse   165.
    to make her eager and ready for sex   227.
    with sexual power   227.
    why most men fail in kissing department   227.
kitchen chair for lovemaking   412.
kitchen counters for making love   413.
kitchen table to make love   402, 411.
kneading   242, 272.
knees   222, 244, 403, 410.
Kobelt, Georg Ludwig; discovered clitoris' true size in the 1800s   201, 202.
Komisaruk, Barry   178, 203.
    study shoots down G-Spot as part of clitoris   183.
    fMRI study   203.
    study validates breast-induced orgasms   294.
Korda, Joanna B.   181.
    female ejaculation study   181, 182.
Kukkoka and female ejaculation   182.

L

labia majora   197.
labia minora   136, 176, 187, 190, 191, 196, 197, 198, 205, 229, 232, 234, 245, 247, 253, 254, 266, 267, 268, 277, 345, 349, 350, 352, 356, 357, 358, 361, 363, 369, 373, 395. *See also* pussy lips.
    Erotic Lip Spreading Technique   277.
    inner circles technique   277.
    inner rims of each labia minora lip   197.
    Labia Tease Technique illustration   354.
    More Fun With Her Pussy Lips   277.
    origin in female fetus   190.
    stretching them open during oral sex   232.
    velvet touch technique   277.
labioscrotal folds   190.
Lassek, William   144.
Lee, Peggy; one of the sexiest songs ever   143.
leering letches   55, 57
    undesirable to women   55.
legs   113, 117, 239, 240, 242, 243, 253, 260, 267, 397, 403, 404, 406, 409, 410, 412, 413.
Lesbians   399, 401.
    bondage Queen   401
    Lesbian sex educator Betty Dodson   191.
    and pornography   153.
"Let It Be"; as great oral sex pace setter   251.
lidocain- and prilocain-containing creams may help delay ejaculation   128.
lifestyle, attitude and mindset issues   14.
limbic cortex; bigger in women   47.
lips   345, 366, 372, 373.
locations for lovemaking   381–386, 382–386, 383–386, 384–386, 385–386. *See also* sexy locations to make love.
    choosing creative locations   381–386.
    Some Locations To Avoid   385.
London's Primal Health Research Center   122.
Long Island; posh North Shore   388.
Long Self-Tease Exercise   104, 105, 107.
long-term relationships   32–40, 145, 149.
    bigger challenge than one-night stands   11.
    Loving Touching For Men In Relationships   258.
    unique challenges   31–40
Looking Good For Her Pays Off   160.
looking handsome   144.

lotions   264.
lousy lovers   168. *See also* bad lovers.
love   236, 237, 240, 248, 254, 256, 343, 348, 351, 352, 353, 354, 355, 356, 357, 358, 359, 375, 387, 388, 389, 390, 391, 394, 395, 399, 400, 405, 408, 416.
    expression of love in lovemaking   29.
    higher love   41.
love fluids   136.
Love Is The Drug   122.
love juices   5, 8, 9, 356, 358, 361.
    vaginal areas that can trigger   214.
love life   389.
    adding variety to your love life   381.
lovemaking
    after lovemaking   379.
    After The Lovin'   379–380.
    anal intercourse   218.
    an emotion in motion; says Mae West   348.
    as a lifestyle   29, 55.
    a means to a higher consciousness and joy   41.
    a selfless act   24.
    a slow steady rhythm is all you need   372.
    as nonverbal communication   30.
        communicating loving, warm, feelings   29.
    a woman sleeps with you and stays with you only if she loves you   65.
    butterfly technique   370.
    Chinese Taoists spiritual view   42.
    deep penetration; don't try until she's tented   214.
    Deep Trigger orgasms; how to produce   370.
    don't discount your role in lovemaking   171.
    edgy lovemaking   387–408.
        anal beads   406.
        food play   406.
        gentle bondage   398–403.
        Going Too Far   407.
        Make Her Your Sex Servant   404.
        pushing the envelope   407.
        Pussy Shaving   404.
        role playing   399, 404, 405.
        sex swings   406.
        Sex Toys   390–397.
        should be done in moderation   407.
    emotions, as a guide   29.
    expressions of love in lovemaking   29.
    four lovemaking processes   132, 135.
        choreographed by woman's brain   135.
        physical changes you can produce   136.
    glans *See also* cocksmanship.
        as a big tickler   370.
        as a massager   370.
    great lovemaker   11.
    has many aspects to it   22.
    her desire depends upon how you treat her   22.
    Hindu Kama Sutra spiritual view   42.
    how it makes women feel   29.
    how your attitudes toward women relate to it   22.
    in public places   383.
    intermittent pressure technique   370.
    Introducing Her Vulva Cleft Zone   351.
    Introducing Targeted Lovemaking   367.
    Introducing Vulva Love   351–358.
    is about your lover's soul, heart, mind   24.
    is like dancing   40, 50, 373.
    is not just about penetration   130.
    is on a higher level than sex   12.
    It's A Celebration   44.
    it's all about her   408.
    it's also about being a good partner   11.
    lengthy lovemaking   343.
    less is more; illustration   369.
    Lovemaking 101 Rules #1 and #2   65.
    lubrication; wettening activities should not end after penetration   141.
    making love, at its best   24.
    master plan   297.
    missionary-style; good for AFE Zone access   216.
    motion-inches

lovemaking (continued)
    Introducing The Concept Of Motion-Inches 368.
    Understanding Motion-Inches: G-Spot
        Techniques illustration 369.
    need to work on skills 32–40.
    non-penetrative sexual activities; should not be
        confined to pre-intercourse period 130.
    not supposed to be predictable 341.
    Old Testament view on lovemaking 44.
    penetration See cocksmanship and penetration.
    Plateau Rule 364.
    Precision Lovemaking: How To Target Her
        Orgasm Triggers 371.
    private secret naughty places 414.
    producing a pulsating sensation 370.
    putting her into a joyful haze of ecstasy 28.
    Putting The Love Into Lovemaking 23–30.
    rear-entry sex; for biggest orgasms 212.
    romance as necessary precursor 59.
    sensitizing her 365.
    shallow lovemaking See cocksmanship.
    should be a beautiful undivided process 130.
    Should Be More Exciting With Time 32–40.
    skills 35–40.
    spiritual and emotional heights 24, 29.
    spiritual side 348.
    targeted lovemaking 367.
    techniques
        Too Hot Technique 371.
    the difference between sex and lovemaking 12.
    the love in lovemaking 12.
    the power of great lovemaking 16, 18.
    the premium women place on it 23.
    The Spiritual Side To Lovemaking 41–44.
    The Three Physical Processes 134.
    the ultimate goal 24.
    the whole lovemaking experience 204.
    through clothing or while clothed 130.
    Transcendental lovemaking 42.
    vaginal lovemaking 351.
    very shallow sex; might trigger clitoral bulb
        orgasms 213.
    Vulva Love See cocksmanship.
    what it's about 24.
    what it's all about 30.
    what not to do afterward 380.
    when you should enter her 139, 141.
    where your joy should come from 30.
    while you're driving 388.
    your best way of making love 374.
lovemaking experience; hundreds of women 6.
love of women 20.
    what makes Casanovas so successful 19.
lovers
    edgy female lovers
        Exhibitionists, Voyeurs, Sex Kittens &
            Submissives 387–389.
        safe ways to fulfill their fantasies (list) 388.
        sex kittens 389.
        submissives 389.
        voyeurs 388.
        exhibitionists 387.
lover's high 122.
Lovett, Lyle; putting Julia Roberts above him 171.
loving 144, 148, 149, 385, 389, 399, 400, 405, 407, 408, 416.
lovingly 165, 167.
loving touching 218, 257–278, 258–278, 259–278, 276–278, 278. See also sexual love touches.
    artful touch 258.
    blindfold; enhances effect of touching 399.
    butt cheeks; separating them 269.
    butterfly tapping on her clit 416.
    Clitoral Body Massage Technique 274.
    Clitoral Ring Orgasm Technique 274.
    "Come Here" G-Spot Technique 273.
    communicating love and a fascination 262.
    Covered Vulva Orgasm Techniques 267.
    cranberry twist and shake techniques 276.

loving touching (continued)
    Erotic Lip Spreading Technique 277.
    Extreme Clitoral Orgasm Techniques
        Sorrento & The Clit Shake 274.
    feather light to super strong 262.
    finger motion 269, 403.
    furtive fingerwork 265.
    great way to stimulate multiple hot spots 267.
    G-Spot Circles 273.
    G-Spot Press Technique 272.
    G-Spot Pulsations 272.
    G-Spot Wiggle Technique 273.
    Her Bottom - For Double-Penetration 269.
    Introducing the Niche Tickle Technique 270.
    Killer G-Spot Crunches 273.
    Killer U-Zone Techniques 268.
    Knock-Her-Socks-Off G-Spot Techniques 272.
    learning to use every one of your fingers 266.
    lightly rubbing the back of her neck as seduction 258.
    Loving Touching For Men In Relationships 258.
    make her come with slightest of touches 166.
    Massages Within A Relationship 259.
    massaging her hairline as seduction 258.
    More Fun With Her Pussy Lips 277.
    Multiple Erogenous Zones For Big O's 267.
    Nook Press for incredibly quick orgasms 270.
    offer of a massage to speed relationship 258.
    pace to make her come; associate with a song 262.
    Power Of Furtive Fingerwork 265.
    Pressure Point Orgasm Techniques 268-272
    sensitizing her to your touch 166.
    sexual love touches; multitude of strengths 262.
    Sexy Ways To Use Lubricants 263.
    Spread-Lips Clitoris Technique 266.
    The G-Spot Tease 273.
    The Many Kinds Of Erotic Touches 262.
    the most exciting multitasking method 269.
    The Perineal Pinch - For Quick Results 271.
    The Titillating V-Spot Massage 271.
    Vulva Orgasm Massage Techniques 267.
    Vulva Vibrations Massage Method 268.
    what is having "great hands" all about? 262.
    when you're going for her orgasm 262.
    wiggling (finger motion) 269, 270.
lubricants 134, 140, 263, 264, 271, 345.
    artificial lubricants 134, 140, 141.
    not sufficient to prep untented vagina 182, 188.
    oils; olive oil 140.
    petroleum-based; don't use inside her 140.
    quality oils 264.
    the best love touching lubricants 263.
    water-based lubricants; often dry out 140.
    what you need; lubricant dispensers 264.
    When She Needs Help Getting & Staying Wet 140.
lubrication 182, 183, 205, 206, 214, 216, 263, 275, 393.
    during oral sex with olive oil 235.
    for fast slippery lubrication 272.
    lubrication glands 352.
    slippery kind of wetness; helpful kind 271-272.
    to produce a torrent of lubrication 363.
    women with poor lubrication response 183.
Lust Doesn't Work In The Sack 56.

M

MacLaine, Shirley; on male lovers 339.
Madonna's Express Yourself 23, 51.
    lessons to be learned, for a man 51.
make her horny 265.
make her more reactive 166.
make love to her breasts 293.
making love 162, 164, 165, 168. See also lovemaking and sex.
    at its best 24.
    in public places 383.
    your best way of making love 374.
making love to her mind 150.
    motivate her to make a move 165.

making sexy sounds; as a turn-on to her   162.
male friends who'd sought author's advice   1.
males aged 18-59 years   144.
manhood   120.
Manilow, Barry; "Somewhere In The Night" lyrics   223.
manly   144, 171.
man's role   146.
manual sex   130.
Mardi Gras celebration   388.
Marina Plastic Surgery Associates (of Marina del Ray, California)   286.
marriage   34–40, 339.
   dependent upon good sex says Bette Davis   339.
married man's route   33–40.
married men   33–40.
   how they fall short   11.
   mistakes   33–40.
Mars And Venus In The Bedroom   15, 17, 59.
Martin , Chris. See Coldplay.
masculinity
   Bedazzled; scene razzing "sensitive" men   49.
   Being Handy And Helpful Is Sexy Too   51.
   easy masculine confidence   258.
   Forget about getting into your "feminine side."   49.
   Get into your masculine side!   49.
   masculine presence   148.
   masculine, to roar   165, 168.
   powerful masculine sexual energy   151.
   role models
      Sean Connery   56, 78.
      Cary Grant   56, 78.
      Sidney Poitier.   56.
   traditional sex roles; pitch in around the house she'll become a better partner   51.
massage   240, 242, 245.
   erotic massage   259, 260, 261, 263.
      how to give a great erotic massage   260.
      Rule #1 in giving a great erotic massage   260.
      Rule #2   260.
      Rule #3   261.
      Rule #4   261.
   Massages In A Relationship To Please & Learn 259.
   offer of massage; to speed along relationship   258.
   offer of a shoulder or neck massage   257.
   sensual massage   259.
   Swedish massage   259.
massagers   394.
massaging   258, 259, 261, 264, 268, 272, 274.
   breast massaging   281.
mastering control   110.
Masters and Johnson   174.
   forgot a sexual process: seduction   132.
   four-phase "human sexual response" model 131.
   misinformation: "All orgasm involves...the clitoris."   174.
   squeeze technique for premature ejaculation 100.
masturbate   388, 390, 391, 405, 406.
masturbating   99, 101, 103, 104, 107, 390, 397, 406.
   ask her to masturbate for you, for pointers   89.
   Edgy Masturbation; she for you   390.
   first rule of smart masturbation   103.
   fourth rule of smart masturbation   104.
   mastering control during masturbation 101, 110.
   Masturbation The Smart Way   102.
   onanistic pleasures with shower massager   395.
   relaxed masturbation   108.
   second rule of smart masturbation   103.
   Seinfeld "The Contest" episode   107.
   third rule of smart masturbation   103.
   wrong way; training yourself to come quickly   101.
Match.com survey   17.
mattresses   409, 410.
   new mattresses' higher surface; great for rear-entry sex (while standing up)   410.
   old mattresses that are way too bouncy bad for lovemaking   410.
   pillow-top; good for lovemaking   410.

mattresses (continued)
   "space-age"; not usually great for sex   410.
   spring in a mattress; desirable   410.
   which ones are good for lovemaking?   409.
   Why is a good mattress important?   410.
McKenna, Dr. Kevin E.   210.
mechanical sex   341, 342, 348.
media; oversexed   30.
median length of time before men come   95.
Medical Breakthroughs For Men With PE   128.
medications
   that interfere with her orgasms   178.
   that have bad sexual side-effects   36–40.
membrane   358.
memorable romantic moments   385.
men
   Becoming Type Of Man Women Desire   45.
   desirable male traits; being forgiving   54.
   example of kind of man not to be, on Shalom In The Home   61.
   grooming   70–78.
   in relationships; not getting enough sex 145.
   Lust Screws You Up   54.
   multi-orgasmic   132.
   muscular men vis a vis bedding women   144.
   uncircumcised; special hygiene needs   75.
   what it means to be a man   45.
   What You Don't Know About Hygiene & Grooming   69–78.
   who are attractive to women   21.
   who know how to seduce women   143.
   who neglect their wives   34–40.
   whose behavior is offensive   22.
   who seem to dislike women   20.
   why women are different than men   47.
menopause   280, 283, 284.
men's fashion magazines   145.
menshealth.com   161.
mental illnesses can interfere with a healthy sex life   36–40.
men who've run out of sexual ideas   40.
methyl paraben   140.
middle-aged women; a decline in lubricity   140.
middle finger 265, 266, 267, 268, 270, 272, 273, 275, 276.
milk glands; as sexual organs   280, 281, 284.
Miller and Byers   97.
mindless sex   53.
mindset   53, 56, 127.
   worst mindset   56.
mirrors; sexy uses for edgy lovemaking   388.
misinformation   174, 179, 183.
   Brunhild Kring disputes G-Spot's existence   180.
   CNN story: "The G-Spot: Is it real?"   181.
   G-Spot as a "recent discovery"   179.
   questionable study by King's College   181.
missionary position   216, 299, 304, 312, 315, 318, 328, 338, 347, 357, 373, 376.
   best for G-Spot orgasms   347.
   graphic representation; tented vagina   195.
   modified missionary   403.
   variants   315, 318, 326, 327, 403.
moaning   225, 366.
monogamy   387-389.
   comes with a price   38–40.
   creative male monogamist   387.
mons pubis   192, 193, 194, 205, 278.
morning sex   146, 149.
motion   339, 340, 341, 347, 348, 355, 364, 365, 368, 369, 370, 371, 372, 373, 374, 375, 376, 378.
   pendulum-like motion   326.
   rocking-type motion   326.
   sympathetic motion   326.
motion-inches   368, 369, 370, 373, 374, 375.
   for Deep Trigger or AFE zone orgasms   368.
   for G-Spot orgasms   348, 368, 369.
   Introducing Motion-Inches   368.
mound   193, 205, 278.
MRI study of the human anatomy during missionary position and rear-entry sex   187, 189, 212.

M Spot 8, 279, 280, 282, 283, 284, 288, 291, 292, 293.
    M Spot Massaging   291.
    M Spot Pulsations   291.
mucous-like lubrication   141.
mucous membranes in vagina   214, 377.
multi-orgasmic   132.
multiple erogenous zones 208, 267, 268, 351, 363, 367, 420.
    Covered Vulva Orgasm Techniques   267.
    mixed multiple erogenous zone area   363.
    Multiple Erogenous Zones For Big O   267.
    Vulva Orgasm Massage Techniques   267.
    Vulva Vibrations Massage Method   268.
multiple orgasms 5, 9, 36-40, 94, 268, 272, 342, 351, 363, 367, 375-377.
    powerful and rapid-fire multiple orgasms   272.
multiple orgasm triggers   179, 363.
    study that proves existence of   179.
Multiple Spots = Bigger Orgasms   206.
multitasking   130, 208, 245, 267, 269, 288, 322.
    great way to stimulate multiple hot spots   267.
    most exciting multitasking method ever   269.
muscles   224, 225.
    contractions   137, 224.
        vaginal walls, pelvis, anus, uterus   137.
    spasms   137.
myth that the vaginal orgasm was a falsehood   174.

N

nails; why trim them   75.
naked   148, 149, 152, 163, 164, 167, 242, 256, 384, 385, 387, 388, 389, 399, 400, 405, 406.
naked men; as a turn-on to your lover   389.
nakedness   170.
naked women   104, 108.
nape of neck   221.
narcissism; does not make for great lovers   416.
National Health and Nutrition Examination Survey   144.
naughty   389, 411, 414.
neck   166, 229, 243, 330, 366, 403.
    massage   257.
neglect   34–40.
    a big sexual turn-off   22.
    as cause for women to end relationships   62.
nerve endings
    in her clit, lips and vulva   232.
    in your frenulum (aka "Trigger")   101.
    unexplored   29.
nerves   179, 196, 198, 199, 202, 203, 208, 209, 210, 213, 214, 280, 282, 286, 294, 341, 345, 346, 347, 359, 363, 364, 365, 368, 375, 392, 399.
    fatigue   336, 364.
    hypogastric nerve   179.
    in breasts   280, 282, 286, 294.
    injured by breast reduction procedures   286.
    nerve input   399.
    nerve sensitivity   398.
    pelvic nerve   179.
    pudendal nerve   179.
    sexual nerves   262, 368.
    Shallow Sweet Place; two kinds of nerves visceral and somatic   363.
    thoracic intercostal nerves   179.
    vaginal nerves   208, 346.
nervous system   135.
neuron activation   294.
neuroscientists   128.
neurotransmitters   135.
never gush   170.
never make it seem she's above you   170.
New Discoveries On Sexual Positions   338.
Nexus   194, 371.
    graphic   194, 195, 203, 213, 216, 217.
Niche   8, 177, 192, 193, 194, 198, 245, 267, 268, 269, 270, 351, 352, 354, 355, 356, 357, 358, 375, 420.
    graphic representation   177, 192, 193, 194, 198.

Niche (continued)
    Introducing the Niche Tickle Technique   270.
    Niche orgasms   198.
    Niche to Nook Technique; illustration   354.
Nicks, Stevie; on "lousy lovers"   168.
nipples   30, 103, 107, 116, 126, 136, 137, 139, 245, 261, 263, 279, 280, 281, 282, 283, 284, 286, 287, 288, 289, 290, 291, 292, 293, 294, 322, 330, 366, 392, 404.
    after reduction operations; less sensitive   286.
    as orgasm trigger; proven by study 179, 220, 221.
    during breast reduction procedure; separated from milk ducts   286.
    erect   280.
    Her Nipples As Special Case Orgasm Triggers   220.
    Nipple Circles   291.
    nipple clips and clamps; as sex toys   395.
    Nipple or M Spot Clamping   291.
    Nipple Pulls   292.
    Nipple Pulsations   291.
    nipple sensitivity   284, 286.
    Nipple Shakes   292.
    Nipple Twists   291.
    teasing her nipples through clothing   292.
    What Can Make Breasts Less Sensitive?   283.
    Which Nipple Is Most Sensitive?   290.
non-clitoral orgasms   175.
non-clitoral orgasm triggers
    AFE zone   178, 183, 203, 215, 216.
    breast-induced   178.
    Nook 177, 178, 192, 193, 194, 198, 199, 208, 213.
    perineal sponge   178, 184, 198, 199, 208.
    scientifically identified centuries ago   175.
    vaginal ball   178, 199, 200, 203, 206, 208, 214.
    vaginal ring   178, 203, 214, 215.
    voice-induced orgasms   178.
    V-Spot   177, 178, 192, 193, 194, 198, 199, 208.
non-intercourse sexual activities   129, 130.
non-visual sensory stimuli   399.
Nook   8, 177, 178, 192, 193, 194, 198, 199, 208, 213, 245, 270, 271, 352, 272, 354, 356, 357, 358, 361, 363, 375.
    graphic representation   192.
    Nook Press technique; for quick orgasm   270.
norepinephrine   122.
North by Northwest; seduction scene   150.
Northwestern University Medical School   210.
nucleus accumbens   135.
nude; partially-nude   403.
nude beaches as edgy lovemaking locations   388.
nudity   132, 134, 153, 154, 389.
    using it to seduce her   148, 149, 152.
nymphomaniacs   126.

O

obsession   408.
O Calcutta   295.
O'Connell, Helen
    made many aware of true size of clitoris   201.
    study includes warning on pelvic surgery's threat to clitoris   202.
    study on anatomy of clitoris   202.
    theories on clitoral bulbs   213.
office desk as a location for making love   414.
oils   263, 264, 275.
    as lubricants   140.
    quality oils   264.
    that heat up; warning on their use   395.
olive oil   159.
    as natural lubricant   140.
    as oral sex lubricant   235.
onanistic pleasures   395.
one-night-stand   34–40.
one of the sexiest songs ever   143.
oral sex (for *her*)   113, 130, 231–256, 384.
    69 position   241.
    alarm clock, to prolong the tease   247.

oral sex - for her (continued)
 approaches to try, clit and stem together 252.
 as diversion to keep from coming too soon 113.
 ask her to kneel on the floor 405.
 Bad Odor 238.
 big, bushy beard; gave wife leg burns 231.
 Butterfly-Light Vulva Tongue Technique 250.
 Clitoral Sensitivity And Over Doing It 234
 Clit Stemming 252.
 Communicate Some Excitement 236.
 don't make her clit sore! 235.
 Ecstasy Clitoris Stem Technique 252.
 Ecstasy Vulva Technique 252, 254.
 female grievance 233.
 flattened top of your tongue 240.
 Flutter-Tonguing 249.
 for her whole body 243.
 giving her a show and a feel 244.
 Good Lovers Use Drama 247.
 G-Spot; stimulating with tongue 240.
 Hands-Free Clit Exposer 245.
 have her "sit on your face" 242.
 how to make her come faster and harder 232.
 it's all about nonverbal communication 236.
 It's A Two-Step Process 248.
 Knock-Her-Socks-Off Head 252.
 location counts 255.
 men who are in rush to get to penetration 233.
 novel oral sex technique 231.
 one thing men get wrong 233.
 one-way strokes 251.
 Oral Sex That Will Drive Her Wild 231–256.
 path your tongue takes 244.
 penetrating her with your fingers 242.
 places to tease 234.
 Play With Her Mind 249.
 Pulsar Tongue Technique 251.
 pussy lips 240, 247.
 range of skin covered 244.
 requires understanding of female anatomy 247.
 rub, tickle, pinch, stretch, pull, massage, outline, knead, hold, touch and shake 242.
 saliva; as oral sex lubricant 235.
 scratchy tongue work 235.
 Sex and the City episode
  importance of being good at oral sex 233.
 69 position for oral sex 241.
 skin 243.
 Stretching Her Pussy Lips Open 232.
 technique; you usually want to start small 232.
 The Cunnilingus Artist's "Palette" 240.
 The Thrill of Surprise 255.
 thoughts, emotions; what to communicate 236.
 tongue baths 229.
 tongue patterns 245.
 tongue tip; use during oral sex 240.
 tonguing her bottom 256.
 Turn Off The Clock 237.
 two more common complaints 234.
 Using A Mantra 251.
 U-Spot 240.
 vaginal canal, with tongue 245.
 vary a range of factors 244.
 vulva approach 247.
 wetter the better 235.
 What Are You Communicating? 234.
 What If She Doesn't Like Direct Stimulation 246.
 what women smell like "down there" 238.
 When To Do It 255.
 with or without exposing clit 244.
orbitofrontal cortex 135, 138.
orgasms 35, 40, 94, 96, 100, 101, 104, 106, 107, 109, 112, 113, 121, 122, 123, 124, 131, 224, 225, 232, 234, 244, 246, 249, 254, 262, 264, 265, 266, 267, 268, 269, 270, 271, 272, 275, 277, 278, 279, 280, 282, 288, 294, 304, 322, 328, 330, 332, 335, 338, 351, 355, 359, 360, 361, 363, 364, 367, 368, 372, 373, 375, 376, 377, 392, 415.

orgasms (continued)
 AFE orgasms
  couch positions great for 414.
  motion-inches to produce 368, 376.
 anal beads; to make her orgasm bigger 406.
 anal sex orgasms
  orgasm trigger is being debated 219.
 A Toy For Double Penetration 394.
 bigger orgasms 267, 269.
 biological events during a climax 85.
 breast-induced orgasms 5, 279, 280, 282, 288.
  How To Give Breast-Induced Orgasms 290.
  Rutgers University study validates 294.
  breast-triggered vaginal, uterine or clitoral orgasms 282.
 brought on by vocal suggestions
  30-year-old actress experienced one 161.
  ear canal is sensitive to vibration 161.
  Eastern proof it's possible to have an orgasm just from sound 161.
  trained to come to vocal command 161.
  woman had orgasm listening to my voice 161.
 caused by tension in your sphincter 112.
 cervical orgasms; existence proven by Rutgers scientific study 179.
 Choosing The Right Rhythm And Intensity To Make Her Come 372.
 Clitoral Body Massage Technique 274.
 Clitoral Ring Orgasm Technique 274.
 cranberry twist and shake techniques 276.
 Deep Trigger orgasms 368, 370, 371, 372, 376.
 entry-only orgasms 361.
 exotic orgasms 5.
 Extreme Clitoral Orgasm Techniques 274.
 genital orgasms 350.
 great lovers give women more orgasms 40.
 G-Spot orgasms 347, 375.
  and motion inches 348, 368, 369.
  missionary position best 347.
  techniques 272, 273.
 huge orgasms 265, 274.
 Is She Faking It? 79–92.
 many kinds
  "It's amazing how many kinds of orgasms you've produced in me!" 175.
 multi-orgasmic 132.
  most women are 222.
 multiple orgasms 5, 9, 94, 268, 272.
  Giving Her Multiple Orgasms 342, 375.
 Multiple Spots = Bigger Orgasms 206.
 muscle spasms 137.
 muscular contractions
  contraction rate during her orgasm 137.
  vaginal walls, pelvis, anus, uterus 137.
 Niche orgasms 198.
 non-clitoral orgasms 175.
 orgasm boosters 8, 161, 185, 217, 221, 267, 278, 292.
 Orgasmic Mind 154.
 orgasm process 141.
 orgasm simulations 85.
 orgasm size varies 203.
 oxytocin; brain-produced, role in orgasm 122.
 pace to make her come; associate with song 262.
 Perineal Pinch technique; for female ejaculation and orgasms in seconds 271.
 powerful and rapid-fire multiple orgasms 272.
 powerful orgasm 360.
 pressure point orgasms 268-272
 quickest and sloppy-wettest of orgasms 270.
 quick orgasm 356.
  can be shallow and unsatisfying 360.
 Reaching Her Orgasmic Potential 222.
 rear-entry sex; might produce biggest orgasm 212.
 recovery period 85.
 repeat orgasms 217.
 telltale sign with breast reduction 137.
 the hotter she gets, the bigger her orgasm 344.
 there are many types, of differing sizes 40.

430

orgasms (continued)
   through seductive suggestion alone   133.
   union-only orgasm   367.
   vaginal 174, 177, 178, 208, 209, 212, 215, 219.
   vary per lovemaking location   381, 382.
   vary greatly in size, quality and duration   141.
   very biggest orgasms   269.
   very shallow sex; might trigger clitoral bulbs 213.
   V-Spot orgasms   199.
   vulval orgasms   178.
   Windshield Wiper Orgasm Technique
      352, 355.
   with only shallow penetration   9.
   without clitoral stimulation   9.
   with the slightest of touches or penetration   8.
   with vibrators; making them bigger   392.
orgasm trigger complexes   208, 267.
orgasm triggers 5, 8, 29, 40, 101, 106, 134, 141, 161, 173, 174, 175, 177, 178, 179, 184, 186, 187, 197, 202, 203, 204, 206, 208, 212, 213, 215, 219, 221, 222, 246, 267, 268, 271, 272, 279, 280, 292.
   AFE zone   178, 183, 203, 215, 216.
   alleged anal orgasm trigger   219.
   breasts   178.
      M Spot 8, 279, 280, 282, 283, 284, 288, 291, 292, 293.
   cul-de-sac   219.
   deep orgasm triggers   215.
   deep spot   219.
   epicenter   219.
   exact location is moot   217.
   Introducing Her Deep Trigger And Nexus 216.
   Introducing New Orgasm Triggers
      Deep Trigger, Nexus, Fornix, Nook 194.
   Introducing Special Case Orgasm triggers 186.
   multiple orgasm trigger   363.
   Nook 177, 178, 192, 193, 194, 198, 199, 208, 213.
   orgasm trigger complexes   208.
   orgasm trigger locations; exact?   213.
   perineal sponge   178, 184, 198, 199, 208.
   posterior wall of the vagina; has most reactive
      orgasm trigger   210, 212, 213.
   Pouch of Douglas (recto-uterine excavation) 219.
   special case orgasm triggers 186, 198, 199, 206, 220.
      vaginal ball   272.
   vaginal ball 178, 199, 200, 203, 206, 208, 214, 272.
   vaginal ring   178, 203, 214, 215.
   voice-induced orgasms   178.
   V-Spot 177, 178, 192, 193, 194, 198, 199, 208.
   women have many   177.
ottomans; as a location for making love   413.
outdoor sex   140.
ovaries   194.
Over-The-Top Seductions   148.
Ovid   1, 123, 127.
oxytocin   122, 293, 294.
oxytocinergic neurons   294.

P

pace 262, 269, 270, 273, 274, 276, 352, 355, 356, 358, 359, 360, 364, 374.
pain   389, 395, 400, 402, 407, 408.
palm   261, 265, 267, 278.
panties   393, 400.
   as bondage toy   400, 403.
pantyhose   398, 403, 404, 405.
   as bondage toy   403.
Pappalardi, Felix; example of how not to be   408.
paracentral lobule   294.
paracentral lobule neurons   294.
pars intermedia   202.
passenger seat of your car as location to make love   384.
passion   22, 30, 32-40, 59, 133, 134, 143, 151, 166, 169, 170, 262, 342, 348, 361, 377.
   need for   28.
   women want   50.

Patrick, Donald L.   95, 96, 97.
Pauls, Dr. Rachel   209, 210.
Pause Method   114.
pauses   355, 376.
Pavlov's bell   385.
PDE-V inhibitors   128.
Pelvic Floor Institute, Graduate Hospital in Philadelphia 293.
pelvic nerve   179.
pelvic surgery; threat to clitoris' integrity   202.
penetration 115, 116, 124, 130, 139, 140, 141, 175, 188, 197, 202, 213, 214, 230, 267, 269, 272, 273, 278, 299, 309, 312, 319, 328, 331, 332, 333, 335, 336, 338.
   cocksmanship; don't need to go deeply   341.
   complete penetration; value of delaying   343.
   Creating Expectations   359.
   deep penetration; don't do until she's tented 214.
   each millimeter of penetration   346.
   measured penetration   367.
   orgasms produced by   175, 188, 197, 202, 213, 214.
   requires wetness   134.
   wetness and lubrication issues   139, 140, 141.
   when you should enter her   139, 141.
penis 9, 15, 77, 100, 102, 106, 113, 117, 136, 154, 157, 159, 166, 167, 168, 187, 188, 189, 190, 191, 196, 199, 201, 202, 204, 210, 215, 230, 234, 244, 252, 267, 268, 269, 273, 304, 309, 313, 336, 338, 393, 394, 395, 406, 414. (Includes "cock.") *See also* cocksmanship.
   as cause of control problems   100.
   blood vessels   345.
   boomerang-shaped during sex, MRI study   338.
   components when hard 344, 345, 346, 352, 357, 361.
   coronal ridge   101.
   corpora cavernosa illustration   346.
   Cowper's gland   106.
   erection; to make your erection bigger   105.
   frenulum; as source of control problems   100, 101.
   glans   105, 106.
   nerves   103, 115.
   origin in fetus   190.
   pre-ejaculate   106.
   some cannot produce vaginal orgasms?   175.
   shaft   140.
   to express how you feel   348.
   Warning: A Penis Can Be Broken   313.
   what makes it hard 340-348, 352, 355, 356, 357, 360, 366.
   you reach different places inside her with front and rear entry says MRI study   338.
Penthouse   404.
perineal sponge 177, 178, 184, 192, 193, 198, 199, 208, 271, 272.
   graphic representation   177, 192, 193, 198.
   Perineal Pinch technique; for female ejaculation and orgasms in seconds   271.
perineum   76, 193, 240, 245, 271.
Perry, John D.   179.
petroleum-based lubricants   393
   destroy latex   140.
   warning: don't use inside her   140.
pharmaceutical companies; medicines for PE   128.
phenylethylamine   122.
phobias that can hurt a woman sexually   36–40.
Phone Sex   162.
physical problems can hurt a woman sexually 36–40.
physicians   140.
physiologists   198.
pillows   402, 413.
pinch   242.
pinky   265, 266, 268.
pituitary gland   135.
Plant, Robert   98.
   advocate of lengthy lovemaking   343.
   role model as a lover, confidence in lyrics   343.
plateau effect   262, 263, 364, 392.
   plateau scale   365, 368.
      After Orgasm: How Plateau Scale Works 367.
   nerves dulled somewhat by her first orgasm 368.
platform beds   411.
Playboy Reader Sex Survey, faking orgasms   81.

playfulness   144, 146, 150, 152, 401, 405, 407.
Play Her Like An Instrument   223–226.
pleasures   163, 168, 394.
    erotic pleasures   406.
    more intense with bondage   402.
    of being entered   197.
    pleasure zones   184, 185, 197, 204, 221, 345, 367.
politically-motivated "clitoromania"   174.
pools to make love; drawbacks   385.
poor lovemaking   38–40. See also bad sex.
porno; for the lover who's a voyeur   389.
positions   295–338.
    Art of Changing Positions   334.
    Attitudes   304.
    basic principles   296.
    best ones for men with premature ejaculation   333.
    Contrary Positions   309.
    cozy-type positions   315.
    depth   309, 330, 331, 332.
    doggy-style   328.
    entry angles   403.
    Entry Choices   302.
    ergonomic positions   326, 327.
    Examples Of Artful Position Changes   337.
    Examples Of Attitude Choices   307.
    Examples Of "Being Taken" Positions   325.
    Examples Of Entry Choices   306.
    Examples Of Full Frontal Positions   310.
    Examples Of Hot Spot-Specific Positions   319.
    Examples Of In-Line Positions   308.
    Examples Of Position Variants   314.
    Examples Of Romantic Positions   316.
    feng shui of it   299.
    finding ones that work for your body types   299.
    front entry   403.
        where penis arrives inside her   338.
        position facilitated by modern beds   411.
    How Many Positions Are Enough?   302.
    How To Use Her Favorite Positions   332.
    How, When & Why Of Position Changing   334, 335.
    In-line Positions   305.
    It's All About Her   297.
    lying on her side   403.
    missionary   299, 304, 312, 315, 318, 328, 338.
        variant   315, 318, 326, 327, 403.
    Nerve Fatigue   336.
    New Discoveries On Sexual Positions   338.
    not the be-all and end-all of lovemaking   296.
    novel and fun positions for the couch   414.
    pendulum-like motion   326.
    Position Myths   298.
    Position Types   302.
    propulsion   327.
    rear-entry positions   299, 304, 305, 318, 319,
        327, 338, 402, 403, 406.
        where penis arrives inside her   338.
    Reasons To Choose A Position   315.
        Because it's one of her favorites   332.
        For her desire to feel she's being taken   323.
        For the ability to multi-task   322.
        For the depth you can achieve   331.
        For your ease in making her come   328.
        For the special moves you can do   330.
        For the speed you can achieve   320.
        For the unique propulsion options   326.
        For the way it makes her feel   327.
        Other Reasons   333.
        To fulfill her desire for romance   315.
        To massage specific areas   318.
    rocking-chair positions   327.
    romantic positions   317.
    sideways positions   318, 403.
        best in maintaining control   115.
    sitting up on your knees   403.
    spooning position   415, 416.
    standing positions   376, 403.
        facilitated by modern beds   411.
    sympathetic motion   326.

positions (continued)
    Three Best Positions For Deep Vaginal Orgasms   329.
    vaginal canal shortening positions (VCS)   331, 332.
    Warning: A Penis Can Be Broken   313.
    wheelbarrow position   326.
    with big-bottomed woman   299.
    woman-on-top positions   116, 309, 312.
Posterior fornix   194.
posterior wall of the vagina   210, 212, 213.
    has most reactive orgasm trigger   210, 212, 213.
    posterior wall orgasms   338.
Pouch of Douglas   219.
Pounders   339.
Precision Lovemaking   371.
pre-ejaculate   106.
pre-intercourse activities   129, 130.
premature ejaculation   333. See also control.
    Advances in Treatment   128.
    a problem especially among younger men   95.
    as cause of a divorce   4.
    causes
        celibacy   111.
        control problems we all confront   118.
        frenulum responsible for "hair trigger"   101.
        getting yourself overheated   121.
        Glamour magazine   107.
        her sexy body   110.
        Her sexy reactions   110.
        Looking at women lustfully   55.
        masturbating the wrong way   101.
        orgasmic thoughts   106.
        peekaboo clothes   119.
        putting on a condom   111.
        sexually provocative stimuli   104.
        tension in your sphincter muscle   112.
        two organs that often cause problems   100.
        vaginal heat, tightness, and wetness   110.
        woman-on-top positions   116.
    famous bon vivant and playboy might have it   2.
    scientific study: groups: temporary, dysfunction   99.
    singer-songwriter suffering from   2.
    solutions
        Affirmations & Visualizations   120.
        attitude adjustment   118.
        Big As You Can Get Game   105.
        choosing safe rhythm, intensity, motion   115.
        Clear Fluid Game   106.
        control excitement in your head   120.
        dealing with "Oh no!" moments   110-111.
        defeat your automatic response syndrome   108.
        Desensitization Exercise   108.
        don't be goal-oriented   121.
        exercises   100-114.
        lidocain- and prilocain-containing creams
            may help delay ejaculation   128.
        Long Self-Tease Exercise   104.
        Medical Breakthroughs   128.
        Pause Method   114.
        Positions That Enable You To Last   115.
        power of your mind   105.
        Short Diversion Method   113.
        slow masturbation exercise   108.
        Sphincter Relaxation Technique   112.
        Stay Within Yourself   114.
        Surviving The Big Teasers   116.
        Take Back The Power   118.
        tame your Trigger   101.
        Think Of Something Not Sexy   124.
        Think Of The Mechanics   124.
        Tune Out Her Reactions   123.
        tuning out the negative voices   121.
        willpower   109.
    stopwatch studies   95.
    study by researchers Miller and Byers   95, 97, 104.
    study by sex therapists Corty and Guardiani   97.
    University of Washington study (Patrick)   95, 96, 97.
    Y Tu Mama Tambien; on bad masturbation and
        control problems   102.

pressure   355, 366, 368, 370.
    what works on her Deep Trigger   368.
Pressure Point Orgasm Techniques 268-272
Pretenders; lyrics show way to tease   276.
primal desire   399.
private secret naughty places   414.
prolonged sex   107.
propulsion   410. *See also* motion.
prostate; homologous to her G-Spot   180, 190, 207, 215.
psyche of women   64, 349.
psychological component   399, 407.
pubic bone   395.
pubic hair   76.
public places as locations to make love   383, 388.
pudendal nerve   179.
pulling   235, 241, 242, 245, 246, 247, 251, 252, 253, 256, 265, 266, 271.
Pulsar Tongue Technique   251.
pussy   233, 266, 385, 395, 404, 405, 406, 414.
    See also vagina.
    lips   232, 240, 247, 253, 254, 256, 266.
    during oral sex   240.
    More Fun With Her Pussy Lips   277.
Pussy Shaving   404.

Q

qualifications (author's)
    anatomical and sexual discoveries   8.
    facilitated a successful marriage   5.
    feedback from lovers *See* feedback (under "F")
    hands-on experimentation   6.
    Helped So Many Others   3-5.
    identification of orgasm and wetness triggers, erogenous zones and orgasm boosters never before documented   8.
    decades of hands-on experience and secrets   6, 10.
    informal but intense scientific studies   6, 8.
    invented shallow techniques so men of all sizes can give women vaginal orgasms   9.
    lovemaking experience; hundreds of women   6.
    no long-term lover has ever left   10.
    practical experiments with scores of lovers   8.
    sexological breakthroughs   8.
    the guy everyone turns to for sexual help   4.
    university-trained in biological research   8.
    unofficial sex, romance and relationship counselor   4.
    what he's achieved as a lover and researcher   3.
    what makes him qualified to write a book   3.

R

radical feminists; sexual disinformation   174, 175.
Rambam Medical Center (Israel)   211.
range of motion   114, 115, 116, 124, 262, 276, 340, 341, 372.
rash, sexual   137, 141, 225.
Reaching Her Orgasmic Potential   222.
reaching your sexual potential   9.
Real Sex   390.
rear entry   299, 304, 305, 318, 319, 322, 327, 329, 338, 370, 371, 395.
    graphic representation; tented vagina   195.
    kitchen counters good for this   413.
    might produce biggest orgasms   212, 217.
    some mattresses are great in aiding this   411.
    using a vibrator for double-penetration   395.
reassurance   170, 401.
recto-uterine excavation   219.
Rectum   194. *See also* anal canal.
Reiser, Paul; on sex in marriage   31.
relationships
    break-ups: causes
        man fell short as a man   26.
        man was a lousy lover   26.
        true story: a lack of *lovemaking*   27.
    Massages In A Relationship To Please & Learn   259.
    require chemistry   14.

relinquishing control; as a role-playing turn-on   387.
researchers Korda, Goldstein and Sommer   42.
rhythm   115, 232, 234, 240, 244, 245, 248, 249, 251, 266, 268, 269, 271, 341, 355, 358, 372, 373, 374, 375, 376, 378.
    pulsating   273.
    regular   273.
    to make her come   262, 270, 273.
    vis a vis oral sex   244.
right moves   147.
right timing   151.
right woman   30.
ring finger   268.
risk of infection   269.
risky thrills   266, 383.
robe   261, 264, 406, 407.
robe belt   406.
    as a sex toy   406.
rocking-chair positions   327.
rocking-type motion   326.
role playing   389, 399, 404, 405.
romance   1, 3, 4, 12, 13, 14, 16, 21, 33–40, 59–68, 366.
    acts that produce a feeling of closeness   59.
    An Essential Everyday Act: Affection   60.
    as a lifestyle   61.
    Commit Random Acts Of Affection   67.
    five most romantic things to do in bed   68.
    is a necessary precursor to lovemaking   59.
    list of romantic things to do for her   63.
    most women hard-wired for the romantic   22.
    "old fashioned" romantic relationships women want them   21.
    Print Ritter (Robert Duvall) view on it in the movie *Broken Trail*   41.
    Togetherness Is Where It's At   66.
    "woman wants to be the center of...attention."   22.
Romance novels   33–40, 119.
    represent a deep-seated desire   49.
    Romance novel hero
        knows how to seduce, romance, make love   50.
        manly, sensual and sexual presence   50.
        women will measure you against   50.
    warning: they're programming women   50.
    why they're so popular among women   49.
romantic   114, 144, 151, 154, 340, 367, 382, 384, 385, 389, 394, 399, 400, 409, 411, 413, 415.
Romeos   33–40.
    secret that makes them successful   21.
ropes; stay away from   398.
Ross, Carlin   279, 283.
    women are stimulated by sexy visuals   155.
Ross, Dr. Rachael   279, 283.
    says larger breasts have less sensitivity   284.
Rutgers University, sexual studies   178, 203, 294.

S

sadomasochism   399, 407.
saliva   134, 140, 141, 263.
    as oral sex lubricant   235.
San Francisco Plastic Surgery And Laser Center
    about risks of breast surgery   286.
scars; due to breast procedures   286.
scarves; as sex toys   398, 401, 403.
scenarios   387, 389, 399, 402.
schlump   145.
Scientific American; "The Orgasmic Mind"   154.
scientific sexual studies   10.
    on anatomy of clitoris
        O'Connell: internal structure quite big   202.
    on arousal by visual stimuli
        Psychologist Meredith Chivers of Toronto's Center for Addiction and Mental Health proves women are aroused by sexual visual stimuli   154.

scientific sexual studies (continued)
    on breast-induced orgasms
        Rutgers University fMRI (Barry Komisaruk) validates breast-induced orgasms   294.
    on breast sensitivity after breast reduction
        University of Brussels (Hamdi, Greuse, De Mey, and Webster)
            sensitivity is harmed   286.
    on breast size and sensitivity
        University of Vienna (Tairych, Kuzbari, Rigel, Todoroff, Schneider, Deutinger)
            inverse relationship between breast size and sensitivity 283.
        Johns Hopkins Medical Center
            bigger breasts have less sensitivity 284.
    on breast stimulation
        University of Pisa
            makes woman feel more loving and bonded to you   293.
    on differences in male and female brains
        Center for the Neurobiology of Learning and Memory (U. California)   47.
        Harvard Medical School study   47.
    on female ejaculation
        Austrian urologist Florian Wimpissinger
            female ejaculate is not urine   207.
        researchers Korda, Goldstein, Sommer
            "History of Female Ejaculation" 42.
            female ejaculation known centuries ago 181.
    on G-Spot
        King's College London disputes existence 181.
    on how long men last during vaginal sex
        Netherlands' Marcel Waldinger
            5.4 minute median time   95.
    on how long sex should last
        sex therapists Corty and Guardiani
            define how long is "too short," "adequate" and "too long"   97.
    on how long women want sex to last
        Canadian researchers S. Andrea Miller and E. Sandra Byers   95, 97, 104.
    on men - what kind women sleep with most   144.
        by William Lassek (of the University of Pittsburgh) and Steven Gaulin (of the University of California, Santa Barbara)
    on multiple orgasm triggers
        Rutgers University fMRI (Barry Komisaruk)
            gives credence to orgasm triggers in her vaginal walls, cervix area, nipples 179.
    on neurophysiology of female sexual function
        Northwestern University Medical School Professor Dr. Kevin E. McKenna
            "a field...in its infancy" 210.
    on penis - where it winds up inside her in front- and rear-entry positions
        CMC Beausoleil MRI study 187, 212.
            suggests there are two types of vaginal orgasms 212, 338.
    on premature ejaculation
        Recent Scientific Studies Offer Hope 128.
        University of Washington (Donald Patrick) stopwatch study   95, 96, 97.
    on vaginal orgasms
        University of Amsterdam (Stuart Brody)
            proved vaginal orgasms occur   178.
        Dr. Rachel Pauls of Cincinnati's Good Samaritan Hospital
            validates vaginal orgasms 409-410
        Caldas University Manizales (Heli Alzate)
            confirms existence, believes triggered by anterior wall not G-Spot   211.
        various vaginal erotic sensitivity studies
            confirm vaginal orgasm but do not locate exact location of trigger 209.
        Israel's Rambam Medical Center (Zwi Hoch)
            validates; anterior wall is trigger   211.

scientific sexual studies (continued)
    on vaginal walls' sensitivity/ennervation
        Hilleges, Falconer, Ekmon-Orderberg, & Johanson
            anterior wall most reactive   210
        Dr. Rachel Pauls of Cincinnati's Good Samaritan Hospital
            nerves evenly distributed 409-410
            validates vaginal orgasms 409-410
    on women's brains during orgasms
        Gert Holstege and colleagues at University of Groningen (Netherlands) 137.
scientists 8, 10, 13, 173, 178, 182, 183, 184, 198, 202, 207, 208, 209, 213, 215, 349, 399.
scrotum   76, 186, 190, 191, 196, 395.
Sean Connery as masculine role model   56, 78.
sea water; location to make love, drawbacks 385.
sebaceous glands   280.
second widening event   377.
secret designations women use to rate men   12.
seduction 131, 132, 133, 134, 136, 143–152, 385.
    acceptable teaser   150.
    Casual Seductions   151.
    charm her   150.
    create intense and impatient desire   151.
    creates desire, an essential element   132.
    examples   152, 164.
    Excite Her With Sexy Visuals   153–160.
    Feeler-Outer Talking Tease Line   164.
    form of making love, in and of itself   133.
    how to seduce when in a relationship   143.
    how to make your lover wet, aroused, horny 162.
    how to get her in the mood   133, 146.
    how to seduce your lover   146.
    lightly rubbing back of a woman's neck   258.
    making love to her mind   150.
        the first essential sexual deed   133.
    massaging a woman's hairline   258.
    "Nice necklace!" seduction   258.
    one that was ruined by bugs at the beach   385.
    Peek-a-boo Seductions In Relationships   149.
    plausible denial   152.
    pre-sex kissing   229.
    provoke interest   150.
    Quick-Acting Seductions   151.
    seduce without seducing   152.
    Seduction Lesson #1: Dress seductively   145.
    Seduction Lesson #2: Make things happen 145.
    Seduction Lesson #3: Sneak attacks   146.
    Seduction Lesson #4: seducing the first time 147.
    Seduction Lesson #5: Over-The-Top   148.
    Seduction Lesson #6: using nudity   149.
    Seduction Lesson #7: Using words   149.
    Seduction Lesson #8: a sexy influence   151.
    Seduction Lesson #9: Stripping her   151.
    Seduction Lesson #10: keep her on simmer 151.
    Seduction Lesson #11: Take her places   152.
    Seduction Lesson #12: Playful seductions. 152.
    seduction scene in North by Northwest
        lesson on how to seduce a woman   150.
    Sexy "Welcome Home" Scenario   157.
    slow-acting seduction by suggestion   149.
    verbal seductions   146.
    with sexy artwork   158.
seduction process   132, 133, 134, 136.
seductresses   118.
Seinfeld   107, 108.
    Elaine tells Jerry she faked her orgasms   79.
    George isn't confident "below the equator" 173.
    sex begins "with the appearance of the nipple" 132.
    The Contest (masturbation episode)   107.
semen 346.
sensations   347, 349, 351, 363, 364, 394, 399.
    and lovemaking location   382.
senses; more vivid with bondage   398, 399, 402.
sensitivity 262, 269, 282, 283, 284, 285, 286, 287, 288, 290, 291, 292, 398, 399, 403.
sensitivity scale   283.

434

sensitizing her   166, 264, 272, 342, 365.
sensual   29, 144, 145, 149, 151, 387, 398, 399, 400.
sensual clothing   145.
sensual massage   259.
sertraline   128.
sex   31–40, 387, 390, 393, 395, 400, 404.
   attitudes on talking about   1.
   bad sex   129.
   Can You Have Too Much Sex?   96.
   does not have to include clitoris   204.
   Fingerwork During Sex   266.
   good sex   129.
   mindless sex: boring   53.
   non-intercourse sexual activities   129.
   pre-intercourse activities   129.
   prolonged sex   107.
   sexually unsatisfied Hamptons crowd   3.
   sexual secrets   6.
   sexual unhappiness   2.
   Sex Vs. Lovemaking   12, 23, 23–30.
      purely physical sex an empty experience   28.
   shallow sex   *See* cocksmanship
   through clothing or while clothed   130.
   while you're driving   388.
   without an orgasm   131.
Sex and The City
   Samantha: most men are lousy lovers   339.
   Samantha leaves lousy lover   17.
   Samatha's lover has a small penis; Charlotte:
      How's he with his tongue?
      importance of being good at oral sex   233.
sex education, author's, as a kid.
   Earle became a mentor   7.
   father's advice: "You get a tickle."   7.
   friend's father had trove of sex manuals   7.
   sexy newspaper   7.
sexiest movie   154.
sex in public places   388.
sex kittens   118, 389.
Sex Machine   98.
sex manuals   174, 182.
sex museums; as turn-on for voyeurs   389.
sexological breakthroughs author made   8.
sexologists   30, 283.
sex-positive feminist Carlin Ross   155.
sex servant   389, 404, 405, 406.
sex "slave"   389, 405.
   woman who was one for six months   161, 407.
sex surveys
   11% would give up a kidney for great sex   17.
   ABC News American Sex Survey   18.
   Indiana University's National Survey of Sexual
      Health and Behavior   80.
   Match.com survey   17.
   online poll by Dr. Keith Ablow   96.
   Playboy Reader Sex Survey   81.
sex toys   390–398.
   anal beads   406.
   as an adjunct to your lovemaking   390.
   bathroom sex toys   395.
   chains   400.
   cock rings   395.
   For Double Penetration   394.
   fuzzy handcuffs   398.
   G-Spot vibrators   393.
   handheld mirror   388.
   massagers   394.
   nipple clips and clamps   395.
   scarves   398, 401, 403.
   shower massager   395.
   spout of your bathtub   397.
   swings   406.
   toy handcuffs   400, 403.
   using an alarm clock to tease   165.
   vibrating "eggs"   393.
   water jets   397.
   Where To Find Sex Toys   393.
sexual bondage; definition   387.

sexual continuum   132.
sexual Dark Ages   173.
sexual discovery   279.
sexual education, need for   37–40.
sexual energy   151.
sexual entrances   196, 348, 349.
   emotional, psychological, spiritual significance   197.
   should be treated specially   197.
sexual excitement that fizzles out   31–40.
sexual information; not happily passed along   6.
sexuality issues   180.
sexualizing her   264, 390.
sexual love touches to make her come   262.
sexually reactive areas   213.
sexual nerves   173, 262, 368.
   dulled somewhat by her first orgasm   368.
sexual experience to get closer to God   42.
sexual potential   36–40, 162.
sexual power   162, 227, 278.
sexual problems.
   married man's route   33–40.
   older men not attracted to women their age   30.
   premature ejaculation
      See premature ejaculation (under "P")
   running out of sexual ideas   40.
   sex losing its spark over time   31–40.
   that lead to relationship disasters   2.
   Women Who Pose Challenges   36–40.
sexual roles
   man's role   146.
   sexual role confusion   49.
   traditional female role   120.
   traditional sexual roles
      to make her a better partner   51.
sexual satisfaction   95, 96.
   significant predictor of relationship satisfaction   18.
sexual tingles   345.
Sex Vs. Lovemaking   23-30.
sexy   143, 144, 145, 146, 147, 148, 149, 150, 151, 152,
   161, 162, 164, 165, 166, 167, 168, 169, 170, 171, 172,
   381, 382, 383, 384, 385, 388, 389, 391, 393, 394, 395,
   396, 397, 398, 400, 404, 405, 406.
sexy ads, movies, music videos   119.
sexy artwork; as a turn-on for her   158.
sexy clothes
   make her feel sexy   152.
   make her horny   265.
sexy films   108.
sexy locations to make love   381–386.
   back of a movie theatre or plane   383.
   beach parking lots   383.
   cave   384.
   considerations to keep in mind (list)   384.
   desert mesa   403.
   forests   382.
   for exhibitionists   383.
   good general rule   383.
   her office desk or chair   385.
   hotel balcony overlooking a beach   384.
   in front of a window   388.
   in the backyard   388.
   naughty   383.
   passenger seat of car on a highway   384.
   public places   383.
   risky   383.
   romantic   382.
   sexy   381, 382, 383, 384, 385.
   Some Locations To Avoid   385.
   suggestions (list)   384.
   suited to quick oral sex or fingerwork   384.
   Unusual Locations You Might Try (list)   386.
sexy material   108.
sexy memories   383, 414.
sexy ruses   169.
sexy sounds   224.
sexy talk   244.
sexy topless babes   105.
sexy TV shows; as a turn-on for her   389.

sexy visuals
    examples of women getting hot over
        anticipation of seeing him nude got her hot   159.
        "Do you know what that does to me?"   160.
        due to sexy artwork   158.
        "I just love that sexy bulge!"   156.
        scenes of naked people primed her to come   154.
        sex-positive feminist Carlin Ross blogs about   155.
        she gave author see-through thermals   159.
        she bought author thong underwear   159.
        "When I see your cock hanging down..."154.
        "You're half naked!"   157.
    Excite Her With Sexy Visuals 153–160.
    your body writhing   168.
sexy vocalizations; produce sexual effects   161.
Sexy Ways To Use Lubricants And Lotions   263.
shaft   140, 252, 344.
shake   232, 241, 242, 255.
shallow lovemaking techniques *See* cocksmanship.
Shallow Sweet Place   361, 362, 363, 364, 375.
Shalom In The Home
    how not to be as a husband and partner   61.
she should come before you   342.
She's So High; as example of how not to be   170.
Short Diversion Method   113.
shoulder massage   257, 258.
shoulders   221, 229, 403.
shower massager   163, 395, 396, 403, 406.
    As Sex Toy   395.
    creative use before oral sex   239.
    techniques   396.
    tips   396.
sideways positions   115, 273, 318, 330, 403.
Sidney Poitier; as masculine role model   56.
single men   143, 145, 147, 148, 149, 164.
    especially need to intrigue a woman   164.
    Touching Ruses For Single Guys   257.
sitting up on your knees   403.
Skene's glands   184, 185, 205, 206, 207, 467, 268, 420.
    ducts   137, 352.
        graphic representation   192.
skin   139, 140, 176, 190, 196, 198, 200, 206, 208, 210, 212, 221, 235, 241, 243, 244, 245, 247, 252, 253, 254, 258, 259, 260, 261, 263, 264, 266, 268, 270, 271, 272, 275, 277, 419, 420.
    during oral sex   243.
    her largest sex organ   139.
    of her neck   221.
sleeping in the buff
    as a turn-on to her   156, 160.
Slow Hand; lessons to be learned from lyrics   127.
slow masturbation exercise   108.
slow squeeze technique   371.
S&M   407.
smaller-breasted women   284, 288, 293.
small of her back   229, 243.
smegma   75.
sneak attacks   146, 147, 265.
Society for Sex Therapy and Research   97.
Song of Solomon; Bible's exalting lovemaking   44.
Sophia Loren; her take on sex and love   29.
sophisticated repartee   150.
sophistication   149, 150, 155, 156, 395.
Sorrento technique   274, 275, 276.
spanking   402.
special case orgasm triggers   271, 272.
special challenge of the long-term lover   38–40.
speed   244, 341, 342, 355, 356, 372, 373, 374.
spermicide; tastes bad during oral sex   140.
sphincter   112, 113.
Sphincter Relaxation Technique   112, 113.
spine   221, 243, 330, 403.
spiritual side to lovemaking   348, 416.
spooning   149.
spooning position   415, 416.
Spread-Lips Clitoris Technique   266.
squeeze technique   100.

squeezing   272, 273, 397.
SSRIs   128.
Stairway To Heaven; people making love to it   98.
standing positions   403, 411.
stealth attacks   265.
stem   252, 267, 270, 276.
sternum   293.
stimulation   342, 355, 356, 359, 363, 364, 368, 373, 389, 392, 393, 399.
Sting; false claims of sexual longevity, as joke   93.
stomach   403, 404.
Straighten Up And Fly Right; pointers on sex   98.
strap-on   389, 393.
strategy, sexual   364, 365.
    smart sexual strategy   365.
street cred. *See* qualifications.
stretching   232, 241, 242, 271.
    increases arousal   346, 347.
stripping her   151, 256, 403.
stroke depth   352.
suave guys   258.
submissive women   389, 398, 399, 404.
sub-U   268, 269, 420.
sucking   279, 283, 284, 288, 289, 290, 291, 397.
Sundahl, Deborah   207.
surprise; importance of, in lovemaking   54, 351, 416.
suspensory ligaments   280.
Svengali   133, 166, 167.
Swedish massage   259.
sweeping her off her feet; playing to fantasies   400.
sweet talking; as a turn-on to women   161.
swingers   37–40.
sympathetic motion   326, 327.

T

Talking To Her During Sex
    examples of comments author made during sex   168.
    examples of women getting aroused by words
        "As if you were already in me."   163.
        "Don't ever stop talking to me during sex!"   169.
        "Do you know what that does to me?"   162.
        She groaned and came then and there!   165.
        To my amazement   166.
        "What you said was incredible!"   163.
    She wants to know a number of things   170.
    Talking like a Svengali   166.
    Talk To Her About The Sexual Event Later   171.
    What Not To Say   170.
    #1: tell her what you'll do to her the next time   165.
    #2: Talk to her about what you're doing to her   166.
        examples   163, 164, 167.
    #3: Engage her in conversation   167.
    #4: Play into her fantasies   167.
    #5: egg her on to her climax   167.
    #6: Let out some moans and groans   167.
    #7: Express your honest sexiest feelings   168.
        examples   168.
targeted lovemaking   367.
Tarzan; strips Jane naked, plays to women's fantasies   400.
tease   144, 150, 158, 159, 163, 164, 165, 229, 234, 259, 260, 261, 278, 344, 355, 356, 357, 360, 361, 364, 365, 366, 392, 401, 402, 403, 404, 405, 406, 417.
    Feeler-Outer Talking Tease Line   164.
    long nipple tease   364.
    pre-sex kissing   229.
    slow entry tease   364.
teaser to provoke interest   150.
teasing   224, 262, 268, 276.
    act of delaying   344.
    slow-tease approach   366.
    when you strip her panties off   278.
teeth; creative use when giving her oral sex   240.
tempo   262, 355.
tented vaginal canal   189.
tenting process   187, 216.
    How The Vagina "Tents" With Arousal   188.
    how to verify she's gone wide   187.

testicles. *See* balls.
thigh   258, 265, 266, 404.
thighs   222, 403, 407.
    pre-intercourse kissing, for effect   229.
thong   159.
thoracic intercostal nerves   179.
thoughtfulness   144.
    Thoughtful acts show her you care   68.
threatening harm; never to be done   407.
three anatomical systems involved in sex
    nervous, endocrine, vascular   135.
thumb   258, 266, 268, 271, 272, 274, 275, 276.
tickle   242, 247, 248.
Ticklers   339.
tickling   259, 260, 262, 265, 269, 270, 277.
ties   398.
    in massaging her before or during sex   264.
timing   151.
today's women   39–40.
toes 117, 208, 221, 244, 312, 318, 322, 326, 330, 403, 406.
    sucking   403.
togetherness
    act that produces this feeling   59.
    Togetherness Is Where It's At   66.
to keep your lover happy for a lifetime   38–40.
Tombstone; romantic quote by Wyatt Earp   19.
tone of your voice; powerful sexual effects   161.
tongue 113, 117, 166, 283, 287, 288, 290, 291, 292, 403, 404.
    during oral sex   235, 240.
tongue baths   229.
tongue patterns   245.
Too Hot Technique   371.
topless   388, 405.
torso   403, 406.
total honesty   169.
touch   232, 236, 242, 244, 246, 247, 249, 254.
touches   399.
touching *See also* loving touching
    The Many Kinds Of Erotic Touches   262.
Touching Ruses For Single Guys   257.
toy handcuffs   400, 403.
toys; as an adjunct to your lovemaking   390.
traditional sexual roles
    female role   120.
    man's role   146.
        to make her a better partner   51.
tramadol   128.
Transcendental lovemaking   42.
tribal rape ritual   399.
Trigger   100, 101, 102, 103, 105, 139, 190, 194, 195, 198, 203, 213, 216, 217, 219. *See also* frenulum.
    responsible for "hair trigger response"   101.
turn-offs   144.
    baggy unisex athletic warm-up clothes   145.
    being a bad kisser   228.
    if you're repressed   168.
    Lousy lovers - never cry out loud   168.
    never gush   170.
    never make it seem she's above you   170.
    Pounders   339.
    speedy entrance   350.
    Stroke, Stroke, Strokers   340.
    their husbands don't talk to them in bed   169.
    What Not To Say   170.
turn-ons   30, 144.
    a woman made hot by the word "fuck"   162.
    being responsive during sex   168.
    cashmere sweaters   145.
    confidence   165, 171.
    gentle bondage   400.
    Looking Good For Her Pays Off   160.
    making sexy sounds while making love   162.
    naked men   389.
    sexy bulge   156.
    sight of your balls and cock hanging   244.
    sleeping in the buff   156, 160.
    sweet-talkin'   161.
    Ticklers   339.

turn-ons (continued)
    visual   156–160.
    when you react audibly and visibly   168.
    your body writhing   168.

U

uncircumcised males; special hygiene needs   75.
underwear vent hole; as sexy tool in sex   160.
undocumented erogenous zones   173.
undocumented orgasm triggers   173.
unpredictability; as desirable element   147.
urethra   176, 183, 185, 192, 193, 194, 205, 206, 207, 239, 245, 267, 268, 344, 346, 420.
    graphic representation   192.
urogenital folds   190.
urogenital groove   190.
Using A Mantra To Communicate Thoughts   251.
using nudity to seduce her   149.
    Excite Her With Sexy Visuals   153–160.
    study shows that "wearing something sexy"
        leads to more sex   160.
    Visuals Require The Element Of Surprise   158.
    "Have something else I need to wash?"   164.
U-Spot   177, 178, 192, 205, 206, 207, 234, 240, 245, 246, 253, 268, 269, 352, 356, 357, 420.
uterine contractions   282, 294.
uterine orgasms; possibly breast-triggered   282, 294.
Uterus   194, 195, 216, 219.
U-Zone; Killer U-Zone Techniques   268.

V

vagina   136, 137, 139, 140, 174, 178, 179, 183, 187, 188, 189, 191, 199, 202, 206, 209, 210, 211, 212, 213, 214, 216, 217, 218, 232, 239, 242, 244, 245, 253, 256, 345, 346, 349, 350, 351, 352, 359, 366, 368, 375, 377, 393, 402, 403, 406.
    anterior wall of the vagina   209, 210, 211, 213.
        greater number of sexually reactive areas   213.
    aroma (her vagina's)   238, 404.
        problems; A Solution   239.
    arousal process; makes her vagina go wide   139.
    a variety of orgasm triggers   178, 222.
    bad vaginal odor
        indicator of infection   238.
        IUDs, cause of   238.
    canal   136, 137, 140, 141, 176, 177, 187, 189, 199, 210, 213, 214, 215, 216, 234, 273, 347, 395.
    it needs to be "prepped"   187.
    never enter her before vagina tents   187.
    changes during her orgasm   85.
    do not use petroleum-based lubricants 136, 137, 139, 140.
    entrance   371.
        graphic   194.
        entry hole (introitus)   196, 214.
        warning: never blow in!   240.
    "erotic sensitivity" studies   209.
    fluids   85.
    grows in size during the arousal process   9.
    heat   110, 225, 366, 403.
    inelasticity, with age   140.
    membrane separates vaginal and anal canals   254.
    muscle throbbing   110.
    muscles   141, 200.
    nerve study   209.
    nerves   346.
    posterior wall of the vagina   210.
    second widening event   377.
    sharp nails can cause cuts   75.
    side walls; might react to shallow sex   213.
    tenting process   187-189, 195, 216.
        how to verify she's gone wide   187.
    Untented Vagina   188, 194.
    vaginal ring *See* below.
    walls   136, 137, 141, 179, 189, 202, 203, 208, 214, 216, 346, 347, 377.

vagina/walls (continued)
    anterior wall   294, 338.
    muscles, nerves and mucous membranes   214.
    nerves inside her vaginal walls   208.
    produce mucous-like lubrication   141.
vaginal ball   8, 178, 199, 200, 203, 206, 208, 214, 240, 245, 267, 272, 349, 352, 357, 361, 362, 363, 371, 372.
    as special case orgasm trigger   272.
    during oral sex   240.
    graphic representation   192.
    Vaginal Ball Tease Technique illustration   362.
    Vaginal Ball Wetness Technique   271, 272.
vaginal orgasms   5, 9, 174, 175, 177, 178, 189, 203, 204, 208, 209, 210, 211, 212, 213, 214, 215, 219, 296, 328, 329, 336, 338.
    breast-triggered   282, 290, 294.
    controversy about orgasm triggers   208.
    deep orgasm triggers   215.
    Easy - For Longer & Shorter Men   177.
    erogenous zones that trigger   203.
    existence proven by Rutgers study 175, 177, 179, 192, 193, 194, 199, 202, 203, 208, 211, 214.
    MRI study suggests two vaginal orgasm triggers   212.
    muscle throbbing   110.
    posterior wall orgasms   338.
    precise trigger location is unknown   213.
    shallow intercourse can produce   341.
    vaginal orgasm trigger study by Dr. Zwi Hoch of Israel's Rambam Medical Center   211.
vaginal ring   8, 178, 203, 214, 215, 361, 362, 363, 364, 372.
    graphic representation   193.
vaginal sex; median time   95.
Vagina Makes A Come-back   174.
vaginismus   36–40.
variety   381, 408.
vascular system   135.
vent hole as sexy tool in sex   160.
ventral pallidum   135.
vestibule   184, 192, 194, 197, 198, 199, 214, 268, 349, 350, 352, 361.
    graphic representation   192.
vibrating "eggs"   393.
vibrators   384, 388, 390, 391, 392, 394, 395, 406.
    danger in using   392.
    discover her comfort level   392.
    give her unique orgasms   394.
    if she has trouble coming; use to cure her   392.
    lubrication   393.
    pocket-book sized vibrators   393.
    speed, motion and location   391.
    strap-on clitoral vibrators   393.
    tips   392.
    types (list)   393.
    warning for men with control problems   395.
    watching her use one   391.
videotape   388.
virginity   144.
visualizations   120.
visual stimulation; extreme   389.
vixens   119, 389, 405.
vocalizations   161, 168.
vocal sounds   163, 165.
Voice, yours, as a sexual instrument   167, 168, 264.
voyeuristic lover   389.
voyeurs; female   388.
V-Spot   8, 177, 178, 192, 193, 194, 198, 199, 208, 245, 253, 267, 268, 271, 272, 351, 352, 356, 357, 358, 361, 362, 363, 364.
    graphic representation   192.
    V-Spot Massage technique   271.
    V-Spot orgasms   199.
vulva   9, 30, 113, 146, 166, 232, 234, 235, 236, 239, 240, 241, 242, 245, 247, 249, 250, 251, 253, 254, 261, 262, 263, 265, 267, 271, 275, 278, 304, 319, 345, 349, 350, 351, 352, 355, 356, 357, 359, 363, 365, 368, 393, 397, 415, 419.
    cleft of her vulva   146, 265.
    Covered Vulva Orgasm Techniques   267.

vulva (continued)
    Every Vulva Is Different   191.
    Her Vulva   190–195.
    keeping it lubed during oral sex   235.
    techniques for complete vulval stimulation   206.
    vulva cleft zone (VCZ)   351.
    vulva erogenous zones   177, 191.
    vulval orgasm triggers   178, 208.
    Vulva Love   *See* cocksmanship
    Vulva Orgasm Massage Techniques   267.
    Vulva Vibrations Massage Method   268.
    Vulva Vs. Vagina: Do You Know The Difference? 191.

W

Waldinger, Dr. Marcel D.   95, 99, 128.
warm fuzzies   172.
Warning: A Penis Can Be Broken   313.
Water-based lubricants   140.
water beds; mixed bag for lovemaking   411.
water jets   397.
waterproof mattress cover   207.
way to a woman's heart   23.
West, Mae; comment on sex   348.
wetness   139, 140, 183, 214, 268, 272, 273, 275, 277, 352, 366.
    slippery kind desirable   271.
    wetness issues   139.
        dryness problems as she gets older   140.
        hormone replacement therapy   140.
        hysterectomies and dryness   140.
        solutions to dryness problems   140.
        your job as a lover   214.
    wetness triggers 5, 8, 173, 177, 185, 196, 222, 271.
        Bartholin's glands   184, 206, 216.
        great wetness triggers   222.
        Skene's glands   184, 185, 205, 206, 207.
        The Vaginal Ball & Bartholin's Glands Wetness Technique   271.
        vestibule   184, 197, 198, 199, 214.
    what parts make her wet   134.
wet spot   207.
wettening process   131, 132, 133, 134, 136, 139, 141, 162, 277.
    mucous-like lubrication by vaginal walls   141.
    should not end after penetration   141.
    What Wettening Is All About   139.
wetter the better vis a vis oral sex   235.
what a woman needs to know, every day   64.
What Can Cause Breasts To Be Less Sensitive?   283.
what it means to be a man   45.
    Being Handy And Helpful Is Sexy Too   51.
What Not To Say   170.
what women want   36–40.
wheelbarrow position   326.
when you're tired or ill   392.
Whipple, Beverly   179, 180, 215.
why women are different than men   47.
why women leave men
    a lack of lovemaking (not sex)   27.
    Bad Hygiene: Real Stories   70.
    she wanted to be treated like a woman   49.
    she wanted him to write a love song for her   62.
    her lover fell short as a man   26.
    he was a lousy lover   26.
    no romance once she got married   62.
    true story   26, 27.
wideness   167, 2268, 272, 277, 366.
    wideness triggers   5.
    second widening event   377.
wife   31–40, 51.
    after me to complete On Loving Women   1.
    hardest lover to please   31–40.
    wife's endorsement   2.
Wiggle Technique   355.
wiggling   269, 270.
wikimedia commons graphic with mistakes   176.

wild sexual proclivities   408.
willpower   109.
wimp; not manly   171.
Wimpissinger, Florian   207.
Windshield Wiper Orgasm Technique   352, 355.
   illustration   353.
woman-on-top positions   116.
woman's sexual entrances   348.
   anal canal opening   349.
   from a woman's perspective   349.
   introitus (vaginal)   349.
   labia minora   349.
   there are three (listed)   349.
woman's sexual response
   medications that can interfere with   178.
women.
   a woman's sensuality   29.
   beautiful at every age   30.
   Becoming Type Of Man Women Desire   45.
   being "taken" fantasy
      Clark Gable In Gone With The Wind   48.
      especially liked by submissives   389.
      Tarzan and His Mate; sex scene   400.
      women in Romance novels are "taken"   50.
   big teasers   116.
   brains   179.
   can tell if you're a great lover   18.
   can read your mind   20.
   crave great lovers   15.
   don't leave great lovers   15–18.
   fantasies   269, 388, 394, 399.
   good bullshit detectors   168.
   great women; they're out there   20.
   hard-wired for all things romantic   22.
   her body as an instrument   32–40.
   kind of man and lover a woman craves   5.
   kind of man women don't ever leave   6.
   leave bad lovers   17.
      Match.com survey   17.
      Sex & The City: Samantha leaves one   17.
   love intercourse   175.
   Love Sweet Talkers   52.
   most are multi-orgasmic   222.
   primary reason for loss of interest   59.
   psyche   64.
   secret labels women use to rate lovers   12.
   still prefer traditional sexual roles   21, 48.
      flowers for no reason   62.
   turn-offs
      disrespect   22.
      neglect   22.
      offensive, cold and insulting behavior   22.
   turn-ons
      men who demonstrate a mastery   52.
   want to be the center of a man's attention   22.
   want to settle down   32–40.
   what most women want through intimacy   25.
   what they want   36–40.
   why women are different than men   47.
   with poor lubrication response   183.
   with the wildest sex drives   393.
women's brains   179.
women's complaints about men   32–40, 49.
   "97% of them can't fuck you!"   339.
   about oral sex   233.
   bad hygiene   70.
   becomes predictable   38–40.
   don't like Pounders   339.
   lack of romance once married   62.
   men stopped being as assertive romantically   49.
   husband's feminine side became dominant   49.
   inability to show affection   61.
   lousy lovers   26.
   most men fail in the kissing department   227.
   scratchy tongue work   235.
   Stroke, Stroke, Strokers   340.
   their husbands don't talk to them in bed   169.
   their partners don't give them oral sex   233.

Women's Movement; as cause sexual role confusion   49.
woods; as a location to make love   403.
words
   acceptable teaser   165.
   are like powerful caresses to her   169.
   clever sexy banter   165.
   implied invitation   165.
   powerful sexual effects   161, 162, 163.
   provocative comments   165.
   to provoke interest   165.
   velvety bedroom voice enhances them   165.
World Journal of Urology   210.
wriggling   225, 366.
writhing   225, 366.

Y

Yin Yang   42.
your learning process   415.
your own body   344
   information crucial to being a great lover   4.
   insights essential to reaching your potential   9.
Y Tu Mama Tambien
   on bad masturbation and control problems
      102.

About The Author

James Moore has accomplished many things in life - not the least of which has been pleasing hundreds of women as a much sought after ladies man (that is, before he found the love of his life, his wife). He has also traditionally been the guy to whom other guys turn for sexual advice.

Having been university-trained in the biological sciences, James applied the lab skills he learned to a more sexy kind of research after college. As you'll see, his efforts have furthered the art and science of pleasing women.

He did have to earn a living, too, though. Having earned a Master's degree in journalism, he became an award-winning journalist and author. His articles appeared in such publications as the Boston Globe, the Chicago Reader, Downbeat Magazine, the Boston Herald and others and his books have graced the bookshelves of the nation's finest bookstores. He is also an award-winning public speaker, has appeared on hundreds of radio shows and TV shows nationwide and has been written up in many of the nation's finest newspapers and magazines. He was also an uncredited story development editor for the sexy *Baring It All*, edited by Layla Shilkret (ISBN 978-0-9742845-4-5, retail $9.95 - available at all fine bookstores and now also at **www.helixeye.com**).

James divides his time between doing public speaking events, writing books, movie scripts and plays, and spending time with his wife and his four-legged fuzzy family.

For more info on James, his workshops for couples and singles, and his public appearances worldwide, visit **www.onlovingwomen.com**.